LANDSLIDE

LANDSLIDE

THE UNMAKING OF
THE PRESIDENT,
1984–1988

Jane Mayer

and

Doyle McManus

Houghton Mifflin Company

BOSTON

FOR OUR PARENTS

LIBRARY OF CONGRESS CATALOGING-IN-PUBLICATION DATA

Mayer, Jane.
Landslide : the unmaking of the President, 1984–1988.

Bibliography: p.
Includes index.
1. United States — Politics and government — 1981–
2. Reagan, Ronald. I. McManus, Doyle. II. Title.
E876.M38 1988   973.927′092′4   88-13178
ISBN 0-395-45185-X
ISBN 0-395-51757-5 (pbk.)

PRINTED IN THE UNITED STATES OF AMERICA
D 10 9 8 7 6 5 4 3 2 1

Contents

Prologue

EARLY ON A SUNDAY morning in March 1987, a gray-haired man wearing only pajamas and tortoiseshell glasses padded down the hall to his study and switched on his computer. It was not yet light outside his Georgetown home, but Jim Cannon hadn't been able to sleep. Now that he faced the blank screen of his computer, he couldn't quite bring himself to write, either. Cannon was still too shaken by what he had learned earlier that weekend while carrying out a confidential mission inside Ronald Reagan's White House.

In the transient world of Washington politics, Cannon had been around a long time, and, at sixty-nine, he was not usually disturbed by the ups and downs of political fortunes. As a former aide to Vice President Nelson A. Rockefeller, domestic policy adviser to Gerald Ford, and finally as counselor and confidant to former Senate majority leader Howard Baker, he had seen a good stretch of history. By now, not much surprised him. Though not especially well known outside moderate Republican circles, Cannon had earned a reputation as a smart, tough operator. Engaging but unsentimental, he was cool under pressure and decisive when faced with a hard choice.

That was why Howard Baker had turned to Cannon for help a few days earlier. Baker was about to become Ronald Reagan's third chief of staff, and he wanted a wise and trusted aide to scout out the territory before taking over on Monday, March 2. Cannon was already familiar with the White House and the unique landscape of the West Wing — the hushed hallways, the armed Secret Service agents, the tense buzz of fluorescent lights, the complex network of computers and military communications systems, the self-consciously harried occupants, who seemed so captivated by the building's heady promise of history and power. Superficially, little of this had changed since the Ford days, when Cannon himself had an office in the building. But in less obvious ways the Reagan White House was startlingly different. In fact, Cannon had not been at all prepared for what he had found. And so now, on Sunday morning, he was trying to write a confidential memo to Baker, his patron and closest friend in politics, warning him about what he had learned.

Cannon stared at his computer screen for a moment, then pushed back his chair. With professional detachment, he realized that the information he needed could come from only one source — the United States Constitution. He found a copy on his bookshelf, thumbed through its pages, and began to weigh recent events.

On Friday, February 27, just two days earlier, Donald T. Regan, the president's second chief of staff, had stormed out of the White House in humiliation and anger after having learned that he'd been fired. But the news had not been delivered by the president; instead, Regan heard about it from another White House official, who had himself seen a news report on television. The first public word of Regan's removal had come from Nancy Reagan's office, and Cannon had little doubt that the shrewd First Lady was behind the shake-up.

On that Friday evening, while attention was riveted on the unseemly and irresistible spectacle of Regan's graceless departure, Cannon had quietly slipped into the White House to begin his confidential mission. Baker assumed there would have to be major changes in the staff. But before he made them, he needed to understand how the old White House team had functioned — or not functioned.

At Baker's instruction, Cannon embarked on a series of exhaustive interviews with the members of the White House staff, trying to determine what had gone wrong. It was like interviewing witnesses in a political mystery. For six years, Ronald Reagan had been the most commanding presence in American politics, a president of apparently limitless popularity and success. But for the past four months, ever since the news had broken that he had secretly sold weapons to the government of Iran, his presidency had seemed lifeless, a hollow shell. Reagan had been elected by a forty-nine-state landslide only twenty-seven months earlier, but the polls now showed that his popularity was plummeting. He had been praised for having restored the credibility of the office, but more than half the country thought he was not telling the whole truth about either the arms sales to Iran or the diversion of money to the Nicaraguan contras. More than any recent leader, Reagan had shown an instinctive ability to please the American public, yet he had blundered into a misbegotten set of policies that no one, no matter where they stood on the political spectrum, could support. How, Cannon wanted to know, could this have happened?

Cannon had talked with the president's aides late into Friday evening and through most of Saturday. By the time he returned home quite late on Saturday night, he had been tired, dispirited, and very worried.

Now, in Sunday's early light, he began to draft his report for Howard Baker. He looked again at the notes he had taken during the two days of interviews. The picture they presented of Reagan's White House was nothing short of astounding.

Cannon later recalled his impressions: "Chaos. There was no order in the place. The staff system had just broken down. It had just evaporated.

There was no pattern of analysis, no coming together. Individual cabinet members were just doing whatever they wanted to do — the ones who were smart had realized that the White House really didn't matter. They could go around the White House, and no one would retaliate.

"I took a look at some of the staff's paperwork and was stunned at their incompetence. They were rank amateurs."

But more chilling than anything else was the portrait these aides drew of the president they served. They spoke with Cannon in confidence; one by one, he recalled, "they told stories about how inattentive and inept the president was. He was lazy; he wasn't interested in the job. They said he wouldn't read the papers they gave him — even short position papers and documents. They said he wouldn't come over to work — all he wanted to do was to watch movies and television at the residence.

"They felt free to sign his initials on documents without noting that they were acting for him. When I asked a group of them, who among them thought they had authority to sign in the president's name, there was a long, uncomfortable silence. Then one answered, 'Well — everybody, and nobody.' "

Sifting through his notes, Cannon couldn't shake his astonishment. He was of course an uninitiated outsider; he'd had only a brief glimpse into the inner workings of an enormously complex organization. But he had seen enough to find the situation frightening — for him, for the party, and for the country.

Cannon reopened his copy of the Constitution and found, almost at the end, what he had been searching for: Section Four of the Twenty-fifth Amendment.

AMENDMENT XXV. SECTION FOUR. Whenever the vice president and a majority of either the principal officers of the executive departments or of such other body as Congress may by law provide, transmit to the president pro tempore of the Senate and the speaker of the House of Representatives their written declaration that the president is unable to discharge the powers and duties of his office, the vice president shall immediately assume the powers and duties of the office as acting president.

Cannon stared hard at the provision. It had never been invoked; deceptively simple, it was a straightforward procedure for removing the president from office if he were no longer competent to govern. All it would take would be the agreement of the vice president and a majority of the cabinet. After a good deal of thought, Cannon reached a conclusion that would seem extreme, maybe even bizarre, to those who only knew the Ronald Reagan they saw on television and who hadn't heard all that he had over the past two days. But Cannon wasn't concerned with public perception; his primary loyalty was to Baker, to whom he felt he owed his unvarnished judgment. So he carefully typed out his first recommendation:

"Suggested priorities, March 1, 1987:

"1. Consider the possibility that section four of the 25th amendment might be applied."

That evening Cannon took the finished memorandum — which included several recommendations for immediate action — to Baker's home in a posh wooded enclave of Northwest Washington for a confidential meeting. Two of Baker's other trusted aides had also been asked to attend: A. B. Culvahouse, a bright young lawyer who had cut short his vacation to take over the next day as the White House counsel, and Thomas Griscom, another transplanted Tennessean who had been Baker's press aide and would soon become the White House's director of communications. Griscom already knew what Cannon thought. He too had been asked to interview the White House staff over the weekend, and he had been similarly appalled. By Friday night, he was so shocked by the stories he was hearing that he kidded Cannon that they should be given medals for even daring to go back to the White House the next morning. The two had exchanged notes on their findings during a late lunch at the Old Ebbitt Grill on Saturday, and although they had thought they were starving, by the time they had realized the magnitude of the crisis they were facing, neither had had any appetite left.

In the privacy of Baker's home on Sunday night, Cannon warned Baker and the others that what he was about to say was extremely serious. Baker assumed his practiced poker face and waited. Sparing no details, Cannon then repeated what he had heard from the president's aides. The man they described, he told Baker, had no interest in running the country. In his estimation, and as the only one in the room who had previously worked in the White House, Cannon told Baker that his first decision should be whether to set in motion the involuntary retirement of the president on the grounds that he was no longer fit to discharge the duties of his office. Such a move could cause a constitutional crisis, Cannon realized. But, he said, if the president was as incompetent as his aides indicated, invoking the Twenty-fifth Amendment could be the only way to serve the national interest.

There was a long, sober silence. During Watergate, Howard Baker had been a senior member of the Senate's investigating committee, and he understood as well as any politician in the country the implications of Cannon's words. But neither Baker nor his aides dismissed the constitutional remedy as beyond the realm of possibility. Instead, after hearing Cannon out, Baker finally said in his Tennessee drawl, "Well, it doesn't sound like the Ronald Reagan I just saw, but we'll see tomorrow."

On Monday morning, March 2, Cannon, Baker, Culvahouse, and Griscom gathered in the West Wing of the White House. They planned to watch the president closely, to determine whether he appeared mentally fit to serve. First they observed him from across the room as he chaired a formal cabinet meeting. Then they accompanied him to one of the weekly "issues luncheons," a free-flowing discussion with members of the White House staff that was also held in the Cabinet Room.

One of Donald Regan's aides guided them to seats alongside the French doors that lined the side of the room and led out to the Rose Garden. But Cannon insisted on four seats at the table; he wanted a closer look at Reagan. The four men deliberately bracketed the president: Baker on his right side, Griscom on his left, and Culvahouse and Cannon directly across from him, so that they could look into the president's eyes.

Reagan seemed relaxed and animated. He swapped a few familiar jokes with Baker. There was the one about the lady from Tennessee who was a stern teetotaler. A friend had protested, "Even Jesus drank a little wine," to which she had replied, "I would think more of him if he hadn't." Everyone laughed. The tension evaporated. Then Reagan reminisced a bit about being governor of California. He seemed so alert and attentive that Cannon began to wonder about everything the White House staff members had told him.

Perhaps Donald Regan's henchmen had exaggerated the president's frailties, he thought. Perhaps they were trying to justify an internal coup, an arrangement whereby the chief of staff would make others believe he had been forced to act as a kind of regent for a disabled president. Could the president they described — the inattentive, incurious man who watched television rather than attending to affairs of state — be the same as the genial, charming man across the table?

What the hell is going on here? Cannon wondered. The old fella looks just dandy.

And, through it all, Ronald Reagan always did.

I

MANDATE

I

Morning in America

FOUR MONTHS BEFORE election day, five men gathered in a small conference room at the Reagan-Bush headquarters and reviewed an oversize calendar that marked the remaining days of the 1984 presidential campaign. It was the last Saturday in June, an unusually bearable summer day in Washington, and at ten o'clock in the morning the rest of the office was practically deserted. Even so, the men kept the door to the conference room shut and the drapes screening it off carefully drawn. The three principals and their two deputies had come from around the country for a critical meeting. Their aim was to devise a strategy that would guarantee Ronald Reagan's resounding reelection to a second term in the White House.

It should have been easy. These were battle-tested veterans with long ties to Reagan and even longer ones to the Republican party, men who understood presidential politics as well as any in the country. The backdrop of the campaign was hospitable, with lots of good news to work with: America was at peace, and the nation's economy, a key factor in any election, was rebounding vigorously after a recession. Furthermore, the campaign itself was lavishly financed, with plenty of money for a top-flight staff, travel, phone banks, and television commercials. And, most important, their candidate was Ronald Wilson Reagan, a president of tremendous personal popularity and dazzling communication skills. Reagan had succeeded more than any president since John F. Kennedy in projecting a broad vision of America — a nation of renewed military strength, individual initiative, and smaller federal government.

But even with these advantages, the president's campaign strategists found that something was missing. They couldn't have foreseen the po-

3

litical predicament that would face Reagan in 1987, but already, in the summer of 1984, this inner circle sensed that the White House was strangely adrift. Ordinarily, to win an election, a candidate needed to show voters some blueprint for the future. The problem, as the president's men were rapidly discovering, was that, for the most part, the Reagan White House had none.

So far, the omission had not made much difference. Until the June 30 meeting, the campaign had pursued a standard Rose Garden strategy, sticking to events that underscored Reagan's presidential stature without being overtly partisan. But the strategists knew that after July's Democratic convention, Reagan would face a determined opponent who would almost surely challenge him to articulate a more definite political agenda. For several days they had been groping for ideas, interviewing cabinet officers, White House officials, and the president himself. Yet they were stumped.

Now, in the privacy of the conference room, they were expected to draft a strategy. The meeting was highly confidential — the kind of high-level session whose secrets are usually kept forever. But in this case the discussion was tape-recorded, and although the participants intended that the tapes stay secret, they did not. The four hours of tapes capture an exchange that reveals not only the strategists' worry over the unformed agenda, but also — and perhaps more important — the way the president's men viewed their candidate.

"The problem is, we've been talking to everybody at the White House over the past few days — and the Reagan administration fired all its bullets very early and very successfully in the first two years," the tape begins. The speaker was Stuart Spencer, who chaired the meeting and served as the campaign's chief strategist. "All their plans, all their priorities, all their programs. They've run out of ammunition.

"The most striking thing I discovered is that they don't have a goddamn thing in the pipeline," Spencer said. "They don't have an idea."

The two other advisers at the table, pollster Robert Teeter and speechwriter Kenneth Khachigian, readily agreed.

"Days digging around, and we found nothing," Teeter said. "This is a national election. We've got to find something to say."

Reagan had charted an overall direction, of course, one that seemed clear and strong to most of the country in the summer of 1984. But it was more an attitude than a program. Although his administration had accomplished a great deal in its first term, a number of unfinished tasks remained. But most of them had already proven politically impractical then; it made little sense to believe that they could provide an agenda for the second term. As Reagan approached his bid for reelection, his campaign strategists sensed that the White House was running on empty. For the rest of the day they did their best to create a presidential campaign that would bring Reagan to victory anyway. Journalists would later conclude that its lack of specificity was a stroke of genius, in the great tradition of cautious incumbent campaigns — and it may have been. But the truth, known to few outside the conference room, was that it was not just a strategy of choice. It was also a strategy born of sheer necessity.

The three men around the table that day were eminently qualified for the job. Spencer, the first among equals, was a profane and irreverent political consultant from California who had helped transform Reagan from a B movie actor into a national political figure nearly two decades earlier. Spencer had taken Reagan on as a client during the 1966 California gubernatorial campaign, and, other than assisting Gerald Ford in 1976, he had worked with Reagan ever since. He was now Reagan's oldest and most trusted political adviser — a Westerner who preferred cowboy boots to Gucci loafers and who, more than any other aide, knew how to deal with Ronald and Nancy Reagan in a way that they found entirely comfortable. Spencer ran the meeting; after it ended, he would sell the 1984 plan to the Reagans and, with their approval, to the rest of the campaign hierarchy.

Seated next to Spencer was Khachigian, probably the only top campaign adviser whose office boasted an ARMENIANS FOR REAGAN poster. Khachigian was another Californian; he too had been tested in earlier campaigns. A slight man with bushy eyebrows and a ready smile, he was an eloquent polemicist and a conservative true believer who had served Richard Nixon both in the White House and in exile. Loath to leave Southern California, he had nonetheless written occasional speeches for Reagan since 1980. Throughout the 1984 campaign, he was technically in charge of issues and "opposition research" — the political euphemism for compiling dirt on opponents. But his broader role was to serve as a resident ideologue.

Finally there was Teeter, an unassuming and widely respected political pollster from Detroit who once worked for Gerald Ford. He was gifted not only at crunching numbers but also at divining trends and strategies from long computer columns of voter data. Although Teeter was not the campaign's official pollster, he was one of its most thoughtful analysts, and he added a good deal of intellectual firepower to the campaign.

Together, these three men searched for an agenda that could animate Reagan's quest for reelection. The tapes show that much of the day was spent working through an unusual process of elimination. They considered the many issues that Reagan had championed in the past and, one by one, they discarded them as either irrelevant or too politically risky to fit a winning campaign plan.

One of the first to go was defense spending. Although restoring the nation's military strength had been among Reagan's clearest objectives in 1980, Teeter warned, "We've got rapidly decreasing numbers there." His polls showed evaporating support for continuing the arms buildup because, as he put it, "the public has this sense that we haven't subjected defense spending to the same kind of scrutiny as other spending." Spencer chimed in that he had been talking with the navy secretary, who told him "horror stories — he says he's found so much crap going on over there, he could run the Navy Department on the cost-of-living increases alone."

Khachigian added Social Security to the list of taboos. Cutting government spending had long been a central goal of Reagan's; he had once even suggested that Social Security ought to be voluntary. But any threat of cutbacks there would be political poison. "We should have the next person who even mentions the word fired," Khachigian said. "Yeah," sighed Teeter. "The group we're hurting worst with is women over sixty-five. For Chrissake," he added, "if Ronald Reagan had any constituency, you would think that would be it, but Social Security is the problem. There's absolutely nothing good to say about it."

Abortion was another unmentionable. "It's one issue we ought not to talk about," said Teeter. "They [antiabortion groups] know where we stand, and we've got a lot of people on the other side."

The Treasury Department was working on a plan for overhauling the tax code, but that was untouchable too. "We have to put it off until after the election," said Khachigian. "It's a question of politics, not policy. If there's any uncertainty about it, it can hurt us." Ironically, several Democrats had charged that Reagan had a secret plan to raise taxes after the election in order to close the widening federal deficit. But the truth was, as his campaign aides knew, that on taxes, as in so many other areas, there wasn't really any presidential plan at all. "We'd have to get five people with brains to sit down and cast a position by the president," Khachigian acknowledged.

In the absence of any new, compelling presidential initiatives to run on, the group toyed with a few of their own. Spencer suggested that perhaps they could have Reagan say something about "acid rain and all that stuff," since he was vulnerable on environmental issues. But Khachigian threw up another red flag. "We're better off without it. If you get the old man going on it, he does 'killer trees,' " he warned, referring to Reagan's embarrassing assertion in 1980 that trees caused pollution.

Instead, Khachigian thought that Reagan might attract women's votes by talking about "wife-beating." He suggested, "You just get the old man . . . so upset, he tells [Health and Human Services Secretary] Peggy Heckler I want you to spend $30 million on it right now. I don't care where you find it."

"You take it away from poor people," came the answer, prompting guffaws.

Soon their conversation became serious again, and by the end of the day, Reagan's political advisers had fashioned a way to win the election even without the help of a clear blueprint for the future. Despite the policy vacuum, they devised a strategy that would spare Reagan the task of resolving the fundamental question of where to take the country over the succeeding four years. After the election, Democratic nominee Walter Mondale would say he lost because of his evident unease on television in the face of an acknowledged master. But Reagan's landslide had less to do with medium than with message. Reagan won because his skilled campaign team succeeded in framing the election as a choice between the bad old days of what Spencer called "the Carter-Mondale past" and Reagan's own effervescent celebration of the present, which was characterized by good times for most voting Americans. Given that focus, there was little need to think about the future. The overarching theme for this campaign, Spencer thought, would be leadership — neatly placing the spotlight on Reagan's record rather than his plans.

The three men had no doubt that Reagan would agree to their campaign strategy, even though he hadn't helped draft it. Reagan's public image was that of a strong and decisive leader, but the private reality was quite different. The president's political career was in many ways the product of a revolution in American politics, which well before 1984 had turned campaigns into sophisticated marketing operations run by experts more professional than the candidates themselves. Reagan supplied the broad vision and vocal cords. But from the start, Spencer's consulting firm had done the coaching and packaging, marketing him brilliantly to the most media-oriented state in the country and, later, to the most media-oriented nation in the world. In Reagan's view, campaigns were literally their business. They were true professionals; as a candidate, he saw little reason to interfere.

This detachment from the daily decisionmaking suited Reagan's temperament. Unlike most of his predecessors — men like Lyndon Johnson and Richard Nixon, who were obsessed with controlling all the facets of power, including the politics that endowed them with it — Reagan was aloof, even disengaged. He had little vanity or curiosity, which enabled him to stay serenely removed from most of the machinations around him. Although they took care to portray him publicly as forceful and vigorous, his campaign advisers saw the other side.

"The president was never really involved in any of the planning or strategy of the campaign," conceded his campaign manager, Edward J. Rollins. "He would make small talk some of the time relative to what was going on with Mondale or [Democratic candidate] Gary Hart. But there was never any real inquisitive effort to get to the nitty-gritty on his part. I don't think he ever focused on it. The truth of the matter is that Ronald Reagan is the perfect candidate. He does whatever you want him to do. And he does it superbly well."

If the president's participation in his own campaign was considerably smaller than most outsiders thought, his wife's role was greater than most people knew. Reagan might not be attentive to details, but his wife kept a close eye on things; she sometimes even rationed the number of handshakes she would allow him to give, setting a limit on the number of supporters allowed in the receiving line — two hundred was usually the maximum — and reprimanding the advance men for wearing him out if they allowed more. "You're trying to kill him," she would sometimes charge.

Over the years, Nancy Reagan successfully played down news accounts that suggested she meddled in serious affairs of state. Her role inside the White House was difficult to document, and staff members were fired for being indiscreet. But no one who knew Nancy Reagan well underestimated her influence. As the actor Jimmy Stewart, an old friend of the Reagans', once summed it up: "If Nancy Reagan instead of Jane Wyman had been Ronald Reagan's first wife, he never would have gone into politics. Instead, she would have seen to it that he got all the best parts, he would have won three or four Oscars, and been a real star."

Spencer, who conferred frequently with the First Lady by phone, had described her many years earlier, in a cool moment in their relationship, as "a lot tougher than the image America has of her. . . . Nancy is ambitious, very ambitious." By 1984, in the interest of harmony, he kept such thoughts out of the public domain, but insiders knew that, with growing practice and success, Mrs. Reagan had become emboldened to play an even greater role in both politics and policy. She was her husband's closest friend, of course, but she was also his chaperone, prompter, nurse, and theatrical manager. Some people came to believe she was his hatchet man. With the protection and assistance she gave him, Reagan sometimes called her "Mommy."

During the June 30 strategy meeting in the campaign's conference room, the tapes capture Spencer, Teeter, and Khachigian treating Mrs. Reagan as a force to be reckoned with. At the time, their particular concern was her resistance to their proposal to have Reagan do a two- or three-day campaign trip before the Republican convention in August. "What's her reasoning?" asked Khachigian. "Her reasoning is, you don't put the actor onstage before the show starts," answered Spencer. "She thinks the convention is the show. I tried to make her see that you're talking about two different shows, two different nights. I think I finally got through to her."

Mrs. Reagan rarely explained her decisions about the campaign schedule. Only later did anyone learn the reason for her reticence: by 1984, she was secretly consulting an astrologer about which days were propitious for her husband's speeches and appearances — and, more important, which were not. But the campaign strategists knew nothing of this, so her decisions often seemed maddeningly arbitrary.

Mrs. Reagan's grip on her husband's campaign was not enough to allay concerns about the potentially grave political problem that Reagan's detachment posed. Teeter had heard through the political grapevine that Mondale was going to make an issue of Reagan's lack of attentiveness. "They're working on some examples that he doesn't know what he's doing," Teeter warned. And so the advisers spent a considerable amount of time that day trying to devise a strategy to protect him from charges that he was an absentee president.

Among the tactics they considered was having Reagan give three or four "sophisticated speeches," as Spencer put it, "to talk about things like sound money, constitutional reform, education. Things that when he gets through, people will think he sure as hell knows something — without really saying something."

Another possibility, Khachigian suggested, was to have "the old man make some visible phone calls, reversing a policy or something. Some conspicuous ass-kicking of cabinet members would help."

Teeter suggested doing presidential events with young people. "It will help inoculate against the idea that he doesn't know what's going on," he suggested, "but it can't be seen as something . . . cooked up."

The arms control talks in Geneva provided another opportunity. Khachigian suggested that Reagan could meet in front of the television cameras with the negotiating team before it left. "That's good, hands-on," agreed Teeter. For full effect, the session would have to last hours, but Teeter pointed out that Reagan wouldn't have to actually do anything. "I mean, you can play dominoes during the session." But Spencer was still worried. "He probably shouldn't be shooting his mouth off while it's going on, it could jeopardize it," he said.

A favorite idea was to have the president take advantage of improvements in the tone of U.S.-Soviet relations, giving the public the impression that he was a forceful and commanding world leader. Khachigian remembered that Reagan was due to speak at the opening session of the U.N. General Assembly in the fall, and he suggested that they could cue the president to point to the Soviets, seated only a few feet away, and say, "See, there isn't such a big gulf between us." As Khachigian imagined the moment, "You could have it programmed into the speech, but literally look like an ad lib."

"He'd probably point at the Puerto Ricans," Spencer jibed.

Though his handlers worried about Reagan's detachment, what was known of it in the summer of 1984 did not seem to concern the voting public. Reagan somehow operated on a different plane from most politicians; he moved in a world of myths and symbols, not facts and programs. Even after four years in the White House, the government wasn't his responsibility; it was still his adversary, a position that had insulated him almost completely from mishap.

Eighteen years earlier, as governor of California, Reagan had astounded not just critics, but even some of his own advisers, by being unable to tell a reporter a single item in his own legislative program. But his inattention hadn't stopped him from going on to win a second term in Sacramento, and it seemed unlikely that it would stop him now.

Teeter warned that after four years in the White House, Reagan might be seen as more vulnerable than before. Second presidential terms were historically more perilous than first. For two centuries the American electorate had shown a deep ambivalence about the amount of power it wanted its chief executive to wield over any prolonged stretch of time; even George Washington saw the overwhelming popularity he enjoyed in the first term dissolve into factional fighting and accusations of "monarchistic" behavior in the second. For Reagan, whose success in the first term was based in part on his status as an outsider, this could be a particular hazard, should the public now hold him more responsible for the government he headed.

"You might have a problem," Teeter said. "People are beginning to believe that what's in place in Washington is Ronald Reagan's."

But Spencer, who had worked with Reagan the longest, argued, "He can pull it off. In 1970 he pulled it off. He ran against the fucking government he was running. I mean, he believes he's above it all. He believes it. That's why *they* believe it. I can't believe it. But they do."

The advisers who knew Ronald Reagan intimately may have joked privately about his deficiencies, but the image they presented to the public was completely different: Reagan appeared to be a decisive, self-confident, and unusually good-humored leader. Born eleven years into the twentieth century, America's oldest president seemed to be a reassuring link to a simpler past, an imaginary realm of small towns, wholesome values, and happy endings. Even those who helped to keep him in power, like Spencer, clearly didn't believe in all of Reagan's myths, but as he so acutely observed, the magic was that Reagan believed in them, and so he was extraordinarily good at inspiring the rest of the country to similarly suspend disbelief. His opponents tried to dismiss him as a mere actor memorizing lines, but this view underestimated Reagan's substantial skill as a professional trained in the dramatic art of make-believe.

It was a talent that he shared with many of his most successful predecessors in the White House, some of whom were scorned in language surprisingly similar to that used against Reagan, often by those who lacked the same gift. "If he was not the greatest president, he was the best actor in the presidency we have ever had," was the crabbed way in which John Adams dismissed George Washington. "Efficient government does not interest the people as much as dramatics," concluded a sour Herbert Hoover, explaining the popularity of Franklin Roosevelt. But in Reagan's case, there was a crucial difference. He was a master of stagecraft before he ever took up statecraft, blurring the line between the two professions. From the outside, the Reagan presidency looked like most others, if a bit more polished; but on the inside, it was like no other presidency in modern history.

Part of Reagan's success as a leader lay in the fact that most of the myths he created were preferable to reality. He told an affluent country beset by stubborn social ills that as far as "the complex problems we have been told are beyond our control" are concerned, there "are simple answers, just not easy ones." He said it was possible to have it all — to cut taxes and increase defense spending at the same time, to fight terrorism, roll back communism, and end the threat of nuclear war, all without risking American lives. Reagan seemed to be offering a miracle cure. Opponents and other experts warned that his remedies were suspect, delaying pain instead of dealing with its causes. But his performance was hard to beat. His advisers could afford to construct a strategy calling for him to coast; most people thought he had a great deal to coast on.

By midsummer 1984, when the campaign was under way in earnest, Reagan had confounded his critics and was by almost every measure riding high. He could boast of a dramatic economic recovery. When he entered office in 1981, unemployment stood at 7.5 percent, inflation topped a ravaging 12 percent, and interest rates seemed out of control. In his first year in office, Reagan overwhelmed Congress with his conservative agenda, enacting sweeping cuts in domestic spending and income taxes and winning the biggest peacetime buildup ever in the defense budget. By 1982, these steps (along with the Federal Reserve Board's tight money policy) had plunged the country into one of its deepest recessions, setting, at its worst, a postwar record of 10.6 percent unemployment.

But two years later, well in time for the election, the economy had bounced back, and Reagan seemed miraculously close to flattening the Phillips curve, the traditional economic principle posing a tradeoff between high inflation and high unemployment. Thanks to a growing work force, record numbers of Americans now held jobs. And for the first time in twenty years, partly because of the falling price of oil, the recovery was accompanied by low inflation. As long as the voters ignored the ballooning federal deficit (and the huge amounts of borrowed foreign capital funding it), Reagan had a domestic record virtually unassailable by the Democrats.

In foreign affairs, too, Reagan had foiled his critics' most potent charge: that he would be a trigger-happy warmonger. There were no foreign policy triumphs to point to by the end of the first term, but, more important for the campaign, American soldiers had been kept out of any lengthy war. Reagan could sound bellicose — he joked into a microphone in the summer of 1984 that he was about to bomb Russia — but in practice he had responded calmly to real provocation, such as the Soviets' shooting down of a Korean airliner in 1983. It would later be a cause of his undoing, but now this gap between rhetoric and reality was a campaign asset. Reagan could straddle the public's own conflicting desires between showing strength and conducting a risk-free foreign policy.

Reagan had also been spared the kind of humiliation that Jimmy Carter had suffered at the hands of Iran's Ayatollah Khomeini. Reagan drove this point home in 1984 by boasting, in a televised address on election eve, of a "new patriotism" that "began . . . when after 444 days our hostages came home from Iran to breathe American freedom again." The reference to Carter's hostage problem was fine for a quick political hit, but it was not a point that the White House wanted to push too far. In the final weeks of the campaign, for instance, the Reagan team made a TV commercial that showed rabid-looking Iranians shredding the U.S. flag and emphasized how far the United States had come. But White House chief of staff James Baker quietly spiked the ad, knowing that the truth about this complex issue was less of a selling point than the campaign rhetoric revealed. After all, pro-Iranian terrorists in Beirut had taken three U.S. citizens hostage in 1984, including the CIA's station chief, William Buckley.

To be sure, the Reagan administration had had some foreign policy setbacks. Just a year before the election, on October 23, 1983, 241 U.S. servicemen had been killed by a terrorist bomb in an ill-conceived "peace-keeping" mission in Beirut. But the public didn't seem to hold the president responsible, giving further currency to his reputation, in Colorado congresswoman Patricia Schroeder's phrase, as the Teflon president — nothing stuck to him. The hasty U.S. withdrawal from Beirut had left behind an unintended legacy of anti-American sentiment and as fecund an environment for terrorism as existed anywhere in the world. The problem would come back to haunt Reagan, but in 1984, the polls showed that the president's tough rhetoric, combined with his evident unwillingness to risk further U.S. bloodshed, almost perfectly mirrored the public's own contradictory impulses.

Reagan seemed to have what his 1976 campaign manager, John Sears, called "a perfect sense of the appropriate." He seemed to know instinctively how to stay in tune with the electorate and how to sidestep damage that could have ruined other politicians. Reagan's popularity didn't suffer when the barracks in Beirut were bombed, but it soared when the U.S.

invaded the Caribbean island of Grenada, just two days later. It was Grenada, not Beirut, which he revisited in his August speech to the Republican National Convention in Dallas. The victory over a small group of Communist insurgents in Grenada became a metaphor for nothing less than the country's willingness to overcome the paralysis regarding the use of force that had followed the Vietnam War. "America," the president proclaimed to the enthusiastic throng, "is standing tall."

As his campaign advisers had hoped, Reagan again proved his masterful ability to present a broad vision of a shining America. He seemed to float airily above specifics: in the final days before the election, former White House communications director David Gergen declared that "Reagan has become a father figure — he transcends the party." His popularity did seem to rise above and beyond partisan politics. This was not necessarily reflected in his job approval ratings. For the first two years of his term, Reagan had lower job approval ratings than any other president elected since World War II, including Jimmy Carter, according to statistics compiled by the Gallup poll. His standing recovered with the economy, and by January 1984, more than 50 percent of the public approved of the way he was conducting his presidency — higher than Richard Nixon's rating, but, surprisingly, still lower than either Carter's or Eisenhower's at a similar point in his presidency.

But Reagan seemed to share a strange kind of alchemy with the American public. It was visible in the tear-streaked faces of the cheerleaders who lined his parade routes, in the hurting farmers who said they'd vote for him despite their economic devastation, and in the southern Democrats who set aside traditions held since the Civil War and flocked to the party of Lincoln. Reagan evoked the romantic myth of American superiority, as old and powerful as the country itself. Reagan was larger than life, yet voters had an extraordinary affection for him as a man. They were inspired by his optimism, and they responded to his warmth and humor. They felt he was more trustworthy than other politicians. They thought he had backbone — whether they approved of his programs or not. Most of all, they respected the fact that he said what he meant, and meant what he said. By 1984, even his political opponents stopped trying to attack him directly.

The grace and humor Reagan showed after the attempt to assassinate him in 1981 had, more than any other single event, added a mythical quality to his leadership, revealing his character in a way that made it almost impossible to dislike him. This effect didn't escape the 1984 campaign team's notice. In a flash of black humor during the June 30 session, Spencer suggested that even with a weak political agenda, they might get lucky: "If he got a bullet in the toe, it would help the election."

Unable to define the future or even expound on present risks, by midsummer the Reagan campaign resorted to the political equivalent of mood music. Taking the cue, the campaign's "Tuesday Team" from Madison Avenue, whose members had marketed everything from Gallo wine to Pan American airlines, now churned out reels of feel-good ads. As an announcer intoned, "It's morning in America," Americans were shown bathed in butterscotch morning light, building skyscrapers, holding hands, and applauding the passing of the Olympic torch.

To bolster the campaign's broad theme of leadership, cinematic paeans to the Reagans were prepared for their introductions at the Republican National Convention in Dallas. The little films were so effective that the president became teary at the private screening of the eighteen-minute tribute to himself, and some of his Secret Service men blinked back tears of their own.

The First Lady was less pleased with the first attempt to capture her own legacy on film. Although it was widely known that she was obsessively concerned with her husband's image, she was evidently concerned about the image the public had of her as well. The campaign had proposed a six-minute tribute, but their subject found such brevity insulting; she wanted at least ten or twelve minutes. A delicate week-long battle ensued, with the campaign insisting that the president's wife couldn't be toasted for more than half as long as the president himself. Deputy chief of staff Michael Deaver, Mrs. Reagan's usual emissary in such matters, kept saying, "That's what the First Lady wants." A compromise was finally struck: eight minutes. With the extra time, the First Lady's staff added footage of a romantic scene she shared with Reagan from their 1955 movie, *Hellcats of the Navy*. They also added a track of Frank Sinatra crooning "Nancy with the Smiling Face."

On August 23, Reagan accepted his party's nomination with a speech that was in many respects the apogee of his campaign. The mood in the Dallas Convention Center was nothing short of ecstatic. At almost every pause, the crowd roared either "Four more years! Four more years!" or Olympic-inspired chants of "USA! USA!" Reagan's eyes sparkled, and his perfectly modulated voice resonated as he delivered an uplifting peroration that skillfully evoked all the pitfalls of the Carter-Mondale past without describing his own program for the future. His speech made no reference to any plans to cut government spending further — Social Security or otherwise. It made no explicit promise to continue the defense buildup. It never mentioned either Nicaragua or Lebanon. Instead, Reagan delivered a moving soliloquy on the Olympic games taking place that summer, likening the runners' torch to "another torch, the one that greeted so many of our parents and grandparents . . . Miss Liberty's torch." The speech wove together many strands of the nation's lore, entwining his presidency with hope, excellence, athleticism, and patriotism, and finally placing his reelection bid on a symbolic plane completely above partisan politics. It was everything the strategists of June 30 could have hoped for.

Some in the Reagan camp bridled at the notion that the most conservative president in the twentieth century was being packaged with a pitch that might just as easily have sold beer. Ken Khachigian later said, "I thought we needed to at least convey something of the sense that this election was an epic ideological conflict," he said. "For me, Walter Mondale is the Darth Vader of American politics. But instead of engaging him, we were just waltzing through the campaign. It was like we were heading for a dignified coronation."

But as the June 30 skull session had established, there was method to this vagueness. Behind the red, white, and blue bunting, not only was the Reagan camp short on new ideas, but the polls showed that support was eroding for most of the old ones. By 1984, fully a third of the voters approved of Reagan personally but disapproved of his policies. People were comfortable with the status quo, but didn't want to push the so-called Reagan Revolution further. The truth was that beneath the pleasing myths and images was a political foundation less solid than it seemed.

Reagan had become, in the words of political scientist William Schneider, "a victim of unintended consequences." The very success that Reagan enjoyed in the first term had, by 1984, undermined the conditions that brought him to power. Once alarmed over its perceived military weakness, the country now felt the defense buildup had been accomplished, and there was a growing eagerness for arms control. Similarly, the tide of antigovernment feeling that had swept Reagan into office had been replaced by a sense that domestic spending had been cut far enough. So, even as this hugely popular president coasted toward a massive electoral victory, the public was already moving beyond his first-term agenda.

Nowhere was public opinion less in tune with Reagan's policy than on the issue of Nicaragua. Reagan was deeply committed to supporting the contras, the rebel army, in their effort to overthrow the leftist Sandinista government, but his passion for their cause cast a shadow on the campaign's otherwise sunny picture of "morning in America." Richard Wirthlin, a presidential pollster who had been tracking public opinion on the subject for years, told others in the campaign that the issue was "pure poison." Khachigian recalled, "He would go bananas at just the mention of the word *contras*." By late 1983, an internal White House memo showed that only 37 percent of the public had heard or read anything about Nicaragua. But of those who had, only 18 percent supported Reagan's handling of the issue. The greatest problem by far was that nearly three quarters of those polled — and an even higher percentage of female voters — feared that the U.S. role in Nicaragua would lead to another Vietnam War.

For the duration of the campaign, therefore, Nicaragua became the site not only of covert operations, but also of a full-fledged covert foreign policy. When Langhorne A. "Tony" Motley was named assistant secretary of state for Latin American affairs in 1983, both Secretary of State George P. Shultz and White House chief of staff James A. Baker III made it clear that part of his job was to keep Central America from turning into a campaign issue.

In 1964, a weak opponent had allowed Lyndon B. Johnson to coast into a landslide, saying to voters, "I just want to tell you this, we're for a lot of things, and we're against mighty few." Barry Goldwater had been too weak to pin Johnson down on such specifics as his plans to escalate the Vietnam War. Similarly, in the final months before the 1972 election, George McGovern was so overpowered by the incumbent, Richard Nixon, that he never managed to make the issue of the Watergate burglary stick. In 1984, voters had a general sense of how Reagan felt about Nicaragua, but Mondale was likewise too weak to flush Reagan out on many specifics.

In the final weeks before the election, however, the unpopular war momentarily ruptured the carefully controlled campaign, causing some of the president's advisers to panic. On October 17, four days before Reagan's second debate with Mondale, the Associated Press reported that a training manual written by the CIA for the contras advocated the "selective use of violence [to] neutralize carefully selected and planned targets such as court judges, police, and state security officials." Clearly, the CIA was recommending assassination, a tactic prohibited by an executive order Reagan had signed in 1981.

In the presidential debate, reporter Georgie Ann Geyer asked the president, Didn't this amount to "our own, state-sponsored terrorism?" Reagan grew flustered and responded, "We have a gentleman down in Nicaragua who is on contract to the CIA, advising supposedly on military tactics of the contras. And he drew up this manual. It was turned over to the agency head — of the CIA in Nicaragua — to be printed. . . ." At a time when the CIA was legally barred by Congress from giving military aid to the rebels, the president's response raised more questions than it answered.

"Are you implying, then, that the CIA in Nicaragua is directing the contras?" Geyer asked.

The president flushed visibly and stammered, "I'm afraid I misspoke when I said a CIA head in Nicaragua. There is not someone there directing all of this activity."

Mondale made a halfhearted effort to keep the subject alive. But the president simply ignored his question, saying, "I have so many things to respond to, I'm going to pick out something you said earlier. . . ."

Well after midnight, pollster Wirthlin frantically began calling other top campaign aides. The numbers in his computerized tracking polls showed a hemorrhage of support among young voters, the prize catch of the new Reagan coalition. Wirthlin was sure it was because of Nicaragua. But by the next day, his fears subsided when it became clear that the consensus in the media was that the president had "won" the second and last presidential debate. The reason: his good comeback on a reporter's question about whether, at seventy-three, he was too old to handle the job. Reagan had gravely promised "not to make age an issue in this campaign." Then, after a perfectly timed pause, he deadpanned, "I am not going to exploit, for political purposes, my opponent's youth and inexperience."

On election day, three weeks after Reagan had assured the country that the CIA was not really playing a military role in Nicaragua, a little-known marine officer on the staff of the president's National Security Council met with a contra leader just across the street from the White House. The purpose of Oliver North's meeting in the Old Executive Office Building was to provide tactical military advice to the insurgents. But the debate, like the rest of the campaign, had proved that there was no need to tell the rest of the country what the White House was doing, or where it was going, in order to win. In fact, it was smarter politics not to.

Critics could carp about the hollow rhetoric, but no one could quibble with the results. The campaign strategy was unqualifiedly successful: by 11:07 P.M. EST on November 6, Ronald Reagan had swept forty-nine states, all but Walter Mondale's native Minnesota and the District of Columbia. The oldest president in U.S. history had convinced millions of young and blue-collar ethnic voters to sever their customary ties to the Democratic party. In terms of percentage, Reagan's margin of victory fell slightly short of earlier records set by Roosevelt in 1936, Johnson in 1964, and Nixon in 1972, but in absolute numbers of votes cast, both popular and in the electoral college, Reagan's reelection established new records.

No president since Dwight Eisenhower had achieved back-to-back landslides, and Reagan's triumph brought tremendous promise. The returns brought serious possibilities of a Republican realignment, altering the majority party status the Democrats had monopolized since Franklin Roosevelt's day. For the first time in twenty-eight years and after four failed presidencies, it seemed possible that the country's chief executive could once again be both popular and effective. "The idea that the job was too big for one person has little currency now," wrote *Time* magazine's columnist on the presidency, Hugh Sidey, in a tribute printed in the official inauguration guidebook. "We enter these next four years with the knowledge that the presidency works."

Like the earlier record landslides of Roosevelt, Johnson, and Nixon, Reagan's victory conferred a sense of limitless mandate on his followers. History cautioned that such victories could be dangerous. They tended to bring both opportunity and hubris, a heady but combustible combination. Roosevelt stumbled in his second term when he tried to pack the Supreme Court; Johnson expanded an unpopular war; and Nixon tried to operate above the law. In 1984, some of the same temptations were already in the air. On election night, when the Republican faithful in Washington crammed into the Shoreham Hotel to watch Reagan's acceptance speech live from Los Angeles, "there was an incredible feeling of invincibility," recalled Mary Jo Jacobi, a former White House aide. "I think we misread it from the start," she added later. "We had this historic landslide, and everyone, depending on their own bias, thought it meant something different. The ideological people thought it meant the president could do anything. That's when the hubris problem began."

Out on the West Coast, the Reagans had dined for good luck at the Bel Air home of the industrialist and longtime supporter Earle M. Jorgensen and his wife, just as they had the night of the 1980 election. Now, the huge dimension of the landslide brought both a sense of relief and a renewed feeling of power. Nancy Reagan, exhausted from the wear and tear of the campaign and nursing a lump on the head she'd suffered after tripping in an unfamiliar hotel bedroom the night before, wore her most gracious smile at a cocktail party for big backers in the luxurious Tower of the Century Plaza Hotel. But later, she confided to a longtime aide that she and Reagan had "swallowed enough and taken enough." The aide recalled her saying, "From now on, we're going to do it our way."

They wasted little time: that night, breaking tradition, Reagan didn't pay tribute to Mondale in his acceptance speech. Newspaper accounts the next day suggested that it had been an oversight. But Reagan had been so angered by Mondale's final attacks, characterizing him as old and disengaged, that he told his speechwriters he wanted to see how gracious Mondale's concession speech was before striking a conciliatory tone himself. The Mondale bow — "We didn't win, but we did make history" — didn't pass the test in Reagan's eyes, and with forty-nine states on his side, he was going to play by his own rules. The next morning, taking needling questions from reporters about when his next press conference would be, the president was clearly savoring the spoils of victory. With a winning smile, he said, "Look, I won. I don't have to subject myself. . . ."

Before the celebrating was even over, however, John Sears, Reagan's incisive former campaign manager, concluded that Reagan was in for a very tough term because of the kind of campaign it had been. "If you're very popular," he later explained, "you can seduce yourself into thinking that the best way to get reelected is to traffic on what's popular already, and not say anything else. But you get real power by sharing with voters what you want to do — and then afterward being able to tell Congress, the press, and the bureaucrats: 'Well, I told them I was going to do this, and they voted for me.' In 1984," he said, "there was none of that."

Some members of Reagan's entourage were affected by a strange kind of letdown. Campaign manager Ed Rollins, who had first joined forces with Reagan in 1980, felt unexpectedly depressed the morning after the election. In part, it was the thudding realization that the last Reagan campaign was over. But there was also a sinking sensation that reality, which had been so gloriously suspended during the campaign, was about to return with a vengeance. The administration's future seemed disturbingly unsettled. "We'd run an issueless campaign," Rollins recalled later. "There was no second-term plan. During the time when they should have been thinking one up, the White House was practically paralyzed."

But the president felt "invigorated and completely at peace with himself," according to an aide. He had forty-nine states and a wide-open future. Many serious and intelligent advisers had supported the idea of a vague campaign; it was their theory that once Reagan had proven his popularity, they would have more clout and plenty of time to define the next term's agenda.

Reagan's national security adviser, Robert C. "Bud" McFarlane, was among those aides who saw the landslide as an enormous opportunity. The first term had been devoted largely to domestic concerns, but McFarlane felt it would now be possible to press for some of the foreign policy goals that had previously been deferred. On a bright November morning only a few days after the election, he drove up to the president's ranch in the Santa Ynez Mountains north of Santa Barbara, his hopes high.

Although Reagan was resting up from the strenuous final weeks of the campaign, McFarlane brought with him a thick black binder. Intended for the president's eyes only, it contained a detailed list of foreign policy initiatives for the president to consider in setting the goals for his second term. It was by any measure an extraordinary selection: a dozen ambitious proposals ranging from holding a summit with the Soviet Union to seeking to establish an Asian common market, from reopening the Middle East peace process to attempting to reverse the economic decline in Western Europe.

McFarlane was excited at the prospect of taking on these important projects. The achievement of any one of them, he thought, would be a triumph of statecraft and would provide the foreign policy coup that had eluded the Reagan administration so far. But McFarlane was also experienced enough to know that no president, no matter how powerful, could successfully break ground in more than two or three areas; if he tried to do too much, he would inevitably spread himself too thin. Reagan would have to choose.

Certainly, there could be no better time. The campaign was over, Reagan dominated the political landscape. But if he wanted to put his stamp on foreign policy, the president had to make hard choices now, before the aura of the landslide vanished and the reality of his lame duck status, which had so crippled other second-term presidents in the postwar period, set in. To underscore the point, McFarlane added a note to the binder. In his usual deferential prose, he explained that in the weeks before the election, he and Secretary of State George Shultz had drafted a list of "possible achievements for your second term." Because of their complexity, "we'd invite your identifying two or three at most."

McFarlane left the packet with the president's military aide. Not until the end of the week, on the trip back to Washington aboard *Air Force One*, did he get a response. As he opened the familiar black binder, his heart sank. There, scrawled in the margin in the president's unmistakable hand, was the reply: "Let's do them all!"

The sentiment was charmingly optimistic — but breathtakingly naive. Trained as a marine to follow the military chain of command, he wondered what direction to take. It was as if Reagan actually believed that government could be run on the airy rhetoric of the campaign that had lifted the entire government into a bright and cloudless sky. As McFarlane scanned the binder for some hint of presidential guidance, he came to a realization: if a clear foreign policy was ever going to be set, "I'll just have to do it myself."

2

The No-Hands Presidency

IN THE HEADY DAYS after the 1984 election, Bud McFarlane was not the only presidential adviser with his own plans for Reagan's second term. Treasury Secretary Donald T. Regan, a man with an uncommonly keen appetite for power, had his eye on an even more influential job. Even before the campaign was over, Regan had begun work on a plan that would enable him to swap jobs with the White House chief of staff, James Baker, the man closest to the president on a daily basis. The way Regan planned his own promotion to the most critical job in the administration — without consulting the president whose alter ego he was to become — explained precisely why the changing of the palace guard was among the most decisive events of the second term.

Regan, like many others, recognized that the president was the sort of leader who delegated a great deal of authority to those immediately around him. As secretary of the treasury, he had been surprised to find that the president never once talked with him privately or explained his economic goals beyond the broad phrases of campaign rhetoric. In Reagan's permissive White House, policymaking was literally up for grabs; proximity to the president was tantamount to power itself. Regan understood this early on: more than three years before the swap took place, he had already begun to eye the top White House staff job, confiding to a trusted Treasury aide that Baker had the only perch he considered "better" than his own. As the second term began, Regan saw his opportunity and took it.

On November 7, the day after Reagan was reelected, his advisers specifically denied that there would be a second-term house cleaning. The last president elected to a second term, Richard Nixon, had immediately and dramatically reasserted his authority by demanding the resignation of every member of his cabinet. But Jim Baker told inquiring reporters that Reagan had no plans for any kind of staff change. "He doesn't want to break up a winning team," Baker said. "That means everybody."

Nine days later, however, Regan deftly planted the idea of trading places when Baker confided that he was dispirited. The treasury secretary suggested, "You know, the trouble with you is that you're tired. . . . We should swap jobs — that would serve both of us right." His tone was light, but his intentions were serious.

Regan's ambitions might have gone nowhere had it not been for Nancy Reagan. Thanks in no small part to the First Lady, Baker was already looking for a way out of the White House. As patrician as Texans come, Baker was both too smart and too genteel ever to discuss it publicly, but two of his closest confidants said that her constant complaints and commands had made his job, already difficult, nearly impossible. Mrs. Reagan had pushed Baker, his confidants later said, beyond the point of no return after the president's disastrous performance in the first of two debates with Walter Mondale. The president had fallen into a rare but deep slump over his meandering performance. Mrs. Reagan, in turn, became fearful and enraged, excoriating those who had prepared her husband for "brutalizing him" with too many facts. Baker and his aides became primary targets of her wrath.

Mrs. Reagan's barrage struck Baker at the wrong time. For four years he had served the president well. But the endless hours had taken their toll; Baker was so exhausted that he'd even considered becoming commissioner of baseball just to get a break. The criticism now coming from the president's wife was more than he cared to take. Her tirade, he told others, crystalized a hard truth for him: in the White House all staff members, no matter how talented or devoted, were ultimately expendable. Many felt this particularly keenly in the Reagan White House, where the president — though charming and amiable — was always remote, an unknowable star, a man who formed few lasting attachments. And his wife, as one senior adviser conceded, "viewed us all as servants — some were house servants and some were field hands — but we all had dirty fingernails."

Baker may also have sensed that the bumpy ride toward the end of the campaign foreshadowed what would undoubtedly be a rough second term. Others had evidently had the same premonition: many of the brightest lights of the first term — including Office of Management and Budget director David Stockman and Baker's assistant, Richard Darman — were similarly anxious to leave. Ed Rollins, looking back, suggested a reason: "The last thing they wanted to do was spend four more years in the White House. They could see the size of the deficit, and they knew Reagan wasn't going to raise taxes and Congress wasn't going to cut much more spending. They thought that the whole thing was just going to crash and burn."

So Baker was immediately interested in Regan's proposal, and by Thanksgiving he had fully endorsed the swap — apparently feeling no more need to inform the president than Regan had. In a series of meetings, one at Baker's house, the two men worked out the fine points. Regan would become chief of staff, retain his cabinet status, and take a seat, as Baker would, on the National Security Council. Baker would become treasury secretary. Eventually, they were joined in their discussions by Baker's ally, deputy chief of staff Michael Deaver. And they agreed that Deaver would sell the plan to the Reagans.

All of the pieces of the swap were in place in mid-December, yet it would be almost a month before the president was informed. It was a time when news accounts described the White House as "curiously drifting" and the president's top advisers as "sleepwalking." Budget preparations were weeks behind schedule, and it was already clear that it would be very difficult to live up to the president's recent promise to reduce the federal deficit to $100 billion by the time he left office in 1989. The White House seemed confused about the Treasury Department's recently released tax overhaul plan, changing its position almost daily. Old hands wondered why so little planning was being done for the State of the Union address. Pundits warned that these early months were crucial if Reagan was to take control of the political agenda — always a struggle for second-term presidents. It would be especially difficult in 1984 because, despite the landslide, Reagan had actually lost two Republican seats in the Senate and now commanded only a narrow 53–47 majority (the House remained a fortress of Democratic opposition). Four years earlier, the first hundred days of the first term had been a frenzy of planning. Thanks to Baker and his staff, the administration had seized the initiative and put its stamp on economic policy for years to come. But after Reagan's reelection, the days slid by, with the president strangely quiescent.

Deaver was waiting to make his move, his eye not so much on the president as the First Lady. He knew that Reagan would do almost anything to avoid personnel conflicts; he had once required the family lawyer (and later attorney general) William French Smith to settle a dispute with a troublesome maid. But Deaver also knew that Mrs. Reagan was as active in these matters as her husband was not. He wanted to wait until just the right moment, after the Reagans had had time to relax with their friends over the New Year's holiday in Palm Springs. "The timing was left up to Deaver," said one participant in the plan, "and he specifically wanted to cut the First Lady out as long as possible." As for the president, Regan later recalled thinking at the time, "He's tired. Why bring this one up?"

In the end, Deaver informed Mrs. Reagan before he told her husband, according to two others familiar with the process. Her reaction was favorable. And so back in Washington, on the morning of Monday, January 7, at the beginning of a busy week when Secretary of State Shultz and Soviet foreign minister Andrei Gromyko were set to announce resumed arms control talks, Deaver finally broke the news to Reagan in the Oval Office.

"Mr. President," Deaver recalled saying of Regan, "I've finally found you a playmate your own age."

Reagan's reaction was not to ask how the critical deal had been arranged, or why he hadn't been consulted earlier, or even what the merits were. Instead, he asked only, "Do you think Don [Regan] would do it?" Just as four years earlier he had agreeably accepted Deaver's and his wife's recommendation of Baker as his first White House chief of staff, Reagan raised few questions now. He told Deaver he wanted to think about it overnight. But soon Regan and Baker were ushered into his office. Regan briefly explained the audacious plan. The president asked no questions. "Reagan nodded affably," Regan later recalled. "He looked at Baker and Deaver as if to check the expressions on their faces, but asked them no questions either." Regan was baffled. "He seemed to be absorbing a fait accompli rather than making a decision."

Reagan's casual acceptance of a shake-up involving two of the most sensitive positions in his administration was emblematic of his operating style. It was this remarkably passive approach to running the most powerful office in the Western world that made the matter of who was at his elbow almost as important as who won the election. The chief of staff's job derives all of its power from presidential delegation; in the Reagan White House, the job was enormous.

Reagan was unabashed about delegating many of the daily responsibilities of the presidency. When he cared deeply about an issue, he was outspoken and stubborn. His views were often strong, even radical. But his involvement in day-to-day governance — the actual running of the country — was slight. Since his days in Sacramento, he'd grown accustomed to letting others translate his goals into programs, much in the same way that he'd allowed others to run the 1984 campaign. Reagan portrayed this as a deliberate "management style," explaining to *Fortune* magazine (in an interview that pleased him more than most) that "I believe that you surround yourself with the best people you can find, delegate authority, and don't interfere."

Others in the office had delegated where possible, but Reagan's style of governing was unlike that of any other postwar president — each of whom had, in different ways, been strong chief executives who dominated not just the formation of policy but also its implementation. To a great extent, Reagan left the job of implementing his ideas to others —

shunning personnel issues, rarely engaging in discussions about congressional strategy, and routinely following his subordinates' advice on media plans. Instead, he mastered the ceremonial and symbolic functions of the office so that he could act presidential even when he wasn't, in the traditional sense, functioning like one.

Reagan's day generally began between 7:00 and 8:00 A.M., when the White House operator would put through a wake-up call. By nine o'clock, after a light breakfast and a glimpse at the morning papers and television news shows, Reagan would ride the elevator downstairs from the second floor of the 132-room residence to the State Floor. There, a cadre of Secret Service agents would escort him out across the flagstone colonnade bordering the Rose Garden, past a well-disguised emergency box containing an extra pistol, and on through the armored door of the Oval Office. His chief of staff would greet him, and they would sit down for his first meeting of the day. If it was cold, the stewards would have a fire blazing; in the summertime, they would have already plumped the pillows on the wrought-iron chaises that graced the patio outside.

By the time he arrived in the Oval Office, Reagan had usually memorized most of the lines he would deliver in his public appearances that day. His nearly photographic recall — sharpened by his training as an actor — was an enormous asset. The night before, at seven, the staff would have sent an usher to the residence with a packet of the next day's instructions — whom he'd be meeting, for how long, and what he was expected to say. On carefully typed index cards, the staff composed most of his remarks, down to the greetings and banter. They wrote out stage directions as well — where to turn and when. (One such cue card was accidentally released publicly, directing Reagan to greet a member of his own cabinet and identifying him as the gentleman sitting under Coolidge's portrait.)

Reagan carried the cards with him when he came into the office in the morning, informing the staff of any changes he thought should be made. The cards were coded by size and filed by color: green for unclassified action, yellow for unclassified information, red for classified information, white for his statements. He had one size for his breast pocket, another, always folded in two, for his outside pocket. Longer remarks were typed in large print on what he called "half sheets." The president used these cards, not only for large meetings, but also for small gatherings of regulars, such as the congressional leaders, whom he usually saw weekly. Frequently he used cards to introduce members of his own cabinet, and, in one instance, he relied on them during a ceremony honoring James Brady, the press secretary wounded beside him in the 1981 assassination attempt. He also had "phone memos," which spelled out what his end of telephone conversations should be and left space for him to jot down what the interlocutor said, so that the staff could keep

track. As he moved from one event to another, his staff first gave him
a briefing on every move he would make. Over the years, many advisers
tried to convince Reagan to dispense with his cue cards, but, conceded Regan, for the president "they were sort of like Linus's blue
blanket."

By the standards of most other presidents, Reagan's office hours
weren't long. After a 9:00 A.M. meeting with his chief of staff, Reagan
attended a nine-thirty national security briefing with his national security
adviser, the chief of staff, and frequently the vice president. After that
the schedule varied, though usually the staff tried to give the president
some private time late in the morning for reading; after lunch, some
aides like David Stockman learned to avoid scheduling important business because the president was prone to nodding off. He was often finished for the day by four o'clock, and he usually took both Wednesday
and Friday afternoons off. But he was organized and orderly in his
habits. He spent about an hour almost every day lifting weights in the
private gym — a habit developed under doctor's orders after the 1981
assassination attempt. Where other presidents grew gray in office, Reagan managed to put an inch and a half of muscle on his chest, and he
loved to have visitors feel the tone of his biceps. Inside the Oval Office,
though, Reagan was formal. He felt awed enough to say "I couldn't take
my jacket off in this office," and aides said he never did. They also said
he never left at the end of the day without first straightening his desk —
a great slab of dark wood as imposing as its donor, Queen Victoria,
who had it made for Rutherford B. Hayes from the timbers of the H.M.S.
Resolute.

At the end of the day, Reagan usually returned upstairs with paperwork
and spent the evening with his wife — both in their pajamas, eating
supper from trays in his study, reading, studying the next day's lines,
and watching television. Nancy Reagan said her husband generally fell
asleep within minutes of going to bed, usually around 11:00 P.M. Just
before he did, he would alert the thirty-six-person domestic staff, one
of whom would then quietly turn off any remaining lights in the family
quarters.

But Reagan was more complicated than liberal caricatures would suggest. He liked to joke about his image, using such lines as: "I hear hard
work's never killed anyone, but I figure, why take a chance?" Yet those
around him found to their surprise that he could be diligent — even
compulsive — in performing the tasks they gave him. He was always
immaculately dressed, and he was so punctual that he could time a statement or an appearance down to the second. His delivery and stage presence were honed by years of training. He would follow his daily schedule
meticulously, drawing a line through each completed event with an arrow
pointing to the next, exactly the way screen actors mark off completed

scenes on a script. The president brought self-discipline and myriad skills to the White House; they simply were not the skills usually associated with the job.

Reagan's self-confidence was an important part of his appeal. In a complex world, he trusted his instincts, frequently to surprisingly successful effect. Although he occasionally worried about appearing ill informed in front of experts, he was generally relaxed about his ability to handle the job, perhaps because, as he once explained to Deaver, he thoroughly believed that "God has a plan for me." The American public is especially intolerant of hesitation in its presidents, and Reagan simply wasn't agonized by self-doubt, as Carter had been. Nor was he needlessly concerned with controlling minor aspects of the office. Early on, Jimmy Carter's chief of staff Jack Watson had warned that by getting involved in too much, Carter was risking blame for too much. No one needed to give that lecture to Reagan. Both his strength and his weakness rested in an ability to leave the details to others.

White House communications director David Gergen had marveled at Reagan's similarity in this respect to Dwight Eisenhower, whom Reagan admired. But the Princeton historian Fred Greenstein, in his groundbreaking reassessment of the Eisenhower era, has termed Eisenhower's a "hidden-hand presidency" and has suggested that the former military commander ran his administration more forcefully than was immediately visible. By contrast, Reagan's rule bordered — far more than anyone wanted to admit — on a no-hands presidency.

A fundamental contradiction lay at the heart of the Reagan presidency: in public Reagan pursued the ideological agenda of an activist, but in the Oval Office he was just the opposite. As long as his record of achievements seemed strong, the way he ran the White House did not seem to matter to much of the press and the voting public. But many of those who worked on the inside — close enough to observe the inner workings of the presidency under these strange conditions — were privately astounded.

They found that Reagan was not just passive, he was sometimes entirely disengaged. He did not delegate in the usual sense; he did not actively manage his staff by assigning tasks and insisting on regular progress reports. Instead, he typically gave his subordinates little or no direction. Usually, he provided the broad rhetoric and left them to infer what he wanted. When it came to the fine points of governing, he allowed his staff to take the lead. "He made almost no demands and gave almost no instructions," conceded former adviser Martin Anderson. "Essentially, he just responded to whatever was brought before his attention." He seemed to have unquestioning trust in many of the small and large decisions others made for him — and when his staff could not reach a decision, he frequently made none either unless events forced him to do so. As Ed Rollins, who worked with Reagan for five years, concluded, "The job was whatever was on his desk."

Reagan's former campaign manager, John Sears, attributed this trait to Reagan's first career, as a movie actor in an age when the studios discouraged independent thinking. As such, Sears noted, Reagan had become professionally accustomed to learning his part and "following the prescribed rules — doing what they told you to do." If something went wrong on the set, Sears said, Reagan would most likely think, Hey, I'm just the star. I'm the performer. Others were supposed to worry about the rest of the show.

This complacency was evident in cabinet and staff meetings, where Reagan was a wonderful raconteur — frequently speaking as if he were still governor of California — as well as a good listener. But he rarely made substantive points. A staff member who had also served in the Ford White House said, "Ford led the discussion; Reagan followed it." When the public began to learn of Reagan's lack of involvement in meetings, aides explained it by saying the president wanted to hide his thought process in order to avoid leaks or that he was trying to spare the feelings of those with whom he disagreed. But, as Don Regan later admitted, Reagan "sent out no strong signals. It was a rare meeting in which he made a decision or issued an order."

If the president rarely played the leading role in meetings, his aides found he was even less likely to question the paperwork they sent him. Reagan obligingly read whatever he was given — all of it — at least in the early years. One aide early on was surprised to find that the president was staying up until the early hours of the morning trying to read all the materials his staff had sent him. "He read indiscriminately," the aide marveled. "If you gave him eight hundred pages, he read every word. He used no judgment." Nancy Reagan finally stepped in and explained that her husband's workload needed to be reduced. Similarly, the staff had to monitor the amount of information they sent him to prepare for press conferences. As former communications director David Gergen recalled, "If you gave him too many pages, as good as his photographic memory is, he tries so hard to remember what he read that he sometimes gets mixed up." He was particularly susceptible to whatever arguments he had heard most recently. White House spokesman Larry Speakes used to joke that "the last thing you put in is the first thing that comes out."

Unlike other presidents, Reagan seldom requested information beyond the briefings and talking points his aides gave him. He enjoyed occasional luncheons with outside experts when they were brought in, but he rarely initiated invitations. He watched what Regan later called "a lot" of television and read a number of newspapers, although he claimed, possibly for effect, that he turned first to the comics. He was quite impressionable, particularly when it came to such arch-conservative publications as *Human Events*. After Reagan had seen it, Regan later said, "the goddamnedest things would come out of him — we had to watch what he read." He took great interest in the clippings and letters people sent him in the mail: one senior aide estimated that he opened more than half of his fifteen-minute national security briefings by reading selections from them.

Despite his position and power, Reagan often appeared to be living in contented isolation. Nancy Reagan was an inveterate telephone talker, and, in addition to acting as her husband's eyes and ears, she would occasionally put him on the line. But the president rarely initiated calls unless his staff asked him to. Nor did he keep in touch in other ways with those who were reputedly his oldest friends and advisers, on or off the White House staff. Holmes Tuttle, one of the few surviving members of Reagan's original California kitchen cabinet — the informal group of millionaires who financed his early campaigns — was usually advertised as one of the president's best friends. "We've had many years of togetherness," Tuttle affirmed. Yet when pressed he admitted, "No, he doesn't ask for advice. And as for picking up the phone and calling me, no." Similarly, Reagan's closest political friend in Washington, former Nevada senator Paul Laxalt, conceded that despite having known Reagan since 1964, "campaigning together, socializing together, camping together. . . . Do we talk about personal matters? Not at all."

Even on purely physical terms, Reagan's operating style was passive. Although he had 59 rooms in which to roam in the West Wing alone, he seldom ventured far beyond the Oval Office. In part, it was a necessary fact of life after the 1981 assassination attempt. Much as Eisenhower's schedule was restricted after his heart attack in 1955, the Secret Service became a protective wall around the president after the 1981 shooting, inevitably limiting his movement. He attended cabinet and congressional meetings and delivered speeches in the rooms set aside for those activities, but one senior White House official doubted whether, beyond these ceremonial rooms, the press room, and the barber shop, he knew his way around the West Wing complex. He even seemed unsure about the location of most of his aides' offices, and he only visited his chief of staff, who worked a few yards down the hall, two or three times a year on special occasions, like birthdays.

Likewise, White House officials rarely wandered into the Oval Office except on official, prescribed business. In the second term only six officials — the chief of staff, the vice president, the national security adviser, the military aide, the White House doctor, and the president's personal aide — had walk-in privileges, meaning they could see the president without an appointment. And even those who could drop in seldom did so, in part because the president's workday wasn't all that long, and his time was filled by an unusually large number of ceremonial functions.

A telling example of Reagan's isolation came out of the Iran-contra hearings, when the White House counsel's office tallied all the time the president had spent alone with his national security adviser, John Poindexter. The total — over eleven months and twenty-three days — came to eighty-one minutes.

The obvious danger was that Reagan could easily lose touch with political reality. It was always a peril of the office. As Woodrow Wilson noted, "Things get very lonely in Washington sometimes. The real voice of the great people of America sometimes sounds faint and distant in that strange city." But for Reagan, the hazard was exacerbated by his personality, which habitually screened out discord in order to paint the rosiest possible picture. One of his own children confided that "he makes things up and believes them." As a former senior White House official said, "He has this great ability to build these little worlds and then live in them."

In the first term, the single greatest safeguard against the president's losing touch was a staff structure as unusual as the president it served, an odd system that came to be known as the troika. It consisted of an uneasy triumvirate of top White House advisers — three extremely different men, with extremely different views and backgrounds — who policed not only each other but, in the process, the president too.

Chief of staff James A. Baker, a Princeton graduate, was the scion of one of Houston's most distinguished families, a former "Tory" Democrat who converted to the GOP in time to become under secretary of commerce for Gerald Ford and campaign manager for George Bush in 1980. A dealmaker in pin stripes, he was as smooth as any political operator in Washington. Unlike Donald Regan, who would take his place, he enjoyed the hurly-burly of politics — having made an unsuccessful run for attorney general of Texas in 1978 — and counting a handful of congressmen and senators among his close friends. He never gained the trust of the president's more conservative backers for being too "pragmatic," but the alliances he forged so skillfully in Congress were the backbone of the first term's many legislative successes.

Deputy chief of staff Michael Deaver, the son of a gas station owner at the edge of the Mojave Desert, had come to know the Reagans through his administrative work for the Republican party in California. Uninterested in the substance of policy, he'd proved a master at the imperative of the eighties: producing the presidency for television. He had a sixth sense about how to play to Reagan's strengths and cover his weaknesses. And, more than any other White House hand, he understood how to deal personally with the president and his wife; legend had it that he'd once run through a glass door in his eagerness to retrieve a purse that Mrs. Reagan had left behind. Having spent all but four months of the previous nineteen years serving them, he was one of the few people who knew how to tell both of the Reagans when they were wrong and get away with it — a skill that would be lost to the White House with his departure.

Edwin Meese, the presidential counselor who would soon be attorney general, had attended Yale as an undergraduate and law school at the University of California at Berkeley; he went on to serve as deputy district attorney in California's Alameda County. Active in crushing the student demonstrations at Berkeley in the sixties, he had a fascination with law enforcement all his life. In Sacramento, he'd been Reagan's chief of staff, and in the White House he ran the Office of Policy Development. Though the office was ridiculed for its bureaucratic inefficiency and arch-conservative agenda, it nonetheless played an important role by translating Reagan's views into programs — a function largely abandoned with Meese's departure. If Baker was the political expert and Deaver the loyal retainer, Meese was the conservative conscience.

Many complained that the troika system was divisive and inefficient, since none of the three men could make a decision on his own. But in their jealousy, each helped ensure that before the president put his imprimatur on a decision, either there was a rare consensus or he heard all their views. The system was built on mutual distrust and, although no one said so, on the premise of an impressionable president vulnerable to whatever argument he heard last.

Each member of the troika thus spent much energy trying to neutralize the others. For instance, when in 1982 Meese got Reagan to back the Treasury and Justice departments' move to reestablish tax-exempt status for racially segregated schools, Deaver, recognizing the racist image it could give the administration, went into high gear. He successfully shepherded the few blacks serving in the White House into the Oval Office to change Reagan's mind.

At times the troika worked as a protective shield around the president, preventing interlopers from getting too close to him. Baker and Deaver, for instance, often became temporary allies in the fight against CIA director William J. Casey and other "hard-liners" on foreign affairs. After each of Casey's visits to the Oval Office, Deaver would saunter in casually and ask the president, "Did Bill have anything interesting to say?" Reagan would naturally tell his loyal retainer, and if the news was alarming, Deaver would notify Baker. Together they would then marshal some expert to make a counterargument — a congressman, family member, or longtime backer — to try to turn Reagan around. One issue given special surveillance was Casey's promotion of the secret war in Nicaragua, which Deaver believed "played to Reagan's dark side" in a dangerous way.

Baker had an equally great distrust of those serving as national security adviser — a post with a long history of back door communications aimed at getting the president's support. Baker attended the 9:30 A.M. national security meetings with the president and McFarlane. Even though Baker and McFarlane got along well, if the president nodded appreciatively during the briefing, as was his habit, Baker, according to a senior NSC aide, made a point of tracking McFarlane down later and saying, "If you think that was a go-ahead, think again."

Baker's deputy, Richard Darman, a skilled bureaucrat who had served in four federal agencies since 1971, set up what he proudly called "an authoritarian system" to monitor the NSC and others who sent paperwork to the president. The president's Out box became Darman's In box. If the president was out of the Oval Office and received, for instance, emergency correspondence elsewhere, Darman demanded that he get a facsimile immediately. If something was sent to the Executive Residence after hours, he insisted that the White House ushers deliver a copy to him by seven-thirty the next morning. The system was rigorous, but it wasn't foolproof.

One breakdown of the system resulted in the Strategic Defense Initiative. Two of the president's old political backers, Joseph Coors and Karl Bendetsen, managed to slip the nuclear scientist Edward Teller in to see Reagan without explaining to Baker and Deaver what the meeting was about. By the time Teller was done, the president had become a fervent convert to the untested and perhaps unfeasible notion that a shield could be built against nuclear weapons. It was a utopian concept that privately struck many of Reagan's arms control advisers as crazy; some privately rolled their eyes and called it "the dream." But once Teller had reached Reagan, the dream was policy.

When it worked, however, the troika forced Reagan to be exposed to diversity. Even if he raised no questions about an issue, his battling aides would. Moreover, they frequently forced him to play an active part in policy disputes. Ordinarily, a president would naturally serve this function, but as White House aide Johnathan Miller concluded, "Reagan is like a great race horse that performs well when you have a jockey that knows how to use a whip. If you don't use the whip, he'll just loaf." The troika wielded the crop that kept both the government and the president running.

Of course, Reagan wasn't completely pliant, as his first budget director, David Stockman, learned when he asked him to raise taxes. But those who knew him best, like John Sears, discovered that "you can't argue with him on the general, but on the precise you can see a tremendous amount of malleability." This characteristic inspired a maneuver that some staff members called "the Reagan argument." Its purpose was to persuade the president to change stubbornly held views by convincing him, in the face of contradictory evidence, that a switch in policy was only a change in tactics, not principles.

In order to make "Reagan arguments," former labor secretary William Brock recalled, senior advisers kept "Reagan files" — clips documenting his earlier stands, which could be marshaled to support whatever new position was being considered. Thus, levying $14 billion in new corporate taxes, which Reagan opposed on strong philosophical grounds, could be sold to him as "closing loopholes" in the Treasury's initial 1984 tax reform plan. Government surcharges on the price of gas could be sold, not as tax increases at all, but as "user fees" for highway use. The conservative social agenda — abortion, school prayer, and the other high-risk moral issues — was not being neglected, it was being postponed, so that his top priority, the economic program, would not be compromised.

By 1984, the more able advisers were masters of the technique. They liked to think they were saving Reagan from his own excesses — and frequently they were. But in the process, they ran the risk of manipulating the facts to fit their argument, politicizing intelligence, stretching rhetoric, and deluding a president not given to performing rigorous analysis of issues.

The troika also mastered techniques for managing the president in public. From Reagan's earliest days in politics, his advisers always feared the unpredictable results of his "going live." Although his aides never told him, they had engineered his most famous 1980 primary triumph — his insistence on opening a New Hampshire debate to all the candidates, not just front-runner George Bush — partly as a damage control manuever. It was clear by the time of the debate that Reagan would win a narrow victory if nothing went wrong. But with Reagan, as his campaign aide James Lake explained seven years later, "if he went one-on-one against George Bush, there was a fifty-fifty chance he'd screw up." So they invited the other candidates, knowing that "if there were six guys, the risk would be spread out to one in six."

In the White House, Reagan's aides continued to limit his live exposure. They dispensed with an earlier idea of having him hold frequent "mini–press conferences," invented a rule trying to ban press questions at the daily "photo opportunities," and vetoed various proposed give-and-takes with youth groups because, as White House spokesman Larry Speakes explained, "he was too loose." Of course, spontaneous exchanges were sometimes unavoidable, but when the president's comments strayed too far afield, the White House press office sometimes managed to clean up his oral meanderings before a text was released for public consumption, thus altering the historical record along the way. In an Oval Office interview with the *Wall Street Journal*, in February 1985, for instance, Reagan mentioned that he had been talking "just this morning" about the biblical Armageddon. Some fundamentalists believe that it refers to an impending nuclear war, a provocative (and to some unnerving) notion for the president to entertain. "I don't know whether you know," he said with animation, "but a great many theologians over a number of years . . . have been struck with the fact that in recent years, as in no other time in history, have most of these prophecies been coming together." When the official transcript of the interview was released, the comments about Armageddon were gone. The White House later suggested that they had been "accidentally" omitted.

Similarly, his aides went to great lengths to conceal potentially embarrassing quirks. They were secretive about such matters as the president's and his daughter Maureen's apparently sincere belief that a ghost haunted the Lincoln Bedroom (Maureen claimed it had a "red aura"), the president's assertion that he had seen a flying saucer, and his acquiescence to Mrs. Reagan's reliance on astrology to determine his schedule.

Press access to the president was more tightly controlled than ever before, but complaints from journalists stirred little sympathy, perhaps because the problem was as old as the office. The question of how open the presidency should be to the public in this most democratic of governments was contentious right from the start. When George Washington announced that he would open his doors to the general public only twice a week, one senator fumed, "For him to be seen only in public on stated times, like an eastern Lama, would be . . . offensive." Despite such grousing, the presidency has grown progressively more closed to public inspection ever since. Herbert Hoover was the last president to set aside time once a week to receive any citizen who wanted to shake his hand. After that, the public had to rely on the press to serve as its eyes and ears — and there, too, access was progressively narrowed. Franklin Roosevelt used to give two press conferences a week, Eisenhower averaged more than two a month. Kennedy turned his frequent news conferences into witty jousting matches and took some members of the press into his closest confidence, getting protection in the bargain. But Reagan was the most remote. He didn't socialize with the working press, and he only gave five news conferences during all of 1984. Although a rotating pool of reporters traveled with him on *Air Force One* during the campaign, he never once came back to talk with them, though occasionally he waved from the Secret Service compartment. David Hoffman of the *Washington Post* used to joke that "covering Reagan means having to say you never saw him."

Yet the staff devoted huge amounts of energy to controlling and shaping the little the public did see of Reagan. This, too, was only new in the degree to which it took place. Many presidents before Reagan had harnessed public relations techniques to promote the office: Theodore Roosevelt may have created the modern "photo opportunity" by staging a press trip out West simply to dramatize his interest in conservation. The Nixon White House, more than any before it, perfected the art of controlling the press in the television age both by limiting access to the president and by planning no event without imagining the headline, photo, and story that would follow it. This system tried to ensure that every story was advantageous to the White House, no matter what the facts. This practice simply reached its apogee in Reagan's time, when in contrast to the Nixon era, the system served a consummate performer.

The result, as political essayist Leon Wieseltier described it, was that for the Reagan administration, "the truth was a problem to be solved." The solution was an art form known as "spin control," which referred to the "spin" the White House public relations experts put on news to make sure it bounced the desired way. Enterprising reporters tried to detect the spin and dig out the real story. Occasionally they were successful, but not without risking revenge. Press secretary Larry Speakes gave what he called "death sentences" to those reporters he deemed too critical or otherwise uncooperative. He would threaten to "put them out of business" by making sure their phone calls went unreturned and questions unanswered, putting them routinely at a competitive disadvantage. Speakes explained proudly, "The idea was to be subtle. They thought they were being screwed, but they were never quite sure." He froze out some reporters for years, but it is debatable how much they missed. Speakes later confessed to having fabricated several presidential quotes; even before his confession stirred a controversy, he admitted that he misled the public about how disengaged the president was. "As a rule," he said, "I did not think it was lying to suggest that the president might be aware of something when he wasn't."

These strategies shaped not only the written record but the photographic one as well. The official White House staff photographers shot an estimated eight to ten thousand pictures of Reagan every month, the best of which were released to the press. Mrs. Reagan usually determined which images the public saw, particularly when they included her. She personally went through the thousands of pictures, signing "O.K. per N.R." when they could be released and tearing off the corner of each of those she deemed unflattering.

Despite these many protective layers, someone close to the Oval Office would occasionally break ranks, providing a glimpse of a place that sounded quite strange. Terry Arthur, a staff photographer who spent countless hours quietly observing and documenting the president alone and with others, said he took the job partly "to find out who was running the show." After two solid years of traveling with the president, following him through meetings and on his weekend retreats, he concluded, "I never found out." Reagan, he said, "was like a Buddha. People would say, 'He wants this' or 'He wants that,' but you'd never really see him say so. He'd be shown the decisions others had made, and would say, 'Uh-huh.' "

Alexander Haig, Reagan's first secretary of state, was equally puzzled by the president's operating style. In his White House memoirs, he wrote: "To me, the White House was as mysterious as a ghost ship; you heard the creak of the rigging and the groan of the timbers, and sometimes even glimpsed the crew on deck. But which of the crew had the helm? . . . It was impossible to tell."

On January 7, 1985, the Reagan White House, with its many fault lines and delicate counterbalances, was turned inside out. In place of the competing centers of power, the multiple sources of information, and the extraordinary mechanisms designed to police the president, there was now just one man: Donald Regan.

Just before Reagan went to the press room to announce the job swap, he sat with Regan and the members of the troika in the Oval Office, kidding around. Regan studied the three men whose jobs he'd soon single-handedly replace. Until becoming treasury secretary, Regan had spent his whole professional life on Wall Street. Unlike the others, he was neither ideologue, political pro, nor a longtime Reaganite — in fact, when he headed Merrill Lynch, its political action committee gave campaign contributions to both Reagan and Carter. But Regan was smart, and above all he was competitive. As the banter continued, he broke in to point out his own most important qualification.

"Mr. President," he said with a twinkle in his brown eyes, "you might as well realize it. I got something these other guys haven't got. Jim Baker's got some of it. Meese doesn't have it, maybe never will. And Deaver will try to get it."

"What's that?" asked the president, swallowing the bait.

"I've got 'fuck you' money," bragged his new chief of staff with a bluntness that kicked off a whole new era. "Anytime I want, I'm gone."

With his smoothed-back silver hair, strong chin, French cuffs, and banker-gray suits, Regan looked born to his $40 million blind trust. But he wasn't. In many ways Donald Regan was the living proof of Ronald Reagan's American dream. He started life much as Reagan had: an Irish American, born to a Democratic household not on the wrong side of the tracks but, as Reagan liked to put it, "close enough to hear the whistle blow real loud." Their shared heritage, as well as a mutual ability to enjoy a good joke, soon made the two men fast friends.

But there was an important difference between Reagan's early years in the Mississippi River towns of northwestern Illinois and those of Donald Regan in Cambridge, Massachusetts. Reagan's world was more or less homogeneous, modest but middle class, a grounding that gave him the common touch he carried with him throughout his whole life. During his presidency, the rich grew richer and the poor grew poorer, but he paid tribute to ordinary Americans. In his movie roles, he played a clean-cut Everyman, and in politics, he capitalized on a populist antiestablishment strain and delighted in using his past as a common denominator with the blue-collar Americans who swelled his constituency.

In contrast, Regan grew up with his Irish nose pressed against the old Yankee panes of Boston. He learned early on what it was like to be excluded for lack of social status and power, and he fought not just to gain these credentials but to outdo everyone else in their attainment. The grandson of a horsecart deliveryman and the son of a policeman fired during the great Boston police strike of 1919, Regan was born on December 21, 1918 — almost eight years after Reagan — into a town of sharp class distinctions, where the Irish were still barred from many prestigious jobs. When Regan attended public school in Irish-Catholic North Cambridge, a slightly older boy named Thomas P. "Tip" O'Neill lived in the neighborhood too. O'Neill was also aware of divisions within the city; as he recalled in his memoirs, "Although I could walk home from Harvard . . . in about 20 minutes, North Cambridge might just as well have been on the other side of the moon."

Class was a threshold Regan would cross eagerly, but not without tremendous drive and tremendous costs, jettisoning his blue-collar roots — and some would say the kind of compassion essential to political sensitivity — along the way. Later, when asked if he thought anyone could do as well as he had, he answered, "Sure, they can do it. It can be done. If they don't, it's their choice."

At the city's prestigious public high school, Cambridge Latin, Regan was a good student despite many hardships. His adored older brother died when he was ten, and he had to help support the family by working as a movie usher in his free time. Nevertheless, he was active in many extracurricular pursuits. Showing the flair for self-promotion that would later push him to the top, in his senior year he edited the school yearbook, which called him "a youth of marked and rare ability distinguished by his versatility." Regan also ran for class president that year and came close to winning. One of his classmates, George Quint, remembers feeling that this political failure revealed a lot about Regan's character. He said, "I was never sure Don could be elected to anything. He was the kind of person who would have to be appointed. He didn't want to put in the effort of running for office; he never asked for help, even from people like me who could have swung votes. I think there was some pride there. He was reasonably popular, but he didn't have the ability to make people love him."

Even so, Regan made it to "the other side of the moon," entering Harvard as a day student with the class of 1940. The university was branching out from its patrician past and actively soliciting poorer students from nearby ethnic enclaves, both Irish and Jewish. Although he took pride all his life in making it on his own and staunchly opposed government social programs, Regan was in fact assisted by a Cambridge-Buckley Scholarship, which paid the tuition for local boys in need. Harvard still maintained conspicuous social distinctions. The historian Theodore White, who graduated two years before Regan enrolled, described a universe inhabited by "white men, gray men, and meatballs" — aristocrats, the middle class, and day students. White and Regan fell into the third category and, in White's words, had "come to Harvard not to help the working classes, but to get out of the working classes." Regan did not attract much notice in a class that included John Fitzgerald Kennedy — another Boston Irishman, but one endowed with enough wealth, fame, and charm to enter the exclusive Hasty Pudding Club. Regan "was a guy who never entered my ken, nor that of any of my friends," confirmed his impeccably "white" classmate, J. P. Morgan II. Regan had little time to socialize; he worked as a tour guide to cover his expenses and lived with his family in a modest apartment on nearby Ware Street.

Though Regan didn't make a big impression on Harvard, it made a big impression on him. In his senior year, the ambitious young man with dark hair, dark eyes, and a broad Boston accent broke with his family's tradition and registered as a Republican to vote for Wendell Willkie. He graduated with a degree in English and headed straight to Harvard Law School. But in 1941, as he wrote in his class notes, "the war clouds and the draft made me decide to enlist in the officers candidate class of the United States Marine Corps. That changed my entire life." In a short time, Donald Regan had compiled an outstanding war record; he saw action with the artillery in four campaigns, including Okinawa. Harvard's elitism had been hard to penetrate, but Regan showed a flair for real combat.

His taste for battle served Regan well in 1946, when he began selling stocks on Wall Street. He was also served well by his marriage, in 1942, to a young Washington woman he'd taken on a blind date to a dance at Quantico, Ann Gordon Buchanan, a niece of the wife of Winthrop Smith, one of the managing partners of Merrill Lynch. There's little doubt that Regan would have done well by dint of his own talents, even as a bachelor. But many at Merrill Lynch thought that he was marked for particularly rapid promotion in part because of the powerful uncle his wife reportedly called "Daddy."

In thirty-five hard-driving years, Regan worked his way from being a lowly stockbroker trainee to chairman and chief executive officer of the largest brokerage empire on Wall Street. He oversaw a work force of thirty-two thousand, earned a salary of $500,000 a year, and had a colorful reputation as a supersalesman, an ingenious innovator, and a tyrannical boss. He proudly described himself as "a bomb thrower," shaking up the WASP establishment. In time, some of the short-term innovations he was given credit for — including the diversification of Merrill Lynch into such full-service financial fields as real estate — proved to be long-term losers. But Regan was as good at selling himself as anything else, and while he headed the firm, all of his innovations were promoted as financial breakthroughs.

Detractors called Regan "an absolute dictator" who surrounded himself with yes men. He seemed almost to enjoy cultivating a ruthless image, admitting bluntly that "I've chewed up an awful lot of executives . . . either they couldn't stand the heat, or I couldn't stand their performance." One of Regan's most quoted sayings at Merrill Lynch was: "I don't get ulcers — I give them."

Regan had long sought his government appointment. As early as the 1960s he showed restlessness at Merrill Lynch, confiding to Clark Clifford, the well-connected Washington lawyer, an interest in getting government experience in what was at that time the Kennedy administration. When Nixon became president in 1968, Regan actively pursued the top job at Treasury, reportedly using five Merrill Lynch public relations men to help push his prospects and becoming privately deflated when he was passed over. But during that administration he became friends with another Irish "bomb-thrower," William Casey, head of the Securities and Exchange Commission. The two men enjoyed swapping gossip between Wall Street and Washington, and when Casey became Reagan's campaign manager in late 1980, he urged Regan to hold a fund-raiser in New York for Reagan. Soon after, the Casey connection helped a man only slightly known to the Reaganites to at last get the Treasury post, after two other candidates had failed to work out.

At the Treasury Department, Regan's greatest triumph was launching the overhaul of the tax code, which lowered rates and closed a number of unproductive loopholes. His greatest failure, however, was doing little to stem the staggering growth of the federal deficit. As it mounted — and as his chief competitor as the administration's top economic voice, David Stockman, privately and publicly lost faith in "Reaganomics" — critics accused Regan of doing too little to avert a political disaster.

A bright and decisive executive known as one of the quickest studies on Wall Street, Regan entered the White House eager to apply corporate principles of rational management to the disorderly process of democracy. By the time he joined the White House staff, many criticized the troika system as hopelessly inefficient. The White House was plagued by constant news leaks and slowed by endless argument. Regan, said a friend of his, "couldn't wait to straighten things out." He announced on his first day that he'd be the new "chief operating officer" of the United States — drawing a parallel to business that presumably left Reagan as the chief executive officer or chairman of the board. Regan assured those familiar with his military take-charge style that he would not be "grabbing power." But some inside the White House soon began to wonder about this promise from a man whose subordinates said he liked to be called "Chief."

Although Regan had had very limited experience in politics, he was supremely self-confident. The executive office of the president was just some sixteen hundred officials — small when compared to the size of Merrill Lynch. While the troika had functioned somewhat in the manner of Franklin Roosevelt's loosely defined and often overlapping staff, allowing the president to benefit from the clashes of viewpoint, Regan fashioned himself in a different mold, more like Eisenhower's aggressive chief, Sherman Adams, or Nixon's strongman, H. R. Haldeman. His primary concern was efficiency, and he set out to create a system streamlined for action, one that allowed the president to be only as involved as he wanted to be.

Regan soon reduced the number of assistants to the president from seventeen to eleven and collapsed seven cabinet-level domestic policy discussion groups into two: one for economic policy, the second for domestic policy. Although the president technically presided over these groups, as time went on, he attended less and less frequently. Regan downgraded much of the apparatus that had kept the president engaged in a so-called permanent campaign, scaling back the public liaison office from fifty-six to twenty-four people so that its chief administrator soon admitted, "We can't really do constituent services the way we used to." Similarly, Regan gutted the political office that had been used to mobilize outside support for Reagan's programs even in nonelection years. He placed himself in charge of long-range strategic planning — his forte on Wall Street — thus becoming the supervisor of an entire group of legislative, communications, and advance men who had met weekly and sometimes daily during the first term to chart the administration's agenda. Now, they were forced to wait for Regan to be available, and sometimes they went a month between meetings.

Regan also took steps to improve the perquisites attached to his office. By law, he wasn't entitled to Secret Service protection unless facing an explicit threat, but he became the first chief of staff ever to surround himself regularly with government guards. In order to persuade the White House to support the expensive extra security, he had to ask the Secret Service, which was run out of his old Treasury Department, to give frequent assurances to the White House counsel that he was physically at risk. It was noted wryly in the counsel's office, however, that Regan demanded enough security to provide a driver for his car but not enough to fend off attackers. He was on the verge of having a private bathroom constructed for himself — the only private one besides the president's in the overcrowded West Wing — when a secretary convinced his aides that the plan for what wags were calling "the royal flush" was beginning to create an image problem.

Although Regan hadn't had much formal political experience, he wasn't worried. He'd seen enough of Washington to become impatient, even contemptuous of the time-consuming political process and its emphasis on negotiations and consensus. James Madison's delicate separation of powers, with its inherent inefficiencies to slow the process of change, could scarcely have been more alien to someone used to the fast pace and brute force of Wall Street. This problem became apparent almost as soon as Regan took over, when, accompanied by his new congressional expert, longtime White House hand and assistant to the president Max L. Friedersdorf, he paid his first courtesy call on the congressional leaders. He proceeded to lecture the leadership, many of whom had decades more political experience than he. "It was just embarrassing," recalled Friedersdorf, who concluded that "Regan had little respect for politicians as a class. What he respected was wealth." As Senator Paul Laxalt said, "He thought Congress was a damn nuisance."

But Regan did not seem to worry about alienating Congress. He brought to the White House a lesson he had learned at the Treasury: he said he had "only one master." He served not the public, not the press, not Congress, not this or that political orthodoxy — his only master was the president of the United States. Unlike the troika, which guarded Reagan from his own worst instincts, Don Regan believed that the 1984 landslide carried one main message: "The American people wanted Reagan to be Reagan. It was my job, as I saw it, to make that possible." He intended to run the White House along hierarchical lines, in accordance with the marine code. As he put it, "I believe in loyalty up, and loyalty down."

At the Treasury, this strict and dogged concept of loyalty as acquiescence had caused some critics to castigate Regan as a yes man. They noted that although he had shown distinctly Keynesian sympathies in his own book about Wall Street, *A View from the Street*, he instantly became a supply-side advocate at Treasury, raising questions about his ideological sincerity. But Regan's performance was pitched to please his one boss, who, not surprisingly, had no such complaints. "I don't know how anyone can complain about him ideologically or philosophically," the president told the *Dallas Morning News* in January 1985. "He's been as loyal to everything I've wanted to do as anyone I could name."

Former White House chiefs of staff warned that the job called for more than obedience. The post shouldn't be compared, they said, to a corporate command on Wall Street. Ford's much-admired chief of staff Richard Cheney said that "you have to build consensus in Washington — it's very different." Another important distinction noted by Ford's first chief of staff, Donald Rumsfeld, was the necessity of ensuring that the president was "exposed to all points of view — even the unpopular ones."

A hazard was that Regan shared many of the president's political blind spots — and with Baker, Darman, and Meese gone and Deaver and Stockman on the way out, there were few to broaden the debate. He was no more prone to second-guessing himself than Reagan was, and his political antennae were less sensitive. (He had a tendency to make impolitic statements about women and minorities. He once suggested that "Negroes" would like the new tax reform bill's increased personal exemptions because "they have such big families." He also tried to dissuade two non-Jewish White House employees from joining "Jewish" firms on Wall Street.)

The president, though, was more comfortable with his new "chief operating officer" than with almost any previous staff member. The two men swapped jokes like locker room buddies. Many of them were off-color in an old-fashioned sort of way. The two elderly men, for instance, were observed on one occasion elbowing each other like schoolboys after savoring an intelligence report detailing the improbably active sex life of the octogenarian Tunisian president, Habib Bourguiba. Even in jest, however, Regan had ulterior motives; he once confided to an aide that he had stumbled on a key to Reagan's heart: "I always let him tell his joke first." By Easter, Regan got the supreme compliment of being invited socially to the ranch. "Reagan admired Regan," said Deaver, "because, in a sense, he was exactly what Reagan wasn't: hands on."

In fact, an unspoken dividend of "letting Reagan be Reagan" was that this allowed the president to delegate so much to Regan. Reagan was fond of telling his staff, "Don't bring me problems — bring me solutions," and Regan was happy to comply. Before long, critics began to believe that Regan had cast himself in the role of prime minister. As Ed Rollins saw it, "He figured, if Ronald Reagan didn't want to be president all the time, he would be. Probably eighty percent of the decisions made during his era were made by Regan."

This concentration of power put a great strain on Regan and his staff, a staff not particularly adept or experienced. Regan methodically filled crucial White House posts with loyalists, many from his Treasury staff. Observers like Max Friedersdorf, who had worked with five chiefs of staff before Regan, described the staff as "obsequious yes men" who "would laugh at all his jokes. It was just sickening." A more generous view was that they were a well-meaning and able enough group of mostly young men who were simply cast in the wrong roles. They inherited a second-term White House badly in need of fresh political thinking, but, in the words of one of their own members, Christopher Hicks, "we were implementers, not thinkers, organization guys, not policymakers." Moreover, Regan didn't like being contradicted. It did not take long before the bolder, more seasoned aides dubbed these timid, colorless young men "Regan's Mice."

Regan was a bright man and, recognizing his vulnerabilities, tried to bring in several more experienced aides. Ed Rollins, Reagan's former campaign manager, became head of the White House Office of Political and Governmental Affairs, and Friedersdorf, the congressional liaison director during the successful 1981 tax cut blitz, rejoined the White House as a special legislative strategist. But both had their own ideas, and both soon paid for their independence with their jobs.

Regan also brought in Patrick Buchanan, a former speechwriter for Richard Nixon and a conservative zealot who, despite great personal charm, had been called "combative" so often that it seemed his nom de guerre. Regan, who had witnessed the hard-core conservatives' crusade against Baker, hoped that Buchanan would protect his right flank. Deaver warned that he was too strident and would jeopardize the administration's successful blend of hard-line policy and smooth salesmanship. But Regan went ahead with the appointment anyway, and it caused euphoria among the president's most conservative backers.

Less noticed at the time was another personnel shift, one that would prove the bane of these same conservative ideologues. It did not involve the hiring of a new adviser but, instead, the gradual increase in influence of someone already serving the president, pollster Richard Wirthlin.

Wirthlin was a formidable backstage presence at the White House, a private businessman whose services cost the Republican National Committee, which shared the polls with the White House, an estimated $1 million per year — far more than had ever been paid to a pollster before. The father of eight children, Wirthlin was a devout Mormon; but, as his yellow Porsche suggested, he also had a taste for the temporal things in life. Like a palace soothsayer, he had a talent for making his clients feel good, and, in turn, he enjoyed a position of special trust with both of the Reagans, who apparently took great comfort in his generally upbeat reports. "It was like getting a [good] report card at the end of each month," said Regan of the Reagans' attachment to the polls. Not surprisingly, Wirthlin was resented by his competitors, some of whom derided him as "Old Numbers" and begrudged him his high fees. They also questioned his political acumen, noting that before he became a political pollster and signed up his most famous client in 1968, he had been chairman of the economics department — not the political science department — at Brigham Young University in Utah.

With Regan's encouragement, Wirthlin quietly brought what Alexander Hamilton had called "the small arts of popularity" to new heights of sophistication in the White House. Wirthlin met with the president approximately every three weeks, and within a few months of Regan's arrival he was consulting with either Regan or his staff almost daily.

Wirthlin, whose company conducted between 16,000 and 20,000 polling interviews a year, found Regan "a very sophisticated user of public attitudes." His polling soon went well beyond traditional applications. In the second term, Wirthlin began to incorporate into the daily operations of the White House a novel system that he had pioneered during the 1984 campaign. Called "speech pulse," it allowed him to market test every presidential phrase. He would gather forty to eighty people (usually drawn from the heartlands) in a room where they were each handed sensitive, computerized dials that enabled Wirthlin to chart their instant response to presidential speeches moment by moment. The system could measure their positive or negative reaction, interest or boredom, understanding or confusion, as well as their view of the speaker's credibility. The information, once processed, was printed out with the text of the president's speech in one column and a number measuring second-by-second approval ratings in the other. So precisely calibrated was the system, Wirthlin exulted, that "it's not just phrase by phrase, it's word by word!"

Wirthlin analyzed the results to determine something called a "speech rate," which measured the effect of the rhetoric on the audience's mood. He also found what he called "power phrases" or "resonators," the lines most effective in altering public feeling. His system was useful, he said, because "it tells us what themes we can play after the speech, what phrases we can use again, and the tonality of speech that makes sense." It also allowed the White House to "do some pretesting so that we can fine tune the [president's] message."

Political campaigns had experimented with versions of this direct-response polling, and it bore a resemblance to market research done in the entertainment business by movie and television producers. But as a tool for governing, this state-of-the-art system was something quite new. Some of the speechwriters, whose speeches were subjected to "speech pulse" analysis, privately objected. "If anyone had tried this in the first term," said speechwriter Peggy Noonan, "he would have been laughed right out of the White House."

In the first term, in fact, Wirthlin's numbers were weighed with some skepticism by a staff with enough political experience to recognize the limitations of polling. As Deaver once put it, he would no sooner "launch a political campaign without a poll than perform an operation without an X ray." However, Deaver understood that the information was diagnostic, not prognostic; polls are by nature reactive and can't be expected to provide a blueprint for leadership. But Regan, whose background was in sales, was simply fascinated by the numbers. Just as new computers allowed him and his staff to follow the financial markets, so Wirthlin allowed them to follow the political markets. Regan's staff would soon talk about who was following the welfare "account" and how to "invest the president's political capital." And inevitably Regan and those around him would think and talk about Reagan's popularity as "the bottom line."

"As a former marketing guy," Rollins later said, "Don Regan thought he understood polls. What he didn't understand was that popularity is only a portion of how a president's doing. Someone can be liked but still not be politically effective." The distinction was not drawn by the new staff, which, without its own political moorings, soon came to see the polls as its guiding compass.

Ronald Reagan's second term as president officially began on Monday, January 21, 1985. Outside, a killing cold front had frozen the capital in brilliant, crystalline splendor. It was a beautiful but impossibly cold day to celebrate the nation's fiftieth presidential inauguration. The president took one look at the 30 mph winds gusting the snow across the south lawn and started to rummage through his closet for the pair of long johns he hadn't worn since the New Hampshire primary back in 1980. It wasn't a romantic picture, but for both Reagans the morning was filled with anticipation and emotion, so much so that Mrs. Reagan said it reminded her of the day they got married.

This inaugural would call for an unusual amount of improvisation, for all the carefully laid plans had been literally frozen out. The day before, just after the president's private swearing-in in the White House, inaugural manager Ron Walker had been ushered into the family quarters, where he told the Reagans that a team of military arctic weather specialists had been charting the coming cold front. They believed that with the wind-chill factor, the temperature would reach − 50 degrees by three o'clock the next morning. At that hour, in order to meet the Secret Service's security standards, the 40,000 parade participants would have to pass through metal detectors in the Pentagon parking lot — some of them high school band members wearing sneakers and nylon windbreakers. There was also the problem of the Secret Service snipers who would be positioned along the parade route, stuck for hours on crusty, frozen rooftops in the path of the fierce winds. Walker believed the weather could literally kill somebody. He told the Reagans they'd have to call the parade off and move the inaugural address indoors to the Capitol Rotunda.

The First Lady, who hated cold weather anyway, was relieved. But the president had two worries, one compassionate, one political. "Where are all the kids going to go?" he asked Walker with genuine concern. And under the new arrangements, asked the best political performer in the country, "where will the television cameras be?"

The president's advisers had another question: What about the speech he was to give shortly? It had been drafted late and in an unusually haphazard way. The problem was that during the fall, when new initiatives would normally have been thought up, the president's staff had been preoccupied with the election. Only the Treasury Department had produced any forward-thinking plan — an ambitious overhaul of the tax code that the White House had yet to endorse. "The inaugural address, the State of the Union, and the new budget have to be beat out in September, October, and November. But instead, we were concentrating on politics then," said speechwriter Ken Khachigian. "Baker and Darman were traveling with the president, and really no one was behind, thinking."

Nonetheless, as the president delivered his midday address on Monday, hushing his voice dramatically to accommodate the acoustics of the Capitol's dome, spirits were high. "In this blessed land, there is always a better tomorrow," the president said. " . . . Our nation is poised for greatness." His familiar recitation of optimistic themes was generally well received. One *New York Times* reporter noted that it seemed "more a celebration of the 'American Renewal' of his first term than a driving call for action in the second."

But such skepticism was lost in the general jubilation. The stock market soared. The Dow Jones Industrial Average closed up 34 points, the greatest single increase since January 19, 1984, when the president announced he'd be seeking a second term. Despite the flickering doubt of its reporter, the *New York Times* ran its inauguration day coverage under the headline: A MASTER'S MARK ON POLITICS.

And that evening, in the confetti-filled Fiesta Room of the Washington Hilton, where one of nine glittering inaugural balls was under way, tomorrow was no more real than the next morning's hangover. The Xavier Cugat band struck up a rumba. The president, as handsome and poised as a movie star in his jet black tuxedo, took the First Lady by the hand, smiled at the cheering crowd, and promised, "There'll be a hot time in the old town tonight!"

3

A Dangerous World

IT WAS A TIME, in the wintry weeks just after the inauguration, when anything seemed possible. The economy was roaring ahead, with both unemployment and inflation dropping magically in tandem; the morning after the official swearing-in, White House spokesman Larry Speakes announced 1984's results with a grin — 6.8 percent growth, 3.7 percent inflation. On the political landscape, Reagan's record-breaking electoral majority was still the biggest news in town. "We can read," Tip O'Neill, the crusty, partisan Speaker of the House, told Reagan at a postinaugural reception. "In my fifty years in public life, I've never seen a man more popular than you with the American people."

The only apparent danger to the Reagan revolution was complacence. "There's an understandable tendency, when a second term begins, to think that all the great work is behind us, that the big battles have been fought and all the rest is anticlimax," Reagan told a conference of his political appointees. "Well, that's not true. . . . Our greatest battles lie ahead. All is newness now.

"We can change America forever," the president declared to a rolling crescendo of applause. "From here on, it's shake, rattle and roll!"

One major new battlefront, the president and his advisers promised, would be foreign policy. Under the pressure of the reelection campaign, Reagan's international agenda had been toned down, his rhetorical fervor against the Soviet Union, Nicaragua, and terrorism put on hold. Instead, Michael Deaver and his staff had reduced Reagan's foreign policy to three marvelously evocative but essentially empty words: "America is back."

So it was intentionally symbolic, in that first week after the inauguration, that Reagan spent much of his time working visibly on foreign initiatives. His first formal meeting of the second term was with his new arms control negotiating team, and he took the opportunity to declare: "I have no more important goal than reducing and ultimately eliminating nuclear weapons."

It was also symbolic that Reagan's first public speech after the inauguration focused on a region that ranked high on his list of priorities: Central America. One of the major goals for the new year was to breathe new life into the flagging insurgency of the Nicaraguan contras — "the freedom fighters," as he had taken to calling them. The president wasted no time in castigating Nicaragua's leftist regime as a menace to the entire Western Hemisphere. "The Sandinistas have been attacking their neighbors through armed subversion," he charged, and added that the Managua regime had established ties with the world's most radical powers — even Ayatollah Khomeini's Iran.

Foreign policy was one field in which Reagan's battles were far from won. He had entered office in 1981 with sweeping international ambitions: to halt Soviet assertiveness, to reshape the nuclear balance of power, to stamp out terrorism, to reverse the tide of revolution in Central America. He boldly declared an end to the "Vietnam Syndrome," the allergy to U.S. intervention abroad that had dominated the 1970s. And he had happily quoted Tom Paine, the firebrand of the American Revolution: " 'We have it within our power to begin the world again.' "

But where Washington was susceptible to Reagan's charm, the world outside resisted. Neither the Soviet Union nor terrorists in the Middle East nor guerrillas in Central America cooperated. There had been some successes: Reagan won a massive increase in military spending, launched an audacious new program to study strategic defenses against nuclear attack, and sent nineteen hundred troops to topple a fragmenting Marxist regime on the Caribbean island of Grenada. But the frustrations of the first term were much larger than these small triumphs, especially when measured against the ambitions of beginning the world anew.

In U.S.-Soviet affairs, Reagan's hard line on arms control produced a long freeze between the two superpowers and made him the first president since Harry Truman to let four years pass without a summit meeting. Nor did the administration achieve any appreciable progress toward a nuclear weapons agreement, although his more hawkish aides considered that a sign of success in resisting the siren call of arms control, not a failure.

But Nancy Reagan wanted her husband to be seen by history as a man of peace, aides said, not merely a builder of missiles. And the 1984 campaign, if nothing else, prompted Reagan to display a hitherto unseen enthusiasm for arms control. When the Soviet Union walked out of arms talks at the end of 1983, Reagan's advisers recognized the public relations boon and adroitly turned the stalemate to the president's benefit.

"*We* will never retreat from negotiations," the president announced.

Once the Soviet leadership saw that Reagan was both immovable on major issues and certain to be reelected, they came back to the table. And Moscow, too, had a new leader with ambitious goals and intriguing ideas. So one of the first issues on the new term's agenda was a summit meeting with the new Soviet leader, Mikhail S. Gorbachev.

In Central America, Reagan had long declared the Marxist guerrillas in El Salvador and the Sandinista regime of Nicaragua to be serious threats to U.S. security. But his administration's response to that ostensibly vital threat was ill defined and inconstant. When Congress and the public reacted with fear that Reagan's hawkishness would lead toward "another Vietnam," Baker and Deaver, the guardians of the president's image, banned any display of military interest in the area. Instead of armed action against Cuba or Nicaragua (which both Alexander Haig and Henry Kissinger noted would logically follow from Reagan's rhetoric), the president chose a "low-cost" solution, a secret war run by the CIA. When the secret war became a public embarrassment, the same president who pronounced the Sandinistas a serious threat proved unable to wheedle a few million dollars from Congress to finance the Nicaraguan rebels.

It was in the Middle East that Reagan suffered the most spectacular failure of the first term — the debacle of U.S. intervention in Lebanon. Initially a modest mission in which a battalion of marines landed as impartial peacekeepers, the administration's objectives in Beirut grew almost willy-nilly. As officials convinced themselves that they had a chance to remake divided Lebanon — and to wrest the country away from its powerful neighbor, Soviet-backed Syria — the marines' mission expanded to include the ill-defined job of supporting the Lebanese government. That was a laudable goal, but the Lebanese government was dominated by Christians who were at war with Muslim factions. Throwing the marines into the fray made them partisans, not peacekeepers.

The fatal error came in September 1983, when the government's army came under fierce attack from Muslim forces only three miles from the presidential palace in the hills overlooking Beirut. Lebanese army officers convinced Reagan's special envoy, Robert C. McFarlane, that their men were in danger of annihilation. McFarlane sent a plea for intervention directly to the White House in a fevered message that more skeptical Middle East hands quickly dubbed the "sky-is-falling" cable.

"We may well be at a turning point which will lead within a matter of days to a Syrian takeover," McFarlane warned, citing reported Muslim atrocities and likening the shelling of the presidential palace to an attack on the State Department from Capitol Hill.

"Faced with this threat which cannot be contained by the [Lebanese army], we must decide whether the U.S. will, by withholding direct support, allow the fall of the [government]," he cabled. He urged that

U.S. Navy ships off Lebanon use their artillery and airplanes against the Muslim rebels. Secretary of State George Shultz supported the idea, and Reagan agreed. The guns of the cruiser *Virginia* and three other navy ships opened up on Muslim villages — making the United States a party to the eight-year-old Lebanese civil war.

Reagan insisted, and apparently believed, that the navy was shooting merely in a kind of extended defense of the marines. The Lebanese knew better. One of their leaders warned that with the shelling, "the marines turned into a fighting force against the Muslims in Lebanon."

The following month brought a terrible retaliation. A Muslim suicide bomber rammed a truck full of explosives into the center of the main marine barracks at the Beirut airport. The massive explosion caused the building to collapse, killing 241 American servicemen at a single blow.

Reagan's initial reaction to the outrage was to escalate his rhetoric, as if to show that the marines' sacrifice had been for a worthy cause. When asked why the troops were in Beirut at all, the president replied, "It is vitally important to the security of the United States and the Western world. . . . If Lebanon ends up under the tyranny of forces hostile to the West, not only will our strategic position in the eastern Mediterranean be threatened, but also the stability of the entire Middle East."

Reagan's cabinet, however, was bitterly divided. Shultz and McFarlane insisted that the bombing made it even more important for the marines to stay in Beirut; a retreat, they argued, would show that the United States could be intimidated by terrorist bombs. Secretary of Defense Caspar W. Weinberger and the Joint Chiefs of Staff wanted to get the marines out; they saw nothing but danger in Lebanon, with few possible gains. After weeks of wrangling, aides produced an uneasy middle way, a plan to withdraw the marines while escalating the use of naval guns in support of the Lebanese army. But by the time the plan was ready, Lebanon's army and government were already collapsing. Radical Muslim militias took over half of Beirut; the marines were hastily "redeployed" to the fleet offshore. Lebanon, which Reagan had declared "vitally important" to the West, was lost. The president and his advisers did their best to forget the misadventure. But Beirut's Muslim terrorists, who had longer memories, continued to attack Americans — both in Lebanon and abroad.

"The sad thing in Lebanon is that you had two philosophies of what we should be doing — Weinberger's and Shultz's — and the White House wanted to split the difference," a senior foreign policy aide said later. "The president found it hard to choose. The president was torn. We never did choose which it was going to be. That's not how you make a strategy."

•   •   •

The debacle in Lebanon was an object lesson in the way Ronald Reagan approached problems of foreign policy. His reach frequently exceeded his grasp; his enthusiasms exceeded his understanding of the facts. His sweeping rhetoric often outstripped his willingness to bear real costs. And, although his basic goals were clear, he often gave his aides no useful guidance on how he wanted to pursue them.

Part of the problem was the scope of Reagan's ambitions. His rhetoric acknowledged no half solutions, no limits to American power. His immediate predecessors in the White House saw America's power in the world as shrinking, and they perceived their task as adjusting gracefully to the new constraints of a lesser role. Reagan rejected the premise and argued that a revitalized America could still make the world bend to its desires. But the president also argued that his new, assertive America could pursue its mission at little cost in money, lives, or political disruption. The defense budget ballooned to buy a six-hundred-ship navy and bombers for the air force, but Reagan was never eager to send American troops to fight the enemies he condemned. His right-wing supporters fretted that the hawkish leader they knew had been caged by dovish advisers, but they misunderstood their man. "Few seemed willing to grant that Reagan was always Reagan, trusting more to words than actions, to weapons bought than to weapons used," wrote Garry Wills. "He actually believed that if one just took a tough stance, then bullies would scatter."

Thus Reagan declared his devotion to freeing Poland in 1981 but did little when the Soviet-backed regime declared martial law. In Central America, he denounced the Sandinistas and their sixty-thousand-man army but insisted that a CIA-run force of ten thousand rebels could overthrow the regime. In the Middle East, he promised to respond to terrorism with "swift and effective retribution," but in practice he turned down every proposal for retaliation until 1986, when Libya's Qadhafi finally presented an irresistible, low-risk target.

The paradox stemmed at least partly from Reagan's striking lack of interest in international issues. Unlike every other president in modern times, he showed little passion for the details of foreign policy. Nixon, Ford, and Carter all spent hours plotting strategy with their foreign policy advisers, but not Reagan. Alexander Haig, his first secretary of state, once sent Reagan a memo proposing that he set aside just one hour a week to study foreign issues. "There was no reply," the baffled Haig recorded.

Reagan's detachment from international affairs took several forms. His inattention to the facts was legendary, from his garbled accounts of Lebanese history to his confession that he had never realized that the Soviet Union's nuclear forces were concentrated in land-based missiles. His concentration during meetings of the National Security Council and the smaller National Security Planning Group (NSPG) could waver visibly, depending on the subject. When terrorism, Nicaragua, or South Africa came up, aides said, the president was often animated and lively, but on the arcana of arms control or less compelling issues, his mind appeared to wander. His aides became accustomed to his daydreaming gaze, which one described as "a glassy look [that] would come over his face." But to an outsider, his inattention could be disconcerting. John Horton, the CIA's national intelligence officer for Latin America in 1983 and 1984, described one such NSC meeting. The meeting, held in the Cabinet Room, "was formal, staged, more a ceremony than a discussion," Horton said. "The president told anecdotes. I'd heard about this, but was shocked to see it was the case. He talked about a letter from a little girl he'd gotten; it was totally irrelevant. Shultz and Weinberger looked patient, bored, not quite tolerant while the president carried on this way. Then they shifted in their chairs and got down to business. The president seemed quite uninvolved."

When kings and presidents visited the White House, Reagan's entire knowledge of the issues was sometimes contained in the index cards his aides typed to hold his "talking points." "The three-by-five cards — ninety percent of his performance is that," said one official who helped prepare the president for these meetings. "He has a grasp of the big truths, but not the details. He's a political animal, an ideological animal . . . not a foreign policy thinker."

As a result, Reagan reversed the pattern of all the other modern presidents and left most foreign policy decisions to his top aides. In the second term, that meant the members of the National Security Planning Group: Vice President Bush, Secretary of State Shultz, Secretary of Defense Weinberger, chief of staff Regan, CIA director William J. Casey, the chairman of the Joint Chiefs of Staff, and the national security adviser — who by 1985 was the man who had urged the navy to use its artillery in Lebanon, Robert McFarlane.

"Foreign policy wasn't terribly important to the president," McFarlane said later. "He was defensive about foreign policy, didn't know a lot about it himself. His instincts were pretty good in terms of East-West competition and what deters and what doesn't; but that really doesn't go beyond 'strength,' period. When you get into the nuances of how you use strength for negotiation or deterrence, or beyond that for coercion, he didn't really know much about that. So he preferred to leave matters to his cabinet officers."

But the system had a major flaw that nearly crippled the administration's ability to carry out a coherent foreign policy: the cabinet officers were chronically divided. Reagan's idea of cabinet government turned out to be a recipe for gridlock as the members of the NSPG feuded almost constantly.

"The problem was that the cabinet officers disagreed," McFarlane said. "I don't think the president knew that when he appointed them, or he wouldn't have appointed them. But having done it, his quality of loyalty or of not liking conflict at all, and finally of not being terribly interested in the substance, led him just to say 'No, I prefer to let them work it out among themselves.' "

In the absence of clear direction from the Oval Office, Shultz, Weinberger, Casey, and McFarlane all interpreted the president's will according to their own, often conflicting, inclinations. Each insisted that he alone knew the true mind and meaning of the president; each insisted he was doing what the president truly wanted.

The conflict was most bitter between the secretaries of state and defense. Shultz wanted more flexibility in arms control talks with the Soviet Union; Weinberger resisted doggedly. Shultz wanted to keep the marines in Lebanon; Weinberger and his military officers took the marines out. Shultz wanted military strikes against suspected terrorists, even if innocent bystanders might be hurt; Weinberger said his armed forces would fight only in wars that had clear support from the American public, and that kind of war didn't.

The battle over the proper response to terrorism drove the two cabinet officers out into the nation's pulpits like feuding medieval theologians debating a point of doctrine.

"We must be willing to use military force," Shultz thundered at New York's Park Avenue Synagogue. "We cannot allow ourselves to become the Hamlet of nations, worrying endlessly over whether and how to respond."

"The United States should not commit forces unless vital interests [are] at stake," Weinberger responded at the National Press Club; no military expedition should be launched without "reasonable assurance that the mission would be supported by the American people and Congress."

To that, Shultz, at Yeshiva University, replied, "There is no such thing as guaranteed public support in advance."

It was an extraordinary public display of fundamental disagreement. In private, the debate was even more personal; the two men simply did not like each other. At one heated White House meeting, Shultz reportedly snapped at Weinberger: "If you're not willing to use force, maybe we should cut your budget." Weinberger replied with an acid tirade of his own on uses of force that would be "irresponsible." Back at the Pentagon, the angry defense secretary told aides that Shultz had become unreasonable and that he, not Shultz, "knew what the president wanted." An arms control expert left one NSC meeting astonished at what he had seen. "They were fighting like a couple of kids in there," he said.

Part of the conflict was a genuine difference in ideology. Weinberger was the more conservative Reaganite, preternaturally suspicious of any deal with the Soviet Union, while Shultz was a product of the GOP's Nixon-Kissinger wing, a more supple conservative. But much of it, McFarlane said later, was "just animus." The two men were markedly unlike in style: Shultz was a former business professor at the University of Chicago and Stanford, deliberate, stolid, and colorless; Weinberger was a lawyer educated at Harvard and Oxford, dapper, glib, and feisty. Each was clearly convinced he was smarter than the other. And they had been competing this way for more than a decade, first in the Nixon administration, where Shultz was secretary of the treasury and Weinberger director of the Office of Management and Budget, then at Bechtel Group, the giant international construction firm, where Shultz was president and Weinberger general counsel.

"These people were very bitter, and I don't pretend to really know the antecedents of it," McFarlane said. "Cap was very willful in opposing George Shultz on virtually every issue. And I think that he used improperly his defense of knowing better what the president wanted."

Reagan's wishes were rarely ambiguous, but he framed them broadly. When it came to providing concrete direction for the national security bureaucracy — on which of his goals were most important or how they should be pursued — the president was often reluctant to choose, as in November 1984, when McFarlane went to Rancho del Cielo in search of priorities for the second term.

McFarlane, the man in the middle of the Shultz-Weinberger fight, often tried to cajole Reagan to intervene, but with minimal success. The president preferred to stay out of the fray, even when he was annoyed at one of the cabinet antagonists. Once, when Weinberger publicly criticized an arms control position that Reagan had already endorsed, the president shook his head and asked, "What is Cap trying to say?" But he didn't take the matter up with Weinberger himself.

"He should have picked up the phone and said, 'Cap, I don't want you saying that anymore,' " said a White House aide who was present. "He never did."

"Occasionally we'd coach [Reagan] to say something to the cabinet on arms control," said another. "Sometimes we'd get him to sign a letter. . . . But it kind of cheapened the currency. The letters would be so complex, so ridden with technical language, that they couldn't have come from the president. The cabinet guys knew that, so the letters didn't have clout. The president's signature was not enough."

And even when Reagan agreed to deliver a tough message in person, the aide noted, it didn't always work. "We had a rule," he said. "If you want to get a stern message to a head of state, get a written message — don't put the president on the phone. He won't do it; he'll wimp out. He doesn't follow the script."

Much of the time, Reagan simply stayed out of the way — and the problem remained unsolved. When McFarlane pressed him for a decision between the competing positions of state and defense, the president normally asked whether he couldn't split the difference. It fell to McFarlane to cobble together policies that combined elements from both camps, even when their arguments were polar opposites. Often the result was either incoherence — different parts of the government moving in different directions — or paralysis, no movement at all. As a system for making decisions, McFarlane said later, Reagan's style was "intrinsically unworkable."

The persistent gridlock moved Shultz to offer Reagan his resignation twice during the first term, both times with the underlying aim of strengthening his putative position as first among equals on the NSPG. The first time, in 1983, Shultz discovered that Weinberger and national security adviser Clark were making decisions behind his back — launching naval maneuvers off Nicaragua and negotiations in the Middle East — and went straight to the Oval Office to put the matter on Reagan's desk.

"Mr. President, you don't need a guy like me for secretary of state if this is the way things are going to be done," Shultz said.

That time, Shultz not only got a promise that the other cabinet members' competitive diplomacy would end; he was also formally given walk-in privileges in the Oval Office. And Shultz was promised a private hour with Reagan each week, a session in which he could brief the president on whatever issues he chose. That was no small concession; other aides knew well that Reagan often acted on whatever information he received in the short briefing time on his schedule.

But the deadlock continued, and as the second term approached Shultz decided to lance the boil again. At the end of 1984 he brought up the problem at one of his regular meetings with Reagan.

"Mr. President," he said bluntly in the quiet of the Oval Office, "I think you will do better in the second term if you build your strategy around Cap or around me — but the two of us, together, will lead to paralysis. I have strong views, and I think mine are correct. But I think you would do better even if you adopted Cap's views and not mine."

Reagan tried to protest, but Shultz went on.

"The two of us are unable to work congenially," he said. "You should take one or the other."

In effect, Shultz was urging the president to fire Weinberger. But Reagan, characteristically, sidestepped the ultimatum.

"George," he said, "I'll think about it. But I definitely want you on my team. Make no mistake about that."

McFarlane, who sat in, was dismayed. In November, at the ranch, Reagan had blithely declined to choose among the foreign policy alternatives Shultz and McFarlane had given him. Now, when Shultz tried to force another kind of choice — even offering to give up his own cabinet seat — the president ignored the problem.

Shortly before the January 1985 inauguration, McFarlane resolved to push the president toward a solution. Sitting with Reagan in the forward compartment of *Air Force One* on the long flight from California back to Washington, he repeated Shultz's complaints. The deadlock in the cabinet couldn't go on, McFarlane said. It was blocking the administration's chances of achieving any major goals.

"I don't want to make any change," Reagan said stubbornly. "I think we can work with both George and Cap."

"Well, that implies one of two courses," McFarlane replied. "Either you delegate to someone within the White House" — in other words, give more power to McFarlane himself — "or, if that is not a choice that appeals to you, and I would understand that, then you've got to expect to become far more involved yourself in decisionmaking."

Fine, Reagan said, embracing the second option. If that's what it takes, then that's what I'll do.

There was little more McFarlane could say. He was not convinced that Reagan was about to change his habits. He was a little disappointed that the president had not chosen to put him in charge. And he was tired, McFarlane thought as *Air Force One* streaked eastward — tired of being ground down between two strong cabinet officers and their bureaucratic warriors, tired of running into obstacles, tired of being treated as a paper carrier instead of a major player.

For a week or so after their talk on the plane, McFarlane agonized over his dilemma. Maybe the president simply needs a new national security adviser, he thought; maybe I'm part of the problem.

"I went back to him," McFarlane said later, ". . . and told him that I thought I wasn't serving any particular purpose."

"No, Bud, that's not true at all," Reagan replied. The president liked his team the way it was; he didn't want to change anything.

"I will never accept your resignation," he told McFarlane, "except for personal reasons." Somehow he made it sound like both a presidential command and a personal appeal.

McFarlane was still unhappy. None of his problems had been solved. But he mentally saluted his commander in chief and went back to work.

McFarlane's friends would later shake their heads and wonder how the man had managed to contain all the pressure so well. He was like a volcano beneath the ocean, one friend said, a mass of seething energy hidden by depths of seeming calm. Now and then, a burst of pressure might explode through the surface, but even the few who saw it could only guess at what lay below.

"Bud McFarlane may be the most dedicated yet complicated man I've ever met," said Robert M. Kimmitt, who worked for him on the staff of the National Security Council. "He seemed to be searching constantly for the right way to serve. But he spent a lot of energy preserving that unflappable exterior."

"He's a very, very, very private person," said Richard Fairbanks, who worked with him at the State Department and NSC. "I think he constructed the McFarlane persona. He wasn't that way as a young major. He would be laughing and joking, and we'd walk into a hearing room and the mask would fall into place. It's something he worked on. A protective thing."

Consumed by a vision of public service as an unremitting duty, gnawed by fears of inadequacy, McFarlane was at once hard-nosed and sentimental, guarded and vulnerable. A competent but far from dazzling diplomatic strategist, he yearned to be recognized as another Kissinger. But his successes rarely measured up to the impossible standards he set for himself.

McFarlane was born in Washington, D.C., in 1937, the youngest child of a New Deal congressman from Texas; his mother died when he was only eight months old. McFarlane later credited his father for bequeathing to him a sense of public service, but he was reared largely by his older sisters and a stern, Calvinist housekeeper, whom he later listed (along with the Methodist Church and the United States Naval Academy) as the formative influences of his life. As a junior at Annapolis, McFarlane wondered whether he had chosen the wrong path and thought seriously about the ministry. "Don't be silly," his father said. So he went on to graduate and took the uncommon choice of a commission in the marine corps instead of the navy.

Vietnam defined McFarlane's military career and shaped his adult life. He landed near Danang in the spring of 1965 and commanded an artillery battery that was among the first U.S. combat units in the war. After a year of duty, he won a fellowship to study international affairs in Geneva. But he could not help brooding about the war. He was back in Vietnam for the 1968 Tet offensive.

"I went back," McFarlane said later, "because I had a very strong attachment to the Vietnamese people. . . . I felt they needed me." But by the end of his second tour, he found the war more troubling. "Close friends were getting killed, and I wasn't," he told the *Washington Post*. "How do you justify inflicting violence and being vulnerable to it, especially when you know the whole enterprise is unlikely to be successful?"

He cast about for a new direction and, this time, landed a White House Fellowship. At the age of thirty-four, McFarlane was working for Richard Nixon's top aides. Within two years he was a military assistant to

Kissinger, who was then at the height of his secret diplomacy. And in 1975 McFarlane, working from the White House Situation Room, helped run the final U.S. withdrawal from Saigon.

A decade later, Vietnam was still with him. McFarlane saw part of his mission at the NSC as ending America's reluctance to intervene in the Third World. Through his church in suburban Maryland, he was also working to resettle Vietnamese refugees. And he was still struggling to draw some benefit from the lessons of defeat. "The most relevant lesson I learned is what is and what isn't sustainable by the American people," he said. "No administration can expect to succeed in any major policy undertaking unless it succeeds in building [a] clear understanding of its goals and strategy. The administration clearly failed to do that in Vietnam." The war also had a lasting emotional impact on the taciturn marine. He would later speak reluctantly but with deep feeling about the experience of combat, a kind of stress that even working in the White House couldn't match. "It was unpredictable," he once said haltingly. "If you witness enough violence, if you hold enough people in your arms as they die, that's about as bad as it gets."

McFarlane rose steadily through jobs at the Senate Armed Services Committee under John Tower of Texas, at the State Department under Alexander Haig, and back at the White House in 1982 as deputy to William Clark. It was in his NSC role that McFarlane went to Beirut in 1983 and demanded the use of naval gunfire — an unusual hands-on role for a deputy national security adviser.

"The NSC became operational when McFarlane became the Mideast envoy," said Howard Teicher, an NSC aide who accompanied McFarlane on his foray into Lebanon. "On the ground in Beirut, we figured out how to move the bureaucracy." One of the keys, Teicher said, was a portable satellite communications transmitter that enabled McFarlane to communicate directly with the White House — without going through the State Department or any other agency.

In the fall of 1983, Clark, exhausted by White House infighting, weary of a job for which he had been ill prepared — and suffering from recurrent nightmares — abruptly told Reagan that he wanted to quit. James Baker and Michael Deaver quickly cooked up a proposal: Baker could take the NSC job, and Deaver could succeed him as chief of staff. Reagan happily approved the scheme without consulting Clark or anyone else in the cabinet. But on his way downstairs to the Situation Room to announce the change, the president confided his plan to Clark — who immediately organized a revolt. Clark, Weinberger, Casey, and Attorney General Edwin Meese all considered Baker too moderate, not enough of a hawk. Reinforcing each other's agitation, they told the president they might all resign if the changes went through.

Upstairs, Deaver could see that something was wrong; the electric board that tracks the president's whereabouts in the building showed Reagan waylaid in the basement. Deaver called Clark's secretary and, only half joking, demanded, "What have you done with him?" When the president finally emerged, he was shaken and abashed. "Sorry," he told Deaver and Baker. "I had no idea the fellows would be so adamant." Deaver, who had already told friends that he would soon become chief of staff, was livid.

The NSPG then debated who should succeed Clark at the NSC. Casey wanted the hawkish and prickly Jeane Kirkpatrick to step in, but there was little support for her. Instead, the cabinet members settled on a compromise candidate, a man who would be even-handed and, equally important, bureaucratically unthreatening: Bud McFarlane.

McFarlane's tenure did not begin well. He was Reagan's third national security adviser in less than three years, and the press quickly learned that he had won the job almost by default. And he had no time to settle in: in McFarlane's first nine days on the job, the marine barracks in Beirut were bombed and the United States invaded Grenada. "This job is way beyond me," he told a friend in a moment of doubt. "They should have gotten somebody better, like Kissinger."

The national security adviser to the president of the United States has virtually no formal powers. The job is not even mentioned in the National Security Act of 1947, which set up the basic machinery of foreign policy after World War II. Legally, the adviser is one of a half-dozen aides who carry the deceptively simple title of assistant to the president. His influence depends entirely on how the president chooses to exercise his power. It is, inherently, a courtier's job; its holder is powerful only if he has the president's ear and carries the president's proxy.

The National Security Council consists of the president, the vice president, the secretaries of state and defense, and anyone else the president adds to the list. In the second Reagan administration, the NSC's membership grew to include Casey, Meese, Baker, Regan, and the chairman of the Joint Chiefs of Staff.

In theory, the national security adviser merely coordinates the work of the NSC. In reality, however, the adviser and the NSC staff act as the president's personal foreign policy arm. Every president since Kennedy has chosen to make the national security adviser a powerful figure, a guarantor of the chief executive's will. Reagan had explicitly downgraded the job at first, banishing his first national security adviser, Richard Allen, to a basement office and a second-rank position on the organizational chart; but William Clark quickly restored the office's clout, and McFarlane took it one step further, reclaiming Henry Kissinger's first-floor quarters down the hall from the Oval Office.

Unlike Clark, who had been at Reagan's side since the 1966 gubernatorial campaign in California, McFarlane was barely known to the president when he took over the daily 9:30 A.M. national security briefing. But Nancy Reagan quickly took a shine to the new adviser. "She was crazy about Bud at first," a friend said. "She thought he was good-looking, close-mouthed, and one of the few people in the White House who hadn't overplayed his hand." The First Lady invited McFarlane and his wife, Jonda, to the White House residence for dinner along with two other guests — only six people at the table, chatting like intimates. During the evening, the president and Mrs. Reagan listened attentively to McFarlane's comments on the international scene, a heady experience for the forty-eight-year-old former marine. "McFarlane seemed in awe of the president — and they were very high on him, too," another guest recalled. At the Reagans' annual New Year's Eve gala in Palm Springs, the First Lady even made a point of praising McFarlane's ballroom skill — a clear signal of high favor.

McFarlane's soldierly reserve, the quality Nancy Reagan so admired, also made him acceptable to the feuding cabinet secretaries, Shultz and Weinberger. And initially McFarlane was satisfied to work as a low-key mediator, not a policymaker in his own right. "My greatest frustration before coming into this job was to see disagreements linger," he said in 1984. "Whenever there are strong-willed cabinet officers and disagreements, it must be the job of this person to resolve them. It is the measure of whether you succeed or fail whether you do that."

But his deferential instincts also restrained McFarlane from pushing Reagan too hard. Unlike Clark and Deaver, he was mortally uncomfortable with the idea of telling the president that he was wrong. "When you've got a president of the United States, there are very few people who will take him on, tell him exactly what they really think," Deaver recalled later. "I used to have to . . . beg Bud to do it. He'd come to me and say, 'You know, our position on this or that is terrible.' And I'd say, 'Bud, for God's sake, go tell him that.' Well, he was a soldier, you know. He'd say, 'You can't talk to the commander in chief like that,' and I'd say, 'Yeah, but you're not a soldier anymore. He hired you to give him the best advice.' "

Although McFarlane never found it easy to second-guess the president, he had little hesitation about challenging other members of the administration. Over time, he gradually expanded his policymaking role. As a mediator, he helped organize weekly breakfasts and lunches for Shultz, Weinberger, and Casey, hoping to clear the air. And when the cabinet members' conflicts festered, he began to use his own office to cut through the deadlocks. He began drafting presidential orders — National Security Decision Directives — without waiting for the members of the NSC to request them. He reshaped the NSC staff to promote "action officers" over ideologues; he sent his aides on clandestine missions that he kept secret even from the State Department. And White House orders began to appear with an unusual signature: "FOR THE PRESIDENT: Robert C. McFarlane."

As McFarlane quietly acquired more influence, his little-known staff became a center of power as well. Clark, his predecessor, had expanded the NSC staff from about 120 at the end of the Carter administration to more than 180, turning the organizational chart into a forest of senior directors, directors, and deputy directors. He insisted that his people carry the same ranks and privileges as White House aides, including the right to eat in the White House Mess, the most prestigious lunch spot in Washington. Most important of all, Clark brought the NSC into the computer age.

When Reagan took office in 1981, one NSC aide recalled with some exaggeration, "the average newspaper office had more robust communications capabilities than the federal government." The White House had its own high tech military communications office, which kept the president and his aides within reach of secure telephones, but that was about it. In stepped a computer wizard named Richard S. Beal, a veteran of Wirthlin's polling operation in the 1980 campaign. The former Brigham Young University professor first proposed to computerize the flow of information around the Oval Office, but James Baker's aides refused to allow a technician inside their closely guarded process. So Beal made his pitch to Clark and was permitted to set up a new facility in the Old Executive Office Building: the Crisis Management Center, more often known simply as Room 208.

Beal's idea was simple but powerful: to collect all the government's foreign policy information in one central location. The State Department, the Pentagon, the CIA, and the National Security Agency (which eavesdrops on international communications) all had sophisticated computer systems full of intelligence, but each operated autonomously. Beal wanted to give the NSC staff direct access to the other agencies' raw data — an important source of bureaucratic power.

Thanks to Beal and some $10 million worth of computer and communications equipment, within four years the NSC had engineered a technological coup d'état. The NSC staff, using video terminals in Room 208, could now tap directly into Pentagon data banks. They could, for instance, identify flight paths and refueling stops for military aircraft, an ability that proved crucial in planning both the 1983 invasion of Grenada and the 1986 bombing of Libya. The NSC never gained access to all the data it wanted, but it got enough to shift the balance of power within the bureaucracy. Before Room 208, the Pentagon and the CIA could slow down a White House proposal for covert action simply by choking off the flow of information; now NSC aides could plan operations themselves in a cockpit of glowing computer screens and electronic maps.

Beal also turned out to be an ingenious bureaucrat; he assembled an entire staff for Room 208 by borrowing employees from other agencies. No one in the White House was quite sure how many aides Beal had or what they did; they were all on loan, and their funding came from accounts outside the White House. "Millions of dollars were being spent, dozens of people were working twenty-four hours a day . . . and there just weren't that many crises," said Christopher Hicks, who ran the White House office of administration during 1985. "There was nobody asking if this was necessary. This is ultimately a civilian government, but here was this growing military operation — part of the White House, but the White House had no oversight."

Even within the NSC staff, only a few people knew much about Room 208. McFarlane's staff resembled a series of concentric circles; of the forty-five top professionals, about fifteen did most of the policy work and only five or six worked closely with the national security adviser. Around the outer circle was an astonishing amount of deadwood, including several hard-line right-wingers installed to protect the administration's ideological purity. They could not be fired without a political flap, so McFarlane simply added new people he wanted to the old ones he didn't.

"It was a very strange management system," said Raymond F. Burghardt, who was senior director for Latin America. "There were some people who didn't do anything; there were others who worked all the time. There were no job descriptions — none. Eventually, people defined their work for themselves."

The result was a staff of unprecedented size — a record high, ultimately, of 186 — and a certain degree of disorder. "McFarlane saw the ideal system as one in which members of the staff would work directly for him and would get their motivation from the satisfaction of knowing that they were working for the national security adviser," said Kimmitt. "But he couldn't deal directly with every member of the staff. It was simply too big. The result was that there were about five people with whom Bud dealt constantly . . . and everyone else went through the structure."

The inner circle included McFarlane's deputy, Rear Admiral John M. Poindexter; his chief strategist, Donald R. Fortier; and Howard Teicher, his thirty-year-old director of political-military affairs. And it included a marine lieutenant colonel who worked on terrorism and special operations, Oliver L. North.

The men of the inner circle found that the new technology helped them get around even their own tiny bureaucracy. Officially, NSC aides could not send messages directly to McFarlane; instead, Kimmitt, as executive secretary, was supposed to sort out what McFarlane needed to see. But in 1984 the NSC acquired a new computer message system called PROFS, an IBM product whose name meant simply "professional office system." Kimmitt, seeing a potential for chaos, insisted that the system move memos up the ladder step by step, just as if they were still on paper. But McFarlane and Poindexter short-circuited Kimmitt's rule, allowing members of the inner circle to communicate among themselves instantly — and privately.

One of the aides most adept at manipulating all this new technology, from Room 208 to the PROFS message system, was Oliver North. "Before PROFS, Bud would often encourage Ollie to bring things directly to him without going through the system, but it wasn't easy," Kimmitt said. "He had to come across the street into the White House, walk the paper into the first floor — and hope that nobody else saw him. But once we had PROFS, he could get anything he wanted straight into the office. He didn't even have to leave his desk."

When Donald Regan replaced James Baker as White House chief of staff in January 1985, McFarlane expected that his own hard-won power would remain intact; after all, he had three years of seniority on the president's staff, and Regan had no real experience in foreign policy. Nevertheless, to McFarlane's dismay, Regan set out to demonstrate his control of the entire White House almost as soon as he settled into the spacious corner office at the other end of the corridor from the national security adviser's slightly smaller quarters.

It was an odd struggle for dominance, a duel of one-upmanship fought over perks and perceptions more than policy. Regan had few, if any, strong ideas about foreign affairs; he cheerfully admitted that his ideology began and ended with "the belief in and practice of capitalism." But he cared passionately about being number one. It was no accident that Regan's men had the White House computer terminals renumbered to make their chief's "Executive Office of the President 001."

Regan knew that his preeminence rested on one thing: an intimate working relationship with Ronald Reagan. As it happened, that was precisely McFarlane's sore spot; after more than a year on the job, the national security adviser was still a little insecure about his relationship with the man in the Oval Office. When Regan arrived, an NSC colleague recalled, McFarlane had "just begun to build up a social and working trust with the president, working under enormous pressure, when a new fellow came in with a whole new toy box, asking questions and getting in the way."

Regan quickly made it clear that while McFarlane had the right to deal directly with the president, he also reported to the chief of staff. Regan reinforced the point almost every morning during the president's national security briefing. "Baker rarely talked in the nine-thirty briefings," an aide recalled. "Regan commented on everything."

But the real battle was not so much over power as over public perceptions. In time, McFarlane took on a higher profile; the self-effacement that had worried Deaver began to disappear. The national security adviser began acting increasingly as the administration's chief spokesman on foreign policy issues, overshadowing even George Shultz. In a move that drew snickers from other Reagan aides, McFarlane took to strolling through the White House press room to buy candy from a vending machine, only to be "surprised" by the presence of reporters.

And he began, with increasing audacity, to criticize his seniors in the cabinet. In an impromptu briefing on New Year's Day of 1985, after his ballroom prowess had so impressed the First Lady, McFarlane bluntly told reporters that Weinberger had "misspent" much of the military buildup and dismissed the defense secretary's beloved MX missile as "a turkey system." Later that spring, while Shultz was briefing reporters on arms control, McFarlane nudged an aide. "This isn't right," he whispered. "I'll do a backgrounder." As soon as Shultz was out of the room, McFarlane mounted the podium to offer his own, slightly different version of the administration's policy.

For his part, chief of staff Regan seemed to crave recognition of his power more than the actual use of it. And when events failed to match his boasts, Regan could erupt in a fearsome rage — as McFarlane soon learned. On the night of March 10, 1985, McFarlane woke the president with a telephone call to tell him that Soviet leader Konstantin Chernenko had died, but he neglected to call the chief of staff as well. The next morning, Regan walked into the Oval Office to be greeted by the president with: "Boy, wasn't that something?" The chief of staff, livid at being caught uninformed, dressed McFarlane down "in that tone people reserve for servants," said one former White House aide. McFarlane, chastened, wrote Regan a formal letter of apology.

Only two weeks later, it happened again. This time McFarlane woke the president to tell him that a U.S. Army observer in East Germany had been shot by Soviet troops. At a staff breakfast, Regan learned about the incident from an aide. He was "stone-faced," the aide recalled. "Don hated surprises." Unwittingly adding insult to injury, the president cheerfully told reporters later that day: "When I hear the phone ring in those early morning hours, I know that all I have to do is pick it up and say, 'Hi Bud,' and there he is on the other end." Regan turned a visible pink around the ears; the message he heard was that the one man who talked with the president day and night was McFarlane.

Regan retaliated by injecting himself further onto McFarlane's foreign policy turf. In April, as McFarlane was working toward a U.S.-Soviet summit meeting, Regan breezily told reporters that the president wanted assurances of "results," not "meetings for meetings' sake." The offhand remark was taken in Moscow as a serious signal of U.S. hesitation about a summit, and McFarlane had to give a counterbriefing the next day to retract what Regan had said.

Not long afterward, when McFarlane was preparing to head up to Congress to lobby for money to build more MX nuclear missiles, Regan said curtly, "I'll go — they don't want to hear from you."

As the gamesmanship escalated during the spring of 1985, McFarlane began to think again about leaving his job. The problem of extracting a foreign policy from a passive president and a feuding cabinet hadn't been solved. The president was still ducking the task of choosing clearly among foreign policy priorities. If anything, with the arrival of the opinionated and assertive Regan, the problem was worse.

"It had become not as much fun in comparison to the first term," McFarlane said later.

And so, just as after the 1984 election, McFarlane decided to make the decisions himself. In effect, he guessed what the president wanted, and acted on that.

"Based upon his daily reactions and comments, you can't help but get a sense of what's important to him," McFarlane recalled. "So, reflecting on what seemed to be important in morning briefings for the past three years, I decided that the Soviet Union ought to be the leading priority, and Shultz agreed. . . . We devoted most of our efforts in 1985 to getting the two of us back to the table and developing an agenda that the American people might understand and support."

As the year went on, McFarlane's decision to push for arms control talks slowly bore fruit. The Soviet Union agreed to return to the negotiating table; so did Weinberger's Pentagon. NSC meetings were still "pretty starchy," with Shultz and Weinberger battling over how flexible the U.S. position should be. But Reagan, under McFarlane's increasingly assertive counsel, was slowly coming around to a more moderate view.

"Cap made his points very firmly; George did too. And the president's habit was never to decide during the meeting," McFarlane recalled. "The next day I would go in, talk to him about it, and he ended up coming down on George's side."

Reagan still wasn't playing the more active role in foreign policy that he had promised McFarlane on *Air Force One* back in December 1984. But he was listening more closely to McFarlane, and that had tipped the balance: McFarlane decided to stay. The national security adviser still saw a chance to achieve some of his foreign policy goals, and he believed that he and his aides were the only ones who could do the job.

4

Cowboys

IN FEBRUARY 1985, a routine scrap of intelligence about a Nicaraguan cargo ship landed on the desk of a young marine officer on the staff of the National Security Council. To most officials in Ronald Reagan's White House, the news that the freighter *Monimbo* was picking up weapons in North Korea was merely another sign that Nicaragua was slipping into the Soviet camp. But to Oliver L. North, the NSC's deputy director for political-military affairs, the voyage of the *Monimbo* was a golden opportunity — a chance for an audacious stroke on behalf of the contras, the Nicaraguan rebels dear to Reagan's heart.

"There is no apparent armed security detail aboard the *Monimbo*, despite the sensitive nature of her cargo," North quickly wrote in a Top Secret memorandum to his boss, national security adviser McFarlane.

"There appear to be three options: The shipment could be seized and the weapons delivered to the FDN [the largest contra faction]; the ship could be sunk; or the shipment . . . could be made public as a means of preventing the delivery."

To North, the best choice was the boldest — seizing the ship and stealing its cargo, even though, his memo acknowledged, that amounted to "piracy." The operation could be carried out without leaving any U.S. fingerprints, he suggested. South Korean naval commandos could intercept the freighter on its return voyage somewhere in the Pacific, swarm up its sides with grappling hooks, and overpower the crew.

"If such an operation were undertaken, it would be best to seize the vessel as it cleared the East China Sea enroute to Nicaragua's Pacific port at Corinto," North wrote. "If time does not permit a special operation to be launched, [contra leader Adolfo] Calero can quickly be provided with the maritime assets required to sink the vessel."

North's immediate superior, deputy national security adviser John Poindexter, thought it a fine idea. "We need to take action to make sure [the] ship does not arrive in Nicaragua," he scrawled across the bottom of North's memo. But McFarlane and others worried the idea to death. "When the moment of truth came — that we would have to do it ourselves — the spleen just ran out of them," a senior official recalled. The *Monimbo* made a safe passage; the Sandinistas got their North Korean rifles.

North, disappointed, went back to the drawing board. But the proposal to seize the *Monimbo* was vintage Oliver North: the dramatic, unorthodox idea, the breathless, not-a-moment-to-lose tone, the loving attention to operational detail — and the cavalier disregard of possible pitfalls. And North soon came up with even more audacious schemes to help the contras. The same day he proposed seizing the *Monimbo*, North was working on schemes to raise money for the rebels from right-wing foreign governments, to hire British mercenaries to train the contras in special operations, and to float the rebel leaders to Philadelphia on a cruise ship to unveil a Nicaraguan declaration of independence. Dramatic ideas and quick action were the tools North used to make his name on the NSC staff. He was everything a national security adviser could want in a special operations aide: impossibly energetic, a true believer, and an unstoppable bureaucratic commando.

"Ollie was a great action officer," said Tony Motley, then assistant secretary of state for Latin America. "You could depend on Ollie to bust through a paperwork logjam."

North also knew how to impress his superiors; he was a relentless self-promoter and a spellbinding storyteller, almost as good as Ronald Reagan himself. One of the stories North told most often was about the 1983 invasion of Grenada — the only instance in history, he noted, when democracy had supplanted a Marxist regime.

North had spent four days and four nights in the NSC's Room 208 helping to plan the invasion, and he was the man who actually got Reagan's signature on the order dispatching the marines. But once the troops had landed and evacuated some 350 American medical students from the island, North realized that no one had told the students why they had been rescued. They might walk off the air force planes and announce that they hadn't felt any danger in Grenada at all, bringing the entire operation into question.

North bolted into the West Wing in search of McFarlane, he said, but found only Ronald Reagan, sitting in the Oval Office.

"What's the matter, Ollie?" the president asked.

"The medical students," North replied breathlessly, explaining the dilemma.

"Come with me," Reagan said. He led North into a room with a television monitor.

As the president and the young marine officer watched together, the air force jet landed and the students streamed down the stairs. The first one to reach the runway fell to his knees and kissed the ground.

"You see, Ollie," the president said, "you ought to have more faith in the American people."

North told the anecdote to several friends and acquaintances. It was a perfect parable: it tugged at patriotic heartstrings, it showed the wisdom of Ronald Reagan, it put Oliver North at the center of great events. And, as far as anyone can determine, it was made of whole cloth.

North did help coordinate the Grenada landing, and he did carry the marines' orders to the president — as McFarlane's messenger. A day before the highly secret invasion, he also absent-mindedly left a placard marked ST. GEORGES under one of the clocks in Room 208. A visitor horrified the staff by asking, "What are you working on, an invasion of Grenada?" But North himself, in his later testimony before Congress, had to admit that he had never met alone with Ronald Reagan.

"Ollie was about thirty to fifty percent bullshit," said one of his colleagues at the NSC. "He was notorious for constantly exaggerating his role in things. He was always 'coming from a meeting with the vice president.' We checked once, and he hadn't been in to see the vice president at all."

North even exaggerated his official NSC biography, claiming experience in "unconventional warfare operations in Southeast Asia" and a stint running a "Special Operations Training Detachment." His Marine Corps records showed no formal special operations work at all. Yet North succeeded in making himself indispensable to two national security advisers, first McFarlane and then Poindexter. "He was a guy of tremendous energy, a quick study, and he had terribly important bureaucratic skills — good writing, a good voice, no self-doubts at all," said Rodney McDaniel, the NSC's executive secretary under Poindexter. "He learned where the levers of power were . . . and played them like a violin." And North simply worked harder than almost anyone else. "He stayed around a long time, and he worked eighteen-hour days," McDaniel said. "There aren't many people on the NSC staff who work that hard and stay around that long."

North's five years at the NSC were composed of manic days, weekends at his desk, and vacations not taken. On the fifth birthday of his daughter Dornin, one friend recalled, "she called him three times — at seven o'clock, at eight o'clock, and at nine o'clock — and in essence said, 'Daddy, when are you coming home?' And Ollie said, 'Don't worry, honey. Daddy's coming home as soon as he can. I've just got to finish this work.' By the time he got home, she was already asleep. But he was willing to take the time to get the job done."

Not everyone admired this trait. "He was always scheduling meetings on Sundays, just to distress everyone else," CIA analyst John Horton grumbled. Others worried less about his workaholic devotion than his manic intensity. "I used to keep Ollie out of Reagan's office because he was dangerous," Michael Deaver recalled. "He scared me. . . . He'd fly to Beirut, be back twenty-four hours later, and brief the president. Reagan loved him, [loved] the style."

To North, foreign policy was a continuation of war by other means; the president was the nation's commander in chief, even in peacetime. "And if the commander in chief tells this lieutenant colonel to go stand in a corner and sit on his head, I will do so," he later told a congressional committee.

Behind that parade-ground view of the world, North, like McFarlane, harbored searing memories of commitment and betrayal in Vietnam. The son of a businessman in upstate New York, North had made his way through the U.S. Naval Academy on sheer determination after a devastating automobile accident. Neighbors at his boyhood home remembered watching the young midshipman jump repeatedly off the garage roof during his recuperation to try to strengthen his legs, and a classmate at Annapolis said North once plotted to surreptitiously remove records of a knee problem from his file so that he could make it into the marines. His persistence was rewarded: upon his graduation in 1968, North made the corps and went almost immediately to Vietnam. He won a Silver Star and a Bronze Star for bravery in combat just south of the demilitarized zone, in one instance leading his platoon on an eight-hour assault in the face of almost constant machine-gun fire. According to one of his men, North also led a brief, unauthorized, and possibly illegal foray across the DMZ to seize a North Vietnamese prisoner.

Yet, despite heroism and sacrifice, the United States lost its war in Vietnam, and North took the defeat badly. He was hospitalized briefly for "delayed battle stress" in 1974 after a superior officer discovered him naked, roaring incoherently and waving a pistol. The worst thing about America's withdrawal from Saigon, North said later, was not just defeat, but the betrayal of allies who had put their confidence in Washington's commitments. "We didn't lose the war in Vietnam," he insisted in his testimony. "We lost the war right here in this city."

But if North was a passionate anti-Communist, he was also a shrewd and practical bureaucrat. He engineered his rise to power, like many ambitious young men in Washington, by attaching himself to a series of patrons. His first lucky break came when a paper he wrote at the Naval War College was noticed by another Vietnam veteran, Navy Secretary John Lehman. In 1981, as the Reagan administration was getting under way, Lehman recommended North for a staff job on the NSC. Eventually, North joined a top-secret study group planning "government continuity in national crisis" — a euphemism for keeping things running during a thermonuclear war. North, as a thirty-seven-year-old major, was little more than an "easel carrier" at first, but his bureaucratic talent quickly earned him a reputation in the small world of the NSC. National security adviser William Clark put him to work on a grab bag of military projects, beginning with terrorism and special operations. Beginning in 1982, North gradually expanded his turf into El Salvador and Nicaragua, neatly fleecing the less agile bureaucrats of the NSC's office for Latin America. "He could be very Machiavellian," one colleague recalled. "Having figured out in his own mind what he wanted to do, he'd use whomever he needed to get it done."

When McFarlane became national security adviser in October 1983, North acquired a new mentor. In time, North almost seemed to play the role of the younger brother McFarlane never had: six years his junior, a fellow Annapolis graduate, a marine who agreed that the lessons of Vietnam hadn't been learned. And North was working on the fun part of foreign policy, the action part — not McFarlane's endless treadmill of mediating among cabinet members. It was as if the impetuous North were the person McFarlane secretly yearned to be. North could be "a romanticist," McFarlane admitted later, and some of his memos were "rather lurid . . . but I don't fault him for it. . . . I don't fault him for being an imaginative, aggressive, committed young officer."

Most middle-level NSC aides rarely dealt directly with McFarlane, but North often did. His twenty-five-year-old secretary, Fawn Hall, was the daughter of McFarlane's secretary, and she could easily learn when the adviser's schedule had a few minutes open for a young marine officer to slip in the door.

But North was also an effective advocate for his ideas, even the hare-brained ones, because he conveyed, like Ronald Reagan, an impression of absolute sincerity. And the issue he was most passionate about, week after week, was the struggle of the contras in Nicaragua. Even North's colleagues found themselves touched by his talk of "the brave boys and girls" fighting in the mountains of Central America. "He could make you feel very guilty for not going to the hilt," the CIA's John Horton said.

It all went back, again, to Vietnam. "For people who went through that, and Colonel North surely did, you come away with the profound sense of very intolerable failure," McFarlane said later in a television interview. "That is, that a government must never give its word to people who may stand to lose their lives and then break faith."

A congressman intrigued by that theme once asked North what he saw as the major difference between the two wars. "Ten thousand miles," North replied. "In Nicaragua . . . you're talking about something right next door. That's the major difference."

With fewer people than Arizona, a primitive economy, and the squalid history of a banana republic, Nicaragua until recently seemed just one more backwater among the sad little countries of Central America. Even the Sandinista revolution of 1979 aroused little attention from Americans, most of whom were not sure where to find the country on a map.

But Ronald Reagan paid attention. Even before his 1980 campaign for president, he denounced Jimmy Carter for abandoning the Nicaraguan dictator, Anastasio Somoza, who remained a faithful U.S. ally even as his misrule drove his citizens to revolt. After the Sandinistas came to power, they proved to be students of Cuba's Fidel Castro: they openly declared their sympathy for the Marxist guerrillas fighting a U.S.-backed government in neighboring El Salvador, and there was evidence that they were providing guns and other aid to the rebels as well. To Reagan and his conservative supporters, Nicaragua was thus turning into "a second Cuba," a Soviet base on the mainland of Latin America. However poor and weak Nicaragua looked now, they argued, the Sandinistas' alliance with the Soviet Union was a genuine threat to the United States.

It did not take the Reagan administration long to begin acting on those convictions. Within five weeks of Reagan's first inauguration, in 1981, CIA director Casey proposed a covert action program targeted against Cuban advisers in Nicaragua. Later that year, Reagan signed a secret order authorizing the CIA to fund a small guerrilla army of Nicaraguan rebels. The aim, Casey told Congress in December 1981, was not to overthrow the Sandinistas but merely to interdict Nicaraguan arms shipments to El Salvador. Congress's intelligence committees were worried because Reagan's "finding" — the official charter for the operation — was not nearly that precise. But Casey pointed out that the contras had only five hundred men under arms; a force so small couldn't dream of toppling the Sandinista regime.

At first, the contra war was indeed a puny affair, but under the prodding of Casey and his energetic chief of operations in Latin America, Duane "Dewey" Clarridge, the little war quickly grew. By 1983, the CIA had recruited political leaders and swelled the contras' ranks to more than six thousand. The rebels began striking deep inside Nicaragua, attacking military patrols, Sandinista officials, and not a few innocent bystanders. Casey himself flew down on impromptu inspection tours, turning up at secret bases in colorful resort clothes, an American diplomat recalled, "like a tourist who'd lost his way." Clarridge and other veterans of the CIA's operations directorate were exultant. For the first time since Indochina, they were running a war.

Congress's two intelligence committees, on the other hand, weren't exultant at all. Created after a series of scandals in the 1970s, the committees were charged with monitoring the CIA's operations and making sure they didn't exceed their authorized bounds. This operation, members complained, didn't seem to have bounds at all. Casey still claimed that his objective was merely to stop Sandinista aid to the guerrillas in El

Salvador, but no arms had been interdicted. The contras themselves were forthright about their goal: despite their CIA handlers' pleas for discretion, they said they aimed to overthrow the Managua regime. But Casey and the rest of the administration never openly sought public support for that objective; instead, they sought the path of least resistance, which meant insisting that their aims were strictly, if illogically, limited. Over the long run, the result was a crippling loss of credibility.

The first of many congressional battles over Nicaragua began in 1982. The House Intelligence Committee, run by Edward P. Boland of Massachusetts, voted to put a limit on funding for the contras. But the Senate Intelligence Committee, chaired by Republican patriarch Barry Goldwater of Arizona, supported the CIA. They settled on a compromise that took Casey at his word: the CIA could support the contras, but not "for the purpose of overthrowing the Government of Nicaragua." The measure was called the Boland amendment.

At the CIA, there was jubilation. As long as the agency declared that its "purpose" was within the law, Casey's aides reasoned, they could do almost anything they wanted. A few months later, reporters asked Reagan whether the administration was doing anything to overthrow the Sandinistas. "No, because that would be violating the law," the president replied. "What I might personally wish or what our government might wish still would not justify us violating the law of the land." But when a U.S. ambassador abroad, confused by the shifting rationales for the Nicaragua program, asked Casey for a private answer, he got one.

"What's the real goal, Bill?" the ambassador asked. "What are you trying to do?"

Casey replied without hesitating. "Get rid of the Sandinistas," he said.

Still, in the rugged mountains and jungles of northern Nicaragua, the contras' war did not go well. The rebels ranged through the backwoods of three provinces, ambushing trucks and attacking remote farms, but they were not winning the kind of victories they needed to attract a following. And while the contras struggled, the Sandinistas gained ground, cementing control over the population and expanding their Soviet-equipped army.

The failure of the CIA's covert program to produce immediate results made Congress increasingly restive. The intelligence committees could see that the contra war, which Casey had sold as a small and limited effort, was pulling the United States toward a deeper involvement. In July 1983, the House voted to stop the project entirely; in a compromise, Congress placed a limit of $24 million on what the CIA could spend on the war.

Casey would not be deterred. His first response was to try to evade the spending cap, asking the Defense Department to give the contras $28 million worth of weapons and aircraft free of charge. The Pentagon delivered three small airplanes and some night vision equipment, but then decided the arrangement was probably illegal and refused requests for more. The CIA's next move was to press for more action in Nicaragua — for spectacular victories that could seriously weaken the Sandinista regime. A working group reported to the NSC: "Given the distinct possibility that we may be unable to obtain additional funding [from Congress], our objective should be to bring the Nicaragua situation to a head in 1984." CIA officers in Honduras, where the contras were based, came up with an ebullient rallying cry: "Managua by Christmas!" But the contras couldn't win by themselves; the CIA had to help.

When the resulting offensive began in September 1983, the Sandinistas were startled to see that the contras had suddenly acquired a well-equipped navy and air force. CIA "Q-boats" sped into Nicaragua's harbors and set fuel tanks ablaze. At least one battle drew a U.S.-crewed CIA helicopter into direct combat with Sandinista gunners. Other CIA helicopters strafed Sandinista positions to support contra troops on the ground. A contra-piloted Cessna tried to bomb the military airfield at Managua International Airport but crashed into the passenger terminal, inflicting embarrassing civilian casualties.

But none of this was turning the tide of the war. "We've got to hit the Sandinistas where they hurt," Casey said. "Where are they vulnerable?"

His chief strategist, Dewey Clarridge, came up with the answer: oil. All of Nicaragua's fuel was imported through three small ports. Clarridge had studied the Russo-Japanese War of 1904–5; the Japanese paralyzed the czar's navy in port by mining his harbors. It was the Sandinistas' weak point too. "You don't need to sink the ships — just scare them," he explained to Motley, the assistant secretary of state. "If Lloyd's of London pulls the insurance from ships going in to Nicaragua, that's it — they don't get any oil."

Motley, Casey, and McFarlane were all enthusiastic. It seemed a devilishly clever ploy. Reagan reviewed the plan at an NSPG meeting on January 6, 1984; the participants remember no special reaction from the president, merely his usual approval of what his advisers had prepared. The magnetic mines, custom made in North Carolina to produce maximum noise and minimum damage, were already waiting aboard a CIA-run "mother ship." On January 7, the first charges splashed into Nicaragua's harbors. But the "firecracker" mines didn't seem to faze merchant seamen; the freighters continued to deliver guns and fuel to Nicaragua's ports. "It was a basic miscalculation on our part," a State Department official mourned.

The mines' only real impact was in Congress, where the Senate Intelligence Committee realized with a start that the CIA was committing acts of war. Casey had mentioned the mining briefly in two appearances before the committee, but most of the members either weren't paying attention or didn't understand what he was talking about. Not until April did the senators realize belatedly that it was the CIA, their CIA, that was dropping mines into Nicaraguan harbors. Casey's defenders on the committee felt betrayed. "This is no way to run a railroad," a livid Barry Goldwater stormed in a letter to Casey. "I am pissed off!" Republicans offended at the slight to senatorial prerogatives joined anticontra Democrats to condemn the mining by the extraordinary vote of 84–12. On April 26, 1984, Casey was summoned to an unusual secret session of the Senate and formally apologized.

After two years of struggle, the debacle of the mining finally enabled the Democrats to halt the funding for Reagan's contra war. The CIA's money ran out in June. Many of the contras began moving out of Nicaragua, wading back across the Coco and Poteca rivers into squalid camps in Honduras. The contra war was "dead," Speaker O'Neill said triumphantly.

To Casey and his loyalists, the lesson was that Congress could not be trusted. They felt they had done what they were supposed to do; they had not been forthcoming about the mining, but they had in fact provided details to any member of Congress who asked. Now they were receiving only punishment in return.

But Casey, a canny, bare-knuckled New York lawyer and veteran of the World War II spy agency, the Office of Strategic Services (OSS), was not easily denied. If Congress refused to give the rebels the help they needed, the entrepreneur who ran the CIA would simply look somewhere else.

Like Ronald Reagan, William J. Casey had assumed office with a goal that was simple but audacious: he wanted to turn back the clock and undo the constraints on covert action that Congress imposed on U.S. intelligence agencies during the 1970s. "The CIA is something unique in the world," Casey said. "Its depth was created over twenty-five years. Then it went through a time of bad criticism — sensational, inaccurate, unfair, and distorted. The government turned its back on intelligence and the process of gathering it. I want to restore the earlier, good days."

That was no small order. The CIA Casey inherited was no longer the organization that had run daring, cold-blooded covert actions around the world during the 1950s and 1960s. The operations directorate was still hung over from the scandal days and budget cuts of the 1970s. The men who ran covert action were split into two camps: those who had risen mostly by caution and deference to Congress, and those who yearned, like Casey, for a return to "the earlier, good days." Each faction had a derisive name for the other. The men of caution were called "shoe clerks," the risk takers, "cowboys."

Casey's highest priority was restoring the luster of covert action, the range of clandestine operations — from anonymous propaganda and political funding to undeclared wars — by which the United States seeks to influence the affairs of other countries. In the mid-1970s, Congress had actually considered outlawing covert action altogether, and while the idea never came to serious debate, it was a measure of the bad odor into which the clandestine service had fallen.

Reagan's support for anti-Communist rebels in Afghanistan, Nicaragua, and elsewhere demanded a more aggressive CIA. On this point the warring members of the NSC, Shultz and Weinberger and McFarlane, all agreed: covert action was an indispensable "third option" between mere diplomatic pressure and overt military intervention. To Reagan's political lieutenants, secret intelligence operations, which could always be denied, set off fewer domestic alarm bells than sending troops. Covert action seemed to promise great results at minimal cost.

So Casey flew around the world, bringing CIA station chiefs the word that taking risks was back in fashion: it was okay to be a cowboy again. Results were what counted, he said. According to one tale that flashed instantly through the brotherhood of clandestine operators, Casey himself demonstrated the new rules of the game by planting an electronic listening device in a foreign leader's office during an official courtesy call. "Bill Casey was the last great buccaneer from OSS," his deputy director for operations, Clair George, said admiringly. "He was dropping agents into Germany and France and saving lives when most of us were doing nothing. This was a great guy."

Casey played his role in Reagan's cabinet cannily as well. In World War II, he had seen how intelligence policy was made in Washington: "Anyone with access to Roosevelt could get a charter for himself." Casey made sure he was one of the few members of the NSC with regular, direct access to Reagan. He called himself "the president's intelligence officer" and told others that his most important job was keeping Reagan constantly informed. Sometimes that meant shuttling to the White House with intelligence on the latest crisis; sometimes it meant regaling Reagan with tales of CIA derring-do or detective work, like the agency's success in tracing a load of terrorist guns back to Cuba or showing him CIA films on foreign leaders and international issues. As Shultz and McFarlane noted jealously, all that access to the president gave Casey an unusual opportunity to press his own hawkish views — especially to a president as susceptible to vivid arguments as Reagan.

The first CIA director ever to hold a cabinet seat, Casey thus played a forceful double role, first presenting the intelligence community's analyses and then his own passionate opinions as well. He would later be accused, especially by George Shultz, of "cooking" intelligence to promote his policy recommendations; but most other officials maintained that Casey didn't distort the formal CIA analyses as much as wield his command of secret information as a weapon of advocacy.

On the question of Nicaragua, for example, intelligence was frequently a focus of the administration's internal debates. Partisans of the contras trumpeted reports of success; skeptics called attention to the rebels' failings. Analysts fought regularly over competing estimates of how many contras were in the field, with the CIA's numbers frequently at the high end. The agency once triumphantly presented irrefutable evidence of a contra victory: an intercepted order from a Sandinista army officer for seventy-eight coffins. An American diplomat visited the town in question and found it full of empty coffins; the army had simply ordered too many. But the CIA stuck to its claim of seventy-eight dead. "The intercept was just too sexy," one aide recalled.

More important, the information that Casey and others took to Reagan was not always the product of careful, dispassionate analysis. Good news about the contras reached the president's ear quickly; bad news, grudgingly or not at all. A U.S. Army general once told White House aides that the contras were so popular inside Nicaragua that the peasants were volunteering to feed them; within minutes, he was in the Oval Office telling his story to the president. "General," Reagan said emotionally, "you've just made my day." The general's story turned out to be dead wrong, but it made a deep impression on the president all the same.

Casey played the secret-information game on a subtle, even clandestine level. He cultivated allies on the White House staff — agents, in the parlance of espionage — who could keep him informed and help press his arguments. One was speechwriter Tony Dolan; another was Oliver North; and another was no less than Donald Regan, an old friend and political protégé from Wall Street days.

Regan's arrival as White House chief of staff marked an important change from Casey's point of view. The CIA director had never gotten along with James Baker, the first chief of staff; the two men had accused each other of lying in 1981 in a flap over the theft of a briefing book from Jimmy Carter's presidential campaign. But Regan was a longtime ally of Casey's who could guarantee the director's access to the Oval Office. More than once, when Casey and McFarlane were at odds over policy, the CIA chief simply went around the national security adviser and asked Regan to arrange his meetings with the president. The Reagan-Casey tête-à-têtes were torture for McFarlane; he was never sure whether Casey was delivering intelligence or extracting secret presidential decisions. And between meetings, the CIA chief wrote notes to the president and to Regan — fervent pep talks urging steadfastness on Nicaragua and other issues. Some closed with a special Casey touch over the signature: "God Save America!"

By 1985, Casey's drive to restore the CIA's power and prestige had at least partially succeeded. According to informed estimates (the actual figures are resolutely secret), Congress more than doubled its appropriations for intelligence during Reagan's first term, enabling the CIA to expand its operations around the world and hire as many as three thousand new officers. Even Casey's adversaries gave him credit for skillfully managing the agency's growth and for energizing the intelligence directorate, which reports and analyzes information.

As for the effort to make covert action respectable again, Casey's record was mixed. His men were working on a half-dozen secret wars around the world — some massive and covert only in a formal sense (Afghanistan, Nicaragua, Angola), others smaller and hardly noticed (Ethiopia, Chad). But success did not come easily.

On the outside, the press persisted in exposing covert operations whenever reporters stumbled across them. On the inside, even some members of the NSC displayed what Casey viewed as a disturbing tendency toward softness — Weinberger's resistance to using military force and Shultz's interest in negotiations in Central America, an exercise Casey considered not only futile but potentially dangerous. And as for the president himself, Casey was occasionally baffled and dismayed by Reagan's unwillingness to decide on a clear course.

But of all the barriers in Casey's path, Congress was the worst. Casey oozed contempt for the House and Senate, Republicans as well as Democrats. He saw no useful role for the intelligence committees and as much as told them so. The congressmen, with little real power to find out what was going on inside the agency, put Casey through long secret hearings, testy sessions that ended in a few minutes of studied camaraderie, after which the legislators shook their heads in wonder and Casey stalked away muttering, "Assholes."

Casey believed he was fighting the most important war on the planet: a shadow war against Soviet expansion. "This is not an undeclared war," he told audience after audience. "In 1961, Khrushchev, then leader of the Soviet Union, told us that communism would win — not through nuclear war, which could destroy the world, or conventional war, which could quickly lead to nuclear war, but by wars of national liberation in Africa, Asia, and Latin America. We were reluctant to believe him then — just as in the 1930s, we were reluctant to take Hitler seriously."

Nicaragua was the most important battleground, Casey said, the beachhead for Soviet inroads on the nation's southern flank. The Democrats might try to stop him from supporting the contras' war, but the crusade was too important for him to drop. Congress could pass laws to its heart's content; Casey, who had made his fortune as a tax lawyer, considered it a challenge to find a way around them.

If the contras were to keep fighting, the first requirement was money. Even before the uproar over the mining of Nicaragua's harbors, it had been increasingly apparent that Congress wasn't going to approve the funding needed to run a war. Casey and McFarlane both hit on the same solution: find a friendly foreign country to keep the rebels supplied with guns, boots, and food. Casey even had a list of candidates, three countries that all depended heavily on the good will of the United States: Israel, South Africa, and Saudi Arabia.

McFarlane sent an aide to Israel to seek a contribution, but Prime Minister Shimon Peres didn't want to defy Congress on an emotional issue like Nicaragua. Casey sent his man Clarridge to South Africa on a similar mission, but he could not immediately close the deal. No one at the CIA seems to have worried whether asking South Africa to bail out Reagan's contra project would dilute the administration's proclaimed goal of pressing for reform in the country's racial system.

Several newspapers soon reported fragments of the search for foreign aid for the contras, and the House Intelligence Committee summoned Casey for an explanation. The CIA chief, fresh from his apology for the mining, assured the congressmen: "We have not been involved in that at all."

"Is any element of our government approaching any element of another government to obtain aid for the contras?" asked Wyche Fowler, Jr., of Georgia. "No, not to my knowledge," Casey replied — an outright lie.

On June 25, 1984, the NSPG met with Reagan to consider ways to keep the contras alive. Casey urged the president to encourage other countries to send money to the rebels, but Shultz disagreed sharply. "You can't do indirectly what you can't do directly," he said. He warned that it could be "an impeachable offense" for Reagan to act as a conduit for other countries' money.

Reagan apparently said little and, as usual, made no decision at the meeting. But, in fact, McFarlane had already asked Saudi Arabia to donate $1 million per month to the contras — and Reagan knew it. Faced with Shultz's blunt opposition, Reagan, Casey, and McFarlane kept secret what they had already done.

In May, McFarlane had gone out to see Prince Bandar bin Sultan, the Saudi ambassador to Washington, at his elegant home overlooking the Potomac River. The Saudi prince's main concern, McFarlane remembered, was the war in the Persian Gulf. The Saudis had asked for fourteen hundred portable Stinger antiaircraft missiles to protect their oil tankers but Congress objected. Only four Stingers had been sent — to protect King Fahd's new yacht.

McFarlane, who considered the young prince a personal friend, told him about his main worry, Nicaragua. "It was almost inevitable that the administration would fail in getting any support for the contras," he said. "It would represent a substantial loss for the president." It wasn't an outright solicitation, McFarlane insisted later — but he did mention explicitly that the contras needed at least $1 million per month. The prince, a sophisticated man, knew what he was driving at.

Within a few days, Bandar told McFarlane that his uncle, King Fahd, had agreed to give the contras the monthly stipend of $1 million. And within a few weeks, on May 22, Reagan sent a message to Fahd that his army would get the Stingers it wanted, despite the political heat on Capitol Hill. Over the Memorial Day weekend, with Congress safely out of town, the president invoked an emergency rule and secretly flew four hundred missiles to Saudi Arabia without waiting for legislative approval.

There was no explicit quid pro quo; the administration was genuinely concerned over Saudi Arabia's air defense needs and had already offered the Stingers before the contra issue arose. But there was also little doubt why the Saudi king felt a sudden urge to bankroll an insurgency in Central America, a part of the world that had never piqued his interest before. In the world of Arab royalty, just as in Washington, favors are investments; they are expected to produce returns.

McFarlane slipped a note for Reagan into the president's morning briefing memos: thanks to Fahd, the Nicaraguan rebels were in business again. The card came back from the Oval Office with a reply scrawled in the president's looping hand: "Good News!"

McFarlane hoped that the Saudi contribution would be only a short-term stopgap to keep the contras alive until Congress allowed the CIA to rejoin the war. But Congress remained adamant, and it soon became clear that $1 million a month simply wasn't enough. King Fahd would have to be asked for more.

Luckily, the monarch was making a rare state visit to Washington in February 1985. Reagan and his cabinet showered every attention on the Saudi king — several long meetings, a state dinner, a private breakfast in the White House residence, and a special session with just Reagan and Fahd alone together.

There was more than simple courtesy to the private meetings, and more than simple friendship in the smiles on Fahd's and Reagan's faces when they emerged together from the White House family dining room. Even before Reagan could raise the issue, the king had volunteered to send another $24 million to the president's rebels.

Few secrets were more closely held. Casey, McFarlane, and Weinberger knew, and there may have been one or two others. But nobody told the secretary of state, presumably because of Shultz's legal objections to begging other countries for a bail-out. When a Shultz aide asked McFarlane where the contras' money was coming from, McFarlane simply looked blank and said he wasn't sure.

And, of course, nobody told Congress. Saudi Arabia had contributed money to U.S. covert operations before and was giving gigantic sums, hundreds of millions of dollars, to the war in Afghanistan. Congress's intelligence committees had been told of those U.S.-Saudi understandings, at least in general terms. But this one was different. This time, Fahd was giving Reagan money for a project that Congress had explicitly banned, the war in Nicaragua. There could be no notification on this one, not even to the secretary of state.

King Fahd could well smile. At a price less than one tenth of what he was paying for the war in Afghanistan, he had just rescued Ronald Reagan's favorite cause.

The administration continued to assure Congress that it was not asking foreign governments to fill the gap in support to the contras. Reagan himself, when asked about the contras' supply needs two months after his $24 million breakfast with Fahd, feigned ignorance. "I have a feeling that they are not well fixed enough to provide any of these things for themselves," he told reporters. "I think that they are close to desperate straits."

Even after King Fahd's contributions, the administration still needed someone to provide the contras with some of the operational support they had received from the CIA — help in handling foreign aid, advice on strategy, and access to U.S. intelligence. When Congress barred the agency from that role, the logical successor was the NSC staff. And the logical man was one who both had a zest for secret operations and was already working on the contra issue: Oliver North.

"Your mission," McFarlane told him, "is to hold the resistance together, body and soul."

He sent North off to the CIA for a quick orientation course in the spring of 1984, but it turned into far more than the usual round of training: director Casey himself came down to meet the man who was taking over his favorite account. Casey and Clarridge introduced North to the contra leaders at the White House's own "safe house," a town house on Lafayette Park, across Pennsylvania Avenue. (Officially a pied-à-terre for former presidents, the house contains a conference room for clandestine meetings.) And in May, North traveled to Honduras and Costa Rica to meet the contras' military chieftains.

He quickly became devoted to his new cause. "I've got a commitment to those guys," he earnestly told colleagues on his return. "I told them I'd come through for them."

That summer, Congress passed an even tougher version of the Boland amendment, banning the CIA or "any other agency or entity involved in intelligence activities" from spending money to support the rebels, "directly or indirectly." Congressman Boland had tried to make the wording airtight. The law "clearly ends United States support for the war in

Nicaragua," he told the House triumphantly. "There are no exceptions to the prohibition."

But Boland didn't know that Casey and North had already hit on a novel — but secret — legal theory. As North explained brightly to his colleagues: "The White House isn't covered by Boland." By then, North had already taken over the contra account. He was advising the rebels on strategy, helping them assemble shopping lists for weapons, and providing them with intelligence from the CIA and the Pentagon. He was, as Poindexter later said in testimony before Congress, "the switching point that made the whole system work."

He was also moving imperceptibly from McFarlane's orbit into Casey's. North was changing mentors again, and this would be his most fateful switch. "Ollie needed to be on a very short leash," the State Department's Motley observed. "McFarlane had him on a leash, and tried to hold on. At some point, the leash just disappeared."

McFarlane, with all his internal conflicts and self-doubts, had begun to sour on the contra crusade. He still believed the cause was just, but he was growing impatient with the contras' inability to produce military victories, political impact, or even internal unity. They just weren't very good guerrillas, he concluded. "Where I went wrong was not having the guts to stand up and tell the president that," he later admitted in testimony to Congress. "To tell the truth, probably the reason I didn't is because if I'd done that, Bill Casey, Jeane Kirkpatrick, and Cap Weinberger would have said I was some kind of Commie."

Instead, McFarlane alarmed both North and contra leader Adolfo Calero by giving the rebels an ultimatum. The war couldn't go on forever, he warned. The contras had to show more political imagination and more military skill. If not, McFarlane warned, "We owed it to them and to ourselves to cut both our losses."

Calero and North were startled. Had McFarlane gone defeatist? Casey, whom Calero jokingly called "My Uncle Bill," never displayed such corrosive doubt about his course.

Others at the NSC and CIA can't remember when they first noticed it, but North soon had an unprecedented direct line to Casey. Sometimes North turned up in Casey's offices at Langley or in Room 345 of the Old Executive Office Building, on the same floor as his own quarters in Room 392; more often, they simply talked on the secure telephone.

"I remember sitting in the office and hearing Ollie North call Casey and talk to him, and Casey would talk to him," Clair George marveled. "He had guts in approaching anybody, anywhere, anytime, in any conditions, without any concern about their title or rank. You know, we all grew up that you don't just storm into the CEO's office the third day with the company, and Ollie did it."

And Casey reciprocated, George said. "He loved North very much.

He liked action people." It all went back to Casey's swashbuckling days in the OSS of World War II: "He saw in Ollie North a part of that." In August 1984, Casey squired North to a major meeting, in Panama, of his Central American station chiefs, making it clear that the NSC aide had the director's blessing. "It really solidified Ollie's credentials," an impressed CIA man recalled. And Casey even invited North to the Pumpkin Papers dinner, the annual Halloween gala of American conservatism. North was dazzled.

"Bill Casey was, for me, a man of immense proportions," he later testified. "A teacher . . . a philosophical mentor."

Over time, and apparently without McFarlane's knowledge, Casey unfolded his vision of the future to North. Congress could stop the CIA from helping the contras, North recalled Casey saying, but it couldn't stop Ronald Reagan. Working at Casey's direction, North could set up a private covert operations network, funded entirely by foreign contributions — but secretly run from the Old Executive Office Building, next door to the White House. And it could go well beyond the contras, Casey said. There were plenty of other wars in the world.

"It was always the intention to make this a self-sustaining operation," North testified later. "There [would] always be something there which you could reach out and grab when you needed it. Director Casey said he wanted something you could pull off the shelf and use at a moment's notice."

North signed on enthusiastically. Bill Casey, the old spymaster, had acquired his newest agent. And North's little office on the third floor of the EOB, as its tenants call it, became the unlikely nerve center for covert operations on three continents.

The office was a cramped, unimpressive room with windows on an inner courtyard, and North made it even more crowded by eagerly acquiring all the machinery that Beal's Crisis Management Center could supply. Eventually, he had not one computer terminal but three, grouped around his leather chair like the instrument panel of a global command post.

All were "Tempest" secure — sheathed in protection against electronic eavesdropping by foreign agents. One screen was the PROFS machine, over which NSC memos and messages moved in pale green characters. A second offered a menu of secret cables between Washington and U.S. diplomatic and military outposts all over the world.

But the third computer terminal was the rarest and most envied by others on the NSC staff. Called a Flashboard, it linked North's desk to the National Security Agency's secret counterterrorism center at Fort George Meade, Maryland. Whenever the NSA picked up the scent of terrorist activity anywhere in the world, a little bell sounded from the terminal, a global fire alarm.

Next to the terminals sat three telephones. One was a standard black multiline phone with North's regular business line, 395–3345, and an internal NSC line. A second, beige phone was his "secure unit," linked to the NSA network of eavesdrop-proof telephone lines between the White House, the Pentagon, and the State Department. A third was even more secure: the "gray line," a link to the CIA and NSA.

It was not unusual, NSC aides said, to see North juggling his beige secure phone in one hand and his gray line in the other — while his flashboard beeped its early warnings of terrorist threats somewhere in the real world.

Into this impromptu command center streamed the contra leaders, who still had a war to fight. The rebels had little experience in the international arms market; they had depended almost entirely on the CIA to handle the mundane but crucial matters of supply and logistics. And organizing the delivery of weapons and provisions was unusually complicated because the rebels were technically outlaws, operating from bases in countries that officially denied their presence.

To buy weapons, for example, the contras needed end-user certificates, the licenses for international arms deals that certify that a shipment of weapons is solely for the use of a legitimate, recognized government. North wheedled several fraudulent EUCs for the contras from Guatemala's rightist military regime; the certificates claimed that the contras' guns were going to the Guatemalan army. He later asked McFarlane to increase U.S. military aid to the regime "to compensate Guatemala for the extraordinary assistance they are giving."

On the supply side, North sent a retired U.S. Army general to Taiwan to ask the nationalist Chinese government for aid to the rebels. John K. Singlaub, jug-eared and crew-cut, was an anti-Communist true believer who had fought in guerrilla wars since 1944, when he parachuted into southern France for the same OSS that employed the young Bill Casey. Now he was chairman of the World Anti-Communist League, a global alliance of the far right, and a leading public booster of the contra cause. Singlaub reported back to North that Taiwan was ready to make a contribution once it received a signal from the administration that the general's plea was legitimate. But McFarlane refused to send the signal, and Singlaub returned home puzzled and annoyed.

North offered the contras advice on their military operations too. He sent their leaders packets of U.S. intelligence information about Nicaragua. And he introduced the rebels to a British mercenary who proposed a plan to infiltrate guerrillas into Nicaragua and destroy Sandinista helicopters on the ground.

In time, Room 392 became a center of Nicaraguan political intrigue as the administration tried to reshape the contras' civilian leadership — to make the movement more attractive to Nicaraguans and, equally important, to Congress. The CIA had been paying a salary to Arturo Cruz, a moderate anti-Sandinista, but members of Congress questioned the arrangement. So the CIA tossed Cruz into North's lap, and North secretly supported him with Saudi money from Adolfo Calero's accounts, even though the two Nicaraguans were bitter political rivals.

Eventually, North stashed more than $150,000 in cash and traveler's checks in the little safe in his office. He once threw open the strongbox drawer and boasted that it held $1 million. "It was more money than I've ever seen in one place," an awestruck colleague said.

There was even a touch of romance: Cruz's son Arturo Jr., a voluble ex-Sandinista, struck up a dramatic love affair with North's secretary, Fawn Hall. North, ever vigilant, asked the CIA to investigate to be sure young Arturo wasn't a Cuban agent in wolf's clothing.

Even a man as tireless as Oliver North found it difficult to carry on all these duties himself, so he recruited a series of unofficial aides, earnest young conservatives who thrilled to the contra cause and volunteered to do their part. One was Johnathan S. Miller, a thirty-two-year-old lawyer who had come to Washington with George Bush's 1980 campaign and worked on Central America at the State Department. Another was Robert W. Owen, also thirty-two, a conservative former Senate aide who quit a lobbying job to work for North full-time.

Their lives soon took on the qualities of a spy novel: midnight telephone calls, clandestine meetings, secret missions, and envelopes of cash. Owen found himself standing in a Chinese grocery on Manhattan's lower West Side, uttering a code word that he remembered as "mooey"; the grocer responded by producing, from inside one trouser leg, a fat roll of $100 bills. And one rainy April night, Owen stood on the sidewalk in front of North's office, only steps from the floodlit White House, waiting for a blue BMW 320 to emerge from the mist. The car roared up, its right front window slid down quickly, and Owen handed an envelope to the dark-haired woman in the passenger seat. She handed it to a small, dark man in the back, and the car roared away. The man in the back seat was Wycliffe Diego, a leader of Nicaragua's Miskito Indian tribe; the envelope contained traveler's checks and cash from North's safe.

"It sounds strange now, I know," Owen said later with a rueful smile. "It didn't at the time."

North and his acolytes joked about going to jail for what they were doing. At one point, one of them said, North waved a copy of the Boland amendment in the air and scornfully declared, "This is the law I'm breaking every day." North later denied that account, but he acknowledged — as did the others — that he felt justified in skating on the edge of the law when the president's cause was at stake.

Still, they knew they were taking risks, at least political risks. North worked in a blaze of self-conscious secrecy, hinting coyly to colleagues (and a few trusted reporters) that he was running operations of enormous sensitivity — but refusing to offer any details. "Exercise absolute stealth," McFarlane instructed before one of North's trips to Central America. "No visible meeting. No press awareness of your presence."

The particulars of stealth and diversion had also been laid down by Dewey Clarridge, the CIA's contra chief, as North was taking over the contra account in 1984. North took dutiful notes of the conversation. "Keep mouth shut," they read. "Never mention North."

Even the new chief of the CIA's Central America Task Force, Alan Fiers, was kept in the dark. Fiers, a burly former linebacker from Ohio State, had just returned from the prestigious job of CIA station chief in Saudi Arabia. The seventeen-year agency veteran couldn't fathom what was going on at the NSC or why he was subjected to constant demands from a young lieutenant colonel.

"I didn't know who Oliver North was and what he was up to," Fiers said later. "I [was] like that cat running around in the dryer, trying to find out where I was."

But Fiers knew enough to recognize that North was on what should have been his turf. He complained to Clair George, his CIA superior, that he couldn't do his job without knowing what North was up to. Fiers's befuddlement was no accident; Casey himself had told North and Poindexter to conceal their operations from the CIA man. Finally, though, Casey called the two combatants into his office to clear the air.

"Ollie, are you operating in Central America?" Casey asked.

"No," North said, according to Fiers. "I'm not operating in Central America."

If some at the NSC and the CIA were confused about what was going on in Nicaragua in the spring of 1985, so were Congress and the public. The administration's policy was a tangle of contradictions, a public policy with a covert core. Reagan and Casey and his men were still doggedly concealing their true goals; they professed a willingness to negotiate but planned secretly for war. One course or the other might have produced a coherent approach, but both at once were difficult to sell. Ironically, when Reagan himself got directly involved in selling his crusade in Nicaragua, the problems only got worse.

One morning in February, White House speechwriter Peggy Noonan had been putting the final polish on a presidential speech appealing for contra aid when she received a note that almost knocked her off her chair: the president had a suggestion.

Like the other presidential speechwriters, Noonan rarely heard from Reagan himself. Normally, he spoke the words she drafted almost verbatim. Reagan's aides often assured reporters that speechwriting was one job the Great Communicator did for himself, but his speechwriters knew otherwise. In the first term, the president had drafted some of his public statements, but by 1985 he had given up the exercise. One new wordsmith on the staff wondered whether the president saw his speeches at all before he actually gave them. Drafts came back from the Oval Office with only tiny changes, usually to make the speech easier to read aloud; the ringing rhetoric that shaped the nation's policy was unaltered, but a "do not" might change to a more fluid "don't."

Noonan, a gifted writer and dedicated conservative, was delighted with Reagan's suggestion. The president thought it might be effective to compare the Nicaraguan contras to the French Resistance of World War II or the American revolutionaries of 1776. Noonan quickly banged out a strong new passage and inserted it in her text. "They are our brothers, these freedom fighters, and we owe them our help," Reagan would read fervently to the Conservative Political Action Conference a few nights later. "They are the moral equal of our Founding Fathers and the brave men and women of the French Resistance. We cannot turn away from them. For the struggle here is not right versus left, but right versus wrong."

Noonan, a diehard supporter of the contra cause, lived to regret her hyperbole. Liberal Democrats seized on "the moral equal of our Founding Fathers" to make the contras' character the central issue of national debate — and a beauty contest against Jefferson and Madison was one the rebels were doomed to lose. "In the first term, where they were sensitive to the political implications of these things, it would have been caught," the speechwriter said later of her fatal phrase. "What I was trying to say was that the contras were like the Founding Fathers in the sense that they both faced a monolith. I didn't mean to imply that the Founding Fathers were rapists and murderers."

But the speech had slipped right past Don Regan and his new White House staff. James Baker, Richard Darman, and their bureaucratic filters were long gone; instead, the watchword was to let Reagan be Reagan. As a result, in the Founding Fathers speech, the president led with his chin in the 1985 contra battle, and his handlers did nothing to stop him.

The problem was compounded by Reagan's confusion over the facts of the issue and his vacillation from one strategy to another. In April 1985, when Reagan sent his formal request to Congress for contra aid, he attached a secret policy statement warning that if the rebels failed, U.S. military force would be an "eventual option." That disturbed Lee Hamilton, the new chairman of the House Intelligence Committee, who asked Reagan at a White House meeting, "Did you review that sentence?"

Reagan, for all his passion about Nicaragua, was caught unaware. No, he said, he didn't know about that. Hamilton went around the table, to

Bush and Shultz and McFarlane; all said they had not seen the passage suggesting the use of American troops.

Confusion dogged the president on other counts as well. He suggested that Pope John Paul II had declared his support for U.S. policy, only to have the Vatican stiffly deny it the next day. He spoke emotionally at a gala fund-raising dinner for Nicaraguan refugees and hugged an eight-year-old girl who was said to have fled her ravaged homeland — but the girl turned out to be the U.S.-born daughter of a banker, and the $219,000 fund-raiser turned out to be a fiasco, netting a grand total of $3,000.

The lack of clarity at the top stemmed from basic disagreements within the White House on both strategy and tactics. Cabinet members continued their long-running arguments over policy; rival factions on the White House staff battled over the tactics that would best win the congressional fight. The great divide was between voices of caution, who didn't want to damage the president by tying him to a losing cause, and hard-liners, who felt the issue was so vital that it demanded bold action despite the political risks.

"There were rival baronies," said communications director Patrick J. Buchanan, a leader of the hard-liners. He wanted the president to barnstorm the country with hair-raising speeches about Nicaragua: "We had to drive up the fear factor," he proclaimed. The White House polls showed that people were afraid of a torrent of Central American refugees, so Buchanan urged the president to stoke public concern with a series of speeches in border states. He pushed for a giant evening rally in Miami's Orange Bowl, which would be filled with conservative Cuban Americans to show that at least some parts of the country shared Reagan's anti-Sandinista fervor. There would be bonfires, Buchanan said, and wildly cheering crowds, and the president leading public opinion, not following it.

But Buchanan faced an implacable opponent in the internal debate: Wirthlin's numbers. The pollster's computer printouts still didn't like Nicaragua. The contras, Wirthlin warned, were simply not a popular cause; whenever the president so much as mentioned Nicaragua, his popularity went down. (Arms agreements with the Soviet Union were exactly the opposite: almost every time Reagan made a positive speech about working for nuclear peace, his numbers went up.)

The clash between ideology and popularity reached a peak in April, only weeks before Congress was to vote on contra aid. Nicaragua was an issue that Reagan felt deeply about, and Buchanan, the chief ideologue, wanted the president to come out swinging. His vivid proposal for Cubans and bonfires had been vetoed with the excuse that Mrs. Reagan thought there were too many security problems. So now Buchanan had another plan: he wanted the president to go on national television with a good, tough speech to move public opinion on the contra issue. Other advisers were dead set against the idea. Reagan was about to leave for Europe, and the trip was already embroiled in controversy over his plan to lay a wreath at a cemetery in Bitburg, Germany, where SS troops were buried. The furor over this incident had plunged Regan and his aides into what one called "pure panic," virtually paralyzing their work on an already cluttered legislative agenda — the kind of jam James Baker had successfully prevented during the first term. And Wirthlin's polls had turned up a sobering new fact: in the midst of the tenth anniversary of the fall of South Vietnam, the war in Nicaragua set off even worse negatives than before. "A direct televised address might even be counterproductive," a memo from the White House Political Office warned. Instead, the soft-liners proposed, the president should give his speech on a safer subject, the federal budget.

In the morning senior staff meeting, Buchanan locked horns with political director Ed Rollins, who had the polling memo in hand. No single speech was going to turn the public around on the contras, Rollins argued. The president would have to fight a long war against prevailing opinion, and at this point it was smarter simply to stick with old-fashioned arm-twisting in Congress. Buchanan disagreed forcefully. Their fight continued from the meeting in the Roosevelt Room down the hall and into Regan's office. As Rollins and Buchanan debated, Regan suddenly spoke up.

"The president will make the budget speech," he said.

Buchanan and Rollins stared. "Don't you think the president should make that decision?" Rollins recalled asking.

Regan's face reddened. "I've made the decision. That's the recommendation I'm taking to the president."

Rollins didn't like the way the decision was being made, even though it was in his favor. "With all due respect," he told the chief of staff, "I campaigned in fifty states, and I didn't see your name on any ballot."

But Regan had made the call. He took his recommendation to the Oval Office, and the president, insulated from his advisers' debate, quickly agreed. "The president definitely was not given a choice," Rollins complained.

But while the White House soft-liners won this battle on tactics, their conciliatory approach came too late to save contra aid in Congress. Reagan had launched the spring campaign on Nicaragua with the moral equals of the Founding Fathers, switched to a test of U.S. ability to halt Soviet expansion, and finally changed key again to embrace a hastily devised "peace plan." A week before Congress was to vote, the president bowed to pressure and promised that the proposed $14 million in aid would be used only for "humanitarian" purposes, not guns or bullets. But the underlying intentions remained suspiciously unclear. "The administration has yet to produce a policy which enjoys sufficient support of the American people and the Congress to make it sustainable," complained Senator Sam Nunn of Georgia, a conservative Democrat who supported the contras. "Right or wrong, the American people perceive that the military option, through the contras, has been on the front burner and is the president's course of first resort." In votes on April 23 and 24, 1985, the House rejected the president's request.

"Abysmal handling," Casey complained to Bob Woodward of the *Washington Post.* "The White House can't do two things at once. . . . The president is uninterested. He still has his instincts, but he will not even focus on the objectives, let alone the way to get there."

But Reagan vowed to come back for aid "again and again," and in the stinging defeat his aides found some seeds of hope. The House had been deeply divided on the Nicaraguan issue; a compromise approach built around the new concept of "humanitarian aid" might yet win. Better still, the long debate had refocused from the contras' moral character (a debate the rebels could not win) to the nature of the Sandinistas (a debate the regime couldn't win). Less than a week after the vote, Sandinista president Daniel Ortega flew to Moscow to seek more Soviet aid. The news crystalized a shift in sentiment that had already been building. "Daniel Ortega is a swine," railed one border state Democrat who had voted against contra aid in the first round.

This time, the House Republican leadership put together a bill with $27 million in humanitarian aid. Reagan weighed in with a letter to fence-sitting Democrats, pledging, "We do not seek the military overthrow of the Sandinista government."

Tip O'Neill derided the president's promises. "He can see himself leading a contingent down Broadway, with a big smile on his face, kind of like a grade B motion picture actor, coming home the conquering hero," the Speaker said bitterly. But the Democratic warhorse had lost control of his own party. On June 12, the House approved the $27 million in humanitarian aid by a comfortable margin.

There was little jubilation at the White House. Nearly four months of Ronald Reagan's time and energy had been invested, and the result was a paltry sum of aid that couldn't buy guns or bullets.

North was disgusted. Pat Buchanan had been right, he said. You can't win if you don't fight for what you want. He raged around his little office, cursing Democrats and Republicans alike.

"It's bullshit," he told Owen. "It's bullshit. You can't win a war with blankets and Band-Aids." There had to be a way to get more money for the contras, he said. There had to be a way.

5

A Hard-liner's Soft Touch

ON THE AFTERNOON of Sunday, June 16, 1985, Reagan returned early
from a weekend at Camp David and strode directly into the Situation
Room in the basement of the White House for a hastily called meeting
with his National Security Council. As his aides took their places around
the conference table, Reagan unfolded a letter he had brought with him
and began to read it out loud. This wasn't unusual; one NSC official
estimated that Reagan opened three of his five weekly national security
briefings by reading snippets from his mailbox. But this was neither an
ordinary meeting nor an ordinary letter. It was a desperate plea written
under extreme duress.

Halfway around the world, on a darkened runway at Beirut International Airport, the twenty-nine signers of the letter were barricaded inside
the belly of TWA passenger flight 847, which Shia Muslim gunmen had
hijacked on its way from Athens to Rome on June 14, two long days
before. Armed gunmen were still guarding the jet. Members of Lebanon's largest Shia militia, a group known as Amal, had sealed off the
airport and were manning its control tower. Six more American passengers — those with Jewish-sounding names or government passports —
had already been separated from the others, abducted by their captors.
They were taken into Beirut's nearby Shia slums — a no man's land
overrun by goats, cats, and ragged children, some barely in their teens
but already wielding machine guns.

The hijackers had threatened to execute the thirty-nine American pas-
sengers and crew unless a list of demands was met. Foremost was that
Israel release some seven hundred prisoners, most of them also Lebanese
Shia, from its Atlit prison, near Haifa. One day into the ordeal, to prove

they meant business, the hijackers had cold-bloodedly killed one passenger, shooting a young U.S. Navy diver named Robert Dean Stethem
in the head and then throwing his bloodied body onto the tarmac for all
to see.

In the Situation Room, Reagan read out loud from the survivors' letter.
"We implore you not to take any direct military action on our behalf.
Please negotiate quickly our immediate release by convincing the Israelis
to release the 700 Lebanese prisoners as requested. Now."

It was in many ways Ronald Reagan's worst nightmare come true.
The situation was not threatening on a global scale, but for the president
it was fraught with political peril. Five years earlier, he had run Jimmy
Carter out of office, in part because of his weakness in the face of another
Middle Eastern hostage crisis, Iran's 444-day incarceration of fifty-two
Americans. As a candidate in 1980, Reagan had charged that Carter's
"foreign policy helped create the entire situation that made their kidnap
possible. I think the fact that they've been there that long is a humiliation
and a disgrace."

On January 27, 1981, a week after his inauguration, the president held
a gala welcoming ceremony in the White House's Rose Garden for the
just-released hostages. There he vowed, "Let terrorists beware: when the
rules of international behavior are violated, our policy will be one of
swift and effective retribution." The ceremony was meant to mark a
break with the past, yet in an unanticipated way it repeated one of Carter's greatest mistakes. By receiving the hostages in the heart of the White
House, Reagan, like Carter, elevated their welfare to the highest level
of national concern. As Terrell Arnold, a member of the administration's
Terrorist Incident Working Group, later concluded, "Where did we first
go wrong? Nineteen eighty-one. Once we had the Rose Garden ceremony, we had attached huge political benefit to the return of U.S. hostages. After that, it was only logical to welcome home [the others]. And
when the TWA hostages were returned, we took them to our bosom."

For the four years after 1981, Reagan had talked tough, vowing never
to yield to terrorist demands and boasting of America's renewed military
strength. But by the summer of 1985, the expectations he stirred with
such ceremonies and rhetoric had yet to be backed by visible action or
a coherent policy against terrorism. In fact, Reagan's rallying cry of
"swift and effective retribution" was the phrase of a young aide, who
added it to Reagan's Rose Garden speech, he later said, simply because
"it just sounded good."

A whole series of terrorist outrages followed this cry, yet Shultz and
Weinberger never agreed about what would comprise appropriate retaliation, and in the midst of the policy gridlock, the only presidential
response seemed to be more words. In April 1983, when the U.S. Embassy in Beirut was bombed, Reagan proclaimed: "Let this serve notice

to the cowardly, skulking barbarians of the world that they will not have their way." Six months later, after the bombers of the marine barracks had exposed the hollowness of his warning, Reagan said it again: "Those who directed this atrocity must be dealt justice, and they will be." Yet in September 1984, a truck bombed the supposedly safe U.S. Embassy annex in Beirut, and then two American foreign aid officials were murdered on a hijacked Kuwaiti jet — all with no U.S. response beyond more threats.

In fact, the administration's efforts in the Middle East had misfired badly, and the TWA hijackers were living proof of the bitterness the earlier U.S. failures in Beirut had engendered. Reagan had deftly withdrawn from Lebanon in 1984, cutting his political losses and shifting U.S. attention elsewhere. But he had left behind a cauldron of anti-American sentiment. This lingering rage was reflected in the TWA hijacking. At one point the hijackers, Mohammed Ali Hamadi and Hassan Ezzedine, shouted "Marines" and "New Jersey" at the confused hostages, most of whom failed to understand their angry references to the military role the marines and the battleship *New Jersey* had played in Beirut in 1983. Hamadi also demanded, "Did you forget the Bir al Abed massacre?" The hostages didn't know what he was talking about. But Bir al Abed was the site of the apartment building where more than eighty civilians were killed in March 1985, when it was blown up by Lebanese operatives reportedly working indirectly for William Casey. Until now, Reagan's response to terrorism had successfully rested on defiant words. But, suddenly, it was as if events were conspiring to call his bluff.

The truth was that the dark and dirty war of terrorism was far more difficult than Reagan's rhetoric suggested for an open and civilized nation like the United States to fight, let alone win. As Noel Koch, the Pentagon's top counterterrorism planner, put it, "Our virtues are our vulnerabilities." In fact, the United States did not have the political appetite, much less the precise intelligence or military ability, to carry out Reagan's promises.

Reagan's rhetoric rested on an ideal of America so respected and feared around the world that no one would dare take its citizens hostage. Reagan invoked this inspiring vision in his 1980 campaign when he fondly recalled a newsreel he had seen of the Spanish Civil War, in which an American naval company went "through the streets at double-time" to rescue American citizens trapped in a Spanish coastal city. "You can't help but thrill with pride at that," he told an interviewer, explaining that America was so greatly respected that the war had been miraculously suspended in order to let the Yankees go home safely.

But like so many of Reagan's most compelling visions, this ideal seems to have owed more to Hollywood than history. American scholars of the Spanish Civil War have expressed no familiarity with the historic moment the president was referring to, and several doubted that the incident could have taken place. But two scholars suspected the account might be based on a Henry Fonda movie called *Blockade*, which depicts such a rescue in a northern Spanish port town during the civil war. With the president resting his terrorism policy on heroic myth — of a particularly implausible kind — it wasn't surprising that it didn't correspond well to the real world, a world in which the role of U.S. power abroad had been greatly complicated since the Vietnam War.

It was not unusual for a president to find the realities of public office quite different from the rhetoric of the campaign. Franklin Roosevelt campaigned against the costs of big government before going on to build the foundations of the modern welfare state; and Kennedy campaigned against a nuclear "missile gap," only to learn upon taking office that it hadn't really existed. Reagan, unlike his predecessors, clung to his original rhetoric even as the empirical evidence invalidated it, straddling rather than solving the contradictions, unwilling or unable to admit to the nation that there might indeed be limits to the uses of U.S. power.

Turning the political pressure up even further as Reagan faced the situation in Beirut were the expectations created by advances in worldwide television news coverage — and by the administration's own attitude toward television performance as the benchmark of political success. The same media that had purveyed Reagan's polish and charm so well on the screen were now bombarding his White House with breathless bulletins from a faraway crisis, demanding an instant presidential response. When Reagan's helicopter touched down that Sunday afternoon from Camp David, droves of journalists were waiting on the White House lawn with their cameras rolling and notebooks open.

For the first two days after the hijacking, the White House had tried to maintain the appearance of normalcy, hoping not to repeat Jimmy Carter's mistake of holding the entire government hostage to a hostage situation. On Friday, Reagan had delivered a standard tax reform speech in Baltimore. In the afternoon, he had taken the helicopter *Marine One* to Camp David, appearing to the world unruffled enough to go about his usual weekend activities — quiet horseback rides with Nancy, Saturday night movies in the retreat's Aspen Lodge. But by Sunday, the pretense was useless. With the gruesome murder of the U.S. Navy diver, the situation had become too explosive to pretend to ignore, and the president had returned early for the emergency meeting with his staff.

After he finished reading the hostages' letter, Reagan looked up at his national security advisers and asked simply and unabashedly what he needed to do to free the Americans. He sounded pragmatic and understated, like the negotiator who had represented the Screen Actors Guild thirty years earlier. He noted the captors' demand concerning the prisoners in Israel and wondered if there was a way to pressure Israel subtly.

Perhaps, he suggested, the United States could tell the kidnappers that if they released the hostages, it would then push Israel to release the Amal prisoners.

George Shultz was incredulous. He pointed out in his steeliest professorial tone that the United States had a highly visible and principled policy of not making concessions to terrorists — a policy that Reagan himself had articulated on numerous occasions. That policy precluded pressuring allies to make concessions on behalf of the United States. To Shultz, the hard-liner, the talk of cutting a deal now was preposterous.

But even he realized that the options open to the administration in this situation were few and poor. Since some of the hostages had been dispersed — and more would be soon — any kind of military intervention would simply invite retaliation. Off Lebanon's coast two huge American warships, the aircraft carrier *Nimitz* and the guided missile destroyer *Kidd*, floated about as usefully as bathtub toys. It was left to McFarlane to point out that for the time being, there really were no reasonable military options. All they could do was to keep channels of communication open and bide their time.

The meeting broke up inconclusively. But as his immediate impulse to read the terrorized hostages' letter had hinted, the president was an impressionable and sentimental man. When confronted with real-life anguish, there was no telling where his compassion would lead him. To McFarlane and several others, one lesson was clear: as much as possible, Reagan had to be kept away from the daily hostage drama.

This was both smart policy and smart public relations. After leaving the White House, Jimmy Carter admitted that one of his greatest regrets was having become embroiled emotionally in the Iranian hostage issue. His close personal involvement had made it almost impossible to make cool and detached decisions. The Carter misfortune had taught other lessons as well. Presidential involvement inevitably intensified the heat of the crisis, exaggerating both its importance and the public's expectations of what a president could do.

Looking at the crisis from a public relations perspective, White House pollster Richard Wirthlin had reached the same conclusion. Four days after the hijacking, he appeared at the White House with a briefcase filled with his latest statistical samplings. As was so often true, he'd found a silver lining in the dark cloud. Extracting a useful lesson from Carter's experience, Wirthlin said the president had at least a ninety-day grace period during which the country would rally around the flag without demanding action. In this early stage, the country wouldn't likely blame the president. The numbers suggested that the less Reagan was personally seen to be involved — or responsible — the less the episode would hurt his standing in the polls. If it was handled right, he might even become more popular.

Don Regan quickly deferred to the White House pollster. The chief of staff always relied heavily on the polls, and after the public's negative reaction to Reagan's visit to the Bitburg cemetery, just a month earlier, he was even more loath to run any public relations risks than usual. A diary entry from a senior staff member noted, "Regan appears taken with the reams of Wirthlin data that say leave RR out."

Soon afterward, when it became clear that the body of the slain sailor Robert Stethem would be returned to the United States, these concerns about public relations dominated the debate over whether Reagan should attend the burial. White House political director Ed Rollins and communications director Patrick Buchanan — who had been dubbed "the Mad Bombers" for their thirst for retaliation — thought that Reagan should go to the burial in order to show the world how strongly the country felt about Stethem's murder. Regan said he would bring these views to the president, but he clearly opposed them, fearing that the bad news about Stethem would be associated with the presidency. "It was not an upbeat issue," Regan argued, "and obviously, you try to keep [Reagan] as far away as you can from downbeat issues . . . from the point of view of influencing his popularity." Besides, Regan continued, "why that guy's funeral? . . . It's an unusual occasion when the president goes to someone's funeral. Many people die — ex-senators, ex-cabinet members. Almost anybody could get killed in an automobile accident. Would you have the president then go to their funeral? Why go to this guy's?"

Regan and the publicity experts prevailed. On June 20, six days after the hijacking, Vice President George Bush — not Reagan — represented the U.S. government at Stethem's burial in Arlington National Cemetery, just across the Potomac River from the White House.

This cautious plan of keeping the president politically and emotionally apart from the hostage drama remained in effect for the better part of two weeks. Reagan was of course informed of his aides' efforts to resolve the situation, and he kept in close contact with McFarlane and other advisers. "He was quite attentive," said one such adviser, "unusually so." McFarlane later noted that "there were two weeks of television coverage — and Reagan watches television quite faithfully — it elevated his interest." But other than asking the vice president to head a task force on terrorism and quietly working with the Israelis, Iranians, and Syrians to gain the release of the hostages, the White House tried to maintain a distance from the situation. It wasn't easy.

From the start, the panicked relatives of the TWA passengers pushed for a meeting with the president. Twice in the midst of trips to promote his tax reform plan, Reagan had hurriedly met backstage with relatives who lived near his stops and who demanded to see him. "We couldn't very well freeze them out," explained one presidential aide. "Besides, it was what the president wanted to do." But the White House had tried to limit such contact as much as possible.

However, toward the end of June, a series of complicated, behind-the-scenes maneuvers put the White House on the verge of breaking the hostage deadlock — and changing its public posture. Israel, with the acquiescence of the United States, had quietly agreed to start freeing its disputed 766 Shia prisoners. Outwardly, the administration continued to maintain that it had made no concessions to terrorists and had put no pressure on Israel. But when asked what the president wanted the Israelis to do, Don Regan had replied with a heavy wink, "They'll just have to read our minds." It was the kind of blunderbuss remark that infuriated the more discreet foreign policy officials, fueling the NSC's distrust of the White House domestic policy staff.

But for the domestic White House staff, the imminent breakthrough was cause for huge relief — and big plans. As the news became more promising, the public relations–minded staff ignored its earlier caution and began gearing up for a triumphant hostage return. It now seemed less risky to have the president hold a formal meeting with the families. "There was a debate about whether it was a good idea, and basically it was decided as a PR thing," explained William Henkel, the head of the White House advance office, which handled Reagan's schedule. "We were getting hammered for not meeting with them, so we went ahead." Don Regan, who had the ultimate say over Reagan's schedule, apparently agreed that the White House now had more to win than lose from the image of Reagan's involvement. He agreed to have the president meet en masse with the relatives of the hostages on June 28 in Chicago Heights, Illinois. If he saw any long-term political liabilities, they didn't deter him.

In his first term, Reagan had been surrounded by men who instantly understood what a combustible mix the president and hostages could be. In one little-known episode, Reagan had actually wanted to get on the telephone with a domestic kidnapper who said he would release his hostage only if he could talk with the president. Reagan believed that his personal intervention could resolve the situation, never considering the likelihood that such a concession would spur more such demands or the impropriety of allowing the presidency to be used as part of a package deal at gunpoint. It took both Meese and Baker to talk the president out of it — but, significantly, they did. It was one of those instances in which, as an official close to Baker later said, "sometimes it's best not to let Reagan be Reagan. You owe him your sternest judgment."

By June of 1985, that was a lesson apparently forgotten by Reagan and not yet learned by Regan, who had been chief of staff for only four months. Both Meese and Deaver — those with the longest Reagan ties — had departed. And although Baker was just across East Executive Avenue in the fortress-like Treasury building, Regan never asked his advice on the TWA crisis (or virtually anything else) — and Baker never volunteered it. Regan's aides liked to boast that they were doing much better than Baker had, and it was a point of pride with them that they needed no help.

The danger, as former national security adviser and longtime Reagan hand William Clark saw it, was that "there was no one left who understood Reagan" — and how to protect him from his own peculiar weaknesses. One of these was that Ronald Reagan might toe a hard line in theory, but when confronted with adversity before his very eyes he was, as family friend Nancy Reynolds put it, "the softest touch in the whole world." His sentimentality made him extraordinarily susceptible to individual human appeals. When Reynolds, a savvy Washington lobbyist who had worked for Reagan in Sacramento, heard that the president had actually met the hostages' relatives in person, she knew immediately where it would lead. "The day I saw that the hostage families had gotten to him, I thought, 'Here we go again.' If you can just get a personal audience with Ronald Reagan, he's hooked."

From his earliest days in politics, Reagan had shown an irrepressible tendency to be sympathetic when dealing with individual hardship cases while pursuing policies that slashed government largesse to the unseen masses. In part, this was an outgrowth of Reagan's belief that private philanthropy was preferable to the public dole. But sometimes it seemed simply a function of his laying eyes on the needy. Thus, although he campaigned for tougher law and order in California, Reagan couldn't bear to see a pregnant woman picketing in the street outside his office about her husband's long jail sentence. He quickly invited her in and promised, after a half-hour chat, that he would help ease her plight. While he campaigned against welfare, he sent his friend Frank Sinatra to deliver Christmas toys to a single welfare child who he heard was without gifts. Former budget director David Stockman wrote of Reagan: "He always went for hard-luck stories. He sees the plight of real people before anything else. Despite his right-wing image, his ideology and philosophy always take a back seat when he learns that some individual human being might be hurt." He seemed oblivious to the clash between his actions on the particular and his policies in the abstract.

Reagan's ability to connect emotionally with individuals who suffered before his eyes had never been a political liability: in fact, in an important way it humanized the president. Almost all of those who worked closely with Reagan found him amazingly considerate for an ostensibly busy man. He never learned many of his newer aides' names — they liked to kid about whether they could pass "the name test" — but he treated them all kindly. He could forget whether the U.S. nuclear advantage was on land or at sea, but he remembered to take care of the White House squirrels, filling his pockets with acorns collected for them at Camp David. He didn't like to impose, and he worried about the inconvenience his every move became for the staff. He once refused to go along with a stunt that called for him to dump confetti on a visiting athlete's head because he didn't want anyone to have to pick it up. (Aides settled on popcorn for the outdoor event, so that the birds could do the cleanup.)

The danger was that left to his own good intentions, the president would confuse the human interest with the national interest, mistaking gestures for policies, romantic themes for strategy, and immediate emotional gratification for long-term strategic gains. There was no clearer example of this danger than in his approach to the hostages. But those around him should have seen plenty of warnings in the unique way in which Reagan turned the presidency into a case-by-case philanthropic pursuit — seemingly disconnected from his own broad policies.

Reagan's view of himself as First Caseworker of the Land was institutionalized in the White House Correspondence Office, a little-known but extraordinary shop in the basement of the Old Executive Office Building, a few hundred yards from the West Wing. It was a sprawling empire managed by an energetic blonde named Anne Higgins, who liked to turn up the volume on the office tape to the Simon and Garfunkel song "Bridge Over Troubled Water" — which expressed how she saw her mission. As anyone who worked closely with the president must have realized, it was Reagan's sentimental view of his own role too.

In a rare lapse from good Samaritanism, Higgins once described the office as the Schlock Capital of the World, buried as it was in needlepoint inspirational sayings, stained-glass doodads, and other offerings Americans felt compelled to share with their commander in chief. During Reagan's tenure, it employed a staff of 130 people and 500 part-time volunteers to handle as many as twenty thousand letters and packages a day — much more mail than any other president had ever received. While most presidents had dismissed the public mail as a nuisance, Higgins said of Reagan, "It's hard to believe when you get that much mail, but he actually likes it."

Every week Higgins selected thirty representative letters for the president to read, many of them appeals for help or tales of heartache, and just about every Friday afternoon he took the time to answer them in longhand on sheets of yellow legal paper. It was a habit he had picked up in Hollywood, where he had often answered his own fan mail. Some aides snickered privately at the amount of time and energy Reagan gave to this epistolary pursuit. George Shultz had had to fight strenuously to get two half-hour meetings a week with the president, but if Reagan spent only five minutes on each letter, he was still devoting more than twice as much time to strangers' letters as to his secretary of state. When a program to adopt a school-aged pen pal was introduced, Reagan was the only senior official who took it seriously, corresponding through much of his tenure with Rudy Hines, a young black boy from Washington's Southeast slums. But Higgins observed, "I think it's one of the keys to his success as a man in public life: he doesn't take the average person lightly."

Frequently, though, this empathy seemed to place Reagan at odds with his own policies in the White House, just as it had in Sacramento. This conflict between the particular and the abstract was endemic to the correspondence unit, which was, after all, a central switching point between the presidential cocoon and the real world outside. Thus, while Reagan was moved by one letter to make a televised appeal for a liver donor for an eleven-month-old girl in Texas, his administration pushed to eliminate spending for a new national computer network designed to match organ donors with patients in need of transplants. In another such case found by Higgins's office, Reagan ensured that a young girl in Hawaii got a waiver from his administration's own toughened eligibility requirements for welfare benefits because she had won a new automobile, which put her family over the new $1,700 limit for possessions. (The White House helped the girl's family sell the car and place her prize money in a trust — thus resorting to the kind of dodge Reagan had accused "welfare cheats" of doing for so many years.) One member of the correspondence unit, Sally Kelley, said, "He loves having that stuff done, especially when it's a deserving youngster against the huge bureaucracy" — no matter that the bureaucracy was now his own.

Aides who knew Reagan well recognized that his episodic sentimentality left him open to manipulation. Some realized that if they could harness it, they could alter whole policies. In the summer of 1982, when Israel's air force was bombing residential neighborhoods in Beirut, killing hundreds of civilians, Reagan's deputy chief of staff, Michael Deaver, took action. Deaver had no experience or responsibility in the area of foreign affairs, but he didn't like the civilian casualties, and he knew that the Israeli attacks using U.S. weapons were potentially harmful to Reagan's image at home. Reagan, in contrast, hadn't reacted much to the air strikes, but he generally supported Menachem Begin's government.

In the middle of August, after an especially bloody raid, Deaver reached his limit. He stormed into the Oval Office by himself and declared emotionally, "I can't stay here any longer."

"What are you talking about?" the president asked.

"I don't want to be part of this," replied Deaver. "You sit here and listen to these guys, and you don't know what they're talking about. And you let Begin bomb Beirut every day, and they're your bombs. And the result of that is children without arms." Deaver was referring to a horrifying news photograph showing a Lebanese baby bound in gauze from the shoulders down, the caption explaining that both arms had been severed by an Israeli bomb.

"For what?" stormed Deaver. "Just to make the Israelis happy? It hasn't got anything to do with anything else. And you are sitting here, the only man on the face of the earth that can stop it, and you won't do it. I can't stay any longer and be part of it."

The president looked at his distraught aide for a moment and then asked bewilderedly, "How do I stop this?"

"You pick up the phone and call Menachem Begin," Deaver replied. "And," Deaver said later, "he did." Within twenty minutes, Begin called back to say that a cease-fire had been imposed. Reagan then put down the phone and said, "It's over with." Two and a half years into his presidency, he then looked at his longtime aide and said, "Gosh! I didn't realize I had that kind of power."

It later turned out that the caption under the UPI photograph had been mistaken. Israeli authorities went to the trouble of finding the injured child, who had indeed been hurt, but not by Israeli bombs, and who under the bandages still had the use of both arms. Yet, as was so often true with Reagan, the facts didn't matter as much as the emotional impact.

Before the TWA hijacking in 1985, Reagan had little occasion to display his soft side in the realm of foreign policy, if only because he was so rarely face to face with the individuals affected by his views abroad. His views on terrorism, for instance, were largely insulated from his sentimentality. But that changed dramatically on June 28, when he flew to Chicago Heights, Illinois, to meet for the first time en masse with many of those whose relatives had been taken hostage on his watch. They and their relatives, more than any other group, were placed in the greatest jeopardy by his hard-nosed rhetoric. The skirmish with the families left what another White House participant called "an indelible impression" on the president's already receptive mind.

It was ultimately Regan's decision to have the president meet with the hostage families. Nonetheless, McFarlane later blamed himself for having ever let it happen. The national security adviser had at first argued against the meeting, but before long he gave in. Even at the time, he later said, he knew the risks. "I knew that the president was not a person who took decisions on the basis of analysis . . . of insisting upon a range of optional courses of action [and] rigorous examination of the pros and cons of each. He was more an instinctive decisionmaker," McFarlane later said. "The president has a romantic view of leadership. He worries about human suffering. He's moved by human misery, human interest. He would put that above the national interest in almost any circumstance.''

The library of the Bloom High School in Chicago Heights had been transformed into a waiting room for despairing families — the young, the old, sisters, brothers, parents, children, and spouses of ordinary citizens who'd suddenly disappeared and who now were being held hostage in the lawless sprawl of Beirut. All but one of the families in the room had relatives who had been hijacked on TWA's Flight 847. For them, the meeting was an occasion for comfort and reassurance, since by June 28 the White House was all but certain that the thirty-nine surviving passengers would be released any day. The president was there to do one of the things he did best — give hope. Since he had basically good news, the meeting wasn't supposed to be grueling. And in fact, before Reagan had entered the room, McFarlane had spent some time explaining to the families just how promising the situation now looked.

But the staff had overlooked one key detail. Illinois was the home not just of many of the passengers aboard the plane but also of Father Lawrence Martin Jenco, a Catholic priest who had been taken hostage in Beirut five months earlier. He was one of seven captives who appeared to have little hope of coming home now with the others. As one local official involved in arranging the meeting put it, "Some genius of a White House advance man said, 'Hey, wouldn't this make a great photo op?' but forgot that a handful of these guys, including Jenco, had been over there for a good bit more than two weeks."

The Jencos were not easily overlooked. They may have started out, as one State Department official put it, as "a large, basically unsophisticated, blue-collar Catholic family" from working-class Joliet, but their five months at the edge of the limelight had been a crash course in power politics. They were no longer unsophisticated about the media, nor about the levers of political pressure. As a huge extended family from a closely knit town with five Catholic churches, the previously apolitical Jencos soon learned that they had plenty of muscle to flex. The relatives united and enlisted the help of their congressman, Republican George M. O'Brien, who insisted on their being added to the president's Chicago Heights guest list.

Sensing potential trouble since there was little the president could offer the Jencos, State Department officials objected. But the White House knew that if the Jencos complained, their exclusion could prove politically embarrassing. As it turned out though, their presence may have marked the beginning of the end of Reagan's resolve on terrorism.

By the time the president entered the Bloom High School library with Regan at his side, the Jencos, who sat on thin metal chairs in a semicircle around him, were already upset by McFarlane's hopeful intimation that the TWA hostages would be home soon. The Jencos wanted to know now, from the president, why the government was leaving their brother and the other longtime American hostages behind. How could the president agree to bring home thirty-nine Americans and leave seven others stranded?

The Jencos also wanted to know why it looked as if the United States had cut a deal on the release of the 766 Israeli prisoners but would not make a similar deal for their brother, a selfless missionary who had volunteered for every hardship post from Bangladesh to Beirut. The administration had repeatedly spurned the demand, made by the kidnappers of the original seven Beirut hostages, that seventeen terrorists backed by Iran be released from prison in Kuwait, where they had been convicted of bombing the American and French embassies in December 1983, killing five and leaving many more wounded. Kuwait, the United States had said, was a courageous example of how not to give in to terrorism.

Unprepared for anything but a sympathetic audience, the president was taken aback by the Jencos' tough questions. After listening to what they had to say, Reagan responded in an uncertain, quavering voice, "Everything that can be done is being done."

"I want more detail," demanded John Jenco, striking an emotional tone the president seldom heard.

"We're doing touchy things we can't talk about," Reagan answered, his voice now cracking. "We don't want to jeopardize it by talking about it."

"Why won't you at least try to negotiate?" demanded a second Jenco brother, Joe.

The exchange continued, back and forth, the president shuffling in his uncomfortable chair, stumbling under fire, and becoming visibly downcast. His aides worried that he was badly shaken. It was painful just to watch. Finally, the son of one of the TWA hostages, staring at the president's crushed expression, blurted out, "Mr. President, I don't know how you can stand your job!"

Don Regan, who had sat silently for thirty-three minutes, fidgeting impatiently with his watch, abruptly grabbed Reagan by the arm and literally pulled him out of the school library, asking him as they went whether he needed time to "compose" himself. The Secret Service guards led the president quickly down the locker-lined corridor — with the Jencos hopelessly trying to trail after him — to an improvised sanctuary made from the principal's office.

In the calm of the paneled office, Reagan, still shaken, turned to McFarlane and said, "It's an awful thing that these parents and loved ones have to live with." The president could just as well have been speaking about himself.

"It was just brutal," said presidential assistant William Henkel. "The Jencos just excoriated the president — they were real motherfuckers. It was a tough, tough thing for him. It made an indelible impression."

In truth, before the TWA hijacking, there was little evidence that Reagan had focused much on any of the U.S. hostages. Michael Deaver, who had worked at the White House until a month before the hijacking, couldn't remember the president's ever bringing up the subject of their welfare. Peggy Say, the sister of hostage Terry Anderson, said, "They didn't want to acknowledge they even had a hostage problem." Some White House and State Department professionals felt that the American hostages had known the risk of staying in Beirut, so they were largely on their own.

In fact, most of the hostages had been tied to Beirut for some time through their work, and while that argued for their understanding the danger, they had almost all arrived under far less hazardous circumstances — staying on, perhaps inured, as conditions around them deteriorated. Jeremy Levin, who was seized in 1984 and released in February 1985, was the Beirut bureau chief for Cable News Network. Similarly, Terry Anderson, who was taken captive on March 16, 1985, was the chief correspondent for the Associated Press, used to the relative protection that a press pass bought in Beirut. A tough former marine who had served two tours of duty in Vietnam, Anderson hadn't wanted to desert the story, even though almost all the rest of the Western press corps had finally abandoned Beirut to unreported anarchy. A Presbyterian minister, Benjamin Weir, who was kidnapped on May 8, 1984, had lived in the area for thirty years and, as a missionary, felt deep ties. And David Jacobsen, who was kidnapped on May 28, 1985, and Thomas Sutherland, who was kidnapped on June 9, 1985, were, respectively, director of the American University Hospital and dean of its Agriculture School at a time when the university had largely been a sanctuary from violence. Peter Kilburn, an older man of frail health, similarly may have been lulled into a false sense of security at the American University, where he had been a librarian for decades. Only Father Jenco, who was kidnapped on January 8, 1985, was a relative newcomer, and he, like Weir, felt committed to the region through his missionary work.

In a category by himself was William Buckley, the CIA's Beirut station chief, who was taken captive on March 14, 1985. Thirdhand reports of his torture were said to have affected not just Reagan, but Casey too. Although he was normally cold-blooded, as his profession demanded, Casey felt a special horror and rage about Buckley. He had personally sent Buckley to rebuild the agency's Middle Eastern intelligence network after the catastrophic embassy bombing of 1983. Moreover, there were reports that Buckley had broken under pressure and divulged the agency's secrets in a lengthy confession. These reports, while unreliable, drove Casey to distraction, since he was unable to know which of his assets had been compromised, which agents needed to be pulled and protected, and how much the Soviet Union had learned. There was a rumor that an Iranian agent had witnessed Buckley's interrogation — raising further questions about how far the information may have spread. But until the TWA hijacking, Buckley appears to have been the only hostage the president really focused on.

After the hijacking — and the meetings it prompted with the relatives — Reagan began to show an entirely new level of concern for the others and their families. Before long, what had largely been Reagan's concern for the welfare of one CIA agent, William Buckley, was becoming both a public spectacle and a private ordeal.

Even after the disastrous Chicago Heights meeting, the White House public relations experts couldn't resist having Reagan do yet one more "good news" hostage event. When it became certain on July 1 that the TWA hostages were on their way out, the White House's image-conscious advance office went into overdrive to plan a spectacular reception.

Originally, TWA had planned to send one of its own planes over to pick up the hostages and then reunite them with their families in a TWA maintenance hangar at New York's Kennedy Airport. But Henkel, an impeccably dressed former Merrill Lynch employee who had "advanced" trips for Nixon, Ford, and Reagan's campaigns before rising to head the office under Reagan, knew immediately that this was too good a moment for the White House to miss. Henkel had replaced Deaver as the top advance man in the White House by the summer of 1985, a job that, as he put it, entailed not just the planning of all trips but overseeing the "critically important stagecraft of the presidency." Though taken to new heights during the Reagan presidency, the art of presidential advance in the television age was born during the Nixon presidency, when chief of staff H. R. Haldeman recruited clean-cut, zealous, corporate go-getters for volunteer assignments setting up presidential events. The events were organized along the so-called HPS precept — each one had a specific Headline, Photograph, and Story or "Sound bite" in mind, all maximizing what Henkel unabashedly called the final goal: "press manipulation."

When the hostages appeared to be routed to New York, Henkel saw irresistible HPS possibilities about to slip away. As he later recalled, "Everything in me said it's too important to do that. I said we've *got* to shift it to Andrews." One problem was that the hostages had already been told their families would be waiting for them at JFK. And the TWA vice president for Europe was outraged at the White House's insensitivity, screaming at Henkel over the crackling overseas phone line that the hostages' psyches were "far too fragile" to take another shift in plans. "He went ballistic," chuckled Henkel. "We ended up prevailing."

The following morning, July 2, the day that the TWA hostages would

return, Don Regan proudly brought Henkel into the Oval Office to brief
the president on the welcoming ceremony at Andrews Air Force Base.
Both Henkel and Regan were jubilant. The horrible specter of a prolonged hostage drama had lifted without even a dip in the president's
approval ratings. They were laying out the plan — how the transportation would work, what the president would say, how long it would
take — when to their surprise Reagan interrupted them.

"There's only one thing missing in this," the president said quietly,
almost apologetically. "That poor young man. Do you think it would be
all right if we went to Arlington before Andrews?"

Henkel was completely taken aback. No one else had even thought
of it. While Reagan's aides worried about how to boost his image, the
president was still grieving for Robert Stethem, whose sacrifice he considered his personal responsibility and whose memory he'd been unable
to honor on their political advice. Clearly, they had underestimated the
depth of his emotional involvement.

Henkel scrambled over to Arlington, found the fresh grave in Section
59 — just fifty feet from a plaque dedicated to "victims of terrorism
throughout the world" — and tried to contact the family for an impromptu service. The White House operators, who are renowned for their
skill in tracking down the recipients of phone calls from the White
House, eventually located the sailor's sister at work. A White House car
was sent to her office, and she was whisked to the gravesite just in time
to be met by the Reagans.

The president and his wife laid wreaths of red and white carnations
on the grave. Everyone — Reagan, Nancy, and Stethem's sister —
cried. The ceremony was supposed to last only a few minutes, but they
stayed there for nearly three quarters of an hour. Before leaving to welcome home the surviving passengers at Andrews Air Force Base, across
the river, the president vowed to Stethem's sister, Sherry Sierralta, that
he would bring her brother's murderers to justice.

As president, Reagan had seen many steel caskets and comforted many
grieving relatives. These were the kind of ceremonial roles he played
well, but his aides said such experiences took a genuine toll. "You could
tell he really felt it — he wasn't just acting," said one aide who traveled
with him often. "He'd get back in the car or back on the plane, and
there would just be silence."

At three twenty-eight that afternoon, in the tropical summer sun, the
TWA hostages' jet touched down on American soil at Andrews Air Force
Base. A cheering crowd of some four hundred people carried signs like
AMERICA IS #1 and waved American flags. But Reagan's brief remarks
were tinged with anger. After welcoming the former hostages home, he
said, "There are promises to be kept. The day your plane was hijacked,
the terrorists focused their brutality on a brave young man who was a

member of the armed forces of the United States. They beat Robbie Stethem without mercy, then shot him to death. . . . We will not forget what was done to him. There will be no forgetting."

When it was all over, the president declaimed his harshest attack on terrorism yet. "Let me make it plain to the assassins in Beirut and their accomplices that America will never make concessions to terrorists," he told the American Bar Association on July 8. "The American people are not going to tolerate . . . intimidation, terror, and outright acts of war against this nation and its people. And we're especially not going to tolerate these acts from outlaw states run by the strangest collection of misfits, Looney Tunes, and squalid criminals since the advent of the Third Reich."

It was great rhetoric, crafted largely by Bill Casey's hard-line point man on the White House speechwriting team, former investigative journalist Tony Dolan. But when one senior White House aide asked Dolan whether there was a policy, as he put it, to "backfill" the speech, he was told only, "We'll have to push one." As everyone around the president knew, there was still no consensus.

And, in fact, as a handful of key advisers knew, Reagan had already made concessions even while he was swearing not to. His NSC was actively violating Reagan's public pledges in a far-flung, ultimately unsuccessful effort to buy back the CIA's kidnapped Beirut station chief, William Buckley, with ransom money borrowed from Texas billionaire H. Ross Perot. The architect of this scheme was McFarlane's aide Oliver North. His rationale was that this was private money meant for "bribes," not government-funded ransom. Although Reagan later said he couldn't recall whether he had known about this scheme, he sent a note thanking Perot for his "discreet assistance," on which he said he had been "fully briefed."

Both Reagan and Casey were said to be deeply moved by the rumors of Buckley's torture. Casey had shown Reagan a videotape of Buckley that had been made by his captors to document his deterioration. If that was not enough, the CIA's hostage team posted two photographs on the wall of a conference room at Langley. One was of Buckley before he left for Beirut: craggy good looks, cool professional eyes, and the barest hint of a smile. The other was a blurry, haggard image of their colleague in the hands of his torturers. No matter what the administration's rhetoric said, Buckley was Casey's man, and Casey was determined to get him back.

But again, just as with the TWA hijacking situation, the ideological principle had been overpowered by compassion for one individual. By treating counterterrorism as a matter of words, not policy, to be solved by public relations, not strategy, the administration could temporarily have it both ways. But the danger, conceded State Department expert

Parker Borg, was that "we were in a position of talking loudly and carrying a wet noodle."

Despite such long-range problems, by early July, the euphoria over the return of the TWA hostages had catapulted Reagan some ten points in the public opinion polls, as Wirthlin and Regan had hoped. It wasn't nearly the twenty-point boost Jimmy Carter had experienced in the first thirty days of his hostage crisis, but it successfully lifted Reagan out of May's Bitburg-inspired slump. And in an effort to capitalize on his increased popularity, the White House image-makers now took credit where before they had tried to avoid blame. The Regan team provided the newspapers and television networks with fourteen photographs showing the president in charge of the TWA crisis, as well as a blow-by-blow chronology of events. Aides even talked triumphantly about capitalizing on Reagan's more "activist" image to push other programs like his flagging tax reform plan.

But this new presidential image had an unintended consequence. Once the White House had portrayed Reagan as critical to solving the plight of the hostages' families, it was almost impossible to keep him away from the increasingly distressed families of the seven original hostages, who had watched the yellow ribbons come down while their relatives were still being held captive and, for all they knew, beaten and tortured.

Television, like the White House, is driven by a thirst for high ratings, and by issuing dramatic pictures and flamboyant speeches, the White House had helped make the hostage crisis a highly rated news event — one easily prolonged by the families of the "forgotten seven," as the earlier captives now came to be called. "It was clear [that] world attention was finally focused on it," said Peggy Say, the articulate and persistent sister of Terry Anderson. "At this point, the families went public. For me it was just a blur. I did probably every major TV show. The media turned it around for us. . . . They did the job for us."

The supposedly unsophisticated Jencos stormed the country with a media plan so ambitious that a presidential candidate would have been proud of it. Thirteen Jenco relatives sat down and divided the entire nation among themselves like conquering generals. "We crisscrossed the country, trying to hit every state we had relations in," explained Father Jenco's brother John, "and we had relations in forty-seven states. Our local relatives could do all the media setups — there wasn't an area we touched that didn't have local media for us." The result was what he called a national "awareness campaign to keep the hostages in the eyes of the American public. If it wasn't for the media," he conceded, "the plight of the hostages would have been dormant."

As the families had hoped, their appearances generated a great number of sympathetic stories, some of them highly critical of the White House. Gannett's *USA Today*, ordinarily a national cheerleader, ran one such editorial a month after the TWA hostages' release, chastising the country for being "ignorant, insensitive," and "uncaring" about the "forgotten seven" and asserting that the U.S. policy of "quiet diplomacy has failed."

Inside the White House, where everything from self-importance to public criticism tends to be magnified, the anguished families and the taunting media coverage took a heavy toll. It was during this period that Reagan began to ask about the seven remaining hostages in "ninety percent of his daily briefings," according to Don Regan. Day after day, the president would turn to his advisers and ask, "Anything new?"

II

ENTERPRISE

6

Drifting into a Deal

LESS THAN TWO WEEKS after the TWA hostage crisis ended, the White House was plunged into another unwelcome drama. In an antiseptic room in Bethesda Naval Hospital, Ronald Reagan was recovering from surgery. A day earlier, a physical examination had revealed a cancerous growth in his intestines. Surgeons had removed it, and now, as the president began to regain consciousness on the afternoon of July 13, 1985, his aides were trying to decide whether he was ready to reclaim his office.

For the first time in history, the vice president had been designated the acting president, in accordance with the transfer of powers outlined in the Constitution's Twenty-fifth Amendment. For nearly eight hours, George Bush had "command authority" — a complete set of the codes and equipment controlling the country's nuclear arsenal and augmented communications status — so that he could command the military to launch its nuclear weapons in just fifteen seconds.

The transfer of powers had been problematical. The White House counsel and the vice president had conferred by telephone until nearly three o'clock on the morning of the thirteenth, debating whether they would be setting an unfortunate precedent. But when at last they had settled on a plan, Reagan good-humoredly delegated his powers to Bush with a warning that the First Lady did not come with the title. The president signed the papers transferring his powers at 10:32 A.M. on Saturday, July 13, although because of a misunderstanding between the lawyers and doctors, Bush wasn't told that he was the acting president until 11:28 A.M. — by which time Reagan was already well under anesthesia, accidentally leaving the country for a short time with no functioning president.

Now, as the minutes ticked past seven o'clock on that summer evening after the surgery, Reagan's aides were left with a difficult and delicate task: determining whether the president was competent to resume control. The general anesthetic had largely worn off, but the president was still numb from the waist down. As White House counsel Fred Fielding pointed out to the president, his condition was reminiscent of his former movie line and autobiography title, *Where's the Rest of Me?* Tubes carrying antibiotics ran into Reagan's veins, a tube removing gas and liquid from his stomach ran out from his nose, and although the doctors said he seemed to be "responding remarkably," his aides wondered whether he was lucid.

Despite the tremendous advances in modern medicine, the chief surgeon said there was no standard method of determining whether the president had fully regained all his faculties. It was a judgment call. The aides — Fielding, Don Regan, and press secretary Larry Speakes — looked at one another dubiously and debated whether to wait until the next morning. Then, in the absence of any scientific test, they devised their own. "How about asking him to read a letter . . . ?" asked Fielding. "Wouldn't that be evidence that he was lucid?" The surgeon agreed. So they decided to see whether Reagan could coherently read the two-sentence statement they had prepared for him to sign upon reclaiming his powers.

The three men gathered around his bed, handed him the piece of paper, and watched in suspense. Reagan lifted it before his eyes, then stammered, faltered, and blinked. "His eyes," said Fielding, "were shutting and opening, and it was obviously going like this, like he was turning his eyes. And I thought, 'Uh-oh,' and Don Regan and I looked at each other." For an awful split second, it seemed possible that the seventy-four-year-old president might be seriously impaired.

"I guess I need my glasses," Reagan said pleasantly.

The aides let out a collective sigh of relief. When Reagan, who usually wore contact lenses, put on his bifocal reading glasses, he read the passage perfectly.

The false alarm had been sobering. The world would never know it from the public rendition Speakes gave of this episode, describing Reagan as so feisty, he'd demanded, "Gimme that" pen when they asked whether he was ready to take back his powers. But Reagan's skirmish with cancer made a deep impression on all those around him. If they had been protective of him before, they now grew fiendishly so. If they had sometimes slyly made decisions without him before, they now justified doing so openly. They didn't want to strain him with the burdens of his office. In their eagerness to shoulder some of the responsibilities, though, they inadvertently made him more detached than ever from his job.

Drawing the protective curtains around the president most of all was Nancy Reagan. Her husband jauntily downplayed his health problems — while the rest of the country became intimate with his intestines, thanks to nightly diagrams on the news — and he asked the doctors virtually no questions about his condition. But the First Lady became a knot of worry. She sat in the hospital with a fixed stare as Reagan recovered consciousness following the surgery, and she insisted that no photograph of him be released for twenty-four hours. She was focused so entirely on him, she left it to the staff to call the couple's children about their father's condition. Her concern for Reagan's health was all-consuming, and as a doctor's daughter, she viewed medical orders as sacrosanct. In an effort to guard his recovery, she argued vehemently against anyone's disturbing his rest, no matter what their official business.

The chief exception to her iron rule was Donald Regan, who soon made a public display of his exceptional access. Presidential hospitalizations, like trips abroad and long vacations, throw all of the rules that order the White House into disarray, testing the character of the staff. When Reagan had been hospitalized four years earlier, following the assassination attempt, and his condition was far graver than anyone let on, his top aides closed ranks to try to convey the impression that he was still very much in command. The troika of Baker, Meese, and Deaver met with him daily at the hospital, conveying the impression that he was still controlling affairs of state. Years later, one of them admitted that the hospital visits had been window dressing. In reality, the troika paid only brief respects to the ailing president, spending the rest of the time in the hospital cafeteria, quietly keeping the government going for him.

But Don Regan's approach to Reagan's hospitalization was entirely different. He walked out of the hospital and breezily boasted to the press that he had "tried to test him, to see was he alert." Then, after personally pronouncing the president fit, the chief of staff went on to show every sign of running the government himself. Regan's posturing did not go unnoticed. Larry Speakes related that after each visit, "I noticed that he would always make a strategic pause just outside the hospital to confer with either me or one of the advance men in full view of the photographers. [It] helped create the 'I'm-in-charge' image."

It was not until three days after the operation that the vice president managed to see the president, and then Regan made a point of ensuring he was there at precisely the same time. "We were already at the hospital, and [a Regan aide] kept telling us, 'Hold on, he'll be here any minute' — like the vice president couldn't possibly talk to the president alone," said one of Bush's aides. The display deepened the vice president's staff's thinly veiled contempt for Regan, whom they saw as boorishly power-hungry. Bush and Regan maintained cordial relations, but the fault lines ran deep. Bush was exactly the kind of Yankee aristocrat Regan had spent his life trying to dethrone, and Regan was the kind of unmannered upstart who made Bush clench his jaw.

While Reagan lay in the hospital, his wife and chief of staff also barred Robert McFarlane for the first four days. Instead, Regan himself brought national security paperwork to the president — mixing it with Reagan's reading matter, a Will Rogers anthology — even though the national security adviser felt he had urgent business to communicate. Mrs. Reagan was probably as much to blame as Regan. But the delay fueled the growing bad feeling and rivalry between Regan and McFarlane.

During this period, Nancy Reagan too began to chafe at Regan's passion for appearing omnipotent. An aide said that "Mrs. Reagan's eyes were opened wide" when Regan suggested he take a presidential helicopter up to the hospital for one of his visits. Not only would this upstage Mrs. Reagan, who was being driven to the suburban hospital, it also would have set a precedent in the perquisite-conscious White House: until then, the landing pad on the South Lawn of the White House was reserved for the president and other heads of state. The idea died almost as quickly as the First Lady picked up the phone and asked Regan if what she had heard was true. He told her it was. She then got off the phone and said with amazement, "He's still going to do it!" In fact, Regan took the hint and came by car.

Shortly after the surgery, Regan became still more offensive to Mrs. Reagan when he hired an aide supposedly to "handle" the First Lady, whose daily calls drove him to distraction. To Regan, Mrs. Reagan's intrusiveness was no joking matter. Ed Rollins claimed he had once kidded the chief of staff that "we've all got our burdens in life. Dawson's [Regan's executive assistant] is to take your bags. And yours is to take Mrs. Reagan's shit." Rollins recalled that Regan had exploded: "I've never let any broad push me around before, and I'm not about to start now." By October, a close friend of Nancy's confided that "she hasn't spoken to Regan for weeks." The problem, one aide close to the First Lady surmised, was that "Regan doesn't understand Nancy. Among the things he doesn't understand is that, no matter what, he's just staff."

Regan's actions and statements during the president's hospitalization hinted at a problem more serious than an insensitivity to protocol. Max Friedersdorf, the seasoned White House congressional affairs director, watched with alarm as Regan proceeded to run roughshod over everyone else as he consolidated his power. Friedersdorf, who had worked for six chiefs of staff, said he had never seen anything like it. It was as if Regan viewed himself as a regent for the president, first in sickness and later in health. Regan, as Friedersdorf put it, "built up a staff that was completely loyal to himself. . . . The president was just an appendage."

In Ed Rollins's view, "Regan's style was not to bother the president, not to pull him in to decisions — instead to tell him 'Mr. President, we've decided this. Don't worry, we'll take care of it for you.' " The result, he said, was not just that Regan had far too much to handle, but also that "Reagan seemed more and more distracted and detached."

As Regan increasingly allowed the president to drift away from the daily details of governance, he apparently justified this to himself and others as a form of protectiveness. One aide to Regan argued with him that it would be more efficient if he sometimes allowed the president to attend events by himself so that Regan could use the time for other matters, such as the growing heap of unanswered phone calls from congressmen and senators. But Regan explained that he believed the president needed him, as both a friend and a counselor. Regan told the aide that "the president looks to me for reassurance. At meetings or whatever, I think it makes him feel better to see that I'm there." Much later, in a candid moment, Regan described the president as having "a remarkably retentive memory" but basically "the mind of a movie actor." That view apparently infused much of Regan's thinking about why, increasingly, he was needed as the president's understudy.

During Reagan's week in the hospital, Regan stood in for the president at some White House meetings — a role that George Bush had played after the assassination attempt in 1981. And, significantly, Regan announced to a reporter after the surgery, "We'll try to make as many decisions as we can without involving him [Reagan]. Where we can't get agreement, and if there's a difference of opinion and it can't be ironed out, we'll make it crisp and succinct and take it to him for a decision. But we will try to spare him as many of the details as possible."

It was in this unsettled environment, one in which top aides presumed to act in the president's stead, that Ronald Reagan embarked on the foreign policy adventure that would turn out to be the biggest public debacle of his career.

The seeds of the weapons sale were first sown just down the hall from the Oval Office in the emotionally charged days immediately following the TWA hijacking crisis. On July 3, the morning after Reagan had wept at Robert Stethem's grave at Arlington National Cemetery, he spent more than an hour directing a postmortem of the TWA incident at an NSPG meeting in the Situation Room. Reagan was deeply frustrated at the inability of the United States to get better intelligence on the terrorists holding the hostages in Beirut. One participant later said that Reagan asked if the United States couldn't work with its allies to strengthen the intelligence-gathering. Everyone in the room knew that the ally with the most expertise on terrorism was Israel.

Reagan's concern made a big impression on his aides, most of whom were accustomed to his more usual passivity. No one at the meeting had a workable plan for bringing the hostages home. But Reagan's dictum to his staff had long been, "Don't bring me problems, bring me solutions." It was a command that Bud McFarlane — groping for a way to live up to the heavy mantle he'd inherited — took to heart. He left the meeting determined to find a plan.

That very afternoon, as if sent by providence, David Kimche, an urbane former Mossad spy, walked into McFarlane's office. Kimche had elevated covert action to an art form and, in an unusual move for an intelligence operator, risen to the top civil service job in Israel's foreign ministry. McFarlane had long admired him and envied Israel's prowess in counterterrorism. Now Kimche brought with him three other Israelis — and an intriguing idea of how to crack the deadlock surrounding Shia terrorism in Lebanon. The idea was named Manucher Ghorbanifar.

The Israelis explained that Ghorbanifar was an Iranian, a man who seemed to have wondrous contacts within the tightly closed hierarchy of the Ayatollah Khomeini's Islamic revolution. He represented a faction of pragmatists, Kimche said, who feared that chaos would overwhelm their country when the eighty-five-year-old ayatollah died and so wanted to open up discreet contacts with the West — even with the United States, the Great Satan in their leader's demonology. And, Kimche continued, the man might even be able to gain the release of the CIA's captive station chief in Beirut, William Buckley. All it would take, Kimche claimed, was the opening of talks with his pragmatic faction in Iran and — speaking as if it were an afterthought — a hundred U.S. antitank missiles. They would just be a gesture, a token of friendship.

This meeting was McFarlane's introduction to the fateful deal. For the other players, however, it was not the beginning but the culmination of years of intrigue, each phase bringing the idea of a U.S. arms deal with Iran one step closer to the susceptible Reagan White House.

In fact, four distinct elements came together in McFarlane's corner office on that July afternoon. Three were governments: the first was Iran, the world's only revolutionary Islamic state, wracked by six years of Khomeini's zealous despotism and five years of war with neighboring Iraq; the second was Israel, the constantly embattled Jewish state, forever caught in a bare-knuckled struggle to prevail in the Middle East; and the third, of course, was Ronald Reagan's United States, grasping as yet unsuccessfully for a counterterrorism policy. Yet as much as these governments had an interest in exploring a secret deal, they never could have tied the knot without the fourth party — the arms merchants.

Far beyond the shelter of the White House, the arms merchants inhabited a universe driven by private profit, indifferent to the public weal. As if compelled to prove Adam Smith's lesson about the market's invisible hand — a lesson Reagan's men loved to cite — they did what all good merchants do: they provided a link between a buyer and seller who could not reach each other directly. If buyer and seller had different aims, no matter. To the merchants, the deal was everything.

There are 159 sovereign governments around the world, and every one of them buys weapons. So do guerrilla groups and private armies from Ireland to Lebanon to the Philippines. The international arms bazaar never closes: it is open every day of the year in New York, Washington, and Miami; in Hong Kong and Johannesburg; in London and Paris; in Tel Aviv, Beirut, and Tehran.

The mechanics of the market are simple. Basic infantry weapons like rifles and machine guns are easy to buy. But only a handful of countries make sophisticated arms: antitank or antiaircraft missiles, artillery, precision-guided rockets, and aircraft — the kind of weapons that can mean victory or defeat in most wars, big or small. These few countries try to control their sales tightly. The scarcity not only keeps prices up but also reaps additional political benefits: arms sales can be doled out as a form of political patronage.

Not surprisingly, the demand for advanced weapons constantly exceeds the supply. And such weapons are expensive: a single HAWK antiaircraft missile can cost as much as $437,700 — and most users buy hundreds at a time. Because the potential profits are so large — and because most of the buyers and sellers are governments — the arms market is one of endless intrigue, of deals and double deals, where influence and bribery are currencies as common as money and guns.

The deal that Kimche brought to McFarlane began in one of the arms bazaar's most venerable markets, in Hamburg, Germany, in June 1985. The old port city, with its stately brick warehouses, had seen crates of weapons change hands at least since the 1860s, when Alfred Krupp, the young munitions manufacturer, hit on the brilliant innovation of selling guns to both sides of the same war. Hamburg's harbor on the Elbe was no longer what it had been, but the ancient city remained a major trading center. It also housed a thriving community of Iranians, from pro-Khomeini merchants to exiles plotting to put the son of the late shah back on the throne.

It was in one of the ancient warehouses, over a pile not of weapons, but of Persian rugs, that Ghorbanifar got his break. He was looking for a deal on behalf of someone high up in Iran. But little more about his intentions or his background was clear. Tall, dark-eyed, and glowering, he said he was about forty, but he looked a decade older. He claimed to be the chief of intelligence operations for Khomeini's prime minister, but he had worked for the shah's intelligence agency as well. He said he was an Iranian patriot, but CIA officials said he worked for both U.S. and Israeli intelligence, too. (The CIA evaluated him in 1980 as "a rumormonger of occasional usefulness," but soon decided he was working only for financial gain and dropped him.)

Ghorbanifar had been unusually agile in profiting from both sides of

Iran's 1979 revolution. Before the fall of the shah, he cooperated with the regime and served as a partner in Starline Iran, a joint Israeli-Iranian shipping firm that reportedly served as a cover for Israeli intelligence operations. After Khomeini came to power, Ghorbanifar was accused of participating in an abortive military coup in 1980, and he fled the country. But he quickly surfaced as a commercial and political agent for leading figures inside Khomeini's regime, causing some of the air force officers who had planned the coup to wonder whether he was the one who had betrayed them.

He was a gifted salesman, a master of sweeping promises who convinced otherwise skeptical men that he could deliver great things. He spoke the languages of the West, wore exquisite French suits, and appeared perfectly at home in the most elegant hotels and restaurants of Europe. But he ran his business according to an ancient Middle Eastern code. "People betray me, I betray them," he said. "People are honest with me, I give them everything. If not, I cut their throat."

This time, Ghorbanifar had a prize customer in his pocket: Ayatollah Khomeini. The ayatollah's regime had authorized Ghorbanifar to go into the global bazaar and buy American weapons.

Iran — the first nation behind the deal — desperately needed more guns and spare parts for the war with Iraq, then in its fifth terrible year. The army was still fighting with U.S. weapons originally sold to the shah, but ammunition and parts were critically low. For Khomeini and his rival in Iraq, President Saddam Hussein, the war had become a struggle for survival; each had vowed to overthrow the other. For the outside world, it was a matter of who would be the strongest power in the Persian Gulf, the most important oil-producing region in the world. At the moment, the war was a bloody stalemate. Iraq had stopped several Iranian offensives with its tanks and Soviet and French warplanes. Iran, relying on its much larger population, had made small gains, but at a horrendous cost in lives; many assaults were simply waves of teenage boys riding motorcycles straight into Iraqi minefields and shouting "God is great!" The tactic unnerved the Iraqis, but it could not win the war. To do that Iran had to catch up to Iraq's technological advantage — by buying more advanced weapons.

And the only way to resupply an army the size of Iran's with U.S. weaponry was to persuade the United States to sell the weapons directly. That was Ghorbanifar's task, and he knew well the kind of profits that could result. With luck — and the right connection in Washington — a thousand antitank missiles could be bought from the United States for a little more than $5 million and sold to Khomeini for at least $10 million, perhaps more.

But Ronald Reagan had come into office reviling Khomeini's Iran.

His advisers, believing that U.S. interests lay primarily with Iraq, had imposed a worldwide (if leaky) embargo, Operation Staunch, on the sale of U.S. arms to Iran. It thus turned out to be exceedingly difficult for Ghorbanifar to make his Washington connection. He had begun in 1984, approaching the CIA with two stories designed to pique its interest: he knew who was behind the Buckley kidnapping, and he claimed that he knew of an Iranian plot to assassinate both of the presidential candidates in the United States. The CIA promptly put him on a polygraph, popularly known as a lie detector; he failed. Three months later, he popped up with an offer to set up secret talks with an Iranian leader; the CIA polygraphed him again, and again he failed. This time, the agency issued a Burn Notice, warning its officers that Ghorbanifar was "an intelligence fabricator and a nuisance." The CIA had concluded, operations chief Clair George said later, that "Mr. Ghorbanifar's information, intelligence, regardless of the subject, was inaccurate, incomplete, and dishonest."

Ghorbanifar did not give up. In late 1984 he arranged to meet Theodore G. Shackley, a former CIA station chief in Tehran who had been pushed out of the agency during the Carter administration. Iran was willing to act as a broker in a deal to release the hostages, Ghorbanifar told Shackley. "The transaction would be simple," he said. "Money for people." Shackley, who was worried about the fate of his old CIA colleague Buckley, made sure the message reached the State Department; but "money for people" ran contrary to Shultz's tough line on terrorism, and the offer was ignored.

Not until his fourth attempt did Ghorbanifar make the right contact. This time, his pitch was slightly different: now he represented a moderate faction in Iran which wanted to move the country away from the Soviet Union and back toward the West. And this time his connection was an old friend and client of CIA Director William Casey's, a New York oil broker named Roy M. Furmark. For years, Casey had been his lawyer, and the two men were in intermittent touch. It was a crucial connection, for it was Furmark who began the chain of opportune introductions that ultimately brought Ghorbanifar, the CIA's "fabricator and nuisance," past the cement antiterrorist barricades and the computer-scanned ID checks inside the White House complex.

Furmark was an international dealmaker operating on the fringe of the world oil market from a suite of grimy offices on New York's lower Broadway. Furmark had spent much of his time in a series of joint ventures with Adnan Khashoggi, the flamboyant Saudi arms dealer once known as "the world's richest man." Khashoggi had made his fortune as the Saudi Arabian agent for the U.S. aerospace giants Lockheed and Northrop, who paid him enormous sums for smoothing their sales to Saudi officials in the 1960s and 1970s. But the Saudi royal family eventually decided that it didn't need him as a middleman. Khashoggi continued to cut a grand figure on the diplomatic scene, but his business never did as well. He still traveled in his own custom DC-8 with a squadron of aides, but his financial empire was slowly collapsing. He desperately needed a big new deal to stay afloat.

Although they were in the same trade, Khashoggi and Ghorbanifar had never met. It fell to Casey's old friend Furmark to make the crucial introduction, so the three men met together for the first time on a rainy June day in Hamburg during a friendly bout of haggling over a heap of Persian rugs. Exquisite tapestries of wool and silk were piled unceremoniously on the floor of a rented warehouse, and the arms merchants argued at some length over quality and price. Mostly it was just for the game; Khashoggi, the wealthiest among them, bought only two prayer rugs the size of bath mats. The traders' minds were elsewhere, on their real business. But it was over this pile of Persian rugs, as they told the story later, that Ghorbanifar's connection was finally made.

As Khashoggi recalled it, "There was this gentleman who represented himself as the head of intelligence for the prime minister of Iran. First time I met him. And he took me aside and started telling me how awful, what's happening in the Middle East, and this war between Iraq and Iran, and all this Muslim brother blood is being shed for six years," the arms merchant said. "And he was talking language that I could understand and accept." Furmark recalled the conversation somewhat differently. "In [Khashoggi's] mind [was] that if we could get Iran closer to the West, and Ghorbanifar was the person doing it, we could then go to a $10 or $20 billion contract," he said. "That was ultimate in Khashoggi's mind." In any case, Ghorbanifar told Khashoggi that the key to peace was a new relationship between Iran and the United States, and the key to a new relationship was access for Iran to U.S. weapons. He wanted Khashoggi the statesman to make a connection for him in Washington. Any connection but the CIA, Ghorbanifar had said; the agency couldn't be trusted.

"We don't have to deal with the CIA," Khashoggi had said with his customary bravado. "We'll deal directly with the president of the country."

"Very good," Ghorbanifar had said admiringly. It was, no doubt, a line he wished he could have used himself.

In fact, Khashoggi did not have a direct line to Ronald Reagan. But he did have a direct line to Shimon Peres, the prime minister of Israel and the Americans' closest ally in the Middle East. Within a week, with Khashoggi's help, Ghorbanifar was meeting with Israelis who had direct ties both to the arms trade and to the Israeli government. Upon first hearing about the proposed deal, Prime Minister Peres was skeptical, but when he heard that Ghorbanifar's name was on a $100 million Swiss bank account (along with those of three ayatollahs), "people's eyes lit up," one of the Israeli intermediaries said. They set up a $50 million deal to sell Israeli mortar shells to Iran.

Israel's willingness to sell deadly weapons to Khomeini through Saudi and Iranian arms dealers — the second nation behind the final deal — surprised most Americans when they learned about it almost two years later. But it was nothing new to the practitioners of the trade. "We have to sell our arms," one of Ghorbanifar's Israeli contacts told a *New York Times* reporter. Speaking of Ghorbanifar, he said, "Sure he is a liar. But what do you expect to find in this business? Sons of rabbis?"

But Israel's history of selling weapons to Khomeini had roots more tangled than a simple desire to make a profit. Since its founding, the Jewish state had looked to the non-Arab states around the Middle East — of which Iran is one — as natural allies against its Arab enemies. Iran's Khomeini had sworn enmity toward Israel, but his war was with Iraq, an Arab country that had sent troops marching toward Jerusalem in 1948 and 1967. Some Israeli leaders candidly expressed a desire to keep the Iran-Iraq war going as long as possible, to bleed both sides. But most viewed Iraq as a greater threat to their security than Iran would ever be.

So Israeli arms dealers had quietly kept up their contacts in Tehran after Khomeini came to power in 1979. When Iraq invaded Iran in September 1980, the Israelis sold U.S. airplane parts to Khomeini, even as the Iranian regime held fifty-two Americans hostage in the U.S. Embassy in Tehran. (President Carter was furious when he learned of the sale after it had occurred and insisted that the sales stop.) But as the new Reagan administration prepared to move into the White House, the Israelis decided to try again. They enlisted the American Jewish leader Morris Amitay to meet with Richard V. Allen, Reagan's national security aide. Would Reagan allow Israel to resume arms sales to Iran?

Allen responded with deliberate ambiguity: "Tell your friends I heard what you said," which Amitay took as a go-ahead — "an amber light."

Some Israelis said they got similar go-aheads from Secretary of State Alexander Haig and his counselor, Robert McFarlane. Haig and McFarlane did agree that Israel could sell its own weaponry to Iran, but both insist that they told the Israelis that sales of U.S. parts would be illegal. The Israelis continued the sales anyway.

When Israeli defense minister Ariel Sharon came to Washington in 1982, Haig planned to confront him with the secret shipments. But Sharon preempted him; Israeli intelligence had discovered that the United States had secretly allowed Egypt to sell artillery guns to Iraq. Sharon heatedly protested the shipments, and Haig fired back with his own strong words about Israel's dealings with Iran. But his righteous indignation now sounded a bit tinny and the argument ended in a standoff.

State Department officials said they believed Israel finally bowed to American pressure and stopped selling U.S. weapons to Iran in 1982, when George Shultz put Operation Staunch into action. But the Israelis never stopped selling their own arms.

The erratic U.S. protests, of course, were only a small part of the complicated U.S.-Israeli relationship, a sometimes rocky marriage of two very different partners who viewed each other with mingled trust and mistrust, admiration and impatience. In the areas of special military operations and counterterrorism, especially, the Americans admired Israel's prowess — and felt a touch of envy at its ability to retaliate decisively against terrorism.

One of those who was most impressed was Bud McFarlane, who had first worked in the Middle East in 1982, when Haig was promoting the idea of "strategic cooperation" between Israel and the United States. That was also when McFarlane first worked closely with David Kimche, as sophisticated an exponent of Old World intrigue as the Middle East could offer. Israelis like Kimche argued for more "flexibility" in both Jerusalem and Washington for secret payments and weapons sales to influence other governments, no matter how repugnant they might appear at first. After two decades of secret negotiations with Arab leaders who publicly vowed to destroy Israel even as they met, the Israelis were used to the idea of doing business with an enemy. They viewed Iran in cold geopolitical terms: it was a regional power that could line up with either the United States or the Soviet Union and could either help the Arabs or hinder them. And they knew that finding a supply of advanced weapons was, as Kimche put it, Iran's "biggest problem today."

The Israelis had one other important interest in Iran that they kept doggedly quiet: the rescue of the eighty thousand Iranian Jews. Only long after the fact were officials willing to divulge even part of the story. Jews had lived in Persia since the Babylonian exile of the sixth century B.C., sometimes freely, sometimes oppressed. But Khomeini's revolutionary Islamic regime was explicitly hostile to all non-Muslims. It put Jews under the control of the Ministry of Internal Security, restricted their rights to travel abroad, and stamped their passports with a red seal forbidding travel to "occupied Palestine." In 1979, after the fall of the shah, Menachem Begin's government decided to get as many Jews out as wanted to leave. But exit visas took money and influence. One solution was crassly commercial: to buy the Jews' freedom with weapons — hence Begin's secret sale of aircraft parts to Khomeini in 1980, in the midst of Jimmy Carter's hostage crisis. During the next few years, Israel continued to work assiduously to rescue Iranian Jews, and by 1985, some fifty thousand had left Iran. But some thirty thousand were left behind, and the repression was getting worse. And so the Israelis stepped up this secret exodus by increasing the sale of arms. In the fall of 1985,

Oliver North excitedly told colleagues that he had stumbled across an astonishing arrangement: an Israeli arms-for-hostage deal. Israeli cargo planes carried weapons to Iran, North said, then brought Jewish refugees back. Other officials have said that they think North's account an exaggeration. Nevertheless, rescuing Jews from potential pogroms was Israel's trump card — clearly its basic duty as a nation. Although the Americans could complain about their weapons going to Iran, the Israelis had a simple reply: "We are getting our people out before they are slaughtered."

As it happened, by the spring of 1985, the United States was particularly receptive to unorthodox approaches to Iran, thus becoming the third and final nation necessary for the deal. It was a geopolitical shift actively promoted by a free-lance antiterrorism consultant to the NSC, Michael A. Ledeen, whose close ties to Israel and position as a private contractor eventually led even McFarlane — his original sponsor — to question his suitability as a go-between. But McFarlane's misgivings were not strong enough to overcome his fascination with the new ideas about Iran coming from Israel, since McFarlane secretly sent Ledeen to meet with senior Israeli officials in early May. Ledeen returned to Washington with word that the Israelis wanted to work with the United States on new approaches to Iran — approaches that might include Israeli arms sales to Iranian "moderates."

Given the administration's hard-nosed posture toward terrorism in general and Iran in particular, one might have expected such a scheme to be met with horror. Instead, it instantly appealed to a small but influential clutch of policymakers at the NSC and CIA for a variety of reasons. In part, these men were eager for a breakthrough because of their compassion for William Buckley and the other hostages. They were also drawn to the view that Iran could be a key counterbalance to Soviet expansion. And as was usually true at the White House, personal ambition also played a part.

Both the president and the CIA were increasingly concerned about Buckley — an anxiety fanned not inconsiderably by the speculation about Buckley's torture that frequently turned up in the president's daily briefing material. But, according to one authoritative account, the reports exaggerated Buckley's true condition. Buckley was indeed in bad shape, but the cause was medical neglect, not torture. McFarlane and others at the NSC were also motivated by an ill-informed global calculation that, in its eagerness to make Iran an ally of convenience in the struggle against the Soviet Union, underestimated the complicated politics of the fundamentalist Islamic state. And finally, it appears that McFarlane saw the opportunity for some creative diplomacy, perhaps even along the lines of his mentor Henry Kissinger's opening of relations with the People's Republic of China. "Bud was Kissinger's military deputy — he sat there and watched Kissinger become a hero with China. He defended this as the same thing," said an NSC colleague. In McFarlane's eyes, the initiation of new and fruitful relations with Iran would earn him a place in history.

Thus in mid-May, McFarlane asked Graham Fuller, the CIA's national intelligence officer for the Near East and South Asia, to study the options. The result was a report, a new Special National Intelligence Estimate, painting a grim picture of Iran approaching the end of the Khomeini era with every reason to turn to the USSR instead of the United States. In a blandly stated passage, Fuller suggested a solution: the United States could encourage closer relations between Iran and countries like France, China, Japan, and Israel — countries which, the SNIE noted delicately, "can fill a military gap for Iran."

That reference to arms sales was so gentle that it aroused no major controversy within the bureaucracy. McFarlane quickly endorsed the proposal, and the NSC reformulated it into a National Security Decision Directive, to be circulated to the members of the NSC, and sent on for presidential approval. The NSDD made the proposal explicit: the United States should actively encourage Israel and other allies to sell weapons to Iran.

Casey, ever the Cold Warrior, gave it his enthusiastic endorsement. But Weinberger and Shultz were astonished by the suggestion. "This is almost too absurd to comment on," Weinberger scrawled in a fury on the margin of his copy. "It's like asking Qadhafi to Washington for a cozy chat." Shultz wrote that he agreed that Iran policy should be reassessed, but added, "Its proposal that we permit or encourage a flow of Western arms to Iran is contrary to our interest both in containing Khomeinism and in ending the excesses of this regime."

Shultz was even more upset about Ledeen's secret mission to Israel, which he had learned of by the end of May. The secretary of state angrily told McFarlane that he would not accept that kind of "back channel" action. And, Shultz warned, "Israel's agenda is not the same as ours." McFarlane, caught red-handed, lied; he told Shultz that Ledeen had been in Israel "on his own hook" and promised that he was "turning it off entirely." But he didn't. Instead, on June 3, McFarlane approved a second Ledeen trip.

Within the month, during the height of the White House's panic over the TWA hijacking, the same U.S. officials who favored new relations with Iran also announced that Iran had, to their surprise, tried to ease the crisis. They said that the speaker of Iran's parliament, Rafsanjani, pressured the Lebanese terrorists to release the last hijacked hostages — those with Jewish-sounding names or government affiliations. Shultz was not convinced by the evidence, but Casey and the NSC staff convinced Reagan that there were rational players in Iran willing to help. On June

30, they encouraged Reagan to send a secret note of thanks to Rafsanjani, who was then on a visit to Tokyo. The message was relayed by Japan's prime minister, Yasuhiro Nakasone.

Looking back some time later, McFarlane admitted that he and others may have wanted to read more into the Iranian help than the situation merited. People on the NSC staff "hyped" the amount of help from the Iranians, McFarlane later conceded. "And I think, to be fair, there is, in terms of Western logic, a very good case that there ought to be moderates in Iran. That is logical. It is not, I think, the reality."

But such doubts came to McFarlane only much later. At the time, despite knowing the strong objections of the secretaries of both defense and state, McFarlane told Ledeen to authorize a single small Israeli arms sale to Iran — the mortar shells that Ghorbanifar had wanted.

By mid-June, the shells were on the dock, their Israeli markings carefully erased, when Ghorbanifar suddenly turned up in Israel. "We will buy the mortars later," he had said. "Now we must have TOWs." TOWs, the Israelis knew, were tube-launched, optically tracked, wire-guided missiles, one of the most effective antitank weapons in the world. And they came from only one source: the United States.

The moderates in Iran, Ghorbanifar said, needed five hundred TOW antitank missiles. The Israeli defense minister protested that the loss of five hundred TOWs would drop Israel's supply to a dangerously low level. He agreed to an initial shipment of a hundred instead. Prime Minister Peres called David Kimche to his small office on the second floor of the Ben Gurion Government Compound. Kimche was already scheduled to go to Washington for talks with the Americans; now, Peres said, he had a new mission: to present the Iranian arms merchant's lengthening proposal to Bud McFarlane.

When McFarlane opened his White House door to Kimche and his confederates on the afternoon of July 3, the four elements necessary to clinch the deal came together at last. Ghorbanifar had already brought together the Iranians and the Israelis; now, thanks to Khashoggi's contacts, the Israelis were taking his offer within a few footsteps of the president of the United States.

The Iranian offer that Kimche presented to McFarlane on July 3 was somewhat vague. It may not have included a specific number of weapons. But the basic elements were clear: a desire to oppose the growing Soviet influence in Iran; a chance to make contact with pragmatic Iranians who wanted to deal with the West; U.S. weapons; and American hostages. There was one further condition, a demand made by Ghorbanifar after his unsettling experience with the polygraph: the CIA was not to be involved. This operation would have to be run by the NSC staff itself.

McFarlane signed up almost immediately. "I was very much open to somebody giving me a basis for conducting a probe [into Iran]," he said. "The second important influence . . . was Kimche's visit, because I had enormous respect for David, and I still do. . . . So because David believed in this guy, I was willing to believe in him — almost entirely because of that."

Within a day or two, McFarlane said, he mentioned the opening to Reagan — complete with possible arms sales to Iran — at one of their 9:30 A.M. briefings in the Oval Office. This was the same week that Reagan delivered his bellicose speech against terrorism, castigating "outlaw states." But when McFarlane talked to Reagan about opening relations and sending arms to these same "outlaw states," with the hostages' release as a goal, the president's reaction was agreeable. Reagan was immediately "quite enthusiastic, and perhaps excessively enthusiastic, given the many uncertainties involved. But it was expressive of his attitude," McFarlane later recalled. "The president had no hesitancy about it at all."

It was not, however, until some ten days later — on July 18, during Reagan's hospitalization — that McFarlane, who had finally gained admittance into the president's hospital room, sought Reagan's explicit approval for specific negotiations with Ghorbanifar. The meeting lasted twenty-three minutes, but there were only about ten minutes for the complicated Middle Eastern initiative. There was much ground to cover, and five days after his surgery Reagan was still weak. But the hostages were very much on his mind — in fact, their welfare was one of the first things he spoke of upon regaining consciousness. So McFarlane quickly outlined the Iranian deal.

Don Regan was present during this encounter but only vaguely recalled it later; he believed that the discussion covered only new relations with "outsiders" in Iran but never covered arms shipments. Although Regan liked to tell his aides that the key to his own success was his ability to "anticipate," in this instance he asked no questions about a scheme that had instantly horrified Shultz and Weinberger. Also, as was his custom, Regan took no notes.

Thus the only available detailed account of the meeting is McFarlane's. But McFarlane has provided somewhat contradictory accounts. The first version suggested that the president had spoken at length about Iran's geopolitical significance, but McFarlane later admitted that Reagan had, instead, focused almost entirely on the hostages: practically as soon as McFarlane had outlined the Iranian proposition, the president, excited that it might bring back all seven captives, responded with characteristic optimism, saying, "Gee, that sounds pretty good."

The proposed arms deal was potentially illegal; a set of export control acts barred U.S. arms sales to countries supporting terrorism unless the president specified otherwise for national security reasons, and then notified Congress. Laws similarly restricted the resale of U.S. weapons from one country, like Israel, to another without congressional authorization. But McFarlane later said that he had explained some of the complications to the president, who wasn't deterred.

"The weapons issue is a problem," McFarlane claimed the president said. "I guess we can't do the weapons or something like that ourselves. But isn't there a way that we can get at trying to keep this channel going?" From Reagan's question, McFarlane inferred that the president seemed to be saying that the United States could not sell weapons directly to Iran, but it might be possible for Israel to sell its own weapons that came from the United States. McFarlane thus told the Israelis that the president had approved the deal in principle.

But, almost from the start, the initiative started changing in strange ways. Soon after McFarlane had conveyed Reagan's approval, Ghorbanifar had reopened the terms of the deal. He asked, not only for TOWs, but also for spare parts for antiaircraft missiles; and he said he might succeed in winning the release of only some of the hostages, not all seven. On July 31, Kimche returned for a second meeting with McFarlane, and this time he brought news of another possible snag. The Israeli defense minister was being cautious; he refused to move the TOWs to Iran without specific assurance from Reagan that he had authorized the sale and would replace the missiles. The Israelis, at least, sensed the political danger posed by the deal and wanted explicit approval from the top. McFarlane had no choice; he would have to take the issue back to the president again.

On August 6, now back in the White House, Reagan heard the details of the first concrete plan to ship weapons to Iran. Accounts differ about when these meetings occurred and who participated in which ones, but almost all agree on the basic arguments that were made. According to White House records, in the morning the president met with Weinberger, McFarlane, Regan, and George Bush as well as General John Vessey, chairman of the Joint Chiefs of Staff. Bush later insisted that he was never at any meeting at which Shultz or Weinberger argued against the arms sales. But McFarlane and Weinberger both recalled a discussion of the arms deal, and Weinberger recalled attacking the proposal head-on and heatedly, saying, "This would undercut everything we were going to do in the Mideast."

None of the participants recalled Don Regan's saying anything. In his own testimony, Regan suggested that what struck him most at the time was the mispronunciation of the Latinism *bona fides* by his colleague McFarlane, who was using the term to describe the weapons. Regan fancied himself "an old Latin scholar." His silence about the larger issue of the politically explosive Iranian proposal wasn't unusual. In many meetings, Regan often played his cards close to the vest, knowing that he could discuss issues alone with the president later. A Regan aide described this method as "straightening the president out, once the others had gone." But in this instance there is no record that Regan did so.

Bush, the former CIA director and recently named head of the anti-terrorism task force, expressed no opinion either. This also was not unusual. According to dozens of officials, Bush seldom spoke out in policy debates, either feeling no urge to express himself or reserving his thoughts for the confidential luncheons he and the president shared almost weekly.

The discussion resumed in the afternoon, at one of Shultz's weekly meetings with Reagan, which was also attended by McFarlane. Here the president apparently heard McFarlane propose the deal in the most explicit terms yet. McFarlane emphasized an argument that Reagan used later: that it was not a U.S. deal but an Israeli deal. That meant that if something went wrong, the United States could deny any authorship of the operation. And McFarlane added one more humanitarian plea: the shipment might win freedom not only for the American hostages in Lebanon, but also for the Jews of Iran.

But Shultz was not convinced, saying that it was "a very bad idea." An opening to Iranian moderates would be fine, he said, but "as far as arms sales are concerned, it's a mistake." It could be a sting. No matter what was being said about a new relationship with Iran, he warned, "we were just falling into the arms-for-hostage business."

As was his custom when his aides were in conflict, the president listened to the arguments that day but announced no formal decision. And, as often happened, each of his advisers read what he wanted into the vague and ambiguous responses that Reagan did make. It was as if his passivity became a reflecting glass for his willful advisers. Both Shultz and Weinberger came away thinking that they had stopped the deal from going ahead. McFarlane later said he believed that Reagan had accepted his own arguments. However, all agreed later that the president never really gave any definite response — at least not in this meeting.

But McFarlane, in what later became one of the most hotly contested aspects of his testimony, said that in the end, Reagan did declare his unambiguous support for the initiative. McFarlane's account remains uncorroborated, but he testified that the president called him at home "a day or so" after the meeting on August 6. In a later interview, McFarlane said that he remembered the conversation distinctly and that Reagan was calling from Camp David. According to McFarlane, their conversation proceeded as follows:

"Bud," said Reagan, "I want to go ahead with the Iranian matter we discussed."

"Two of your cabinet officers are against it," McFarlane replied.

"Yeah, I understand that," Reagan said. "But . . . we've got to try to find out if there are any people in Iran who are ready to change. And we've got to get the hostages back."

"All right," said McFarlane. "I'll notify the others."

If this was, in fact, the manner in which Reagan approved the initiative, his method was odd in many respects. There was no formal directive, no presidential memo — not even a note of the telephone call by either Reagan or McFarlane. But that, McFarlane said later, was how Ronald Reagan, fully apprised of the risks, agreed to sell American weapons to Iran's Ayatollah Ruhollah Khomeini. The decision meant violating the core of his stated policy on terrorism and possibly a host of laws. So McFarlane went ahead and called Kimche, who was delighted to hear that the deal could go forward.

More than a year later, when Reagan was asked about his decision, he could not remember when or how he had made it, and he couldn't recall the telephone call with McFarlane at all nor did the White House have a record of the call. Although McFarlane said he notified Shultz and Weinberger of the decision, neither recalled being told. Stranger still, Reagan was never at Camp David during the period in which McFarlane said the telephone call occurred. From Tuesday, August 6, the day of McFarlane's proposal, until Saturday, August 10, Reagan stayed in Washington — and McFarlane was at the White House every one of those days, including Saturday. On Sunday, August 11, Reagan flew to his ranch in California, and McFarlane went with him on *Air Force One*. So there was no obvious reason for Reagan to call his aide at home, something he rarely did in any case.

In short, there is much evidence to rebut McFarlane's version and little to support it. Yet both the Tower board and congressional investigators believed McFarlane. To this day, it remains uncertain whether Ronald Reagan gave his explicit approval for the scheme. If he did, then McFarlane was uncharacteristically casual in his handling of the approval; under standard procedure, a decision of this importance would be formally recorded. If he did not, then McFarlane clearly took the liberty of converting the president's broad inclinations into a specific policy that he happened to favor.

A favorite story of Reagan's described a little boy who, when presented with a pile of manure, instead of complaining said excitedly, "There must be a pony in here somewhere." The president was a self-described optimist, and journalists credited him with lifting the spirits of the whole country. But aides knew the flip side of this trait: when faced with unwanted, unpleasant facts, Reagan would keep digging for the pony rather than acknowledging pure manure.

So when McFarlane mentioned the jumbled, complicated proposal from Ghorbanifar, there is every reason to believe that Reagan characteristically screened out the bad news and grasped at the good. McFarlane's complex rationale for the deal was tailored to Reagan. It was like a menu; he could choose whatever parts he liked. The aim of opposing the Soviet influence in Iran was sure to appeal to the old Cold Warrior, and the idea of helping anti-Khomeini moderates was also congenial, even though McFarlane warned that the presence of moderates could prove illusory. Reagan reiterated these arguments, as it turned out, even long after everyone else knew them to be unfounded.

Selective thinking was a mental trick that Reagan used often. His early life was marked by instances of his rearranging and even denying unpleasant facts. For instance, his biographer, Lou Cannon, noted that well after his first marriage ended in divorce, Reagan "acted as if he had not really been divorced at all" because he hadn't wanted the divorce. Similarly, at the same time that Reagan eagerly accepted McFarlane's packaging of the arms-for-hostage deal as an opening to Iranian moderates, he screened out unwanted news about his health — so much so that it bordered on self-delusion. After returning from the hospital on July 20, he was preparing for a press conference about his bout with cancer when a telling answer popped out of him. He told his aides, assembled for the practice session in the family theater, that if asked about cancer, he wanted to say "I appreciate all these cards, but I never suffered from cancer."

He reasoned that since the cancerous growth had been removed, *it* had cancer, but he didn't; and since he'd felt no pain, he had never actually suffered from the disease. It was the sort of comforting self-denial that Reagan's more seasoned aides had learned to correct gently, and one tried at this session. Afterward this same aide, John A. "Jack" Svahn, argued with Regan that he must emphasize to the president that he should not use the phrase. But for all his celebrated power, Regan was apparently loath to tell the president no. Reagan went ahead and told the *Washington Post*'s Lou Cannon, "I didn't have cancer. I had something inside of me that had cancer in it and it was removed." Sure enough, it set off ripples of press stories, making Reagan look like an escapee from reality.

Don Regan, unlike some aides who had been with Reagan longer, either didn't see that it was his job to persuade the president to keep such fictions to himself, or else he was inadequate to the task. By the summer of 1985, examples were proliferating. Shortly before Reagan entered the hospital, Regan had indulged the president in another of his most cherished fantasies: the notion that the gaping federal deficit could be conquered without cutting middle-class entitlements like Social Security payments, without cutting the Defense Department's annual budget increase, and without raising taxes. This unrealistic position assured the White House's irrelevance to the budget process, abdicating leadership to Congress on the most crucial domestic issue of the day, a move that political scientist and *Los Angeles Times* columnist William Schneider later called "the worst domestic policy mistake of the second term."

The way that Regan indulged the president's unrealistic position, scuttling any meaningful budget reform, was an object lesson in the problems afflicting the second-term White House. Reagan came close to backing a Senate proposal to freeze the cost-of-living increases, COLAs, in Social Security payments, which would have made a substantial dent in the deficit. But when House Republicans attacked the cuts as unnecessary and politically costly, the president broke his commitment to the Senate, leaving its leaders hanging. Behind the flip-flop was Don Regan, who assumed personal command over relations with Congress, in the process botching relations with the members and any chance of getting the president to support a responsible budget package.

White House political director Ed Rollins, in a panic over the situation, told Regan that Congress was in an uproar. Rollins said that Regan replied, "Fuck Congress!" Within twenty-four hours, the remark had circulated about the Hill, bringing the White House's congressional relations to a new low. When the Senate and House negotiators worked out a plan for a budget compromise on August 1, the White House was relegated to observer status. Not only had it forfeited its political clout, it had also alienated Congress, at least temporarily disrupting any real chances for cooperation on the crowded political agenda ahead. Beneath the rancor lay a serious problem: Regan's White House was increasingly pandering to Reagan's whims, dismissing opponents on the Hill as hopelessly hostile. Instead of considering the possibility that the lawmakers sometimes had legitimate concerns that ought to be heard, to the White House's fortress mentality, Congress was becoming the enemy.

That summer Regan also indulged Reagan's delusions on another major issue: South Africa. As the Pretoria government of P. W. Botha declared a state of emergency and clamped down on black political unrest, Congress moved to pass economic sanctions. But in a breathtaking leap into wishful thinking, Reagan cheerily declared on August 24 that South Africa — where blacks had no voting rights, where many public facilities were still segregated — had "eliminated the segregation that we once had in our own country, the type of thing where hotels and restaurants and places of entertainment and so forth were segregated — that has all been eliminated." Regan's staff, blindly absorbed in economic issues, was not perturbed. Much of the Republican party perceived potentially damaging racial overtones in the White House's position, and the congressional movement for economic sanctions was gaining force. But Regan's executive assistant, Thomas Dawson, reflected the White House outlook at dinner one night, declaring that as far as South Africa went, "I couldn't care less."

However, Reagan's statements horrified McFarlane. On August 11,

McFarlane had flown with Reagan and most of the presidential staff to Santa Barbara, where the president was taking a twenty-three-day post-operative vacation in the isolation of his ranch. Nancy Reagan was still so protective of his health, she forbade almost all visits, postponed press interviews, and limited Regan and McFarlane largely to written communications and phone calls. McFarlane suspected that Reagan's ramblings on South Africa owed much to right-wing clippings that he believed communications director Patrick Buchanan was sending the president. Moreover, McFarlane thought that, increasingly, Regan was sanctioning such unorthodox communications on delicate foreign affairs matters partly in an effort to undercut McFarlane's own authority.

Under his streamlined management system, Regan and McFarlane were the only White House aides with regular direct access to the president. But the two men were increasingly locked in a debilitating rivalry, and by the summer of 1985 their fighting had descended to such a mean and petty level, McFarlane's aides believed that Regan was spreading spurious rumors about McFarlane's having an extramarital affair with NBC's well-informed White House correspondent, Andrea Mitchell. The rumors were bound to raise questions about his judgment; they might even jeopardize his job.

By mid-August, the rumors grew so rampant, they seemed to have taken on a virulent life of their own. McFarlane, the tormented, self-contained Methodist soldier, was at a loss to know how to quell a story that he insisted to his close friends was not true. On August 11, the issue crossed the threshold from private gossip to public humiliation when *Parade* magazine printed a supposed letter from a reader in its personality column, asking, "Just what's keeping the lid on the sex scandal involving a married White House official and a White House reporter?" The magazine answered, "The gossip has been hushed about in print and broadcast journalism circles. There's no conclusive evidence that it's true."

That evening, out in Santa Barbara, several members of the White House staff were having cocktails in Don Regan's bungalow in the Biltmore Hotel, a lush seaside enclave of Spanish stucco and red tile roofs where they all stayed when Reagan was at the ranch. Outside, hotel employees in white jackets crossed the beautifully manicured garden paths on bicycles, delivering room service, but inside the talk was less genteel. One aide's wife had called him from Washington about the *Parade* item, telling him it was all anyone in the capital was talking about and asking who it referred to. He didn't know, so at the gathering in Regan's bungalow he asked. According to several people present, the chief of staff snickered and said, "It's Bud and Andrea Mitchell!"

It was a nightmarish experience for McFarlane, and a few days after, he later said, he asked to have lunch with Regan. Over cheeseburgers in the little resort town of Montecito, just down the coast from Santa Barbara, the issue of the rumors came up. As McFarlane later recounted, "I told Don it was of concern to me, and I was sure to him, but that the *Parade* magazine piece was false." He said Regan replied with surprise, "It never occurred to me it was you. I thought it was someone else!" They agreed to bury the hatchet, but soon the issue came up again. Regan had returned to the capital and was attending an off-the-record editorial luncheon at *Newsweek*'s Washington bureau. He was thrown a light question about the gossip, and several of those present were surprised that rather than dismissing it in some anodyne way, Regan slyly told the group of national journalists, "I've tried to counsel Bud about it . . . but these things happen. You know how these things are."

Meanwhile, the president remained aloof at his ranch. In a reenactment of the process McFarlane had gone through in November 1984, by August 1985 Regan's staff had prepared a detailed set of options and legislative goals for the president's consideration, which they left for him to study on his vacation. Regan thought of it as a recipe for "an activist presidency." The plan focused on three central areas: economic recovery, foreign policy, and legislation. Regan thought that presenting the plan to the president would be the first phase of a process meant to define the next year's goals. "I expected that the president would read it, decide on his priorities, and call for more detailed suggestions" and eventually issue "marching orders," he later wrote.

But when the president returned to Washington to start the new legislative season after Labor Day, he handed the plan back to Regan without any comment. "What did you think of it?" asked his baffled chief of staff. The president said only, "It's good, really good, Don."

"I waited for him to say more," Regan later wrote. "He did not. He had no questions to ask, no objections to raise, no instructions to issue. I realized that the policy that would determine the course of the world's most powerful nation for the next two years . . . had been adopted without amendment."

McFarlane had other worries: the Iranian arms deal. After nearly two months of talk, the first shipment of U.S. arms to the ayatollah was finally ready to go through. On August 20, Israeli soldiers loaded sixteen wooden crates onto a chartered DC-8 at the military side of Ben Gurion Airport. Each box contained a cluster of six TOWs, made by Hughes Missile Systems in California; there were ninety-six missiles in all, and the agreement was that four hundred more would be forthcoming. Ghorbanifar clambered aboard, and the unmarked plane took off onto a secret flight path that began west over the Mediterranean, turned north to cross the friendly territory of Turkey, and then abruptly went east to skirt Syria and Iraq and enter the airspace of Khomeini's Iran. Within hours, the plane was on the ground at Mehrabad, the international airport on the western edge of Tehran.

Now it was the Iranians' turn to deliver. McFarlane had designated Oliver North to work out a plan to receive the freed hostages, and the State Department had issued North a passport in the name of William P. Goode. But the hostages did not come. Ghorbanifar had many excuses. He told the Israelis that his Tehran contacts wanted all five hundred missiles at once, and he wasn't shy about applying pressure. "Do you want the Iranians to send an arm and a leg of Buckley as an advance?" he threatened. He told the Americans that the radical Revolutionary Guard had seized the first ninety-six missiles. In any case, Ghorbanifar said, the hostages would be freed only if four hundred more missiles were shipped.

McFarlane was stuck. "We might as well go ahead and do the whole thing and see what comes of it," he said. Reagan agreed. On September 14, the DC-8 was again loaded, this time with 408 TOW missiles. The airplane took the same circuitous route as earlier but landed this time in the northwestern Iranian city of Tabriz, to make sure the missiles went to the army instead of the Revolutionary Guard.

But McFarlane was now suspicious of Ghorbanifar; he wanted more information about the arms merchant. Breaking his promise not to involve the CIA, he asked Casey over to the White House and briefed him on just enough of the operation to explain why North would be asking for intelligence about a certain arms dealer. McFarlane said the CIA reports should go to North, to himself, and to the military chiefs of staff at the Pentagon, but not to Weinberger or Shultz.

Casey went back to the CIA and called in his top aides. "I've just had a strange meeting in the White House," he said. "Bud McFarlane informs me that the Israelis have established a contact with Iranian interests, and these contacts could lead . . . to release of the hostages. But the Israelis have one demand: [that the] CIA not be informed." Casey seemed both intrigued and nettled. He fixed his men with a clear, blue-eyed stare. "I wonder what in hell this is all about," he mused.

Meanwhile, David Kimche telephoned McFarlane with more bad news. "It looks as though we've been deceived — the dealers can't deliver all the hostages," he said. "We can expect only one." It was up to McFarlane to choose, Kimche said. Which hostage did he want? Which of the seven would go free? McFarlane was speechless for a moment, then anguished. "I was being asked to play God," he said later.

The choice itself was easy: William Buckley, the CIA station chief who had been held the longest, reputedly tortured most cruelly, and for whom McFarlane felt a special responsibility, since the government had sent him to Beirut. But the act of choosing — of "playing God" — preyed on McFarlane's mind for months.

"I asked for Mr. Buckley," McFarlane said later. But Ghorbanifar relayed word that Buckley was "too ill" to be moved. Instead, on Sunday, September 15, word came from Beirut that a hostage had been released on the street outside the bombed-out hulk of the U.S. Embassy: the Reverend Benjamin Weir, a Presbyterian missionary who had been imprisoned for more than a year. Weir was taken by helicopter from Beirut to Cyprus, then flown to a naval hospital in Norfolk, Virginia. The White House delayed an announcement, hoping that more hostages would still be freed. But when no others emerged, finally, on September 18, Reagan himself announced Weir's release to a cheering crowd in Concord, New Hampshire.

White House spokesman Edward P. Djerejian, who was assigned to give details to the press, had carefully asked North, "Can I say there was no ransom, no blackmail?" North said he could, and Djerejian obediently took that line; Weir's release, he said, was brought about by the humanitarian intercession of foreigners like Terry Waite, the special negotiator sent to Beirut by the archbishop of Canterbury. "The United States government has made no deal," he said.

"Then why does it look like you're claiming credit for something?" demanded ABC's Sam Donaldson, a reporter with a sharp sense for obfuscation.

"We're not, Sam," Djerejian replied.

In fact, the White House was trying to have its news three ways at once. Reagan's announcement of Weir's release made the president the mouthpiece of good news. To the press, his aides could deny righteously that there had been any deal. But not only had there been a deal; in private, Reagan, Regan, and McFarlane knew they had been taken. They just didn't know how badly.

Three months earlier, terrorists in Beirut had seized David Jacobsen, an administrator at the American Hospital. They blindfolded him and put him in a room with a man who was ill. Jacobsen put the clues together and realized that his cellmate was William Buckley. "He was delirious. He was regurgitating. He obviously was running a very high fever," Jacobsen told a television interviewer after his own release in 1986. "The guards came to me because I was a hospital director and said, 'What can we do?'

"And I said, 'You better take him to see — get him to a hospital or get a doctor to him.'

"They said, 'We can't do that.'

"I could not see him. . . . We were not permitted at that time to see one another." Eventually, Jacobsen couldn't hear anything, either. "There was just a long, long silence. When you're in a small room — and there are certain noises that are associated with death. . . . I firmly believe that William died the evening of June third."

The outcome of McFarlane's secret negotiations could hardly have been worse. U.S. arms had been shipped to Ayatollah Khomeini's Iran as part of a tenuous arrangement to secure the release of seven American hostages. Iran got its much-needed weapons, but only one hostage was freed. Even then, it wasn't the hostage the administration was most eager to get back, for William Buckley had died three months earlier.

The first deal, in short, was the first swindle.

Benjamin Weir returned to Washington on September 20 with a chilling message: the remaining six U.S. hostages in Beirut would be killed if the United States didn't pressure Kuwait to release its Shia prisoners. But for the first time, Weir also brought firsthand confirmation that at least four of the six — the Reverend Lawrence Martin Jenco, Thomas Sutherland, David Jacobsen, and Terry Anderson — were very much alive. The families flocked to Washington to meet with Weir and demanded to see the president. But Reagan had spent the earlier part of the day at the Bethesda Naval Hospital, getting a postoperative checkup, and then had taken off the afternoon, as he usually did on Fridays. Instead, the families were presented with a surrogate, George Bush.

Newly aware that her brother was still alive and disappointed at not seeing Reagan himself, Peggy Say exploded at Bush for not showing more concern.

"How can you accuse me of not caring?" the vice president retorted hotly. "I'm a Christian man."

"You'll have to excuse me, Mr. Bush," she replied acidly, "but don't tell me you're a Christian, show me. When the TWA hostages were released, I was in a motel room watching the TV, waiting for my brother's face, and instead I got a call from some peon in your office telling me he wouldn't be released with the others. The Christian thing would have been to call yourself."

"Maybe we've made some mistakes —" allowed Bush.

"If you hadn't," interrupted Say, "you wouldn't be facing an angry mob."

Bush appeared stunned. Both Jenco sisters were crying, as was their habit. ("One of them," said a State Department official, "could cry on command. It was . . . just incredible." Peggy Say agreed: "Each of us had our roles — they were our criers.") The vice president, momentarily losing his composure, angrily pointed his index finger at Benjamin Weir and said in a high-pitched voice, "We are responsible for getting him out. I don't care what you think!" In his outburst, Bush came close to revealing the covert dealings the White House had taken pains to deny just two days earlier.

Finally, on October 28, four months after Reagan first met with the Jencos, the other relatives of the so-called Forgotten Seven got what they most wanted: an audience with the president. The meeting, like so many White House events, was thrown together quickly in reaction to outside pressures. The media had generated much heat on behalf of the hostage families, and it had been felt keenly in the Oval Office. "I remember the president saying, 'I'd like to meet with them — let's do it,' " recalled McFarlane. Regan went along with the plan, but by now he had learned a little about Reagan's vulnerabilities. Instead of allowing the president to become ensnared as he had in Chicago Heights, when he had been surrounded by a semicircle of family members, the chief of staff set up this event so that Reagan could not even sit down. The session would take place in the Roosevelt Room. Rather than providing a seat for Reagan, his aides carried in a podium. The president would have to remain at arm's length from the families.

"We staged it so that after expressing a few words, we were able to get him out," Regan later explained. "First of all, we didn't want it to be too emotional. Secondly, there wasn't much he could say, and for the president of the United States to face distraught families and say, 'I'm sorry, there's not a damn thing I can do for you' — the man just couldn't bring himself to say that type of thing, and who knows what sort of promises or things he might have said."

But the families had done some planning too. The meeting was supposed to be a brief, late afternoon photo session; they were to give the president an oversize yellow ribbon as a reminder of the hostages and then leave. But before entering the Roosevelt Room, they had plotted for several hours, hoping to turn the event into a serious exchange that would somehow draw the president deeper into their crusade. They chose a reasonable spokesman — Jacobsen's son Paul, a teacher — and drew up a list of tough questions. By the time the president entered the handsome room with its memorabilia of Theodore Roosevelt, the families were ready.

Peggy Say recalled that she saw "deep concern" when she looked into Reagan's eyes, and she and others remembered his saying with evident sincerity, "Not a day goes by that the hostages aren't the first question on my lips." But when it came down to details, except for reiterating that it would be wrong to strike a deal for the Kuwaiti prisoners, Reagan passed most of the questions on to McFarlane. "Reagan seemed very uncomfortable," said Jenco's sister Sue Franceschini. "It was as if he had really mixed emotions. He seemed like he cared about the hostages, and he said he was doing everything possible, but he didn't seem on top of the details. It wasn't like he was trying to be evasive, it was more like he just wasn't that up on things. He seemed to want to get out of there, to leave as soon as possible."

And despite the families' long list of questions, within twenty minutes — as Regan had planned — the president did leave. He apologized to the group, explaining that he had to go because "Nancy is waiting for me in the parking lot." But as he left, Reagan surprised some of the relatives by taking with him the yellow ribbon that they had brought as a prop for the photo opportunity. "The ribbon was just a little bit of harassment," said Peggy Say, "but he seemed to take it quite seriously." Later, at the president's insistence and over the objections of his aides, it was tied in a large bow above the polished brass handles on the main entrance to the West Wing.

After the president left, McFarlane took over and, to the astonishment of the families and the few officials present, spoke for an hour and a half. It grew dark outside, but he kept on talking about the complexities of Middle Eastern politics and the perils of dealing with terrorists, all in his inimitable monotone. Peggy Say recalled being touched because "he wasn't talking down." But Sue Franceschini got completely lost in his elliptical syntax. "He just talked in circles," she said. "He didn't seem to say anything. It was a monotone. We couldn't even figure out enough sense to know what to ask questions about."

Robert Oakley, the director of the State Department's counterterrorism office, hoped fervently that it would stay that way. He could scarcely believe what he was hearing. Amid the jumble of phrases and theories, McFarlane told the families that the government was pursuing contacts with "Iranians who were close to the ayatollah, but who wanted to move the country in a more moderate direction." Not only had Oakley not known this, but he was convinced that there were no "moderates" in Khomeini's regime.

Amazed at what he'd heard, Oakley went back to the State Department shaking his head. "Well, now all the families have been briefed," he told an aide. "Let's hope they didn't understand."

For the moment at least, thanks to the miracle of McFarlane's impenetrable delivery, Oakley's wish seemed answered. The families went out into the chilly autumn night still unaware that some two months earlier, in the emotionally charged days after the TWA hijacking, Reagan had already bent under their pressure and begun a desperate gambit to buy back their loved ones.

7

Project Democracy

THE INSPIRATION STRUCK, Oliver North said later, on the morning of October 10, 1985, as he dashed across the private drive from the Crisis Management Center to McFarlane's office in the White House: *We can do a Yamamoto.* Over the Reagan administration's protests, Egypt was about to release four terrorists who had hijacked a Mediterranean cruise ship, the *Achille Lauro*, and murdered an American passenger. U.S. intelligence agencies had learned that the terrorists were about to board a plane for Tunisia.

At that moment, North said, he suddenly remembered a piece of World War II lore: when U.S. radiomen overheard the flight plans of Japan's Admiral Isoroku Yamamoto, Navy fighters ambushed the enemy sea lord over the South Pacific and shot him down. North glanced at his watch: 8:30 A.M. There was still time to try. Inside the White House, North breathlessly outlined the idea to McFarlane and his deputy, John Poindexter: U.S. jet fighters could force the hijackers to land in Europe, where they could be arrested and tried. McFarlane, who was on his way out the door to join the president for a trip to Illinois, told his aides to work up a plan.

En route to Chicago on *Air Force One*, Reagan pointed angrily at an editorial in that morning's *Washington Times*: "Fish or Cut Bait, Mr. President!" The conservative newspaper complained that Reagan had failed to keep his promise to strike back at terrorists. Sooner or later, it said, "his constituents will want to know why they sent him back for a second term." Reagan was always nettled by criticism from the right. We can't just strike out blindly and kill innocent bystanders, he told McFarlane. We've got to wait for a clean shot.

Reagan arrived at the giant Sara Lee bakery plant in Deerfield, Illinois, for his scheduled speech on tax reform shortly after noon. As bakers and salesmen and inventory clerks waited in the auditorium, the president stopped in a conference room. McFarlane briskly outlined the plan Poindexter and North had developed for intercepting the hijackers, noting its chances for success (unknown) and its potential dangers (few). According to several aides, Reagan asked no substantive questions — and did not hesitate. "Permission granted," he said.

It was evening over the Mediterranean. The aircraft carrier *Saratoga* sent its F-14 Tomcat fighters aloft with an E-2C Hawkeye command and control plane. The squadron found the terrorists' jet off Crete and boxed it in — one fighter in front, one off each wing, a fourth behind the tail. The navy commander's voice burst onto the startled Egyptian pilot's radio: "Egyptair 2483. Be advised you're being escorted by two F-14s. You are to land immediately at Sigonella." Less than an hour later, the terrorists were on the ground and under arrest at a NATO air base on Sicily. It was the first successful "clean shot" in Reagan's otherwise frustrating war against terrorism.

At nine-thirty the next morning, as McFarlane and Poindexter walked into the Oval Office for the daily national security briefing, the president sprang to his feet and snapped off a crisp, movie-style salute. "I salute the admiral!" he said, grinning. Congress, the newscasts, the editorial pages, had nothing but praise for Reagan, his decisiveness, and his rebuilt military machine. Some quoted Weinberger's extravagant tribute: "He has better judgment than all the rest of us put together." Even Democrats joined in. "He's never had a finer hour," New York's governor Mario Cuomo said.

But Don Regan seemed a little nettled by the McFarlane-Poindexter triumph. At *his* morning staff meeting, he gruffly called on Poindexter for a two-minute report on the capture of the hijackers, then moved on, without comment, to economic news. Eyebrows of surprise lifted around the table, but chief economic adviser Beryl Sprinkel obediently swung into his recital: Retail sales up 2.7 percent, auto sales up 9.6 percent. "It was a horrible letdown," one aide recalled. "There was no sense of euphoria."

At the end of the meeting, press secretary Speakes suggested that the president try an impromptu news conference to extract one more public opinion boost from the *Achille Lauro* adventure. Regan, who usually reveled in such exercises, replied, "We don't need an additional boost." But the president wanted one anyway, and he bounded to the briefing room podium that afternoon to offer "a message to terrorists everywhere": "You can run, but you can't hide."

The episode sent an equally powerful message to the rest of the White House and the foreign policy bureaucracy: McFarlane's NSC staff knew how to run covert operations. Credit went to North and Poindexter as well as to Israel, whose intelligence service located the hijackers at a crucial moment when U.S. electronic trackers had lost them. North boasted openly of his authorship of the idea and even made sure that the vivid story of his Yamamoto inspiration was leaked to the press. In fact, other officials said, the idea came from a lower-ranking navy officer on the staff; North merely appropriated it.

But North's self-inflating version impressed Reagan himself, and so, with purloined glory, a new hero was made. By October 1985, North's little office on the third floor of the Old Executive Office Building was an increasingly important nerve center for covert operations on three continents. Some days the crisis was in Central America, other days Lebanon or Iran, still others at home on Capitol Hill. The entire world, it seemed, had descended onto the shoulders of Oliver North. On paper, he was still an anonymous deputy director for political-military affairs, but in fact he was now working directly for Casey, McFarlane, and Poindexter. Poindexter even gave him a password to slip his computer messages past the NSC hierarchy directly to the admiral's desk. The password, appropriately enough, was "Private Blank Check."

Most of North's work still centered on Nicaragua, where he had run the contras' secret supply operation for more than a year. There was still no sign that Congress would turn around and give the rebels military aid. In the interim, the contras needed not only constant infusions of money, they needed help in spending it — in buying the right mix of weapons, organizing a system to deliver supplies to the troops, and simply running their little war on a day-to-day basis.

The job was too big for one man, even a man with the frenetic energy of Oliver North. Casey and North gradually recognized that they needed a field marshal for the rebels, someone outside the government who could run a supply system for the contras the way the CIA had before Congress threw the agency off the battlefield.

It was a critically important job; whoever ran the supply lines would hold the contras' fate in his hands. It had to be someone trusted, someone committed to the cause, someone who knew secret operations — and someone who was at least officially outside the U.S. government. Casey and North knew exactly whom they wanted: Richard V. Secord.

"He's a man who has experience," Casey said. "He's a man who gets things done. And he's been poorly treated."

In the secret fraternity of unconventional warfare, Dick Secord was universally recognized as a master of covert air operations inside enemy territory, from Vietnam in 1962 to the never-attempted second Iranian rescue mission of 1980. His peers acknowledged him as an expert in the art of clandestine war — if a little frightening in his cool intensity. "A man of ice," one of the contras called him. "Cold blue steel," said Noel Koch, who worked with him at the Pentagon.

Secord was not just a man of action, but also a man with ideas. Once mentioned as a potential air force chief of staff, he sat on the Defense Department's advisory group on special operations. He wrote his master's thesis at the Naval War College on covert operations as an instrument of foreign policy, and his conclusion was blunt: "The unconventional warfare instrument of national policy is so important that bureaucratic obstacles should be dismissed out of hand." The CIA should be given free rein, Secord argued, subject only to direction from a single higher authority — "probably the National Security Council."

Those conclusions came from twenty-eight years of combat in both the guerrilla battlegrounds of the Third World and the corridors of Washington. Secord flew combat missions in Vietnam, ran air operations in the CIA's secret war in Laos, and headed the air force group in Iran which built the shah's air force. By 1981, he was a major general and a deputy assistant secretary of defense, an unusually high policy post for a uniformed officer. But then Edwin P. Wilson's secret arms-dealing network fell apart, and Secord's brilliant career disintegrated along with it.

Wilson, a CIA officer turned arms broker, latched onto Secord through a mutual friend, another veteran of the covert wars named Thomas G. Clines. With a keen eye toward future business, Wilson entertained Clines and Secord in the Virginia hunt country, lent them a private plane, even bought a town house from Secord when the general was in a financial squeeze. But then Wilson was convicted of conspiring to sell plastic explosives — the type used for terrorist bombings — to Libya's Muammar Qadhafi. As part of the case, the FBI investigated an allegation that Secord had profited from the Libyan deal, but the general was never charged with a crime.

Then a second scandal erupted around Wilson: a company he had formed to ship U.S. military aid to Egypt was convicted of overcharging the Pentagon by $8 million. One of the partners in the company was Tom Clines, and Wilson claimed that Secord, too, had been a "silent partner."

Secord denied the charge, but the allegations cut short his career. He retired in May 1983 with a major general's pension (and a $240-a-day consulting deal at the Pentagon) and joined a small military equipment trading firm run by an Iranian he had met in part through the ubiquitous Wilson. The company was called Stanford Technology Trading Group; the Iranian-American owner, who brought Secord in as a fifty-fifty partner, was named Albert Hakim.

Hakim, whose outward manner was as courtly as Secord's was blunt, had already made a fortune in the cutthroat, bribe-ridden world of Iranian government contracts. He had represented several major American firms at the court of the shah, companies like Motorola, Hewlett-Packard, and Winchester Arms, and also worked closely with the CIA. In 1976, one of his better years, an associate estimated that Hakim grossed $15 million in commissions. He freely acknowledged paying money to Iranian officials to win government contracts. "I was wheeling, I was dealing," he testified in a 1983 federal court proceeding. Still, he added with dignity, "we have more class than using the word *payoff*."

Hakim left Iran well ahead of Khomeini's 1979 revolution, settled on a ridge in California overlooking Silicon Valley, and built a business selling security equipment to Third World governments. His first prospects included South Korea, Saudi Arabia — and the United States Congress, which needed a new security system for the Capitol's secret hearing rooms. Hakim's employees and consultants over the years were often drawn from the small, closed world of clandestine operations — former CIA officers like Edwin Wilson, Tom Clines, and Theodore Shackley.

So when William Casey sent Oliver North to ask Secord for help with the contras, he was also sending him into the middle of an existing fraternity of retired covert operations specialists. Secord was the manager, Hakim the financier, Clines the arms buyer. For help on the Central American side, Secord would recruit Rafael "Chi Chi" Quintero, a Bay of Pigs veteran who had worked for both Clines and Wilson. Clines and Quintero, in turn, would recruit Luis Posada, a folk hero among anti-Castro extremists for allegedly blowing up a Cuban airliner over the Caribbean, killing seventy-three innocent passengers.

Following Casey's advice, North first enlisted Secord in the summer of 1984 for a simple mission: to buy guns for the contras. With Saudi Arabia's donated money, the general bought $9.7 million worth of armaments in 1984 and 1985 — SA-7 antiaircraft missiles from the People's Republic of China, ammunition from Communist Romania, and plastic explosives from Portugal, a NATO ally. (Secord rarely let politics interfere with profits; one of his middlemen turned out to be a Syrian who also supplied guns to Palestinian terrorist chieftain Abul Abbas — the leader of the *Achille Lauro* hijackers.) Secord enlisted Clines to scout the arms warehouses of Europe and chartered cargo planes from Southern Air Transport, a freight carrier founded by the CIA that, while officially independent, had never lost its agency credentials.

As time went on, Secord received discreet — and apparently illegal — help from the U.S. Army as well, according to several witnesses. On June 2, 1985, a small Danish freighter called the *Erria* landed at the steamy Honduran Caribbean port of Puerto Barrios with a cargo of AK-47 rifles from Poland and plastic explosives from Portugal, bought for the contras by Secord and Clines. Shouting Honduran troops cleared civilians from the dock. A crewman from the *Erria* said he was startled to see a group of tall, fair-skinned men in U.S. Army uniforms, with armbands reading MP, suddenly arrive to supervise the unloading. "They seemed to be in a big rush," he recalled. The army denied it had anything to do with Secord's guns; but a Honduran official who examined the port records said it appeared that the U.S. government reserved the dock for a military shipment.

That spring of 1985, North wrote a three-page report to McFarlane, marked TOP SECRET, crowing about the supply operation's success. "Since [U.S.] funding expired in May 1984 . . . $17,145,594 has been expended for arms, ammunition, combat operations, and support activities," he boasted. "The resistance has grown from 9,500 personnel in June 1984 to over 16,000 today . . . and has become an effective guerrilla army in less than a year." North asked McFarlane to relay the good news to President Reagan. McFarlane put a big check mark in the space marked Approve and briefed Reagan on what he later called "the general conclusion" of how the contras were doing.

North's optimistic picture of the contras' prospects did not mention that the rebels had failed to mount a single effective military operation against the Sandinistas, a record that worried more sober strategists. Even the contras' military commander, Enrique Bermúdez, was less sanguine. "We have grown," he said, "but we haven't improved." "The training of the contras was, when I last saw them in 1985, abysmal," testified General Paul F. Gorman, then commander of U.S. forces in Latin America. "I didn't regard them as a very effective military organization based on what I could see in reflections of battles, in communications on both sides. The Sandinistas could wipe them out." North attempted to prevent Gorman from communicating his assessment to the Joint Chiefs of Staff and members of Congress. "He was doing his damnedest to get me to shut up — 'Old general, put a cork in it,' " Gorman said later.

North also didn't mention that the resupply effort had taken seven long months to get under way. Secord's first shipload of antiaircraft missiles, which the contras needed desperately, took so long to arrive that rebel leader Calero called it "the slow boat from China." Nor did North mention that Secord and his partners had collected a commission of some 29 percent on the cost of the weapons they shipped. Secord, as it happened, was not the lowest bidder for the contras' business; that distinction went to North's other retired general, Jack Singlaub, who was also soliciting contributions for the contras from South Korea and Taiwan.

In March 1985, Singlaub heard the contras' complaints about the long wait for antiaircraft missiles and volunteered to set up a new arms deal through a former Miami radio hostess and beauty queen named Barbara Studley. Calero, who had grown uneasy with Secord's control over his arms procurement, agreed, and later that spring met with Singlaub at Washington's elegant Sheraton-Carlton Hotel. When Singlaub showed Calero a price list, the Nicaraguan was dumbfounded. Singlaub's prices were markedly lower than what he had been paying Secord: $135 for an AK-47 rifle instead of $260; $165,000 for an SA-7 missile instead of $180,000. "At least in the case of the AK-47s, that price was about half of what we had previously had to pay," Calero said later. "We were getting twice as many weapons for the same amount of money." The reason was simple: unlike Secord, Singlaub was working on a nonprofit basis.

But North's orders from Casey were to give the business to Secord. In this operation, maintaining control was more important than competitive pricing. North also worried that Singlaub was too outspoken. "Ollie's biggest concern was that General Singlaub could never tell a lie, and he talked too much," Rob Owen said. Even so, Calero insisted on making one deal with Singlaub to take advantage of his low prices, and he bought ten thousand bargain-basement Polish AK-47s. Singlaub approached Casey twice to tell the CIA chief that his deal for the contras had been both successful and cheap. But the earnest, too-honest general never heard back.

Buying weapons was only half the battle, though. Once the guns arrived in Honduras, they had to be trucked to the rebels' camps along the country's southern border, a tangle of steep green ridges and narrow gorges. Some of the camps could be reached on spectacularly bad roads, bone-jarring tracks of dirt and mud that snaked up ridges and across creek beds. But others were beyond the reach of any road. Even worse was the problem of getting supplies into Nicaragua, where the rebels were supposed to be fighting. Their primitive little air force couldn't do the job; it consisted of seven aging, ill-maintained cargo planes flown by pilots who sometimes refused to take the risk of crossing into Nicaraguan airspace. So the rebels fell back to an older form of transport: the mule train. But with some units a three- or four-week march away, supply missions were long and chancy. More than one mule driver ran out of food and resorted to eating the transport.

The contras could have spent some of King Fahd's $32 million to equip an air delivery fleet. North, in fact, had urged them to put aside $10 million for logistics. But the rebel leaders had never run a war before; in their experience, the CIA had always taken care of such mundane details. They foolishly spent the money on guns and ammunition instead — and ended up with stacks of weaponry in their warehouses, but no way to move it to the troops in the field.

Finally, there was persistent talk of corruption within the contras' ranks. Saudi Arabia's millions had gone straight into the hands of Calero, a former manager of Coca-Cola of Nicaragua who had schemed his way to the top of the rebel leadership. Calero ran the rebels' cash fund from his hip pocket, handling millions of dollars with little accountability. His garrulous brother, Mario, ran the rebels' procurement operation from a warehouse near New Orleans International Airport, and some of the troops complained that he was buying second-rate boots at first-rate prices. And there were persistent rumors of links between the contra leaders and South American cocaine traffickers.

There was no proof of corruption, but North worried about the appearance; it just didn't look good to have Calero in total control. He decided to confront the problem, and on the evening of June 28, 1985, just after the release of the TWA hostages had been arranged, he flew to Miami on an air force executive jet. It was almost ten o'clock when he walked into the airport hotel. There, awaiting him, were Secord, Calero, and several others.

North shook hands all around, took a chair, and made an announcement: Gentlemen, he said, we've got a problem.

"He had been receiving reports that the limited funds they had might be getting wasted, squandered, or, even worse, some people might be lining their pockets," Secord recalled later. "If anything like this was going on . . . the image of the resistance could be badly damaged. It could ruin us, in fact. He was very, very hard on this point. It surprised me a little bit."

"It was a showdown," said Rob Owen, who talked with North soon after the meeting. "Ollie had finally realized that it was crazy to put all that money in Calero's hands with no real control."

Calero, the supposed leader of the cause, stalked out of the meeting after several hours, but North and Secord talked until dawn. North said that the Nicaraguans just didn't have the know-how to run their own rebellion, and he asked Secord to take over the contras' supply system. As part of the change, he added, Secord — not Calero — would administer the money as well.

We need you, North said fervently. The president needs you.

"I'll think about it," Secord replied.

As North flew back to Washington to start another workday without sleep, Secord's partners advised him to turn down the offer. The profits were in making arms deals with a 29 percent commission, Clines and Quintero pointed out; trying to "manage" the contras was a losing proposition, a major headache without a major payoff. But running operations was what Secord knew and loved. It was the career he had wanted, the career that he felt had been stolen from him. Now, after he had spent two years in the wilderness, the president of the United States and the director of central intelligence were turning to him for help. If he could make this project work, he would be untouchable no longer.

Secord called North and told him his answer was yes. Then he called

Albert Hakim and told him to open a new dummy account in Geneva. The company was already "on the shelf," a disembodied name in a lawyer's files: Lake Resources. On July 19, Secord's Swiss financial agent opened an account for Lake Resources — number 386430-221 — at the Eaux Vives branch of Geneva's Crédit Suisse bank.

The opening of the account marked the birth of a secret conglomerate that Secord, the icy operations man, would simply call "the Enterprise." North, with his more dramatic bent, gave the undertaking a far more appealing name: Project Democracy.

Casey and McFarlane had instructed North that secrecy was a key to success in all covert operations — in counterterrorism, in negotiations with Iran, in organizing Project Democracy. But by the middle of 1985, reporters in Washington and Central America were already onto the scent of the NSC's secret contra aid operation. Beginning with a virtually unnoticed article in the *Miami Herald*, several newspapers identified North as the administration's point man for private aid to the contras. Not until the *New York Times* revealed that North was giving the rebels "direct military advice," however, did Congress pay any attention to the reports that the White House was flouting the Boland amendment.

The *Times* article, printed right in the middle of the front page on August 8, was impossible to ignore. It did not identify North by name, but it threw a severe scare into the men of Project Democracy. An agitated McFarlane, then in the midst of putting together the first Israeli arms shipment to Iran, assured the White House and NSC staffs at their morning meetings that he had asked North about the article, "and there's no truth in it." (McFarlane had, by then, received dozens of memos from North outlining his secret contra program.)

President Reagan dismissed reporters' questions with a single sentence: "We're not violating any laws." But Lee H. Hamilton of Indiana, chairman of the House Intelligence Committee, and Michael D. Barnes of Maryland, chairman of a subcommittee on Latin America, wrote to McFarlane, demanding an explanation of his staff's activities. "Congressional intent in passing the Boland amendment was to distance the United States from the Nicaraguan rebel movement while the Congress and the nation debated . . . our involvement in Nicaragua," Barnes wrote. "The press reports suggest that, despite congressional intent, during this period the United States provided direct support to the Nicaraguan rebels."

McFarlane, Poindexter, and North launched a frantic cover-up to protect their operation. "My objective all along was [to] withhold information," Poindexter acknowledged later in his testimony before Congress. An aide searched NSC files for any documents, pulled out hundreds of memos, and found six that would cause an uproar if Congress saw them. Three described efforts to nail down aid for the contras from China, South Korea, Taiwan, and Guatemala; three more described U.S. military advice to the rebels, including North's proposal to "pirate" the Nicaraguan ammunition ship, the *Monimbo*.

North suggested that he rewrite the six documents, months after they were dated, to make them appear to comply with the law. McFarlane agreed. Then McFarlane sat down and drafted a dignified reply to the congressmen. "I can state with deep personal conviction that at no time did I or any member of the NSC staff violate the letter or spirit of the law," he wrote. "We did not solicit funds or other support for military or paramilitary activities either from Americans or third parties. We did not offer tactical advice for the conduct of their military activities or their organization. . . . There has not been, nor will there be, any such activities by the NSC staff." All four denials were untrue.

On one letter, he added a plaintive postscript: because of the newspaper articles about North, someone had poisoned the North family's dog. Administration spokesmen solemnly told reporters that this was what happened when a man's name was used carelessly in print. It turned out, however, that the poisoned dog was merely an Ollie North flourish. "The dog died of cancer," a friend said.

McFarlane repeated his denials in face-to-face meetings with the House and Senate intelligence committees. The legislators questioned him closely, but his standing on Capitol Hill was still high. "I, for one, am willing to take you at your word," Chairman Hamilton said after the House Intelligence Committee session.

Barnes, who relished confrontation more than the conciliatory Hamilton, pressed a little further with his request for memos North had written on Central America. This time, McFarlane resorted to an old lawyer's trick: he piled all the North documents, hundreds of them, on his desk. Then he invited Barnes in for a meeting. "There they are," he told the congressman. "You're welcome to read them. But I'm afraid I can't let them leave my office."

Barnes looked at the foot-high stack of papers and shook his head.

"I'll have my staff go through them," he said.

"I'm afraid we can't do that," McFarlane replied. "Some of these documents include highly sensitive, highly classified information."

"We have procedures for dealing with highly classified information," Barnes countered.

"I'm sorry," McFarlane said. "We can't do it."

"I can't accept this," Barnes said stiffly.

McFarlane shrugged as impassively as he could.

"You'll hear from us," Barnes said. Then he turned and walked out of the room.

Barnes returned to his office on Capitol Hill and told his aides how nervous McFarlane had seemed. "I've just met a man who's afraid he's going to go to jail," the congressman said.

But McFarlane heard only once more from Barnes, in a letter proposing that the documents be turned over to the House Intelligence Committee. McFarlane simply ignored the request, and Barnes never pressed it.

No other member of Congress took up the fight. The public, seemingly exhausted with the debate over Nicaragua, wasn't interested. "The news that there is a *comandante* in the White House, a staff member who expedites the contra war against the Nicaraguan government, has caused not a ripple in the pond of public opinion," columnist Mary McGrory of the *Washington Post* complained. "As a source of opposition, the Democratic House has flopped." All but a few reporters turned to other, more alluring issues. The White House press corps never really pursued the matter, never asked the president if he knew where the contras were getting their money. The White House chief of staff and the White House counsel asked no tough questions.

In a matter of weeks, the issue faded. Oliver North and his new Project Democracy had dodged a bullet.

As North later explained it, Casey saw the beauty of a private covert action organization like Project Democracy in its magical ability to evade the laws of Congress while drawing secretly on all the resources of the U.S. government. Despite its name, Project Democracy would answer to no elected official; it was accountable to no one but its creators. Formally, all its organs were merely private businesses. "It was . . . almost drawn up by Director Casey how these would be outside the U.S. government," North testified later. "The two criteria that Director Casey and I talked about [were] that these had to be stand-alone, offshore commercial ventures — [and] that they ought to be, ultimately, revenue producers; that they would generate their own revenue and be self-sustaining." But the project also relied heavily on CIA intelligence, State Department aid, Pentagon logistics, and White House fund-raising to carry out its mission of running the contra war.

That meant getting help from the bureaucracy. By October 1985, a new triumvirate was running U.S. policy on Nicaragua: the Restricted Interagency Group, or RIG. Officially, the RIG had from twelve to fifteen members, but the real work was done by only three: North, the NSC coordinator for Project Democracy; Elliott Abrams of the State Department, a combative former Democrat who led the administration's ideological charge on Nicaragua; and Alan D. Fiers, chief of the CIA's Central America Task Force.

The RIG met most Wednesdays in Abrams's comfortable sixth-floor office in the State Department building. "The meetings themselves were bland," said an NSC official who sometimes attended. "Ollie would always come in late, theatrically, with his military greatcoat. But it was basically an informational meeting. Those three guys — Ollie, Elliott, and Alan — were the only ones who took action. No one else was expected to do anything. After the meeting, you'd see Elliott talking with Fiers or with Ollie; that was where the action was."

Secretary of State Shultz had asked Abrams to keep an eye on North; the old bureaucratic warrior had sensed that the young lieutenant colonel was someone who needed to be watched carefully. Abrams dutifully scrawled a reminder in his notebook: "Monitor Ollie." But Abrams, a Harvard-trained attorney who served Shultz assiduously in all other respects, later admitted that he purposely neglected this duty: "I was careful not to ask Colonel North what questions I thought I did not need to know the answers to."

Instead, Abrams walked a lawyer's thin line. He publicly praised private help to the contras, and he told his ambassadors to press other governments to help the contras too. When, later, he was accused of approving private and foreign aid to the rebels with a wink and a nod, he responded characteristically, "A wink and a nod, hell. We think it's been fine." But he insisted that he knew nothing of what North had been up to, and he even denied the existence of the three-man RIG (or "RIG-let," as one of his aides dubbed it).

Nevertheless, several of Abrams's ambassadors in Central America said the RIG gave them clear instructions to help the contras and their "private benefactors" in any way they could. The ambassador to Costa Rica, a quirky conservative historian named Lewis Tambs, joined in enthusiastically. "When you take the king's shilling, you do the king's bidding," he explained. The ambassador to El Salvador, career diplomat Edwin Corr, also cooperated, though a bit more discreetly. But the ambassador to Honduras, John Ferch, resisted. Congress had not made its will clear on the contra issue, Ferch believed, and he had serious doubts about the war himself. In late 1985, Abrams summoned him before a session of the RIG.

"There's a perception in town that you don't support the contras," Abrams said, with North and Fiers at his flanks. "We've got to have somebody on the ground take responsibility for the contras. That's part of your job."

Ferch yielded to the pressure from his boss. "Okay," he said. But his doubts persisted, and a week or so later he sent Abrams a secret cable: he was willing to carry out the RIG's wishes, he said, but only if his instructions were put in writing. No such instructions ever came; instead, a few months later Ferch lost his job.

"It was part of the duties of all of our ambassadors to Central America to support the resistance," Abrams later explained. "And Congress had just approved $27 million for us to distribute to support a fighting force. So it was the duty of every ambassador to support U.S. policy, to try to get the government of the country to which he was assigned . . . to support that policy."

Abrams also gave North considerable influence over the way the State Department ran the $27 million fund of nonlethal aid that Congress approved in 1985. When North sent his acolyte Rob Owen to apply for a contract with the new Nicaraguan Humanitarian Assistance Office, Abrams endorsed the bid despite the resistance of NHAO's director. NHAO gave North's courier a $4,350-a-month contract, but noted in a cautious (and apparently knowing) proviso: "Mr. Robert Owen shall not during the term of this grant perform any service which is related to the acquisition, transportation, repair, storage, or use of weapons."

The third member of the RIG, the CIA's Alan Fiers, had a newly strengthened position thanks to a secret agreement reached with Congress's intelligence committees, allowing the CIA back into the contra war. The CIA was still prohibited from funding or directing the war, but under the new agreement it could give the contras communications equipment and intelligence. After months with his nose pressed against the window, Fiers finally had some operations to run. Equally important, Congress allowed the agency to begin funding selected contra leaders with millions of dollars of clandestine political aid, funneling roughly $200,000 per month into the rebels' political operations. The amount was small, and Casey portrayed it as intended to help the contras become more democratic. But, in fact, the money was vitally important to Calero and his rivals for political leadership within the rebel movement, so it gave the CIA leverage over all their decisions. Within months, the contra chieftains would complain, in the words of one, that "the agency people . . . are trying to run things again, instead of letting us run them."

The U.S. bureaucracy helped Project Democracy on the ground, too. North's secret warriors installed themselves in each of the countries surrounding the Nicaraguan battlefield — Honduras and El Salvador to the north, Costa Rica to the south — and the U.S. government lent a hand in all three.

In Honduras, the contras were already well established. They had a comfortable political base in the capital of Tegucigalpa and a growing military base near the misnamed hamlet of Las Vegas on the border of Nicaragua. And they had a packed-dirt air base — built by the U.S. Army Corps of Engineers as a "training exercise" — halfway between, at Aguacate. North secretly recruited several former marines to help the contras with training, and the CIA sent its own men to help with intelligence and communications.

The main problem was the Honduran government, which, depending on its mood, alternately helped the contras and impeded them. When the first plane of U.S. "humanitarian aid" for the rebels arrived in Tegucigalpa in October, Honduran officials were astonished to see it unload, not only crates of combat boots, but an NBC television crew as well — Mario Calero had imprudently invited the newsmen on his inaugural flight. The Hondurans, who insisted on maintaining a façade of secrecy around the effort, impounded the cargo and refused to allow any more shipments for months.

Then the Hondurans added another glitch: they told the State Department that none of its diplomats could observe the final delivery of the nonmilitary aid, ostensibly because that too would acknowledge the contras' presence. Fiers quickly volunteered his CIA men for the inspection, and the Hondurans agreed with suspicious alacrity. The State Department could pay for the aid, but the Hondurans, the contras, and the CIA ended up with day-to-day control over how it was used.

In part because of the Hondurans' unpredictability, North and Secord decided to base their new airdrop operation in neighboring El Salvador. Their key contact there was another of Quintero's old Bay of Pigs comrades, a Cuban American named Felix Rodriguez. A legendary figure in Latin American covert operations, Rodriguez had fought for the CIA in a dozen secret wars, helped hunt down Cuban revolutionary Che Guevara, and joined the Salvadoran air force as a volunteer adviser at the age of forty-three. He was also a friend of Vice President Bush, whom he credited with saving his pension when Bush was director of the CIA. In September 1985, North asked Rodriguez to help Secord set up Project Democracy's air base in El Salvador. Rodriguez, who was acting as a personal adviser to the Salvadoran air force chief of staff, agreed with enthusiasm. Now Project Democracy had an airfield of its own.

Secord also needed an airstrip to use in moving guns to the contras' planned Southern Front. Costa Rica, to the south, was the obvious choice, and North turned for help to Ambassador Tambs and the CIA's station chief, Joe Fernandez. In August, at about the same time President Reagan was recuperating from his cancer operation at his ranch, Fernandez took North's courier Rob Owen up to Costa Rica's northwestern corner to scout an airstrip site. Owen described the plan to North in a memo addressed to him as BG — for "Blood and Guts." "The cover for the operation is a company owned by a few 'crazy' gringos wanting to lease the land for agricultural experimentation and for running cattle," Owen reported. "Cattle will be purchased, as will some farming equipment, and some land plowed. . . . The colonel [a Costa Rican officer] will provide a cook, the *peones* to work the farm, and security."

Back in Washington, Secord recruited another air force special operations veteran, Richard Gadd, to buy cargo planes and hire crews. Gadd owned a number of small companies that did secret air charter work for the Pentagon; now he put them at Project Democracy's disposal. He drew up plans for a fleet of planes and arranged for Southern Air Transport to maintain them in Miami.

Until the fleet was assembled, Gadd offered the services of his own charter freight company, Airmach. It owned no planes and had no known track record. But after North took up his case, Gadd quickly won a contract from the State Department to deliver nonlethal aid to the contras. Eventually, Project Democracy "piggybacked" its weapons flights onto the State Department's "humanitarian" missions; State conveniently paid for the long flights from the United States to Central America, and Project Democracy paid for the short flights within the isthmus.

By October, North was a very busy man. Between masterminding the capture of the *Achille Lauro* hijackers and helping McFarlane arrange another arms deal with Iran, North met with Secord, Hakim, and Gadd to review the progress of Project Democracy. At last the pieces were falling into place, he said. There were airplanes now, and airstrips, and the nucleus of a crew to run the resupply operation. "The president may not be able to tell you this himself for a while," North told his team of covert managers. "But he's grateful for what you're doing."

The contras were not winning their war yet; but from a business standpoint, Project Democracy was already a success. By the end of 1985, Secord's companies had received $9.4 million of King Fahd's money from Calero for weapons and kept $2.7 million, or 29 percent, as profit. And money was still coming in. North had never given up the idea of canvassing other foreign governments for contra aid; the United States had plenty of small allies who might be interested in buying good will by donating to the contra cause. In the summer, North and the NSC's Asia expert had made another pitch to Taiwan; over tea at the Hay-Adams Hotel, North told Taiwan's representative in Washington that Reagan himself "would be very grateful" if his government gave. Within a few days, Owen carried a three-by-five card with Lake Resources' Swiss bank account number up to Taiwan's mission, and $2 million soon appeared in the Geneva account.

In fact, Project Democracy was awash in money — so much that North got careless with it. He still had some of Calero's traveler's checks in his office safe, and as his life grew more hectic he mixed his accounts, using his own money for secret operations and paying himself back from the contra treasury. Some traveler's checks went for groceries, some for dry cleaning, and some — King Fahd's money, originally — bought leotards for North's daughters Sarah and Dornin. One Friday that fall, Fawn Hall worked late and had no cash for a weekend at the beach; no problem, said North, and he handed her $60 in traveler's checks from the exotic Banco del Pichincha. And on October 29, North drove down to Owen's wedding in Virginia. At the reception, he embraced his young aide and handed him an envelope containing $1,000 in Calero's traveler's checks.

"I don't feel comfortable taking this," Owen said.

"No," North said grandly. "We want you to have it."

Still, North wanted more. The $32 million from Saudi Arabia had been a godsend, but Calero had already spent most of it on weapons. North's plans for the air cargo fleet, the new Southern Front, even a force of British mercenaries to mount sabotage raids deep inside Nicaragua were all expensive projects. And North wanted to give more money to Calero's moderate rivals within the contra movement, Alfonso Robelo and Arturo Cruz; he had already slipped them some of Calero's Saudi cash, but it was an arrangement none of the feuding Nicaraguans liked.

One answer, North had discovered, was right at home: wealthy conservatives in the United States. They had given millions to Reagan's campaigns and millions more to right-wing outfits like the National Conservative Political Action Committee (NCPAC). It was only logical that some would want to give money to Ronald Reagan's favorite cause, the contras. And North knew just the man to find that money.

In March 1985, as Congress was debating the administration's request for contra aid, North had proposed putting Reagan on television to make a nationwide appeal for contributions to a new Nicaraguan Freedom Fund. The speech was never made; "the Mice knocked it down," North complained. The idea of the president's conducting a telethon for the contras made Regan's aides squeamish. But the Mice did allow the president to speak at a more traditional event, the Nicaraguan Refugee Fund banquet. The benefit was a financial disaster, but it handed North an unexpected and unlikely dividend: Carl Russell Channell.

"Spitz" Channell was a strangely gifted right-wing salesman in search of a product. He had come from the West Virginia hills to work as a fund-raiser at NCPAC and discovered a striking talent for wheedling big-ticket contributions from wealthy conservatives. After the first million or so, Channell realized that he could raise the same kind of money on his own, and he left NCPAC in 1982 to form a series of tax-exempt "educational foundations," culminating in the sonorously named National Endowment for the Preservation of Liberty.

It was whispered widely in Washington that the thirty-nine-year-old Channell, like a few other young conservatives-about-town, was a closet homosexual. One would-be donor, an ambitious young Republican real estate man in North Carolina, was amused, after meeting with Channell, to hear the fund-raiser exclaim to a sidekick, "Didn't I tell you he'd be gorgeous?" But Channell's soft West Virginia voice and fastidious manners never hurt his work. One Texas donor actually gave him money on the understanding that Channell would use it to combat the gay rights movement.

In fact, Channell was happy to raise money for any issue, as long as it inspired donors to give. He had made a profitable business of soliciting contributions to promote Reagan's budget policies, nuclear rearmament, and the Strategic Defense Initiative; he paid himself well, moved around Washington in limousines, and always flew first class. But not until he was drafted to help sell seats for Reagan's speech at the April 1985

Nicaraguan Refugee Fund dinner did he realize that the contra issue could be a gold mine: it was the one issue that could offer access to Reagan himself — and Reagan's personal blessing, he knew, could produce a flood of contributions. A few days after the dinner, Channell called John Roberts in the White House political office.

"Mr. Roberts," the soft voice said, "I'd like to help with the president's priorities. But I have a question: What are they?"

Roberts, nonplused, stammered something about SDI and the contras. Channell asserted that he could get donors to give $10,000 or more to help the president's causes "just by asking" — an extraordinary amount by normal fund-raising standards — and he sent the White House aide a draft of a proposed mailgram for big contributors. "The president needs your help in securing congressional passage of the administration's proposal to support the freedom fighters," it said. "Your positive response and immediate financial support for the president on this issue is of invaluable significance for him. . . . A personal meeting between the president and you in the Oval Office will be arranged and scheduled as soon as Congress has completed action on the aid proposal."

Roberts cautiously checked with the White House legal office; the lawyers said no, Reagan couldn't promise donors a meeting or endorse a pitch like that. But Channell was determined, so Roberts gave him another name. "Talk to Rich Miller," he said. "He fronts for the State Department on public diplomacy projects."

Richard R. Miller, a thirty-three-year-old public relations man, had worked on the 1980 Reagan campaign and as a spokesman for the government's foreign aid agency. In a minor league example of Washington's revolving door, Miller's private firm had now won a State Department contract to sell the president's Central American policy to the public.

When Miller met Spitz Channell, he didn't quite know what to think. "Who's this five-hundred-pound purple canary you sent me?" he asked Roberts. But he was quickly impressed by Channell's ability to produce real money. "Spitz came up with $250,000 for television commercials inside of four days," he said. "I had never seen anybody do that before." So he arranged an introduction for Channell to North — and Channell finally had what he wanted, an entrée to the White House.

Three times that spring, Channell asked North if he couldn't raise money directly for whatever the NSC staff was doing; three times North turned him down. Finally, in June, North needed cash to help the moderate contra leader Alfonso Robelo in his political operation; it was only a modest amount, but because of the contras' feuding he didn't want to ask Robelo's rivals for the money. This time he turned to Channell, who persuaded a donor to come up with a quick $10,000. "At that point," said Miller, "Channell was in the fund-raising business for Ollie North."

North got official encouragement for his private fund-raising efforts from another source, CIA director Casey. On June 18, 1985, Colorado beer magnate Joseph Coors visited Casey at the Old Executive Office Building with a question: What can I do to help the contras?

"I can't do anything for you," Casey said; the Boland amendment had officially tied the CIA's hands. But he added helpfully, "Ollie North's the guy to see."

So a Casey aide set up the appointment, and Coors walked down the hall to North's office in Room 392. Where Casey had been circumspect, North was expansive. He told Coors that the contras needed airplanes; he showed him a brochure for the Maule M-7, a short-takeoff-and-landing plane that was available for only $65,000. And he gave Coors a three-by-five card with what he said was the contras' bank account number: Crédit Suisse, Geneva, account 386430-221. "If you would send the money to the Swiss bank account, I could send it back [to the aircraft dealer] and pick up the plane right away," North said. Coors agreed, and the $65,000 went to Geneva.

A week later, North gave his first briefing for Channell's contributors in the Old Executive Office Building. He showed slides of Soviet tanks and aircraft, talked of the millions of Central American refugees who would flood into the United States if the Sandinistas remained in power, and gave an emotional (if exaggerated) description of how Congress had deserted the freedom fighters in the field, just as in Vietnam.

"Every CIA officer giving aid of any kind to the freedom fighters was yanked out overnight," North said in his husky baritone. "They were gone — overnight!"

The finale really clinched it, many in North's audiences said. The last few slides showed teenagers in contra training camps, youthful rebel units preparing for battle, and, finally, a crude wooden cross over the grave of a fallen fighter. "They are fighting for their own country and the freedoms we believe in," North said quietly in the dark of the auditorium, a slight catch in his voice. "We've got to give them more" — he'd pause — "than just the chance to die."

Then the sobered group filed out of the building for dinner at the Hay-Adams — and the direct pitch from Channell. Two weeks later, Channell had several hundred thousand dollars in hand. He asked North where to send the money. North told him to give it to Rich Miller, who sent most of it to Lake Resources' Swiss bank account.

The first successful briefings touched off a whirlwind of fund-raising by North. He solicited $160,000 from donors in Pittsburgh and Philadelphia. He flew to Dallas on a private jet to dine with oil billionaire Nelson Bunker Hunt, showed him a list of military equipment, and left the room while Hunt wrote checks for $475,000. At Dallas–Fort Worth Airport, North talked with Ellen Clayton Garwood, a land heiress who had already given $60,000 to General Singlaub for a contra helicopter. This time, North told her, the rebels needed trucks to move supplies that were stranded on the docks, just like the shipments "to feed the starving people of Ethiopia." Mrs. Garwood sent $32,000. For the sake of the contras, she explained brightly, "I just gave up going on cruises and fancy dresses."

The biggest donor was Barbara Newington, a conservative widow from Greenwich, Connecticut. In November, North and Channell walked across Lafayette Park to the Hay-Adams and gave Mrs. Newington a private briefing on the contras' need for a defense against the Sandinistas' Soviet-supplied Mi-24 helicopters. Within six weeks, Mrs. Newington sent Channell more than $1 million worth of stock.

"Channell was just fabulous at it," one of his associates said. "He invoked the president's name constantly. He implied that he had a personal relationship — 'The president has asked us to undertake this effort; the president asked me to contact you.' Ollie did the same thing. They were both quite adept at moving people emotionally — but to the point where, instead of pulling out a handkerchief, they'd reach for their wallets."

By the end of October 1985, the team of North and Channell had rustled up almost $2 million in contributions — and it was only the beginning. They made an odd couple, the marine and the soft-voiced fund-raiser, but each had what the other needed. North had found a reliable money machine that could produce untraceable cash at a moment's notice; Channell had found the fund-raiser's perfect product.

Beyond that, Channell was not especially concerned. A Channell associate once tried to explain to the fund-raiser why it was important to reform the contras, but Channell responded with a blank gaze.

"Tell me," he said. "Does it really matter who collects your garbage?"

But Channell, for all his eccentricities, gave Project Democracy something essential: its first independent revenues. Oliver North's "stand-alone, self-sustaining" covert operations network now had everything it needed: money, airplanes, and airstrips; a cadre of enthusiastic managers; the quiet sponsorship of William Casey; and, to free it entirely from control by the "official" government of the United States, its own source of income.

8

Sea Change

As 1985 DREW TO A CLOSE, Bud McFarlane appeared to be at the height of his career. The *Achille Lauro* exploit in October had proven his NSC quick, capable, and ready to act, a dynamic alternative to the lumbering bureaucracies of State and Defense. By autumn, McFarlane and Regan said they had reached an accord, and they encouraged news stories celebrating a new "spirit of détente" between them. And in November, for the first time, Reagan met Soviet leader Mikhail Gorbachev for a summit — a historic opening made possible largely through McFarlane's persistence. Only Nancy Reagan had shown equal tenacity on the subject — buttonholing her husband's foreign policy advisers about the importance of a summit at ostensibly social occasions, including her own birthday party.

Breaking the deadlock on arms control had not been easy. All summer long, a paper war had raged between Shultz, who was anxious to see an arms control agreement, and Weinberger and Casey, whose only real confidence was in continuing the military buildup. But by September, with the First Lady's help, McFarlane had convinced the president to side almost exclusively with Shultz. When the summit began on November 16, Weinberger hadn't been invited.

Yet beneath this temporary breakthrough lay a swarm of unresolved issues. Reagan had brought to Geneva a willingness to consider strategic arms reductions, yet he was completely unwilling to compromise his dream of building a space-based nuclear defense system, the Strategic Defense Initiative. The Soviets had repeatedly warned that they would accept no agreement so long as the United States pursued the defensive system, which they feared would confer destabilizing superiority. Reagan's hybrid position typically tried to have it all: yes to strategic arms reductions and yes to SDI. But his stance, some White House advisers whispered, was inherently contradictory, making genuine progress difficult to achieve.

Reagan's allergy to detail — which in arms control is everything — led to ill-informed pronouncements as well as inconsistent positions. McFarlane tutored Reagan assiduously with books, videos, and even a popular Soviet feature film, but despite his efforts, Reagan's grasp of the issues was shaky. Three weeks before the summit, Reagan confidently told the BBC that the Russian language had no word for "freedom" (it does: *svoboda*). Then Reagan stunned his arms control aides by telling Soviet reporters that the United States would wait to deploy SDI "until we do away with our nuclear missiles, our offensive missiles." If he meant it, he was handing the Soviets a perfect way to block SDI — simply agree to no offensive missile reductions. But the statement was, in Larry Speakes's gentle term, a "presidential imprecision." It bore no resemblance to the policy his cabinet had agreed on, nor to the one he himself espoused.

At the summit, Reagan did make his own unique contributions. One in particular illustrated his genius for symbol and ceremony. It was his inspiration to take off his overcoat when first meeting outdoors with the more heavily garbed Gorbachev, presenting to the world a picture of American leadership that was vigorous, youthful, and open. "It was the president's own idea!" marveled White House advance man William Henkel, with oddly singular emphasis.

In the end, although the two leaders met one-on-one for almost five hours and spent another three hours with the full delegations, the SDI paradox blocked any real progress on strategic arms reductions. The best the leaders could do was to endorse a previously reached agreement to make 50 percent reductions in strategic weapons their long-term goal. But neither Reagan nor Gorbachev wanted to return home from a failed summit, so their subordinates drafted a joint communiqué that was, in essence, an agreement to disagree on all but cultural and educational exchanges and a promise to try again. Given the historic nature of the meeting and the importance of bettering relations, that alone was treated by the White House staff and the press corps as a triumph — adding luster to McFarlane's image.

Even at the height of his public success, however, McFarlane was hitting new personal depths. He seemed to internalize all the contradictions, frustrations, and disappointments of directing foreign policy in the Reagan administration. Throughout the fall he told his friends that he was deeply unhappy and thinking about leaving. He had been passionately committed to achieving at least one great foreign policy breakthrough. Yet a year after he had gone up to the ranch to ask Reagan to choose a course, the administration was still rent by division and disorder. The summit had been largely an exercise in public relations because the president had refused to make a choice between apparently contradictory goals. Similarly, confusion clouded the Nicaraguan policy, where the president hadn't resolved the contradiction between espousing negotiations and expanding the covert war. And the president's counterterrorism policy was secretly riddled with contradictions — with Reagan's public hard line dissolving in his private concern for the hostages.

McFarlane had come away, exhausted and dispirited, from the exercise of trying to make foreign policy decisions where Reagan wouldn't. He had wanted so much to shine, but instead every day brought new evidence that he was in over his head. One White House aide, paraphrasing Hemingway's *Snows of Kilimanjaro*, said the question was, "What was this leopard doing at that altitude?" Another simply described McFarlane as "a spent force."

"What bothered Bud as much as anything else," said NSC counsel Paul Thompson, "was the fact that on a small scale and large, from who was to be his spokesman on TV to whether to abide by SALT II, the president simply wouldn't decide things. And without presidential authority, Bud couldn't."

By the end of the summit, the contrast between the glowing success the public saw and the private disappointment McFarlane felt was too much. What Reagan called the Fireside Summit had been a public relations triumph. Most polls showed that the president had regained the peak of popularity he'd enjoyed immediately after the 1981 assassination attempt. Wirthlin's private polls showed an astonishing 83 percent approval rate among those who watched or read Reagan's dramatic address to Congress following Geneva — a speech that was partly the product of Wirthlin's "speech pulse" system. Gilding the president's image were news accounts throughout November describing him as having mastered the issues of global strategy through long hours of study — a picture that helped his position both in Geneva and at home.

Larry Speakes later admitted that because of his concern that Reagan was "losing the media version of Star Wars" to the articulate new Soviet leader, he and an aide manufactured two lines, which he told the press Reagan had said to Gorbachev. Although the quotes were eminently forgettable — "There is much that divides us, but I believe that the world breathes easier because we are talking together," and "Our differences are serious, but so is our commitment to improving understanding" — Speakes clearly felt that Reagan's performance was not good enough. Evidently Speakes felt no need to show the president the statements; he assumed that Reagan would "certainly . . . not have disavowed the words." After leaving the White House, Speakes confessed that "clearly it was wrong to take such liberties," although the chief reason he cited was the risk that he might be caught.

McFarlane too had been uneasy about his part in the Geneva public relations effort. "We got all that support [from the press]," he recalled in an interview, "but it took a lot of blue smoke and mirrors. I portrayed Ronald Reagan as a Soviet expert. The president went in very confident, mostly because of his immense confidence in his own abilities to persuade. And the press wrote that he really was pretty much on top of things. But I misled the press. When it was over, I just didn't want to be any part of that struggle anymore."

McFarlane's qualms about presidential promotion at such a late date seem curious, given the Reagan White House's well-established preeminence in this old and honorable field. It was, though, an observation made in hindsight, and it seems likely that it was at least partly prompted by a sense that his own hard labors — which, after all, had made the summit possible — were too little appreciated in a White House where taking credit had become a competitive sport, one McFarlane thought he was losing.

The summit had provided one of the most egregious examples of this phenomenon. After their final dinner in Geneva, Reagan and Gorbachev settled onto a red sofa waiting to receive the text of their joint communiqué while their aides mingled politely in the room. The final sticking point was over the phrasing of the two countries' joint goal of reducing strategic arms by half. Shultz and McFarlane had negotiated the compromise with their Soviet counterparts and returned to the parlor to present it to the leaders. The deal was struck, the photographers were ushered in, and both the Soviet and American aides moved politely back from their leaders — all except Regan. The chief of staff blithely leaned over from behind the couch, planted his elbows on the cushions, and posed midway between the president and the Soviet general secretary, forming the apex of a trinity.

Regan had not been a central figure in the talks. In fact, his ignorance of arms control combined with his thirst to look like an expert in the press had created gaffes and confusion, to the unending consternation of the NSC staff. His assertion that most women would find the summit dull because "they're not going to understand throwweights or what is happening in Afghanistan or what is happening in human rights" created an international embarrassment, as did his fumbling description, later, of what throwweights were. But Regan had no appreciation for the cardinal rule of White House etiquette, which held that staff members were supposed to display "a passion for anonymity." In his newsmaking blunders as well as his photographic forays, Regan seemed to be upstaging everyone, including the president.

In an odd way, McFarlane thought, the Geneva photograph was a metaphor for Regan's image-oriented approach to foreign policy. "I couldn't say that Don interfered on the substance of the policy," he later said. "But he did want to be visibly kind of associated with the image of power and the presidency — Oval Office pictures and things like that."

As the friction at Geneva hinted, the talk of reconciliation between McFarlane and Regan was just for show; the discord was, if anything, growing worse. The president seemed oblivious to it: rather than resolving the power struggle, Reagan created the vacuum in which it flourished. His aides sensed a huge amount of tension building between the two former marines, each of whom now commanded rival fronts in the White House. The hostility was usually tamped down. Occasionally, it was reflected in barbs, such as the references to McFarlane by some members of Regan's staff as "Henry Kissinger, Jr.," and "Loverboy."

There were also continuous squabbles over presidential access. McFarlane complained in a memo to Regan that a stream of notes and visitors on sensitive foreign policy matters was reaching the Oval Office without his permission. Many of these backdoor contacts were from hard-liners like Casey, Buchanan, and Weinberger; Casey met with the president alone twice that fall without giving McFarlane any indication of the subject. Access to the president was tightly controlled, and these overtures could not have reached him without first getting cleared through Regan's office. The chief of staff, appearing surprised by McFarlane's complaint, promised it wouldn't happen again. But McFarlane said it did. He thought that either Regan's claims of running the tightest ship outside the U.S. Navy were wildly inflated or Regan was purposely undermining his authority.

Once that fall, presidential assistant Linda Chavez recalled, "it all exploded out in the open." The occasion was one of the regular 8:00 A.M. senior White House staff meetings in the Roosevelt Room. Typically, ten minutes before it started, the less important aides, who had no claim to seats at the large mahogany table, began their ritual of musical chairs, angling for the few unclaimed spots. Where the officials at the table were served coffee in White House china by a Filipino steward, those who were relegated to one of the Queen Anne settees scattered around the periphery of the room drank from Styrofoam cups. Promptly at eight, Don Regan, freshly primed with overnight intelligence cables and financial reports, assumed his customary spot at the western end of the table. Bud McFarlane, his face puffy and pasty-looking from his fourteen-hour days, took his place directly opposite, with his back to the hallway leading to the Oval Office — which at that hour was empty.

The main topic that fall morning was the proposed Gramm-Rudman-Hollings budget reduction plan. Almost instantly, Regan had hopped on the congressional bandwagon, without, McFarlane thought, analyzing its likely impact. More important, he believed that the chief of staff was unilaterally putting the White House's stamp of approval on the bill and not bothering to fully explain the risks to the president.

The legislation was still evolving. But already it was clear that it would call for automatic across-the-board cuts in all government spending, other than entitlement programs, unless Congress somehow broke its habit and met vastly reduced budget targets. Legislators on the Hill wanted to support the bill because it had the dual appeal of making them look responsible about the growing deficit while absolving them of blame for specific painful cuts. Regan and his aides saw the bill similarly as irresistible public relations, placing the White House on the side of the fiscal angels and possibly repairing frayed relations with Congress.

But the budget targets set out in the bill were extraordinarily ambitious. McFarlane's problem was that with entitlement programs and tax increases off the table, it was obvious that the only item left to cut was his own turf — the defense budget — which was, after all, the platform on which Reagan's hawkish foreign policy perched. Weinberger and Shultz were for once united in opposition to the bill, which they saw as a greater threat to defense spending than the doves on Capitol Hill. The measure could mean an automatic cut of $10 billion or more for the Pentagon.

"I think we need to discuss this," said McFarlane, his voice steely with contempt. "If the president's priorities have now shifted so that the two things he wants are no taxes and protecting Social Security, that's fine. If he wants to abandon national defense, that's fine. But I ask that he knows that this is exactly what he's doing. It's a watershed piece of legislation. It's not my decision, but I think he ought to know what the choice is."

At that challenge, an aide recalled, Regan "flipped out." "No!" he yelled, pounding his fist on the great oblong table, Gramm-Rudman would result in "no such choice!" Another aide, Max Friedersdorf, said, "There were a lot of angry words. Regan was getting red in the face. Then he started pounding on the table. I remember thinking, 'This is an act — a power play. It's meant to frighten us, because nobody loses control like that.' He was like a little child having a tantrum. I thought, 'Jesus Christ, I never saw anybody act like that in the fifth grade.' "

Fueling Regan's anger was the sense that he legitimately had the president's imprimatur. Reagan had emerged from his three-week summer vacation at the ranch with the demand that his aides find some way to cut the budget — he'd leave the details to them. The obvious problem, though, was that Reagan's contradictory goals — a continued defense buildup and a reduced deficit — left his warring aides to argue both sides. Once again, indecision above caused a power struggle below. And once again, from McFarlane's standpoint, the resolution was being reached with the president in absentia.

"Don't worry about it," said the exasperated chief of staff. "The president won't make a final decision without fully understanding the issues. And it's not going to be decided today."

But as McFarlane recalled it, later that same day Reagan committed himself to the bill. "To this very day," McFarlane later asserted, "I don't think the president understood the issues. The president was not well served."

McFarlane's suspicions about Regan's running roughshod over everyone else in the White House, including the president in the instance of Gramm-Rudman, may or may not have been correct — and Regan's aides maintained they were not. Yet the fury that Regan unleashed against anyone who dared to challenge his authority had two undeniable effects. The first, as a senior aide to the vice president observed, was that "the friction was so intense, it destroyed the ability and trust necessary to discuss issues in the open," driving dissent underground and encouraging the NSC to become even more secretive. The second effect was to undermine morale, McFarlane's most of all. The one-upmanship and rumormongering about his sex life preyed on him, playing on his insecurities and eating away at his ability to function in an enormously demanding post.

As the fall wore on, McFarlane was having more and more trouble keeping his inner turmoil in check. Others watching him saw a psychological drama unfolding. At Merrill Lynch, Regan had been known for his ruthless elimination of weaker competitors, which he summed up in what was said to be one of his favorite sayings, his so-called sled dog theory. It held that "in order to get ahead, you don't just need a team of strong dogs, you also need a puppy — to throw to the wolves." White House aides had the sense that McFarlane was about to be jettisoned.

Friedersdorf, who had worked smoothly with five earlier White House chiefs of staff, later suggested that "the basic problem was that Regan consciously or unconsciously set out to destroy any threat to his rule. People like myself and Bud, who thought we were assistants to the president, not assistants to the chief of staff, became immediately in conflict. There were numerous challenges. I really didn't understand that at the time. I didn't know why there was such ill feeling there. I understand perfectly now that Bud had to go because Bud was a threat, and Regan didn't want any independent centers of power."

Indeed, by the end of 1985, almost all of the senior White House aides who had independent ideas and power bases — apart from those the press had dubbed Regan Inc. — had resigned their posts or been "cut off at the pass," as Friedersdorf put it, so that their input was ignored. Deaver had left before the summer. Budget director Stockman was gone by August, political director Rollins by October. Congressional relations director Friedersdorf had left by November. Domestic policy adviser Jack Svahn was derided by Regan's staff and was rarely consulted or assigned important work. Collectively, this group represented more than forty years of experience with Reagan. It also numbered most of those who had played a part in his presidential campaigns — an experience that taught much about the importance of winning public support for policy and staying in touch with the electorate.

To be sure, some of this turnover was natural in a second term, and in some cases the veterans were replaced by able men, like the new political director, Mitchell E. Daniels, Jr., and the new congressional relations director, William L. Ball III. But Rollins and Friedersdorf had been brought into the White House by Regan specifically to augment his political skills. Now they had left, bitter about their relations with him and bleak about the White House's contracting center of power. "All his life, Ronald Reagan had been lucky to be protected by people who had his best interests at heart," concluded the disappointed Rollins. "That changed."

McFarlane was teetering on the brink of joining this group of exiles. Both professionally and personally, his self-confidence seemed shot. Inside the White House, Regan was a tough and cunning competitor, instinctively able to sense others' psychological vulnerabilities. The president admired wealthy, successful men, and Regan capitalized on this in a way McFarlane couldn't. A career bureaucrat, McFarlane had never amassed a fortune outside the government. In a cabinet of millionaires, he was the only one who worried about whether his wife, Jonda, a high school teacher, had enough dresses for the state dinners.

"My relationship with [the president] was a curious one," McFarlane later said. "He clearly didn't see me as a person of qualification, deserving of respect. In his set, you had to be a self-made success with money and standing. Unlike Don, I was not a man of means. It's just the way he dealt with us together. He'd pointedly ask George [Shultz], 'What do you think?' He'd be very attentive to Cap and Don. And then he'd say, 'Well, Bud, take care of that.' It's like a child with a parent — you can tell when you're being supported or not."

Increasingly, McFarlane seemed paralyzed by doubt, utterly unable to make up his mind about what to do. His indecision worried friends, who wondered if the pressures were pushing him toward emotional collapse. He confided to the Saudi ambassador, Prince Bandar, that he couldn't take working with Regan anymore and wanted to become ambassador to Japan. He then absolutely denied this to two reporters, insisting that the rumor was "an utterly fictitious falsehood." A sure sign of his nervousness, said one longtime aide, was that he began smoking again after years of abstinence. Another sympathetic official contended that McFarlane broke down and sobbed more than once in his final weeks at the White House. "He was pretty strung out," the official said. After an argument during which McFarlane angrily ordered him out of the office, NSC consultant Michael Ledeen asserted that "McFarlane after 1985 [was] not the same person as the McFarlane prior to 1985. He had a very tough time in that period. . . . He went through a period where, in the old days, people would have said he had a nervous breakdown."

It was during this turbulent time that the second and most legally questionable arms shipment to Iran got under way. August's sale of antitank missiles had yielded one hostage. Ghorbanifar now announced that before freeing the others, his Iranian "moderates" needed sophisticated antiaircraft missiles capable of hitting high-altitude planes, like the Iraqi air force bombers, which were attacking Tehran almost every night. At first McFarlane was skeptical, telling a colleague, "I have a bad feeling about this whole operation. My intention is to shut it down." But he was preoccupied by other matters, and his resolve soon wavered in the face of Ghorbanifar's persistence; by November he relented, approving a shipment of 120 HAWK missiles. North's notebooks record McFarlane's bottom line: "not one single item" of weaponry should go to Iran unless they first deliver "live Americans."

As he was preparing Reagan for the Geneva summit, McFarlane mentioned to the president that the Israelis were planning another arms sale to Iran. In fact, McFarlane had already told the Israelis that the president would approve this second shipment. Again there was no formal meeting, only what McFarlane recalled as "a passing reference" and what Regan recalled as a vague mention of "something up between Israel and Iran [that] might lead to getting some of our hostages out." Neither Regan nor the president asked any questions about renewing the program that had proven so disappointing just two months earlier. Instead, according to McFarlane, Reagan said merely, "Cross your fingers, and hope for the best."

In truth, that was about all McFarlane could do; as he took off for Geneva with the president, he was far too busy to oversee the shipment himself. Instead, he left it in the hands of his aide, Oliver North. Almost immediately, North ignored his insistence that no weapons move before hostages were freed. North also ignored Ghorbanifar's warning that not all five hostages, or "Amcits," in North's shorthand for American citizens, could be released at once. He simply jotted down:

> 120 HAWKs = 1) 5 Amcits
> 2) Guarantee that no more.

On November 18, in Geneva, McFarlane told the president and Regan that the sale was going ahead. The president again expressed no objection, saying only, "Well, let's see what happens." But when McFarlane telephoned Shultz in "the box" — a metal booth that makes telephone conversations secure — Shultz was outraged. "It was a straight-out arms-for-hostage deal," Shultz testified later, "and I told him so. I was upset that he was telling me about it just as it was about to start, so there was no way I could do anything about it." But McFarlane told him that he had the president's approval, and Shultz let it go.

The remotely supervised mission soon ran into trouble. The Israeli 707 carrying HAWKs was supposed to stop in Lisbon, but the Portuguese authorities denied it landing rights. With McFarlane abroad, North was left on his own. After clearing it with McFarlane, he called on his contra airlift confederate, Richard Secord, for help. Secord knew Portugal because he'd bought many of the weapons for the contras there. At North's direction, he flew to Lisbon under the alias John Copp. But even he couldn't convince Portugal's new socialist government to yield landing clearance, so the missiles went back to Tel Aviv. North grew increasingly desperate; he had already dispatched the State Department's hostage reception team to Wiesbaden, Germany, where the officials were killing time at the military base day after day and, said one, "beginning to feel like hostages ourselves."

At this point, North took a step that created lasting legal and political problems for the administration: he brought in the CIA. With the help of his old cowboy colleague from the contra operation, now CIA European operations chief, Dewey Clarridge, North got permission to use an airline owned by the CIA, St. Lucia Airways. He also got the agency's station chief in Turkey to arrange overflight clearances for a "humanitarian" flight to Tehran without even notifying the American ambassador in Ankara. The operation was run directly out of Clarridge's office at CIA headquarters. With this expert help, on Monday, November 25, the unlucky 707 at last touched down in Tehran with its HAWK missiles. North sent Poindexter a jubilant PROFS note: "Clarridge deserves a medal. So does Copp."

But on that same Monday morning, when deputy CIA director John McMahon learned what Clarridge had done, he was beside himself with fury. "Goddamn it!" he raged at the officer who had approved the use of St. Lucia Airways, "I told you not to get involved. For Christ's sake, we can't do that without a finding. Not only did you send the cables, you let the goddamn airplane go to Tehran!" He stormed down the hall to the office of Clair George, deputy director for operations. "You will not support this activity without a finding," he ordered George. "Get me those damn cables," he demanded. Then he called Stanley Sporkin, the CIA's general counsel, and said, "I want a finding — and I want it retroactive to cover that flight."

In McMahon's eyes, Clarridge had flouted the most basic law on covert operations since the scandals of the 1970s, the Hughes-Ryan amendment, which says the agency must have a presidential order, or "finding," before it acts. Within the agency, too, there was the Liddy Rule, which said that requests from the White House staff had to be approved by the director or his deputy. To reformers like McMahon, these rules establishing accountability were the CIA's political shield. Hughes-Ryan protected the agency from congressional critics who were always ready to call it a rogue elephant; and the Liddy Rule protected it from overzealous White House staffers, like G. Gordon Liddy in the Watergate days.

On Tuesday morning, November 26, Sporkin delivered the legally dubious, after-the-fact finding to Casey. On a single typewritten page, it said nothing about improving long-range relations with Iran nor about helping "moderates." In blunt terms, it simply described a direct swap of arms for hostages. One clause was especially unusual: "Because of the extreme sensitivity of these operations, in the exercise of the president's constitutional authorities, I direct the Director of Central Intelligence not to brief the Congress . . . until such time as I may direct otherwise." The National Security Act requires the CIA to notify the congressional intelligence committees of all significant intelligence activities. But Casey had been on the warpath about leaks, which he invariably blamed on Congress. He got Reagan so upset about them that the president proved perfectly amenable to cutting Congress out — even if it stretched the law.

By the end of November, Reagan was eager to keep alive Operation Recovery, as the hostage rescue effort was dubbed. Upon returning from Geneva, even before he had seen the CIA's hastily drafted finding, he had urged the NSC to continue pursuing the hostage deals. North's notebook from those frantic days offers an odd juxtaposition. On one page, from Monday, is an account of McMahon's fury over the HAWK shipment: "This is criminal!" On the next page, for Tuesday, is the laconic note, "RR directed op to proceed."

Reagan had been deeply moved by a letter he had received earlier in November from four of the hostages, appealing for action — their first communication with the outside world in months. "We know of your distaste for bargaining with terrorists," they said, "but do you know the consequences your continued refusal will have for us? It is in your power to have us home for Christmas. Will you have mercy on us and our families and do so?" At the bottom were the signatures of Terry Anderson, David Jacobsen, Father Lawrence Martin Jenco, and Thomas Sutherland. With his usual madcap intensity, North told colleagues, "This thing is really eating away at Reagan, and he's driving me nuts about it," implying that he was meeting frequently with the president. "He wants them out by Christmas." No one else could recall the president's saying that, but nonetheless, the word was spread around the bureaucracy that on this matter, the president really cared.

By the end of November, however, Ghorbanifar was hysterical for an entirely different reason. Although he had ordered the HAWKs, he called with news that "the most horrible thing has happened. The missiles arrived, and they were the wrong missile!" The Iranians had three problems with the HAWKs. They had telltale Israeli markings; about half even sported the Star of David. They were an outmoded model. And they weren't designed to shoot down high-altitude jets as the Iranian had wanted. Ghorbanifar was furious, accusing Reagan of "cheating us." There would be no more hostages at all this time, he swore. The deal was a complete bust. Reagan had approved another shipment of arms to Iran but got no hostages in return. The Iranians were angry. And the CIA had become entangled — probably illegally.

But for Oliver North there had been one unintended benefit of the disastrous shipment. On that harried November weekend when North had brought in Secord to push the missiles through Portugal, an unusual financial transaction had occurred. North had prevailed upon one of the Israeli arms merchants involved, Al Schwimmer, to put $1 million in the Lake Resources account for expenses (which congressional investigators later concluded probably meant bribes). But Secord had spent little of the money; more than $850,000 remained in the account so North and Secord decided to divert it to their other major venture: the contras. "I assumed they would ask for their money back, but they didn't," Secord later recalled. "So," he said, grinning slyly, "Mr. Schwimmer made a contra-bution."

The day after the second arms shipment ended, Tuesday, November 26, 1985, McFarlane returned from the summit in Europe less certain of his fate than ever. His indecision had become a full-fledged melodrama. NSC aides were writing him impassioned memos, begging him to stay. Even David Kimche, the Israeli strategist, made a brief attempt to dissuade his friend from quitting. McFarlane told them all that he wanted to go out to California, where the president would be at the ranch for Thanksgiving, so that he could ponder his fate alone. On Thanksgiving Day, his press aide, Karna Small, sent him a one-word PROFS note: "Well?"

There was no definitive answer. McFarlane was still agonizing. Privately, Small agreed with other staff members that it looked as though he'd probably stay. But she underestimated both McFarlane's fragility and a reporter's tenacity.

Thomas M. DeFrank, a reporter at *Newsweek*, had been told by a friend of McFarlane's that after the summit, McFarlane planned to quit. It was DeFrank who finally put in motion the series of events that forced McFarlane's wavering hand. He was sworn not to print the news until the summit was over. But the following week — Thanksgiving week — he prepared a story.

That Tuesday, DeFrank tried to reach McFarlane and instead got Karna Small, who said her boss had "not talked with the president about resigning." DeFrank took the denial as less than definitive and reconfirmed the story with his original source. By Friday, the day that *Newsweek* generally "closes" stories, locking them into print, DeFrank was out of town for the holiday, and the item was set to run in the Periscope section on Monday. Small thought *Newsweek* would call her for one more comment if it was going to be used. But signals had become crossed in all the holiday travel, and *Newsweek* thought she just wanted a courtesy call before it hit the stands on Monday.

So it was Saturday before Small got *Newsweek*'s call saying the story on McFarlane's impending resignation would run. By then, the magazine was already locked up. She was frantic when she called her boss in California to give him the bad news. McFarlane just sighed. "Well," he said, sounding to her as if he were only just that moment making up his mind, "maybe it's just as well. I better go talk to the president." He drove up the rutted, winding road to the president's ranch and handed his letter of resignation to a military aide, not wanting to disturb the president's holiday. It wasn't until Sunday, after the president had flown to Los Angeles to tape a benefit variety show, that the two men talked. The conversation in the president's top-floor suite in the tower of the Century Plaza Hotel lasted only a few minutes. Unlike a year earlier, when Reagan had refused to accept McFarlane's resignation, this time he accepted it on the spot — to what others said was McFarlane's great disappointment. One longtime Reagan aide, observing the drama, recounted that "I made a pact with myself long ago never to go before Ronald Reagan with my guts hanging out, hoping that he'd offer to put them back in. He just doesn't reach out like that, and it was Bud's mistake to expect more."

McFarlane regretted his resignation almost instantly. His stoic façade had begun to crumble, revealing a man both complicated and emotionally troubled. When he told his NSC staff of his decision, he "was bawling like a baby," one aide said. He had made no contingency plans for his own employment — he had never before worked outside the government. Within a half hour of resigning, he later said, his life seemed "bent on a downward cycle." He immediately blamed himself for quitting; more than a year later, he was still rebuking himself, saying, "It was a cop-out. If I'd stayed in the White House, I'm sure I could have stopped things from getting worse."

Instead, McFarlane recommended as his successor his own deputy and former military aide, forty-nine-year-old Vice Admiral John M. Poindexter.

Poindexter's promotion was rushed through quickly, but not quickly enough to avoid some political jockeying. When McFarlane handed in his resignation, Regan was not with the president in California. But within a few days the chief of staff was at the center of the hurried process of choosing McFarlane's replacement. As usual, no two of the president's foreign policy advisers could completely agree — nor did the president himself have much to say about the process. In a contest where each adviser had his own candidate, Poindexter's advantage was that he was, as Regan later confirmed, "everyone's second choice," the perfect "compromise candidate."

But at least one member of the old troika was alarmed. Michael Deaver, now formally out of the White House but still in constant contact, raised a tiny last-minute flurry of opposition. He was in New York on business when he heard that Poindexter would be the next national security adviser. Although Deaver thought Poindexter had been loyal and capable, he was afraid that the admiral was too pliable for the post. He got to a pay phone and called the White House, asking for the resident most concerned with personnel issues — Nancy Reagan.

"It's a big mistake," Deaver warned. "He's a classic number two guy. He's too weak to mediate between Defense and State." Moreover, he said, "you shouldn't put a military guy in that post."

"I think it's too late," Mrs. Reagan replied. "It's already settled. But call Shultz."

Deaver immediately placed a call to Shultz. The secretary of state came on the line and said, "I think you're wrong. I think John will be just fine." His tone of satisfaction deepened Deaver's suspicions.

But the president — the man responsible for the appointment — had no reservations of his own. The admiral would become his fourth national security adviser in six years. Henry A. Kissinger, the best-known occupant of the post, had warned that even in the best of circumstances, "the national security adviser has no safety net." And with a president only intermittently interested in resolving policy and personnel disputes, these were not the best of circumstances. But with customary cheerfulness, the president turned the event into a little jest. On his endorsement of McFarlane's recommendation of Poindexter, which had included the option of promoting Poindexter in the navy instead, Reagan scrawled lightheartedly, "Hope it doesn't hurt his future career!"

Reagan had accepted the choice of Poindexter without asking probing questions or launching a serious talent search; the year before, he'd accepted Regan in much the same way. The process was simply improvised. All other postwar presidents had devoted considerable thought and effort to attracting aides who they believed were "the best and the brightest."

But Reagan was almost entirely aloof from the personnel process. He rode into the White House on a tide of resentment against the eastern establishment's foreign policy professionals, who he felt had weakened and humiliated the country in the seventies. More generally, he had long campaigned against the power of government itself. He had staffed one department — Education — with the goal of abolishing it, and another — the National Security Council — hoping to weaken it in relation to the cabinet.

If Poindexter did not have the incandescence of his predecessors — men like McGeorge Bundy, Henry Kissinger, and Zbigniew Brzezinski — it did not concern Reagan. Neither he nor his advisers had made more than a passing pretext of valuing the counsel of these Washington alumni. In fact, although he was a conservative, Reagan showed extraordinarily little appreciation for recent history and those who had shaped it. He might have profited from their mistakes as much as their advice. But instead of being bound by the gloomy lessons of the past, Reagan liked to quote Thomas Paine about building the world over again. He brought his trademark blend of optimism and naiveté to every corner of his administration, and nowhere more fatally than at the NSC, where a military man who was virtually untested in the realm of foreign policy was about to take the helm.

In just one year and one month after Reagan's reelection, the White House was about to complete a profound transformation. It had begun with a new chief of staff; it was about to finish with a new national security adviser. Both men had come to the epicenter of political power to serve a notably inattentive president, yet neither had more than a passing acquaintance with democratic politics. One came from the feudal world of corporate America, the other from the hierarchical world of the military. One knew sales, the other knew operations, but neither had any experience in making policy, winning votes, or forging a consensus. Both men shared an executive view of power which held that Congress was at best an annoyance. Both men had succeeded in their respective fields, and neither was prone to either introspection or humility. And both had been chosen to help run the most powerful democracy in the world principally on the basis of convenience.

Pipe-smoking and quiet, with trifocals and a balding pate, John Poindexter at first glance seemed the embodiment of competence and continuity. "He has everything," wrote Poindexter's superior in one internal naval fitness report. "A fine manly appearance, splendid military bearing, a warm engaging personality, the manners of a gentleman, a calm and pleasant disposition, a photographic memory, brilliant mind . . . I cannot recall an error of judgment or omission on his part."

Until he became Reagan's national security adviser, everything about Poindexter's career had been neat, linear, and predictable, much as everyone thought he was. Born in the small, Protestant farm town of Odon, Indiana, he was the eldest son of a strait-laced, Republican bank president. His mother once said, "He was never a little boy. He was born an old man." Serious and studious, he was a stickler for rules even as a small child, scolding bigger children about their behavior in a movie house, where he worked after school as an undersize usher. He was a cautious and conservative boy, the type who, as a cousin recalled, would always wear his trunks when the others went skinny-dipping. But as a student, particularly in mathematics and science, Poindexter won respect: he was extraordinarily good at solving problems. His academic record easily won him entry to the U.S. Naval Academy in Annapolis. By the time he graduated, he had four years of straight A's and was not only the top student in his class but also brigade commander — a dual honor only one other man, Douglas MacArthur, had ever achieved (at West Point).

Upon leaving Annapolis in 1958, Poindexter accepted his naval commission as an ensign on a destroyer in the Atlantic fleet, but the job called for a technical knowledge of electronics, which he lacked. So in 1959, on a prestigious Burke scholarship, he shipped off to Caltech for a doctorate in nuclear physics. While his colleagues argued politics and philosophy, Poindexter remained apart, a technocrat among theoreticians. His dissertation — "Electronic Shielding by Closed Shells in Thulium Compounds" — was narrow and technical. There was never any doubt about Poindexter's intelligence, but as far back as his graduate school days, professors like Felix Boehm questioned whether he possessed the breadth or independent judgment necessary to become a leader. "He didn't give me the impression he would be a great man in the future," said Boehm in an interview with the *Los Angeles Times*. "He just didn't strike me as a man who was outstanding in his overall judgment or perspective."

Nonetheless, in the military Poindexter, who was loyal, calm, and methodical, did extraordinarily well. He progressed through a series of assignments at sea and in Washington, where he served as an administrative assistant to three secretaries of the navy before going on to command a guided missile cruiser. In 1980, he was promoted to rear admiral; in 1985, at the NSC, to vice admiral. He was in line for the coveted assignment of commander of the Sixth Fleet in the Mediterranean when McFarlane tapped him as his successor.

Although Poindexter was the candidate of continuity, he had a strikingly different approach from that of McFarlane, which soon resulted in profound changes in the NSC. Unlike the professorial McFarlane, who liked to hold forth in policy debates, Poindexter was not just discreet; he was, as one colleague said, "quiet as a church mouse." Some thought he preferred computer communication to conversation. Indeed, he was a confirmed computer buff: he won the navy's Legion of Merit for his computer work; later, he oversaw the creation of the NSC's computerized Crisis Management Center.

Unfortunately, Poindexter's taciturn style played to one of Reagan's weaknesses. Many years earlier, Nancy Reagan had warned political aides that her husband functioned best when he could engage in a free-wheeling give-and-take with advisers. But with Poindexter's promotion, the president was now flanked by a chief of staff who liked everything in writing and spent little time on foreign policy and a national security adviser most comfortable dealing in computer messages, not with extensive discussion. Poindexter was considered pleasant enough company, but his behavior — whether because he felt pressed for time or for other reasons — bordered on the reclusive. He often ate all three meals in his office. (He once explained to a colleague that the reason he moved from a corner table to his desk for dinner was that "variety is the spice of life.") And, whenever possible, he avoided large meetings.

This tendency also had an immediate effect on how policy was made. Where McFarlane had tried (at least at first) to forge consensus by mediating endless bureaucratic bargaining sessions, Poindexter's style, according to another NSC official, was "secretiveness applied to all issues. He changed the NSC routine from constant meetings to one-on-one negotiations where only he saw all the cards." McFarlane had led the NSC into an operational role in his frustration with both bureaucratic and presidential paralysis. Poindexter took what had been a dangerous malfunction of the system and transformed it into standard operating procedure. While McFarlane believed in "compartmentalization" to protect covert operations — and had, for instance, cut Shultz out of the details of the deals with Iran — Poindexter saw secrecy and compartmentalization as proper modes for pursuing virtually all foreign policy.

Given his background, this view wasn't really surprising. At the White House, Poindexter had followed directly in McFarlane's footsteps, rising from military assistant to deputy and on to the top job. But unlike McFarlane, who had graduated from Annapolis a year behind him, Poindexter had had no experience in Congress or the State Department, no occasion to develop policy or political skills. He was not a strategic thinker; when he came to the pivotal national security post, another former NSC aide, Geoffrey Kemp, said of him, "John's forte was paper flow. He was a bureaucrat's bureaucrat."

Other military men before him, like Ford's national security adviser, General Brent Scowcroft, had done well in the post. But Scowcroft, Bundy, Kissinger, and Richard Allen had pursued graduate degrees in government and politics; Poindexter's training had been technical and narrow. Scowcroft himself once told McFarlane that he thought the admiral was so seriously in over his head in the deputy's job that he should be transferred out of the NSC altogether. Scowcroft specifically warned that Poindexter seemed too enamored of covert operations, pursuing them at the expense of overall policy. But although Scowcroft had been McFarlane's mentor, his warning went unheeded. Instead, the admiral was promoted.

Not long after Poindexter assumed the helm, complaints started to surface from the political hands in the White House about his impatience with political affairs. The congressional liaison team frequently found to its consternation that Poindexter fought any advice to see key swing voters on the Hill, arguing that it was a waste of time. He was equally insensitive to diplomatic niceties: he resisted meeting with foreign leaders, and stood up at least one foreign minister from South America. The administration's other foreign policy experts soon became frustrated with Poindexter's lack of political vision. One former official said, "You couldn't explain things to Poindexter. . . . He had an engineer's mind." Poindexter's briefings tended to be so dry that an old family friend of the Reagans' said, "I always heard Reagan fell asleep in them, Poindexter was so boring." Reagan's short attention span was already familiar to Poindexter. After one sensitive briefing, in which Casey won the president's approval to use foreign operatives for preemptive strikes against terrorists, Poindexter told a colleague that despite the highly controversial subject matter, "Casey mumbled, and Ronald Reagan nodded off."

When McFarlane recommended Poindexter, he knew some of these liabilities. But he assumed that, in part, the admiral's blind spots would be offset by his more politically experienced deputy, Donald R. Fortier. But Fortier was stricken with liver cancer and died nine short months after Poindexter's promotion. Unwilling to appear to have given up hope of Fortier's recovery, for many months Poindexter refused to fill the post, depriving himself of much-needed help.

A clear example of Poindexter's lack of political sophistication was his underestimation of the role played in Washington by the press. It was hardly new for a national security adviser to dislike or mislead the press. Kissinger had been a master at it, and Bundy had scribbled a famous note to press secretary Pierre Salinger during the Vietnam War, reminding him that "a communiqué should say nothing in such a way as to feed the press without deceiving them." But even the arrogant Bundy had seen the advantage of cultivating the town's important columnists.

As soon as Poindexter took over the national security slot, other White House officials urged him to do the same — if only to buy some good will. But he soon made it clear that interviews would have to wait. "Poindexter," said Larry Speakes, "thought the press was unpatriotic." This attitude emerged when the United States was on the verge of invading Grenada, in 1983. A rumor about the invasion swept up to Washington from the Caribbean, where correspondents had seen American troops on the move. White House reporters asked Speakes if there was any truth to the rumor, and Speakes in turn asked Poindexter. "Preposterous" came back the unambiguous reply. Twenty-four hours later, U.S. troops went ahead and took the tiny island by force — exposing the lie for what it was. Poindexter apparently saw the world, in Oliver North's memorable line, as a choice between "lies and lives." Truth was the casualty of choice, whether in war or — as it later became clear — when pursuing unpopular policies at home. What this view failed to comprehend was the inevitable toll that lies — not evasions, shadings, deflections, or any of the other time-honored Washington techniques for sidestepping the truth — would ultimately take on the president's credibility as well as Poindexter's.

Poindexter seemed to think that building public support for the administration's policies was a waste of time. In contrast, McFarlane had talked often about what he said had been a central lesson of the Vietnam War: the recognition that U.S. foreign policy couldn't be conducted successfully without public support, and public support couldn't be won without the press. These ruminations later appeared disingenuous when details of his lies to both reporters and Congress emerged. But in retrospect, the time he put into manipulating reporters paid off handsomely. While McFarlane was running the secret NSC operations, the White House press corps portrayed him as capable, wise, and steady, even as he was sliding toward emotional collapse. This dynamic began to change the day of Poindexter's promotion. Reporters covering the announcement in the White House press room on December 4 shouted to him, "Admiral, will we ever see you?"

"Maybe," came back the tight-lipped reply.

McFarlane's departure provided Oliver North with a superb opening. McFarlane had not only held him back, he had also recommended that North be transferred out of the White House because he was becoming "too emotionally strung out." North's relations with the admiral were formal — nothing like the father-son relationship he'd enjoyed with McFarlane — but far from being transferred, North soon made himself indispensable to Poindexter. And, with Poindexter struggling to get a grip on the operation, North had less supervision than ever, which allowed him to expand his role in new, unchallenged ways. "Bud kept Ollie on a chain," explained NSC aide Johnathan Miller. "Don Fortier was another chain. He was Mr. Caution — it drove Ollie nuts. Poindexter let go of the chain. Ollie went from being a good staffer to being almost a megalomaniac."

Within days after Poindexter took over, North was running circles around him. To impress the admiral with his expertise, North persuaded him to take a two-day trip to Central America. In a dizzying round of short plane rides, they held quick meetings in Panama, El Salvador, Costa Rica, and Honduras before their executive jet turned back to Andrews Air Force Base. As the plane headed up the eastern seaboard at dusk, North was struck by an idea: Why not give the admiral a public relations boost? He picked up the cabin radiophone and called Miller.

"It's important to show that Poindexter's taking charge," North explained over the radio.

"Ollie, are you still on the plane?" Miller asked in disbelief. He had pulled off the George Washington Parkway to answer his White House beeper — just so North could flatter his new boss?

"You got it," North said from the air force jet. "Get to work."

With a sigh, Miller called a dozen reporters. "Poindexter's really taking charge," he said, dutifully echoing North. "This is sensitive information — but he's on his way back from a secret trip to Central America."

The next morning, Don Regan was annoyed to read of Poindexter's secret travels in the newspapers, and at the eight o'clock senior White House staff meeting, he demanded to know who had leaked. "NSC," Larry Speakes said, a half smile on his face. Regan turned to Donald Fortier. "Well?" Fortier, embarrassed, had to admit that he didn't know anything about it.

Afterward, Miller grabbed North. "Ollie," he pleaded, "that was an authorized leak, wasn't it?"

"Hell, no." North grinned. He knew how to play White House politics with the best of them.

On Wednesday, December 4, the day that Poindexter's promotion was announced, North sat down and wrote his new boss a long memo proposing a third arms-for-hostage deal. North had an uncanny knack for manipulating people and events, and in his memo he made the one argument sure to propel the president onward: if they didn't send more weapons to Iran, the hostages would probably be killed. In his overblown prose, North wrote, "We are now so far down the road that stopping what has been started could have even more serious repercussions. If we do not at least make one more try at this point, we stand a good chance of condemning some or all [of the hostages] to death and a renewed wave of Islamic Jihad terrorism. While the risks of proceeding are significant, the risks of not trying one last time are greater."

In fact, the hostages' captors had made no such threat. With the exception of Buckley, who apparently died of illness and neglect (and not under torture), Islamic Jihad had never killed any of its captives. The idea that the terrorists would murder the hostages if the arms shipments stopped, U.S. officials later concluded, was simply invented by Ghorbanifar, the man who stood to profit most from the sales.

Accompanying North's portentous assessment was a helpful chart, as guaranteed to impress the mathematically oriented Poindexter as the death threats would Reagan. Each additional hostage would be released following a weapons shipment:

H-hr:	1 707 w/300 TOWs	= 1 AMCIT
H + 10 hrs:	1 707 (same A/C) w/300 TOWs	= 1 AMCIT
H + 16 hrs:	1 747 w/50 HAWKs & 400 TOWs	= 2 AMCITs
H + 20 hrs:	1 707 w/300 TOWs	= 1 AMCIT
H + 24 hrs:	1 747 w/2000 TOWs	= French hostage

Although only one hostage had been released in the two prior deals, North wanted to send an additional 3,300 TOWs and 50 HAWKs. In exchange, his chart showed, they would get five American citizens and one French hostage (standing in for Buckley, who was now known to be dead).

North's pitch worked. In one of his first official actions, Poindexter gave North permission to fly to London and pursue the deal. Poindexter was, after all, an operations man: his strength was in getting from A to B, not in evaluating the greater wisdom of the task, and so without a known second thought he renewed the secret Iran policy.

The next morning, his second on the job, Poindexter strode across the creamy yellow carpet of the Oval Office and gave Reagan his first nine-thirty briefing as national security adviser. In the middle of the half-hour session, he handed the president the one-page finding that the CIA had put together after the fact to cover its November shipment of HAWKs. The order described the deal baldly as an exchange of arms for hostages, and nothing else, and included the unusual clause directing that Congress not be told of the action. Both politically and legally, the finding was a time bomb.

But the president signed it on the spot. No one remembers Reagan — or Regan, who was also there — asking what the document meant or discussing the issues it raised. Poindexter placidly returned the page to his folder, took it back to his office, and gave it to his counsel, Paul Thompson, to keep in his safe. Normally, copies went to the director of the CIA, the secretary of state, and a few other offices, including the NSC's secret archives. But Poindexter was a great believer in sharing information only on a need-to-know basis. This piece of information was never shared.

On Saturday, December 7, three days into his tenure, Poindexter reluctantly relented to pressure from others to hold the first top-level meeting since August about the secret policy on Iran. Shultz, Weinberger, McFarlane, Regan, and the CIA's deputy director, John McMahon, all joined the president for an informal session in the family quarters. (Bush chose to attend the Army-Navy football game. Casey was traveling.)

By all accounts, it was a tough meeting. McFarlane, who had been cleaning out his office, took the chair and gave a brief outline of the initiative thus far. His presentation omitted some crucial developments, but none of those familiar with the full story of the operation — Poindexter, Regan, and the president — insisted that he provide a complete account. No one mentioned the November HAWK shipment, which neither Shultz nor Weinberger knew had gone through. (Shultz had been specifically told that it hadn't.) No one mentioned that the president had just signed a retroactive finding authorizing such arms-for-hostage deals. Nor did anyone tell the secretaries of state and defense that North was already in London pursuing a third arms deal with Secord, Ghorbanifar, and the Israelis.

Even though he knew only a little about the operation, Shultz was glowering. He stated his arguments in his habitual blunt tone: selling more arms to Iran would "negate the whole policy" of no deals with terrorists. The United States had just spent months hammering on its European friends to crack down on weapons deals with Iran; the allies would be "shocked if they knew we were helping Iran in spite of our protestations to the contrary."

Reagan turned to Weinberger. "Cap?"

Weinberger hesitated. "Are you really interested in my opinion?" he asked.

"Yes," Reagan said.

"I think this is a terrible idea," Weinberger replied fiercely. He then launched into a thirty-minute lecture. The United States should be denying arms to Tehran, not shipping them; there was "no one of any reliability — or, indeed, any sense — with whom we could deal in Iran"; the Iranians couldn't be trusted to keep their end of the bargain; and even if they did, they could then subject the administration to blackmail. "It won't accomplish anything," he warned, "and the Iranians will undoubtedly continue to milk us. And there are legal problems here, Mr. President, in addition to all of the policy problems," Weinberger, a lawyer, continued. He launched afresh into a dissertation on several arms export laws that, he said, these shipments would break.

But legal impediments did not impress the president. Reagan cut him off. "I want to leave no stone unturned" to get the hostages out, he said. "The American people will never forgive me if I fail to get these hostages out over this legal question," he added a little heatedly. With a forty-nine-state mandate and popularity ratings to match, the president clearly wasn't about to worry about the kind of bureaucratic red tape he'd run against throughout his political career.

Then, as he so often did, Reagan lightened a serious conversation with a joke. Imagining the worst case possible — that laws might be broken and that people might go to jail — he grinned and added, "But visiting hours are Thursday."

Don Regan and John McMahon also expressed objections.

"Cut your losses," Regan said, sounding like the Wall Street pro he had been. He thought he could sniff a sour deal. "We had taken a chance," he later testified. "It didn't look like it was going anywhere. Why bother?"

McMahon noted quietly that the agency didn't believe there were any real moderates in Iran: "Most of the moderates had been slaughtered when Khomeini took over," he said.

Poindexter, taking charge, offered a proposal that showed both his political myopia and his interest in reviving the program now that he was in command. McFarlane, he suggested, could ask the Iranians to return all the hostages without any more arms sales; if the Iranians refused, the president could ask Britain's prime minister, Margaret Thatcher, to sell them weapons.

Shultz was astonished at the specious reasoning. "That would be the same misguided policy," he snapped.

The president made no final decision, except that McFarlane should go to London and tell the intermediaries that the United States wanted the hostages back without trading arms. Both Shultz and Weinberger felt that they had made an impact. But, as was so often true in meetings where Reagan was forced to deal with conflict, no single participant had quite the same understanding about what the president wanted. Weinberger went back to his office at the Pentagon and triumphantly told his deputy, Colin Powell, "This baby has been strangled in its cradle."

But Shultz was troubled. He sensed that Reagan "was somewhat annoyed at me and Secretary Weinberger because . . . he was very concerned about the hostages." It was axiomatic among his oldest advisers that Reagan didn't like being told an absolute no. He was an optimist, and he stubbornly discounted naysayers. Long after David Stockman had begun to preach gloom and doom about the widening deficit, the president had refused to abandon "Reaganomics." Well after others had developed qualms about SDI, Reagan remained a true believer. In the first term, the troika learned that the key to changing Reagan's mind was to realize that he was unmovable on long-term goals but flexible about tactics. To talk him out of a foolish plan, you simply needed a different approach to the same end. The absolute worst tack was to tell him that something was too politically risky; it was like waving a red flag at a bull. In this case, Reagan's heartfelt goal was to get the hostages out. None of the opponents in the meeting had offered a different tactic from the one being pursued by the NSC. And Reagan wasn't about to give up. "He was being pulled and tugged to do something about the hostages," Regan later explained. "The State Department said it was unable to do anything. The Defense Department said it would take thousands of troops. The only avenue open to him was this thing. So he starts down a slippery slope."

That evening McFarlane, hoping to make a final judgment on the Iranian operation before leaving the government, took off for London to join North and see Ghorbanifar. At three in the afternoon on Sunday, December 8, McFarlane and North walked into a palatial West End apart-

Los Angeles, election night, 1984. (*Jack Kightlinger, the White House*)

Reagan meets in the Oval Office with his new chief of staff, Donald Regan, February 11, 1985. (*Michael Evans, the White House*)

Reagan meets with his pollster, Richard Wirthlin, in one of their regular Oval Office sessions. (*Pete Souza, the White House*)

President and Mrs. Reagan relax for a typical evening of dinner and television in the residence. (*Michael Evans, the White House*)

On his birthday, the president meets with his pen pal, Rudy Hines. (*Pete Souza, the White House*)

President Reagan meets the Nicaraguan contra leaders Alfonso Robelo, Arturo Cruz, and Adolfo Calero at the White House, April 1985. Oliver North is at the far right. (*White House Photo, courtesy Peter Kornbluh*)

Reagan meets on Sunday, June 16, 1985, in the Situation Room with his national security advisers about the TWA hijacking. Left to right: the chairman of the Joint Chiefs of Staff General John Vessey, Defense Secretary Caspar Weinberger, Vice President George Bush, the president, Secretary of State George Shultz, CIA director William Casey, and chief of staff Donald Regan. (*Terry Arthur, the White House*)

Reagan talks with chief of staff Donald Regan and national security adviser Robert McFarlane aboard *Air Force One* on June 21, 1985, the day he met with the relatives of the hostages in Dallas, Texas. (*Bill Fitz-Patrick, the White House*)

President Reagan comforts Sherry Sierralta at a memorial service for her brother, slain navy diver Robert Stethem, at Arlington National Cemetery on July 2, 1985. (*Bill Fitz-Patrick, the White House*)

Reagan at his morning national security briefing in the Oval Office, January 7, 1986. Later that day he would attend the first and only full National Security Council meeting on the question of arms sales to Iran. Left to right: chief of staff Donald Regan, the president, Vice President George Bush, national security adviser John Poindexter, and NSC aide Donald Fortier. (*Pete Souza, the White House*)

President and Mrs. Reagan lead Independence Day festivities marking the 1986 centennial of the Statue of Liberty, on Governors Island, New York. (*AP/Wide World Photos*)

Reagan, chief of staff Donald Regan, and aides gather in the Blue Room before the November 19, 1986, press conference on the secret arms sales to Iran. (*Pete Souza, the White House*)

Above: Iranian parliament speaker Ali Akbar Hashemi Rafsanjani displays the Bible with Reagan's signature and inscription for reporters in Tehran, January 28, 1987. (*AP/Wide World Photos*)

Above left: As the Iran-contra scandal grew, Reagan became less accessible to reporters and photographers. On December 13, 1986, he briefly covered his face with a teddy bear given to him by Heisman Trophy winner Vinny Testaverde. (*AP/Wide World Photos*)

Below: Retired air force Major General Richard Secord (*left*) and businessman Albert Hakim were the civilian managers of Project Democracy, the covert operation directed by Oliver North. (*Bernie Boston, Los Angeles Times*)

President Reagan, following prostate surgery, meets with his chief of staff, Donald Regan, and his new national security adviser, Frank Carlucci, at Bethesda Naval Hospital on January 6, 1987. (*Terry Arthur, the White House*)

Reagan's second meeting with the Tower board in the Oval Office, February 11, 1987. At left, the panel members: John Tower, Edmund Muskie, and Brent Scowcroft. Also present were several members of Reagan's staff, including White House counsel Peter Wallison (to Scowcroft's left) and special adviser for the Iran-contra affair, David Abshire (to the president's immediate right). (*Terry Arnold, the White House*)

ment owned by one of the Israeli arms dealers. McFarlane had brought a long list of points for discussion and expected to hold a polite dialogue on geopolitics that might gain the hostages' release without arms in return. He had never before laid eyes on their middleman.

In front of him was the apparition of a wheeler-dealer from the arms bazaar angling to make a killing. Ghorbanifar didn't want to hear McFarlane's earnest geopolitics. He had spent three weeks working on what he thought was going to be another arms deal, and now he wanted to talk TOWs — to be exact, how many each hostage would cost.

When it became clear to Ghorbanifar that McFarlane was not interested in another arms deal, Ghorbanifar stunned him with a bitter, half-hour tirade. The United States had "cheated" by sending the wrong kind of missiles in November, he said. His people in Iran were very angry; it had jeopardized the chances for a relationship. And now the Americans were asking for the hostages without offering any weapons?

"What the hell is this?" Ghorbanifar demanded. "You just left a mess behind and you want something else? Better you cut off," he growled in his Persian-accented English. "And don't put the blame on us . . . because then there will be fire back on your interests."

McFarlane had heard enough. "Go pound sand!" he told the startled Iranian. Then he walked out of the room — and, he hoped, out of the operation forever.

When McFarlane returned to Washington to brief the president, Poindexter, Weinberger, Casey, and Regan on his experience, he was, not surprisingly, highly negative. Ghorbanifar was "a borderline moron," he said, "the most despicable character I've ever met." This effort wouldn't work unless they made contact with someone more trustworthy.

Weinberger agreed.

Casey sighed. "So be it," he said.

But in what was probably the fatal flaw in his presentation, leaving open exactly the crack that would draw the president in, McFarlane acknowledged that, as North's memo had stated, there was some risk of reprisal against the hostages. McFarlane's change of heart about Ghorbanifar seemed to make very little impression on the president; but he was deeply concerned by McFarlane's admission that the hostages might be executed if the gambit were abandoned. "Why can't we go back to letting Israel manage this program?" the president asked in frustration. Whether Israel or the United States was in charge didn't particularly matter to him. The details of the implementation weren't important. He wanted the hostages home, and he wasn't concerned about the legal fine points.

By the end of the December 10 meeting, Reagan still had reached no definite decision on how his aides should proceed. In a broad sense, however, they knew what he wanted. One barometric reading of this feeling was that Don Regan had begun to retreat from his negative counsel of three days earlier, when he'd advised that the president should "cut his losses." This time, Regan left the Oval Office downcast, like the president, and troubled by the poor presidential image that the festering hostage problem projected. "We were going to spend another Christmas with hostages there," he remembered thinking, "and he is looking powerless and inept as president because he's unable to do anything to get the hostages out."

Although he maintained that he tried to scuttle the plan, McFarlane made sure that he could stay involved should the negotiations continue. Before he left, the NSC staff pleaded with Christopher Hicks, the head of the White House Office of Administration and one of Regan's former Treasury aides, to retain the secure telephone line, the signal phone and a PROFS terminal in McFarlane's suburban Maryland home. Hicks, a stickler about spending government money, resisted stubbornly, saying that they would have to give him a good reason why private citizen McFarlane needed the sophisticated equipment. Finally, an NSC aide told Hicks that "it has to do with the hostages. I can't say much more, but it will only take a month or two more." Hicks gave in; and so, with the approval of Regan's staff, McFarlane remained electronically connected to the White House even if he no longer worked there. And he continued to work the hostage account despite his reservations.

McFarlane may have expected to kill the program, but he had underestimated Oliver North, who returned from London with a new way to keep the program alive. In a bureacratic end run around McFarlane, North brought his brainstorm directly to his new boss, John Poindexter, sidestepping the more politically sophisticated old one. North's idea was to eliminate the complications caused by working through Israel and instead run the operation himself: simply merge the Iranian operation with Project Democracy, his secret contra operation. He wrote to Poindexter that they could deliver the weapons themselves, using Secord as their intermediary with Ghorbanifar.

The plan was audacious. It didn't eliminate any of the political risks of going forward; in fact, it increased them — by eliminating the fig leaf of Israeli participation and putting the United States in a direct deal with Iran. Moreover, instead of choosing the CIA or the Defense Department to handle the sales, they would use a network of freebooters led by a disgraced covert operations officer, Richard Secord. But it put the administration in control, and that appealed to Poindexter. After seeing Reagan's frustration at the December 10 briefing, the admiral knew that the president wanted the hostage initiative to continue. He told North to proceed.

But it was clear that the new operation would require a new finding. On Sunday, January 5, 1986, North and CIA general counsel Stanley

Sporkin went to Casey's large, French Provincial house off Foxhall Road, in an expensive development carved out of Nelson Rockefeller's former estate. They sat with Casey, an avid bibliophile, in a study crammed full of books and looked over the new one-page text. In addition to the rationale about opening relations with moderates in Iran by providing arms, North had inserted the words *third parties* among those who would be involved, specifically to cover Secord. Again, as with the December 5 finding, the order included a clause that Congress should not be informed. Casey read the finding and nodded his approval. North and Sporkin prepared to leave. But on their way out, Sporkin was struck by a glaring omission. "Tell me why we're not putting hostages in this document," he asked North.

"The secretary of state doesn't want it in," North volunteered. In fact, Shultz didn't even know that the finding existed. But North knew that omitting any mention of the hostages might protect the operation from his wrath if Shultz happened to discover it. In effect, he was trying to word the classified document so that it could serve as a piece of internal disinformation.

"Well, you know, it doesn't sound right to me," Sporkin said. "Let's go back and see the director." They marched back into Casey's study. "This is going to be a very sensitive finding," Sporkin pointed out. The hostages were an important part of the program, so they ought to be mentioned.

Casey benignly agreed. So Sporkin and North scribbled in a clause adding "the release of the American hostages held in Beirut" to the purposes of the operation.

The next day, January 6, at the regular morning briefing, Poindexter showed the president, Regan, and Bush a draft of the proposal for the revamped operation. To Poindexter's surprise, the president took out his pen and signed it. The new national security adviser had meant to introduce the finding only as an issue for discussion. But Reagan often signed papers by mistake. "When the president is reading something, whether it is a final or a draft, if he agrees with it he'll sign it," said Poindexter. As Rodney McDaniel, one of his top aides, put it, Reagan characteristically initialed documents without necessarily reading them. "Poindexter would go in and say, 'Shultz thinks this, Cap thinks this, and we think this.' The president would say, 'Where do I sign?' "

Even though Reagan had already signed his approval, on the morning of January 7, the NSC met in the Situation Room for the first and the only full meeting it ever held on the issue of selling weapons to Iran. It was the last time the president would be exposed to debate or even dissent on the subject until the policy surfaced publicly, some ten months later.

In addition to the men who'd been there the day before — Reagan,

Bush, Poindexter, and Regan — also present were Shultz, Weinberger, Casey, and Meese. Although Treasury Secretary James Baker was supposed to be invited to all such meetings — one of the conditions of his transfer to Treasury — Poindexter never notified him of any of those dealing with the sensitive Iranian arms deals. Much later, when this exclusion surfaced publicly, Poindexter apologized profusely to Baker, who smiled in his patrician style and drawled, "I don't think you'll ever know how truly grateful I am."

The full NSC meeting was in many ways a rerun of the less formal ones that had already taken place: Shultz and Weinberger argued bitterly against the deal. But now it was increasingly clear that the president wanted to go ahead, and now, despite growing evidence that the plan was going dangerously off the tracks, he had more support, not less. As had been true earlier, not all of those participating had all the information. Neither Poindexter nor Bush mentioned to the others that a finding had already been drafted — and even signed mistakenly by the president. Nor did anyone mention the two Israeli weapons sales in 1985; Shultz and Weinberger still had not heard the full story.

In place of McFarlane's tortured second thoughts was Poindexter, arguing for the policy on the dubious ground that it would be deniable.

Attorney General Edwin Meese too favored further deals and shot down all of Weinberger's legal arguments with a broad interpretation of executive privilege. The president, he said, has "inherent powers as commander in chief"; if he signed a finding, it was legal. Nor did the president need to comply with the law requiring that he notify Congress of the finding if he decided that telling Congress would be dangerous. It wasn't a novel interpretation of the powers of the president; it just hadn't been made quite so brazenly since Watergate. Following that constitutional crisis, Richard Nixon had been asked, "When the president does it, that means that it is not illegal, by definition?" And he had answered, "Exactly, exactly. If the president approves something for national security . . . then the president's decision is the one that enables those who carry it out, to carry it out without violating the law." Meese's approach to the issue was essentially the same.

Regan was now all for the policy as well. A month earlier, he had adamantly opposed it. But he had promised to let Reagan be Reagan; now, seeing quite clearly where the president's heart was, he had completely switched sides.

Bush, who had been absent the previous month, now too was also on board, according to Shultz, who looked around the room and found only Weinberger on his side. To Shultz "it seemed almost unreal."

And where, a month earlier, the CIA's McMahon had expressed polite skepticism in the December meeting, now Casey was talking up the intelligence benefits that he said would come from an opening to Iran.

Casey's own operations men had warned that Ghorbanifar was unreliable. Casey had insisted that Ghorbanifar was useful and told the professionals to evaluate him again. Four days after the NSC meeting, the CIA polygraphed Ghorbanifar, and of fifteen questions he showed deception on all but two: his name and nationality. But Casey wanted to go forward.

More enthusiastic than anyone else was the sentimental president, who wanted to revive the operation no matter what.

The green light for a third deal was immediately conveyed to North, who notified the Israelis that the United States was ready to move ahead. "Joshua has approved proceeding as we had hoped," he said in the schoolboy code he had worked out. "If these conditions are acceptable to the Banana, then Oranges are ready to proceed."

While the November shipment had resulted in an unexpected profit for Project Democracy, this deal had one built in. Within two days, North had discussed with the Israelis how they would split up the proceeds from the arms sale. His notes showed a $10 million total sale, of which $1.5 million would go to Ghorbanifar and $6 million would pay for the 1,000 TOWs, leaving a healthy $2.5 million profit. This time, following North's new plan, the Israeli middlemen were out of the deal; instead, the CIA "bought" the missiles from the Pentagon.

At the Pentagon, Weinberger told the deputy assistant secretary of defense, Noel C. Koch, to set up the details of the arms transfer. The secretary seemed unhappy, even edgy.

"Do we have a legal problem with this?" Koch suddenly asked. "Is somebody going to go to jail?"

There was a very short pause. "Yes," Weinberger snapped at his astonished aide.

The morning of Friday, January 17, almost as an afterthought at the very end of the regular Oval Office meeting, Poindexter made the reborn policy official by giving Reagan the finished text of the finding, a draft of which he had already mistakenly signed. The president, Bush, Regan, and Poindexter's aide Don Fortier were all standing, ready to leave the office. North had written a three-page memorandum explaining the plan. But Poindexter didn't circulate it for anyone else to see, and Reagan didn't read it. Instead, Poindexter quickly reminded everyone of the main points. The TOWs were going to Western-oriented factions, and these factions could come to power with the right encouragement. As he explained the scheme, the swap of arms for hostages was explicit. But he said it would be carefully limited: "If all the hostages are not released after the first shipment of a thousand weapons, further transfers would cease."

"Well," Poindexter later claimed that Reagan said, "if we get all of the hostages out, we'll be heroes. If we don't, we'll have a problem." Reagan then signed the single-spaced, one-page finding.

That noon, the so-called Family Group of Shultz, Weinberger, Casey, and Poindexter met for lunch in the Family Dining Room. When the subject of Iran came up, Shultz launched into his objections all over again; selling arms to Khomeini, he complained, was "unwise and illegal." There was an uncomfortable silence around the table. Reagan had signed the finding only three hours earlier, but nobody had told the secretary of state. Nor, when Shultz met with Reagan on another matter that afternoon, did the president tell him what he had done.

Shultz, whose experience had led him to denounce the plan as dangerously flawed, was being kept in the dark. In part, he had withdrawn from the conflict. When he saw that negotiations with Iran were going to continue despite his objections, he told Poindexter that he did not want to know any of the details of this operation.

His rationale arose from a peculiar fear that permeated the Reagan White House — being accused of leaking. Over time, the president had become increasingly fixated on news leaks, which he believed were undermining his administration. The hard-core conservatives, for whom it was politically useful to bait the press anyway, had managed to turn the accusation into a powerful weapon against those they saw as "disloyal." Reagan's first education secretary, Terrel H. Bell, disclosed in his memoirs that zealous conservatives successfully targeted and removed high-ranking members of his department whose views they didn't like by accusing them, sometimes falsely, of leaking to the press. It is strange that such a fear could have afflicted an official as powerful as the secretary of state, but the same ideologues had long been out to get Shultz, whom they saw as insufficiently loyal to Reagan's conservative agenda. In truth, all quarters of the administration leaked regularly in an effort to sway public opinion, tip internal debates, and aggrandize their own roles; it was as much a part of the job as signal phones and chauffeured cars.

But the secretary of state was especially vulnerable because of his outspoken opposition to one of Casey's recurring pet ideas — applying polygraph tests to those in a position to leak. Shultz's opposition stemmed from a prickly, old-fashioned sense of personal honor that was rare among the Reaganites. It had stopped him before from cooperating with zealous presidents. As secretary of the treasury in the Nixon administration, he had stubbornly rebuffed White House demands to launch Internal Revenue Service investigations against the president's political adversaries, earning him the Nixonian accolade, captured on the Watergate tapes, of "that candy-ass."

In November 1985, Reagan had signed a secret directive approving a new counterintelligence effort that included a "national polygraph program," authorizing lie detector tests for anyone with access to highly secret information. Shultz had objected, but Casey, Weinberger, and Meese pushed the polygraph clause through. Unable to torpedo the plan privately, Shultz made an unusual public display of his dissent. Asked by reporters if he would submit to the polygraph if the president so ordered, Shultz replied, "Yes — once." Then he would hand the president his resignation. "The minute in this government I am told that I'm not trusted is the day that I leave," he told reporters heatedly on December 22. And privately, toward the end of December, he halfheartedly offered his resignation to Reagan, who didn't accept it.

Casey had responded with a highly unusual, pointed attack, issuing a rare public statement: "There is an acute need [for] selective use" of polygraphs to protect the nation's secrets. In the end, largely because of the secretary of state's objections, Reagan backed down and abandoned the idea of the tests. But Shultz knew that he was under a cloud of suspicion; the episode, he said later, "put me at odds with the intelligence and national security community, to put it mildly."

And so, a month later, when it was clear that his opposition to the Iranian arms deal was not widely shared, instead of fighting further, he told Poindexter to spare him unnecessary knowledge. "I wanted to be informed of the things I needed to know to do my job as secretary of state," Shultz testified later, "but he didn't need to keep me posted on the . . . operational details. . . . It seemed to me, in the light of the suspicions cast on me as a result [of the polygraph flap] and the hostility, that I would [rather] not know that." He explained that he "felt it would probably leak — and then it wouldn't be *my* leak."

By cutting himself out of the policy loop, the man who proclaimed he would resign if he wasn't trusted was surrendering a piece of his honor. He knew, deep down, that the others didn't trust him; but if they didn't force the issue, neither would he. It was exactly the opening that Poindexter needed to conceal the NSC's dealings with Iran from the secretary of state for ten months. Twice during 1986, Shultz received reports that arms were being offered to Iran in exchange for American hostages, but Poindexter repeatedly told him that no such deal was under way. And although he saw the president privately on a weekly basis, for those ten months Shultz never again took it up with Reagan — who never mentioned it either.

The two men close to Reagan who had expressed serious qualms about the arms deals were now either cut out (Shultz) or gone (McFarlane). Of those who were left — Bush, Poindexter, Casey, and Weinberger — only Weinberger had misgivings about the policy, and he kept them largely to himself. Bush later said he might have opposed the deals if he had known about Shultz's objections, or if he had realized that they had become arms-for-hostage transactions, but he acknowledged giving full support to the arms sales to Iran. (It is difficult to understand how Bush failed to realize that the deals were swaps of arms for hostages, since he attended at least two dozen national security briefings where the terms were outlined; but aides said the vice president only learned about the issue in bits and pieces, and never stood back to analyze the entire picture.)

On the evening of January 17, when Reagan took his gold-tooled leatherbound diary in hand, none of this turmoil was reflected in his entry for that date. In the eye of the hurricane, all remained clear and calm. In a simple, seven-word sentence, the president wrote in pen: "I agreed to sell TOWs to Iran."

9

"A Neat Idea"

AS OLIVER NORTH TOLD THE STORY later, the idea was whispered in a bathroom in London's Churchill Hotel, a slightly flashy modern hostelry favored by wealthy Middle Eastern travelers.

It was January 22, 1986, and North was negotiating another sale of U.S. weapons to Iran. It would be the Reagan administration's third arms-for-hostage deal and the third time the promise of freedom for the hostages proved empty. But first North faced a round of haggling in a hotel room full of arms merchants. Every man there had his own agenda: Ghorbanifar, the glowering Iranian, was pursuing gigantic profits; Amiram Nir, the Israeli, was promoting his own government's interests; Richard Secord, the American, was seeking a way back into the covert operations game. In the company of such schemes, North's aims seemed almost straightforward: a sale of a thousand TOW antitank missiles in exchange for five hostages and a better relationship between Iran and the United States.

Not that North liked that kind of swap, he insisted later in his testimony before Congress. "I was, after all, the person who, in the United States government, had the responsibility for coordinating our counterterrorist policy. I had written the president's words: 'We will not make concessions to terrorists.'" So, North said, he told Ghorbanifar that a simple swap of arms for hostages was not enough.

"I went in there," he testified, "and I said, 'Look, these things aren't going to work. It's not going to get us from where we are today to where we want to be tomorrow.'

"Mr. Ghorbanifar took me into the bathroom. And Mr. Ghorbanifar suggested several incentives to make that February transaction work. Mr. Ghorbanifar offered me a million dollars."

"Out of the question," North recalled replying.

"And it was then that he came up with what I considered to be a far better idea," North recounted. "He suggested, 'Well, look, we'll just use some of that money to support the Nicaraguan resistance. . . . Why don't you use some of this money for that purpose?' "

It was an inspired notion. "For the very first time, in January, the whole idea of using U.S. weapons . . . was made more palatable," North said during his testimony. "I saw that idea — of using the Ayatollah Khomeini's money to support the Nicaraguan freedom fighters — as a good one. I still do. I don't think it was wrong. I think it was a neat idea."

Oliver North's story of the conversation was arresting, even convincing. And it was almost certainly not true.

North's "neat idea" would explode spectacularly ten months later, ending his career and destroying the credibility of the president he served. The revelation of the diversion of Iranian arms profits to the contras would touch off more than a year of investigations and virtually paralyze the White House. At the height of the crisis, members of Congress would even consider the possibility of the impeachment of the president, the same president who had won forty-nine states only two years earlier.

So it is worth pausing to consider Oliver North's "neat idea": where it came from, who approved it, and how an idea so flawed could become the secret policy of the United States.

A neat idea should have a thousand fathers, but this one turned out to be an orphan. Both North and Ghorbanifar disowned its authorship, even though the idea should not have required too much energy to conceive: it was an obvious paradox that North's contras were running out of money while his Iranians were awash in cash.

The one clear fact about the diversion idea is that it was born well before January 22, 1986, and not in a bathroom of the Churchill Hotel. By December 1985, North and Secord had already realized that the arms sales to Iran could help fund the contras, for they had quietly diverted $850,317 of an Israeli middleman's money to pay for the Nicaraguan project (the transaction Secord had dubbed "a contra-bution").

Weeks before his epiphany in the bathroom, North told an Israeli official that he intended to use the profits from the next Iranian arms sale to help the contras, according to the Israeli. And about the same time, Ghorbanifar told a CIA officer that arms profits could be used for "Ollie's boys in Central America" — a phrase that suggests that the Iranian had already discussed the idea with North. (The CIA man dutifully jotted the offer in his notebook — "Can fund contras" — but said it didn't seem serious enough to report to headquarters.)

North made a tape recording of the January 22 meeting at the Churchill

Hotel, but instead of furtive whispers it reveals North and Ghorbanifar openly discussing the projects they could undertake with their imminent profits. "I think this is now, Ollie, the best chance, because . . . we never get such good money out of this," Ghorbanifar said on the tape with a deep laugh. "We do everything. We do hostages free of charge; we do all terrorists free of charge; Central America free of charge."

Ghorbanifar himself called North's account of their meeting in the bathroom "a real lie" and said North was the one who came up with the idea of a diversion. Ghorbanifar's record of credibility does not inspire confidence, but in this case the evidence is on his side: the idea appears to have been North's.

North, in his boundless enthusiasm for secret schemes, apparently never seriously considered whether the diversion was legal or proper. In his view, as long as the money had not been appropriated by Congress and wasn't in the U.S. Treasury, there could be no objection to his siphoning some of it to Central America. "We diverted money out of the pocket of Mr. Ghorbanifar," he insisted. But as a question of constitutional law, the diversion was an abomination: a decision to finance "private" covert operations by selling government property — U.S. Army missiles — at a profit.

"On the formal level, the case is obvious," former secretary of state Henry Kissinger wrote. "The executive branch cannot be allowed — on any claim of national security — to circumvent the congressional prerogative over appropriations by raising its own funds through the sale of government property."

"You cannot spend funds that the Congress doesn't either authorize you to obtain or appropriate," George Shultz agreed. "That is what the Constitution says, and we have to stick to it."

Without that congressional check, any president could use the government as a personal fief, selling federal assets to endow private projects at whim. In the blunt words of the congressional committees that investigated the Iranian arms sales: "That is the path to dictatorship."

The question is more than academic. The power of Congress to deny money is often its sole effective restraint on presidential power. "The power of the purse," James Madison wrote in 1788, was the "most complete and effectual weapon . . . for obtaining a redress of every grievance." But exactly two hundred years after Madison, Ronald Reagan's men said they recognized no such restraint. John Poindexter dismissed Congress's laws on Nicaragua as mere "outside interference" in the president's work. "The point was, and still is, that the president has the constitutional right and, in fact, the constitutional mandate to conduct foreign policy," Poindexter testified. "His policy was to support the contras."

Thus, when North brought his diversion idea to Poindexter in January

1986, not only did the president's top foreign policy adviser see nothing wrong, John Poindexter admired the elegance of the idea.

"I think I have found a way we can provide some funds to the democratic resistance," North told his boss in the West Wing of the White House.

"Let me think about it for a few minutes," Poindexter replied. But by Poindexter's account, at the end of the same meeting — after no more than half an hour — he told North to go ahead.

The decision was momentous. It launched an audacious new covert operation; it added an entirely new objective to the Iranian arms sales; it was an important new factor in the contras' supply line. For all of those reasons, it was the kind of decision that normally should have been approved by the president.

Reagan, of course, repeatedly denied even knowing about the diversion, much less authorizing it. "They just didn't tell me what was going on," the president said.

Yet North said later that at the time, he understood that Reagan did approve the diversion. He testified that he wrote at least five memoranda outlining the plan for the president. Only one such memo survived; it ends with a line headed "RECOMMENDATION": "That the president approve the structure depicted above." But it does not bear the president's signature.

"I assumed that the president was aware of what I was doing and had, through my superiors, approved it," North testified. He acknowledged that none of his memos ever came back "with the president's initials on it, or the president's name on it, or a note from the president on it," but that was not unusual. Reagan often approved proposals orally and relied on aides to take care of the required paperwork.

Poindexter's account was quite different. The admiral testified that he approved North's diversion plan on his own, without ever mentioning it to Reagan or anyone else. "I made a very deliberate decision not to ask the president, so that I could insulate him from the decision and provide some future deniability for the president if it ever leaked out," he said. "If the president had asked me, I very likely would have told him about it; but he didn't.

"On this whole issue, you know, the buck stops here with me," Poindexter added, turning Harry Truman's model of presidential accountability on its head. "I made the decision. I felt that I had the authority to do it; I thought it was a good idea; I was convinced that the president would, in the end, think it was a good idea.

"I must say," he added, "that I don't believe that I estimated how controversial it would be."

During much of 1987, the mystery of whether Reagan knew about the diversion perplexed Congress and the nation. The diversion was not the only dubious decision made in Reagan's White House, of course, but it became a symbol, a test of the president's guilt, his complicity — or the extent of his detachment. It was the one crime in the Iranian affair for which there might be, in Watergate jargon, a smoking gun in the Oval Office. And it was the one crime for which members of Congress could conceive of demanding the president's impeachment.

Poindexter's testimony — that he had approved the diversion on his own — saved Ronald Reagan's presidency from instant ruination. Yet the admiral's account of his decision was baffling and, at times, contradictory. Poindexter contended that the diversion was both too trivial to bring to the president's attention — "a matter of implementation" — and, at the same time, too controversial for Reagan to touch. Poindexter said he withheld knowledge of the diversion from Reagan to provide him with "deniability." But the admiral neglected to create any record of this decision at the time that could serve as evidence that he had indeed kept the president in the dark.

Poindexter insisted that he knew that Reagan would have approved the scheme. When a White House spokesman said Reagan would have done no such thing, Poindexter calmly responded, "I would have expected him to say that. That's the whole idea of deniability." In effect, he was saying politely that the White House was lying to protect the president.

Given such frank appreciation of official deceit, it is little wonder that Poindexter's own credibility was suspect. In his 1987 testimony to Congress, the admiral acknowledged that he had lied to Congress, the press, even the secretary of state and the attorney general. Some of his testimony was difficult to believe, like his dogged inability to recall important conversations and his insistence that the only memo that mentioned the diversion was the one that survived. ("If you've got [another] memo, maybe I can remember it," he offered.)

North testified that Poindexter had discussed a "fall guy" plan under which one or both of them would take the blame if the diversion were discovered. Poindexter denied knowing of such a plan, but he played the role convincingly just the same, assuming responsibility for everything North did while shielding the president from blame. As Senate counsel Arthur Liman observed, North's account of the fall guy plan created a classic paradox: without more evidence, it was impossible to determine what was true and what was a cover story. "This man will never say anything that reflects adversely on his commander in chief," Liman said of Poindexter. "How do we know he's not still protecting the president?"

In the summer of 1987, twenty-six members of Congress heard Poindexter's account in stunned silence. In public, most struck attitudes of polite skepticism; but in private, many of them concluded that the account was almost certainly untrue. The chairman of the House Intelligence Committee, Louis Stokes of Ohio, said flatly, "I don't believe it. I just don't believe it." But others held their tongue. In a capital where deception is admired as an art, *lie* is perhaps the last dirty word.

In their formal report, the majority of the committees did not take Poindexter's sworn testimony as credible proof and confessed that they were still unable to decide whether Reagan knew of the diversion. "In light of the destruction of material evidence by Poindexter and North and the death of Casey, all of the facts may never be known," the report said.

Even Poindexter's own friends and colleagues found it difficult to square his account with the record of the meticulous, chain-of-command officer they knew. To some, like McFarlane, it was almost inconceivable that the admiral had made such a decision without consulting the president, whom he saw nearly every working day. To others, it was difficult to imagine that Poindexter had resisted telling Reagan the extraordinary news that he had solved the contras' financial problem.

Some offered alternative theories to try to explain the inconsistencies. McFarlane speculated that Poindexter might have learned about the diversion only after the fact and decided not to tell the president out of embarrassment. Another former official wondered whether Poindexter hid the diversion from the president because he did not want to risk having the plan turned down — or even because he had grown a little contemptuous of Reagan. Congressional investigators offered another hypothesis: Poindexter did not tell the president about the diversion, but CIA director Casey did. Or one of them might have told Reagan of the diversion, but only in elliptical terms, so that the president either did not understand what he was being told or chose to pretend that he did not. Even George Shultz, who said he had "no doubt" that the president did not know of the diversion, gave some credit to the elliptical briefing theory. "In this case, the decision was not to tell him at all," he said. "But you can imagine people going in and sort of passing something by the president in a way that he doesn't quite see, in a busy schedule, the significance of it."

In the White House of any other president, the idea that such a decision could have been made without the chief executive's knowledge would have been unthinkable. But in the White House of Ronald Reagan, where accountability was nonexistent, the unthinkable was entirely possible. Because of the compartmentalization and autonomy of the NSC staff, North knew he had a blank check to negotiate a deal like the diversion. North was accountable only to Poindexter. And Poindexter — at least according to his own testimony — was accountable only to himself.

Finally, others who met with Reagan and heard his denials at first hand found his protests convincing. Donald Regan, who was present in November 1986 when Attorney General Edwin Meese informed Reagan of the diversion, said it was clear from the president's shocked reaction: "He couldn't have known it."

The members of the Tower Commission, who interviewed Reagan in the Oval Office at the end of 1986, also leaned toward believing the president. "I can't say that he did or did not know," one member of the panel said in an interview. "But I walked out with a gut sense that [Reagan's disclaimer] was correct. It was reinforced by his general sense of confusion — one which you would not have expected him to show if he had really been the architect."

In the end, the one man who knew most about Reagan's knowledge of the scheme was, ironically, not Reagan himself but John Poindexter. Yet, after all the investigations and all the sworn testimony, some of Poindexter's own friends and colleagues — the people who knew him best and wanted to accept his story — still found it difficult to believe. Did Poindexter really withhold the good news of the diversion to provide Reagan with deniability? Or was he playing the fall guy, hiding the fact that the president knew in order to save the government he served? The questions remain unanswered — and, perhaps, unanswerable.

With Poindexter's approval for the diversion in hand, North went to work on the proposed third arms deal with Iran with new enthusiasm. On January 24, 1986, he wrote a memorandum for Poindexter outlining the swap: Iran would get 4,000 TOW missiles and a package of U.S. military intelligence about Iraq, and all five American hostages would go free. Along with those basic terms came a five-page schedule with the dramatic heading: "Destroy After Reading." It was Oliver North's Christmas list, one month late. The schedule described, day by day, a fifty-nine-step transaction including the delivery of the TOWs to Iran; the release of the American hostages as well as Italians, a Briton, Lebanese Jews, and fifty Shia Muslims; the return of William Buckley's body, seven months after his death; and, finally, the payment of $40 million by Iran to Ghorbanifar and Secord. The plan included one last item, drawn entirely from Ghorbanifar's inventive promises and North's grandiose fantasies. Under the line marked "February 11," North's schedule noted: "Anniversary of Iranian Islamic revolution. Khomeini steps down."

Compared with the earlier arms deals, this swap was no bargain. After two deals that had failed to free the hostages, the Iranians had actually increased their price from 500 TOWs to 4,000. And only shreds remained of McFarlane's original rationale: there was little here to build a broader U.S. relationship with Iran except for the donation of military intelligence to Khomeini's war effort. North's intention to charge exorbitant prices for the weapons could hardly strike the Iranians as a gesture of good faith. But North and Poindexter seem hardly to have noticed the growing contradictions. "The hostage plan is still working," Poindexter wrote to McFarlane in a message to his predecessor's home computer terminal. "George [Shultz] and Cap [Weinberger] still disagree on policy grounds, but are cooperating. More importantly, president and VP are solid in taking the position that we have to try."

The covert bureaucrats of the CIA and the Pentagon, on the other hand, were outraged by North's plan. CIA deputy director John McMahon told Poindexter directly that he was appalled by the idea of giving military intelligence to the ayatollah. "Giving them TOW missiles is one thing," McMahon protested in a meeting in Poindexter's White House office on January 25, 1986. "Giving them intelligence would give them a definite offensive edge. . . . That can have cataclysmic results." If Khomeini's armies defeated Iraq, McMahon explained, Iran's radical regime would control the entire Persian Gulf.

"We have an opportunity here that we should not miss, and we ought to proceed to explore it," Poindexter replied. "If it doesn't work, all we've lost is a little intelligence and a thousand TOW missiles. And if it does work, maybe we can change a lot of things in the Middle East."

McMahon steamed back to his office at Langley. The lunatics have taken over the asylum, he thought. He fired off a cable to the traveling Casey; asking for permission to resist the White House orders. His message was pleading, almost desperate. "We have been asked to provide a map depicting the order of battle on the Iran/Iraq border showing units," he wrote. "Troops, tanks, and what-have-you. . . . Everyone here at Headquarters advises against this operation, not only because we feel the principal involved is a liar and has a record of deceit, but secondly, we would be aiding and abetting the wrong people." He asked for Casey's confirmation of the White House order before turning any secret intelligence over to North. The cable came back from Casey: "Confirmed."

From that point on, the CIA reduced itself to providing facilities and expertise for North's adventures but accepted no responsibility for how they were conducted. Over the next nine months, at least four CIA officers would stumble across evidence that Secord was diverting profits from the arms sales to the contras, but none of them blew the whistle.

"We took directions," McMahon said later. "We followed directions." But after thirty-four years in the CIA and nearly four years as Casey's deputy, McMahon himself had reached his limit. That spring, he resigned and moved to California.

In February, the agency's intelligence analysts issued a new Special National Intelligence Estimate on Iran. Back in 1985, another estimate had helped launch the Iranian deal by predicting imminent chaos in Tehran and Soviet moves to exploit the situation, a warning that had impressed Casey and Reagan. This time, the conclusion went in the other direction: Iran now held the upper hand in the Persian Gulf war, and the country appeared more stable than before. But these findings ran against what the men at the top wanted to hear, and they were largely ignored. Despite the new intelligence, Casey and Poindexter continued to tell the president that Iran was in danger of losing the Persian Gulf war.

At the Pentagon, Weinberger reluctantly ordered his military aide, Major General Colin L. Powell, to arrange the sale of TOWs for North's new deal. The task bounced through no fewer than four generals before it landed on the desk of a lowly army major. The major, no expert on missile sales, flipped open a price list and quoted a figure for the most basic TOWs: $3,469 each. He didn't notice that the number was outdated and that the current price was $8,435. The difference, for the 2,008 TOWs that were eventually shipped, came to just over $10 million. Project Democracy, in other words, got a bargain.

On February 15 and 16, two Southern Air Transport cargo planes rolled past the mock-Spanish arms warehouses at San Antonio's Kelly Air Force Base and lumbered into the South Texas sky. The planes carried a thousand TOW missiles, the first weapons officially sold by the United States to Ayatollah Khomeini.

"Operation RESCUE is now under way," North told Poindexter in a computer message. "If all goes well . . . our schedule for releasing the Americans [is] on for Sunday, February 23. Something to pray for at church that day."

The first planeload of 500 missiles reached an air base in Iran within a day. But North's Sunday prayers went unanswered; the Iranians abruptly raised a new condition for the release of the hostages — they wanted to see the promised military intelligence first. North, Secord, and retired CIA officer George Cave were distressed, but nevertheless took off for Frankfurt to deliver the intelligence to Khomeini's agents.

It was their first meeting with an official of the Khomeini government — and it was a disaster. The Iranian was Mohsen Kangarlou, the radical prime minister's chief aide for weapons procurement — a purchasing agent, not a diplomat. They met at the Frankfurt Airport Sheraton on February 25 and 26. Secord brought his business partner, Albert Hakim, hastily disguised in a wig lest the Iranian recognize him as an old retainer of the shah. After only minimal courtesies, the negotiations began — and went immediately downhill. Hakim discovered that Ghorbanifar was deliberately translating falsely between English and Persian, misleading both sides into thinking they were on the same track. And the Iranian envoy, Kangarlou, ignored North's offers to talk about political relations and pressed immediately for a weapons deal.

"Mr. Ghorbanifar has told me that you promised to deliver a lot of Phoenix missiles," Kangarlou said.

"We have never heard anything about Phoenix missiles," North responded, aghast. The Phoenix is one of the most sophisticated air-to-air missiles in the American arsenal, far more powerful and expensive than the TOW.

Well, the Iranian replied, if Phoenix missiles could be obtained, "then we will start on the hostages."

North and Secord looked at each other. Start?

"You might not get them all immediately," the Iranian added. "But we will at least start on it."

North protested that he had been promised that all the hostages would be freed once the 1,000 TOWs landed in Iran. The Iranian was doubtful, but after the Americans held firm, he agreed that "a couple of hostages" would be freed after the TOWs arrived. Then, he said, U.S. and Iranian officials could meet for secret political talks inside Iran, and the other hostages would be released. It was a promise.

The CIA's George Cave walked out of the meeting appalled by what he had seen — beginning with the Iranian official's stupidity. "This is a man who . . . is on the low end of the scale of intelligence," he said. "He's full of a little fear and a little trepidation and a lot of distrust of the United States, for we truly are the Great Satan in his eyes." Cave was even more scornful of Ghorbanifar, who had "promised hundreds of Phoenix missiles, howitzers, TOWs — just about anything else he [Kangarlou] wants. . . . This is extraordinary nonsense. Essentially Ghorbanifar, as a negotiating technique, lied to both sides to get them to the table, then sat back and watched us fight it out. It was a real slugging match. It was awful."

Nevertheless, on Thursday, February 27, the second planeload of 500 TOW missiles landed in Iran. Once again, the Iranians reneged on their deal. The day before, Khomeini's man had promised that several hostages would be released when the TOWs arrived, but now he insisted on a meeting with American officials first. The delicately balanced exchange of arms for hostages had come apart again.

Poindexter was angry at the Iranians' betrayal. So was Donald Regan, who demanded, "How many times do we put up with this rug merchant type of stuff?" Nonetheless, Poindexter chose to press on, still hoping to deliver the hostages Reagan wanted. And Regan, the corporate captain who prided himself on his managerial prowess, never demanded a serious review. "At that point, we were deep in the middle of the tax bill and the budget battle, and I sort of lost track of, you know, what was going on," he confessed. "I wasn't paying that much attention to it."

In the February arms deal, the terms that Reagan had approved in his January 17 finding went straight out the window. In January, Poindexter had said that if the first 500 TOWs failed to win the release of the hostages, the rest of the deal was off. But in February, the United States shipped 1,000 TOWs to Iran and gained not a single hostage. The project had veered out of control, and no one in Ronald Reagan's White House was clear-headed enough to grab the wheel.

But there was one major gain: the Iranians paid $10 million into Richard Secord's account in Geneva. Secord paid out about $4 million to buy and ship the TOW missiles; the remaining $6 million was profit for Project Democracy and the contras. So from North's viewpoint, the deal was a partial success. He had hoped for both profits and hostages; for now, profits alone would have to do. He sat down at his PROFS keyboard and wrote an optimistic message to McFarlane at his home computer terminal; the former national security adviser had already agreed to lead a U.S. delegation to Iran.

Despite all that had gone wrong, North was filled with optimism. "I believe that we may well be on the verge of a major breakthrough — not only on the hostages/terrorism but on the relationship as a whole," he wrote. "We need only to go to this meeting, which has no agenda other than to listen to each other, to release the hostages and start the process."

"Roger Ollie," McFarlane typed back. "Well done — if the world only knew how many times you have kept a semblance of integrity and gumption to U.S. policy, they would make you secretary of state. But they can't know and would complain if they did — such is the state of democracy in the late 20th century."

The $6 million profit from the arms sale to Iran came not a moment too soon for Project Democracy. In Central America, the secret contra air force was still having trouble getting off the ground. Not until the beginning of February did Secord's air cargo line make its inaugural flight to the contras, and it carried only supplies, not weapons.

The plane was a C-7 Caribou, a propeller-driven workhorse from the early 1960s, which Secord bought with money from his Lake Resources account. Its cargo included rigging equipment, camouflage-patterned canvas gear, training manuals, and even a refrigerator. The most precious item was a $40,000 replacement engine for a disabled rebel plane. Secord's air operations chief, Richard Gadd, organized a crew of former covert operations airmen, and the Caribou hopscotched across North Carolina, Florida, and Texas, landing at little airfields to pick up bits and pieces of equipment. Then it headed across the Gulf of Mexico to the contras' sanctuaries in Honduras.

While traversing the rugged Honduran ridgetops, the Caribou abruptly lost an engine and began losing altitude. As the trackless mountains loomed below, crewmen frantically shoved cargo out the tail door to lighten the plane. Out went the canvas gear, out went the contras' refrigerator, out into the blue went the $40,000 replacement engine. When the plane finally crash-landed at the contras' air base at Aguacate, Gadd was livid — mostly, crewmen said, because they had jettisoned the extra engine.

Gadd and Secord did get a Maule short-takeoff plane down to Aguacate without mishap, but the tiny craft was too small to carry enough supplies deep inside Nicaragua. So, on February 18, North arranged for Gadd's air freight firm to fly a load of the State Department's "humanitarian aid" down to Central America. Gadd chartered a big L-100 cargo plane from Southern Air Transport and ferried the State Department's supplies from New Orleans to El Salvador. Then the plane stocked up with ammunition, took the short hop over to Honduras, and delivered its load to the contra troops. Gadd billed the State Department for the entire trip — "humanitarian" equipment and lethal weapons alike.

Bit by bit, the CIA was getting back into the contras' war as well. In December 1985, Congress had authorized the agency to provide coded communications equipment to the contras, along with training and advice on how to use it. Casey's men interpreted that permission broadly, considering almost anything permissible as long as it didn't directly assist specific combat operations. The CIA's men in Honduras streamed back into the contra camps, providing the rebels with radios, satellite data, aerial photographs, weather reports, computerized flight vectors, secret intelligence, and training. The Boland amendment still formally barred the CIA from giving the contras material military aid, but in practice, the rebels had access to almost every service the CIA could procure.

At Aguacate, two CIA men known to the contras and Secord's crew only as "Mick" and "Moe" watched over the rebel air force from a hilltop shack bristling with radio antennas. Eventually, they even set up a paratroop training program for the contras, complete with practice jumps. In Costa Rica, to the south, the CIA station chief oversaw construction of the secret airstrip for the private resupply operation there. "Sure they bent the rules," a senior U.S. military officer in the area said later. "It was for a good cause."

The U.S. Army helped the contras surreptitiously as well. In El Salvador, the chief of the American military advisory group, Colonel James Steele, helped arrange the construction of a warehouse for Project Democracy at the Salvadoran air base at Ilopango. And North wrote that the commander of the U.S. forces in Latin America, General John Galvin, knew about the work under way "both in Costa Rica and at Ilopango. . . . Gen. Galvin is enthusiastic about both endeavors."

In public, of course, no one mentioned that North, the CIA, and the army were helping the contras build a clandestine air force. Secrecy was the main reason, but North, Poindexter, and Casey also wanted to maintain the impression that the contras were at the edge of starvation, to keep up pressure on Congress — so that was what they told the president and the cabinet as well.

In fact, the truth was a bit embarrassing. The contras had an adequate supply of guns and ammunition, but they were running the minimum war necessary, waiting for their U.S. funding to be renewed. When the rebels did attempt major guerrilla operations, the results were usually uninspiring. And the rebel leaders seemed to spend more time squabbling with one another than organizing to overthrow the Sandinistas.

To those who could get a close look at the secret war, it was clear that not all was well. In February, at an elegant Georgetown party, the State Department's director of humanitarian aid, Robert W. Duemling, ran into CIA director Casey. Amid black ties and evening gowns, the aristocratic Duemling gave Casey a brief, blunt report on his latest visit to the contras.

"You've got a very thin reed there, Bill," the diplomat warned. "A very thin reed."

North and Secord had one more secret weapon: Spitz Channell, the right-wing fund-raiser. By the beginning of 1986, Channell was a major part of North's effort to fund the contras. The Iranian diversion held out the promise of bigger money, but North knew that the arms deals might always collapse. In that event, Channell's blue-haired ladies and their stock portfolios would still be there.

By the same token, North was central to Channell's ambitions to raise even larger sums of money. Channell used Reagan's name relentlessly in his pitch, for his contributors regarded the president with reverence and awe. But he needed Reagan's blessing in a more tangible way, and North was the man who could provide it.

At first, this meant nothing more than North's help in obtaining a letter of endorsement signed with Reagan's familiar signature. "Dear Spitz," one began. "Your efforts to educate the American public on the true nature of the Communist regime in Nicaragua are vitally important. . . . May God bless you."

Then came more briefings for Channell's donors in the Old Executive Office Building. The White House offered such sessions with minor officials to almost any sympathetic group, but Channell told his wealthy flock that they were extraordinary, solemn occasions and advertised them as "secret military briefings." He sent limousines to the airport to meet big donors and put them up at the elegant Hay-Adams Hotel. "President Reagan is asking for the help of people like you," he told them. "You would not be here unless the president wanted you here."

But what Channell really wanted was Ronald Reagan himself — not just at the bottom of a letter but in the flesh. If the president would attend one of his briefings, speak to his prospects, shake a few hands — that would be, in the donors' eyes, the mandate of heaven. Channell went to his public relations man, Richard Miller, with the question: How do we get a meeting with the president?

It's almost impossible to get a private cause on the president's calendar, Miller warned. But he promised to try, and he soon turned to a former personal aide to Reagan, David Fischer. Fischer, a young lawyer from Utah, had been the president's personal assistant from 1980 through 1985, a job that put him in closer daily contact with Reagan than any other aide. He was the president's coat carrier, pen finder, and Oval Office doorkeeper; he traveled around the world with Reagan, and when the president was in the hospital, Fischer slept on a cot in the room next door. His job, in other words, was one of small tasks and great trust.

Fischer, now in private business, was only too happy to sign a two-year, $480,000 contract to introduce Channell to top administration officials. But when Channell escalated his demand for a meeting with the president, Fischer asked for another $50,000. Channell agreed, apparently believing that Fischer was suggesting a fee-for-service arrangement: $50,000 for every meeting with Ronald Reagan. (Both Fischer and Channell later denied that, but two of Channell's aides insisted that the terms of the deal were clear.)

In January, Fischer followed the White House staff to California to lay the groundwork for the presidential meeting he had promised Channell. On January 2, he visited Don Regan at the Century Plaza in Los Angeles, and described Channell's group as having spent $3 million on television commercials supporting the president's policies and preparing to spend $3 million more. He did not mention that most of the money being raised was intended for Project Democracy's military airlift.

The chief of staff had a soft spot for Fischer. "I always thought he was a great guy," he said. "And he was tireless in his devotion to the president. . . . He went way beyond the call of duty." So when Fischer said his clients needed a few minutes with the president, and all in a good cause, Regan was happy to help. He patted Fischer chummily on the knee. "I hope you're being compensated for this," Fischer remembered his saying. Regan later denied making such a statement, but he acknowledged approving Fischer's request. "If NSC agreed, if our own people agreed, that's the checking we did," the chief of staff explained. It was a long way from the vigilant days of Baker, Deaver, and Meese.

The meeting with the president was set for January 30. Channell was jubilant. He invited all the contributors who had given his organization $30,000 or more — and put his fund-raisers to work persuading less generous donors that they still had time to make the grade.

When the day came, the briefing was held in the Roosevelt Room, the most elegant conference room in the White House. Around the long table sat Channell, his friend Eric Olson, his assistants, and nineteen contributors. Elliott Abrams, the assistant secretary of state, opened with a fervent little talk about Central America and the contras. Then, as Fischer hovered in a corner, Ronald Reagan strode jauntily into the room. Channell and the donors all applauded, wide-eyed. The president spoke for only a few moments, mostly simple words of thanks to the donors around the table for helping the effort to win aid for the contras from Congress. He praised their "selfless devotion to the cause of freedom and democracy" and said, "With your help we can prevent the consolidation of this Soviet client state on the mainland of our hemisphere." Then he was gone.

Of the nineteen contributors at the briefing in the Roosevelt Room, sixteen gave a total of more than $4 million to Channell's organizations. Almost $3 million of that went to North's contra effort; only a tiny fraction went to advertisements for contra aid, the ostensible purpose. Over the following year, Fischer arranged at least seven meetings or photo sessions with Reagan for Channell and his donors. During the same period, Channell paid Fischer and his partner a total of more than $662,000. From Channell's standpoint, the money was well spent.

As North charged ahead on his secret projects in Iran and Nicaragua, the White House speechwriters went to work on the president's annual presentation of his public agenda, the State of the Union address. Not surprisingly, it would include not a word about his hopes for a new relationship with Tehran and only a little about his desire for more military aid for the contras. Secrecy was only half the problem. Most of Reagan's advisers, beginning with pollster Wirthlin, wanted the president to stay away from subjects that the public disliked. "The domestic White House staff wanted the president engaged on positive issues — the ones Wirthlin would say were 'resonators,' " Rodney McDaniel noted. "The NSC agenda wasn't made of resonators." The theory turned into practice when Wirthlin, armed with his "speech pulse" system, joined in the process of refining the president's annual message. People didn't like long speeches, he said, so the maximum length was twenty minutes. Even though tax reform was one of the administration's main priorities, Wirthlin warned that any time a politician mentioned taxes, the public figured he was thinking about raising them. Many in the public were put off by Reagan's social agenda, many more by any specific proposals for cuts in the federal budget. And people were particularly afraid of Reagan's designs on Nicaragua. Wirthlin told the speechwriters bluntly, "It's his worst issue."

Those policies were the core of Reagan's second-term agenda, but Wirthlin urged the speechwriters to soft-pedal them and to stress, instead, Reagan's perennial promise to cut "the national budget — not the family budget."

That left the staff facing the problem of what else to put into the speech. At a meeting in the Roosevelt Room, Michael Deaver, who had been asked back to help on the address, insisted, "You've got to get something sexy." But the White House was just as barren of new ideas as it had been in the 1984 campaign. Donald Regan and his aides had pursued a strategy of keeping the economy strong and Reagan's popularity ratings high; when it came to fresh ideas for the nation's agenda, most of them just shrugged.

"How about catastrophic health?" asked Dennis Thomas, Regan's top political aide, referring to federal insurance to protect people from financial ruin because of massive medical bills. Expanding national health insurance wasn't exactly vintage Ronald Reagan, the foe of big government. But Deaver replied, "Yeah, that's sexy." The program became one of the few legislative promises in the address.

"It was like sitting around a Madison Avenue advertising agency," one speechwriter marveled. "It was just nauseating."

Reagan himself was curiously absent from the process. Most modern presidents have, of course, relied on professional writers to draft their speeches. But Reagan seems to have ceded not only the literary craftsmanship, but much of the basic content, to his unelected staff. The 1986 State of the Union address started, not with a set of ideas from the president, but with a speechwriter's outline — to which Reagan contributed exactly three points. One was a clipping from the conservative *Washington Times*, calling for more boldness in the campaign for aid to the contras. One was a brief note, scrawled in the margin of a draft, explaining why Reagan wanted the power to veto individual items in the federal budget. And the third was a question jotted next to a passage about teenage pregnancies: "Will this get to the subject of pregnancies deliberately sought in order to obtain welfare and independence from the family?"

With that sum of guidance, the White House speechwriters prepared a draft full of tough rhetoric on the president's favorite issues and sent it over to Regan for his approval. Then the text disappeared into a bureaucratic black hole — until Regan's aide David Chew called chief speechwriter Bently Elliott only four days before the address was scheduled. "Mr. Regan has seen a second draft and decided it will be forwarded to the president," Chew said.

The mention of a second draft threw the speechwriters into consternation. They discovered that a Regan aide had secretly rewritten their first draft to bring it into line with Wirthlin's cautious prescriptions. Out came several passages that had responded to the president's requests, including a call for "material assistance" to the contras. In place of the earlier, hard-edged rhetoric was a string of bromides. "Isn't it time for the United States of America to indeed be all it can be?" the new draft asked. "We cannot stop at the foothills when Everest beckons." And, in a double negative that suggested a certain want of craftsmanship, "We cannot perpetuate these problems no longer."

At that, Elliott and the other speechwriters rebelled. A third, compromise draft was produced and sent to Reagan the day before he was to speak. Thanks to Wirthlin's research, the speech was now short and featured the favorite "resonator" comparing the national budget and the family budget, as well as the call for a study into catastrophic health insurance. But it still did not include any of the three modest points that Ronald Reagan himself had suggested. It did not delve into the link between teenage pregnancies and welfare benefits, nor did it include Reagan's detailed language on the line-item veto. And despite the prod-dings of the *Washington Times* and the president's own predilections, its language on Nicaragua was cautious, not bold.

The president delivered his fifth State of the Union address on Feb-ruary 4, 1986. From the Regan team's standpoint, the speech was a smash hit. Wirthlin said its numbers were better than those for any pre-vious State of the Union, both in audience approval and the level of audience interest. But the speechwriters, who saw themselves as the keepers of Reagan's ideological flame, were outraged.

Whatever its drawbacks, rule by "resonator" had one great advantage: it helped keep Reagan extraordinarily popular. That fact did not escape Nancy Reagan, who had regular private sessions with Wirthlin and watched her husband's poll numbers closely. And since the president's popularity was the White House's chief measure of success, Reagan's high numbers in the polls boosted Donald Regan's standing as well. Both the First Lady and the press acknowledged that the chief of staff's ap-proach seemed to be effective.

But beneath the euphoria of success was an uncomfortable sense among some aides that the White House staff system was not working well. Some fretted that there was less openness than in the first term, both in the West Wing and at the NSC. The president was more isolated from the public view than ever; he had held only six press conferences in all of 1985, despite promises of one each month. And Reagan seemed insulated, even withdrawn, from debates within his own White House.

The State of the Union address was just one example. During the first term, speechwriters had sat in the Oval Office and discussed their ideas with the president. "By the time of the State of the Union, we could never get in," said one. "Regan made the final decisions on speeches — Reagan never got the options. It was bloodless, and it was quiet, but it was a coup."

Kenneth Khachigian, who was an old hand at writing Reagan's speeches, thought the new system inhibited the president as well. In the past, he had been able to talk with Reagan "one on one and get some real chemistry going," Khachigian said. But now, under what he called Regan's "imperial system," the sessions were invariably invaded by Re-gan and his aides. "The result," Khachigian said, "was that Reagan shuts up. He gives you no guidance. He feels confined and cornered."

The Iranian initiative provided another illustration of how much had changed. Those who dissented from the idea of selling weapons to Iran were systematically eliminated from discussions of the policy. By February, Poindexter tightly controlled the flow of information to the president about the Iranian deals. It is unclear how much Reagan knew, but it is clear that the president heard only the arguments of those who favored the arms sales, Poindexter and Casey; all others were left in the dark.

In fact, Poindexter and his staff at the NSC were slipping past effective management by Donald Regan or anyone else. Regan's office couldn't even get a count of the number of people who worked for the NSC, which was borrowing aides from other parts of the federal government at an alarming pace.

Oliver North took advantage of the situation to expand his own little staff. After Vice President Bush's task force on terrorism recommended beefing up the NSC's role, North persuaded Poindexter to give him two assistants to handle counterterrorism policy. One was Robert L. Earl, a marine officer and Rhodes scholar who had known North on Okinawa; the other was Craig Coy, a coast guard officer who had studied at Harvard Business School. On paper, neither man worked for North or was paid by the NSC; they were formally assigned to the Crisis Management Center and paid by the Pentagon. But they ensured that North's one-man office became even more of a power center and enabled the voracious lieutenant colonel to handle — at least for a time — the whirlwind of covert operations that he had sown. "Ollie was very clever in getting two staffers working for him," said another NSC official. "That freed him up. They really took care of counterterrorism for him so he was free to devote himself to Project Democracy."

North was also clever about office space. He and his new assistants soon moved from their cramped quarters in Room 392 into Room 302, a two-level, five-room suite with a splendid view of the Ellipse, the same greensward the president saw from the Truman Balcony of the White House.

The topsy-turvy growth of the NSC staff was worrisome to several of Regan's aides, who found it difficult to keep a rein on the demands of the swelling bureaucracy across the driveway from the West Wing. In February, one of Regan's men wrote a long memorandum to the chief of staff with a deliberately blunt warning: "From an administrative standpoint, the NSC is out of control. . . .

"Not only do I question the number of people on the NSC staff, but I also question the type of people," wrote the aide, Christopher Hicks. "Virtually every senior member of the NSC staff is either an active duty or recently retired career military officer or foreign service officer. I do not mean to suggest that these are not bright and able people . . . but I do wonder whether it is wise to rely almost exclusively on people whose past and, in most cases, future careers are in the two departments.

"Although it may not be my place to raise, I can't help but wonder whether or not the virtually unchecked amount of human and financial resources that support the NSC operation are worth it," Hicks wrote. "Is it a policy developer, a policy synthesizer, a crisis manager, or all three, or something else?"

It was time to ask whether a monster had been created, the young aide warned. "If that is not done soon with regard to the NSC, I am concerned that the legacy of this Administration may well be a sprawling bureaucracy . . . that tries to do a little bit of everything, but little of it well."

His words were prescient, but they went unheeded. Regan was too busy with the flood of presidential business he had insisted on handling himself, and he had no desire to pick a fight with Poindexter. The chief of staff never followed up on Hicks's warning, and Ronald Reagan never saw it.

10

Off the Shelf

CAMERAS CLICKED, sound men hustled, and television correspondents elbowed each other to capture the novelty of the moment: on March 12, 1986, Ronald Reagan ventured out from the heavily guarded White House into the open expanse of the front driveway, an exposed area frequented by handymen and journalists but scarcely ever graced by the president.

The stroll down the asphalt drive looked spontaneous, but assistant to the president William Henkel, the White House's resident stage manager, had given it considerable thought. Henkel knew the action would attract news coverage if only because it involved the president's appearance in an unexpectedly public spot. The press was so attuned to Reagan's habits that his use of a different chair in the Oval Office was cause for speculation and suspicion. (In one case, the suspicion was justified: in the summer of 1985, Reagan changed chairs in order to hide a scab on one side of his nose covering his then-secret skin cancer.) Reporters knew that Reagan seldom did anything spontaneous, so even the smallest alteration in his behavior drew photographers' zoom lenses.

On that day in March, Reagan wasn't walking alone. At his side was the veteran diplomat Philip Habib, whom Reagan was sending off to explore peace talks in Central America. The farewell, like most of the events in Reagan's public schedule, was planned by Henkel to put a special "spin" on the news. "We wanted to dramatize the diplomatic track," Henkel explained. "Liberals were saying that our only interests were in war and mayhem. This was scheduled to show that we wanted peace."

Behind the peace imagery was the White House's determination to get

Congress to vote, later that month, for $100 million in new aid for the Nicaraguan contras, $70 million of which was earmarked for military equipment. It had been a year since Congress had grudgingly voted $27 million in nonlethal "humanitarian" aid, and for the White House it was the biggest foreign policy vote of the spring. The administration was still easily thirty votes short in the House of Representatives, and if it took a peace plan to sell the war, they were ready.

In fact, that spring the White House tried a dizzying array of different political pitches in an effort to win the military aid. For a White House famous for sophisticated salesmanship, the message on this issue seemed confused and contradictory. This problem reflected both the amateurishness of the second-term team and the persistent conflict within the administration about the true goal of the policy.

At the center of the conflict was Patrick Buchanan, resident political pugilist. He had come out swinging with a column in the *Washington Post* on March 5, equating opponents of contra aid with supporters of communism. Buchanan, whose childhood heroes included Senator Joseph McCarthy, had been a right-wing standard-bearer in the Nixon White House, and this sally echoed some of the overheated accusations of the Vietnam War years. "With the vote on Contra aid," thundered Buchanan, "the Democratic Party will reveal whether it stands with Ronald Reagan and the resistance or Daniel Ortega and the communists."

Buchanan had sent the inflammatory column to the *Post* after checking it with his friend Oliver North — but without running it by his boss, the chief of staff. Buchanan was a political high roller; he didn't mince words or tactics, and he had been frustrated for more than a year by the timidity of his public relations–minded colleagues. He argued repeatedly that there were times when leaders won by losing — just by fighting for a cause, even one that was unpopular. A year earlier, Buchanan had lost his battle to have Reagan give an all-out, hard-line appeal for contra aid on television — he never even got the chance to argue the issue in front of the president. This time, he was determined to have an impact: if he couldn't get to the president inside, he would shape events from the outside. By firing an unauthorized first shot, one that took an unmistakably hard line, he gambled that Reagan would be forced to take sides — and when it happened, he'd take Buchanan's.

Predictably, the March 5 column caused "a heart attack among the Mice," as an official close to Buchanan later put it. They had hoped once again to win aid for the contras with as little public backlash as possible by quietly twisting a few arms on Capitol Hill. Influencing them was Wirthlin, who argued that Reagan was hurting both himself and the contra cause each time he spoke out. Thus when Will Ball, the ordinarily amiable head of congressional relations, came across the piece while reading the morning paper in his second-floor office in the West Wing, he hurled his bearish form down the narrow carpeted stairs to Regan's office and demanded, "Did you see this in advance?"

Regan, of course, was as surprised as Ball, and he hated surprises. Buchanan had committed a mortal sin: he had ignored Regan's rigid chain of command. This infraction might have enraged Regan more had not President Reagan read the piece after it was published and loved it.

Buchanan's words, after all, had the virtue of reflecting Reagan's own views. Taking Buchanan's Red baiting one step further, Reagan suggested in an off-the-cuff comment that the contras' opponents were unwittingly aiding the Soviet Union, like "fellow travelers" who had defended the Communists in the late 1940s, when Reagan became an FBI informant in an effort to purge them from Hollywood's unions. Said the president, "I've had enough experience with Communist subversives back in my former profession to know that a great many people are deceived and not aware that what they're doing is inimical to the United States."

To the continuing dismay of "the Mice," Reagan had few compunctions about speaking out. For him, the White House provided what Theodore Roosevelt once called a "bully pulpit" — in a way it was an extension of the banquet circuit through which Reagan entered public life. Reagan was a great believer in taking his causes directly to the people, showing a faith in the public not necessarily shared by his aides. As Dennis Thomas put it with a hint of exasperation, "Although history argues against it, Reagan actually believes that if you talk to the people on any issue, they'll make the right choice!" And so Reagan willingly starred in the spring scare campaign. The hard-liners were determined to win the aid this time, whatever it took. As it happened, it called for a level of hyperbole unusual even for the White House. One of the president's speechwriters conceded, "there was a real problem with rhetorical inflation — his words started losing their value."

Thus, on March 16, Reagan delivered a televised address from the Oval Office which marked a high point for heated rhetoric and a low point for presidential accuracy. The speech, accompanied by a dramatic map showing a red tide of communism sweeping Central America and lapping at the borders of the United States, was filled with alarming statements of "fact" — some of which turned out to be fiction. In one of the shakiest inventions, Reagan accused the Sandinista regime of wholesale involvement in the international drug trade. Sitting at his desk in the Oval Office, the president displayed a grainy photograph of an airplane and charged that it showed an aide to one of Nicaragua's top leaders loading cocaine bound for the United States. "No," he said, "there seems to be no crime to which the Sandinistas will not stoop — this is an outlaw regime."

It is doubtful, given his unquestioning acceptance of almost every line written for him, that Reagan knew that most of this account was seriously misleading. In truth, the photograph had been supplied by a convicted drug smuggler who had become a U.S. government informer in the hope that his own sentence would be reduced. U.S. Drug Enforcement Agency officials later acknowledged that the only cocaine shipment they knew of both into and out of Nicaragua had been flown by the informer and that Nicaragua was not a major transit point for drugs.

The Sandinista drug charge, like many other alarming statements in the speech, had been supplied to Buchanan and the speechwriters by Oliver North and the NSC staff; it fell outside the purview of the White House's ordinarily fastidious fact-checkers. (One of the checkers confessed the next day that she had no idea if any of the speech was true.) In his zeal to blacken the image of the Sandinistas, North and his colleagues apparently thought little about the consequences of abusing the president's credibility.

Many of the administration's claims to Congress during this period were similarly hyperbolic at best. Casey, North, Poindexter, and Reagan knew that millions of dollars of private funds had been funneled to the contras from Saudi Arabia and Taiwan — and, as some of them knew, from Iran and Spitz Channell's blue-haired brigade as well. Yet they told Congress that the resistance was destitute. North, who feverishly lobbied Capitol Hill, described vivid scenes of near-starvation; he said some of the troops looked like "survivors of the Bataan death march" and that contra medics had resorted to washing out old bandages in order to use them again. In essence, he was trying the same lines on members of Congress and their staffs that he'd used to such effect on Channell's dowagers. Reagan, too, echoed this desperate line. "Their supplies are running short," he warned in his March 16 speech.

But Congress still had its doubts. As Will Ball had feared, the Buchanan fusillade had incensed the Democrats and offended some Republicans who were important swing votes as well. Congressman Michael Barnes of Maryland, a leading Democratic opponent of the contras, called it "the moral equivalent of McCarthyism." Senator Nancy Landon Kassebaum, a moderate Republican from Kansas, said the White House was arguing "that this is a matter of patriotism — those who love America will support the president, and those who oppose [contra aid] want to abandon San Diego to the Sandinistas. I find this simplistic reasoning to be highly offensive."

On March 20, the House of Representatives rejected the president's aid request by a narrow margin, 222–210. It was a bitter defeat for the White House, especially since they had staked so much of Reagan's personal prestige on the line. But there was a significant consolation: although Buchanan's aggressive approach had not succeeded, it had effectively altered the terms of the debate. Instead of putting the onus on the administration to justify its designs on Nicaragua, the contra issue was pushing Democrats into an uncomfortable defense of an undemocratic, Soviet-backed government. Although the aid had been defeated in the first round, House Speaker Tip O'Neill had to promise members that they would be able to reconsider the issue soon. That meant the White House would get another chance. And momentum was finally building on the administration's side.

In Nicaragua, however, the reality was quite a bit less inspiring than the theatrics. On March 17, the day after Reagan's Red tide speech, North's young, idealistic courier, Rob Owen, sat down in his home in Georgetown and poured out his own disillusionment in a five-page memo.

Owen had worked for North for a year. Calling himself "a foot soldier" in the anti-Communist cause, he had trekked the swampy Nicaraguan jungles in the shadow of an idolized older brother killed in Vietnam. What he'd seen was not all he'd dreamed of. Owen had struggled to arm a Southern Front in Nicaragua, the theory being that opening up a war on many fronts was one way of overcoming the Sandinistas' superior military strength. But his efforts had been hampered by the petty political rivalries within the contra leadership. The Northern forces of Adolfo Calero had brazenly hoarded the weapons that the United States had tried to send to the supposedly allied rebels in the south. There were other problems, too. Owen had a sneaking sense that the idealistic crusade against communism was a romantic illusion. For some of those involved, "the war," as he put it, "has become a business."

Addressing his memo to North, Owen wrote, "If members of the US [government] think they can control Calero, they also have another thing coming. . . . Take a close look at the people around him, those who he intimately trusts. Unfortunately, they are not first-rate people; in fact, they are liars, and greed- and power-motivated. They are not the people to rebuild a new Nicaragua. In fact, the FDN [the largest contra faction] has done a good job of keeping competent people out of the organization."

There was evidence of corruption, too, Owen warned: false receipts submitted to the State Department and black market currency transactions — even apparent profiteering on medical supplies. (The State Department had paid $416,000 for medical purposes, but the contras' chief surgeon said he had received only $102,000 worth of goods.) "There is some money going somewhere," Owen wrote. "I am not saying it is being pocketed, but there are questions unanswered. . . . If the $100 million is approved [by Congress] and things go on as they have these last five years, it will be like pouring money down a sink hole."

He included a particularly sour note about Richard Secord, the resupply operation's secret godfather: there were rumors that Secord and other arms dealers were all making big profits from supplying the contras. "Some people are complaining . . . that the prices they are getting are not as good as they could be," he wrote. The reality of the war was so grim, Owen concluded, that it might be better if he ended his own involvement.

That afternoon, Owen took his letter to North and waited for his reaction. North read the memo and looked at him. "Dick Secord's a great American," North said in his most sincere fund-raising voice. "He's honest. He took his own money to set up the programs and set up the proprietaries. He's not doing this because he's trying to make money, but because he's trying to see a project become successful."

It wasn't surprising that Owen's warning fell on deaf ears: by the spring of 1986, North had a substantial stake in protecting Secord. Secord had given North the ability to live his most ambitious fantasies. Bitter bulletins from the front were about the last thing North wanted to hear — and the last thing he wanted anyone else in the bureaucracy to hear. Owen's worries about the contras apparently never got past North; they almost certainly never reached the president. Just as the CIA analysts' skepticism about the "moderates" in Iran had been discarded, so Owen's firsthand warnings about serious problems weakening the contras — and ultimately Reagan's crusade — were also quickly shelved. The ideological model had no room for facts that didn't fit.

"Nobody tells Ronald Reagan bad news," a State Department official said later. "Nobody's told him that we're going to fall short. Nobody's told him that the contras can't make it by the end of his term."

Nobody told Reagan the hard truth about the contras. And he surely never went looking for it.

An illusion of success distorted the real picture in Nicaragua too, for the contras' chronic difficulties were masked by the robust financial health of Project Democracy. The operation now included ten companies, most of them no more than random names attached to bank accounts: Lake Resources, Albon Values, Defex S.A., Dolmy Business Inc., Gulf Marketing Consultants, Hyde Park Square Corp., Toyco, Udall Research. The only real companies were Stanford Technology Trading Group Inc., the Secord-Hakim business base, and Amalgamated Commercial Enterprises Inc., a company Gadd was using to run the contra airlift. But as evanescent as the companies were, Project Democracy was in the process of acquiring some very real property. It owned an airstrip in Costa Rica, bought four cargo aircraft, and was soon to purchase its own oceangoing freighter. In its accounts in Geneva, in the wake of the February arms sale to Iran, sat the substantial balance of $6.8 million. Oliver North's "off the shelf" covert operations agency was quickly becoming a conglomerate with expanding horizons.

If Project Democracy was a confusing web of dummy corporations, that was exactly the way it was supposed to be. In organizing it, Secord had turned to an international financial mastermind, Willard I. Zucker, a former IRS lawyer who had lived in Switzerland for twenty years. Zucker's specialty was hiding money in offshore accounts around the world, from Geneva to Liberia to the Cayman Islands.

The only problem was that this profusion of private enterprise confused even the agile minds of Oliver North and Albert Hakim. North finally had to ask for an organizational chart, and Hakim labored at a borrowed computer to draw one. At the top were three "collecting companies," like Lake Resources, into which income was to flow. There was no real difference among them, Hakim explained; but if one were ever discovered by the press or anyone else, it could be quickly dissolved and replaced by another. In the middle of the page were four columns. The first was labeled South America — Hakim's grasp of Western Hemisphere geography was uncertain — and included a "treasury company," which would disburse funds to two "operating companies." One of the operating companies owned the contra arms and made payments to contra leaders; the other bought the airstrip and the airplanes. The second column was headed Middle East. It featured the account that handled money from the Iranian arms sales. The third column, labeled Africa, contained only a suggestively empty box. Hakim later explained readily why Africa was there: Secord had told him, "Who knows? If we do a good job, the president may send us to Angola." Finally, off in the right-hand margin, was a fourth column containing the financial services firm that handled the banking and kept the books. This firm would receive the "reserve" — the profits that would turn Project Democracy into a permanent, privately run covert action organization. It would collect the funds that North and Casey had discussed. With this funding they could operate, as they put it, entirely "off the shelf." In March 1986, as Rob Owen was expressing his doubts about Secord and the contras to North, Hakim started the reserves with a $2 million deposit — apparently from the proceeds of the February arms sale to Iran.

The chart was not entirely accurate. It should have shown a fifth column, listing the separate accounts set up for Albert Hakim, Richard Secord, and the firm that they owned. By the spring of 1986, after most of their arms purchases for the contras had been completed, Secord's and Hakim's accounts had each taken in $1.1 million, apparently in commissions on the sales, and their firm had received $360,000. Secord later contested the charge that his account represented his own profits. But Hakim testified that he had understood it to be Secord's. Perhaps more telling, money from it went to Secord's personal bank account in Virginia ($74,600); to Secord as cash ($33,000); to pay for Secord's 1986 Porsche ($31,825); and to pay for the hard-working general's stay at a health farm ($3,075).

North personally got no money at all from Project Democracy's accounts, as far as can be determined. But the "reserves" were covered by a fiduciary agreement: if Hakim should die, control would pass to Secord; and if Secord should die, control would pass to North. More important, North got access to a pool of funds to use for his own rapidly expanding covert operations. In effect, this relatively unknown White House aide now had a global charge account with which he could set up extralegal covert operations anywhere around the world. Despite its flattering name, Project Democracy had no congressional oversight and no public accountability. In fact, it turned U.S. foreign policy into a private venture.

Project Democracy took its first big step beyond the contras and Iran when it bought a ship. The story of its purchase bore all the signs of North's manic ambition. It began earlier that year, when North learned of an administration proposal for the CIA to send a shipboard radio station off the coast of Libya to broadcast propaganda against Qadhafi. Who better to perform such a stunt than Project Democracy? Secord and his friend Tom Clines went looking for a ship and found the M.V. *Erria*, a rusty 163-foot Danish freighter that had already carried a cargo of guns for the contras to Honduras. On April 28, Project Democracy purchased the freighter for $312,000, complete with crew and running costs of $50,000 a month. But when they tried to convince the CIA to choose them for the mission, they found that it had no interest in any deal involving Tom Clines.

The episode, however, brought Project Democracy to the attention of many in the CIA's hierarchy (if they had not known of it before). Some would wonder later how North operated so brazenly without detection by the rest of the intelligence community. In this instance, he was helped by an old friend, the chief of European operations — Dewey Clarridge — who took steps to protect the operation by restricting its visibility within the CIA.

Even so, by the end of May, at least five senior officers at the CIA knew that a low-level White House aide, Oliver North, was running a ship — and had "his own resources" with which to run it: Casey, George, Clarridge, Fiers, and the chief of operations for the Near East, Tom Twetten. But none of them seems to have asked how a lieutenant colonel on the NSC staff commanded the resources to finance a ship — a puzzling lack of curiosity from America's top intelligence officers.

Although Project Democracy was prospering financially, its military operations were foundering. Secord had been working on the contra airlift for nine months, yet he had not dropped a single load of military supplies into the jungle. Even in late March, when a Sandinista offensive had nearly overrun the contras' base camps, Secord was unable to organize a relief flight to the troops. Facing military disaster, the contras appealed to their CIA advisers for help. Congress had explicitly prohibited the agency from participating in military operations; even so, the chief of the CIA mission to the contras, Jim Adkins, ordered his helicopters into the air. The unmarked aircraft evacuated wounded troops and carried supplies to the rebel units — a clear violation of the law.

Finally, on April 1, Project Democracy made its first and long-awaited private supply flight. Using a Caribou, it was a quick flight from Honduras over the border into northern Nicaragua. The crew dropped 3,440 pounds of grenades and ammunition to the contras in the green hills below — the first of many such drops. Over the next ten days, the little Caribou flew fourteen missions into Nicaragua, dropping a total of thirty-seven tons of weapons and ammunition.

They were not comfortable flights. The Caribou was a relic of the early 1960s, a lumbering twin-engine short-takeoff utility plane, the rough equivalent of an airborne jeep. The planes were outfitted with the most rudimentary radar and electronics; eventually, some of the pilots installed standard highway "fuzzbusters," which seemed to do a better job of detecting Sandinista radar. The flights were often hair-raising. Even more dangerous than the Sandinistas was the spectacular jungle terrain. Mountains seemed to shoot out of the clouds, and large sections of the aviation maps for the area were simply blank, bearing the ominous legend: RELIEF DATA INCOMPLETE.

"I couldn't believe the cheapness of the operation," said Iain Crawford, who was the loadmaster on some of the early flights. "The Caribou we were using had holes in the dashboard. We weren't using navigational equipment." On the ground, the Sandinistas had plenty of defensive weaponry: Soviet SA-7 antiaircraft missiles, which could home in on the hot exhaust of an engine as high as 10,000 feet; ZSU 23-4 mobile antiaircraft guns, each with four gun barrels and an efficient radar aiming system. But the planes did get through, and at long last the contras in northern Nicaragua were getting some supplies by air.

Supplying the allied guerrillas on the Southern Front, as Rob Owen had complained in his memo, was quite a different story. In March, the jealous Northern leader, Adolfo Calero, had done everything in his power to block efforts to share the weapons with the others. Finally, in April, North persuaded him to rise temporarily above petty rivalries and let some of his weapons go to the struggling Southern Front.

Reaching southern Nicaragua, however, required a much larger plane. For help, Oliver North turned to the State Department's "humanitarian aid" program, as he had in February. North realized that a cargo plane could deliver its boots and uniforms (which the State Department considered "humanitarian"), then load up with guns for the military airdrop. The State Department, without asking North any questions, chartered a Lockheed L-100, a big four-engine cargo plane known more often by its military designation, C-130. The plane and crew belonged to the CIA's old airline, Southern Air Transport.

On April 10, six men assembled at a safe house in San Salvador to plan the Southern Front mission. Iain Crawford, the loadmaster, walked into a smoky room and found Felix Rodriguez, whose nom de guerre was "Max Gomez." Rodriguez was George Bush's old CIA friend, the operations boss in El Salvador. Also in the room were U.S. Army colonel James Steele, the chief of the U.S. military advisory mission in El Salvador, and the two Bay of Pigs veterans, Quintero and Posada.

"It was a flight planning session," Crawford said in a subsequent interview. "Max . . . did the planning. Colonel Steele helped with information. He told us where the Sandinista radar was, when to turn our lights off, and what kind of radio contact we could have." The crew knew this would be a risky mission. They would fly from Ilopango Air Base, in El Salvador, some 300 miles down the length of Nicaragua's Pacific coast, then cross the top of Costa Rica, perform a quick jog inside Nicaraguan airspace for the drop, and then make their getaway over the Caribbean Sea to Honduras.

Before leaving the air base, Colonel Steele inspected the plane himself. "He came in back with me and wanted to know what the cargo was," Crawford said. "It was written on the boxes — AK-47. He questioned me about the footlockers. I told him they contained G-3 rifles. He questioned me if they were padded properly, said he didn't want any of the barrels to get bent. Just before we took off, he gave us two M-16 rifles and several grenades as personal survival equipment, in case the plane went down," Crawford said, shaking his head at the memory. "I wasn't sure what we were supposed to do with the grenades."

As planned, the L-100 flew southeast from Ilopango, skirted the dark line of Nicaragua's Pacific coast, and turned east over Costa Rica. Then it turned north again, heading across Nicaragua's lightly guarded southeastern border, searching for the drop zone in the pitch black jungle. But something had gone wrong on the ground: the area of the drop zone remained dark. The plane circled for a nerve-racking half hour before the crew decided to quit and fly back out to safety.

The next night, April 11, they went through the same drill: the meeting at Max's house, Colonel Steele's inspection, the takeoff into the night. This time, the drop went like clockwork. Out in the Nicaraguan jungle, visible for miles, blazed a line of primitive beacons: three hilltops on fire. A little farther on was the drop zone, brilliantly lit by torches in the jungle blackness. As the contras waited below, seventeen parachute loads of guns and ammunition came floating down. Crawford called it "a perfect drop."

In San Jose, the capital of Costa Rica, CIA station chief Joe Fernandez had helped plan the mission, despite the legal prohibition on CIA assistance for military operations. He sent a triumphant message to North, confirming that the drop was on target. The mission's success inspired him to look ahead: "My objective is creation of a 2,500-man task force which can strike northwest and link up with [a contra commander] to form solid southern support force. Likewise, envisage formidable opposition on Atlantic Coast resupplied at or by sea. Realize this may be overly ambitious planning but with your help believe we can pull it off."

The successful delivery pleased Secord, as well. On April 20, he and North flew to Ilopango for a half-day meeting with Steele, Rodriguez, the contra leaders, and the commander of El Salvador's air force. It was Secord's first (and only) visit to Central America. That afternoon, Secord and North took Iain Crawford back to Washington with them on an executive jet so that he could regale them with the details of the L-100 flight to the Southern Front on the way home. "Secord talked about how the operation reminded him of Vietnam," Crawford said. North, looking sharp in his white khaki bush outfit, seemed unusually quiet. At one point, he turned to Crawford and said, "Thank God we got away with it."

But there were still problems. For one, Felix Rodriguez was complaining increasingly about the way Secord was running the operation and threatened to blow the whistle on it by calling his old friend George Bush. Rodriguez had become convinced that Secord was making massive profits from the contra war, and was upset to find men who had been linked to Edwin Wilson, the renegade CIA agent, involved.

Rodriguez made sure the others realized that his relationship with Bush was real. He decorated his little office at Ilopango with autographed pictures of the vice president; he made a point of visiting Bush's office whenever he was in Washington. In January, Bush's military aide, army colonel Samuel J. Watson III, had visited Central America with Rodriguez as his guide. Watson toured the contras' camps, addressed a throng of rebel fighters ("You have friends in Washington," he told them), and even accompanied Rodriguez on an aerial combat mission against the leftist guerrillas in El Salvador. (Bush and Watson later denied knowing that Rodriguez was involved in the contra airlift — despite Watson's eight-day visit to the region and despite a Rodriguez meeting with Bush for which the official agenda promised that Rodriguez would give a briefing "on the status of the war in El Salvador and resupply of the contras." Watson, who drafted that agenda, insisted that he never wrote the reference to "resupply of the contras" and could not imagine how it came to be on the vice president's agenda.)

But Secord had other concerns. He also told North that Project Democracy's contra accounts were nearly out of money. If there wasn't a new infusion of cash soon, he warned, he would have to dip into the $2 million reserve he had set aside for insuring arms flights to Iran.

This, he said, would make it difficult or impossible to continue the Iranian operation. Secord apparently did not tell North about the other accounts, which held some $2.4 million at the end of April. Nor, presumably, did he tell North that Project Democracy had just paid him another $50,000 profit on its arms sales.

Alarmed, North began searching frantically for more money. "The resistance account is darn near broke," he wrote to McFarlane. "Any thoughts where we can put our hands on a quick $3–$5 million? Gaston [Sigur, the assistant secretary of state for East Asia, who had helped with an earlier solicitation] is going back to his friends [the government of Taiwan], who have given $2 million so far. . . . The pot is almost empty."

In the end, though, the pot was replenished from two familiar sources. One was Spitz Channell's favorite Texan, Ellen Clayton Garwood. After a particularly emotional appeal from North, who summoned up tears as he told her that the contras might not survive long enough to see Congress restore their funds, Mrs. Garwood turned over $1.6 million in cash and stocks to Channell, most of which went to Project Democracy. The second was North's other major donor: Ayatollah Khomeini of Iran.

In the spring of 1986, as his concern about funding for the contras grew, North launched an effort to put together a fourth arms deal with Iran. But the Iranians didn't seem as eager — or as reliable — as he would have liked. When he asked for a meeting, the Iranians stalled. And it still wasn't clear that these Iranians even had the ability to free the hostages — the rationale for the deals in the first place. "What we may be facing," a CIA officer wrote in March, "is evidence that [Kangarlou] does not have the authority in Tehran to make it work."

The Americans were also dissatisfied with Ghorbanifar. Ever since their meeting in February — when Albert Hakim realized that the arms merchant was deliberately mistranslating their negotiating positions — North and his colleagues viewed Ghorbanifar with a new skepticism. Hakim denounced his countryman as an opium addict. And Secord even told Ghorbanifar that he was recommending that the Iranian be "terminated" — a figure of speech the panicky arms merchant took the wrong way. When he learned that Secord merely wanted to eliminate his role as a go-between, he was mollified only slightly and spent hours telling North that he was absolutely essential to the deal.

Despite problems with the Iranians, the hope of skimming more cash for the contras provided a powerful motivation to continue working toward another deal. Ghorbanifar came to Washington for a series of talks on April 3, meeting nearly all night with North, Cave, and Tom Twetten of the CIA at the drab, modern Ramada Renaissance Hotel, near Dulles International Airport. Shortly afterward, probably on Friday morning,

April 4, a tired North summarized the agreement that had been reached in a memo to the president. His memo would be discovered seven months later by Justice Department investigators and become famous as "the diversion memo." It would cost North his career and shake the foundations of Reagan's presidency, but at the time North apparently saw it merely as a matter-of-fact description of the deal he was assembling. Once again, the plan called for the sale of arms to Iran in return for the hostages. But his memo shows that the release of the hostages was only one of the objectives; equally important, from North's point of view, was the fact that the agreement would result in $12 million "to purchase critically needed supplies" for the contras.

But the deal never came off. Instead, the Iranians continued to haggle. On April 14, they demanded that half of the weapons arrive in Iran before they released any of the hostages. And they asked for another meeting in Frankfurt before a U.S. mission arrived in Tehran.

Poindexter was losing patience. He told North that the negotiations could continue, but he said that all the hostages had to be freed before another U.S. weapon moved to Iran. "None of this half-shipment-before-any-are-released crap," the admiral insisted. "If they really want to save their asses from the Soviets, they should get on board."

Before a new deal could be arranged, however, there was yet one other little interruption: the key mediator, Ghorbanifar, was arrested. The resourceful arms merchant, it seemed, had been working on a side deal — a separate weapons sale to Iran that unfortunately turned out to be part of a U.S. Customs Service "sting" operation. Swiss police, acting on a request from Customs, arrested Ghorbanifar in Geneva and held him in jail for a day. By that time, North and the other Americans were no longer surprised by anything. They heard out Ghorbanifar's complaints about his treatment and kept on negotiating. Although events suggested that the Iranian initiative had strayed seriously off the track, no one at any level of the operation seemed deterred.

The delay in setting up the deal — which hinged on a proposed meeting in Tehran, one that McFarlane would lead — was frustrating to North, but not to George Bush. The vice president was preparing his own trip to the Middle East, and he knew enough about the planning for McFarlane's mission to worry that it might embarrass him while he was visiting Saudi Arabia, one of Iran's Arab enemies. In early April, Bush asked Poindexter to postpone the Tehran trip so that it wouldn't happen while he was visiting the Middle East. He added that he wouldn't insist on a postponement if it would endanger the Iran initiative or the hostages. But the Iranians were so snarled in their own delays that the timing proved to be no problem, and Bush made his visit without incident.

While the public and the press were told only half the truth about

Nicaragua, they were told even less about Reagan's policy on terrorism. All spring, they believed Reagan was taking an increasingly hard line, judging from his highly visible war of words and weapons against Libya's bizarre champion of terrorism, Muammar Qadhafi. The White House's contradictory policies toward the two terrorist states of Iran and Libya escalated in their intensity at the same time, and while one became increasingly secret, the other became ever more of a show.

The despicable Qadhafi was a perfect target, a cartoon character Americans loved to hate. Qadhafi had praised the Christmas 1985 machine gun massacres at the Rome and Vienna airports as "honorable." He had decidedly odd personal habits: he reportedly liked to use makeup, wear women's clothing, and travel with a teddy bear. Most experts said Qadhafi was less important than other sponsors of terrorism; Georgetown University's Robert Kupperman said Syria was really a "planner of the terrorism business," whereas Qadhafi was "merely a theatrical booking agent." And many believed in fact that Iran had been behind the bombing of the U.S. marine barracks in Lebanon. But for an administration looking for a simple victory in its confused war against terrorism, there was no easier mark. Libya was neither strategically nor militarily formidable. Taking Qadhafi on was the counterterrorism equivalent of invading Grenada — popular, relatively safe, and theatrically satisfying. As the spring unfolded, the White House campaign against him quickened.

It was conducted with more than geopolitics in mind. Concerned that its visible initiatives meet with the public's approval, the White House had ensured that it would be popular too. In fact, the campaign against Qadhafi, like so many other policies, was partly guided by a series of secret polls. Some of these polls were conducted at the expense of the Republican National Committee by Richard Wirthlin. But, over time, Don Regan became so covetous of the Wirthlin information that, according to the NSC staff, he refused to share it. In frustration, they resorted to conducting their own polls; they used a Defense Department grant to pay a former White House official, Ronald Hinckley, and his Washington think tank $400,000 to sample public opinion for the NSC in general and Oliver North in particular. Both Wirthlin and Hinckley, though private citizens, were privy to matters of extreme secrecy and sounded out thousands of people on such sensitive questions as how they would feel about a U.S. attack on Libya and under what circumstances they would support it. By mid-March, public opinion favored military retaliation, as long as the strike was seen to be a quick and "reluctant" response rather than one resulting from U.S. provocation.

Meanwhile, Qadhafi declared a "line of death," threatening any who passed within 120 miles of his coast. It was a clear violation of the internationally recognized 12-mile limit; but given the relative insignificance to the United States of navigating freely through the Gulf of Sidra, the reaction from the White House was surprisingly strong. In a March 14 NSPG meeting, Reagan approved plans to send in a virtual armada of 45 ships, 200 planes, and even nuclear-powered attack submarines; in all, some 15,000 U.S. military personnel would be involved. Nine days later, American forces streamed across Qadhafi's "line." As could be expected, Libya attacked the U.S. ships, but with little effect. Within two days, the United States calculated that seventy-two Libyans had been killed without a single U.S. casualty.

This skirmish hardly quelled tensions. In Beirut, Qadhafi's agents retaliated by paying the ransom asked by the kidnappers of American hostage Peter Kilburn, then murdering him. "Qadhafi bought him," acknowledged one senior State Department official, explaining that the NSC had been on the verge of doing so itself with a scheme that would use trick disintegrating dollar bills. "In effect, you might say Qadhafi outbid us."

On April 5, tensions escalated further. Terrorists who were said to be sponsored by Libya blew up a West Berlin discotheque frequented by U.S. servicemen, killing two Americans and a Turkish woman and injuring 230 others. It was all the provocation needed by a president who had told his aides for more than a year that he was looking for "a clean shot" against terrorism. In a press conference on April 9, Reagan used his mastery of communications skills to rally public opinion, denouncing Qadhafi as "the Mad Dog of the Middle East."

Naturally, inflammatory rhetoric heightened expectations of retaliation. The president's aides were indeed working with military planners to prepare a full-fledged attack against the Libyan leader, but they did not want to encourage speculation. So Oliver North went to work. Knowing that NSC aide Johnathan Miller enjoyed good press relations, North told him that the United States didn't want an incident, that the right ships weren't available, and that the French wouldn't approve overflights — a plethora of reasons that there could be no retaliation. At North's direction, Miller called John McWethy, the State Department correspondent for ABC News, with the story, and ABC anchorman Peter Jennings redid his show to include a report saying that action against Qadhafi was unlikely. After the broadcast, North offered his crooked-toothed smile to Miller and said, "That was the best disinformation I've ever seen." Miller was furious.

On April 14, shortly after 7:00 P.M. Washington time, some thirty navy and air force bombers shelled Tripoli and Benghazi, while nine F-111s attempted to drop their lethal cargo of laser-guided bombs on Qadhafi's desert compound. (In the end, mechanical problems intervened and only two planes dropped their bombs inside the compound; one F-111 and its two crewmen were lost.) The raid occurred at 2:00 A.M. Libyan time, and although administration spokesmen denied it, it was clearly aimed at striking the leader in his sleep. Two of his sons were wounded, and an infant he claimed was his adopted daughter was killed. But Qadhafi survived.

The public had been primed for six years for just this sort of action, so the bombing raid was tremendously popular at home — as the NSC had already determined it would be, based on its extensive private polling. Richard Wirthlin's surveys showed that an impressive 75 percent of the public approved of the raid — and a CBS–*New York Times* poll showed that Reagan's overall approval rating shot up to 68 percent, even higher than it had been after the assassination attempt in 1981. After all, the polls also showed that there was only one world leader whom the American public reviled more than Qadhafi: Iran's Ayatollah Khomeini.

Thus, some three weeks after the bombing of Libya, it was not at all surprising that George Shultz was quietly furious when he learned that the administration was taking a very different stance toward Iran. For a man with Shultz's sphinxlike demeanor, the signs were subtle, but his aides knew them well. His mouth would tighten, his face would flush momentarily, and his usual expressionless monotone would take on, for a brief and frightening moment, a genuine edge of anger.

On May 4, Shultz had every reason to be angry. He was in his paneled suite at Tokyo's luxurious Okura Hotel during the annual economic summit of industrial nations, where united allied action against terrorism was the top order of business. The United States had used all its political might to strong-arm its more reluctant European allies, like France, into signing a strong decree calling for cooperative efforts to fight terrorism. In an unusual display of enthusiasm, Shultz himself had taken the podium before hundreds of international news reporters and, with a genuine gleam in his blue eyes, declared that the new policy said to terrorists, "You've had it, pal." The moment, like the summit itself, seemed to belong to the Americans.

But in the privacy of his suite, Shultz had just been handed a secret cable from Washington revealing the hollowness of all he'd been working for. It suggested that the recent triumphs were a sham, that expediency, not principle, and improvisation, not coherence, were the true state of affairs inside the Reagan White House. The cable had been sent by his trusted undersecretary, Michael H. Armacost, and it began with a warning: he was about to offer "a very disturbing report."

The U.S. ambassador in London, Charles Price, had learned that Adnan Khashoggi and the chief terrorism adviser to the prime minister of Israel, Amiram Nir, were trying to persuade a British entrepreneur, Roland "Tiny" Rowland, to invest in an Iranian arms deal. The deal was being arranged by Ghorbanifar, whom the cable described as "a sleazebag of dubious repute." Rowland, who knew Khashoggi well enough to be suspicious, had upset the scheme by checking it out with an acquaintance at the U.S. Embassy. "According to Nir and Khashoggi . . . the scheme was okay with the Americans — it had been cleared with the White House," the cable said. "Poindexter allegedly is the point man. Only four people in the U.S. government are knowledgeable about the plan. The State Department has been cut out." Armacost closed with a caustic comment of his own: "Legal concerns seem not to impose any constraints whatsoever on our friends in the White House."

Shultz took the cable in hand and set off down the hotel corridor in search of John Poindexter. But he was not to be found; instead, Shultz encountered his sometime golfing partner Don Regan, who, when told about the cable, seemed to be alarmed. Regan said he would take it up with the president when he saw him, and later Shultz said he reported back that Reagan had been upset when he heard of the deal. Months later, testifying under oath, Regan admitted he had not in fact spoken with Ronald Reagan. To those who knew him, this wasn't surprising: Regan often told others he would consult with the president. But many of the staff, from the speechwriters to former national security adviser Robert McFarlane, had their doubts about how often and how thoroughly the chief of staff truly involved the president — and how often he chose to "protect" Reagan from what he deemed unnecessary information. This incident proved to be a case in point: during his testimony, when reminded of the cable's serious implications and asked why he had not talked about them with the president, Regan replied, "I'm not sure that I thought that of sufficient importance to involve the president."

Later that day, Shultz did challenge Poindexter about the cable and was told, "We are not dealing with these people. This is not our deal."

Technically, Poindexter was correct: he and others at the NSC were not involved in this particular deal. (In fact, it was Ghorbanifar freelancing again.) But Poindexter did not tell Shultz that the NSC was deeply involved in another Iranian arms deal and that in fact McFarlane was on the brink of traveling to Tehran with a shipment of HAWK missile parts. "There is only a smidgen of truth in it," Poindexter assured Shultz, who went away with the impression that there were no ongoing operations involving the U.S. sale of weapons to Iran.

Similarly, Poindexter personally assured Ambassador Price by phone that there was "only a shred of truth" to the report. Then, as Poindexter later testified, he sent North a message "wondering what in the world Mr. Nir was doing." Poindexter's actual message to North — preserved as an electronic PROFS note — was somewhat more pointed. He wrote, "We really can't trust those SOBs."

The next day, May 5, Poindexter ordered North to London for another meeting with Ghorbanifar. Now especially sensitive to the State Department's concern, Poindexter told North to be sure not to let the U.S.

Embassy know he was in town. On May 6, North and Ghorbanifar met at the Churchill Hotel to pin down the details of McFarlane's impending visit to Iran and the arms deal — now the fourth — that he would complete in person. Ghorbanifar raised North's hopes by announcing that the American delegation would be met by a contingent of Iranian dignitaries, including Iran's president, prime minister, and speaker of parliament — and perhaps even by Ahmed Khomeini, the powerful son of the ayatollah. These men represented most of the Iranian power structure. In return, however, the Iranians insisted that some American weapons had to come on the same airplane as McFarlane. They refused to wait until after all the hostages were released, as Poindexter had insisted so forcefully only two weeks earlier. North readily agreed to the concession.

North's interest in the hostages was apparently being overtaken by his vision of the profit that could be generated for Project Democracy and the contras. North sketched out a truly massive deal. He planned to provide the Iranians with 236 HAWK parts and two sophisticated radar sets. The inflated price he planned to charge would give Project Democracy an instant $13 million profit.

Eventually, the radar deal fell through, and Ghorbanifar was left brokering only the sale of the 236 HAWK parts. Even so, both sides kept their profit margins healthy. Project Democracy would receive profits of about $8.6 million; Ghorbanifar's gross profit would amount to $9.5 million — a cumulative markup of 457 percent.

Ghorbanifar often protested that he was never interested in the trivial profits in these little deals, but $9.5 million must have looked enticing all the same. In fact, this was to be Ghorbanifar's big deal, the one that would pay his bills for the year. The Iranian had only one problem: he didn't have the capital to finance the sales up front. Iran was too suspicious of the United States to pay for the weapons in advance, and the Americans were too suspicious to let Tehran have the missiles on credit. So Ghorbanifar had to find "bridge" financing to pay the CIA for the missiles just long enough for the ayatollah to take delivery and pay the bill. He turned, logically enough, to his friend and partner since their 1985 meeting in Hamburg, Adnan Khashoggi.

By 1986, "King Adnan," as he was proclaimed at the lavish fiftieth birthday party he threw for himself in Spain, was one step ahead of the creditors. He needed a quick deal like this one to stay afloat, but even he didn't have $15 million at hand to pay for it. So Khashoggi turned to his own secret contacts to put the financing together. By the middle of May, the Saudi entrepreneur had deposited $15 million of this money into Lake Resources, Project Democracy's Geneva account. Others said Khashoggi was to receive $3 million for his trouble; Khashoggi said no, he had only been helping out for "humanitarian" purposes, and the cash was for other services.

"I believe we have succeeded," North wrote in a message to Poindexter once his negotiation with Ghorbanifar was completed. "Release of hostages set for week of 19 May in sequence you have specified. Specific date to be determined by how quickly we can assemble requisite parts. Thank God — he answers prayers." This euphoria was at best misleading. As North knew, the Iranians had not committed themselves specifically to release all the hostages. But North told Poindexter they had, and Poindexter so briefed McFarlane — which would lead to one of the major misunderstandings of the Tehran visit.

On May 15, in his regular morning briefing of the president, Poindexter gave Reagan an update on the planned mission. Of Reagan's top advisers, only Regan, Bush, and Casey also knew of the impending trip. The president approved the mission, apparently without any questions. Later, Poindexter said he didn't remember any extended discussion at all.

If the president was ever told about the diversion, this would have been a likely time. North testified that he had prepared — specifically for the May 15 meeting — a memorandum for the president about the diversion. But such a memorandum has never been found; North did not attend the briefing. Poindexter later said he could not remember ever seeing the memorandum, and he testified that he never discussed the diversion with the president — not on May 15 or at any other time. The others in the meeting said the discussion about the arms deals with Iran was brief and that the subject of the contras never came up.

Poindexter later said he felt comfortable keeping information about the diversion from the president, because he was sure Reagan would have approved. After all, Reagan prided himself on avoiding the dangers of micromanagement. Moreover, Poindexter claimed, he'd interpreted Reagan's will by observing the president on the long plane ride over to Tokyo on May 1 — some three weeks before the Tehran trip.

Flush from the popular success of the Libyan bombing raid, the president seemed frustrated with the same old constraints imposed on his conduct of foreign policy by Congress and the Constitution. He had been avidly reading a book on terrorism that celebrated Israel's ability to act swiftly and unilaterally in the name of national security, when Poindexter approached him with a list of possible compromises they could strike with Congress on contra aid.

Reagan spoke enthusiastically about the possibilities of taking bold unilateral action without worrying about congressional approval, the way the Israelis could. Then, according to Poindexter, the president said, "I'm really serious. If we can't move the contra package before June 9, I want to figure out a way to take action unilaterally to provide assistance."

Poindexter, of course, had already found a way. "I was sorely tempted at that point to tell him what we had working — but I thought better of it, and did not," he later said.

For a man nurtured in the military chain of command, this was strange indeed. Yet it also has to be pointed out that around the same time that Poindexter said he decided not to tell the president about the diversion, Regan decided not to tell the president about Shultz's cable, North didn't pass on Owen's suspicions about contra corruption, Ambassador Duemling's warnings to Casey at the black-tie party never penetrated the Oval Office, and no one apparently told the president that the speech he delivered on March 16 had been filled with errors. Somehow, it seemed, the White House was filled with people who, for one reason or another, felt they could literally take the president and his approval of their actions for granted.

If Poindexter did mean to protect the president from any knowledge of the diversion, he had to keep a close eye on North. Not only was North the man most familiar with the details of the operation, he was also — in Poindexter's view — less careful about secrecy than he should have been. The record shows that North was willing and even eager to tell the president and others about his "neat idea." And at least twice during this period Poindexter moved firmly to shut him up.

The first occasion was an NSPG meeting on May 16. The president and others in the room were in despair about the difficulty of finding funds for the contras. Poindexter obliquely summarized the problem and its potential solutions without any mention of the recent help from Saudi Arabia and Taiwan. Instead, the admiral distributed a briefing paper outlining options. One was described as "a direct and very private presidential overture to certain heads of state. Such a step," it said, "would likely allow us to demonstrate the viability of the resistance without having to endure further domestic partisan political debate." But the option, it warned, had a downside: "The foreign contributors would ultimately expect that their largesse would result in some kind of USG concession in their favor."

Shultz, who didn't know that the administration had already secretly followed this plan, suggested it was a great idea if it could be done legally. Reagan, who did know about the Saudi money since he had helped to secure it, did not comment. Instead, he listened intently as the various sources of potential aid were discussed and then asked with seeming innocence, "What about the people who have been giving money for television ads?"

By this time, Oliver North could contain himself no longer. He began to speak up. Poindexter furiously signaled to him to remain quiet. And North obeyed.

But the president's lack of awareness puzzled North. He was apparently confused about who knew what. After the meeting, North went back to his office computer terminal and wrote a note to Poindexter, suggesting that surely "the president obviously knows why he has been meeting with several select people to thank them for their 'support for democracy' in [Central America]." He explained to Poindexter that he'd simply wanted to say that things were not nearly as desperate as they seemed. Thanks to Khashoggi's deposit, "the resistance support organization now has more than $6 million available for immediate disbursement. This reduces the need to go to third countries for help."

North went on to discuss two other issues raised by the meeting. First, Shultz's lack of awareness about the secret solicitations of foreign money could prove to be an embarrassing problem. What if Shultz should start to solicit unknowingly from allies who'd already given? And North was concerned about how to handle the chief of staff, adding, "I have no idea what Don Regan does or does not know re my private operation."

Poindexter wrote back: "I understand your concerns and agree. I just didn't want you to bring it up at NSPG. . . . I guessed at what you were going to say. Don Regan knows very little of your operation and that is just as well."

Poindexter believed, in the words of another NSC official, that "Don Regan had two problems: he talked too much, and he talked too much." He had also become increasingly worried about keeping North's mouth shut. He had been alarmed to learn the week before that another NSC staffer and two CIA men knew of Project Democracy's ship. The admiral had warned North that he was letting his "operational role become too public. From now on," Poindexter ordered, "I don't want you to talk to anyone else, including Casey, except me about any of your operational roles," he said.

Yet on May 19, as the risky Tehran trip approached, North again showed signs of confusion about whom Poindexter had cut off from the flow of information. He made an emotional plea to Poindexter for a meeting that would include McFarlane, the president, and maybe Casey, Shultz, and Weinberger as well. But Poindexter refused. "I don't want a meeting with RR, Shultz and Weinberger," he replied curtly.

The following day, North practically begged Poindexter to have a meeting with McFarlane before dispatching him to the hostile territory of Tehran. Even if no one else seemed to have sensed the danger of sending a former national security adviser, keeper of the nation's most closely guarded secrets, into the jaws of the enemy, North grasped the peril with his usual dramatic flair. "In my humble opinion, [it would] be very thoughtful if you can find a few minutes to discuss the issues above [with] him and say good-bye. While I'm confident he'll be back next week, I could be wrong and it might be a very long time before anyone sees him again." Poindexter saw McFarlane the next day — alone.

Those who might have objected to the risky mission had been successfully cut out. As far as is known, none of those who knew — Bush and Regan and Casey among them — raised any objections or worried aloud about the political perils involved. The United States was about to send another shipment of arms to Iran — the fourth in eight months. And although the previous three shipments had resulted in the release of only one hostage, no one reviewed the policy, set any benchmarks, or demanded any particular standard of performance. There was no contingency planning for the possibility that fewer than all the hostages would be released; there were no formal meetings on the mission held by either the NSC or the NSPG — forums designed to expose the president to all sides. The policy seemed to have taken on a life of its own outside of ordinary channels, outside of thoughtful oversight, beyond discussion and debate.

On May 22, in the final days before the Tehran trip, Peter Rodman, a deputy to Poindexter, sent the admiral a worried memo. It was a warning shot from a seasoned professional suggesting that the NSC had drifted into a dangerous orbit, with no one thinking about its course. "We might be gearing our policy too much to the hostage issue rather than to the strategic menace that the [Tehran] regime represents," Rodman wrote. "The special one-page finding of a few months ago put the hostages in a properly subordinate place among our objectives — but in practice our approach seems to require a hostage release as an early token of good faith."

The admiral never replied.

II

Into Tehran

TEHRAN HAS ALWAYS BEEN an unlovely city. It spills chaotically down a sloping plain in a vast brown jumble, the invention of twentieth-century kings who turned their backs on Persian tradition to ape the industrial centers of the West. Automobiles choke its dusty streets, and a pall of smog often obscures the only relief on the landscape, the long, sere shoulder of the Elburz Mountains rising from the city's northern suburbs. The minarets of Tehran's mosques are outnumbered by the rusting spikes of paralyzed construction cranes, relics of a dynasty that ran out of money, time, and fear. Instead, the city's new landmarks are a grisly fountain of blood, which spouts crimson dye in praise of Muslim martyrs, and ubiquitous posters of Ayatollah Ruhollah Khomeini, the revolutionary who made Tehran the capital of "the world's first government of God" — and, to some, the capital of world terrorism as well.

Into that unwelcoming landscape on Sunday morning, May 25, flew Bud McFarlane and Oliver North. They bore false Irish passports, a brace of gift-wrapped .357 pistols, a chocolate layer cake decorated with a brass key — and suicide pills in case the gifts were ill received. As their unmarked Israeli 707 approached Tehran's Mehrabad International Airport, McFarlane and North believed they might be on the verge of a diplomatic master stroke. For seven years the United States and Iran had been bitterly estranged; there had been almost no communication between Washington and the most powerful government on the strategically important Persian Gulf. In McFarlane's mind, at least, this mission to Tehran had more ambitious goals than winning the release of American hostages in Beirut. If the Iranians agreed to even a modest cooperative relationship with the United States, the Reagan administration could virtually redraw the political map of the Middle East. An Iranian-American entente would be a major vexation for the Soviet Union, which was already worried about Iran's support for Muslim rebels in neighboring Afghanistan.

There had been months of preparation. The airplane carried HAWK missile spare parts, secure communications equipment, maps for an eight-hour intelligence briefing for the Iranians, and an outline of the terms of a new U.S.-Iranian relationship. The HAWK parts were lashed to a pallet behind the passenger seats. "You had to trip over it to go to the head," Oliver North noted. Eleven more pallets — also loaded with missile parts — were on a second plane under Richard Secord's command, waiting on the ground in Israel. None of the parts was to be released until the hostages were freed.

The delegation itself was ready for serious negotiations. In addition to McFarlane and North, as personal envoys of the president of the United States, the plane carried Howard Teicher, the NSC's senior director of political-military affairs; George Cave of the CIA, who spoke fluent Persian and who grew a mustache to disguise himself for the mission; a CIA radioman, who set up a temporary coded satellite link to Washington; and, riskiest of all, Israel's Amiram Nir, posing as an American because of the Iranians' hatred of the Jewish state.

They expected to meet with the very top rank of Khomeini's Islamic government: the president, Mohammed Ali Khamenei; the radical prime minister, Mir Hussein Moussavi; and the powerful speaker of the parliament, Ali Akbar Hashemi Rafsanjani. Back in Washington, Poindexter waited anxiously in the White House. Secord stood by at the Israeli air force base on the military side of Ben Gurion Airport. The State Department's hostage team was on alert, beepers at the ready, to welcome the American captives who would soon be released in Beirut.

The white 707 touched down without fanfare and taxied to a halt near Mehrabad's giant international passenger terminal. McFarlane, North, and the others entered the VIP pavilion and watched as a squadron of Iran's U.S. F-4 jet fighters, relics of the shah's military buildup, took off with an earsplitting roar. In the distance, from the terminal, glowered the unmistakable image of Khomeini, along with a banner bearing one of the ayatollah's favorite precepts in international affairs: AMERICA CANNOT DO A DAMN THING.

But there was no one to meet McFarlane on the tarmac. For one anxious hour, no one came to greet the delegation of the president of the United States except a few curious airport officers.

Finally, the Iranian arms merchant, Ghorbanifar, turned up with the Khomeini government's arms buyer, Mohsen Kangarlou, and a crew of bearded, rifle-toting Revolutionary Guards, troops of Iran's radical, irregular army. With no further ceremony, they scooped up passports, pistols, and cake — as well as the pallet of HAWK missile parts inside the plane. McFarlane and North were displeased when they learned that the parts had come off; they were supposed to stay on the plane until the hostages were freed.

Then the Americans were bundled into cars for a breakneck ride past the shah's giant victory arch, now covered in graffiti celebrating Khomeini, up past Evin Prison, where Khomeini's political prisoners were held, and, with tires squealing, into the driveway of the Tehran Hilton Hotel, now renamed the Independence. Within moments they were on their way to the top floor, where, at least according to Tehran legend, every wall concealed a microphone. The Americans seemed to have the entire floor, a series of suites including one that became the delegation's conference room.

Many months later, Speaker Rafsanjani would reveal the fate of one of the gifts at the hands of the young Revolutionary Guards: "The kids ate the cake." That was partly a result of the Americans' arriving during Ramadan, the month when devout Muslims fast, foreswearing all food and drink (except water) from sunrise until sundown. It is a time when people are generally irritable; many stay home from work, and business slows to a crawl.

For several hours, it wasn't clear whether any Iranian officials would come see the visitors at all. The Americans tried to get some rest, but with their suspense unanswered and a spectacular view out their fifteenth-floor windows — Tehran's mysterious skyline on one side, the Elburz Mountains on the other — sleep was impossible.

"Don't worry," Ghorbanifar said soothingly. "The hostages will be released. Things are going in the right direction."

McFarlane was not impressed. "It may be best for us," he cabled back to Washington, "to try to picture what it would be like if after [a] nuclear attack, a surviving Tatar became vice president; a recent grad student became secretary of state; and a bookie became the interlocutor for all discourse with foreign countries. . . . The incompetence of the Iranian government to do business requires a rethinking on our part of why there have been so many frustrating failures to deliver."

At five o'clock in the afternoon, an Iranian official finally showed up — but instead of the president or prime minister, it was a man who identified himself as Ali Najavi, a deputy to the radical prime minister. (The Americans later discovered that this name was false; they never learned his true identity.) Najavi was bearded, in his thirties, and wearing a suit with no necktie. Kangarlou, Ghorbanifar, and two other aides came with him. The two delegations sat together in the living room of the hotel suite.

These were not the people McFarlane had come to see, but he gave them his best pitch, beginning on a conciliatory note. "I want to express, on behalf of President Reagan, our pleasure to be in Iran to start what we hope will be a sustained discourse between our two countries," he said. "Obviously, we've had disagreements over the past eight years. But the United States recognizes that Iran is a sovereign power, and we should deal on the basis of mutual respect, not intimidation.

"That's why, before we begin high-level talks, we must put behind us the hostage-taking which has occurred in the past," he said. "We are pleased that informal talks resulted in an agreement on the release of American hostages. Once that is completed, we can begin serious talks."

Najavi ignored the invitation to say something encouraging about the hostages and instead launched into a lecture on Khomeini's revolution. "This revolution depended totally on God, on independent Iranian power, and on a unique ideology," he said. "This revolution cost a great deal of blood."

"We don't want to align with East or West, but that doesn't mean we don't want relations. Once a bridge of confidence is established, then other priorities can be addressed and solved," he continued. "We expect from you that the United States will supply physical [material] support to Iran. U.S. support will be with us. This is the best way to build confidence — for the United States to demonstrate that it is with Iran."

McFarlane steered the discussion politely back to the hostages. "Regarding the commitment of the United States to turn a page [in relations], this is expressed by my presence on behalf of the president. The corresponding commitment on the part of your government to put the past behind us is to use your influence to secure the release of captive Americans. They are not held by Iran, but the captors are also subject to Iranian influence. Finally, as an earnest showing of our good faith, we are prepared to transfer certain items which may be of assistance; we have brought some of these with us."

Finally, the Iranian took the bait. "For humanitarian reasons, we have acted on your hostages," Najavi said. "But we expected more [weapons] than what came on the aircraft."

"We couldn't bring it all on the plane," McFarlane said. "But the rest can be brought forward as our talks progress.

"The corresponding act on your side, a humanitarian gesture, involves the release of our people," he repeated. Drawing a distinction fine enough for a theologian of any faith to admire, he added that although the release of the hostages and the delivery of the weapons would occur in tandem, the two events were actually "separate and not related."

Najavi offered what he saw as a concession. "What Iran expected in parts is not here. But as a humanitarian gesture, Iran will send a delegation to Beirut to solve that problem."

The Americans were alarmed. Had the Iranians not even begun to work on the release of the hostages?

"Everything depends on good will and renewed confidence," Najavi went on. "But we were told that one half of the equipment would be brought with McFarlane. You did not bring one half. This behavior raises doubts about what can be accomplished."

McFarlane's temper rose. "Let's be clear," he said. "I have come. There should be an act of good will by Iran. I brought some things along as a special gesture. So far, nothing has happened on your side. However, I am confident it will."

"We are not decisionmakers," the Iranian said, gesturing at his two aides. "We just carry messages. But we told our leaders that you would bring half of the parts . . . and some of the parts you brought are used."

"I have come here from the United States!" McFarlane said angrily. "I did not have to bring anything, and we can leave now!"

Najavi shrugged helplessly. "We promised things to our superior authorities. . . . Now we will have internal problems." But, he added in a conciliatory tone, "we should respect our guests' needs. . . . We will do what we can."

The Iranians filed unhappily out of the room.

"These guys are nobodies," McFarlane complained to North. "If we don't see their superiors, we're going to get nowhere."

"The central message," he cabled Poindexter on Sunday evening, "was how uncertain, timid, and fearful these third- and fourth-level officials were. Further, it has become more and more clear that while Ghorbanifar has brought us to the beginning of a dialogue with the government of Iran, he has done it with considerable hyperbole, occasional lies, and dissembling."

"The fact that Kangarlou's breath could curl rhino hide was no help either," added George Cave.

The next day, May 26, was Monday, and for most of the time the Americans were left on their own. They had had a night of fitful sleep, a morning strategy session, and a bad room service lunch. Finally, in the afternoon, Najavi showed up for another meeting. But this time McFarlane stayed in his room down the hall to make sure the Iranian understood that his anger was real. In his place, North acted as spokesman for the United States.

"We are confused and concerned," North began. "We have tried for months to come to a point where we could talk government-to-government. . . . We have now been here for over a day and no one will talk to us. Where are we going? Nothing is happening."

Najavi was distressed. "I don't understand how we have come to this situation," he said. "We are working to make things happen. I want to see McFarlane," he pleaded.

North padded down the hall to tell McFarlane that his absence was having the desired effect. McFarlane walked into the room to deliver his message directly.

"Before we came, my president and I believed the preliminary problems affecting our mutual trust had been resolved by the staff," McFarlane said tersely. "On your part, bringing about the release of the hostages; on our part, providing some defensive supplies. But upon arriving, I learned that the steps had not been taken by your government. That is disappointing.

"The more important purpose is to share with your ministers how to restore a basis of trust between us," he went on. "There are crucial matters related to the Soviet Union, Afghanistan, and Iraq that we should discuss. But we cannot begin to address these matters until the preliminary problems are solved.

"Perhaps your government is not ready to deal with these larger issues. Maybe we should wait for another day. But I must depart tomorrow night. I would like to meet with your ministers, but I cannot if the preliminary problems haven't been solved. I have no more to say."

The Iranian apologized. "The delay is due to the difficult effort needed to make everything work out," he said. "At four P.M., a gentleman with higher authority will be here."

"As soon as the problems you are working on are solved, I am prepared to meet with your ministers," McFarlane said. "No other meetings are necessary."

"We are having problems arranging a meeting with a minister," Najavi said. "We are trying to build up to that stage."

"I must return to Washington tomorrow night," McFarlane repeated. "The preliminary problem in Lebanon must be overcome. . . . As I am a minister, I expect to meet with decisionmakers. Otherwise, you can meet with my staff."

Najavi urged patience. "At the start of relations, there are always misunderstandings," he said.

"Yes, there are," McFarlane said curtly. "Good luck."

The Iranian had promised a high-ranking official at four, but it was after nine o'clock when the man finally arrived. This senior official was reportedly Hossein Najafabadi (although he too used a false name with the Americans), a close adviser to Rafsanjani and a leading member of the Iranian parliament. Bearded and balding, he seemed older and more self-assured than the other Iranians. After a day and a half of being confined to the top floor of the Independence, the Americans were relieved to be talking to someone in authority. But McFarlane, continuing to insist that he was entitled to see someone with cabinet rank, remained in his room. In his absence, North again acted as chief U.S. negotiator.

"We have a great opportunity," proclaimed North, ever the booster. "The key is in your hands. It is not easy to turn that key." (The guards had eaten the cake, North's intended prop for this line, but he used the metaphor anyway.)

The Iranian was charming, graceful, and glib, a refreshing change from Kangarlou and Najavi. "You have accomplished a great thing in coming here, given the state of relations between us," he said. "I would be surprised if little problems did not come up. There is a Persian saying: 'Patience will bring you victory; they are old friends.' Without patience, we won't reach anything. All statesmen understand that."

North assumed a confidential air. "There are factions in our governments that don't want something like this to succeed," he told the Iranian. "This is why McFarlane grew angry when things didn't take place as I suggested they would. He took a risk urging our president to do this.

"This is not a deal of weapons for release of the hostages," North continued. "What we had hoped was to agree on the direction for a dialogue between Iran and the United States. Political decisions will be required. We may not agree this week or this year. But this process must begin. It can begin in total secrecy."

"Can the United States keep a secret?" the Iranian asked skeptically.

"We can try," North replied.

"We are against kidnapping," the Iranian said. "What happened here" — the seizure of the U.S. Embassy in 1979 — "was exceptional. Because of one exceptional act we should not be considered terrorists. If there is only one other country in the world against the Soviets, it is Iran. We have a famous saying: 'The enemy of your enemy is your friend.' You don't see it this way. . . . Neither the United States nor the Soviet Union likes independent states.

"I am sorry to be so harsh, but I need to be frank," the Iranian said. "We have the same problem that you have. Some here oppose relations with the United States. I am happy to hear that you believe in an independent, sovereign Iran. We are hopeful that all American moves will be to support this dialogue. But we feel the whole world is trying to weaken us. We feel and see the Russian danger much more than you. You see the threat with high technology. We feel it, touch it, see it. It is not easy to sleep next to an elephant that you have wounded."

The Iranian paused to collect his thoughts.

"When we accepted your team with McFarlane, it symbolized a new political development here," he said. "But there has been a misunderstanding. When we accepted his visit, it did not mean a direct dialogue would occur on the spot. It is too early at this stage."

That was the bad news, however gracefully put. McFarlane had come all the way to Tehran, but the Iranians still weren't ready to talk seriously. In fact, it was becoming increasingly unclear whether the Americans' visit had been authorized from the top or they were in Tehran under someone's murky, unofficial auspices — an unsettling thought.

Both delegations were exhausted. They adjourned for watermelon, a traditional Iranian refreshment. Then Najafabadi took up where he had left off.

"Our relations are dark," he said. "They are very bad. Maybe you don't like to hear it, but I must be outspoken. Iranians are bitter. Many Iranians call America the Great Satan."

Only a very few people even knew that an American delegation was in Tehran, he added. Kangarlou worried out loud about the Iranian air force snooping around the Israeli plane at the airport.

"There was no agreement that when McFarlane led the team it would lead to ministerial meetings," Najafabadi said firmly. "Let us turn the key in a way which will work. We don't see the release of the hostages as the key."

So both of the premises on which the Americans had come to Tehran — that there would be top-level meetings and that the Iranians were committed to freeing the hostages — had been empty.

"I told McFarlane that he would meet with your speaker, your prime minister, and your president," North protested. "I was told this would happen."

"Why was McFarlane promised ministerial meetings?" the Iranian asked.

"Ghorbanifar said the U.S. team would meet with your senior leadership," North said.

"We did not agree to such meetings for McFarlane," the Iranian said. "We keep our word."

Both delegations looked at each other. Ghorbanifar had obviously lied to both sides in organizing this meeting.

"I knew Ghorbanifar . . . was a duplicitous sneak," North said later. "But we didn't know that the lie was quite so blatant."

Returning to the hostage issue, Najafabadi offered a glimmer of hope. "We sent a man to Lebanon. We are very hopeful that we can help you and solve this problem. By solving this problem, we strengthen you in the White House. . . . We are working right now. We hope to get you news about the situation right now. We will finish the job without the spare parts."

"Do you think it is possible to convince those who hold the Americans to release them?" North asked.

"I told you," the Iranian said. "They're difficult to deal with. But anything we start, we are hopeful about."

"Can a secret meeting be arranged with McFarlane and your leaders?" North asked.

Not now, the Iranian said. "You know how our people feel about you. . . . We have to prepare the people for such a change step by step."

As for the arms trade, though, there could be "a $2.5 billion deal in it," the Iranian said. "Speed up what has been agreed. . . . A few 747s can carry a lot in one day." Arms sales first, he was saying; improved relations, only later.

It was almost 2:00 A.M. when they finished. After the Iranians left,

North and the others briefed McFarlane, who had remained in his room down the hall the entire four hours. McFarlane was pleased; if Najafabadi was as sharp as he sounded, then perhaps the mission wasn't a total waste after all. He sent Poindexter a long message.

"I believe we have finally reached a competent Iranian official — and that's good," McFarlane wrote. "Nevertheless, we cannot, in my judgment, be swooned by serious dialogue without acts.

"With regard to the hostages, we have and will continue to make clear that their release is the sine qua non to any further steps between us. And if that has not happened by tomorrow night, they are aware that we will leave and that the balance of this shipment will not be delivered.

"It seems clear that we are dealing with people at the top who (1) understand that they have an important interest in trying to establish a dialogue that leads to a measure of cooperation with us, (2) that doing so requires . . . release of the hostages and no further terrorist acts against us, (3) are very fearful for their own vulnerability to factional attack if they are discovered in this dialogue.

"So we are on the way to something that can become a truly strategic gain for us at the expense of the Soviets. But it is going to be painfully slow. As we proceed we cannot be gulled by promises of what will happen tomorrow — at bottom they really are rug merchants. But little by little, we can make progress because it is a matter of self-interest for both of us to do so.

"Hope you had a nice weekend," McFarlane added. "Your guys are doing a fantastic job, as is Cave and the communicator, who is near death."

Tuesday, May 27, dawned warm and springlike. May can be a pleasant month in Iran; the spring winds cleanse the air, the mountaintops still shimmer with snow, the hills show a brief flush of green before the summer heat sets in.

McFarlane had worked until almost 4:00 A.M. the night before, but he was up by eight. Overnight, he had decided to go ahead and meet one-on-one with the senior Iranian, Najafabadi. It was the only way to salvage any significant gain from the trip. The main targets had already evaporated: the hostages had not been freed and no Iranian of cabinet rank was going to appear. But there was a chance that these talks, however disappointing, could still turn into an opening to a new U.S.-Iranian relationship. And after coming all this way, the hostages were still worth one more try.

The Iranians arrived at ten, and McFarlane invited Najafabadi into his suite for a talk. Sitting in two armchairs, they held the first real U.S.-Iranian foreign policy dialogue in six years.

"We believe in nonintervention in the affairs of all states — and we expect Iran to do the same," McFarlane began in his usual deliberate manner. "We believe Soviet objectives in the Middle East are to expand its influence so as to ultimately be in the position to disrupt the resource flows of the area and exploit its geography for self-interest. The Soviets will go to considerable length to prevent Iraq from losing to Iran [in the Persian Gulf war], for if they did lose, Soviet credibility would be catastrophically damaged in the area.

"Our policy remains to seek an end to the war and not to favor victory by either side. In the case of Iran, that is because we are concerned for what your larger purposes are in the Middle East. . . . We are not prepared to provide a level of arms that would enable Iran to win the war.

"That said, however, we are prepared to enter a dialogue to determine where there might be common interests. Afghanistan appears to be a leading case in point. We would also want to discuss Nicaragua and Iran's support for the Sandinistas, as well as Lebanon.

"Here's what we can do to try to inject a little momentum into the process," McFarlane said. "First, both sides can lower the temperature of their rhetoric toward the other — although we will continue to call it as we see it if terrorist attacks are committed against Americans by Iranians. Second, we should commit ourselves now to a sustained political dialogue in an effort to bridge differences where possible, even though some disagreements will probably remain eternal. Another meeting could take place within two weeks, either here in Tehran or in a third country or in the United States."

The Iranian listened attentively. In a brief, low-key response, he outlined Iran's basic objections to American policies in the Middle East. And then he got to the main message he wanted to deliver: the news from Beirut.

"The people holding the hostages have made demands before they release the Americans," he said almost apologetically. "They asked for Israel to withdraw from the Golan Heights and South Lebanon. . . . The prisoners in Kuwait must be freed. All their expenses from the hostage-taking must be paid."

McFarlane's eyes widened in astonishment. How's that for chutzpah! he thought. But before he could deliver a properly outraged response, the Iranian quickly spoke up.

"These demands are not acceptable to us and we are negotiating with them," he said. "We believe the only real problem is when you deliver the items we have requested."

McFarlane took a deep breath. "I'm glad to hear that your government wants to solve problems and set a political dialogue in motion," he said. "But I have to say that the other matters you have stated lead me to believe that such a dialogue will never get started at all."

He recounted how the United States had already made three arms deals based on promises that all the hostages would be released, only to be disappointed each time. "All this has led to an extremely high level of frustration on the part of the president," McFarlane said. "He agreed to this meeting reluctantly, and under a very clear and precise understanding of the arrangements." Those arrangements were that all the hostages would be released as soon as the U.S. delegation arrived in Tehran, he added.

Najafabadi appeared surprised. "Who is it that has agreed to these terms?" he asked.

"Ghorbanifar and Kangarlou," McFarlane replied.

"These are not the terms as I understand them," Najafabadi said. "We expected all deliveries to occur before any [hostage] release took place."

"Misunderstandings can happen," McFarlane said. "But I am confident that they do not come from our side, since we have two witnesses to the agreement that was made.

"In any case, the president has reached his limit of tolerance," McFarlane said firmly. "This visit is the last attempt we will make. My instructions are to return to Washington tonight. We are prepared to call the other aircraft [carrying arms] forward as soon as we receive word that the hostages are released — even within a couple of days from now, after we leave, if the hostages are not released tonight. But there is no possibility of changing the terms."

Najafabadi was agitated: Had he been misled by his own aides? He asked McFarlane if they could take a break.

"Certainly," McFarlane said. "But as I said, I do have to leave tonight." (Actually, he did not have to leave that night; he simply wanted to put some pressure on the Iranians — and it was working.)

After Najafabadi left, McFarlane cabled another report to Poindexter. "I tend to think that we should hold firm on our intention to leave and, in fact, do so unless we have word of [a hostage] release in the next six or seven hours," he wrote. "Please [convey] this to the president, and we will proceed as directed."

On the fringe of the meeting, Ghorbanifar did not seem concerned that his duplicity had been unmasked. The arms dealer had a more pressing worry. He drew George Cave aside and told him quietly that the Iranians were paying a total of $24.5 million for the HAWK parts. Just in case they ask if that's the right price, he said, tell them yes, that's the right price.

Cave was intrigued. He knew that the real price of the HAWKs was far below $24.5 million — more like $6.5 million. Cave asked North what was going on, but North shrugged and looked innocent. So Cave asked Amiram Nir, the Israeli, why the price was so high.

"Don't worry," Nir assured him. "It involves other deals. And there are enormous expenses in this operation."

That Tuesday afternoon, the Americans and the Israeli sat down to their only good meal of the trip — a Persian lunch prepared by Ghor-banifar's mother and brought to the hotel in the arms dealer's car. At five o'clock, after the dishes were cleared away, the two delegations met again. Najafabadi had good news — of a sort.

"The last contact with our man in Lebanon reported that he was able to eliminate three demands," he said. "We will solve the money problem. The only remaining problem is Kuwait. We agreed to try to get a promise from you that [the Shia prisoners in Kuwait] would be released in the future."

But there was also the misunderstanding over timing: Iran had never committed itself to releasing the hostages before the HAWK parts were delivered. "These documents [for the release of the hostages] are in Ghorbanifar's handwriting," he said of the agreements the American delegation showed him. "Maybe Ghorbanifar made a mistake."

McFarlane said he was glad to see someone trying to solve the hostage problem, but he stood firm on the U.S. terms for the deal: there could be no trade for the prisoners in Kuwait, and the American hostages had to come out first. "Unfortunately, we have reached this point after a year and three efforts where we thought we had an agreement," he said. "This has affected the president's view of our ability to reach an agreement. . . . His instructions in sending me here were that if a fourth try did not achieve results, it was pointless to pursue an ineffective dialogue.

"All the items that have been paid for are loaded and poised for release the minute the hostages are in our custody. Their prompt delivery within ten hours is our solemn commitment," McFarlane added.

Najafabadi looked for a compromise. "Since the plane is loaded, why not let it come?" he asked. "You would leave happy. The president would be happy. We feel no guilt based on our understanding of the agreement; we are surprised now that it has been changed.

"Let the agreement be carried out. Your hostages will be freed very quickly. Your president's word will be honored. If the plane arrives before tomorrow morning, the hostages will be free by noon. We do not wish to see our agreement fail at this final stage."

McFarlane made a counteroffer. "Can we separate the issue? As a humanitarian gesture? We have already delivered hundreds of weapons. You can release the hostages, advise us, and we will deliver the [second planeload of] weapons."

"Okay," Najafabadi replied. "But [Rafsanjani] would like the staff to reach an agreement. . . . This will be a difficult task. It might be difficult to get it done tonight. Can you extend your stay?"

"I will seek the president's decision," McFarlane said. "I cannot know what he will say. But I should say that in his most recent communication, he pointed out that I have been here three days. It should have been enough."

The time was approaching for a firm ultimatum. At nine-thirty on

Tuesday evening, Najafabadi and Kangarlou returned to the hotel with the delegation's passports.

North asked for the plane to be refueled. Then he handed Najafabadi the American draft of a joint U.S.-Iranian agreement. Paragraph One said the United States would order the 707 carrying the remaining HAWK parts to take off and arrive in Tehran at ten o'clock Wednesday morning. Paragraph Two said the Iranian government, "in the spirit of humanitarian assistance," would order the release of the hostages six hours earlier, by four o'clock Wednesday morning. Paragraph Three made the arms-for-hostage swap explicit: "If by 0400 Tehran time the hostages are not safely in the hands of U.S. authorities, the aircraft with the HAWK missile parts will be turned around and will not land in Iran." But if the hostages were released, Iran would be rewarded further: the United States would deliver two sophisticated radar sets.

Najafabadi and his aides studied the proposal. "Their faces displayed anxiety," Howard Teicher recorded in his notes. "They each asked about the timing of deliveries. They repeatedly asked each other about the spare parts."

Finally, Najafabadi turned to the Americans. "How are we supposed to free the hostages by four o'clock in the morning?" he asked almost plaintively.

"We *are* negotiating," the more truculent Kangarlou added. "There is still a lot of work to do. We cannot make a final decision on when they will be released!"

"I don't understand the timing problem," North said. "With McFarlane today, you told us they would be free by noon."

"Yes, I said that earlier today, but now it's late," Najafabadi said. "Our dispute now is over the lack of a complete agreement. What can you say about the people held in Kuwait?"

North was willing to be more flexible than McFarlane about the Shia prisoners. "We can give you a statement," he said. "Something like: 'The United States will make every effort, through and with international organizations, private individuals, religious organizations, and other third parties in a humanitarian effort to achieve the release and just and fair treatment for Shiites held in confinement, as soon as possible.' "

Najafabadi and McFarlane met privately once more — a final attempt at finding common ground. After a brief meeting, McFarlane emerged looking grim.

"They're just stringing us along," he said. "Let's pack up and go."

"Can't," North replied. "The plane still hasn't been refueled."

At two o'clock Wednesday morning, two hours before the 4:00 A.M. hostage deadline, Najafabadi showed up again. "Give us until six o'clock," he pleaded. "We will get an answer on the hostages by then."

"If you give us a time [for the hostages' release]," McFarlane replied, "we will launch the aircraft so that it will land here two hours after the hostages are in U.S. custody." He gave the Iranian until 6:30 A.M., then went to bed.

"The American delegation retired to grab a couple hours' sleep," George Cave recorded, "knowing that we had at least outfrazzled them."

But part of the U.S. delegation stayed awake that night and kept the lights blazing atop the Independence Hotel. North, Nir, and Ghorbanifar had something extra riding on the second 707, waiting with its load of HAWKs in Tel Aviv. Ghorbanifar had borrowed $15 million from Adnan Khashoggi to pay for the shipment. Secord had already paid $6.5 million of that to the CIA. If the transaction failed, they would both have to scramble to recover their money.

More important, a huge profit rode on the success of this deal — a profit as large as $18 million. Some of that, perhaps as much as $11 million, was due to Ghorbanifar (although a good chunk, the Americans believed, would go in kickbacks to Kangarlou and other Iranians). And roughly $7 million was intended for the contras and for Project Democracy.

At some point very early on that morning in Tehran, North decided to order the second 707 into the air. The Iranians had, after all, declared their intention to free the hostages. There was no sign that they could do it; in fact, all the signs were that they had less influence over the Beirut terrorists than Ghorbanifar asserted. Nevertheless, North sent a message to Secord: launch the plane. The second 707 rumbled down the runway at Tel Aviv and headed south over the Negev for the Red Sea, the first leg on its circuitous route to Tehran.

When McFarlane awoke on Wednesday morning, he discovered three things: the hostages had not been released; the Iranians were still trying to cut a deal; and someone had ordered the second plane into the air without his explicit approval.

Kangarlou had already showed up at the hotel at six o'clock, half an hour before the deadline, with yet another proposal. He could win the release of two of the hostages now, he promised, and two more after the HAWK parts arrived. To the Iranians, that was a reasonable deal, even a concession; before the Americans arrived, they had understood that they were committed to release only one hostage.

North quickly agreed: in his view, half a deal was better than none. He relayed the Iranian offer to McFarlane. "My advice at the time was to take the two hostages and go home," North testified later. He did not tell McFarlane that he also had $7 million for the contras riding on the delivery of the HAWK parts.

But McFarlane not only held firm, he blew up at North for ordering the second 707 to leave Israel. "That is unacceptable," he barked at

North. "Turn that plane around." The radio message went out to Secord in Tel Aviv: abort the mission. The plane turned back.

North later defended himself by pointing out that the second plane had always been part of the plan. "I didn't even have to make a decision," he said. "The plane launched in accord with the previously established schedule." But that schedule assumed that the hostages' release would be imminent when the second 707 took off. Instead, by Wednesday morning the hostages' release looked as remote as ever; North had ordered the plane to take off anyway.

McFarlane was ready to leave. The architect of Ronald Reagan's strategic opening to Iran had come face-to-face with the reality of the arms deals he had launched, and he didn't like what he saw. McFarlane had come into the tumult of Tehran with promises of meetings with Iran's most powerful mullahs to talk about geopolitics; instead, he found himself dickering over missiles with middle-level bureaucrats.

The Americans ordered cars for eight o'clock. At seven-fifty, Kangarlou dashed in with another hopeful bulletin on the hostages. "They think two can get out now, but it will require joint action on the other two," he announced.

"It's too late," McFarlane said. "We're leaving."

At eight, Najafabadi walked in and repeated the two-hostage offer.

"You are not keeping the agreement," McFarlane said stiffly. "We are leaving."

The Iranians begged the Americans to wait, but McFarlane virtually walked past them and out the door. Kangarlou rode with them to the airport, keeping up his argument: two hostages could be on their way home.

"Why are you leaving?" he demanded of McFarlane over the shriek of the 707's engines.

"Tell your superiors that this was the fourth time they have failed to honor an agreement," McFarlane said grimly. "The lack of trust will endure for a long time. An important opportunity was lost."

And at eight fifty-five on Wednesday morning, the Americans were in the air, en route back to Tel Aviv.

In Washington, Poindexter sat at his desk in the White House that morning and read the cables describing the mission's failure. Then he went to greet a special envoy from the British government, who had requested a brief audience.

The Englishman went straight to his point. Prime Minister Margaret Thatcher's government had gotten wind of Adnan Khashoggi's investment in the arms deals, and London wanted to know what was going on. Only a month earlier, Thatcher had stood staunchly by Reagan in allowing him to use British air bases for the bombing of Libya. In revenge, pro-Libyan terrorists in Beirut had murdered two British hostages as well as the American Peter Kilburn.

"They had accepted risks on our behalf," an American diplomat explained. "And here we were, doing a deal. They could tell what was going on, and they were very upset."

Poindexter heard the envoy out in stony silence. The Briton asked him to reconfirm, categorically, that the United States would never pay ransom — even indirectly — for the release of hostages.

Poindexter tried to turn the question aside. We are looking at a variety of ways to get the hostages out, he acknowledged, playing with his pipe.

But an arms deal?

No, Poindexter said calmly. There's no arms deal in the works.

The Tehran mission should have been a cold bath in reality for both Poindexter and North. Ghorbanifar had lied; it appeared that North had lied too, in his wildly optimistic explanations of what the Iranians had agreed to before the trip. Contrary to what North had said, the Iranians weren't interested in an early opening toward better relations; their only serious interest was in weapons. Nor were they even certain of their ability to deliver the hostages. The key to the hostage puzzle, it seemed, was not in Tehran, nor in a chocolate cake from Israel, but right where Hizballah had always said it was: in the release of the Shia prisoners held in Kuwait.

Given the cardinal rule of Ronald Reagan's counterterrorism policy — no concessions to terrorists — that should have been the end of the negotiations. Instead, Poindexter and North began looking at a new deal, one that might win freedom for the Shia prisoners.

But that was for the future. Wednesday, May 28, was for the exhausted Americans to fly home from Tehran, lick their wounds, and puzzle out what they might have done differently — and to be thankful that they had come out of Iran alive.

The 707 landed at Ben Gurion in the early afternoon. As the Americans stepped onto the sunny tarmac, McFarlane asked the CIA radioman to set up his transmitter: it was time to call Poindexter.

North, seeing that his former chief was depressed by the mission's failure, drew McFarlane aside. "Don't be too downhearted," he said. "The one bright spot is that we're using part of the money in these transactions for Central America."

The CIA radio crackled to life, and McFarlane turned to make his call to Poindexter. When he was finished, North was already gone — off with Secord to work on another attempt to bribe the hostages free.

The next morning, McFarlane reported to Reagan in the Oval Office. He told the president, Bush, Regan, and Poindexter that the Iranians had insisted on the delivery of all the HAWK parts before releasing any of the hostages. Strangely, McFarlane didn't even mention North's comment about the diversion of funds to the contras.

McFarlane said later that he had been startled by North's revelation, but he did not consider it his place to pursue the matter. "It was of a piece with a half-dozen items that I had learned which seemed to me either unorthodox or very risky. But I was not in the government. . . . [I] had no authority to know, nor need to know.

"I took it to be a matter of approved policy, one of which the government was — must be — witting."

12

Success

ON THE FOURTH OF JULY 1986, beneath glorious bursts of fireworks over New York Harbor, Ronald Reagan stood bathed in spotlights on a glittering platform, the chief of state transcendent. The occasion was the hundredth birthday of the Statue of Liberty, the splendid, rebuilt symbol of the American promise.

Standing at the podium, speaking to a crowd of thousands and a television audience of millions, Reagan outlined once again his bright vision of America: "The things that unite us — America's past of which we are so proud, our hopes and aspirations for the future of the world and this much beloved country — these things far outweigh what little difference divides us."

As the seventy-five-year-old Reagan presided over the relighting of Liberty's lamp and a grand, patriotic gala, it was hard to be sure which national symbol was being celebrated more. On that spectacular evening and for the entire summer of 1986, Reagan seemed to rise beyond partisan politics, beyond his own history as a conservative ideologue, to stand as an embodiment of the sentiments he proclaimed. The Reagan presidency, which had long puzzled and confounded its critics, now managed the feat of eluding ordinary criticism altogether: Reagan the man was treated by the press, by scholars, and even by his opponents as a special, almost supernatural phenomenon.

"Ronald Reagan has found the American sweet spot," marveled *Time* magazine, an assiduous barometer of the national mood. "The 75-year-old man is hitting home runs. . . . Reagan is a sort of masterpiece of American magic — apparently one of the simplest, most uncomplicated creatures alive, and yet a character of rich meanings, of complexities that connect him with the myths and powers of his country in an unprecedented way."

Even liberal Democrats conceded that the president had achieved a special, untouchable status in American life and acknowledged that he had succeeded in restoring the majesty of his office. "We've given up running against Ronald Reagan — there's no advantage to it," said Democratic political strategist Robert Squier. "The Democratic party has reduced itself to guerrilla warfare."

Reagan's supporters, of course, were even more sweeping in their claims. "Not since Franklin Roosevelt have we had a president who changed the agenda so much," declared chief White House speechwriter Bently Elliott. "The only question is what his encore will be."

By that summer, a lengthening string of victories at home and abroad gave new credence to the praise. Not every battle was won entirely on Reagan's terms, but there could be no denying that this second-term president was successfully fending off lame duck status through persistence and popularity.

On the domestic front, the economy continued to expand, the stock markets to rise, and the White House to claim credit for both. Each month brought a triumphant announcement of economic statistics: the creation of new jobs, buoyant corporate profits, stable interest rates, and miraculously low inflation. The tax reform bill that Reagan had adopted as his personal project was assured of victory as well. The president and his aides weren't entirely happy with the changes Congress had made in their plan, but it was still a win on an issue that skeptics had called unwinnable. On the Supreme Court, Reagan pulled off a coup by appointing conservatives William H. Rehnquist as chief justice and Antonin Scalia as associate justice, giving the bench a clear rightward tilt without serious opposition from Congress.

In foreign policy, Reagan's men worked steadily toward an arms control agreement with the Soviet Union. By summer, Reagan, the old anti-Communist, was publicly praising Soviet leader Mikhail Gorbachev as a reasonable man, and there was serious talk of another summit meeting before the end of the year. What had sent Reagan's standing soaring highest in the polls was the air strike against Libya back in April; by Liberty weekend, Reagan's approval rating was still up around the 65 percent mark, a sustained high. To the surprise of some of the administration's own experts, the raid on Libya also seemed to achieve its goal of discouraging further terrorism: attacks against Americans overseas dropped off almost immediately.

And, dearest victory of all, after two years of prohibition, the president at last had a mandate to arm the contras again. Reagan had finally prodded Congress into approving $100 million for the Nicaraguan rebels, including $70 million in military aid. The vote in the House came only ten days before the Fourth of July. "As we approach the celebrations of our own Independence Day, we can be proud that we as a people have embraced the struggle of the freedom fighters of Nicaragua," Reagan declared. "The cause is freedom, the cause is just, the cause will triumph."

Needless to say, neither the president nor his aides mentioned that the cause had been maintained by Saudi money, Iranian arms sales, and an illicit network of privateers backed by the White House. But then, the blurring of old distinctions between public affairs and private pursuits had long been the flip side of the Reagan miracle. Even the festivities at the Statue of Liberty illuminated, in their own way, Reagan's exaltation of the profit motive to a place of honor alongside more traditional civic virtues. When the president made his speech about the American dream, handed out the gold medals minted for the occasion, and pressed the button to light Liberty's lamp, the images — except for what was deemed news — were owned by ABC television, which had bought the exclusive right to broadcast the occasion for $10 million (estimated profit: $6 million). Three federal judges refused to participate in a naturalization ceremony for new citizens as part of the pageant because they felt it would be debased by ABC's frequent advertising breaks. Reagan, with no such qualms, handed out the gala's ersatz medals between Texaco commercials celebrating the right to worship.

Reagan had long declared his preference for private enterprise over government bureaucracy, and he had turned to corporations to handle public functions before. In 1966, he called on the Walt Disney Studios to design his first inaugural program in Sacramento, and he "borrowed" legal staff from his old employer, Twentieth Century–Fox. (Fox's interest was more than patriotic: "It never hurts to have a friend in Sacramento," the studio's president noted.) On the level of policy, Reagan's annual budgets invariably suggested that the private sector should take over public enterprises, from the Tennessee Valley Authority to the National Weather Service. Reagan was certain not only that private enterprise would do a better job, but that there was rarely a serious conflict between private interests and the public good. What was good for General Motors or Fox or Texaco was indeed good for the country.

Eventually, Reagan's blind faith in the private sector and his appointments to public office of entrepreneurs with little time for old-fashioned niceties exposed his aides in both Sacramento and Washington to dozens of conflict-of-interest charges. Reagan consistently dismissed the accusations as unfair, gratuitous, or simply unimportant; he openly disdained the post-Watergate "ethics in government" laws, which required officials to keep their private businesses at arm's length from the public business. This president, wrote one early (and largely sympathetic) chronicler, was "astonishingly unconcerned about displaying a keen sense of propriety."

By the middle of Reagan's second term, more than a hundred members of his administration had either resigned or been forced out of office under allegations of wrongdoing. His first labor secretary, Raymond Donovan, became the first sitting cabinet member in American history to be indicted, although he was eventually acquitted. His closest personal aide, Michael Deaver, and a former press secretary, Lyn Nofziger, were both convicted in cases stemming from influence-peddling charges. And his second-term attorney general, Edwin Meese III, spent most of his tenure facing inquiries into his conduct by special prosecutors. (Nofziger's conviction was later overturned.)

Not once did Reagan show any displeasure with these aides accused of using their public office for private gain. He never held any subordinate publicly accountable for his actions; instead, he invariably lent the appearance of support, if only by omission. He defended Deaver publicly against charges of improper lobbying, saying, "He has never put the arm on me," to the point that even Deaver was a little astonished at the president's solicitude. "He seemed even more puzzled than I was by the charges, and less inclined to accept the seriousness of them," the former aide said. Reagan grumbled frequently about "the lynch mob" around his associates. The president wasn't venal himself, but his permissiveness sent his subordinates a message of indifference to high standards.

Most of Reagan's blind spots were compensated by his wife's vigilance, but on this issue the First Lady shared the president's frailty. Since their early days in Sacramento, she had accepted expensive gifts from their wealthy friends, even demanding that old benefactors like Holmes Tuttle come to their financial rescue because, as she pointed out more than once, "you know Ronnie and I have nothing."

When her friends' donations of expensive china and designer gowns led to public criticism during the first term, Nancy surrendered publicly and went on to alter her image effectively with a campaign against drug abuse. But privately she smoldered. When White House counsel Fred Fielding went to explain why she had to give up some of her gifts, an aide recounted, "she made him come to her at the residence, and then she showed up wearing a dressing gown — making clear in every way what an intrusion she thought he and his piss-ant legal ideas were."

It was as if the Reagans felt the rules were never meant to apply strictly to them or to the people who worked for their administration. But in a decade whose cultural heroes included Donald Trump, Lee Iacocca, and T. Boone Pickens, Jr., Reagan's blurring of the distinctions between wealth and commonwealth caused him no political damage. If anything, it simply underlined the extent to which he was the consummate man of his time. American politics moves in cycles of idealism and self-interest; the 1980s (like the 1920s and the 1950s) were years of private, not public, interest. Oliver North's tin cup diplomacy and Richard Secord's profitable bottom line were not anomalies but natural outgrowths of Reagan's privatized politics. And for a time in the summer of 1986, it appeared, at last, as if their entrepreneurial approach was paying off.

When the House of Representatives approved the $100 million in new aid for the contras on June 25, Reagan hailed the vote as signaling "a new era of bipartisan consensus in American foreign policy." In fact, it had been a bitterly partisan struggle, and, at least in the short run, it turned into something of a Pyrrhic victory for the president. House Speaker Tip O'Neill had failed in his attempts to block the aid vote, but the old lion's parliamentary wiles were far from exhausted. He delayed final passage of the appropriation for almost four months, much longer than any of Reagan's strategists had expected. The contras would not receive any military aid until October; in the meantime, the Boland amendment's prohibitions remained in effect. ("It just drove Poindexter nuts," an aide said.) But Poindexter knew that the White House had an alternative. All summer long, Oliver North continued to manage his ostensibly private covert war in Nicaragua through Project Democracy, flouting the old law while the new one was in limbo.

On the ground in Central America, North's secret airlift to the contras was finally beginning to work. In the four months from May through August, the cargo fleet made forty-three successful trips inside Nicaragua, dropping more than eighty tons of guns, ammunition, and other supplies to contra guerrilla teams in the hills.

There were still some problems, of course. One of Project Democracy's C-7 Caribous made an emergency landing in Costa Rica and remained stuck in the mud for two anxious days — a worry because the Costa Rican government wasn't supposed to know about the operation. And in June, George Bush's hot-tempered friend, Felix Rodriguez, flew from El Salvador to Washington to warn North that his field managers, Richard Secord and Tom Clines, were making profits from the contra war. "Colonel, I have learned that there are people stealing here," Rodriguez stormed. "And if this is known and the people which are involved connected to the [Edwin] Wilson case . . . it's going to be worse than Watergate. This could destroy the president of the United States."

North tried to calm Rodriguez. "Secord's a patriot," he said with his trademark sincerity. He pointed to the television screen in his office; the House of Representatives was voting that very day to restore Reagan's military aid to the contras. "Some of those bastards want me," North boasted. "But they can't touch me — because the old man loves my ass."

That was pure North bravado. In fact, both North and Poindexter were worried about a new surge of interest in their secret operations by Congress and the press. All spring, a handful of reporters had been on North's trail; in the summer the pace picked up, each report feeding another. Many of the stories focused on General Singlaub and his efforts to buy arms; Singlaub was deliberately talking in an attempt to draw attention away from Secord's more clandestine operations. But in July, CBS News broadcast a report that one of the men behind the contras' secret air force was, in fact, Secord. The White House and Secord's lawyer both denied the account.

People inside the bureaucracy were beginning to complain about North as well; he had amassed far too much power for a lowly lieutenant colonel. Some were jealous, like Raymond F. Burghardt, the diplomat who was formally the NSC's chief of Latin American policy but who had long since lost control of the Nicaraguan issue to North. Others were alarmed by the glimpses they saw of North's secret operations. At least two NSC officials complained privately through channels that North was stepping beyond the law; one said Poindexter's counsel, Paul B. Thompson, responded that Attorney General Meese had "okayed everything."

There were also complaints, some even from North's friends, that his behavior was becoming increasingly erratic. In his attempt to juggle both the contra war and the Iranian arms deals, North's already long hours had become even longer and more punishing. His wife, Betsy, was putting pressure on him to cut down his seventy-hour work week, but Project Democracy was too important for him to slack off. His moods seemed to swing between manic boastfulness and paranoiac secrecy. One day he proudly showed a videotape of the contra supply airlift to members of the NSC staff and the vice president's aides; at other times he refused to acknowledge the existence of the airlift. He accused Poindexter's executive secretary, Rodney McDaniel, of secretly harboring liberal ideas. And one day he abruptly announced to several colleagues, "Once this all comes out, I'm going to jail." North himself realized that his job had become too much for one man to handle. "This is ridiculous," he complained to one of his aides, "trying to run a war from my desk."

McFarlane had noticed the problem and quietly told Poindexter that it might be time for North to go back to the marines. Poindexter, who was tired of North's theatrics, agreed at least that North's workload was too large. Congress's approval of aid to the contras meant that soon Project Democracy would no longer be needed in Central America. Congress had also given the State Department authority to ask foreign countries to aid the rebels, so North's role there was disappearing too. In June, Poindexter blandly told North that another NSC official would be given primary responsibility for the Nicaraguan account so that North could concentrate on Iran and other issues.

The admiral could not have expected the explosion that followed. North had become emotionally attached to his Central American crusade, and he protested Poindexter's direction in a series of agitated PROFS messages. He was especially insistent that the State Department not take over his fund-raising duties. "I am very concerned that we are bifurcating an effort that has, up until now, worked relatively well," he wrote. "An extraordinary amount of good has been done and money truly is not the thing which is most needed at this point. What we most need is to get the CIA reengaged in this effort so that it can be better managed than it is now by one slightly confused Marine LtCol."

After the *Washington Times* reported that North was being pulled off the contra account by scheming soft-liners, Poindexter pointedly scolded North for the apparent leak — prompting another bathetic message. "I want you to know that it is, for me, deeply disappointing to have lost your confidence, for I respect you [and] what you have tried to do," North wrote. "You should not be expected to retain on your staff someone who you suspect could be talking to the media or whom you believe to be too emotionally involved in an issue to be objective in the development of policy options and recommendations. I know in my heart that this is not the case, but . . . we live in a world of perceptions, not realities."

"Now you are getting emotional again," Poindexter replied. "It would help if you would call [the *Washington Times*] and tell them to call off the dogs. Tell them on deep background, off the record, not to be published, that I just wanted to lower your visibility so you wouldn't be such a good target for the Libs. . . . I do not want you to leave and to be honest cannot afford to let you go."

Despite North's protestations of innocence, two more newspaper columns soon popped up to defend his job. The conservative columnists Rowland Evans and Robert Novak hailed North as "Reagan's star player in the long, hard struggle to keep the contras alive" and accused Poindexter of planning to sacrifice the marine to mollify Democrats in Congress — an argument guaranteed to scuttle any such plan. Suzanne Garment of the *Wall Street Journal* repeated the sad legend of North's poisoned dog and fumed: "For senior officials to turn their backs on a man with Colonel North's record at a time when he is under outside attack is simply not decent behavior."

It was a virtuoso performance. North had often leaked to selected members of the press before — most notably when he created his own heroic version of the *Achille Lauro* incident — but never to such devastating effect. Poindexter, stunned by the onslaught, retreated. North kept his job and all his accounts.

Congress was after the colonel as well. In the wake of the press reports, the chairmen of the House Intelligence and Foreign Affairs committees wrote to Reagan, asking politely whether his staff really was circumventing the Boland amendment by organizing secret aid to the contras. Poindexter replied in writing on behalf of Reagan, "The actions of the National Security Council staff were in compliance with both the spirit and letter of the law."

To satisfy the congressmen's curiosity, though, North met with the House Intelligence Committee in the White House Situation Room. "I gave no military advice and knew of no specific military operations," he said earnestly. All he was doing, he said, was counseling the rebels to make their politics more democratic. At the end of the meeting, Lee Hamilton, the soft-spoken chairman of the Intelligence Committee, declared himself fully satisfied and, according to the minutes, "expressed his appreciation for the good-faith effort that Admiral Poindexter had shown." Hamilton said his committee, which is charged with keeping watch over all U.S. covert actions, saw nothing further to investigate. "Based on our discussions and review of the evidence provided, it is my belief that the published press allegations cannot be proven," he wrote to a colleague.

Poindexter received a full report on North's performance. His response was pithy but eloquent: "Well done."

For North and the others working to win the release of the American hostages in Lebanon, the Fourth of July had not been entirely happy; they had hoped to make a deal for at least one of the hostages in time for Reagan to announce the news at the Statue of Liberty. If the freed hostage could appear at the ceremony, Ghorbanifar told his contact, Kangarlou, in Tehran, "we could exploit it and benefit from it a great deal; we could get the Americans to accept many of our demands."

But the debacle of McFarlane's secret mission to Iran in May had left the hostage effort dead in the water. After the risky gambit of sending five American officials into Iran gained nothing but more flimsy promises, Poindexter decided to halt the talks until all the U.S. captives were freed. He even asked North to start planning a military mission to rescue the hostages; North, uncharacteristically, protested that his negotiations would still work better.

Ghorbanifar was frantic about the arms deal that McFarlane's walkout in Tehran had left hanging. The collapse of the U.S.-Iranian talks left the promised shipment of HAWK missile parts sitting useless in a warehouse, and now Khashoggi wanted his money back. Even worse, the Iranians themselves had stumbled across a Pentagon price list and wanted to know why Ghorbanifar was charging $24.5 million for parts that retailed for only $6.5 million. The middleman was in danger of losing both his money and his customer.

Something had to be done to get the deals back on track. Ghorbanifar warned his Tehran contacts that unless a hostage was freed now, Iran would never see another U.S. missile. "In 1985, there were 45,703 deaths on U.S. highways," he wrote. "We must not put the Americans under such pressure that they end up losing these four [hostages] as part of the above statistics, and we end up losing this historic opportunity."

The message got through: on July 26, Lawrence Martin Jenco suddenly turned up free in Damascus. His captors had blindfolded him, bundled him into the trunk of a car, driven for three hours over mountain roads from Beirut to the Bekaa Valley, and released the dazed priest on the side of a highway. In Joliet, Illinois, the Jenco sisters, who had burst into tears so often at White House meetings, wept again — this time for joy.

The State Department's hostage team scrambled to West Germany to debrief Jenco on his ordeal. North's aide Craig Coy went along too. As the Americans waited at Wiesbaden, Coy suddenly got a phone call from North — who turned out to be only a few miles away, meeting secretly in Frankfurt with Ghorbanifar.

"What the hell is this?" demanded Robert B. Oakley, the chief of the hostage team, who had already deduced that North was making some kind of secret deals.

Coy gulped. "I can't tell you," he said.

In fact, North was getting a startling report from Ghorbanifar. The Iranian announced that he had made a secret bargain for Jenco's freedom — without clearing it with the Americans at all. The middleman, desperate to make another deal, had simply promised Tehran that the United States would deliver the remaining weapons from the aborted May transaction as soon as a hostage was freed. Ghorbanifar, purporting to act for the United States, agreed to virtually the same terms McFarlane had rejected two months earlier: a sequence of arms deliveries in exchange for hostages, one by one.

Poindexter was appalled. "Of course," he noted, "we have not agreed to any such plan." But North, Ghorbanifar, and Casey went to work to convince the admiral to approve the Iranians' deal: to send Tehran more HAWK missile parts as a reward for freeing Jenco. Their argument was familiar but still powerful: if the weapons weren't sent, the hostages would die. Although the Hizballah captors had never resorted to this kind of extortion, North and Casey now proclaimed the murder of the hostages to be a real and imminent threat.

"It is entirely possible that Iran and/or Hizballah could resort to the murder of one or more of the remaining hostages," Casey wrote to Poindexter. "I believe that we should consider what we may be prepared to do to meet [Iran's] minimum requirements that would lead to release of the rest of the hostages."

North added a ghoulish flourish. If more weapons were not delivered to Iran, he said, not only would an American hostage die; Kangarlou would be assassinated by his opponents in Tehran, and Ghorbanifar would be killed by his creditors.

As the secret debate continued, North even attempted to recruit George

Bush to his side. Bush had supported the arms sales to Iran thus far; a former director of the CIA, he had been especially susceptible to the argument that the government had an obligation to free William Buckley. On July 28, North telephoned Bush, who was visiting Israel, and asked him to meet with the Israeli counterterrorism chief, Amiram Nir, for a briefing on the Iranian deal. The next morning, Nir arrived at Bush's suite in the King David Hotel overlooking the Old City of Jerusalem, its walls and towers sparkling in the morning sun. As a steward served breakfast, Bush settled into an armchair and listened to Nir spin what an aide to the vice president later called an "astounding" story.

Nir described the arms sales as a U.S. deal, with Israel playing an essential role. "We activated the channel; we gave a front to the operation; [we] provided a physical base; [we] provided aircraft," Nir said. Israel had worked hard, he added, to protect the United States from any messy involvement in the logistical aspects of the deal, anything that might leak.

The Israeli described McFarlane's May visit to Tehran as an exercise in "total frustration." Before the meeting, he said, there had been a firm deal: all the hostages would be released in exchange for a set number of weapons. He used a merchant's turn of phrase: "the whole package for a fixed price." But the Iranians reneged.

"We are dealing with the most radical elements," Nir told Bush. "The deputy prime minister [Najavi] is an emissary. . . . We've learned they can deliver and the moderates can't.

"Should we accept sequencing?" Nir asked rhetorically, posing the question that Poindexter was grappling with. He explained that he meant consecutive exchanges of arms and hostages. "What are the alternatives to sequencing? They fear if they give all [the] hostages they won't get anything from us. . . . We have no real choice [other] than to proceed."

When Nir left, Bush's chief of staff, Craig Fuller, exhaled. "That was a very remarkable story!" he told his boss.

"It certainly was," Bush replied laconically. But he was in a hurry and discussed the issue no further.

During his 1988 presidential campaign, Bush would claim that Nir's briefing covered only Israel's dealings with Iran, not those of the United States; that it was never clear that arms were being traded for hostages; and that as far as he knew, the negotiations were with Iranian "moderates," not radicals. Fuller's extensive notes of the breakfast with Nir, however, show all of these three contentions to be untrue.

After Bush returned to Washington, his aide prepared a formal summary of the conversation. It was clear that Nir and North were seeking Bush's endorsement for a "sequenced" hostage deal — arms first, then a hostage, then more weapons, then another hostage. "When you look at the questions Nir was posing — Do we withhold weapons and demand all the hostages, or do we sequence the deliveries? — that question was what Ollie was trying to get various officials to deal with," a Bush aide said. "He might have been hoping that the vice president would take some action as a result of hearing it."

Bush, in other words, had a chance to intervene at that point in the arms-for-hostage deal — either to urge that the deals go on or to raise questions and urge that Reagan reconsider what his aides were leading him into. Yet he did nothing. He had the entire deal laid before him in clear, unsparing terms; but Bush, a dogged loyalist above all, raised no objections and forced no review of the policy. Over the entire sixteen-month life of the Iranian deals, cabinet members and White House aides said that the vice president made no visible impact on the Iranian deals at any time.

On the morning of July 30, Poindexter briefed the president on the heightened (if largely invented) fear that Hizballah might kill the hostages if the United States didn't ship a planeload of parts. Not only did this fourth arms-for-hostage deal offer no opening for improvement in U.S.-Iranian relations, it was little more than blackmail. But Reagan had no stomach for the choice that was placed before him. Poindexter scrawled on the bottom of his briefing memo: "7/30/86 President approved."

On August 4, an Israeli 707 delivered a load of HAWK missile parts to Iran. They were the same parts that McFarlane had refused to release in exchange for two hostages in May, but now the United States turned them over as retroactive payment for only one.

The Iranians got their missile parts. Ghorbanifar got his profits. North and Secord got money for Project Democracy. Three hostages remained in Beirut.   •

In the elegant offices of the secretary of state, George Shultz was feeling increasingly out of step with the president he served.

Shultz knew about the arms deals with Iran, but he felt curiously restrained from intervening. His top diplomat, Undersecretary Michael H. Armacost, wrote a heated memo in July charging that deals were still going on and warning: "As this story surfaces, we are going to sow more and more confusion among our friends, who will recall our frequent lectures on no deals for hostages and no arms for Iran."

Shultz read the memorandum, shook his head, and, like Bush, did nothing. "My understanding was [that] the whole thing had been stood down, so this didn't seem to fit with that," he explained later in a congressional hearing. "I don't recall what, if any, conversations I had or inquiries I made on the basis of this. . . . I had been given a pretty firm assurance — and it made sense in terms of 'How many times do you strike out?' — that this had ended."

The response made a kind of sense; it may well be that Shultz believed that the deals really had stopped. But one of his aides offered a fuller explanation in an interview, although he admitted it was partly an educated guess. "Shultz must have said to himself, 'I've got lots of battles to fight. If I go to the mat on this one, the president may hand me my walking papers.' And there may be an element of, 'They've made their bed, let them lie in it.' "

Shultz did have other problems. He didn't get along with Poindexter, who considered the secretary of state too moderate, too prone to soften Reagan's goals. "Poindexter had the view that Shultz was too much a spokesman for the institution of the State Department," an aide to the admiral said. "Poindexter simply didn't like Shultz," another NSC official said. "He would make comments at the morning staff meetings — little snide remarks."

Poindexter's predecessor, McFarlane, had increased his influence as national security adviser by forging an alliance with Shultz. But Poindexter found Defense Secretary Weinberger and CIA chief Casey more in tune with his views and made a point of arranging meetings with Reagan for Weinberger to balance Shultz's two private sessions a week.

Poindexter also began expanding his own role in policymaking. In the summer of 1986, as the administration began negotiating with the Soviet Union over the agenda of the next summit meeting, Poindexter took personal control of internal deliberations on U.S. arms control positions. Where McFarlane, in 1985, agreed on a strategy with Shultz and then jawboned others to join in, Poindexter worked out positions with his own staff and then slowly, methodically — and secretly — brought the other members of the NSC on board one by one.

Shultz began losing fights on the issues, too. He was overruled in June 1986, when he urged Reagan to continue observing the unratified Strategic Arms Limitation Treaty. And he was rebuffed on the appointments of several ambassadors as Regan reasserted the White House's control over those valuable political perks. When Shultz looked around the Cabinet Room, he now saw a powerful lineup all trying to thwart him: Poindexter, Weinberger, Casey, and — perhaps most painful of all, since they had been old friends — Don Regan.

"I felt a sense of estrangement," Shultz said later. "I knew the White House was very uncomfortable with me. I was very uncomfortable with what I was getting from the intelligence community, and I knew they were very uncomfortable with me, perhaps going back to the lie detector business. I could feel it."

In August, when Reagan and Bush announced that they would submit to urinalysis as part of the administration's war on drugs, White House aides speculated sarcastically whether Shultz, who had refused a polygraph, would submit to the indignity of a drug test. "It'll be easy to get

Shultz's sample," political director Mitch Daniels jibed. "We can just wipe it off the president."

"I was not in good odor with the NSC staff and some of the others in the White House," Shultz acknowledged. "I had a terrible time. There was a kind of guerrilla warfare going on, on all kinds of little things."

Under Regan's direction, the White House even refused several State Department requests to pay for Shultz's jet on official trips, as had been customary. Shultz had to go directly to Reagan to ask for reimbursement for his flights. "I hated to do this. I went to the president and I gave him little memorandums: check off 'Yes,' 'No.' And that's no business for the secretary of state to be taking up to the president of the United States," he said.

In any case, the basic message was clear: "I felt that I was no longer on the wavelength that I should be on."

By August, Shultz's discomfiture was especially acute. Early that month, he walked into the Oval Office for one of his regular meetings with the president and made his third offer to resign in three years.

"I'd like to leave," he told the president, "and here's my letter."

Reagan took the note, left it unopened, and stuck it in his desk drawer. He had already dissuaded Shultz from resigning twice; he knew he probably could do it again.

"You're tired," the president said. "It's about time to go on vacation. And let's talk about it after you get back."

Shultz needed nothing more than that to stay on. "Okay," he said.

Even when Shultz did get into step with the Reaganites, though, he won little credit. He had volunteered to seek bridge financing for the contras that summer, money to see them through until the new congressional appropriation of $100 million began flowing in October, but the project produced only headaches.

Shultz had initially thought of asking Saudi Arabia for help because of its limitless wealth. But U.S.-Saudi relations were going through a rough patch, and his advisers did not think Fahd would be receptive to a pitch. And Shultz soon got a startling telephone call from his old colleague Bud McFarlane.

For two years, McFarlane had kept the Saudi contributions secret from Shultz, but did not want the secretary of state to suffer the embarrassment of approaching King Fahd unwittingly.

"George," McFarlane said in a rush, "the Saudis already contributed $31 million to the contras." He hung up with a click.

With Saudi Arabia off limits, Shultz's aides cast about for an obscure, wealthy, anti-Communist country with no obvious political baggage. They came up with the perfect candidate: Brunei. The tiny sultanate on the northern coast of Borneo has an amiable, fervently pro-American ruler, the thirty-nine-year-old Sultan Muda Hassanal Bolkiah; it has money — a treasury of perhaps $20 billion saved from oil and gas revenues; and it has a shortage of worthy causes to spend its money on. The sultan had already built himself a 1,788-room palace, reputedly the world's largest residence; his subjects live comfortably as well. And, as it happened, Brunei was already scheduled to receive a visit from Shultz, who was embarking on a swing through Asia.

The secretary gave his assent to the idea and asked Elliott Abrams to get him a bank account number for the contras. Abrams knew where to go: to Oliver North at the NSC. He stood in North's outer office as Fawn Hall typed up a three-by-five card:

> Acct. #: 368-430-22-1
> Credit Suisse Bank
> Eaux Vives Branch
> Geneva, Switzerland

A few weeks later, Shultz took the card to Brunei. But in the end he did not make his pitch to the sultan; the U.S. ambassador in Brunei warned that a solicitation might strike the sovereign as a little abrupt during a visit of only three hours. Shultz turned the job over to Abrams, authorizing him to meet secretly with General Ibnu, the sultan's closest aide.

On August 9, Abrams arrived in London and, using the name "Mr. Kenilworth" to fool telephone wiretappers, called General Ibnu. Like characters from a John le Carré novel, they decided to do their business walking in a London park.

"He asked me how much money," Abrams recalled during his testimony. "I said: 'Ten million dollars.' I tried to explain to him why I thought they should, just because they should be interested in the security of the United States. He said to me, 'What do we get out of this? What's in it for us?' "

Abrams did not have a ready answer. "Well," he said, "well, the president will know of this, and you will have the gratitude of the secretary and of the president for helping us out in this jam."

"But what concrete do we get out of this?" Ibnu asked.

"You don't get anything concrete out of it," Abrams said.

They continued walking. "I can't make that decision," Ibnu said. He told Abrams that the answer would come from Brunei, from the sultan himself.

Abrams copied the account number from North's three-by-five card onto a slip of paper for the general to take home. They shook hands and parted.

The message came several weeks later: the sultan agreed to do the $10 million favor for Ronald Reagan and George Shultz. No further conversations were required; all they had to do was to wait for the money.

Secord, whose Geneva account number was on the card, had already decided what to do with the money. His financial manager, Hakim, said $3 million was to be spent, not for "humanitarian aid," which would have been legal, but for more weapons, which was not. The other $7 million, for the time being, would go into Project Democracy's bulging reserves.

By August, Project Democracy had achieved a major objective: the contra airlift was a success. After almost a year of work — and only months before the CIA was scheduled to take over — Secord's air force had accomplished its mission of resupplying the contras. There were still setbacks, of course, some of them serious. The planes carried inadequate navigation equipment; in June, the force's biggest plane, a C-123K, went badly off course, clipped a tree, and nearly crashed. The secret airstrip in Costa Rica turned out to be muddy and unusable most of the time. The contras' political leader, Adolfo Calero, still resented Secord's control over the money and airplanes and sometimes cooperated only grudgingly. And Felix Rodriguez, the key man at Project Democracy's base in El Salvador, had complained again to his friends on the vice president's staff that the operation was being run by the wrong people, people from the Edwin Wilson scandal. (Bush's foreign policy adviser, Donald P. Gregg, relayed the complaint to North, but said he never told Bush about the problem because it wasn't "vice presidential." North, in turn, complained to colleagues that Gregg was "coming into his turf.") But the supplies were getting through. Project Democracy's mission reports showed successful drops to the contras, including those deep inside Nicaragua, on an average of once every three days.

By the end of the summer, airlift manager Bob Dutton was sending messages to North asking for more deliveries to his shrinking inventory and joking about life in the jungle. Saturday, September 13, was "a red letter day," Dutton cabled: all five aircraft flew, and supplies were dropped into both northern and southern Nicaragua. "The surge is now in full force. . . . Have now delivered [55,000 pounds] in two days, taking tomorrow off.

"P.S. C-123 now armed with HK-21 7.62 machine gun on aft ramp. Bring on Mi-24 [Nicaragua's powerful Soviet helicopter gunship].

"P.P.S. Send Fawn — Can't continue on milk and cookies."

Officially, however, the contras were starving. All summer long, harrowing tales trickled into Washington about the contras' desperate straits. Calero had gone $2.5 million into debt to buy food for the troops; when there were supplies to deliver, there were no planes to deliver them. North spread the tales assiduously.

"The fact that the contras were receiving supplies was being picked up in the intelligence, particularly in 1986," a former NSC official said. "At the RIG, North would say the contras are broke. The analyst from

CIA would say, 'Wait a minute, we've got reports of ships coming in, missions being launched; how could they be broke?'

"It was never resolved," the official said. "We were trying to carry out a foreign policy with completely distorted intelligence. I was writing memos for the president saying things that were totally incorrect, including the fact that the contras were running out of supplies. It wasn't true. And the president was reading this stuff."

In fact, some members of the CIA suspected that the contras were getting money diverted from the Iranian arms sales, but none of them ever acted on the knowledge. In August, the CIA's Charles Allen, who was working on the talks with Iran, began to wonder about the huge price differentials in the arms deals. He told the CIA's deputy director for intelligence that he believed that profits from the HAWK parts sale might have been diverted to the contras. The deputy director told his superior, deputy CIA director Robert M. Gates, but Gates took no further action. "[My] first reaction was to tell Mr. Allen that I didn't want to hear any more about it," Gates testified later, explaining that he considered all information about aid to the contras out of bounds for the agency.

Had the CIA investigated, it might have discovered that Project Democracy's Swiss bank accounts were flush. The average balance that summer was more than $6.8 million (including $4.2 million that Secord called a "capital reserve"). The contras complained that they still weren't getting enough food, medicine, and boots to sustain their troops; but between June and August Hakim distributed almost $1.2 million in commissions and profits among his partners.

So successful was the enterprise that North, Secord, and Hakim were already planning Project Democracy's future as a "self-sustaining entity" after it turned the Nicaraguan war back over to the CIA. North told Poindexter that his companies would be delighted to sell their airplanes and other assets in Central America to the CIA for only $2.25 million, well below their estimated value of $4 million or more. Poindexter agreed with North that the CIA should buy the assets, but the agency stalled on the deal. It was reluctant, North complained, because some of its officers seemed to think Secord's assets were "tainted."

Instead, North arranged at least two other operations to funnel money into Project Democracy. One was a puzzling sale of contraband guns to the CIA. Secord and Tom Clines had bought a shipload of rifles through Manzer al Kassar, the arms broker they shared with Palestinian terrorist Abul Abbas. But instead of delivering the guns to the contras, they sold them to an arms dealer in Savannah, Georgia, who was connected to the CIA. Secord said he took a loss of $1.2 million on the sale, but he also shared a commission of $860,000 with his partners. Stranger still, a group of CIA-owned companies bought the guns without going through the agency's usual procedures for approving such purchases. Congressional investigators later said it appeared to be a scheme to generate "off the books" profits, much like the diversion from the Iranian arms sales. "Make things right for Secord," Poindexter had urged. In September, he told North that Secord should pick up a shipment of weapons that Israeli defense minister Yitzhak Rabin had offered to donate to the contras. "It can be a private deal between Dick and Rabin that we bless," Poindexter wrote.

Meanwhile, Secord and Hakim were looking into new business opportunities. They invested in a partnership to explore several ventures, including manufacturing submachine guns. And they entered negotiations to buy an interest in a firm that dealt in HAWK spare parts and other military hardware. Secord also planned to buy a Boeing 707 from Southern Air Transport so that he could handle his own secret arms shipments.

The underlying idea, Secord and Hakim later testified, was to set up a structure that could sell weapons and equipment to Iran over the long run. In time, they figured, Tehran would gradually reopen to the West and use its oil revenues to buy even more. When that happened, Secord and Hakim intended to have their noses already inside the tent. It would be the ultimate marriage of private profit and the public good.

Throughout the summer, North and his colleagues in the Iranian arms negotiations came repeatedly to one conclusion: Manucher Ghorbanifar was more trouble than he was worth. He had lied to both sides; he had lured the Americans to a meeting in Tehran that failed because of his false promises; he was driving deals forward for his own financial gain and, apparently, little more. And his enormous markups on the sales had nearly driven the Iranians away entirely.

North asked Hakim to seek out another channel into the Iranian government. He eventually found his way to an up-and-coming young Iranian official named Ali Hashemi Bahremani. Bahremani was a veteran of the Revolutionary Guard's front-line battles in the war with Iraq; more important, he was a favorite nephew of Rafsanjani, the speaker of Iran's parliament. At Hakim's suggestion, Secord met the new Iranian connection in Brussels on August 25 and was immediately impressed. Bahremani "is a very sharp, well-educated young man," he cabled North. He "knew a great deal about McFarlane mission to Tehran. He also knows all about [Kangarlou], Gorba [Ghorbanifar], Israeli connection, and this group's financial greed.

"My judgment is that we have opened up [a] new and probably much better channel into Iran. This connection has been recruited and he wants to start dealing."

But North did not drop Ghorbanifar completely. Among other things, North was worried that the arms merchant might reveal the operation publicly — including the diversion of funds to the contras — if he was cut off too abruptly. And Ghorbanifar had just proposed a fifth arms-for-hostage deal: 1,100 TOWs plus radar equipment for the three remaining hostages.

Then, to their surprise, the Americans discovered that the two channels to Iran, instead of competing, were cooperating with each other. Ghorbanifar's Tehran contact, Kangarlou, said his boss, the prime minister, had approved the Americans' talks with Rafsanjani's nephew. For the time being, North decided to deal with both sets of Iranians, since he wasn't quite sure who represented what.

The first order of business was bringing Bahremani to Washington to hold serious talks. North and his colleagues wanted to start over, to talk openly about weapons, hostages, and the U.S.-Iranian relationship.

The young Iranian met with North, Secord, and Cave in North's office in the Old Executive Office Building on September 19. Bahremani explained Iran's concerns: winning the war with Iraq, warding off Soviet subversion, keeping the price of oil from collapse. He said Secord had assured him that if the Soviet Union ever invaded Iran, the United States would intervene to defend Tehran. "The government of Iran found this interesting and comforting," he said.

The young Iranian brought with him a long shopping list of arms. North assured him that almost all the weapons could be delivered — once the hostages were freed. "We are prepared to continue to provide to Iran items which will help in her defense, but [we] wish to see the hostage issue behind us so that we can move forward," he said. "The issue of hostages and terrorism must be dealt with, since it is a political obstacle. . . . If the president is found to be helping Iran with this obstacle still in the way, it would be very difficult to explain to our people."

Bahremani proposed a joint commission of Iranians and Americans to work on improving relations. North appointed himself, Secord, and Cave to the panel on the spot and promised that President Reagan would publicly praise the Iranian regime for deciding to refuse landing rights to hijacked passenger airplanes.

Bahremani then delivered a report on the hostages. He told the Americans that William Buckley had "died of natural causes" after suffering three heart attacks, not from torture. And he explained a puzzling new surge of kidnappings in Beirut. Two Americans, Frank Reed and Joseph Cicippio, had been abducted in early September. The Iranian said Reed had been seized by an independent group of terrorists, but Cicippio's kidnapping was even more worrisome: he had been taken by radicals reportedly under the influence of Ghorbanifar's contact, Kangarlou. The Americans worried that Kangarlou might be taking new hostages to improve his bargaining power.

The talks continued, but not without at least one necessary interruption. In the afternoon, as the time for Muslim prayers came around, Bahremani went in search of a prayer rug. He finally borrowed a gym towel from North's assistant, Craig Coy. Then, as the Americans kept a respectful distance, he spread the towel on the floor of the office, turned east toward Mecca (which happened also to be toward the Oval Office), and said his prayers.

It was evening when their talks ended. North took Bahremani across the private drive into the deserted West Wing of the White House. With North providing a running commentary, the young Revolutionary Guard was given a private tour of the Oval Office, the Cabinet Room, and the Roosevelt Room as well as the glittering reception rooms of the East Wing.

In the Cabinet Room, North led him to a painting and pointed out an old hound sleeping under a table. "That one's Casey," he said. The Iranian, whose culture and religion abhor dogs, laughed politely.

In the Roosevelt Room, North was more reverent. He showed Bahremani the portrait of Theodore Roosevelt and a medallion on the mantel. "This is a Nobel Peace Prize — in fact, the first one given to an American," North said. "And it was given to a president who saw that it was to the advantage of our country and to world peace to sit down in Portsmouth and have a conference with two adversaries, the Russians and the Japanese, who were fighting a war thousands of miles from us, that had no immediate impact on America, and we solved it."

The next morning, North and his colleagues were exultant. Bahremani, they decided, was the real thing. North sent Poindexter a message recounting his story about the Russo-Japanese War and added buoyantly, "Anybody for RR getting the same prize?"

What impressed Tom Twetten, the CIA's Middle East chief, was that Bahremani didn't overpromise. "He immediately presented bona fides in the sense of saying, 'Look, we can't get all your hostages out. . . . We can get two out, maybe three, but we can't get them all,' " Twetten said. Charles Allen was also impressed, especially because Bahremani told them that they were not dealing with Iranian "dissidents" or "moderates"; they were dealing with officials who were acting with the approval of Khomeini himself. The ayatollah's son, Ahmed Khomeini, "briefed the father in great detail," Allen said, and "the Iranians had decided that it was worth talking to the Americans not just for arms but, I think, for broader reasons."

So the Iranian initiative now stood completely on its head. Launched with hopes of reaching Iranian moderates who could start a new dialogue with the United States and win the release of all the hostages, it now depended on a Revolutionary Guard who proudly claimed Khomeini's blessing — and who said he could free only some of the hostages, not all.

Poindexter briefed Reagan on the meetings with Bahremani on September 23. If he explained to the president that he was now dealing with emissaries reporting directly to Khomeini (as, apparently, he always had been), the president either failed to understand — or chose not to. For more than a year afterward, Reagan would insist that he had negotiated only with Iranian dissidents and moderates.

None of these seeming contradictions fazed North. He was working on another top-level meeting — this time with George Bush as the American emissary. And North wanted to send a gift to Rafsanjani to celebrate the beginning of a new relationship. He sent a Bible in to the Oval Office, and Reagan, following North's instructions, obediently copied out a verse in his rounded scrawl from Paul's Epistle to the Galatians:

> And the scripture, foreseeing that God would justify the Gentiles by faith, preached the gospel beforehand to Abraham, saying, "All the nations shall be blessed in you."
> GALATIANS 3:8
> Ronald Reagan, Oct. 3, 1986.

Poindexter wrote McFarlane a note of delayed congratulations: "Your trip to Tehran paid off. You did get through to the top. They are playing our line back to us. They are worried about Soviets, Afghanistan, and their economy. They realize that the hostages are [an] obstacle to any productive relationship with us. . . . If this comes off [we] may ask you to do a second round after the hostages are back. Keep your fingers crossed."

Almost everything seemed to be working right. After fifteen months of effort, the NSC's secret Iranian connection was finally paying off. The hostages might yet be home in time for Christmas, if not election day. The contras had survived their two lean years, and the CIA was moving back in with $100 million in aid. Project Democracy was a certifiable success, ready to be retooled for new projects around the world.

The broader view from the White House was equally sunny. The economy was booming, the stock market still churning out a message of prosperity. The president's popularity had eased off from its peaks, but not by much: it was still in the high sixties. And his rating was about to get another boost: a second summit meeting with Mikhail Gorbachev had just been scheduled in Reykjavik, Iceland. Congress was still restive, of course; the House and Senate had just overturned Reagan's veto of economic sanctions against South Africa, a sign that the president's magic was not as potent as it had been. But the midterm congressional elections were coming up, and the polls, as well as the strategically timed summit, suggested that Reagan and the GOP had a good chance to hold their own.

On balance, it was a time when the administration could take much pleasure in its successes. Almost everyone in Ronald Reagan's White House could survey the political landscape with satisfaction. And no one could feel more convinced that the hard work was paying off than Oliver North. On Sunday evening, October 5, North left Washington for Frankfurt aboard Pan Am flight 60, on his way to another meeting with his new Iranian contact. It can be safely deduced that on that night, in that airplane, he was almost certainly a happy man.

III

LANDSLIDE

13

Spin Control

THE OLD, CAMOUFLAGED C-123K lumbered down Ilopango's runway at nine-fifty that morning, lifted off into the humid air, and headed southeast across El Salvador toward the Pacific. It was October 5, the end of the rainy season in Central America, and morning was a good time to fly. The sky was already filling with spectacular tall clouds, like schooners in a clear blue sea, but the pilot knew that they would turn to thunderheads by midafternoon.

The plane carried a full load. The cargo deck was jammed with wooden pallets holding crates of rifles, grenade launchers, and bullets. There were combat boots, jungle knives, a 7.62-caliber machine gun, and a box of medicine for treating "mountain leprosy," the fungal malady that strikes all but the hardiest natives after a few weeks in the jungles of Nicaragua. On each pallet was a parachute clipped to a static line secured to the aircraft frame. When the pallet was shoved out the rear of the plane, the static line would play out. When it was taut, it would, in effect, yank the parachute cord and cause the chute to open a safe distance below the plane.

Four men were aboard. Three of them — the pilot, William Cooper; the copilot, Wallace Blaine Sawyer, known inevitably as Buzz; and the loadmaster, or "kicker," Eugene H. Hasenfus — were all veterans of Air America, the former CIA airline based in Taiwan and used in Indochina during the Vietnam War. The radioman, or "talker," whose job was to make contact with the Spanish-speaking troops on the ground, was a local boy of seventeen. It was his first war. The three Americans carried pistols in their belts; the young Nicaraguan was more comfortable with an AK-47 rifle.

The first leg of the flight was uneventful. It followed the same course that each of the crew had flown at least three times before: down the Pacific coast about 300 miles, then east across the northern edge of Costa Rica. The tricky part came next: after passing the southern end of Lake Nicaragua, with its rocky islands, the aircraft plunged to a low altitude to slip north across the border, hoping to escape detection by the Sandinistas' radar. After that came the search for the drop zone, which was never easy: the contras were notoriously bad at reading maps and frequently gave muddled coordinates; the drop itself, a time of tension because so many small things could go wrong; and finally the dash back out, retracing the way in.

This morning, the crew wanted to vary the pattern to keep the enemy guessing, crossing the Nicaraguan border a little to the west of the usual course. Cooper spotted the landmark, a sharp bend in the Rio San Juan with an island and a boatwreck, dropped the plane to 900 feet, and wheeled sharply to the left. Once across, he climbed back up to 3,000 feet, and the crew, breathing more easily, got ready for the drop. The Nicaraguan boy got on his radio, calling for the contras who were waiting, unseen, under the green canopy below. It was 12:45 P.M.

On the ground, a patrol from the Sandinista army's Gaspar García Laviana Brigade, an elite Hunter unit, was astonished to see the plane appear in the southern sky, heading, it seemed, straight for them. A young infantryman hastily lifted his SA-7 tube to his shoulder, tracked the plane for a moment, and squeezed the trigger. The patrol watched open-mouthed as the missile roared off, found the hot exhaust of the C-123K's motor, and exploded with a flash.

"I can't believe I did it!" the boy shouted. "I can't believe it!"

The crew felt a terrible jolt as the missile hit. Crouching with the cargo, Hasenfus looked out a starboard window and saw part of the wing disintegrate. The right engine burst into flames. Hasenfus, steps from an open cargo door, needed little time to think; he had been through this drill before. He was the only one with a parachute. The owners hadn't supplied them, and the other crew members teased him about his dragging the thing along. But he had borrowed the chute from his brother and it made him feel better, so he carried it.

Someone screamed. Hasenfus jumped out the open door. His parachute opened with a reassuring thump, and he turned to look at the plane. It was on fire and plummeting toward earth. He watched, transfixed. Then he concentrated on the bright green jungle rushing up to embrace him.

News of the crash moved north in spurts. It was not until evening that anyone outside Nicaragua began to wonder what had happened to Bill Cooper's plane. It had been due back at three-thirty in the afternoon. Delayed returns weren't unusual, but after several hours Secord's men began to realize that something had gone wrong. A round of telephone and radio calls began between Ilopango, Aguacate, and the U.S. Embassy in Costa Rica. Joe Fernandez, the CIA station chief, began checking the airstrips in northern Costa Rica where a plane with engine trouble might have put down, and he asked the contras' Southern Front commanders to start a search for the plane inside Nicaragua. The commander of the Salvadoran air force offered to launch a search-and-rescue mission.

Late that evening, George Bush's friend in the airlift operation, Felix Rodriguez, had given up. He picked up the telephone in Miami and called Bush's military aide, Samuel Watson, to alert him about the accident. (Watson said he passed the report along to North's office, but not to Bush.)

It was not until the next morning, Monday, October 6, that Poindexter was informed of the crash. The details were still sketchy. No one yet knew if there had been any survivors.

That same morning, in Nicaragua, the Sandinistas were beginning to spread the news that they had shot down a contra supply plane. However, it wasn't until afternoon that they actually found Hasenfus, who had wandered through the jungle and taken refuge in a peasant's hut. The Sandinistas brought television crews in by helicopter and paraded Hasenfus, bedraggled and bewildered, at the end of a rope held by a peasant soldier half his size.

"My name is Eugene Hasenfus," he called to the cameraman. "I come from Marinette, Wisconsin."

In Washington, these ten words hit the White House with the force of the original SA-7 missile. For more than a year, a handful of administration officials had kept the lid on Project Democracy. When Congress had probed about the White House's role in Central America, Poindexter had used Oliver North to lie and afterward praised him for a job well done. When the president had proselytized against concessions to terrorists, neither Regan, Bush, Casey nor Poindexter, all of whom knew about the arms sales, felt any need to set the record — or the policy — straight. Apparently they had all felt invincible, secure in the knowledge that they had the most popular and trusted salesman in America as their spokesman. Indeed, they had almost gotten away with it — Hasenfus's flight was to have been one of the very last — because in only twelve more days, the military aid from Congress was going to start flowing to the contras legally.

It was so close, and they had been lucky for so long, that no one had even thought to do any contingency planning. Until October 5, they had yet to encounter a problem that public relations couldn't fix. It had been a triumph of image over reality. But suddenly, it wasn't just Hasenfus's plane, but Reagan's presidency, with its irreplaceable cargo of credibility, that was about to crash and burn.

·   ·   ·

Panicky aides immediately sought to bolster their deception with more deception. High-level plans for "spin control" began almost immediately. Even on October 5, before the crash was confirmed, Joe Fernandez realized that the entire operation could be in trouble. "Situation requires we do necessary damage control," he wrote Dutton. "Did this [aircraft] have tail number?" With a tail number, he knew, reporters could trace the plane to Southern Air Transport and see in some of its movements the larger pattern of Project Democracy.

In Washington, the confirmation of the crash prompted orchestrated denials. On October 7, Elliott Abrams presided over a meeting of the RIG. An NSC official present recorded the decisions: They would ask the contras "to assume responsibility for flights and to assist families of Americans involved." (Contra leader Adolfo Calero eventually agreed to say that the plane was his, telling other contra officials that he volunteered to take responsibility for one major reason: "to protect George Bush.") The State Department would prepare a statement for the press "which states no U.S. government involvement or connection, but that we are generally aware of such support contracted by the contras." The same day, George Shultz, relying on a briefing from Abrams, insisted that the Hasenfus flight "had no connection with the U.S. government at all."

Not until the following day, October 8, did Poindexter finally brief Reagan on the situation. It was three days since the crash, and for at least a day it had been a major news item, though more a disconnected curiosity piece than a scandal. But senior aides said that Reagan didn't bring it up until Poindexter briefed him. Then he had a question: "Is this General Singlaub?"

Poindexter carefully replied, "No, it definitely isn't Singlaub. And we know it wasn't a government aircraft."

Then, according to another official who was there, Poindexter misled the president. "We don't know exactly who it was," he said. "But I think you should be careful about denying any U.S. role."

Despite this warning, Reagan was not careful. Where Poindexter had been evasive, Reagan was blunt. "Absolutely none," he said in answer to reporters' questions about U.S. involvement. "There is no government connection with that plane at all. . . . We've been aware that there are private groups and private citizens that have been trying to help the contras — to that extent — but we did not know the particulars of what they're doing."

George Bush's office, queried about its connections to Felix Rodriguez, put out a carefully worded statement denying that either the vice president or his staff had been running a resupply operation in Central America. But the statement conspicuously sidestepped whether his office had known of or aided the efforts.

Elliott Abrams was more categorical. Appearing on a television talk show a week after the crash, he was asked if he could completely deny any control, guidance, or connection to the plane.

"Absolutely," he said. "That would be illegal. We are barred from doing that and we are not doing it. It is not in any sense a U.S. operation."

Abrams was equally emphatic to congressional committees, who, spurred on by the press, immediately began to question the phantom plane crash. "Just to be clear," asked Lee Hamilton, the chairman of the House Intelligence Committee, "the United States government has not done anything to facilitate the activities of these private groups. Is that a fair statement? We have not furnished money. We have not furnished arms. We have not furnished advice. We have not furnished logistics?"

"Yes," replied Abrams, "to the extent of my knowledge that I feel to be complete, other than the general public encouragement that we like this kind of activity." Abrams also said he knew of no foreign contributions to the contras — although he had solicited the $10 million gift from Brunei only two months earlier and had been told that Brunei deposited the contribution. He specifically denied that Saudi Arabia had given the contras any money. "We have not received a dime from a foreign government — not a dime, from any foreign government." (Abrams later testified that his denials stemmed from honest ignorance.)

While Abrams and Poindexter were denying the truth, others on the NSC staff began erasing it. Soon after the crash, Kenneth DeGraffenreid, a close friend of North's on the NSC staff, went to see Poindexter. Ollie wrote all those memos for McFarlane, DeGraffenreid reminded his boss. They're still in the system. We'd be better off without them.

"They probably do reveal too much," Poindexter agreed. "Go talk to Ollie about them."

Ironically, Poindexter, who had a more sophisticated understanding of computers than any senior official in the White House, overlooked an important feature of the system. Copies of every message and memo — reams of them documenting the strange life of Project Democracy — had been stored not just in their own terminals, which they purged, but also in a little-known backup system in the main-frame computer.

Poindexter was preoccupied with more immediate concerns. Both the FBI and the Customs Service had launched potentially damaging investigations of Southern Air Transport after the crash. Poindexter persuaded Meese to suspend the FBI's investigation for roughly two weeks. Meanwhile, North took care of Customs. He called its investigative chief and told him that Southern Air's staff were "good guys" who had done nothing illegal and were helping with legitimate covert operations. As usual, North was persuasive; the Customs man agreed to narrow the investigation to the Hasenfus airplane alone and not even look at Southern Air's other activities.

But while the government's investigative efforts proved rather easy to control, this time the press proved beyond control. On October 18, reporters for UPI and the Long Island newspaper *Newsday* finagled the telephone records for the house where the air crews lived in San Salvador. There in black and white was a series of revealing telephone numbers: Oliver North's office in the Old Executive Office Building, Richard Secord's office and home in suburban Virginia, and a number that led to Joe Fernandez's office in the U.S. Embassy in Costa Rica. Project Democracy's Central American operation was about to be blown wide open.

At the Frankfurt Airport Sheraton on October 6, Oliver North was not at his best. Calling his office, he had learned from Bob Earl about the missing C-123. And he couldn't even begin to patch up his Nicaraguan operations because he was facing two days of meetings with Bahremani, the crucial new channel into the Khomeini regime. But things didn't look right on this end, either.

Bahremani brought with him a man named Ali Samaii, an intelligence officer from Iran's radical Revolutionary Guards. What was disconcerting was that Samaii had been present during the disastrous meetings with McFarlane in Tehran which Ghorbanifar had set up. Was there a direct connection between the Ghorbanifar group, which the Americans had concluded was bad, and the Bahremani group, which they thought to be entirely different and vastly more reliable?

There was little time to puzzle it out. North was a little more frantic, his stories a bit wilder, than usual. With a flourish, he presented Bahremani with the Bible with President Reagan's autographed inscription inside the front cover. "We, inside our government, had an enormous debate, a very angry debate . . . over whether my president should authorize me to say 'We accept the Islamic revolution of Iran as a fact,' " North solemnly told the Iranians. "He [Reagan] went off one whole weekend and prayed about what the answer should be, and he came back almost a year ago with that passage I gave you, that he wrote in front of the Bible I gave you. And he said to me: 'This is a promise that God gave to Abraham. Who am I to say that we should not do this?' "

North, who in fact had never met alone with the president, told of bringing the Iranians' shopping list to Reagan at Camp David. "Stop coming in and looking like a gun merchant!" thundered North's fictional president, pounding the table with a good deal more emphasis than the real thing. "I want to end the war!"

Having thus invoked the blessings of both God and president, North presented a seven-point proposal that he said Reagan had authorized. It offered 2,000 TOWs as well as HAWK parts, medical supplies, and "updated intelligence on Iraq." In exchange, North wanted the three remaining Beirut hostages as well as Buckley's body and a transcript of his confession. (North didn't ask for the new hostages who had been taken that fall in the midst of this ripe climate for barter, Frank Reed and Joseph Cicippio, because U.S. officials believed that they were held by another group.)

After North stated his position, the real bargaining began. As the Iranians pressed for concessions, North gave more and more ground. The Iranians asked for artillery to help their infantry attack Iraq; North said that would be fine as long as it wasn't used to seize Baghdad — an outlandish gentleman's agreement. The Iranians also pressed North to get the United States to endorse their aim of overthrowing Iraq's president, Saddam Hussein. North assured them that he had discussed the Iraqi strongman's future in private with Reagan at Camp David, and that Reagan had confided to him: "Saddam Hussein is a shit." ("Do you want me to translate that?" Hakim asked doubtfully. "Go ahead," North urged. "That's his word, not mine.") In his own words, he added, "We also recognize that Saddam Hussein must go" — thus committing the officially neutral United States to a policy it did not have.

North crowned this list by volunteering a concession on the issue of the Shia terrorists held in Kuwait's prisons. He told the Iranians that he and Poindexter had met with Kuwait's foreign minister and given him a pointed message: if Kuwait decided to release the Shia prisoners, the United States — which for more than a year had publicly praised Kuwait for standing firm — would not criticize the action. It sounded like the same gambit the administration had used to pressure Israel during the TWA hijacking in 1985 — a wink and a nod to suggest that another country make a concession to terrorists.

But after twenty-four hours of U.S. concessions, the Iranians said they still couldn't release all the hostages. The desperate Americans conceded that one or two would be enough for a deal. North was frantic to get back to Washington to protect his crumbling Central American operation. Finally, on the afternoon of Tuesday, October 7, he simply got up and left. "Why don't you guys hold this discussion after I'm gone, okay?" he said.

In private, North told Hakim that he had six hours to pin down a deal; he emphasized that Reagan wanted at least one hostage home by election day, November 4. The close midterm elections would determine whether the GOP maintained control of the Senate, a matter of major consequence to the remainder of Reagan's presidency. No one could say for sure if the return of a hostage would make any difference, but the White House was struggling for every advantage.

In North's absence, Albert Hakim, the former Tehran import agent, took over as the chief negotiator representing the United States. He worked out an agreement with Bahremani and Samaii that had nine points, adding more concessions to those North had already approved.

Going even further than North, he promised that the Americans would put together a plan urging Kuwait to release some of the Shia prisoners. North, following Hakim's progress from afar, told Poindexter that the deal was a bargain.

Poindexter, who apparently had no reservations of his own, later testified that he briefed Reagan on the plan. And although Reagan later behaved with shock when he was reminded of the Kuwaiti aspect of the deal, he approved it, his national security adviser said. Exactly what Reagan thought he was approving, though, is hazy. An explanation Poindexter later gave suggests that he obscured the explosive implications of the U.S. concession by suggesting that the pressure against Kuwait was to be applied, not directly by the United States, but indirectly by Iran. With this evasion, he could argue that the deal didn't directly violate Reagan's policy of no concessions to terrorists.

Poindexter's sophistry might have gone undetected by Reagan, but it didn't get by the Kuwaitis, who later confirmed that they had been pressured on the issue but that they had refused. "Have you forgotten that you are the chief advocate for combatting terrorism in the world?" lectured an editorial in one of the emirate's semiofficial newspapers.

On October 14, White House aides reaffirmed their lofty public posture in a formal statement: "We will not negotiate the exchange of innocent Americans for the release from prison of tried and convicted murderers held in a third country, nor will we pressure other nations to do so. To make such concessions would jeopardize the safety of other American citizens and would only encourage more terrorism." But there were strange rumors circulating in the Middle East — not just in Kuwait — putting Project Democracy in jeopardy of unraveling in two hemispheres at once.

Ron Walker, the man who had orchestrated Reagan's 1984 inauguration, had a simple rule of thumb: "As go appearances, so goes the presidency." In the first term, a politically sophisticated team of public relations experts had lived by this rule. In the second term, a less sophisticated team was about to die by it.

Reagan's first-term advisers elevated presidential stagecraft to an art form. They placed tape marks at his feet, they constructed blue backdrops to flatter his complexion, and they produced presidential playlets, complete with scripts, to send his homilies home. To a remarkable extent, they altered political reality simply by altering public perceptions. With the artful use of such techniques, Reagan moved public opinion, enabling him to change the entire direction of American politics.

But by the fall of 1986 something had happened. It wasn't a quantum leap, just an evolution. The tape marks and the backdrops were the same as ever, but the government of public relations men was no longer as good as it looked. This was ironic, since Don Regan was more of a professional salesman than anyone else who had occupied his exalted post. "He could sell it flat, or he could sell it round," said one admiring colleague from the Treasury Department. But, in a sense, he and his eager acolytes had finally oversold their own talents, apparently believing that public perception was infinitely malleable, reality infinitely flexible, and Reagan's popularity a resource so valuable that it alone could substitute for coherent statecraft. If Reagan's numbers were good, they believed their stewardship was good; it was that simple.

In the first term, Reagan's men had mobilized the huge apparatus of White House public relations to sell his very real agenda, coordinating congressional and media strategies to push through such programs as the 1981 tax bill. But by late 1986, for the most part, they were no longer selling Reagan's programs but simply Reagan himself, devising policies that would keep him popular rather than the other way around. The last real effort to rally public opinion for a Reagan program was the 1985 campaign to sell tax reform, which never gained much popular support but was saved by skillful congressional work largely on the part of Treasury officials. In fact, many of the most pointed White House public relations efforts by this time were devoted, not to selling the administration's programs, but to deceiving the public about the nature of those programs — from Nicaragua to Tehran.

With so much of the White House's real agenda relegated to the shadows, what was left to put before the klieg lights was getting pretty thin. But the president's men seemed to think that with "the big cannon" (as they called Reagan) on their side, they could sell anything. They seemed not to notice that the "spin control" machinery was getting so overworked, it was beginning to collapse under the weight of their demands.

For instance, Reagan's hapless effort during this period to help the Republicans maintain control of the Senate showed how far they thought they could go on public relations alone. His pitch, used in rallies across the country, seemed designed with a heavy hand to avoid issues, which in fact it was. The president's former and current political advisers had held a series of dinner meetings at Washington restaurants in the late summer and early fall to work out the best approach. In the recent past, the party had always had a theme, articulated by the president to rally voters. But the consensus at the 1986 meetings was to instead have Reagan give innocuous speeches that would be sure "not to rock the boat," according to Mitch Daniels. The aim was to keep Reagan's popularity high in the hope that it would boost the other Republican candidates for office.

After some casting about, pollster Richard Wirthlin found a safe focus for the campaign. His polls showed a surging public concern about drug abuse, following the death of basketball star Len Bias from an overdose of cocaine, and a greater trust in the Republicans' ability to cure the problem than that of the Democrats. On Wirthlin's advice, this group decided to capitalize on the numbers and have Reagan make a series of speeches on drugs. It was an issue he and the First Lady cared about and was also the innocuous public relations issue his advisers had hoped for — long on emotion but short on specifics.

Kenneth Khachigian, the speechwriter called in to help craft Reagan's campaign against drugs, was struck by how thin it was. He thought the issue had promise, but "there was no follow-up." Follow-up was beside the point. On September 16, Don Regan sent a note to Khachigian which suggested where his true interests lay. "The results are in and you've done it again!" Regan exclaimed about the joint address that the first couple had just given against drug abuse. "From the President and Mrs. Reagan to the Wirthlin polls, all reviews are outstanding. . . . Dick Wirthlin's analysis indicates that never have reactions to one of the president's speeches been more favorable!"

When the Republican party lost control of the Senate on election day, many would look back and wonder about the White House's strategy. Reagan campaigned for thirteen senators in the weeks before the election — and nine of them went down to defeat. In fairness, each Senate race had its own political dynamic, and the president's power to affect local races was limited. Yet, said one Republican strategist, "Reagan failed to give voters a reason to vote Republican, because he never really spelled out what he wanted to do."

Reagan didn't attend the campaign planning sessions. In fact, he played virtually no role in planning for the 1986 campaign, according to several of those who did. Although he traveled 24,800 miles and made fifty-four appearances in twenty-two states, raising more than $33 million for the Republican candidates, he made only one tactical decision himself during the entire campaign cycle: to make one last-ditch extra stop in Nevada for Republican Senate hopeful James Santini. It was something the retiring incumbent senator Paul Laxalt had personally asked him to do, and although Don Regan was furious about yet another appearance for what was clearly by then a losing cause, the sentimental Reagan wouldn't turn down a friend in need.

In contrast, Nancy Reagan played an enormous role in mapping out the '86 campaign strategy, discussing the president's daily schedule with the advance team every afternoon before election day. "She was very concerned about losing the Senate in '86," recalled a White House aide who was involved. "That's the reason he traveled so much, because she was so worried. That kind of decision never would have gone to him. The political staff, the advance staff, and Mrs. Reagan drew up all the plans. But the president played no part in these kinds of things — he just went. He was pretty oblivious. He never knew what was going on."

It took until election day for the shortcomings of this approach to surface fully. But well before then, there were other signs that the White House's spin control operation was out of control. On October 2, three days before Hasenfus floated to earth, the *Washington Post* exposed what seemed to be a particularly sinister strain of the administration's belief that it could control political reality through political appearances.

According to reporter Bob Woodward, the administration had embraced a policy of "disinformation" deliberately intended to deceive the press. The point of the campaign, he wrote, was to convince reporters that Qadhafi was again actively promoting terrorism after having been briefly subdued by the U.S. raids on Libya. Some on the NSC staff — Oliver North among them — hoped these exaggerated reports would scare Qadhafi and perhaps even inspire a coup. To the alarm of Washington's press establishment, Woodward implied that the administration had succeeded in planting this "disinformation" on the front page of the August 25 *Wall Street Journal*, which led with a story declaring that the United States and Libya appeared to be "on a collision course." In an administration that called nuclear-tipped missiles "peacekeepers," tax increases "revenue enhancements," and fatigues for contras "humanitarian aid," the journalists' outcry seemed a bit fatuous. But perhaps because the policy of manipulating the press had now been spelled out in a White House memo, this time it touched off a furor.

The facts were a bit more complicated. Reagan had neither opposed nor endorsed the "disinformation" plan. As was often true when thorny national security issues confronted him, he simply didn't react to a memo about it. Although Reagan had been given a copy of the memo laying out the proposed disinformation plan in alarming detail, the subject never came up during the NSPG meeting on August 14. By October, instead of scaring Qadhafi, the disinformation plan backfired on the NSC once Woodward exposed it. But, far from criticizing the orchestrated policy of deception, Reagan virtually condoned it. "Our position has been one which we would just as soon have Mr. Qadhafi go to bed every night wondering what we might do," he said.

For years, Reagan had shown limited appreciation for the role of the press, a view that allowed his lieutenants' spin control efforts to prosper. He didn't hate the press, like Nixon, but he did not harbor much affection for the three thousand or so reporters — about sixty of them under foot daily — accredited by the White House to cover him. In fact, the Great Communicator presided over an administration that more than ever before systematically restricted media access to government information — from weakening the Freedom of Information Act to applying press-related clauses of the 1950 Espionage Act to closeting off the president himself.

Reagan liked to reminisce fondly about his own apprenticeship in the fourth estate, as a sports announcer for the Des Moines radio station WHO. But significantly, his biggest moment there came when the transmission line relaying a baseball game to him went dead and he was left to fake the plays. The line between fact and fiction, or accuracy and expediency, was one Reagan crossed early.

If he felt remorse for the Libyan disinformation episode, it wasn't displayed publicly — and it would not have been in character. In June 1982, after Alexander Haig's abrupt resignation, Reagan declared in a press conference that "if I thought that there's something involved with this that the American people needed to know, with regard to their own welfare, then I would be frank with the American people and tell them." The implication was clear. The government, not the press corps, ought to be the source of the nation's news, and the president was the best arbiter of what the public ought to know.

One week after the Hasenfus crash and ten days after the disinformation scare, far from being chastened, the White House "spin controllers" met an even greater challenge. The occasion was the Reagan-Gorbachev summit in Reykjavik, Iceland, over the weekend of October 11 and 12, an event that proved to be the ultimate example of substituting stagecraft for statecraft.

The slapdash summit was launched at the same moment in September that Reagan was insisting there had been no swap with the Soviet Union of the Soviet spy Gennadi Zakharov for the American journalist Nicholas Daniloff, even though the reciprocity was obvious. The Soviet foreign minister, Eduard Shevardnadze, carried a letter proposing the summit to Reagan while he was in Washington to discuss the Daniloff situation. In less than twenty-four hours, Reagan agreed to Gorbachev's offer despite a series of prior statements that he would agree to no superpower summit before the midterm elections, and then to no summit without a clear agenda.

Less than three weeks later, Reagan was in Reykjavik, supposedly not to deal with the substance of arms control but just to plan for the real summit, which Gorbachev had previously agreed to hold with Reagan later in the United States. The Reykjavik meeting happened so quickly, and with so few expectations of substantive discussions, that assistant to the president William Henkel admitted sometime later, "Shit — there was no time for preparation."

The results of Reykjavik may be debated for years, but the casual way in which Reagan played at gambling away the West's nuclear deterrent is beyond question and without match. One U.S. arms control expert involved in the summit belatedly described it as having "the giddiness of a college dorm all-nighter." Larry Speakes admitted, "I never get emotional, but I had tears in my eyes about what we were on the brink

of. My second reaction was, 'Do we really know what we're doing?' "
Michael Deaver, who knew the limits of Reagan's understanding of arms
control after helping to prepare him for the Geneva summit, went further:
"The fact that nobody anticipated that the Soviets were going to put a
deal on the table, and that Reagan wasn't given an alternative strategy
just in case, was criminal — absolutely criminal."

So informal were the negotiations, at least on the U.S. side, that when
Reagan returned to Washington on October 12, what he had agreed to
was unclear. The confusion centered on whether he had offered at one
point to eliminate all ballistic missiles by 1996 or whether he had gone
beyond that, offering to eliminate all nuclear weapons — which would
include all U.S. nuclear bombers and cruise missiles as well as land-
and submarine-based ballistic missiles. In one sense, the difference was
academic, because the offer had already foundered on Reagan's unwillingness in the final hours to agree to an interpretation of the 1972 antiballistic missile (ABM) treaty limiting the testing of the Strategic
Defense Initiative to laboratory research. But in another sense, the confusion surrounding Reagan's offer revealed the extent to which the process had lacked even the semblance of coherent planning.

Confusion abounded. Immediately after the summit, according to one
witness, upon hearing that the president had told some U.S. officials
that he'd offered to bargain away all nuclear weapons, not just ballistic
missiles, John Poindexter was appalled.

"Mr. President," said Poindexter, "we've got to clear up this business
about you agreeing to get rid of all nuclear weapons."

"But, John," replied Reagan, "I did agree to that."

"No," persisted Poindexter, "you couldn't have."

"John," said the president, "I was there, and I did."

In the face of such confusion and with the hope of making a triumph
out of a near-disaster, at which even the modest goal of scheduling
another summit was lost, the White House launched the ultimate spin
control operation.

"It was the super blitz of all blitzes," said Larry Speakes with wistful
satisfaction. "I have to hand it to Larry," agreed William Henkel. "That
was a really good sell." "Damn it all," exclaimed Don Regan two days
after returning to Washington and launching the super blitz, "that's planning. That's what you get paid to do."

Regan started drafting the marketing plan on the plane ride home from
Reykjavik, when he called other senior advisers into his cabin on *Air
Force One*. "We can't go back with our tails between our legs, acting
like we lost the World Series," he told the staff. "We've got to turn any
such perception around, starting now." Regan himself had betrayed disappointment just a few hours earlier when, immediately following the
collapse of the talks, he had scowlingly said, "There will not be another

summit in the near future that I can see at this time. The Soviets are the ones who refused to make the deal. It shows them for what they are." Shultz had also been unmistakably grim. But now, Regan declared, Reykjavik could be sold as "Reagan's finest hour." The president himself was not in on this discussion; having recovered from his earlier anger at Gorbachev, he was in the midsection of *Air Force One* playing parlor games that involved guessing the ages of the NSC secretaries.

The spin control planning resumed the next morning at nine-thirty in the Roosevelt Room, where top White House advisers worked out a media plan and mobilized "surrogates" — administration officials — to go out and spread the word that the summit had been a success. Their line was that by not bargaining away SDI, Reagan had proven how tough a negotiator he truly was. By the time it was over, Don Regan alone did fifty-three print and broadcast interviews. Even Poindexter made a few public appearances, speaking on the record for over an hour to the pool of reporters aboard *Air Force One* on the trip back to Washington and, later, appearing on NBC's *Today* show.

The results, at least for the short term, were remarkable. Wirthlin showed Reagan's approval up from 64 percent before the summit to 73 percent afterward; overall approval of SDI moved from 62 percent before the summit to 74 percent afterward. "It's working," crowed Pat Buchanan, an ardent opponent of arms control who genuinely thought Reagan's refusal to sign a deal was his finest hour. "It doesn't have to be all that complex. You know what? By the end of the week, it's going to be the Triumph of Reykjavik."

There was one other central piece of the spin control plan, though, which proved more problematical. Reagan was the key to selling the Reykjavik results. He was supposed to give a speech to the nation at 8:00 P.M. on Monday, October 13, the night after he returned from the summit. That morning, the speechwriters, Poindexter, and a handful of top aides had begun to put together the text as usual. By two-thirty in the afternoon, they sent a draft of the proposed speech over to Reagan, who was in the residence. They heard nothing. At four-thirty they sent over a revised version and waited to hear which he preferred. But there was no response to that, either. Just as the group was trying to figure out which way to go, an usher from the residence appeared in Poindexter's office, with long yellow sheets of paper from a legal pad. The president had sent over his own speech — four and a half pages of handwritten script — with only about five words crossed out.

"Panic set in," said one senior official in the room. "None of us had ever seen Reagan try to write a speech before. It was pretty much unheard of. In fact, that's the only one I can think of."

What Reagan had written was basically a primer on arms control, a run-through for the American public on the ABM treaty and the doctrine of mutual assured destruction. It thanked the public for its support and tried to tell the country everything that had transpired. But, said one official familiar with arms control, "it was full of errors."

Most of those in the room didn't know what to do. Some, like speechwriter Anthony Dolan, thought it was wonderful that the president had written his own speech and were pushing to go with it. But Poindexter was furious. He had already been through the flap over banning all nuclear weapons. "He thought the speech was dumb and full of mistakes," said one participant. "He didn't think the president had done anywhere near as professional a job as the speechwriters had — he thought the speech was a low-level, brainless thing. Basically," said this official, "he thought the president was ill informed and didn't have that much to contribute."

Poindexter picked up the phone and called the residence. "Mr. President," he said, "there's something very serious I must talk to you about." He then strode off to Reagan's quarters, only to reappear about ten minutes later, even angrier. "He wants to use his own draft!" said Poindexter in utter disbelief.

The speech that night was an amalgamation of both drafts (with the president's errors corrected). In later speeches, Reagan continued to vacillate about precisely what he'd offered in Reykjavik. Independent arms control experts, from the Democratic senator Sam Nunn of Georgia to former secretary of state Henry Kissinger, registered alarm at the thoughtlessness of the proceedings. They pointed out that the elimination of nuclear weapons would leave the NATO countries at a disadvantage in comparison with the Warsaw Pact's larger conventional forces. Others wondered at Reagan's inconsistency: at the same time he was proposing to eliminate all nuclear weapons, he was also declaring his intention of exceeding the limits of SALT II. But Wirthlin's tracking polls showed that the public relations effort had saved Reagan from any immediate damage.

The selling of the summit proved that when it wanted to present an authorized account of the news, the Reagan White House was fearless. In fact, the open pride with which Regan and his aides boasted about manipulating public opinion was as remarkable as the effort itself. But as the fall progressed, the barrage of revelations about secret operations would prove too much for even the White House to finesse.

On October 1, four days before the Hasenfus plane crash, CIA analyst Charles Allen went to CIA deputy director Robert M. Gates and warned him bluntly that the Iran deal was heading for a disaster. "This operation is about to spin out of control," Allen told his chief. The problem, he said, was Ghorbanifar: North had dropped the merchant as his main channel to Iran without planning how to prevent his going public. Ghorbanifar was talking about going to the Senate Intelligence Committee and telling all. It was "a running sore," Allen said. "The creditors are demanding payment. . . . This is going to be exposed if something isn't done." Almost as an afterthought, he mentioned another concern. "Perhaps the money has been diverted to the contras," he said, but added, "I can't prove it."

Gates, a career analyst, knew that this was an operation with interest at the top. Taking no action, Gates cautiously asked Allen to brief Casey himself on the problem. The following week, on October 7, two days after Hasenfus's crash, Allen was ushered into the CIA director's office, where he told his story again.

But Casey had heard the story already. Roy Furmark, Casey's old client and Adnan Khashoggi's new business partner, had visited Casey's office earlier that day and told him a different version of the same story. Back in May, Furmark had said, Khashoggi had needed to borrow $10 million so that he could provide the bridge financing for Ghorbanifar's HAWK deal. Khashoggi had turned to two Canadian investors, promising them $2 million in interest for the use of their money for thirty days. But the deal was interrupted by the failure of McFarlane's talks in Tehran. Somehow, Furmark said, the money ended up in some middleman's account in Geneva. Now Khashoggi and the Canadians wanted either the deal to be closed or their money back. If not, he said, they were talking about suing. Furmark had fished around for the name of the Geneva account. "Lake Resources," he had said.

Casey had stared at him in what looked like astonishment. "Lake Resources is not one of our accounts," he said — meaning it wasn't CIA. "I don't know whose it is. . . . Maybe it's an Israeli operation. Maybe it's across the street."

I'll tell you whose operation it is, Furmark had said: "Ollie North's."

The CIA chief had done a convincing job of looking baffled. He had telephoned across the street — to the White House — and asked for Admiral Poindexter. The admiral wasn't in. But Casey had told Furmark not to worry; he'd get to the bottom of this.

So that afternoon, when Charlie Allen came to Casey, he also wanted to share a suspicion: he believed that money may have been diverted to the contras. Casey betrayed no anxiety, no rush to find out what all this meant. "I think I should put all my troubles down in a memorandum," Allen suggested.

"That would be good," Casey placidly agreed.

Two days later, Oliver North drove up to Langley for lunch in Casey's office. He told Casey and Gates about his meetings with Bahremani in Frankfurt. This channel was the real thing, North said; with any luck, two more hostages would be coming out soon, and Buckley's body as well. Gates asked about the Hasenfus crash. Were there any CIA fingerprints on the airlift? Was the agency clean on this one?

"Completely clean," North replied.

Then, as the lunch was coming to an end, North mentioned something that Gates didn't understand, something "cryptic," he said, "about Swiss accounts and the contras." Gates looked at Casey, who said nothing. The cautious deputy restrained himself from asking North what he meant. But after North was gone, Gates returned to Casey's office and asked whether that was anything to worry about. Not at all, said Casey; it was nothing. He didn't look concerned, Gates thought, so he dropped the issue. That afternoon, Casey and Gates went up to Capitol Hill to assure Congress that the CIA had nothing to do with the Hasenfus airplane.

At some point that week, North said later, Casey called him on the secure telephone. "This whole thing is coming unraveled," he growled. "Get rid of things. Clean things up."

On October 14 — the same day the White House released a statement reiterating its policy of no concessions to terrorists — Allen handed in his memo to Casey. Allen didn't say explicitly that he believed Iranian money had been diverted to the contras, but he did point out that Ghorbanifar was charging that "profit was redistributed to other projects of the United States and of Israel."

That was enough to tell Casey that he had problems. He called Poindexter with Allen still in the room. "I must see you right away," Casey said. But Poindexter — just two days back from Reykjavik and preoccupied with putting out the spin — wouldn't see him until the next day.

Casey and Gates took Allen's memo with them to the White House. Poindexter read it as they watched. With Gates in the room, Casey told the admiral to do two things: consult the White House counsel, and devise a plan to divulge what was going on so the thing didn't "leak out in dribs and drabs." (Neither was done.) Then Gates left, and Casey and Poindexter met alone.

The next day, October 16, Furmark tried again, retelling the history of the arms deals to Allen and Casey. At least $3 million had gone astray, he charged. Casey cut the session short. He was flying up to New York in a government jet; did Furmark want a ride? Sitting with Casey on the plane, Furmark again made his pitch on Khashoggi's behalf. "Why can't someone make a partial arms shipment to show the business is still alive?" he pleaded. Casey made no promises but said he was working on it.

On October 22, Allen and Cave both met with Furmark in New York, and this time Furmark managed to finish his disquieting tale. He told them that Ghorbanifar claimed that he had paid $15 million to Lake Resources for the HAWK missile parts. But the Iranian "firmly believed [that] the bulk of the $15 million has been diverted to the contras."

So Allen knew his suspicions, which he had first mentioned to his superiors in August, had been correct all along. If he hadn't been so conscious of the roar of an oncoming disaster, the analyst might have felt pleased. Instead, Allen and Cave returned to Washington to brief Casey. The director looked "deeply upset" at their news but gave no indication that he'd heard it all before. He told them to write yet another memorandum. And as they watched, he called Poindexter again and told him that another disturbing report was on the way.

At some point, Casey also called North. North said that he had kept a ledger of all his financial transactions for Project Democracy — all the cash, the traveler's checks, the political payments to contra leaders. "Get rid of that book," Casey said, according to North. "[It] has in it the names of everybody, the addresses of everybody. Just get rid of it. And clean things up."

North was already shredding as fast as he could, while working on the next arms sale to Iran. The ledger was the only way he could keep track of where the thousands of dollars from his office safe had gone. But he destroyed it.

At the end of October, the CIA's chief of Latin American operations, Jay Gruner, called Elliott Abrams with more bad news. The newspaper reports were right, he said: there were some calls from the safe house in San Salvador to the CIA station chief in Costa Rica and from the CIA station to others involved. The station chief, Fernandez, had apparently tried to destroy his phone records. We're investigating the problem. We'll let you know.

Abrams said he felt sick. He had been the one who marched up to Capitol Hill and into the television studios to swear up and down that the government had no connection to the Hasenfus flight. He went up to the seventh floor to make his confession to George Shultz.

"I [have] been out there for three weeks saying that there was no involvement, and now I am told that there is involvement," Abrams said. "Who could [Fernandez] have been calling? Was he calling Mr. Casey? Was he calling Mr. North?" Abrams himself had discussed the plans for private air resupply with Fernandez back in 1985. But now he insisted that he had been unaware of what North and Fernandez could have been doing. "I did not know, really, what was up," he said, ". . . other than to say that what I had said — which was that there was no U.S. government involvement — now looked wrong."

Shultz and his temple dogs were angry. So the CIA and the NSC had been off on private adventures in Central America, deliberately cutting out the State Department. What other skeletons were in those closets? They were soon to suffer an even greater humiliation. For Shultz had just launched a new campaign to cut off foreign arms sales to Iran and had personally assured America's moderate Arab allies that the United States was serious this time.

There were persistent rumors floating around the Middle East about some kind of U.S. arms deal with Iran, but Shultz's spokesman confidently knocked them down. "The United States, as you know, in the Iran-Iraq war, reflecting our neutrality, does not supply weapons to either party," Charles E. Redman said on October 22. "Nor does it authorize the transfer by third parties to either side of U.S.-manufactured or licensed weapons. And further, we have specifically opposed transfers to Iran of arms from any source, because it's clear that Iranian intransigence is responsible for prolonging the conflict."

Less than a week later, on October 28, North left for Frankfurt again, as an Israeli plane delivered another 500 TOW missiles to Iran — advance payment for the next hostage. The next day, North and Secord met again with their new Iranian contacts, Bahremani and Samaii. It was more like a meeting of allies than enemies. Bahremani graciously brought with him a Persian rug for North, but the lieutenant colonel drew the line. "That's something I can't do," he said virtuously. Bahremani came back with a handful of Iranian pistachio nuts. North accepted them. "And they were good nuts," he added.

The hors d'oeuvres were a prelude to bad news, though. Bahremani warned that a radical group — reputedly a descendant of the same group that had seized the U.S. Embassy in 1979 — had printed what he estimated to be "five million" leaflets exposing McFarlane's mission to Tehran in May. And he also reported that Hizballah had published an account of the negotiations in its own small newspaper in the Bekaa Valley of Lebanon.

Bahremani divulged one other surprise: his uncle, Rafsanjani, had formed a "joint commission" in Tehran months earlier to oversee the secret negotiations with the United States. There had been no "moderates" and no "radicals," it turned out; all of the Iranians reported back to the same government, headed by Ayatollah Khomeini. The commission included both Ghorbanifar's people and Bahremani's. "[That] really blew our minds," George Cave confessed.

For months to come, Reagan and Bush would continue to claim that they had dealt only with "moderates" in Iran. But the claim was false from the start. The Americans involved in the negotiations began to suspect that they were dealing with Khomeini's men as early as February 1986; Ghorbanifar had said so in July; now, in October, there was no doubt.

The negotiators reported the facts to Poindexter and Casey. Reagan and Bush either never saw the information or chose to ignore it. Long after the congressional committees made it public, Reagan and Bush continued to say they had not been dealing with Khomeini, as if saying it was not so would change the reality.

Faced with this news in Frankfurt, North simply stepped up the urgency of his demands. He'd kept his end of the deal, he argued, and had already started pressuring Kuwait to release its prisoners. He'd "already met with the Kuwaiti foreign minister, secretly," he said, "in between blowing up Nicaragua." Now, he said, was the time for another hostage to be released. Bahremani agreed, promising two of the three remaining hostages by Sunday, November 2 — just in time for election day.

North telephoned Poindexter with both the good news and a media plan. He urged that the White House prepare a quick announcement of the hostages' release and get it out "before CNN knows it has happened . . . so that RR is seen to have influenced the action."

After sealing the arms deal in Frankfurt, North and Secord flew to Cyprus, then took a helicopter into battle-weary Beirut with the expectation of freeing one, maybe two U.S. hostages. This time, though, they had a careful cover all worked out. They had dispatched Terry Waite, the special envoy of the archbishop of Canterbury, back to Beirut simply for appearances. If a release took place, they could say the handiwork was his. Waite turned up in Beirut on Friday, October 31, and telephoned the Associated Press bureau. "I'm here," he announced. "Something might happen. Nothing hard yet, but it's moving."

North and Secord landed in the heavily guarded U.S. Embassy compound, conferred with the American ambassador for a little more than an hour, and then took off again for Cyprus. The instructions they gave were curious. The most important thing, they told the ambassador, was that he should stay in touch with Admiral Poindexter at the White House — and say nothing to his superiors at the State Department.

On Sunday morning, November 2, their efforts bore fruit: the Iranians released David Jacobsen, who had been held captive for fifteen months. On Monday morning, North's helicopter arrived at sunrise to spirit Jacobsen out of Lebanon. Meanwhile, North worked from Cyprus, trying to free a second hostage. Television crews at the airport framed him briefly in their lenses, a disheveled figure in a trench coat moving between an executive jet and a limousine. He later told Peggy Say that he had prayed the next man released would be her brother, Terry Anderson, who, like North, had served two tours of duty as a marine in Vietnam. But by Sunday it was clear that only Jacobsen would be released. North told Say that he was so disappointed, he "cried like a baby."

Reagan, at the end of his tiring campaign on behalf of the Republican senatorial candidates, was asleep at his ranch in the Santa Ynez Mountains when, at nine minutes after midnight, Pacific time, on November 2, Poindexter telephoned from his secure bungalow at the Santa Barbara Biltmore.

"We have one hostage out," the admiral said. "We're awaiting a second."

At four-thirty that morning, with the surf breaking across from the hotel, Poindexter began to draft a statement for the president: "I am pleased to announce that two of the Americans held hostage in Beirut have been released." But the statement never ran.

Despite North's cautions about not allowing CNN to scoop the president, by daybreak in Washington, the radio and television networks were already reporting that a hostage, probably Jacobsen, had been freed in Beirut. The White House and the State Department said nothing.

Poindexter and North later insisted that they delayed the news solely in hope of winning another hostage — although it was unclear how announcing one release would jeopardize another. But a participating State Department official charged, "They were . . . holding the announcement so they could make it where the president was, for maximum political effect." The NSC had indeed seemed eager to deliver at the most politically advantageous time. Poindexter had confided a few days earlier to political director Mitch Daniels that he hoped to have "some good news" that might bolster the White House's efforts in the midterm elections. Said Daniels, "You didn't need to be a Nobel laureate to figure it out. Why else would he tell me?"

Finally, at midmorning, Larry Speakes came into the press briefing room in the Santa Barbara Sheraton and issued a presidential statement announcing the release of Jacobsen and giving misleading public thanks to Terry Waite.

United Press International reporter Ira Allen — nicknamed the Iratollah for his abrasive style — asked the obvious. Was this release politically timed for the election?

Speakes flushed with fury. He had once been a sheriff's deputy representing law and order in the face of the civil rights movement in Mississippi, and now he looked the part. His "good ol' boy" drawl became clipped. In place of Reykjavik's spoon-feeding was the darker side of the White House spin control operation, reserved for anyone who questioned too impertinently the authorized account of events.

"Is the president going to play politics with this issue?" repeated Speakes, rolling forward on the balls of his feet. "No." But then, after a hushed pause, he turned to Allen and added in a cool, measured tone, "You're within one inch of getting your head lopped off with a question like that."

The election was just forty-eight hours away.

14

The Shovel Brigade

THE BENCHES AROUND the rodeo grounds in Twin Falls, Idaho, were jammed with more than five thousand of the faithful. "We love Ronnie!" they roared. "We love Ronnie!" Eyes strained for the first glimpse of Ronald Reagan on what was billed as the last glorious campaign of his political career. When he finally appeared, there was pandemonium — for the president rode into the arena on an Old West buckboard, the nation's leader and the old movie hero rolled into one.

"You know," he told the cheering crowd, "America used to wear a Kick Me sign around its neck. Well, we've thrown that one away, and now it reads, Don't Tread on Me. Today, every nickel-and-dime dictator around the world knows that if he tangles with the United States of America, he will have a price to pay."

It was Friday, October 31, four days before the election, and Reagan was nearing the end of a hard campaign swing, a desperate drive to keep the Senate from falling to the Democrats. And he was returning, as if by instinct, to his oldest, simplest themes.

"Do you want to go back to the days of big spending, high taxes, and runaway inflation?" he asked in Twin Falls and at every other stop.

"No!" the crowd roared.

"Do you want to return to policies that gave us a weak and vacillating America?" he asked.

"No!" the crowd roared.

"Would you rather have an America that is strong and proud and free?" he asked.

"Yes!" the crowd roared.

"You just made my day," he said, the crowd laughing with him.

But the world was not really that simple. As Reagan was speaking in Idaho, the events that would unmake his presidency were already in progress. Halfway across the world, in Lebanon, two secret agents from the regime of one of Reagan's "nickel-and-dime dictators" were pursuing a political mission of their own. The two men, agents of a leftist ayatollah within the Khomeini government, threaded their way through the rubble-strewn streets of Beirut to the office of a leftist magazine, *Al Shiraa*, and sought out its editor, a man named Hassan Sabra.

The story they told, Sabra said later, seemed almost too wild to print. The Iranians claimed that Robert C. McFarlane had flown into Tehran as a secret envoy from the White House, negotiated with Iranian officials, and shipped U.S. weapons to Khomeini on President Reagan's behalf.

Sabra was skeptical, but he knew that his Iranian informants were well connected in Tehran. He was fascinated by their story — not because of what it revealed about the Reagan administration but because of what it said about the Khomeini regime. So he wrote a long article about the Byzantine power struggle in Tehran and added the tale of McFarlane's trip at the end, almost as an afterthought.

As *Al Shiraa* went to press that weekend, North and Secord were briefly in Beirut, secretly negotiating the release of hostage David Jacobsen. On Monday morning, as Jacobsen was being flown by helicopter to safety on Cyprus, vans were already delivering twenty-five thousand copies of *Al Shiraa* to newsstands around Beirut.

It was several hours before foreign correspondents in Beirut noticed the little magazine's strange story about McFarlane in Tehran. That same day, the ·faction of Hizballah calling itself Islamic Jihad issued a statement claiming that it had released Jacobsen in response to "overtures" from the White House. Reporters traveling with Reagan, now in Santa Barbara, began asking questions: What was this about McFarlane's making a secret visit to Iran? Had the United States sent weapons to Khomeini? And did it have anything to do with the sudden release, only days before the election, of another hostage?

In California, where Reagan had just two more campaign rallies to go, Larry Speakes fended off the questions with a shrug and said he didn't know anything about it. For a few hours, the focus shifted back to the campaign. There was a speech in Las Vegas: "Today, every nickel-and-dime dictator. . . ." Then it was back to California's Orange County for a final outdoor rally, an extravaganza where skydivers jumped, a live elephant lumbered across the stage, and the crowd cheered wildly.

"Isn't it a great time to be an American?" the president asked in the sparkling sun.

"U.S.A.!" the crowd roared in reply. "U.S.A.!"

But the strange reports about secret missions to Iran kept rolling in. On Tuesday, election day, Rafsanjani told a press conference that

McFarlane had not only visited Tehran, but he had brought pistols, a Bible, and a cake decorated with a key; he had come disguised as an airline crewman, carrying a false passport; and he had been expelled from the country by vigilant Revolutionary Guards. The questions could no longer be shrugged away.

It was Larry Speakes's job to provide the first line of defense, and that morning, as *Air Force One* carried the president and his aides back to Washington, he went to see John Poindexter in the jet's executive cabin. Not at all sure of how much truth there was in the reports from Iran, Speakes asked Poindexter for something — anything — to tell the press. But the national security adviser responded oddly: for more than an hour, he sat hunched over a pad of yellow legal paper, crumpling up one sheet after another as he labored to find the right words. Speakes had never seen him do this before. "He'd write, and tear it up; try again, then tear it up," the spokesman said. "My suspicions were getting aroused by then."

Finally, Poindexter handed his scribbled handiwork to Speakes, who ambled back down the aisle of the Boeing 707 to the tail. There the press pool — the handful of reporters designated to travel aboard the president's plane — sat waiting.

"Poindexter tells me," Speakes began dryly. It was a point of detail he had begun to add after discovering that the admiral sometimes gave him misleading information. "As long as Iran advocates the use of terrorism, the U.S. arms embargo will continue," Speakes read from the scrap of paper. That sounded like a clear denial that arms had been sold, and most reporters wrote it that way. But the statement didn't say anything about McFarlane, and it didn't say explicitly that no weapons had been shipped. The questions continued, but for the time being they went unanswered.

November 4 was not a good day for Ronald Reagan. The nation's voters, uninspired by his antidrug message and less moved than before by the broad themes of his campaign, swung against the president's party — a normal phenomenon in midterm congressional elections, but one Reagan had seriously attempted to avert. By the end of the evening, four Republican incumbents had lost their Senate seats and the Democrats had a solid, fifty-five-member majority. For the first time in Reagan's presidency, both houses of Congress were under opposition control.

Oliver North and Fawn Hall glumly watched the television maps turn Democratic red in a ballroom at Washington's Willard Hotel, its Victorian elegance recently restored. The occasion was a "Conservative Victory Celebration" held by Spitz Channell, the right-wing fund-raiser. Earlier in the evening, before the news turned bad, North had presented Channell with a Freedom Fighter award and summoned up his winningest gap-toothed smile. The Senate might be lost, but Project Democracy would go on. With the help of Channell and his wealthy contributors, the contras had survived, and now the administration had $100 million in official aid to pump into the rebels' war. And despite the sudden burst of unwelcome publicity from Beirut and Tehran, North's Iranian contact had called to say that he still wanted to go ahead with more arms-for-hostage deals.

Reagan and Poindexter discussed the Iranian problem at their regular briefing on Wednesday, the morning after the election. The important thing, they agreed, was to ignore the reports of arms deals; perhaps the questions would go away. "There's no way we can comment without further damage to the chances of getting the other hostages out," the president said. Poindexter consulted Bush, Weinberger, and Casey, and said they all agreed. Shultz warned Poindexter that the only way to defuse the issue was to get the facts out, but the admiral told him he was outvoted. "We must remain absolutely close-mouthed while stressing that our basic policy toward Iran, the gulf war, and dealing with terrorists has not changed," Poindexter cabled Shultz. "Today I have talked with VP, Cap, and Bill Casey. They agree with my approach."

But the story would not disappear. On Thursday, November 6, the *Los Angeles Times* and the *Washington Post* broke the first full accounts of the arms sales, revealing that there had been more than one deal, including some through Israel; that they were aimed at winning the release of the hostages; and that they went ahead over strong objections from Weinberger and Shultz. Congress was up in arms; the leader of the Senate's new Democratic majority, Robert Byrd of West Virginia, said he would insist on a full investigation of whatever the administration had been up to, complete with public hearings.

At a bill-signing ceremony at the White House, a correspondent shouted a question about the arms-for-hostage reports. Reagan looked annoyed. "The speculation, the commenting on a story that came out of the Middle East and that, to us, has no foundation — all of that is making it more difficult to get the other hostages out," the president said.

No foundation? "He knew it was wrong at the time," Speakes admitted later. "But we were trying to get just one more [hostage] out."

It was still not clear how bad the story would be. Poindexter assured a morning staff meeting that the problem would blow over within days. "I wish everybody would calm down a bit," he said. Regan agreed; the worst problem on the horizon, he thought, was the GOP's loss of the Senate. To seize control of the agenda, he summoned reporters to lunch to unveil what he considered an arresting new theme for the administration's last two years: "a more productive America." The chief of staff announced that the federal budget process would be revamped — his own idea, Regan said proudly, although "the president gave it his blessing."

On the afternoon of Friday, November 7, Reagan appeared in the Rose

Garden with David Jacobsen and accepted credit for his release. But reporters spoiled the sunny mood by asking again about the arms deals. "There's no way that we can answer questions having anything to do with this without endangering the people we're trying to rescue," Reagan said.

Did George Shultz support his policy on Iran?

"Yes," Reagan snapped.

Why couldn't he explain what deals had been made?

The president looked exasperated. "Because," he said, "it has to happen again and again and again until we have them all back."

The awkward attempts at evasion did little to staunch a deluge of leaks from officials who had opposed the Iranian deals from the start. Every morning, the newspapers carried new details about the arms sales: the CIA was involved, Israel played an important role, the weapons had affected the Persian Gulf war, other countries used the shipments as an excuse to sell more weapons to Tehran. Congress was demanding answers, and the only ones available were coming from the press, not from the White House. With no strategy to deal with the disclosure of the arms deals, Reagan and his aides were floundering.

In their secret world, Casey, North, and Secord intensified their efforts to cover their tracks. At the CIA, records of the November 1985 shipment of HAWK missiles to Iran mysteriously disappeared from the files. North, under Casey's instructions, destroyed more documents in his office. And, in Geneva, a shadow company called Lake Resources was quietly dissolved.

At the White House staff meetings, Poindexter was still imperturbable. "I think if we can ride this thing out for the next three weeks, we'll be okay," he said.

"What the hell are you talking about?" exploded communications director Patrick Buchanan, whose hard-liner's ideology had not impaired his political antennae. "We can't stand three weeks of this!"

Poindexter fiddled impassively with his pipe. "We've got assets to protect," he said firmly.

Donald Regan, who was beginning to tire of being made the scapegoat for every mishap in the White House he claimed to run, agreed with Buchanan. If Poindexter had a problem here, Regan didn't want to hang for it. He told reporters from the weekly newsmagazines, speaking as "a senior administration official," that the Iranian affair was all McFarlane's idea — drawing a frantic computer message from McFarlane to Poindexter. "This will be the second lie Don Regan has sowed against my character," McFarlane wrote, "and I won't stand for it."

Regan then convened a meeting of the president's inner cabinet, the NSPG, to work out a strategy for surviving the storm. They gathered at eleven-thirty on Monday morning, November 10, in the Situation Room to decide what to tell Congress and the public about the Iranian arms deals. Around the table were Bush, Regan, Shultz, Weinberger, Meese, Casey, and Poindexter.

The president opened the meeting with only a few lines. As a result of all the media speculation, he said, we need to make some kind of public statement. "We have not dealt directly with terrorists," he insisted. There has been "no bargaining, no ransom."

Then Poindexter took the floor and gave a summary of the Iranian initiative. Shultz and Weinberger still knew little of what had been going on, so they listened with some astonishment. They could not have known that the account Poindexter gave them was riddled with inaccuracies and distortions — an attempt to cover up the facts by hiding them from the rest of the cabinet.

The main consideration, Poindexter said, had always been a "long-term strategic relationship" with Iran, with three lesser goals: supporting Tehran's moderates, stopping Iranian terrorism, and winning the release of the hostages. It all began, Poindexter said, when the United States accidentally discovered that Israel was secretly shipping weapons to Tehran in exchange for Iranian Jews. (This was North's version; as far as can be determined, it was false. Instead, the true genesis of the deals had been Israel's approach to McFarlane in July 1985.)

In August and September of 1985, Poindexter said, Israel shipped 500 TOW missiles to Iran without the knowledge of the United States. "We were told after the fact," he said. (In fact, McFarlane had known about the shipment and urged Israel to go ahead with it; the only point that is not clear is whether the president himself approved it ahead of time.)

McFarlane went to Iran in May 1986 with a second Israeli shipment of missile parts, Poindexter continued, but the trip was "not productive." And there was a third transaction, the admiral said: "500 TOWs sent last week from Israel." (This account was wrong on several points. There were five arms shipments, not three; Iran received 2,004 TOWs, not 1,000; and the arms shipped in 1986 were sold by the United States, not by Israel. The admiral did not mention the potentially illegal HAWK shipment of November 1985. Nor, of course, did he mention that profits had been diverted to the contras.)

The results of the effort, Poindexter said, had been positive: no further hostages were seized for more than a year. (He contended that the three new hostages taken in September and October were seized by other terrorists beyond Iran's control.) The initiative had produced "a solid contact with Rafsanjani." And, of course, three hostages had been released.

"Where do we go from here?" the admiral summarized. "We can continue to work in Iran, can continue to get hostages out." But there was "too much talk in the executive branch of the government, too much speculation."

Shultz and Weinberger exploded with angry questions.

"I thought we had agreed that there would be no more shipments after the first 500 TOWs unless we got all the captives," Weinberger said.

"It just always came back to the president," Poindexter said. "He agreed to go forward. . . . It seemed the only way to get the hostages out."

That sounded like a direct swap of arms for hostages. "Be careful of the linkage between hostages and defense equipment," Shultz warned.

"The terrorists have not profited," Reagan replied, launching into his favorite rationale. "We let the Iranians buy supplies and they influenced the terrorists. There were no benefits to terrorists. We are working with moderates, hoping in the future to be able to influence Iran after Khomeini dies."

"I'm not sure what's the difference," Shultz said bluntly. "But we have made more good contacts in Iran than I was aware of. We should pursue this, but we must not gild the lily. . . . We are paying a high price."

Reagan was nettled by Shultz's naysaying. When an American is taken hostage overseas, the president protested, "one purpose of the government is to go to his or her support."

"I agree that a purpose of government is to protect its citizens," Shultz replied. "But our whole purpose is to protect them by discouraging terrorism. My concern is that the juxtaposition does make it appear that we gave weapons for hostages. I can't help but feel that the Israelis suckered us so they could sell what they wanted," he added.

Meese, the president's advocate, tried to persuade Shultz that Reagan's rationale made sense. "Each of these is a set of complex incidents," he said. "They are not related. There was no ransom. There was no money to Hizballah. We were trying to help moderates in Iran who also tried to help us."

Donald Regan was worried about the public relations problem. "We must get a statement out now," he argued. "We are being attacked, and we are being hurt. We're losing credibility. . . . We'll need to say something to thinking people — not the press," he added to chuckles.

Poindexter dismissed these concerns. "The news has peaked," he insisted. "There are no hearings [in Congress] until January, so we shouldn't say anything."

"We have to say something, because I'm being held out to dry," the president replied. "A basic statement has to come out. . . . We have not been paying ransom. We have not been negotiating. We have not dealt with the terrorists; we don't even know who they are. This is a long-range Iranian policy. We can't engage in any further speculation or answers because it might endanger the hostages. But we won't pay any money or give anything to terrorists.

"Avoid specifics," he repeated. "Declare that whatever we've done is consistent with our policy."

"We should say less about what we are doing and more about what we are not doing," Poindexter offered.

"There have been no violations of law and policy in this," Meese added loyally. That was to be the official line: in Watergate terms, a stonewall.

At that point, the vice president spoke up for the first time, to ask about a peripheral issue. A ring of Israeli and American arms dealers had been indicted in New York, and the defendants claimed that Bush was involved in the deal. "Is the New York case a private or public endeavor to sell arms to Iran?" he asked.

"Probably private with government knowledge," someone answered.

"Israel may try to squeeze us," Bush warned.

Shultz was still shaking his head over being cut out of a major policy initiative for almost a year. "The finding was not known to me from January to November," he said aloud. "Amazing."

The question remained: What would they tell the press and the public? Regan still wanted to get some details out.

"Who will issue Q and A's?" he asked, referring to the question-and-answer sheets provided to government spokesmen.

"No Q and A's," Reagan, Casey, and Meese all chorused.

Shultz returned stubbornly to his basic complaint. These deals were unwise from the start, he said. Now that they had been exposed, they threw the U.S. antiterrorism effort into "total disintegration."

"I would appreciate people saying you support the president's policy," Reagan said pointedly, looking at Shultz. "But we will not comment on anything else . . . because of the danger to the hostages."

"I agree," Meese chimed in.

"I support you, Mr. President," Shultz said firmly. "I'm more concerned about the policy."

That afternoon, Poindexter drafted a statement for the press. "As has been the case at a number of similar meetings with the president and his senior advisers, there was unanimous support for the president's decisions," it said. "No U.S. laws have been or will be violated. . . . Our policy of not making concessions to terrorists remains intact."

Shultz, airborne en route to a meeting in Central America, looked at the radioed text of the statement and said, "No." He was not going to sign something that implied that he had supported the president's decisions on this. Poindexter was annoyed, but the secretary of state forced him to change the statement.

For George Shultz, it was the beginning of a quiet mutiny. Before long, his resistance to Poindexter's attempt at a cover-up would turn into a virtual civil war inside the Reagan administration — in Shultz's words, a "battle royal."

.   .   .

Despite the White House statement, the pressure to explain the arms deals in public continued to build. Paul Laxalt, the president's best friend in Congress, warned that the continued leaking of information was becoming a kind of "Chinese water torture" for the administration. Even the normally unflappable Poindexter was getting edgy. At one senior staff meeting, when Regan aide Dennis Thomas asked whether there was "another shoe to drop," the admiral glared at him and snapped, "Don't ask questions about something you know nothing about!" And Patrick Buchanan wrote an impassioned memorandum to Regan: "The appearance of things is that we have negotiated with a terrorist regime . . . that we have paid in spare parts and military equipment for our hostages, that we traduced our policy and violated our principles, that we are now stonewalling. Not since I came here has there appeared such an issue which could do such deep and permanent damage to the president's standing. . . . The story will not die until some much fuller explanation — giving our arguments — is provided. Prediction: If we wait three weeks, the president's approval will be down in the mid-fifties at best." Regan agreed. "We are going to do something," he scrawled in a return note to Buchanan. "It's late, but I hope not too late."

Regan began marshaling support for a televised presidential speech explaining the arms sales. Without waiting for a formal decision, members of the staff began drafting a speech. Poindexter and North joined in; the survival of their Iranian project depended on how convincingly the president could defend it. Even Bud McFarlane, increasingly agitated about the way he was being portrayed as the author of the initiative, weighed in with a draft. Project Democracy was enlisting Ronald Reagan's skill as the Great Communicator to save its own skin.

On Wednesday, November 12, Reagan and his aides briefed the leaders of Congress. "We have not negotiated with terrorists. We have not broken any laws," the president insisted. "It was a covert operation . . . designed to advance our strategic interests in the Middle East." And, contrary to the newspaper reports, he said, "no one" in the administration had been bypassed on these decisions.

Poindexter repeated his inaccurate account of the history of the deals, omitting the potentially illegal HAWK shipment and half of the TOWs.

"Why do overtures to the Iranians not constitute dealing with terrorists?" Senate Republican leader Bob Dole asked.

"We would have continued on this track with Iran even if no hostages existed," Reagan claimed.

"Was the State Department involved?" Senate Democratic chief Robert Byrd asked Shultz.

"The State Department had nothing to do with it," Shultz said.

"Were you opposed?" Byrd pressed.

"I never discuss the advice I give to the president," Shultz said.

"You were left out," Byrd concluded.

After the briefing, the congressional leaders marched out to the White House driveway and told reporters they couldn't buy Reagan's rationale. Byrd called the arms deals "a major foreign relations blunder" and said the president's explanation was "like saying it's all right to deal with the Mafia boss but not the hit man." Dole, in the closest thing to a defense the White House heard that day, dryly pronounced the operation "a little inept."

Shultz was still upset that Reagan wanted the deals to continue. He asked Donald Regan to help him turn the president around on the substance of the issue — to stop the arms sales to Iran, take the negotiations away from the NSC staff, and hand the problem over to the State Department. Regan said he'd think about it. Then he told his aides that Shultz was trying to turn the Iranian dilemma into "a power play" for his own department.

Not until midmorning on the following day, Thursday, did Reagan finally agree to his advisers' pleas for a televised speech. Even then, he told reporters, he had decided to speak only because "I've never heard such dissemination of misinformation since I've been here." Buchanan was assigned to turn out a quick and convincing speech and was handed a draft by Ollie North. He sat down with North and Alton Keel to work out what the president could say.

"We went over the text and the facts," Buchanan said later. "We'd ask him, 'Listen, I know what a C-5 [cargo plane] is. Can all of these things fit into a C-5?' And they said yes.

"I told Ollie: 'Tonight, I don't care what he says, the president of the United States' credibility goes on the line. It's all got to be accurate. I don't care what we've said before or how it's been coppered. It's got to be right.' And they okayed and went over every single line in that thing. Several times, they walked into [the next] office, got up and closed the doors, came back and said, 'Okay, this is okay.'

"We didn't have the foggiest idea whether it was true or false," Buchanan said. "That's why we checked it all."

That afternoon, in an attempt to soften up the press, Poindexter briefed two dozen reporters in the Roosevelt Room. The admiral was the picture of calm, sitting at the head of the long oval table and puffing slowly on his pipe. He acknowledged that he was unhappy that a speech had to be given at all, but said he was sure the people would approve the president's actions once they understood them. As the briefing went on, however, Poindexter — to the surprise of the reporters around the table — got tangled in his own story.

The arms shipments were perfectly legal, he explained, because the president had signed a secret finding in January 1986.

"Any shipments that were made prior to January 1986, you're saying the United States had no role in — either condoning, winking, encouraging, or anything of that nature?" a reporter asked.

"That's correct," Poindexter said.

"Could you say, then, what prompted the release of Benjamin Weir in September 1985?" another reporter asked.

"Well, that was one of the motivations behind the small amount of stuff that we transferred to them," Poindexter said.

But he had said nothing was condoned before 1986, the reporter noted.

Poindexter was caught. "The problem is — and don't draw any inferences from this — but there are other countries involved. . . . There was one shipment that was made, not by us, but by a third country, prior to the signing of [the January finding]."

"You just said, previously, that you did not condone any shipments," another reporter pointed out.

"There was one exception," Poindexter admitted, "and that was the one I just described." (In fact, there were two exceptions; Poindexter was still omitting the November 1985 HAWK shipment.)

Asked how he could argue that the shipments didn't violate the administration's campaign against other countries' arms sales to Tehran, Poindexter responded with a quizzical look.

"We have never said that *we* weren't shipping arms to Iran," he said.

At 8:00 P.M., Reagan delivered his first full public statement on the Iranian arms deals. He spoke from his desk in the Oval Office and began with a dash of ridicule for the press and its sources. "I know you have been reading a lot of stories the past several days attributed to Danish sailors, unnamed observers at Italian ports and Spanish harbors, and especially unnamed government officials of my administration," Reagan said. "Well, now you are going to hear the facts from a White House source — and you know my name.

"The charge has been made that the United States has shipped weapons to Iran as ransom payment for the release of American hostages in Lebanon; that the United States undercut its allies and secretly violated American policy against trafficking with terrorists.

"Those charges are utterly false. The United States has not made concessions to those who hold our people captive in Lebanon, and we will not. The United States has not swapped boatloads or planeloads of American weapons for the return of American hostages, and we will not."

Reagan admitted approving the shipment of "small amounts of defensive weapons," but added, "These modest deliveries, taken together, could easily fit into a single cargo plane. They could not, taken together, affect the outcome of the six-year war between Iran and Iraq. Nor could they affect, in any way, the military balance between the two countries.

"All appropriate cabinet officers were fully consulted," he said. "The actions I authorized were, and continue to be, in full compliance with federal law; and the relevant committees of Congress are being and will be fully informed."

It was clear that Reagan truly believed — or had managed to convince himself — that arms had not been swapped for hostages. But his statements about the weapons he had shipped were simply false. North had fed him the line about "a single cargo plane," but the 2,004 TOWs, 18 HAWKs, and 240 HAWK parts had in fact arrived on eight cargo planes, and while they probably could have fit into a giant C-5A, the air force's largest cargo lifter, it was not certain. As for affecting the military balance, the president himself had told George Shultz only three days earlier that he had approved the arms sales to help Iran's position in the war; and the U.S. military intelligence that North gave the Iranians clearly had some value to the ayatollah.

All the cabinet officers had not been fully consulted; it was not at all clear that everything had been done in compliance with the law; and although Congress was being informed, it was being informed only because the newspapers had exposed the arms deals first.

As an attempt to reassure the nation and put the president in control of the issue, the speech was a bust. "This was a Ronald Reagan never before seen on national TV," *Newsweek* judged. "His jauntiness had turned to strained sarcasm, his easy charm to defensiveness." More important, the public didn't quite believe him. An ABC News poll taken immediately after the speech found that 56 percent believed that arms had been swapped for hostages; 72 percent opposed selling arms to Iran, no matter what the reason. Even conservative patriarch Barry Goldwater, who had introduced Reagan to national politics back in 1964, said the deal was "not moral." Goldwater's diagnosis: "Reagan has gotten his butt in a crack."

To the White House staff, though, the television statement was a watershed event. The president had publicly adopted Poindexter's version of the events, committed himself to the line that no arms had been traded for hostages — and committed himself, as well, to continue dealing with Iran. Now it was up to North, Poindexter, and McFarlane to hold that account together, however difficult it might be to square with the truth.

That evening, McFarlane appeared on ABC's *Nightline* to describe his secret trip to Iran. "[We] held four days of talks that went reasonably well," he said blandly. "We were received hospitably and treated with the normal practice that surrounds meetings like this."

"Did you bring in a cake?" host Ted Koppel asked.

"No, I didn't have anything to do with a cake," McFarlane replied.

"Bible?"

"No Bible."

"Pistols?"

"I don't operate that way, Ted."

On Friday, November 14, the public relations blitz began in earnest. Regan and Poindexter were the designated hitters in three sessions with reporters. But they were no more successful than the president had been.

Regan tried to win some credibility by acknowledging what was already widely known: that Israel had helped with the arms deals. But he insisted that there had been no swap of arms for hostages. Yes, weapons had moved at the same time hostages were released, but "I can assure you there was no linkage of these two facts."

The reporters didn't buy it, and their skepticism angered Regan. "What's a human life worth?" he demanded. "If you were taken, or one of your relatives taken, what would you have us do? Sit as the head of government of the United States and say, Look, we won't even talk about those hostages?" He was as much as confessing that the policy had been arms for hostages after all.

Poindexter stuck more closely to his practice of no disclosures, but he was having little more luck than Regan.

"I can't find in the legislation where you have any authority to operate the way North has been operating, both in Nicaragua and in Iran," one reporter said. "Have I missed something?"

"I am not going to confirm anything that any of the staff officers on the NSC are doing," the admiral said tersely.

But attention had already focused on North. The once-obscure lieutenant colonel had been implicated in the crash of the contra resupply plane in October; now he seemed to be in the middle of the Iran debacle as well. Was he, as one NSC official privately told the press, "the most dangerous man in the United States government"?

North himself was beginning to suspect that the hounds were closing in on him. He joked with friends about being the fall guy, about "taking the spears" in his chest; he said he was thinking about getting a lawyer. A State Department official visited him and found a North with ragged nerves and forlorn mien. "It was obvious things were falling apart," the diplomat said. "It was palpable."

Elliott Abrams came loyally to North's defense. "Ollie can produce and get things done," he told a reporter. "He's totally and completely honest. . . . He has very good judgment. He's worth consulting on a whole range of issues." People just like to attack him, Abrams said. "Partly it's because he's a marine and fits the portrait that people on the left like to think of — a crew-cut marine who runs a secret war. You know, it's everybody's worst fear: a marine colonel takes over the government.

"My only problem with Ollie is that he spends too little time on Central America," he said.

Upstairs at the State Department, Abrams's boss, George Shultz, was becoming more disturbed. Not only was his plea to abandon the arms sales being ignored, the president had publicly vowed that the initiative would go on. Almost everyone else on the NSC — Reagan, Bush, Poindexter, Casey, Regan, and Meese — seemed intent on convincing one another that there had been no swap of arms for hostages when anyone could see that there had been.

That Friday, Shultz had one of his regular meetings with Reagan. "I sought him out to change him around," he said later. And, he added, to take the Iranian project out of Poindexter's hands. "I wanted to get this out where I could see it for myself and get it managed right."

Shultz tried to approach the issue gently, to lead Reagan from his own premises to Shultz's conclusions. "Iran needs us," he said. "So we should work for a better relationship with Iran, but we don't have to pay up front for it. . . . Arms sales, at this point, are not necessary."

Arms shipments linked in any way to hostages were "not a good idea," Shultz said. "Criminals and terrorists see that hostages can be taken for profit. . . . In the eyes of the American people, the most important achievement of the Reagan administration has been the restoration of the stature and dignity and credibility of the presidency. That has to be maintained — or every achievement of this administration will be at risk."

But Reagan was noncommittal. Shultz wasn't getting through.

The next day, Saturday, November 15, Shultz made one more try. He flew up to Camp David for lunch with the president and the visiting British prime minister, Margaret Thatcher. But there was no time for a private word with Reagan, so Shultz handed his draft of a presidential order ending the arms sales to Don Regan. "See if you can't get this cleared," Shultz said, standing on the helicopter pad in the cold, looking faintly ridiculous in a burgundy and gold Washington Redskins stocking cap.

Regan brushed him off. "I don't think there's going to be time, George," he said. "I just can't do that." (The chief of staff later explained lamely that he was afraid of missing his seat on the helicopter back to the White House.)

The next morning, Washington turned to its Sunday ritual of television talk shows. On NBC, Poindexter was on *Meet the Press*, selling the Iran initiative as a laudable strategic move. "I'm basically an optimist," he said. "If the situation in Tehran can stabilize, then it is possible that we can still make some progress in our relationship which will be advantageous in freeing the hostages."

But the government that needed stabilizing that morning was the one at home. On CBS, Shultz was on *Face the Nation*, offering halfhearted defenses for a policy that he violently opposed. The president had sent arms to Iran, he said, as "a signal of a desire for a different kind of relationship. Now, that's controversial, and there it is. And you can argue for it; you can argue against it."

"Will there be any more arms shipments to Iran, either directly by our government or through any third parties?" reporter Lesley Stahl asked.

"It's certainly against our policy," Shultz offered.

"That's not an answer," Stahl said.

"Under the circumstances of Iran's war with Iraq, its pursuit of terrorism, its association with those holding our hostages," Shultz replied, "I would certainly say — as far as I'm concerned — no."

Stahl could see he was still hedging. "Do you have the authority to speak for the entire administration?" she asked.

The barest hint of a smile crossed Shultz's face. "No," he said, making his mutiny public.

When Reagan received his national security briefing the next morning, he was upset about something he had seen on television the day before — but it wasn't Shultz or Poindexter. Instead, the president was exercised about a *60 Minutes* report on a pacifist group that tried to damage a Minuteman missile silo in Missouri by banging on the lid with hammers. "Wasn't this staged for TV?" the president asked Poindexter heatedly. "Isn't there something the television crew can be prosecuted for?" Poindexter dutifully instructed the Pentagon's general counsel to determine whether CBS had broken any laws.

Poindexter and Regan were more alarmed about Shultz. The secretary of state's one-word rebellion on *Face the Nation* had forced the embarrassed White House, finally, to issue a statement promising no more arms deals with Iran and putting the State Department in charge of all further negotiations — precisely the statement Shultz had sought privately for a week. But his victory was not without cost. Not only was Poindexter annoyed, but Regan, Bush, and — most ominous of all — the First Lady were angry at his breaking ranks in public.

"I don't know what's gotten into George," Regan said. "If he doesn't like it, he should quit." Bush, the quintessential loyalist who had defended Richard Nixon until the bitter end of the Watergate scandal, told aides that he thought Shultz's behavior was "inappropriate." And Nancy Reagan complained to friends that Shultz wasn't standing up for her Ronnie.

Regan's aides, picking up the signals, told reporters that the president himself was grumbling about Shultz. The chief of staff would later deny it, but several of the aides said they leaked the stories with his blessing. "The whole idea was to provoke [Shultz] into resigning," said one of the most assiduous leakers. "We were hoping that if he resigned one more time, his resignation would be accepted."

Regan's men recruited Nancy Reagan's chief of staff, James Rosebush, into their plot. One result was a story in *Newsweek*: "The First Lady, already aggravated by the political damage the affair has caused her husband, reportedly is livid with Shultz for publicly criticizing the president's Iranian deal — an act she perceives as disloyal." One story had it that Treasury Secretary James Baker was already lined up to replace Shultz; in another version, it was to be retired senator Howard Baker.

Still other rumors had both Regan and Poindexter also on their way out. Fingers were being pointed in every direction. Bud McFarlane surfaced to insist that Shultz knew more than he was admitting: "I told him repeatedly and often of every item that went on in this enterprise," he said. Regan, in turn, laid the blame at McFarlane's feet: "Let's not forget whose idea this was. It was Bud's idea. When you give lousy advice, you get lousy results."

Regan offered one other comment for the history books, one that revealed more of his view of substance and image — and of managing Reagan — than he may have intended. It also exposed him, more than ever before, to the ire of Nancy Reagan. In retrospect, it seemed to mark the moment when Regan's power began to ebb, the beginning of the end for the imperious chief of staff.

"Some of us are like a shovel brigade that follows a parade down Main Street cleaning up," Regan told the *New York Times*. "We took Reykjavik and turned what was really a sour situation into something that turned out pretty well. Who was it that took this disinformation thing and managed to turn it? Who was it took on this loss in the Senate and pointed out a few facts and managed to pull that? I don't say we'll be able to do it four times in a row. But here we go again, and we're trying."

Despite Regan's best efforts at spin control, Congress was demanding hearings on the arms sales. After the failure of the November 13 speech, the chief of staff and other advisers urged Reagan to give a press conference, to try to seize control of the issue. Pat Buchanan even consulted a retired expert on White House crises, Richard M. Nixon. His hard-earned counsel, Buchanan said, was: "Get the message out. Admit you made a mistake — you tried something, and it turned out badly. But don't cover it up." Regan took Nixon's advice to the president but came back chastened. The president agreed to hold a press conference but rejected any admission of error. "He doesn't think he made a mistake," the chief of staff reported.

The first thing Reagan and his senior aides needed, though, was a detailed history of exactly how the Iranian deals had transpired, a script from which all the administration's spokesmen could read. But as the storm over the deals grew, and as critics began to raise not only political questions but also legal concerns, the once-simple task of producing a chronology became the focus of intrigue — and the center of an attempted cover-up. The job of compiling a chronology had been assigned, logically enough, to the man who knew the most about the negotiations, Oliver North.

It was 8:00 P.M. on Monday, November 17, more than two weeks after the news of the arms deals broke, when North put the finishing touches on the first complete version of his chronology. The paper, marked TOP SECRET — MAXIMUM VERSION, had swelled to eleven pages — and it was riddled with false information.

The chronology mentioned all five arms deals (August 1985, the first shipment of TOW missiles through Israel; November 1985, the CIA-assisted shipment of HAWK missiles; and the three direct U.S. deliveries in 1986). But it left unclear who had approved the two 1985 deals; since they occurred before Reagan had signed any formal authorization, they were both potentially illegal. Faced with that explosive problem, North, like Poindexter before him, chose deception. When describing the August 1985 shipment, the chronology claimed the United States was not even aware of it until after the fact. (McFarlane, of course, had known about it, and the only question was whether Reagan had authorized it.) The November 1985 shipment got similar treatment: the chronology claimed that Israel had delivered the HAWK missiles to Iran over objections from the United States. (In fact, the CIA delivered the missiles on orders from McFarlane and North, without the presidential authorization required by law.)

But North's chronology, even though sanitized, nevertheless created a problem. A copy of one of his drafts had gone to Charles J. Cooper, a young Alabama Republican who served as legal counsel to Attorney General Meese and who had been assigned to scout out any legal problems in the Iranian initiative. When Cooper read the chronology, he realized that the unauthorized 1985 shipments might be a time bomb. If Israel shipped U.S. weapons to Iran, that was probably a violation of the Arms Export Control Act; and if the White House had authorized the sale, that could be a violation as well. Cooper quickly called both Meese and Poindexter's counsel, Paul B. Thompson, to warn them.

Word of the dilemma spread fast. The morning of Tuesday, November 18, White House counsel Peter Wallison, a Harvard-trained lawyer whom Don Regan had brought over from Treasury, convened a meeting of the administration's top national security lawyers.

"We need the facts," Wallison said. "I can't give the president advice without the facts."

The other lawyers turned expectantly to NSC counsel Thompson.

"I'm sorry, but the admiral told me not to tell anyone," he said. "I can't. I'm sorry. I'm not authorized."

The State Department's legal adviser, Abraham Sofaer, was appalled.

"You've got the counsel to the president here!" he said. "How can you not tell him the facts?"

Thompson seemed embarrassed. "The lawyers who need to work on the issue . . . have been briefed," he said.

"There are real legal questions involved, irrespective of what you might think," Sofaer snapped. "And one of them was the [August 1985] transfer. . . . You may have a good explanation for the shipments after January, because they occur under the Intelligence Act [with a presidential finding] rather than the Arms Export Control Act, but what about prior to January? What's your explanation for that shipment?"

Thompson said he couldn't answer.

Wallison and Sofaer didn't yet know about the CIA's November 1985 shipment. Neither Thompson nor Cooper, who did know about it, mentioned that additional problem.

"This is extremely serious," Sofaer told Wallison after the meeting. "It's particularly serious from your point of view. You're the president's counsel. You should act accordingly."

Sofaer didn't leave it at that. He drove back to the State Department and told Shultz about Thompson's stonewall. Unlike Cooper and Wallison, younger lawyers whose careers had been in the genteel worlds of corporate law and conservative politics, Sofaer had tried gritty criminal cases in New York, first as an assistant U.S. attorney and later as a federal district judge. He knew that men who seemed honorable sometimes committed crimes. And after listening to Thompson, he smelled a conspiracy.

Shultz was on Sofaer's side. The secretary of state had already suspected that Poindexter was still concealing the details of the Iranian initiative. He told his aides to redouble their efforts to find out what was going on.

That afternoon, Poindexter reluctantly agreed to brief Sofaer and Undersecretary Michael H. Armacost on the Iranian operation. The admiral showed them Reagan's January 17, 1986, finding — the original, with the president's signature scrawled in blue ink at the bottom of the page. And he told them that Israel had shipped the first TOW missiles to Iran in August 1985 without Reagan's authorization, although he said McFarlane assured the Israelis that the United States would replenish their stocks if they did. Poindexter did not mention the CIA's November 1985 shipment. Sofaer left the White House convinced that he still hadn't heard the whole story.

That same Tuesday, Poindexter telephoned CIA director Casey to talk about coordinating their disclosures on the Iranian deals. The House and Senate Intelligence committees had summoned them to explain the policy in hearings scheduled for the end of the week. Since Casey was traveling in Central America, the call was made over a secure CIA telephone; the agency taped the call.

"I got to thinking about the hearing on Friday and the coordination that the two of us need to do," Poindexter said. "If you can get back on Thursday so we could meet Thursday afternoon, I think it would be very useful, so we make the best possible presentations on Friday, and try to lay as many of these questions to rest as we can."

"Are you going to have a lot of people at the meeting?" Casey asked. "State and Defense?"

"I'd like to spend some time — just the two of us," Poindexter replied. "But Ed Meese indicated he should want to be helpful, and so he would like to be in at least one of the meetings."

"Ah," Casey said. "You set whatever time you'd like for us to get together and have a little talk ourselves. . . . I'll handle a meeting any time you set it."

On Tuesday evening, McFarlane skipped a dinner party to go to North's office and help rewrite the chronology, which Cooper's legal warning had made obsolete. "It was kind of a feverish climate," he recalled. North, Howard Teicher, two assistants, and two secretaries darted in and out with bits of paper to cut and paste.

McFarlane edited both the chronology and a draft statement for Reagan's press conference. He hoped to accomplish two things: first, to deny that Reagan had approved any arms shipments before January 1986; and second, to separate the arms shipments from any clear connection to a release of hostages.

"A principal objective — probably the primary objective — was to describe a sequence of events that would distance the president from the initial approval of the arms sales," McFarlane said later. It "was not a full and completely accurate account." The new chronology not only said Reagan had not approved the Israeli sales, it claimed he had rejected them. And instead of admitting that the United States had organized the troublesome November 1985 HAWK shipment, it claimed that Mc-Farlane had actually objected to the sale.

The next morning, Richard Secord came in to have a look at the chronology. When he reached the section on the November 1985 shipment, he stopped short.

"There's something wrong here," he told North. "This is bullshit."

"Well," North said, "McFarlane drafted it himself."

"Fine," Secord said, realizing that the problem was over his head. "I'll get out of you guys' hair."

A little later, McFarlane stopped by to take a look at the opening statement for Reagan's news conference. The draft said the main purpose of the arms deals was not buying freedom for the hostages but "bringing Iran back into the community of responsible nations."

It looks fine now, McFarlane told North. You have only one other problem, he added quietly: "the channeling of money to the contras."

As the crisis deepened, the White House turned more and more to deception. Don Regan continued his usual attempts to manage the news, but his efforts were dwarfed by those of Casey, Poindexter, McFarlane, and North, who had seized control of the White House's most precious commodity — secret information — and were now attempting not one cover-up but three. McFarlane wanted to obscure the circumstances under which he approved the first Israeli shipment in August 1985, which was almost certainly illegal under the Arms Export Control Act. McFarlane, Poindexter, and Casey all wanted to save the CIA from the consequences of the November 1985 shipment, which the agency had run without legal authorization. And McFarlane, Poindexter, Casey, and North all wanted to save Project Democracy — not just the half-unraveled secret of North's role in running the contra war, but the deeper, glittering secret of the diversion of funds and, most important, the semiprivate organization that was waging covert operations outside the restraints of Congress or the law.

On Wednesday evening, November 19, Ronald Reagan kept his aides' three cover-ups alive with a news conference that, like his speech six days earlier, was riddled with falsehoods and half-truths. There is no question that the president made false statements during his news conference; the only mystery is how many of them were knowing lies — how many of the three cover-ups the president had consciously joined.

That morning, in another of his regular meetings with Reagan, George Shultz tried to tell the president more bluntly that Poindexter was doing him no good.

"We have been deceived and lied to," Shultz warned.

Reagan said he didn't understand.

"You have to watch out about saying no arms for hostages," Shultz said. He reminded the president of the November 1985 shipment, when McFarlane had told them in Geneva that a planeload of HAWK missiles would go to Iran as soon as the hostages were released.

Yes, the president said, I knew about that.

Poindexter told me in Tokyo last May that the whole thing had been stopped, Shultz said.

"You're telling me things I don't know," Reagan said.

"Mr. President," Shultz replied, "if I'm telling you things you don't know, I don't know very much — so something is wrong here."

But the job of preparing Reagan for his news conference fell not to Shultz but to Poindexter. Armed with ten typed pages of sample questions and answers for the president to study, the national security adviser went to the White House family theater that afternoon to put Reagan through his paces.

Doing a news conference was something of a gamble; it had never been Reagan's favorite medium. Unlike the prepared speeches, which he delivered flawlessly, he often responded to questions with misstatements and flubs of one kind or another. His spokesman, Larry Speakes, noted that the president forgot so much in between his infrequent news conferences that prepping him could be like "reinventing the wheel."

In the "prebrief," the president stood at the podium, chatting and joking, while aides fired sample questions at him. When his answers misfired, Poindexter corrected him. "Reagan's the same in all of these, very relaxed," said Pat Buchanan, who attended the session. "Like a first-rate high school quarterback: you tell him all these plays, and he doesn't listen too attentively, but you know when he gets out there he'll do just fine. He takes instruction very well."

Most of Poindexter's prepared questions about the Iranian affair ran over old ground. One of them opened the way for a special endorsement; if Reagan was asked about Oliver North, he was supposed to respond "I can only say that he is a hard-working and honest officer in whom I have a great deal of trust. I might add that that also goes for his boss, John Poindexter, and the entire NSC staff."

The question that caused Reagan trouble, though, was at the center of the legal dilemma facing Poindexter and Casey: Did the United States authorize Israel to ship weapons to Iran?

"No," the president guessed.

Wrong answer, Poindexter said. The admiral read the elaborate response Reagan was supposed to give: "As I have said before, we will not make public any of the details of this matter or name those who did or did not help us in this matter. I will say that on two specific occasions, I authorized an exception to policy by permitting a small amount of defensive military equipment to be transferred to Iran by a third country."

"Mr. President, we can't use the name of Israel, but we can leave the impression that there was a third country," Poindexter explained.

Buchanan jumped in to try to make the distinction clearer. "Mr. President," he said, "here's how we can answer that in a single sentence: any weapons that were shipped to Iran, authorized by us, could fit into a single cargo plane. . . . not to name Israel, but to leave the impression that some weapons were sent and authorized."

"We've never identified Israel," Speakes added. "We've just referred to a third country."

The president tried again — but got it wrong this time by mentioning Israel by name. Another long explanation from Poindexter ensued. By the end of the session, other aides were shaking their heads. "I was confused myself," said one.

The rehearsal over, Reagan took the elevator upstairs to the second floor to nap for an hour. Then, well rested and in a change of clothes, he descended to the Blue Room, an elegant, oval reception area where his staff would watch the news conference on television monitors.

"Twenty seconds," the broadcast technician called out. With a final joke to his aides, Reagan strode down the red-carpeted hallway through a tall set of double doors — an entrance Michael Deaver had designed to convey a sense of the solitude of power — and stepped up to his specially designed podium, complete with sound amplifiers and seating chart, in the East Room.

"Good evening," the president said. "I have a few words here before I take your questions.

"Eighteen months ago, as I said last Thursday, this administration began a secret initiative to the Islamic Republic of Iran. Our purposes were fourfold: to replace a relationship of total hostility with something better, to bring a negotiated end to the Iran-Iraq war, to bring an end to terrorism, and to effect the release of our hostages. . . .

"I deeply believe in the correctness of my decision. I was convinced then and I am convinced now that while the risks were great, so too was the potential reward. Bringing Iran back into the community of responsible nations, ending its participation in political terror, bringing an end to that terrible war, and bringing our hostages home — these are the causes that justify taking risks," he said.

As soon as the questions began, Reagan ran into trouble. Asked why arms had gone to Iran whenever an American hostage was released, Reagan said, "Iran held no hostages. Iran did not kidnap anyone, to our knowledge. . . . I don't see where the kidnappers or the hostage-holders gained anything. They let the hostages go. Now, whatever is the pressure that brought that about, I'm just grateful to it for the fact that we got them."

Didn't the United States "condone shipments by Israel and other nations"?

"We did not condone and do not condone the shipment of arms from other countries," he said, erring on the side of denial.

"Could you explain what the Israeli role was here?"

"No, because we, as I say, have had nothing to do with other countries or their shipments of arms."

"Mr. President," said NBC's Andrea Mitchell, "we've been told by the chief of staff, Donald Regan, that . . . this government condoned an Israeli shipment in September of 1985, shortly before the release of Benjamin Weir. That was four months before your intelligence finding on January 17. . . . Can you clear that up?"

"Well, no," the president said dubiously. "I've never heard Mr. Regan say that, and I'll ask him about that."

"Why shouldn't other nations ship weapons to Iran when they think it's in their interest?" another reporter asked.

"Well, I would like to see the indication as to how it could be in their interest," he said lamely.

"What would be wrong in saying that a mistake was made on a very high risk gamble so that you can get on with the next two years?"

"Because I don't think a mistake was made," the president said. "I don't see that it has been a fiasco or great failure of any kind. We still have those contacts. We still have made some ground. We got our hostages back, three of them. And so I think that what we did was right. And we're going to continue on this path."

In the Blue Room, Reagan's aides were stunned. The president had gotten the question about Israel wrong, not once, but several times. Larry Speakes raised his hands toward the ceiling, as if appealing to the gods.

Speakes and Regan instantly ordered a correction to be prepared. The White House almost never corrected the president's misstatements, although he made hundreds; but this one went to the issue of his credibility, the most damaging question the Iran affair had raised.

The rest of the news conference wasn't much better. Reagan's rationalizations of the arms sales had looked reasonable on paper, but they didn't play when his questioners — press or public — refused to suspend disbelief and agree that weapons had not really been swapped for hostages. Given a chance to admit gracefully that the decisions to sell arms had been an honest misjudgment, the president stiffened his back and said he'd do it all again.

But Reagan didn't understand any of that. When the president walked back down the red carpet from the East Room, he was surprised to find his aides wreathed in gloom.

"You got the third country issue a bit wrong," Poindexter said gently.

"Did I?" asked the president. He looked at Poindexter's handwritten draft of a correction. "Gosh," he said. "I didn't realize I'd said that."

The staff repaired to the Roosevelt Room to undo the damage. Within twenty minutes, Speakes issued a "statement by the president" that still left unclear what the U.S. role had been in those Israeli shipments. "There may be some misunderstanding of one of my answers tonight," it said. "There was a third country involved in our secret project with Iran. But taking this into account, all of the shipments of the token amounts of defensive arms and parts that I have authorized or condoned taken in total could be placed aboard a single cargo aircraft. This includes all shipments by the United States or any third country. Any other shipments by third countries were not authorized by the U.S. Government."

No one was unhappier with the press conference than Don Regan — but his complaint wasn't so much that the president had misstated facts, it was that Andrea Mitchell had accused him, Regan, of breaking the silence on Israel's role. (In fact, while others may have revealed the Israeli role earlier, Regan was splitting hairs: he too had played a part, as NBC's Mitchell had suggested.)

"It's my reputation," the red-faced chief of staff bellowed to the underlings gathered in the Roosevelt Room. "I'm not going to be hung out on a limb, goddamn it!"

Buchanan, Speakes, North, and a half-dozen aides watched agape.

"I want a correction!" Regan said, pounding on the end of the long table. "It wasn't me who did the backgrounder [that revealed Israel's role], it was somebody else."

Pat Buchanan tried to calm Regan down. "Listen, the thing's wrapped up for the night," he said. "Andrea Mitchell isn't going to break into whatever is on TV to say 'I just want to raise a point here, I misphrased my question.' . . . The thing to do is get her to put a correction out in the morning."

But Regan was in no mood for reason. He raged on for perhaps half an hour; he threatened to go out and give a late press conference of his own.

Buchanan, who fled to the calm of the Jockey Club, said later that he had seen Regan throw tantrums before, but never like this one.

"You could tell he'd been getting it for days and days and days and days, and it finally went click," Buchanan said. "But Regan really didn't know the facts in this. Only the NSC did."

Other cabinet officers were also upset, but their fears were for the president's credibility, not Regan's. Ed Meese telephoned Poindexter to ask why Reagan hadn't handled the questions in "the usual crisp, clear way." George Shultz telephoned the president directly. That morning in the Oval Office, Reagan had acknowledged to Shultz that he knew Israel's shipments were aimed at freeing the hostages; but on television, the president had denied any such swaps and any Israeli involvement.

"I felt as this went on that the people who were giving him the information, in a sense, had . . . a conflict of interest with the president," Shultz said later. "They were trying to use his undoubted skills as a communicator to have him give a speech and give a press conference and say these things, and in doing so he would bail them out."

So Shultz told Reagan that he wanted to stop by the next day and explain what was wrong with the briefings he was getting from Poindexter. Reagan told the secretary of state to come on over.

The president seemed to be the only one who didn't recognize that he had walked into a political disaster. The White House staff was frantic, the Israeli government was upset, and even the Iranians were unhappy; one of Khomeini's negotiators had telephoned North's office to tell him that most of the news conference had been fine, but "the talk of moderates and Israelis was not well received."

Political Washington, absorbed by the inside gossip and indulgent of the president's frailties, focused on the failures of the White House staff. The Republican chairman of the Senate Foreign Relations Committee, Richard Lugar of Indiana, said Reagan needed to "bring in some big leaguers to run things." Conservative columnist George F. Will agreed: "The aides in close contact with President Reagan today are the least distinguished such group to serve any president in the postwar period."

Lou Cannon, the *Washington Post*'s acute but sympathetic chronicler of the Reagan presidency, wrote with a tone of almost paternal concern: "The second-raters around the president do not understand . . . that Reagan needs their help and protection. They have scrambled to save themselves and shoved their president, unprepared and uninformed, in front of the American people to take the heat. Don't any of them have the grace to resign?"

But the American public seemed less interested in the administration's internal politics than in Reagan himself. As some aides had predicted, Reagan won a short-term jump in support because of the televised image of a beleaguered president at the mercy of an insatiable press. But his credibility was plummeting; one poll found that 79 percent of the public judged the president's explanations of the Iranian arms deals "misleading." In the past, Reagan had relied on direct appeals to the people, knowing that they were his best audience. Now, however, the magic wasn't working nearly as well.

After fifteen months of self-delusion about Iran, Reagan had been forced for the first time to defend his policy before skeptical questioners. In reply, he had offered only arguments that were untenable or false; under the no-longer-friendly glare of the television lights, his explanations now came across as desperate rationalizations. Far from being "unprepared and uninformed" for the news conference, Reagan had been well prepared and better informed than most of his aides. But he had insulated himself from real-world arguments too long and too well. And as his aides built ever more complex structures of deception, he found it difficult to keep straight which facts he was and was not supposed to reveal. The Reagan qualities that the public had once found endearing — the relentless optimism, the impatience with the dry specifics of policy — now threatened to turn against him.

Over almost six years in office, Reagan had succeeded in restoring credibility to the presidency. But now, in the space of only a few months, he had allowed his personal credibility to slip increasingly away — to the point that his press conference raised questions, not only about his veracity, but about his ability to handle the job as well. To a crisis of credibility was now added a new crisis of confidence. Long hailed as the Great Communicator, a "masterpiece of American magic," Reagan suddenly seemed no longer majestic, no longer in command — a man at the mercy of events and his own subordinates.

15

Battle Royal

ON THURSDAY, NOVEMBER 20, 1986, the battle for Ronald Reagan's government began in earnest. It was a war of memoranda and meetings, of whispered words and late night intrigues — but it was a deadly war, all the same. The battlefield was Washington, but at times it seemed more like the squalid capital of a Third World military regime. For this was, in essence, a struggle between a secret junta inside the heart of the government and a minority of dissidents who stood in its way. The junta made mistakes; the dissidents had some lucky breaks. Otherwise, the outcome might have been different.

At stake was the survival of Project Democracy, the secret covert action network that William Casey, John Poindexter, and Oliver North had built to evade, not only Congress, but the president's cabinet as well. For more than two years, Casey and his allies — the junta — had mounted what was almost a clandestine coup d'état. But now one of their operations, the arms sales to Iran, had been exposed, and the junta was on the defensive.

Casey's principal opponent, George Shultz, now saw a chance to win back some of the ground he had lost in the administration's struggle for power. Shultz did not know what Casey and Poindexter had been up to, did not know what Project Democracy was about, but he knew that his control over foreign policy had been slowly stolen, and he was determined to regain it.

On the sideline stood Ronald Reagan. It was his government that was being contested, but Reagan played a largely passive role in the events of November 1986. It was never certain how much he knew about Project Democracy, but his instinctive sympathies were clear: he favored

Casey, Poindexter, and North. They had freed American hostages, and the president was all for that; they had helped the contras survive, and the president approved of that effort too.

Shultz, on the other hand, fought virtually alone, under fire from Nancy Reagan, George Bush, and others for what they called disloyalty to the president's cause. And as the combat reached its peak during five days in November, it was not only unclear who would win; more than once, it appeared that the junta might succeed in driving Shultz from the field altogether.

As the moment of battle approached, Casey returned early from his trip through Central America to help Poindexter protect their precious secrets. The men behind Project Democracy had already constructed a series of lies to hide their previous actions, but now they were both being summoned to testify before Congress. They needed a single, coordinated alibi that they could present as presidential policy — an official account of the Iranian arms deals that could protect all their undiscovered operations.

Casey, Poindexter, and North spent much of Thursday morning preparing their accounts. At 1:30 P.M., they gathered in Poindexter's West Wing corner office, with its tall windows facing the White House driveway and Pennsylvania Avenue. They were joined by Attorney General Meese, who Poindexter said "wanted to be helpful"; Meese's young deputy, Charles Cooper; Poindexter's counsel, the navy commander Paul B. Thompson; and Casey's deputy, Robert M. Gates.

A draft of Casey's proposed testimony before the Senate and House intelligence committees was handed around the room. The most troublesome question was how to present the CIA's role in the November 1985 HAWK missile sale.

"In late November 1985, a CIA proprietary airline was chartered to carry cargo to Iran at the NSC's request," the CIA draft read. "The cargo was described to us as oil drilling spare parts. . . . We in CIA did not find out that our airline had hauled HAWK missiles into Iran until mid-January, when we were told by the Iranians."

That account, of course, was not true; the CIA had known all along what was aboard its airplane. But now Casey, realizing that its delivery of HAWK missiles to Iran without a presidential order was probably illegal, was trying to obscure the action. "The CIA did not want to go on record [with] the fact that they had done an operation without a finding," Paul Thompson observed.

As the meeting went on, Oliver North spoke up with a series of changes for the draft to disassociate the NSC staff from the shipment as well. First, North said the fact that he and McFarlane had requested the CIA airline flight should be left out. Then he insisted that no one in the entire government, not just the CIA, had known that the cargo included weapons. The NSC, in other words, knew no more about the shipment than the CIA. Those changes were false — but Casey, Poindexter, and Meese simply nodded. Casey and Poindexter, at least, knew that the testimony was false and getting more so. But they copied North's changes onto their texts and accepted a new official chronology, asserting that the arms deals had been "within the limits of established policy and in compliance with all U.S. law." Casey and Poindexter agreed to use the new chronology as the basis for their testimony to Congress the next day. The effect, North later acknowledged, was to commit the president of the United States to a false story.

After the meeting, Casey and Gates returned to CIA headquarters to put the final touches on the director's testimony. The redrafting session was "pandemonium," Gates said later. "Casey [was] going through, making changes in the testimony, updating and changing things we weren't sure of. People were passing comments and conversations and Casey was tearing off pages, and it was just mass confusion."

Amid the fray, one of Casey's aides raised a frightening new concern. "Bill, not only is this chaos," he said, "there is a discussion of a diversion of Iran funds."

"I know absolutely nothing about that," Casey said firmly.

George Shultz had already called out his troops in the wake of Reagan's disastrous press conference. The same morning Casey was preparing his testimony, Shultz summoned his chief diplomat, Undersecretary Michael Armacost, and his legal counsel, Abraham Sofaer, into his offices on the seventh floor of the State Department. The two of you, he said, are going to be given all the information we have on the Iranian arms sales so that we can see where the president is being misinformed.

Shultz's executive assistant, Charles Hill, pulled out his notes from a year before. There in black and white was proof that the November 1985 HAWK shipment had occurred exactly as Shultz recalled it. They were the notes from the telephone call McFarlane had made to Shultz at the Geneva summit, talking about weapons, not oil parts, and explaining that a hundred HAWKs would go to Iran if — and only if — the hostages were released. In other words, it had been a swap of arms for hostages.

In the middle of the meeting, a lawyer from the CIA arrived with that morning's first draft of Casey's proposed testimony — the text that Poindexter and North were at that moment discussing at the White House. Sofaer flipped through the pages and didn't like what he saw. The CIA's account of its November 1985 shipment of HAWKs seemed odd, at best. The agency admitted providing an airplane for the deal, but insisted that it thought the plane was carrying oil drilling parts, not weapons that might be prohibited by the Arms Export Control Act. "That story did not hang together," Sofaer said later. "The whole thing smelled to me like the kind of thing you see in a trial . . . in a narcotics case, for example, where they refer to the drugs as 'shirts' or something."

Two other points aroused his suspicion. "First of all, I saw the prices, the money for the missiles, and it looked low to me," he said in testimony before Congress. "And then I saw the name of Southern Air Transport in the testimony. That made me concerned. . . . To me it was a red flag indicating a possible connection with Central America."

Sofaer called the Justice Department and outlined his worries to Edwin Meese's deputy, Arnold Burns. Burns relayed the question to Meese, who replied that he "knew of certain facts that explained all these matters and that laid to rest all the problems [Sofaer] might perceive."

Not good enough, Sofaer said. "I'm calling the White House counsel," he announced to Burns.

He dialed Peter Wallison at the White House and warned him that Casey was about to give false testimony by contending that the CIA believed the 1985 shipment contained only oil drilling parts. Wallison was stunned. "I'll talk to Cooper and Thompson about it," the president's lawyer said.

At 4:00 P.M., Cooper and Thompson walked upstairs from their meeting on the testimony in Poindexter's office to Wallison's second-floor quarters. Wallison, who had not been invited to Poindexter's meeting, told them the State Department knew that Casey's testimony was false, that the government knew about the HAWK missiles all along. Cooper and Thompson gaped in surprise, and Cooper immediately called Sofaer to ask him what he was talking about.

There was something other than oil drilling equipment on that plane, and we knew it at the time, Sofaer repeated.

But I've just been through a meeting at which everyone agreed that no one in the government knew that, Cooper replied. Everybody thought it was oil drilling bits.

"Impossible," Sofaer said. "Untenable." He explained that McFarlane had told Shultz, before the shipment even happened, that the plane was carrying missiles.

Cooper turned to the NSC's Thompson. "This is a very serious discrepancy," he said earnestly. "It has to be ironed out."

Wallison sighed. "The president keeps getting deeper into this," he said, "because people are operating in his name."

Cooper checked the story of the 1985 shipment with North, who stuck to his account. Cooper called Sofaer again.

"Abe, are you certain that this is the recollection?" he asked. "Ollie North says . . . he had no knowledge of any of this."

"We have notes, contemporaneous notes," Sofaer said emphatically. *"The word HAWKs is in the notes."*

There was a brief silence on the telephone.

"You're shitting me," Cooper said.

Sofaer said he was scheduled to accompany Casey to the intelligence committees the next morning. "I'm scared," Sofaer said. "If that testimony isn't changed and people aren't forced to tell the truth about all this . . . the president will be in trouble."

If Casey gave his testimony as planned and denied any knowledge of the HAWKs, Sofaer went on, he would feel duty bound to stand up and challenge the CIA director. And then, the judge said, "I'll resign."

Cooper swallowed. If that happened, he told Sofaer, "there will be a lot of us who leave the government."

The young Justice Department lawyer quickly telephoned Meese; Meese telephoned Casey, who agreed that his testimony should be changed in light of Sofaer's "new" facts.

It was 11:28 P.M. when Cooper called Sofaer yet again. Casey's testimony had been "adjusted," he said — not to provide a true account of the November 1985 shipment but rather "to avoid the issue." It wouldn't be the whole truth, but Sofaer figured he could live with it for the moment. "We were satisfied with that fix," he said later, "because at least there wasn't a lie out there and the president wasn't at risk."

Earlier that evening, Shultz met with the president in the family quarters of the White House. He carried with him a six-page paper that unsparingly dissected Reagan's misstatements and blunders from the news conference. Don Regan, who attended the meeting, described Shultz as "boiling."

"It was a long, tough discussion," Shultz testified before Congress, "not the kind of discussion I ever thought I'd have with the president of the United States. . . . It was 'bark off' all the way."

Shultz contested almost a dozen of Reagan's statements. Iran had not reduced its support for terrorism around the world, he said. The arms shipments did affect the military balance between Iran and Iraq. And some of the shipments may have been illegal, no matter what other people were saying. "It is very clear to the Iranians that we were exchanging arms for hostages," Shultz said, according to his prepared "talking points." "We are convinced that Iranian-controlled groups in Lebanon have concluded that it is in their interest to kidnap additional Americans — because whatever we may say, America does pay ransom."

Reagan still didn't agree. It wasn't arms for hostages, he insisted. It was "an effort to get an opening to Iran."

Shultz stuck to his guns. "Mr. President," he said, "no one looking at the record will agree."

But Shultz could see that he was getting nowhere. He left the White House and dispiritedly recounted the argument to his executive assistant, Charles Hill. "I didn't make a dent on him," Shultz said.

Deep in the White House bureaucracy, other officials were resorting to Washington's time-honored method of blowing the whistle: leaking to the press. "Ollie has lied to the president of the United States," one angry aide told a reporter on the phone late one night. "He's written a history, a chronology, which is basically a fabrication. There are a lot of people — and I mean a lot of people — who hope this will get out. . . . You have to go back to Watergate to find something this bad." But there were no details, no proof; the story couldn't run that night.

On Friday morning, Poindexter and Casey finally appeared separately, behind closed doors, before each of the congressional intelligence committees. Poindexter stuck carefully to the original version of the cover-up and insisted that no one knew that the CIA's November 1985 flight into Iran carried HAWK missiles. But Casey was more artful.

"Did the CIA know what was on that aircraft?" asked Senator Patrick Leahy of Vermont.

"There is some question about that," Casey said. "I was told yesterday that the CIA didn't know it until later on. . . . As far as I can find out, the agency did not know what it was handling at the time. Now, I am going to inquire further into that."

"Do you understand why somebody raised the questions, wondering whether there was just plausible deniability being set up here?" Leahy asked.

"Hadn't thought about it," Casey replied equably. "I hadn't thought about it."

Sofaer and Armacost, who were there to represent the State Department, let Casey's testimony on the November 1985 shipment go. The only time they objected, members of the committee said, was when Casey claimed that all appropriate cabinet members had been consulted on the decision to ship weapons to Iran.

"Secretary Shultz participated in the discussions," Armacost interjected, but had "no role" in the decisions.

"I thought we were all supporting the president's position," Casey responded acidly.

At some point that afternoon, Casey could see that his story wasn't working. The intelligence committees were openly skeptical, probing everything he said, demanding more specifics. The Senate's Democratic leader, Robert Byrd of West Virginia, even suggested putting the CIA chief under oath.

Before the House Intelligence Committee, Casey suddenly tossed out some red meat for the investigators to chase: an operation that had outlasted its usefulness but would deflect the bloodhounds from his own agency.

The problems at the NSC, he volunteered, all started with "this Central America business.

"The NSC has been guiding and active in the private provision of weapons to the contras down there," Casey said. "It came to McFarlane and he began to develop it. . . . I don't know all the details. I have kept away from the details because I was barred from doing anything. I knew that others were doing it."

In case the congressmen missed the point, Casey repeated it three times. Now that the CIA had its charter back for the Nicaraguan war, he was throwing Ollie North and his contra project to the wolves. Sometimes, Casey must have thought, you have to sacrifice an agent, even a good one, to protect your most important assets.

At eleven-thirty that same Friday morning, as Casey was talking to the intelligence committees, Attorney General Meese went to the White House to tell Reagan that the administration still didn't have control of its own story.

"There seems to be a lot of confusion among the people who were participating [in] the Iranian initiative," Meese told the president, Regan, and Poindexter in the Oval Office. "North knows some things, the people in the CIA know other things, George Shultz knows some additional information, and nobody has put all of this information together."

By then, the attorney general knew that Casey's draft testimony had hidden the CIA's role in the 1985 HAWK shipment and that North had attempted to make the testimony even more deceptive. According to Regan, Meese even said that there was documentary evidence from 1985 that showed that Casey and North had given a false account of their actions. But the imperturbable attorney general described the contradiction between their stories and the documented truth as a simple muddle, a failure of memory.

"He characterized it as being discrepancies, period, that he wanted . . . cleared up so that we had all of the facts," Regan recalled later.

Meese never raised the possibility that someone was lying. Nor did he ask the president, Regan, or Poindexter whether any of them knew the truth about the controversial November 1985 shipment. He merely said it was worrisome that the administration still had no single, coherent account of the arms sales; he said he wanted to "straighten out any wrinkles in our knowledge."

Regan and Poindexter agreed with that. If the administration was to survive the crisis, it had to show that it was in control of its own affairs. The president asked no substantive questions, accepting his advisers' judgment. Meese's proposal to interview all those involved in the arms sales and pull together a coherent account was approved.

Regan pointed out that the NSPG was scheduled to meet in three days, on Monday afternoon, to discuss formally whether the negotiations with

Iran should continue. "We [should] at least know or have common knowledge of the facts, so try to get them by two o'clock on Monday," he urged.

Meese agreed, and the decision was made. "It was just a quickie meeting, not more than ten or fifteen minutes," Regan recalled. "So there was no detailing in it."

This wasn't an inquest; it was merely, as Meese would say, "an attempt to get our arms around the problem." The attorney general was acting not as the nation's chief law enforcement officer but as the president's personal troubleshooter.

That was a familiar role for Meese, who had been at Ronald Reagan's side ever since their days in Sacramento. Like Reagan, Meese could cheerfully bend the facts to fit whatever case he was trying to make. When he was the White House counselor in Reagan's first term, some reporters found his "background" briefings so unreliable that they flipped a coin; the losers got the exclusive session with Meese.

A former county prosecutor from Oakland, Meese shared Reagan's law-and-order view of the Constitution: "You don't have many suspects who are innocent of a crime," he once declared. Yet while he was unsparing toward those accused of common crimes, Meese could be indulgent toward white-collar criminals. He seemed incapable of recognizing what others saw as conflicts of interest. He was the target of almost constant allegations of misconduct, from approving federal jobs for men who had extended loans to his family to providing high-level Washington access for a lawyer-lobbyist friend.

But Meese was indispensable to Ronald Reagan — both as a guardian of Reaganism and as a troubleshooter in time of crisis. When he turned up at the White House on November 20, it was an implicit reproach to Donald Regan, who as chief of staff should have been the one to coordinate the government's stories on the Iranian arms sales. But Regan, although he recognized the gathering force of the Iranian problem, was preoccupied with his own position and had failed to take control of the issue; no one was effectively defending the president. Ed Meese saw that vacuum and filled it. The last survivor of Reagan's original staff, he now rode to the president's rescue.

Back at the Justice Department, Meese called in three of his closest political aides to begin conducting his inquiry. They were William Bradford Reynolds, the conservative ideologue who served as assistant attorney general for civil rights; John Richardson, Meese's aide for intelligence issues; and Charles Cooper, Justice's internal counsel. None had substantial experience as an investigator. Both the director of the FBI and the chief of the Justice Department's criminal division offered to help, but Meese turned them down in favor of his own aides.

"They were people that I could count on to work over the weekend,"

Meese explained later. "There was no reason to select anyone from the criminal division, inasmuch as there were no criminal aspects to this."

As Meese assembled his team of discreet investigators, John Poindexter called Oliver North.

"Meese will be sending people over to review documents," he warned, according to North.

"Don't worry," North replied. "It's all taken care of."

But it hadn't all been taken care of, not by a long shot. Poindexter's warning to North touched off a frenzied weekend of destroying documents and warning confederates in the junta, sometimes only steps ahead of Meese's investigators.

Within minutes of Poindexter's call, North was in a taxi speeding out to the suburban Maryland home of Michael Ledeen, the consultant who had helped set up the initial, potentially illegal arms deals. He swept into the house to find Ledeen and Robert McFarlane closeted in the library, trying to reconstruct what had gone on in 1985.

North announced that Meese was looking into the November 1985 HAWK shipment. "We may all have to get lawyers," he said.

McFarlane was on his way out the door. North got into McFarlane's burgundy Jaguar for the ride back down to the White House.

"[I'm] worried that Ledeen might have profited from this," he told McFarlane.

"What do you mean?" McFarlane asked.

"Well, I don't know," he said. "I just believe that perhaps Schwimmer [the Israeli arms merchant] and Ledeen have made some arrangements that we're just not aware of . . . and I'm worried about it." (Ledeen denied ever drawing any profits from the deal, and no evidence surfaced to support North's fear.)

The two men tried to convince each other that Meese's inquiry would turn out all right. They talked of their families, McFarlane said later, and their faith in God.

North turned to McFarlane. "There's going to be a shredding party this weekend," he said abruptly.

McFarlane was taken aback. "Ollie," he said, "look. You have acted under instructions at all times, and I'm confident that you have nothing to worry about. Let it all happen, and I'll back you up."

North shook McFarlane's hand, got out at the White House, and went in to see Poindexter. They talked about their "fall guy" plan, North said: someone had to take the fall to protect Project Democracy, and at this point that someone was North. He affirmed that he was ready to resign for the sake of the operation. Later, in his testimony before Congress, North said he also assured Poindexter that any documents that mentioned the diversion of funds to the contras had already been destroyed. (Poindexter, who insisted that he didn't know about any such memos at the time, said he didn't remember North's saying that.)

"Does the president know about the fact that we used these monies to support the resistance?" North said he asked the admiral.

"No," Poindexter replied, according to North: the president knew nothing about the diversion. That surprised North. He had assumed that Poindexter had briefed Reagan on every part of the operation.

North calmly crossed the street to the Old Executive Office Building, took the elevator up to the third floor, and began destroying his tracks in earnest.

He later asserted that by that day, November 21, he had already destroyed the most damning documents, the five memoranda that outlined the plan to divert Iranian arms profits to the contras. He had shredded them, he said, because Casey warned him that people in the deal — Adnan Khashoggi and Roy Furmark, to be precise — were beginning to talk. (Lawyers noted that since the diversion documents might be central to any criminal charges growing out of Project Democracy, North's testimony that he destroyed them before any investigations began might neatly absolve him of a possible charge of obstruction of justice.)

The first thing North did was to ask the NSC archives for a series of memoranda on the contra project — the same memos that had been identified as troublesome when Michael Barnes, the inquisitive Democratic congressman, had turned up in 1985. North marked the changes he wanted with a pen — deleting any references to military advice and assistance to the contras — and handed the documents to his secretary, Fawn Hall. The memoranda were a year or more old, but Hall did not ask why she was changing them. "I felt a little bit of uneasiness when he asked me to do it," she conceded. But "it was a policy of mine not to ask questions and just to follow instructions. I believed in Colonel North and what he was doing. I had no right to question him."

Her attempt to alter the documents was amateurish, at best. One of the memos North asked for never came because a clerk didn't look in the right file. Hall retyped several of the papers on a style of NSC stationery that hadn't been used in 1985. On one memorandum from North to McFarlane, she failed to omit a reference to the fraudulent "end-user certificates" that Guatemala had provided for the contras to buy arms. And Hall never finished destroying the incriminating copies that North had marked up. While North sent the altered versions of the memos back to the NSC archives, Hall's own files still contained the original versions.

At two twenty-five, North went back across the street to the White House to see Poindexter. He was carrying one of his old spiral notebooks — the ones in which he jotted notes from conversations and reminders of things to do, the written notes Casey had admonished him against making.

He'd found his notes from the November 1985 HAWK shipment, he told Poindexter. The official story was that Reagan had not even known of the shipment in advance.

North read out loud from the notebook: "R.R. directed operation to proceed." There was a silence in the room. I guess I'd better get rid of this, North said.

Poindexter says he made no response. North said nothing more; nothing more needed to be said.

North returned to his office and began pulling papers from his files — some from the locked drawer in his desk, some from a file cabinet safe — and piled them on the table in his office.

"What's going on?" asked his puzzled deputy, Robert Earl.

"It's time for North to be the scapegoat," he said dramatically. "Ollie has been designated the scapegoat."

He said he had just come from a meeting "across the street" in the West Wing. Attorney General Meese had been there, he said, and told him his assistants would be coming over to examine North's files. North told Earl that he had asked Meese, "Can I have forty-eight hours?" And Meese replied that he didn't know whether he could. (Earl wasn't sure of the wording, wasn't sure whether North had said twenty-four hours or forty-eight, but insisted that he remembered the sense of the sentence. Both North and Meese later denied that such a conversation had occurred.)

Fawn Hall was still altering the old contra memos when she saw her boss begin to feed other documents into the shredder, a compact gray machine in the small storeroom across from her desk. She jumped to her feet. "I joined him in an effort so that he would not have to be wasting his time shredding," she said later.

As North pulled documents from each drawer of the five-drawer file cabinet and piled them on the shredder, Hall fed them into the whirring mouth of the machine, a dozen pages at a time. As she worked, a thought came to her. "Should I go ahead and shred the PROFS notes and the phone logs?" she asked, referring to her own files of messages and calls. North said yes, good idea.

Colonel Earl appeared with yet another set of documents, an armload of printouts from the laptop KL-43 computer that North had used to communicate with Secord and others involved in the secret contra airlift. Hall said she was startled by the size of the pile.

"If the idea is to get rid of all these things, it's going to be impossible," she warned. There just wasn't enough time. But Earl began handing her the messages, and she fed them into the shredder as well.

Still, there was no sense of frenzy, Hall remembered. "This was a very relaxed atmosphere," she said. "It wasn't . . . close the door, lock the windows, pull down the shades."

North, burrowing through his files, held up a letter from the insistent

Felix Rodriguez, one of his many complaints about the way the airlift had been run. Rodriguez had already been identified in the newspapers as a key figure in the operation; that very morning, Casey had openly steered Congress toward an investigation of the NSC staff's role in the contra operation. North contemplated the Rodriguez letter for a moment and grinned.

"They'll have fun with this," he said. And he tossed it back into the safe.

The stack of papers on the shredder grew to a foot and a half. Fawn Hall fed them into the machine, sheaf after sheaf. Then came a high-pitched whine: the shredder had jammed.

Hall dashed across the room to her desk and called the Crisis Management Center. A technician appeared at the door within minutes and, as North, Earl, and Hall did their best to appear nonchalant, shook loose the jam, punched the Reset button, and removed the shredder bag full of paper spaghetti — the remnants of North's archives. An empty bag was fitted into place and the shredding resumed.

To Earl, it was clear what was going on. There had been three phases in the White House's reaction to the discovery of the Iranian arms deals, he said: first, denial, and second, attempting to devise an explanation for Congress which would not endanger the project. The problem, Earl said later, was that "phase two . . . was not washing, was not going over, and that therefore the decision was taken to go to phase three, which was termination of the project; that it was politically embarrassing and that the political mistake, if you will, of the whole Iran operation would be blamed on Oliver North. He was going to be the scapegoat for this failure, this mess of the Iran thing, and so he was doing his duty."

But North did not, in the end, destroy everything. He was going to play the scapegoat, but he also wanted to keep an ace in the hole — just in case. He took the spiral notebooks that he had discussed with Poindexter a few hours earlier and quietly removed them from his office.

Back in the White House, the president's national security adviser was also destroying files and covering his tracks. At about 3:00 P.M., Meese had called to ask that Poindexter gather all the documents he had which might shed light on the Iranian arms sale. The admiral told his counsel, Paul Thompson, to take a look at the files in his safe.

Thompson walked into Poindexter's office with a manila envelope in his hand. Inside were the three presidential findings that authorized the arms deals: the finding of December 5, 1985, which the CIA had demanded to cover its work on the November shipment; the draft finding of January 6, 1986, which Reagan had signed by mistake; and the finding of January 17, 1986, which actually authorized the later shipments.

"The first version of the finding is going to be embarrassing," Thompson pointed out. The first one, which the CIA had drafted hastily in December for the HAWKs shipment, portrayed the initiative as a simple arms-for-hostage deal.

"Let me take a look at it," Poindexter said. He remembered this one; he considered it simply a "C.Y.A." finding — a "cover your ass" effort by the CIA. But it did pose a problem: the president was publicly denying that he had approved a trade of arms for hostages, and here was a finding with his signature that stated he had done exactly that.

Poindexter thought for a moment and realized he was holding the only existing copy of the finding. "This has no future," he said coolly. Calmly and deliberately, as Thompson watched, he tore the presidential order into shreds. Then he ripped up some old PROFS notes that were in the file as well and stuffed the shreds into the "burn bag" behind his desk. There was only one potential problem: at least one other person could reveal the existence of the 1985 finding — the man who signed it, Ronald Reagan. But Reagan never did. For eight months, until Poindexter publicly testified that Reagan had signed the finding, the president either forgot about the document or deliberately refused to acknowledge it. As late as July 1987, the White House officially denied that Reagan had even seen it. "Our position is that it never went to the president, period," a White House spokesman said.

At three-thirty on Friday afternoon, McFarlane arrived at Meese's office in the Justice Department. It was the attorney general's first interview in his informal inquiry into the Iranian arms deals.

"We need the facts," Meese said, "the total chronology." So McFarlane gave Meese and his deputy, Charles Cooper, a quick — and very inaccurate — history of the arms deals.

It all began, he said, when Israel's David Kimche told him of an opportunity to open contacts with moderates in Iran, but added that "a quid pro quo in terms of military supplies would eventually be necessary." In August 1985, Israel went ahead with a shipment of 508 TOW missiles to Iran — with no explicit U.S. approval, McFarlane said. He said he "knew of no one in [the] U.S. government who had contact with Israel" on the shipment of those TOWs, he said. (This was not true; McFarlane had told the Israelis that the shipment would be welcomed by the United States, and he would later claim that Reagan had approved the shipment in advance.)

Then, in November 1985, there was a shipment of HAWK missiles, McFarlane said. At the time, he added, he believed the shipment included only oil drilling equipment, not HAWKs. Meese helpfully told him that George Shultz had notes that showed that he knew HAWKs had been aboard the planes. At that, McFarlane allowed that Shultz might be right, after all. (By telling McFarlane about the notes, Meese enabled him to tell the others involved in the cover-up that their story about the oil drilling parts had been blown before any of them were questioned about it.)

McFarlane knew more than he was telling Meese, but he volunteered nothing. He did not mention that North had announced he was going to hold "a shredding party." Nor did he mention that North had told him about the diversion of funds to the contras.

"He was not a man who was at ease," Cooper recalled later. "He was attempting to project the image that he was at ease. [But] he was very careful about what he said."

In two hours, they were done. As Meese began to leave the room, McFarlane stopped him. "Ed, wait a minute," he said. "I want to talk to you about this."

He said he was worried about stories in the newspapers charging that he approved the first Israeli shipments himself, without explicit approval from the president. "I have taken on responsibility for every bit of this that I can, Ed, and I shall continue to do that," he said.

"Yes, that's been noted," Meese said.

"But I want you to know that from the very beginning of this, Ed, the president was four-square behind it. . . . He never had any reservations about approving anything that the Israelis wanted to do here."

"Bud, I know that, and I can understand why," Meese replied. "And as a practical matter, I'm glad you told me this because his legal position is far better the earlier that he made the decision."

"Well, I don't have any knowledge of that," McFarlane said. "But there was no question about it, Ed."

McFarlane walked out the door of the Justice Department, went straight to a pay phone on the sidewalk, and dialed North's office. Standing in the cold on Tenth Street, he recounted his interview with Meese to North — including the news about Shultz's notes on the HAWK shipment.

Later that evening, McFarlane sent another PROFS note to Poindexter. "Spent a couple of hours with Ed Meese today going over the record with him," he wrote. "The only blind spot on my part concerned a shipment in November '85 which still doesn't ring a bell with me. But it appears that the matter of not notifying [Congress of] the Israeli transfers can be covered if the president made a 'mental finding' before the transfers took place. Well, on that score we ought to be OK because he was all for letting the Israelis do anything they wanted at the very first briefing in the hospital."

After their interview with McFarlane, the Justice Department investigators packed up for the day. Meese did not send anyone to look at the documents in North's office. "There was no urgency to it," he later explained.

But while Meese was taking his time, others were becoming more suspicious. In the White House, Don Regan belatedly realized that something was going on behind his back. "My nostrils were really twitching," he said later. "There was something wrong, and I couldn't put my finger on what it was." Regan demanded a copy of the NSC chronology of the arms deals from Poindexter; when he got it, he took one look and decided, "This doesn't pass my feel test." He asked his counsel, Wallison, to go through it carefully. Later that day, when Poindexter asked him to return the document, Regan evaded the request by saying he was taking it home to read over the weekend.

At the State Department, Abe Sofaer was running a vest pocket investigation of his own. He asked one of his deputies to get him the price of a TOW missile, then compared it with the payment the Pentagon received for the missiles shipped to Iran. Just as he had suspected, the Pentagon's price was well below what a TOW could actually fetch on the market. Sofaer puzzled over the elements of the story and came up with an audacious guess: somebody had been skimming money for the contras.

"I was very concerned about the possibility that there was a surplus of funds," he explained later. "At a minimum, I was scared that Southern Air Transport had been given a lot of money for its arms shipments to the Middle East to subsidize it, in effect, for doing the work it was doing in Central America."

But none of the investigations was moving fast enough to keep up with Oliver North. Back in his office, he worked late Friday night, feeding more of Project Democracy's documents into his shredder. He fed sheet after sheet into the steel maw until, with a grinding of machinery, it jammed again. At that, he finally gave up and went home to bed.

The only one untouched by the turmoil at the top of the Reagan administration, it seemed, was Ronald Reagan himself. He apparently knew nothing about Poindexter's and North's frantic efforts to cover their tracks; he asked for no progress reports from Meese on his informal inquiry. On Friday evening, the Reagans went up to Capitol Hill for a gala dinner with the Republican members of the Senate — both those who had just won reelection and those who had lost. The president's speech was tinged with regret, for the losers outnumbered the new winners; he gave touching political eulogies for the seven Republicans who had lost their seats and the three who were retiring. But, as always, he began with a quip.

"Thank you very much," the president said as the Republicans applauded him. "You don't know how heartwarming that is to just come back from Iran and be greeted like that."

On Saturday morning, November 22, Meese finally stepped up the pace of his inquiry. At eight o'clock, Meese and his aide Cooper interviewed

George Shultz in the secretary's ornate offices atop the State Department. They talked first about the troublesome November 1985 shipment of HAWKs. Shultz insisted he was certain that McFarlane had told him at the time that the shipment was missiles — not oil drilling parts or anything else. His staff had dug up a note he made at the time, and it confirmed that McFarlane had mentioned missiles. Not only that, Shultz said; the president himself had acknowledged knowing about the HAWKs in a meeting with him only three days earlier.

"Another angle worries me," Shultz told Meese, echoing Sofaer's suspicion. The money in the Iranian deals "could get mixed up with help for freedom fighters in Nicaragua. One thing may be overlapping with another. . . . If this gets connected, then we're going to have a problem with our policy in Central America."

But Shultz's suggestion made no apparent impact on the Justice Department investigators. Cooper didn't even jot it down in the five pages of notes he took on the interview. Meese said later that he did not remember Shultz's mentioning a connection between the Iran deals and the contras at all. Their focus, it seemed, was as narrow as possible: the November 1985 HAWK shipment.

A few minutes after noon, Meese's aides Reynolds and Richardson arrived at the White House to take a look at the documents that North had prepared for them. They were met by Paul Thompson, the NSC counsel. Richardson asked Thompson if they could see the documents from Poindexter's files too, but Thompson told him there weren't any because Poindexter never kept copies — all his documents were in the NSC's central archives. (He didn't mention that the national security adviser had destroyed, only the day before, the sole copy of a presidential finding.)

So Thompson took the investigators up to North's office in the Old Executive Office Building. North wasn't there, but Bob Earl was. The investigators told Earl that they wanted to see only documents bearing on the Iran initiative; they didn't mention the contras. They allowed Earl to make the selection. He opened the credenza behind North's desk and pulled out six brown accordion folders and lined them up on the conference table. Then he called North to tell him that Meese's men were there.

Reynolds dreaded this kind of work. "There is nothing in a lawyer's life that is less sexy than document searching," he said later. But he sat down across the table from Richardson, and each of them took a folder, beginning with the most recent from 1986. They were looking for two things, Reynolds said: a better explanation of the 1985 HAWK deal, and some sense of whether the whole thing had been only an arms-for-hostage swap. There wasn't much on the HAWKs, but Reynolds noted with satisfaction that the NSC's memoranda frequently mentioned the hope for better relations with Iran. "They reflected, generally, arms for hostages," he said in an interview. "But they did indeed address the larger picture as well."

The files contained some curiosities too. Some were intelligence reports on the possibility that Libya's Qadhafi might attempt to "buy" one or more of the hostages to murder him (as he did, in fact, buy Peter Kilburn). And there were intercepted telephone conversations among the Iranians and other arms dealers, with surprisingly frequent references to Vice President Bush. "Their sense was that our president was comatose and the guy who really had power here was the veep," Reynolds said.

Then, in the back of a file of intelligence reports, Reynolds found an item that seemed out of place. It was a standard white manila folder with the letters W.H. in red. Inside was a long memorandum, apparently a version of one Reynolds had already run across, setting out the terms of the May 1986 sale of weapons and HAWK parts.

"I was rather bored," Reynolds confessed. "I thought it was the third draft of a document I had seen before. I started turning the pages, and they looked the same. I damn near didn't bother to turn the next page." When he did, though, something caught his eye.

"Holy Jesus!" Reynolds said involuntarily.

Richardson looked up, startled.

"Look at this," Reynolds whispered.

Richardson took the folder and read the passage Reynolds was pointing to. "Jee-sus," he said softly.

It was only one paragraph, but it left them both stunned. "The residual funds from this transaction are allocated as follows," it said. "$12 million will be used to purchase critically needed supplies for the Nicaraguan Democratic Resistance forces. . . ."

Reynolds read through the memo again. Maybe it was only a draft, he thought hopefully; maybe it was some kind of airy think piece, a proposal that was never tried. But much of the memo described arms sales that had already happened, and the rest of it was pretty specific.

Reynolds slipped the memo back into its place in the file and returned it to the conference table. He said later that he thought about removing the memo or clipping it, but decided that it would be better not to draw North's attention to it. Instead, he would tell Meese about it first.

As he returned the memo to the file, Reynolds shook his head in wonder. What a bonehead idea, he thought.

At about 1:45 P.M., Reynolds and Richardson broke for lunch; they had already arranged to meet with Meese and Cooper to compare notes. On their way out the door, they ran into North, just coming in. Reynolds said they hadn't seen many files from 1985, the period of the HAWK shipment. North promised to find them.

Reynolds and Richardson walked the long block down Pennsylvania

Avenue in front of the White House to the Old Ebbitt Grill, a restored Victorian restaurant full of brass rails and mirrors on Fifteenth Street. Meese and Cooper were already at the table. Meese, presiding, began by describing his interview with Shultz that morning. Then he asked Reynolds what he had found in North's office.

"We found a lot of documents," Reynolds said. "We found an awful lot that would confirm this overarching game plan of trying to persuade a faction [in Iran] that they could trust us.

"And this one you won't believe," Reynolds said. "There's a document that says they would take $12 million from the arms sales to Iran and give the money to the contras."

Meese recoiled, his eyes wide.

"Oh, shit," the attorney general said.

"The memo doesn't say this happened," Reynolds added cautiously. "It says it *will* happen. . . . It could be just pie in the sky."

"We have to find out," Meese said. "We have to find out whether that happened."

Reynolds said he had left the memorandum in North's office, but he planned to get a copy.

After lunch, Meese and Cooper rode back to the Justice Department in Meese's official car. That's a real problem, Meese said — not so much a legal problem, but a real political problem. On the other hand, he mused hopefully, maybe it never really happened. Maybe it was only a plan.

Back in the White House, North continued to choose documents for destruction while the investigators were at lunch. With his own shredder broken, he stacked his papers in a pile and took them across the drive to the shredder in the White House Situation Room. During his later testimony before Congress, North explained why he continued to destroy documents even after the Justice Department had begun reviewing them. "They were working on their projects; I was working on mine."

At about 2:00 P.M., North took a break and walked over to Poindexter's office. He found Casey and Poindexter sitting over a long lunch at the little corner table in Poindexter's White House office. The two senior officers of the junta, still guarding the secrets of Project Democracy, had talked for almost two hours. They knew the Justice Department was going through North's files that very day. But eight months later, when Poindexter was asked by congressional investigators what he remembered of his lunch with Casey in the midst of the crisis, the admiral known in the navy for his photographic memory remembered only what they ate: sandwiches.

Reynolds and Richardson returned to North's office at around 3:40 P.M. after their lunch at the Old Ebbitt Grill. North was there to meet them, but the files on the conference table appeared untouched. Reynolds told North to call Meese to set up an interview, which North did. Meese suggested that they meet on Sunday morning; North said he wanted to take his family to church first—couldn't they delay it until the afternoon? Meese relented and set the appointment for 2:00 P. M.

Only six minutes after North's call to Meese, CIA Director Casey called the attorney general. Ed, Casey said, I've got something I want to talk with you about. Meese was accommodating. "Why don't I drop by on my way home this evening?" he replied.

Meese arrived at Casey's house off Foxhall Road a little before six. By now, the attorney general knew that there had been at least a plan to divert money to the contras, and he knew that Casey had probably lied about the CIA's role in the November 1985 HAWK shipment. Clearly Casey was a central figure in the entire strange chain of events. Nevertheless, Meese met with him alone, took no notes, and later had difficulty remembering any details of their conversation.

According to Meese, Casey wanted to tell him about Roy Furmark, the New York businessman who had sought him out with a tale of missing money from the Iranian arms deals. There are some angry investors out there who think Ollie North owes them $15 million, Casey warned. "Furmark [believes] that they are going to go public as a means of trying to get the United States to replace the funds," Casey said, according to Meese. "They might even claim that . . . the money that should have gone to them was used for other United States and Israeli projects."

Casey said he had already asked Poindexter about Furmark's charge of a diversion of funds, and Poindexter had assured him that there was nothing to it. In effect, Casey was warning Meese that the investors might pop up and charge that a diversion of funds had occurred — but the charge, he assured the attorney general, would be false.

Meese testified later that he didn't tell Casey or anyone else that his assistants had already stumbled across evidence that such a diversion had been planned. "I felt it was not appropriate to discuss this with anyone, even as good a friend as Mr. Casey, until I found out what it was all about," he said. Besides, Meese said, he didn't even perceive a connection between North's memo and Casey's warning. "The two . . . did not seem to be directly related," he said.

But Meese apparently did tell Casey one other critical fact: that George Shultz had provided the key piece of evidence that showed that the CIA may have acted illegally when it shipped HAWK missiles to Iran in November 1985. By now it was clear to Casey that this part of the cover-up was slipping badly.

That evening, after Meese left, Casey sat in his study with a pad of paper and composed a letter. The CIA chief's network of private operations was in danger of disintegrating. Only that morning, he had been forced to hurl Ollie North's contra project before the Democrats of the House Intelligence Committee as something they could profitably investigate. But Casey's worst problem wasn't the Democrats or the press; it was inside the administration in the person of George Shultz. The two men had never been friends, and they almost always lined up on opposite sides of internal debates. Shultz had argued against the Iranian arms sales and lost; now he was trying to take his revenge by pursuing Casey on the matter of the HAWK shipment. It was clear from the way Shultz's lawyer, Sofaer, had bulldozed his way into the question of the HAWKs and from the way Shultz's deputy, Armacost, had objected to Casey's testimony in the Senate hearing.

There was only one way to win this war, Casey decided: decapitate the enemy. The solution was to persuade the president to fire George Shultz before the entire structure of Project Democracy was exposed.

"Dear Mr. President," he wrote. "On Friday I spent over five hours discussing and answering questions for the House and Senate Intelligence Committees on *our* effort to develop a relationship with important elements in Iran. . . . The public pouting of George Shultz and the failure of the State Department to support what we did inflated the uproar on this matter. If we all stand together and speak out I believe we can put this behind us quickly.

"Mr. President," Casey wrote, "you need a new pitcher."

Sunday was Oliver North's day to face the Justice Department inquisitors. That morning, he took his family to the charismatic service at the Episcopal church they attended in Great Falls, Virginia, just as he had said he would. But instead of taking his family to lunch, he called Bud McFarlane at home and asked him to meet him downtown.

North arrived at McFarlane's office at the Center for Strategic and International Studies on K Street at 12:30 P.M. McFarlane had been waiting for him since noon and had even put on a pot of coffee. North seemed unhappy, McFarlane recalled.

The president was in a solid position, North said. Everything seemed to be on track. But there was one problem that still worried him, North said: the diversion.

"Well, that was approved, wasn't it?" McFarlane asked.

"Yes, you know it was," North replied. "You know I wouldn't do anything without approval."

"Well, all you have to do is lay it out," McFarlane said. "Do the right thing."

The problem was a memo, North said. "It is a matter of record," he told McFarlane. "I must do — I must see what can be done about that memo."

That was how McFarlane recalled the conversation. If his account is correct, North had somehow learned that Meese's men had found the diversion memorandum. But North later denied that he told McFarlane any such thing.

After he saw McFarlane, North met for about an hour with Secord and his lawyer, Thomas C. Green, to prepare for his interview with the investigators. Then he drove down to the Justice Department and, at 2:13 P.M., walked into Meese's imposing, flag-bedecked office. North, Meese, and the attorney general's three aides sat in comfortable chairs around a coffee table.

"The worst thing that can happen is for someone to try to conceal something to protect themselves or the president," Meese told him. "We want nothing that anyone can call a cover-up."

North nodded and launched into a history of the Iranian arms deals that was a mixture of fact and fiction, drawn mostly from the NSC's fraudulent chronologies. On the November 1985 HAWK shipment, he claimed that Israel's defense minister, Yitzhak Rabin, had personally told him that the cargo was oil drilling parts, not missiles. He insisted that no one else in the government knew about the missiles, either. "Poindexter was totally innocent, knew nothing of it," North said. "I think I can pass a lie detector test" on that issue, he boasted.

As for the flow of money in the arms sales, North said he didn't know anything until January 1986, when Reagan signed his finding. After that, he said, the Iranians paid Israel for the weapons, and Israel paid the CIA. (Both of those statements were false.)

At that point, Meese produced the memorandum that Reynolds had found in North's office. He asked first about the main part of the memorandum, the section explaining the exchanges of weapons for hostages.

We tried to interest Reagan in a strategic relationship with Iran, North said, but "with the president it always came back to hostages. . . . [It's a] terrible mistake to say the president wanted the strategic relationship, because the president wanted the hostages."

"He talked about both," Meese corrected him.

Then the attorney general turned the page and read North the damning paragraph describing the proposed $12 million diversion. Meese and his aides all remembered that North looked visibly surprised.

"His demeanor changed," Reynolds recalled. "He faltered noticeably. . . . He became halting in his speech. It lasted for about a minute — and then he was back on track."

There was a silence. Finally, North said, "I don't know how much was moved to the Nicaraguans. The Israelis made the decision on money to the resistance."

So it did happen, Reynolds thought. Someone sighed.

The Justice Department men had been half hoping that North would tell them no diversion had occurred, that it was all a crazy idea that had gone nowhere. And if he had said that, they would have believed him. "The document was only telling us what was going to happen in the future," Reynolds explained. "From our standpoint, he was the guy that was more credible. He was the guy who told us what had actually happened."

But North, it appears, had a cover story ready for everything but the diversion. He did improvise a quick lie about the diversion's being an Israeli operation, apparently in the hope that Meese would hesitate to expose the secrets of an ally. But he had already told just enough of the truth to ensure that the inquest would have to continue.

Meese pressed for more details of the diversion. Was there any U.S. involvement?

"None," North replied.

How did it happen? Meese asked.

"The Israelis, in January 1986, approached us with two ways to help," North said. "[One was to] arrange to take residuals from these transactions and [transfer them] to the Nicaraguan resistance."

Was this discussed with the president? Meese asked.

"Not with me," North replied. "Admiral Poindexter was the point of contact with the president." He paused for a moment. "Did you find a cover memo?" he asked. A cover memo would have revealed the routing of the document: who was intended to see it, who had actually received it.

"No," Brad Reynolds admitted. "There was no cover memo."

"Why do you ask?" Meese said quickly. "Should we have found a cover memo?"

"No," said North. "I was just wondering."

If the president approved this, you'd have his approval in your files, right? Meese asked.

"Yes," North replied. "I don't think it was."

Are there other files that it could be in, Meese asked, "to verify that it didn't go forward" to the president? (It was a curious formulation, one that North could almost have taken as a broad hint that the attorney general didn't want to find any memos with Reagan's signature lurking in the files.)

"I'll check on that," North volunteered.

The investigators went back over the details of the diversion. North told them, again, that it was "an Israeli idea — they wanted to be helpful." He said that Adolfo Calero, the contra leader, had opened three Swiss bank accounts, and the only role the United States played was when North passed on the contra account numbers to Israel. It was an Israeli operation, not an American operation. (All these denials were untrue.)

"No other U.S. officials were involved," he insisted. "McFarlane and Poindexter were knowledgeable. . . . That's all."

Besides, he said, "hostages' lives are involved. . . . If this gets out, you could have dead bodies over there."

Anything else like this Nicaraguan angle? Meese asked.

"Nothing," North said. "If this doesn't come out, the only other issue is the November HAWKs deal."

He went back to his plea on behalf of the Israelis. Israel's use of the "residuals" to aid the contras was a foreign intelligence operation that we have no right to expose, he said; I hope it doesn't have to be made public. At the very least, we'd better talk with the Israelis before we do anything.

John Richardson jotted in his notes: "Check on getting cooperation of Israelis before anything public."

North's assertion that the money had been handled entirely by the Israelis was contradicted by the very memo Meese had in his hand. It said the Israelis would put $15 million into "a private U.S. corporation account in Switzerland." But Meese and his men ignored that for the time being; as Reynolds said, they considered North "more credible" than the document.

North returned to the White House to report on the damage. He went down to the Situation Room and called Poindexter and McFarlane. Then he called Amiram Nir, his Israeli counterpart, with a last-ditch proposal to rescue Project Democracy.

We need you to take responsibility for this to save our operation, North said. If you say sending money to the contras was your idea, we may be able to keep the whole thing secret.

There was an astonished silence on the other end of the telephone. "I cannot back this story," Nir said.

North stayed in his office Sunday night until at least 4:30 A.M., shredding more documents. When Fawn Hall arrived at work Monday morning, he was already at his desk.

"How was your weekend?" she asked brightly.

"Lousy," North groaned. "I was in here with the Justice Department all weekend."

When Bob Earl came in, North quietly handed him a copy of the diversion memo.

"They showed me this," North said. He gave Earl a blow-by-blow recap of his interview with Meese and said that he ended the session with the investigators by pointing out that nobody had read him his rights and asking, "Does this count?"

But the bravado was growing a little hollow. North knew he had reached the end of the adventure. With luck, other parts of Project Democracy could live on — the continuing Iranian arms deal, Secord's dummy companies, the airplanes, the ship *Erria*, Spitz Channell's fundraising, the projects aimed at Qadhafi and the terrorists — but only if North sacrificed himself to save them.

He typed out a mock-cheerful PROFS note to Poindexter. "There is that old line about you can't fire me, I quit," he wrote. "I am prepared to depart at the time you and the president decide. . . . We nearly succeeded. Semper Fidelis."

Later that day, Rob Owen and a friend stopped by to say hello. The unaccustomed silence in the office seemed eerie. The phones weren't ringing. The usual line of schemers and supplicants waiting for a moment with North was gone. Something was clearly wrong.

"Why don't you go in and see Ollie?" Fawn suggested.

North was sitting at his desk, looking remarkably serene.

"I'm going to be gone inside of two weeks, guys," North said calmly. "I'm going to be the fall guy."

The only thing that worried him, he said, was the future of his hostage negotiations. His Iranian contact was still calling every morning between three and five; North's departure could mean an end to that link.

Nicaragua was a different matter, North said, because of Abrams. "Things are in good hands," he said. "Elliott will still be there."

Monday, November 24, was the critical day for Meese — both to find the truth and to protect his president. "We were sitting on a nuclear bomb," Brad Reynolds said.

Meese and his aides were terrified that the astounding story of the diversion would leak and never intended even to try to hush it up, Reynolds said later. "It wasn't even a close call. . . . The astounding thing was that it hadn't come out already."

For one thing, he said, the Justice Department men assumed that the diversion memo they had found was only one of several. Sooner or later, another one might surface. And from Reagan's point of view, such a leak would be a disaster. "If it came out from any other source . . . the credibility of the administration would have been totally shot," Reynolds pointed out. "I don't know if the president would have survived."

But Meese himself didn't seem sure yet. He testified later that he, too, was immediately convinced that the news of the diversion had to be made public. But on Monday, the attorney general moved rather slowly toward that conclusion. First he had to find out who was entangled in the diversion — and, in a gingerly way, make sure that Ronald Reagan was not among them.

So Meese embarked on a series of quick interviews with the president and his top lieutenants. In his earlier inquiries, the attorney general had taken notes and brought aides to serve as witnesses. This time he did neither. These "interviews" were entirely one-on-one: Ed Meese, the president's friend, tying down the loose ends of the administration.

He spoke briefly on the telephone Monday morning with Regan, Bush, and Weinberger. Then he met with McFarlane, who by then had conferred with both Poindexter and North. McFarlane said yes, North had told him about the diversion — back in May, on the tarmac in Tel Aviv — and had assured him that it was approved by his superiors. Meese did not ask if McFarlane knew who had given the approval.

At 11:00 A.M., Meese went over to the White House, walked into Regan's office, and told the chief of staff that profits from the Iranian arms deals had been diverted to the contras. Regan remembered feeling "horror, horror, sheer horror"; he assumed that Meese meant money had been siphoned directly from the U.S. Treasury. They went into the Oval Office together to tell Reagan. But oddly, according to the chief of staff, Meese — who by now had known about a possible diversion for two days — decided not to tell the president the news and referred only to "serious problems."

"I have got a few last-minute things to button up before I can give you the details," Meese said.

Reagan, as usual, did not react strongly or ask any probing questions. The president was readying his three-by-five cue cards for an eleven-thirty meeting with the chief of South Africa's Zulu nation, Mangosuthu Gatsha Buthulezi.

A few minutes later, as Buthulezi and Reagan sat in the Oval Office for a photo session, reporters bombarded the president with questions: Was he ready to admit that the Iranian arms sales were a mistake?

"I'm not going to lie about that," Reagan said, as the Zulu chief looked on quizzically. "I didn't make a mistake."

What about others in your cabinet? the reporters asked.

"I'm not going to fire anybody," the president declared.

During the rest of that day, Meese met briefly — and alone — with Bush and Poindexter to ask them if they knew anything about the diversion. According to Meese, Bush said he knew nothing about diverted money. Poindexter, in an interview that took just ten minutes, admitted that he had "an inkling" of the diversion but said he didn't know the details. "Ollie has given me enough hints about this so that I generally knew, but I did nothing to follow up or stop it," Poindexter said.

"Does anyone else in the White House know?" Meese asked.

"No," Poindexter said.

Meese never asked Poindexter specifically whether Reagan had approved the diversion. Nor, curiously, did Meese ask the president himself — even though his aides said it was the question uppermost in his mind.

As the time bomb of the diversion ticked away unseen, the guerrilla war between George Shultz and the rest of the administration continued. On Monday afternoon, Shultz's deputy, John C. Whitehead, delivered an extraordinary public attack on the White House and the NSC, bluntly rejecting the president's assertion that Iran had reduced its support for terrorism and calling for an investigation of the NSC.

"We in the State Department find it difficult to cope with NSC staff operational activities . . . particularly when we don't know about them," Whitehead told the House Foreign Affairs Committee.

In the White House, Don Regan turned purple when he learned of Whitehead's charges. It could only have happened with Shultz's blessing, he knew. According to one account, the chief of staff stormed into the Oval Office, slammed a news-ticker report of Whitehead's testimony onto the president's desk, and said, "This is what your secretary of state is up to." Nancy Reagan was annoyed as well, friends said. Her anger at Shultz had been exaggerated earlier, but this time it seemed real. Shultz's other enemies hit the telephones with glee, decrying his public criticism of the president and suggesting that it was time for Reagan to show him the door.

At two o'clock that afternoon, the antagonists in the internal battle gathered uncomfortably around the table in the Situation Room. Formally, the NSPG meeting was called to decide whether the Iranian negotiations should continue. The somewhat stilted discussion concealed a web of rivalries and suspicions. Regan asked whether the issue of the November 1985 HAWK shipment had been resolved; had the president approved it? Poindexter pinned the problem firmly on the absent McFarlane. "Bud handled it by himself," he said. "There's no documentation." It was a statement he could make with confidence, since he had ripped up the sole copy of the arms-for-hostage finding that authorized the shipment only three days earlier. Reagan, who had signed the finding, remained silent.

Poindexter and Casey made a strong pitch to keep the secret talks going, emphasizing the good faith of their new channel to Tehran, Rafsanjani's nephew. Shultz, glowering, went through his familiar arguments against continuing the operation unless it was completely restructured. But, once again, Reagan ignored Shultz's complaints. The negotiations, he said, would go on.

Meese, Regan, and Poindexter all knew that the diversion had been discovered; so, perhaps, did Casey. But none of them mentioned it in front of the others.

At four-thirty on Monday afternoon, shortly after the NSPG meeting broke up, Meese was finally ready to tell Reagan what he had learned. Through three days of internal investigations, he had felt no need to say anything to the president, and Reagan hadn't asked. But now Meese felt he "had his arms around the problem"; his discreet inquiries had established that the diversion seemed to involve only North and Poindexter. The crisis still appeared to be containable.

Meese collected Don Regan and went into the Oval Office. As the president listened, the attorney general briskly outlined his discoveries of the previous few days. Ollie North had been using money from the

Iranian arms sales to aid the contras, he said. It's in a memo. Nobody else knew about it except Poindexter, and he knew only a little.

Reagan reacted with a look of what Regan later described as "deep distress." It was clear, the chief of staff said, that the president was taken completely by surprise. "This guy, I know, was an actor, and he was nominated at one time for an Academy Award. But I'd give him an Academy Award if he knew anything about this," Regan said. "He couldn't have known it."

Regan suggested holding a press conference the next morning to make sure the White House could announce the problem before it leaked. "We've got to get this out right away," he said. "There's no sense in going with it tonight. Let's go with it tomorrow. But we're going to have to get it out."

But Reagan was hesitant; he said he wanted to wait overnight and make a decision in the morning.

"I think John Poindexter's got to go," Regan persisted. "I mean, we just can't have a guy like that around here, if he didn't follow up on this."

The president said nothing.

Regan was secretly pleased by one aspect of the horrendous turn of events, his aides said later: this disaster wasn't his fault. He had been on the run for a month, with the press and the president's friends turning increasingly against him. The discovery of the diversion was a calamity, but it was someone else's calamity. Now he could redeem himself by helping the president survive. It was, one aide said, the "silver lining."

Poindexter, on the other hand, still did not understand the political dimensions of the disaster he had helped to create. That afternoon, he belatedly replied to North's "Semper Fidelis" resignation message. As far as Poindexter could tell, Meese was still on their side. This might not be such a terrible flap in the end; they might not have to resign after all.

"I have talked to Ed twice today on this and he is still trying to figure out what to do," Poindexter wrote to North. "I have told him I am prepared to resign. I told him I would take the cue from him. He is one of the few besides the president that I can trust. If we don't leave, what would you think about going out to CIA and being a special assistant to Bill? This would put you in the operational world officially. Don't say anything to Bill yet. I just want to get your reaction."

Poindexter also called John Whitehead at the State Department. You guys were right, he said tersely; the State Department ought to be included on the Iran policy. In fact, you can run it, if that's what you want. As for me, Poindexter said wearily, "I want to get out of it."

At the CIA, Casey was still plugging the holes in Project Democracy's dike. His old friend Roy Furmark had come by again to press for repayment of the $10 million Khashoggi wanted. Furmark warned again that Ghorbanifar had talked of a diversion of money to the contras through an account called Lake Resources, and said the investors might blow the whole operation if they didn't get satisfaction soon.

Casey picked up the telephone and called North. "There's a guy here who says you owe him $10 million on the Iran thing," he said.

He listened for a minute, hung up the phone, turned to Furmark, and said, "North says the Israelis or the Iranians owe you the money."

After Furmark left, Casey called Chuck Cooper at the Justice Department. The young lawyer was startled; the director of central intelligence had never called him before. "In all of this research you're doing, have you come across the name of a Lakeside Resources?" Casey asked, mangling the name slightly.

"That has some vague familiarity, but I can't place it," Cooper said. "Why do you want to know that?"

The response was just a Casey mumble.

At the end of the day, Casey called Regan and asked him to stop by Langley on his way home. It was a good forty-five minutes out of the way, but even the White House chief of staff was a little in awe of a summons to the CIA. Regan drove out the parkway along the Potomac and went up to the seventh floor of Casey's headquarters.

"Where are we?" Casey demanded. "What's the president's thinking? Why can't we get a story out?"

Regan blurted out the secret: North had been skimming money from the arms sales to send to the contras. Casey's face betrayed no emotion. "What are you going to do about it?" he asked.

"We're going to go public," Regan answered. "We've got to get this story out. We can't sit on this one."

Casey tried to slow him down. "Do you realize the consequences of what you're doing?" he asked. "You're going to blow the whole Iranian thing, and possibly blow the lives of the hostages." Going public was just a bad idea, Casey argued. The Iranians would be upset, he warned, and Congress might stop aid to the contras again.

Regan bristled. "How the hell can we sit on this stuff any longer?" he said. "I mean, this thing is an absolute disgrace. . . . We have this possible criminal act."

Casey could see that Regan was set on his course. "I guess you've got to do it," he said. "But I hope you realize that, you know, this is going to cause quite a few upsets."

"I know it," Regan said. "But it's the only thing we can do."

Regan was out the door and on his way home before he realized that Casey never said why he had so urgently required him out at the CIA.

When he arrived home, in Mount Vernon, Regan returned a call from

Nancy Reagan. The president had been particularly quiet that afternoon when he learned about the diversion, but his wife had plenty to say.

"There will have to be a house cleaning of people who let Ronnie down," she said icily, "starting at the top."

Regan told her he was working "fast and furiously to try to get this information out, to have an investigation and let the facts come out." But he had the unmistakable feeling that Nancy wanted to see heads roll, his own among them. "When people talked about a thorough house cleaning starting at the top," he noted later, "one gets the impression that one may be considered."

In his study, surrounded by framed photographs of himself with Ronald Reagan, the chief of staff drew up a plan of action that would make the most of his silver lining. The only way to survive was to get ahead of this thing and pin the responsibility on someone other than the president — or himself.

"Tough as it seems, blame must be put at NSC's door — rogue operation, going on without president's knowledge or sanction," he wrote. "When suspicions arose, [Reagan] took charge, ordered investigation, had meeting of top advisers get at facts and find out who knew what." (In fact, the president had not initiated the inquest, but only assented to his aides' demands.)

"Try to make the best of a sensational story," Regan continued. "Anticipate charge of 'out of control,' 'president doesn't know what's going on,' 'who's in charge'. . . . Try to get answers to such charges in advance. President should not answer in press room, but others in administration are going to be asked."

To start with, Regan wrote, the president should order North's reassignment to the marines and accept Poindexter's resignation "because of failure to inform president of possible misfeasance by members of his staff."

Then the president should issue a statement ordering Meese to mount a full-scale inquest and "expressing his chagrin and shock," two sentiments Reagan actually had yet to voice.

As for Poindexter's replacement as national security adviser, Regan warned that George Shultz would undoubtedly try to install one of his own men. "It will then be an outpost of State Department." In fact, he wrote, it was time to "muzzle State Department," along with the other agencies, "or else there will be all kinds of stories and malicious gossip that can only hurt Admiral Poindexter."

It was his last attempt at spin control. But Regan was still behind the curve.

As the time to go public approached on Tuesday morning, November 25, Meese had two private meetings — one with Casey, one with Poindexter. It remains unclear why Meese met with either man: there is no independent record of their hurried talks in the hours just before the diversion was made public, only Meese's own testimony. At the time, the attorney general knew that he was staring a political disaster in the face; presumably, he hoped to protect the president from bearing full blame for the diversion. But, according to Meese's account, he sought no new information from either Casey or Poindexter.

The first talk was with Casey. At 6:30 A.M., the CIA director called Meese to ask for a meeting as soon as possible. Meese drove to Casey's house fifteen minutes later and left his assistant John Richardson sitting in the car. Again, there would be no notes, no witnesses, to the attorney general's interview.

By Meese's account, Casey — who until then had worked diligently to keep the diversion hidden — now put himself on record as favoring full disclosure. "We've got to get this out as soon as possible," Meese quoted the CIA chief as saying.

Casey also told Meese that he had heard about the diversion for the first time from Don Regan the evening before — although he had, in fact, heard reports of it for months from North, his own aides, and, most recently, Roy Furmark.

While Meese was still at Casey's house, Don Regan called. The chief of staff said he wanted Poindexter's resignation in hand at 8:00 A.M. Meese put down the telephone, called Poindexter, and asked him to come to the Justice Department first. Again without notes or witnesses, Meese talked with the national security adviser. According to Meese, he met with the admiral to inform him that he should be prepared to resign; they discussed only that, he said.

At a few minutes after eight, Poindexter walked into his office and ordered breakfast from the White House mess. He found the copy of the diversion memo that North had sent him, the memo that had cut short his career. He read it silently, flipped it into the Out basket, and turned to the breakfast tray on the end of his conference table. His assistant Paul Thompson walked in, and Poindexter announced that he was returning to the navy. He was being considered for one of the navy's most prestigious jobs, commanding the U.S. Mediterranean fleet from Naples; he might still have a shot at it if the Iran controversy blew over.

At that point, Regan stormed in and confronted the admiral.

"What the hell happened here?" he demanded.

Poindexter dabbed carefully at his mouth with a napkin, put it down, and adjusted his rimless glasses. He gave Regan his standard, expressionless look.

"Well," Poindexter said, "I guess I should have looked into it more, but I didn't. I knew that Ollie was up to something, but I didn't know what. I just didn't look into it."

"Why not?" Regan sputtered. "What the hell — you're a vice admiral. What's going on?"

"Well," Poindexter said, "that damn Tip O'Neill — the way he's jerking the contras around, I was just so disgusted, I didn't want to know what [North] was doing."

"Well, John, I think when you go in to see the president at nine-thirty, you better make sure you have your resignation with you," Regan said.

"I've been thinking of that," Poindexter said calmly. "I will."

Poindexter made his last telephone calls to Caspar Weinberger and Oliver North. Then, at nine-thirty, he walked into the Oval Office and found the president, Bush, Regan, and Meese all waiting. There was no national security briefing. With hardly a preamble, Poindexter told Reagan that he was "sorry" and said he was submitting his resignation.

Reagan nodded sympathetically. "I understand," Poindexter and Regan remembered him saying. "This is a shame. . . . But it's in the tradition of the navy . . . of the captain accepting responsibility."

Bush, Regan, and Meese all offered sympathy and regrets. No one asked how the diversion had come about or why Poindexter had allowed it to happen. Reagan exhibited no curiosity and expressed no disapproval. There was an awkward silence, and Admiral Poindexter walked out of the Oval Office.

At ten-fifteen, the National Security Council convened in the Situation Room. Just before the meeting, Reagan told George Shultz that he had won the battle for bureaucratic turf: the policy on Iran was now his, and the president wanted him to remain as secretary of state until the end of the administration. The guerrilla war was over, at least for the moment.

At the NSC meeting, Casey remained silent as Project Democracy collapsed before his eyes. Reagan announced that Poindexter had resigned and that a special commission would be named to study the operations of the NSC staff, just as Regan had proposed. Further negotiations with Iran would be taken from the NSC and CIA and put in Shultz's hands instead.

North was almost forgotten in the upheaval. Regan told Weinberger that the colonel should probably go back to the Marine Corps, and the defense secretary agreed. But no one formally told North.

At eleven, after the NSC was done, the leaders of Congress filed into the Cabinet Room. Grimly, Meese told them what he had learned about the diversion and said North had apparently run the operation on his own. Reagan added that Poindexter had not participated but had known about it, and so he had resigned — in the best tradition of the navy.

The House Democratic leader, Jim Wright of Texas, posed a series of questions. Was this done with the knowledge or approval of anyone else?

No, Meese said. Poindexter knew the money was going to the contras, but didn't know the details and didn't look into it.

Did the CIA know? Wright asked.

"No, I didn't," Casey spoke up. But he volunteered that Bud Mc-Farlane had known.

Wright said it strained his credulity that the Israelis thought up the diversion on their own and carried it out without the participation of anyone in the administration. "None of us gets pleasure from the embarrassment" of the White House, he added. But the intelligence committees should have been informed of the operations on Iran and the contras. "I hope we all could be trusted," he said, "rather than have this done by lieutenant colonels."

Reagan bristled at that. Congress had just agreed to aid the contras, he pointed out. The diversion was irregular, yes, and unauthorized. But, the president insisted, "it wasn't contrary to policy."

Across the drive, in the Old Executive Office Building, North was sitting pensively at his desk, surrounded by his computer screens, his secure telephones, and his secret files. He opened his notebook and wrote down a list — his priorities as the world collapsed around him:

1. My country.
2. Presidency.
3. Family.
4. Hostages.
5. Self.

Then he crossed out the last item. In its place, he wrote: "Others who helped."

He walked out to tell Fawn Hall the bad news, which he had apparently learned from someone in the NSC meeting.

"The president has fired me," he said in a hollow voice.

"Oh, Ollie," she said, disbelieving. "Come on."

"No," he said. "I'm serious."

Hall burst into tears.

North went back into his office and turned on the television. The networks had gone live to the White House briefing room, jammed with reporters. Word had gone out shortly after eleven that the president was making an announcement about the Iranian arms deals, but the specifics still hadn't leaked.

Reagan walked in at five minutes after twelve. His face was grim; the usual bounce was missing from his step.

"Last Friday, after becoming concerned whether my national security apparatus had provided me with a complete factual record with respect to the implementation of my policy toward Iran, I directed the attorney general to undertake a review of this matter," he read from a sheet of paper. "And yesterday, Secretary Meese provided me with a report on his preliminary findings. And this report led me to conclude that I was not fully informed on the nature of one of the activities undertaken in connection with this initiative."

"Although not directly involved, Vice Admiral John Poindexter has asked to be relieved of his assignment as assistant to the president for national security affairs and to return to another assignment in the navy. Lieutenant Colonel Oliver North has been relieved of his duties on the National Security Council staff.

"I am deeply troubled that the implementation of a policy aimed at resolving a truly tragic situation in the Middle East has resulted in such controversy," he said. "As I've stated previously, I believe our policy goals toward Iran were well founded. However, the information brought to my attention yesterday convinced me that, in one aspect, implementation of that policy was seriously flawed.

"And now, I'm going to ask Attorney General Meese to brief you."

There was the usual cacaphony of questions, but Reagan stepped quickly out the door to leave Meese before the cameras.

"Let me say that all of the information is not in," Meese began. "We are still conducting our inquiry, but he did want me to make available immediately what we know at the present time.

"What is involved is that in the course of the arms transfer, which involved the United States providing the arms to Israel and Israel, in turn, transferring the arms — in effect, selling the arms — to representatives of Iran, certain monies which were received in the transaction between representatives of Israel and representatives of Iran were taken and made available to the forces in Central America who are opposing the Sandinista government there."

The contras. There was a general gasp in the room.

Then came the questions — slowly, at first, since the reporters hardly knew where to start, but soon at machine-gun tempo.

How much money? "Our estimate is that it is somewhere between ten and thirty million dollars," Meese said.

Did Reagan know? "The president knew nothing about it until I reported it to him."

Who did know? "The only person in the United States government that knew precisely about this, the only person, was Lieutenant Colonel North. Admiral Poindexter knew that something of this nature was occurring, but he did not look into it further. . . . CIA director Casey, Secretary of State Shultz, Secretary of Defense Weinberger, myself, the other members of the NSC — none of us knew."

The CIA? "To the best of our knowledge, no one in the CIA knew anything about it."

Did North commit a crime? "We are presently looking into the legal aspects of it as to whether there's any criminality involved."

Who diverted the money? "No transfers of money went through anyone," Meese said. "Bank accounts were established, as best we know, by representatives of the forces in Central America. And this information was provided to representatives of the Israeli government — or representatives of Israel, I should say — and then these funds were put into the accounts. So as far as we know at this stage, no American person actually handled any of the funds that went to the forces in Central America."

Meese was sticking to North's account — originally devised as a cover-up — that the diversion had been done by Israelis, despite the memo's reference to a private U.S. corporation.

Should George Shultz resign? "I think every member of the administration owes it to the president to stand shoulder-to-shoulder with him and support the policy decisions that he has made," Meese said. "Anyone who is a member of the president's staff or the president's cabinet has an obligation either to support the policy decisions of the president or get out." That was essentially a "yes."

Is Don Regan leaving? "No."

Was Poindexter fired? "Admiral Poindexter resigned, or actually requested reassignment to the navy, of his own accord."

What about North? "Lieutenant Colonel North has requested to return to the Marine Corps and that has been accomplished."

Did the president approve Israel's potentially illegal shipments to Iran in 1985? "There was at least one transaction that we know about in which Israel shipped weapons without any authorization from the United States. There was another transaction [where] there was probably knowledge on the part of people in the United States. . . . Both of those transactions took place between Israel and Iran [and] did not involve, at that time, the United States." Again, it was North's distorted version, even though Meese knew there was evidence to the contrary.

Does the president need to try a more hands-on approach to managing the government? "It's not a matter of having a hands-on presidency. It's making sure that those people who are working for him are following the procedures."

The reaction in Washington and the nation was pure shock. Senators and congressmen redoubled their calls for an investigation. Jim Wright said it looked to him as though Oliver North was being made into "a fall guy." "How could the president not know?" he asked. Senator Dave Durenberger of Minnesota, the Republican chairman of the Senate Intelligence Committee, predicted the end of the contras, the cause that had launched the entire operation. "It's going to be a cold day in Washington before any more money goes to Nicaragua," Durenberger said. "Ollie may have killed off his Nicaraguan program."

Across the street, Fawn Hall and Oliver North watched the news conference on television. When the briefing ended, North drove out to the Virginia suburbs to meet with Secord and his lawyer, Tom Green, at the Tyson's Corner Sheraton, near Secord's office. North had been startled and worried by one thing Meese had said: that the Justice Department was "looking into . . . whether there's any criminality involved." North was willing to take the fall, but he hadn't bargained on going to jail. "After the press conference, my perspective changed," he said later. "It became more and more of protecting myself."

As he discussed legal strategy with Secord and Green, the telephone in the hotel room rang. It was the White House operator; the president was trying to reach a Colonel North.

North took the phone and instinctively stood at attention.

"Ollie," the president said, "you're a national hero." Then, according to North, he added the best consolation he knew: "This is going to make a great movie one day."

North returned to his office to say good-bye to Earl and Coy, his two assistants. He climbed the narrow spiral staircase to their upper-level offices and chatted with Earl, his fellow marine. North recounted the telephone call from Reagan, and Earl distinctly remembered North's quoting the president as saying a curious thing: "It is important that I not know." (North testified that he recalled Reagan's saying only: "I just didn't know.")

Then Coy walked up, and the conversation trailed off. North seemed stunned, Coy remembered.

"I'm sorry it has to end this way," North said. "I didn't mean for it to end this way." He slammed his hand against the banister. "I didn't think it would end this way," he said.

Back in the White House, Paul Thompson found Poindexter calmly cleaning out his desk, picking up the last loose ends. He seemed almost relieved, Thompson thought.

How do you feel? the aide asked.

Poindexter sighed. "I'm very tired" was all he said.

The shock waves from Meese's announcement rippled across Washington and out to Central America and the Middle East.

At the Justice Department, Israel's prime minister, Shimon Peres, was on the telephone for Meese. The two men had dealt directly with each other before: they had exchanged letters in 1985 about an Iraqi pipeline deal that Meese's friend E. Robert Wallach was trying to put together. Now Peres had a message for Meese. We didn't pay anything into a contra account, he said. Some people in your administration have asked us to take responsibility for this operation, but I'm afraid we can't do it.

The contras were upset about Meese's diversion story too. They had been accused of corruption before, but those charges were nothing compared to this business of a missing $30 million in cash. The rebel leaders called an immediate press conference in Miami. "We don't even have a Swiss bank account," Adolfo Calero claimed.

And McFarlane called North from London, where he was giving a speech, to ask what had happened.

"I missed one," North replied, according to McFarlane's later testimony.

On Capitol Hill, Elliott Abrams and the CIA's Alan Fiers had the misfortune to be testifying to the Senate Intelligence Committee on the contra program that afternoon. The press had already disclosed Saudi Arabia's role in funding the contras, but Abrams's $10 million solicitation from Brunei was still a secret.

"Did either one of you ever discuss the problems of fund-raising by the contras with members of the NSC staff?" asked Senator Bill Bradley of New Jersey.

"No," said Abrams. "I can't remember."

"You never said, you know, 'Maybe we could get the money this way'?" Bradley asked.

"No," said Abrams. "We're not, you know, we're not in the fund-raising business."

Abrams's boss, George Shultz, was back at the State Department giving his aides the one piece of good news about the debacle: he had won the guerrilla war. Shultz had won on two counts, it seemed: the policy on Iran now belonged to the State Department, and he was going to keep his job despite the best efforts of Casey and his other enemies.

But Shultz sternly warned his aides: "No gloating." The war had not been easily won. Had it not been for three strokes of luck, Shultz might well have lost, and Casey or Weinberger might have become secretary of state. The first break was the discovery of his own notes that proved McFarlane knew that the November 1985 shipment contained HAWK missile parts; without those notes, Meese might never have opened an inquiry into the arms sales. The second was William Bradford Reynolds's fortuitous discovery of the "diversion memo" in North's files; had Reynolds not read that one page on that one document — as he nearly did not — the diversion might have gone undiscovered (if not forever, at least long enough for Casey and his allies to oust Shultz). Finally there was North's surprised reaction when Meese confronted him with the diversion memo. Had North been ready with a plausible cover story, the Justice Department men might have believed it; as it happened, he confessed that the diversion had actually occurred.

Shultz also knew he had one more basic problem. The Iranian initiative had been thoroughly discredited — except in the eyes of one man: Ronald Reagan. The president still didn't see anything wrong with selling weapons to Khomeini to help win the release of the hostages. Shultz had won a major bureaucratic battle, but he had not won the war after all.

Late Tuesday afternoon, the NSC's security officers arrived to seal up North's office. As they came in the door, Fawn Hall suddenly remembered, to her horror, that she had failed to finish the job of replacing North's altered contra documents in her files. Both the incriminating originals and the new versions were still sitting on the desk next to her word processor.

As the security officers did their work in North's office, Hall coolly scooped up a stack of documents and took them upstairs. Standing outside Earl's office, she folded two bundles and stuffed them into her boots. The security officers were finishing up downstairs.

Hall dashed into Earl's office, a sheaf of PROFS notes in her hand. The marine grabbed the notes, folded them, and began putting them in the inside pocket of his jacket, but Hall stopped him. "No," she said. "You shouldn't have to do this."

She asked him to watch the door. As he turned around, she stuffed the notes into the back of her blouse. Then the former model did a hasty pirouette. "Can you see anything?" she asked. He couldn't.

They walked downstairs. North and Tom Green had just walked in.

"Can you see anything in my back?" she whispered to North nervously.

"No," he said.

The security officers inspected their briefcases as they left the office, but that was all. Halfway down the marble corridor, Hall reached for the back of her blouse.

"No," North muttered. "Wait until we get outside." On the sidewalk on Seventeenth Street, she reached for the papers again, but Tom Green, the lawyer, said, "Wait until we get inside the car."

Once she was in Green's car, Hall extracted the documents from her blouse and boots. Then her face fell. "I left the originals in the office," she confessed. In her haste, she had smuggled out the wrong documents. The ones she left behind would show clearly that North had tried to alter the records.

Tom Green asked what she would say if the investigators asked her about shredding.

Hall thought for a moment. "We shred every day," she said.

"Good," said Green.

On Wednesday morning, November 26, Meese finally turned his investigation over to the Justice Department's Criminal Division, which normally handles criminal cases. But he told his aides that he wanted Cooper, his own counsel, to be a part of the prosecution team, and the new investigators were instructed to report anything "hot" to the attorney general. And that afternoon, Meese's deputy, Arnold Burns, called the White House to ask if the documents in North's office could be secured; it was four days after the diversion memorandum had been discovered. (None of Meese's investigators knew that Wallison, the White House counsel, had already ordered that move.)

That same day, Ronald Reagan appointed a three-member commission to "conduct a comprehensive study of the future role and procedures of the National Security Council staff," the next step in Regan's damage-control plan. But the president turned down a plea from several aides for a speech that would admit some measure of error in the Iranian affair. The aides had drafted a speech that would have confessed that Reagan's heart had won over his head. Regan told them the president wouldn't listen to the idea. "He isn't ready for that," the chief of staff said.

Instead, Reagan took refuge in the familiar rituals of the holiday weekend. He accepted a live Thanksgiving turkey from the National Turkey Federation in the Rose Garden, as he did every year. And in the late morning he took off for California aboard *Air Force One*, fleeing a ruined White House for the safety of a long weekend at the ranch. First, however, Reagan returned a telephone call from *Time* magazine's veteran Washington correspondent, Hugh Sidey. Sidey was as close to a friend as Reagan had in the press; his daughter had even worked in the White House.

"I have to say that there is a bitter bile in my throat these days," the president said. "I've never seen the sharks circling like they are now with blood in the water." He did not blame North or anyone else. "I do not feel betrayed. Lieutenant Colonel North was involved in all our operations: the *Achille Lauro*, Libya. He has a fine record. He is a national hero. My only criticism is that I wasn't told everything."

The only villain in the affair, as far as Reagan could see, was the press — for exposing the operations. "This whole thing boils down to a great irresponsibility on the part of the press," he said. "We got three people back. We were expecting two others. The press has to take the responsibility for what they've done.

"It wasn't us funneling money to [the contras]," he continued. "This was another country. . . . I think we took the only action we could have in Iran. I am not going to disavow it. I do not think it was a mistake. No, it has not turned out the way we hoped. But I don't see anything I would have done differently."

Aboard *Air Force One* that afternoon, Reagan picked up the telephone again. He asked the operator to get him Peggy Say, the sister of hostage Terry Anderson.

Say had been feeling depressed. She worried that the exposure of the negotiations might have derailed any chance of getting her brother back. Once Reagan's severest critic among the hostage families, she made a point of praising the president for trying to negotiate the captives' freedom in a letter published in *USA Today*.

On Wednesday, with Thanksgiving marking the start of a second holiday season with her brother in captivity, Say didn't feel like talking with anyone. She told her daughter to take the phone off the hook, but her daughter forgot about the request until the telephone rang. She picked up the phone and screamed. "It's President Reagan!" she shouted. "He's calling from *Air Force One!*"

The president, his voice crackling across the air-to-ground line, said he had seen Peggy's words of support in the newspaper. He wasn't getting too much support just then, so he wanted to thank her for the kindness.

And one other thing. "I don't care what anyone else says," Ronald Reagan said firmly. "I'm going to bring those men home."

Peggy Say sat down and cried.

16

No One in Charge

BY THE TIME REAGAN arrived for Thanksgiving at his Rancho del Cielo, a remote swath of 688 acres cut from the grassy hills high above Santa Barbara's jagged coastline, he was the clear focus of the nation's concern. The questions raised by the Iran-contra revelations went to the heart of his presidency; suddenly, both his credibility and his competence were in doubt. Only Reagan had the power to reassure the nation and lay the doubts to rest, and the long holiday weekend at his ranch provided a good opportunity to come to grips with the crisis. Ordinarily, the ranch was the one place where he could renew his spirit and regain his perspective on the world below. But now, instead of putting him in touch with reality, it had just the opposite effect. The weekend at the retreat stiffened his determination to deny the problems facing his White House.

By Thanksgiving, almost all of Reagan's advisers felt that a quick explanation and apology would help put the furor behind him. But the president showed a fierce aversion to any display of remorse. He had summarily turned down a draft of an apologetic speech that his aides had crafted, and, during the weekend, he repelled the first effort by his old political cronies to convince him to fire members of his cabinet and staff. Furthermore, his pronouncement that North was a "national hero" had, in a single stroke, completely nullified Regan's plan to lay blame on the NSC — or, for that matter, anywhere else.

It had long worked to Reagan's advantage that he virtually never apologized publicly or privately for his failures. The deficit was Congress's fault; setbacks in arms control were the Soviets' fault; the persistent problems of "sleaze" among his appointees were either the press's fault or no fault at all. Until the arms sales to Iran, the public had largely accepted this sunny reconstruction of reality and admired the president's self-confidence.

But now, the entire political dynamic had shifted in just over a month, turning many of Reagan's formerly celebrated strengths into weaknesses. The Reykjavik summit marked the beginning of the recognition among Washington's policy professionals that his untutored utopianism may have reached dangerous proportions. The loss of the Republican majority in the Senate not only emboldened the political opposition, but also produced a palpable sense in the White House press corps that the president's invulnerability was no longer intact. Finally, the Iran-contra revelations had raised the general public's concern about his basic command of the job, a concern that for the first time couldn't be wholly met by his ordinarily winning response — a dismissive one-liner delivered with an amiable grin.

For the first time in his life, his own integrity was seriously in question. Reagan had capped a relatively successful acting career with a largely charmed political career. He had very little experience with failure. Even his loss of the Republican presidential nomination in 1976 was a victory in the sense that he exceeded almost all expectations, setting himself up handily for 1980. Inevitably, he had suffered some defeats, but he had generally rationalized them, sometimes rearranging the facts of his life to edit out the pain. So the seriousness of the situation facing him by the end of November 1986 — only twenty-four months after he had won his second national landslide — was beyond his experience, and, judging from both the accounts of his aides and his own remarks, beyond his comprehension.

Those who expected Reagan to apologize for his mistakes and take charge of righting his listing administration would have done well to look back nineteen years to 1967, when he faced the first serious scandal of his political career. Reagan was in his first term as governor of California, and there were rumors — of which he was oblivious — that his chief of staff was filling choice administrative posts with homosexual friends. His communications director, Franklyn Nofziger, began to investigate on his own initiative — much as Meese would do almost two decades later. In time, Nofziger found enough in the rumors to have to confront the governor with the bad news.

"My God," exclaimed Reagan, "has government failed?" Reagan did not ask whether *he* had failed, nor did he accept responsibility. Instead, he dismissed those involved without explanation while publicly denying the scandal. Privately, however, he exhibited a strange kind of numbness, withdrawing from the unpleasant reality to such an extent that for four months, as one participant told his biographer Lou Cannon, "the governor cut himself off from a lot of things he shouldn't. The governorship went into receivership."

Now, almost two decades later, Reagan grew similarly despondent. The seventy-five-year-old president again faced a scandal for which he had yet to accept any responsibility. And again he lashed out publicly at the press for publishing false and malicious accounts. Privately, however, it became increasingly clear to those around him that he was again entering a prolonged phase of withdrawal. Just as in 1967, his administration now went into receivership; power and authority shifted almost daily from one competing voice to the next. This time, however, it was not the state government of California but the government of the most powerful democracy in the world that slid toward confusion.

But the president, whose luck had held out for so long, now seemed unable to navigate the changed political landscape. "He just denied everything," a senior aide later said. "It was strange — I mean really strange. He couldn't confront anything. He was living in a dream world."

The president seemed paralyzed by the crisis, but the public was quick to react. Reagan's approval rating fell dramatically; it was as if the fickle American public were jilting a suitor — the romance seemed gone almost overnight. If the loss of the Republican majority in the Senate a month earlier had signaled the beginning of the end of Reagan's long run as the most famous exception to the laws of political gravity, polls taken upon his return from Thanksgiving measured just how ephemeral his earlier standing had been. The secret funding of the contras outraged liberals, but the arms sales to the ayatollah — which exposed the hollowness of Reagan's rhetoric — offended voters along the entire political spectrum. It wasn't the stupidity that shocked people — it was the duplicity.

On December 1, the *New York Times*–CBS News poll revealed the damage to Reagan in terms his staff had trouble dismissing. Reagan's overall approval rating had dropped from 67 percent to 46 percent in a single month; suddenly less than half of those polled approved of his performance. Reagan was still almost twice as popular as Nixon had been during the depths of Watergate — and a substantial portion of the public would never lose its affection for him as a man. But what amazed the pollsters was the speed with which the public lost faith in his leadership. The twenty-one-point drop was the largest one-month collapse in presidential approval ever recorded.

Almost more devastating were the numbers measuring Reagan's credibility — the foundation on which his reputation as a communicator rested. A vast majority of the country — 90 percent in one *Newsweek* poll — did not believe that Reagan was telling the truth about what he knew of the Iran-contra affair. After six years of admiring him for his apparent candor and decisiveness, the country couldn't accept the image of a bungling leader, a president so out of touch that he had failed to notice a private foreign policy conducted by his immediate staff. The polls showed that most people could only conclude that he was lying. The cruelest cut, however, may have been inflicted by a *Wall Street Journal*–NBC News poll, which found that the public now rated Jimmy Carter almost twice as high as Reagan on his handling of Iran. The White House — which had read its temperature by Wirthlin's numbers — ironically found itself in the anomalous position of dismissing the importance of polls. "Polls go up, polls go down, polls go back up again," said a hapless spokesman who had been sent out to deal with the accumulating flak.

The White House did its best to downplay the affair, but it was growing increasingly difficult to do so. On Sunday, November 30, a parade of friends and foes appeared on television talk shows to demand that, as Indiana Republican senator Richard Lugar put it, Reagan must get a new White House staff and "clear the house of all the malefactors." That same weekend, while the president was still up on his ranch, the *Los Angeles Times* ran the first report that North had shredded reams of documents in his office — an act reminiscent of Watergate and one that raised serious questions about criminal obstruction of justice. The administration halfheartedly denied the reports. After the first account in the press, Larry Speakes called Fawn Hall, who informed him blandly, as she had promised North and the others she would, that "we shred all the time." Speakes in turn told reporters, "If there was any shredding, it was very limited." Then, with logic worthy of Inspector Clouseau, he explained, "We have not uncovered any missing documents." But it was not until November 28 — the day after the shredding was revealed — that the FBI was finally given joint custody of the documents with the NSC security office and was for the first time allowed to enter the Old Executive Office Building and the White House to search for and protect potential evidence.

As if sensing the president's new vulnerability — and his potentially contaminating problems — Senate majority leader Robert Dole, a man with his own presidential aspirations, demanded that the White House call a highly unusual special congressional session to deal with the growing imbroglio. The White House quickly rejected Dole's suggestion. But on December 4, House and Senate leaders agreed on their own to form two select investigating committees, which would soon combine to mount a full-scale, nine-month investigation.

As the pressure mounted in the first week in December, Attorney General Edwin Meese reluctantly agreed to the appointment of an independent counsel to look into the controversy. (On December 19, Lawrence E. Walsh, an Eisenhower Republican with a reputation as a dogged prosecutor, was named.) The administration had long argued that the independent counsel statute was unconstitutional, and Meese had initially opposed appointing one. But he relented as demands from subordinates in the Justice Department and critics on the Hill grew with the appearance that the Justice Department had a conflict of interest — a perception bolstered by questions about Meese's slowness to have the FBI seal off North's office. Meese's casual handling of the initial probe had created other problems too. Although some underlings had urged him to issue subpoenas as early as November, Meese had resisted, allowing North and others to argue later that they hadn't obstructed justice by shredding documents, because they hadn't realized a formal criminal investigation was under way. With these questions hanging in the air, by mid-December, all of the machinery of Watergate had clanked inexorably into place.

In the face of the scandal, Regan's minions tried to stave off further political damage with a series of announcements that made the president seem in command. Immediately upon returning from California, Reagan announced his choice of a national security adviser to replace Poindexter: Frank C. Carlucci. And on December 1 he also met for the first time with the members of the special three-man commission that would review the Iran-contra evidence from a policy perspective. The panel, chaired by former Texas senator John Tower, was widely expected to produce a whitewash. It could then be released before the Democratic-controlled 100th Congress, which would convene on January 6, could get far in its own, presumably tougher investigation.

The Tower board was the brainchild not of the president, who had merely signed on to the idea, but of Don Regan's aides, who a year earlier had won praise for recommending the Rogers Commission as a way of dealing with the NASA shuttle disaster. They hoped that a panel of acknowledged wise men would add credibility to the official statements of concern and keep the problem within gentlemanly limits. Few were consulted by Regan about the plan — and some of those who later learned of it were outraged. Pat Buchanan, a veteran of Watergate, heatedly argued that bringing outsiders — including a Democrat — into the heart of the White House to investigate "was like calling in an air strike on our own positions!"

In fact, between Carlucci and the Tower board, Reagan's aides had placed the president in the hands of the very Washington establishment he had promised, in 1980, to displace. Carlucci had been a career foreign service officer under both Democrats and Republicans — not at all the sort of ideologue whom Reagan had promised to bring to power. And the Tower board was made up of three men pulled from the very backbone of Washington's establishment: Tower, who had been the powerful chairman of the Senate Armed Services Committee; Brent Scowcroft,

President Ford's national security adviser; and Edmund S. Muskie, a former Democratic senator from Maine and Carter's secretary of state, who was Don Regan's particular choice for the panel. In part because of their ties to the Washington establishment, and also because they had no subpoena power, few thought they would dig deep enough to do much damage.

Don Regan, the man closest to the president on a daily basis, seemed to believe it would be possible to hang the administration's mistakes on scapegoats less important than himself and meanwhile handle the inevitable questions arising about the president's grasp of the job with yet another campaign of "spin control." Some three weeks into the scandal, Regan had turned to the black binders of Wirthlin's opinion polls he kept by his desk and argued to a visiting reporter, "We've had far worse problems before. Bitburg was worse." Ambushed by reporters on the way out to California, Regan was combatively defiant. "Does a bank president know whether a bank teller is fiddling around with the books?" he asked contemptuously. "No!" But Mrs. Reagan had lost all patience with Regan and what she saw as his second-rate staff. She had been incensed by his "shovel brigade" remark, with its obvious implication that her husband had created the garbage that Regan, in his superior wisdom, had cleaned up. And she was enraged that Regan had supported the policy of arms sales to Iran but now shifted the blame onto everyone but himself. The chief of staff — who had earlier asked, "How much more experience in foreign policy do you have to have than I do to believe you are qualified?" — now seemed to be taking as his motto a gag that was inscribed on a paperweight on his desk: "The buck doesn't even pause here."

Mrs. Reagan was not amused. In an administration in which the ethic had become, as one aide to Regan later conceded, "every man for himself," she was almost alone among those close to the president in putting his survival above everything else. Yet her ability to protect him now from what she judged to be a serious crisis was limited by the constraints that public opinion placed on First Ladies. She was also hobbled by the useful myth that she had helped create about her own lack of influence in anything beyond the traditional wifely realms of domesticity and charity. This portrait had always been false, but for the next three months it would be less true than ever.

After Thanksgiving, she became increasingly agitated. Unlike Regan, she saw that the problems facing her husband went far deeper than public relations — in fact, one family friend said she cried about the prospect that after six successful years, the president would be impeached. Another said, "She was so worried about impeachment, she would have done anything to buy Congress off."

One of the things Congress was demanding was Don Regan's removal. Even Utah's conservative Republican senator Orrin Hatch called for his resignation, saying, "He did not protect the president. He did not inform the president. What is worse, he did not assure that he was informed himself." Regan, the man who had dismissed Congress and the press by saying he had only "one master," was now finding that in Washington this left him with only one friend.

On December 3, Mrs. Reagan told reporters that a decision about Regan's future "has nothing to do with me." But she had quietly arranged for two outside political experts to visit the residence; in fact, they were coming the very next evening. Their job was to tell her husband what she felt he wouldn't hear from Regan. She had worked out the details with Michael Deaver, who, despite facing an independent counsel's probe into his lobbying business, now talked with the First Lady daily about how to remove Regan and save the White House. Reagan had rejected their direct appeals to fire the chief of staff, so the two had devised a plan to bring in both a good cop and a bad cop, knowing that that way the president would be less inclined to think the meeting stacked. The witness for the defense was Nixon's former secretary of state and a golfing partner of Regan's, William Rogers; and, for the prosecution, a former Democratic party chairman and professional Washington insider, Robert Strauss.

"Rogers was no help at all," said one of the First Lady's confidants. "He just sort of said, 'Well, you're the president, and you have to just ride these things out.' " But Strauss was deadly in his own smooth way. "Today, you need two things desperately," he told the president. "You have a serious Hill problem — Don Regan has no allies on the Hill. And you have a serious media problem — Don Regan has no friends there. You have got to get a fresh face in that job." Strauss also pushed Reagan to get rid of Bill Casey, a cause he undoubtedly knew was dear to Mrs. Reagan's heart.

The foursome talked for more than two hours. Mrs. Reagan directed the conversation and posed most of the questions. One account described the president as actively engaged; another said he sat impassively through most of the discussion. But by all accounts, the meeting had little impact on its intended target. After Strauss's analysis, Reagan averred, "Don Regan has been loyal to me. I am not going to throw him to the wolves." The political problem, Reagan insisted, was being exaggerated; it would be over in a week.

Deaver and Mrs. Reagan remained determined to rouse the president to action. Over the next few weeks, Deaver talked to Reagan twice in a general way about clearing the decks and once more directly about firing Regan. But the president told him he wasn't going to fire anyone "to save my own tail." He told Deaver that he shouldn't worry, "my staff is taking care of these things." Deaver, who had served Reagan for nineteen years, could scarcely believe his loyalties were so easily turned on and off; it seemed he simply put his faith in whoever was around him.

It became clear to Nancy Reagan and her allies — who included political adviser Stuart Spencer, among others — that they must take stronger measures. If the president wouldn't yield to private suasion, his wife would secretly generate public pressure, which might force Regan to resign on his own. As one conspirator in the effort put it, "She wasn't gaining with him, so we took it public."

The campaign against Regan turned to orchestrated leaks in the nation's most prestigious newspapers. With Mrs. Reagan's blessing, a former White House aide and a friend of Deaver's, Joseph Canzeri, was designated to spread the news that top officials wanted Regan out. At a party, Canzeri dropped a hint about the story to R. W. Apple, Jr., the chief Washington correspondent for the *New York Times*. An article appeared under Apple's by-line on the front page of the *Times* on December 11, complete with a photograph of a downcast Regan. The following day, December 12, the leak spilled onto the front page of the *Washington Post* along with the first account of the formerly "secret" Strauss and Rogers visit. Nancy Reagan denied having had anything to do with the effort. But one participant said that "she was with us a hundred percent."

In fact, Mrs. Reagan spent considerable time and effort scheming on the telephone with her confederates about how to conceal her increasingly powerful role. In one call, she went into excruciating detail about how to make it appear that her husband was taking the initiative. "It can't look like my idea!" she insisted.

But Mrs. Reagan's efforts to oust the chief of staff were fruitless: Regan stayed on. He probably saved his job for the moment with a masterful performance before a closed session of the Senate Intelligence Committee. On December 16, appearing without lawyers, and without hiding behind executive privilege or the Fifth Amendment, Regan testified under oath for five hours. The chief of staff, who could be almost as charming as his boss when he tried, appeared to gush with sudden candor. He explained that he knew little about the affair because the NSC had kept him uninformed. The senators were impressed. "He told an unbelievable story in a believable way," said Arizona's Democratic senator Dennis DeConcini. Soon after, the demands for his resignation slackened, and stories began to appear suggesting that Regan might in fact provide necessary continuity during the turmoil.

Not everyone in the White House shared this view; one who thought Regan should not continue was political director Mitch Daniels, who had grown increasingly alarmed not only by the public polls, but also by the private ones conducted by Wirthlin. He had been stunned by the outcome of one of the routine telephone soundings his office did of the Republican party faithful. Overwhelmingly and unanimously, these bedrock supporters called for the president to take command, answer questions, fire his chief of staff, and make a clean sweep while there was still time. Aware of the president's reluctance to fire Regan or anyone else, he decided to confront the chief of staff himself.

Daniels, mild-mannered and amiable, steeled his nerves and, armed with the statistical outcome of his research, set up an appointment to see Regan. "I was nervous," he later recalled in his flat, midwestern twang, "but Regan had always been pretty good to me."

He walked into Regan's office, down a narrow flight of stairs from his own West Wing office, with the bad news that the president's staunchest friends were demanding Regan's head. "It's objective fact," he said. "We've got to make some changes. These next few months are critical. Politically, they're the only ones that count. Our best supporters think you've got to resign."

Accounts of Regan's response differ. One of Daniels's friends said that the chief of staff screamed, "Goddamnit! *You* fucking resign!" Daniels denied the rancorous exchange, depicting instead a more artful Regan. According to Daniels, Regan listened politely, then argued quietly that the White House would look more unstable if he resigned at that point. There was, after all, important political business to finish — the State of the Union address was coming up, and the budget had to be completed. But Regan had some other helpful ideas on how to handle the crisis. He agreed that together they needed to come up with changes that would "give the appearance of a fresh start." And so, before Daniels had quite realized that his thrust had been parried, he sat there with his intended victim, trying to come up with the names of other officials whose dismissals would satisfy the public clamor.

Regan had just proven what many suspected: in two years he had eliminated virtually every official who could seriously challenge him.

The president remained completely convinced that he had done nothing wrong and owed no apologies, and his defiance set the tone for others in his administration who were drawn into the controversy. Don Regan went underground, refusing to give any interviews to reporters. And White House press secretary Larry Speakes, serving his last days on the job, refused to answer Iran-contra questions, using one daily briefing to doodle cartoons of the press corps instead. He explained that he was waiting for the White House counsel, Peter Wallison, and the Tower board to dig up the answers. Inevitably, this heightened the sense that the president was either stalling or completely out of touch, since he needed two internal investigations to discover what his own NSC had done.

Adding to the impression of stonewalling were North, Poindexter, and five other figures in the widening scandal, who invoked their Fifth Amendment rights not to testify. Speakes read a statement from Reagan asking for everyone to "tell the full story" when called to testify before Congress, but the NSC aides refused. Appearing in full uniform — his ribbons and medals sparkling in the television lights — and biting his lower lip as if in agony, North broke his silence only long enough to say in a cracking voice that, "I don't think there's another person in America who wants to tell this story as much as I do."

Republican leaders, including the president's best political friend, Senator Paul Laxalt of Nevada, privately urged Reagan to push Poindexter and North harder to talk, before the scandal consumed the administration. But the president held back, saying he would not presume to abridge his former aides' constitutional rights. He dismissed the spectacle of active military officers, who until recently had been high-ranking members of his staff, pleading the Fifth Amendment, saying that it was "not that unusual." In every way possible, he downplayed the proceedings. To his aides, he described the investigations as "a witch hunt." Publicly, he said he only tuned in to the televised hearings "when I can't find a ball game." It wasn't just posturing. An aide said that Reagan had watched George Shultz testify before the House Foreign Affairs Committee on December 8 for only a few moments in the morning "while he dressed."

Meanwhile, the crisis had plunged George Bush into an awful dilemma. On December 3, he was due to give a public address on terrorism at the annual conference of a Washington think tank. Inevitably, the speech would have to confront the treacherous issue of where he, as head of the administration's task force on counterterrorism, stood on the arms shipments to Iran. Bush, who had built his political career on loyalty to his bosses, apparently found the pressure to distance himself from Reagan extremely uncomfortable. The day Meese made the diversion announcement, Bush started conferring with speechwriter Landon Parvin, a felicitous writer who had a knack for extricating politicians from tough binds.

Bush was really worried about this one. Before long, an entire committee was debating how to handle the speech. The central question was whether to put even the slightest distance between himself and the president. The 1988 presidential campaign would soon begin in earnest, and some of Bush's advisers argued that he shouldn't even touch the Iran-contra affair. On the other side was Bush's deputy chief of staff, Frederick Khedouri, who argued that Bush must denounce the arms sales. In a draft of the speech, Khedouri had worked out a line conceding the obvious, that "mistakes were made" — a line that so far the president had conspicuously refused to utter himself. But even this careful construction caused arguments. It was in one draft and out the next; the night before the speech, it seemed out for good. The subject bothered Bush so much that at a private dinner that evening, he gave an impassioned speech of his own to his staff, explaining why he felt it so important to be loyal to the president.

Overnight, however, Bush reversed himself, but only after clearing the line "mistakes were made" with the president and Meese did he restore it to his text. He delivered it early that afternoon in a widely acclaimed address. Temporarily, it took the pressure and the spotlight off the vice president.

Bush was similarly tormented about how to handle Don Regan. Privately he told several confidants that he believed the chief of staff ought to resign. But when an ally of the First Lady's suggested that he tell that to the president, Bush backed off, arguing, "It's not my role." The First Lady's ally retorted, "It's exactly your role." A second attempt by the same person was only slightly more fruitful. After more prodding, Bush agreed to talk with Reagan about it, but he soon returned, saying that "he just didn't want to hear about it, and I wasn't going to push."

In the general chaos, contradictions accumulated with each day's news stories. On Saturday, December 6, the $10 million Brunei contribution — which Elliott Abrams had denied in a blanket disclaimer to Congress — was reported by the *Los Angeles Times*. At the State Department, officials were in a small panic: the sultan's money had somehow disappeared, and for a week they had been desperately trying to track it down. (It turned out that because Fawn Hall had typed the wrong account number on the index card, the money was deposited in the account of a Swiss shipping executive. The shipper, apparently hoping no one would ask about his $10 million windfall, quietly transferred the money into another account. There it stood until congressional investigators found it in 1987 and a Swiss magistrate persuaded him to return his mistaken wealth.)

On Monday, December 8, two days after the news about Brunei was printed, the Senate Intelligence Committee called Abrams back to ask why he had told them in November that the State Department had not raised any money for the contras.

Senator Thomas Eagleton of Missouri displayed an obvious distaste for the brash young Abrams. "If you were under oath, Elliott, you were guilty of perjury," he warned.

"I resent that," Abrams said, bristling.

"Were you, then, in the fund-raising business?" Eagleton asked.

"I would say we were in the fund-raising business," Abrams conceded. "I take your point."

"Take my point?" Eagleton exclaimed. "Under oath, my friend, that's perjury. Had you been under oath, that's perjury."

"Well, I don't agree with that," Abrams said.

"That's slammer time," Eagleton said.

"I don't agree with that, Senator," Abrams said. "You've heard my testimony."

"I've heard it, and I want to puke," the senator replied.

But McFarlane caused the most serious discrepancy to surface, one that only deepened public skepticism. Testifying under oath before the House Foreign Affairs Committee on December 5, he asserted that the president had authorized the first shipment of TOWs but never notified Congress. McFarlane's testimony contradicted the White House's version, which held that the Israelis had sent the first arms shipment in August 1985 on their own without Reagan's authorization. A month earlier, McFarlane too had said that the Israelis had acted on their own, but the Israelis, with good reason, had hotly denied this. McFarlane now offered a new account that also provided him with a cover.

The question of prior authorization had serious political, diplomatic, and legal implications. A variety of laws barred sales of arms to terrorist nations (including Iran) unless the president specifically waived them for national security reasons. If McFarlane had acted without presidential authorization, his own situation was legally dubious. If he had acted with authorization, there was the question of why Reagan hadn't notified Congress, as required by law. Moreover, there was a question of why a number of other White House officials, including Donald Regan, had given contrary accounts — and, more important, of why the president, whose actions lay at the crux of the controversy, had not clarified his own role.

William Casey's position had grown more tangled too. His old friend Roy Furmark had contradicted Casey's earlier professions of ignorance by telling investigators that he had warned Casey about the diversion before Meese announced it. On December 10, Casey returned to Capitol Hill and admitted that Furmark had indeed talked with him on October 7. This, he now said, had been the first he had heard of the diversion. He downplayed the growing discrepancies. When asked whether North had lied to the CIA in describing missile shipments as "oil drilling parts," Casey tamely offered, "Maybe he made a mistake." And when asked about the contra resupply operation, he still professed to know nearly nothing.

In fact, Casey and his men had already been covering their tracks. To head off the mounting political pressure, Casey ordered the agency's inspector general to investigate the allegations that his men had secretly helped the contras when that was illegal. The inspector general, an old CIA man himself, obediently traveled to Central America to find out what the operations boys had been doing. Remarkably, he came up empty-handed. In Honduras, the men who had run a helicopter service ferrying ammunition and other supplies to the contras nonchalantly assured their visitor that they had done nothing of the kind. In Costa Rica, Joe Fernandez, the station chief who had virtually run the supply flights to the contras' Southern Front, admitted that he had had some contacts with the contras' "private benefactors," but nothing improper. "They all lined up and lied to him," a congressional investigator marveled. "Not some outside guy — their own I.G."

At CIA headquarters, two key cables on the November 1985 shipment of HAWK missiles had already disappeared from the secret archives of the Operations Directorate. The men who ran the secret shipment — Dewey Clarridge among them — testified that they did not know the agency's plane was carrying missiles. That was curious, since two CIA lawyers remembered some of the same operations men telling them, only a few days after the shipment, that missiles were indeed the cargo.

Casey's CIA, in short, answered not to Congress, nor to its own inspector general, but only to him. He appeared to have built a secret, parallel network of personal operatives inside and outside the agency, from Clarridge, the operations "cowboy," to the CIA men who reportedly "retired" from the agency to work clandestinely for him on the outside. Others in the agency knew something of what was going on, if not all of it. Some, like deputy director Robert Gates, appear to have been kept in the dark to provide Casey with more cover — or to have deliberately avoided learning about what was happening. But Casey's CIA was beyond the control of its own titular managers.

Astonishingly, despite the public outcry, Reagan still tried to keep the hostage deals going. Although he had halfheartedly pronounced the execution of the policy as a "mistake" in his December 6 radio address, he was so intent on getting the hostages home that, at Casey's instigation, he agreed to press on until they were all out of Beirut. The fact that new hostages were being seized — three in late 1986, three more in early 1987 — did not seem to dampen either Reagan's or Casey's enthusiasm, although a premise of the deals had always been that they would halt further abductions.

Thus, in early December, the CIA's George Cave and Secord's partner Albert Hakim set up another meeting with the Iranians to try to revive the deal after the cataclysm of November. But the CIA had a problem: Reagan had formally handed control of the Iranian policy to George Shultz and the State Department. The negotiations had to be shared. Shultz agreed to another meeting with the Iranians only to discuss possible political relations between the two countries, not hostage deals. Shultz also insisted that the State Department head the negotiating team. And the team had to carry instructions informing the Iranians that any hostage deals were over and that all future contacts would be limited to exchanges of intelligence.

On Friday, December 12, Casey said he reluctantly accepted Shultz's conditions. But later that day, Casey broke his word. He met alone with his old friend from Wall Street days, Don Regan, and told him Shultz's conditions would doom any chances of freeing more hostages. He asked Regan to help persuade the president to overrule the secretary of state. Casey said the CIA should stay involved in the negotiations, and that the talks should cover not just intelligence but the hostages too. Regan helpfully took Casey's message to the president, and Reagan accepted his chief of staff's recommendation. Just that easily, after all of the public outcry and official disclaimers, the hostage negotiations resumed.

Casey and Regan did not tell Shultz that they had overruled him. Instead, without informing Shultz, that night the White House ordered the State Department to cable new instructions to the U.S. negotiators, who were already in Frankfurt for their meeting with the Iranians. "The president intends to continue a channel of communications to the government of Iran for both policy and intelligence discussions," the new instructions said. The key was the inclusion of the word "policy," which Casey knew was code for wide-ranging, open-ended discussions of exactly the nature that Shultz had strictly forbidden. In further violation of the promise to Shultz, the instructions continued to dwell on the hostage situation, saying delicately, "We trust that in furtherance of our mutual goals, you will take it upon yourself to arrange the release of all Western hostages held in Lebanon as quickly as possible."

At Frankfurt's Park Hotel on Saturday, December 13, the Iranian official, Ali Samaii, laid out his understanding of where the deal stood, based on where Hakim had left it in October. Samaii said Iran was still willing to help win the release of the hostages in Beirut, but it wanted the United States to deliver the promised 1,500 more TOW missiles. And Iran wanted the United States to put more pressure on Kuwait — as Hakim had promised — to release some of the Da'wa Shia terrorists in its prisons.

The State Department's new man in the talks, Charles Dunbar, was appalled. He had never heard of Hakim's concessions. As far as he knew, the United States had a firm policy on terrorism that specifically forbade pressuring other governments — like Kuwait — to free prisoners in exchange for hostages. Samaii was polite but confused by Dunbar's protests. The meeting broke up after an hour and a half. Only then, at lunch with the CIA's Cave, did Dunbar learn of the earlier negotiations. "Poindexter told Cave et al. that he personally had asked the Kuwaitis to do something about the Da'wa prisoners," Dunbar reported in amazement to the State Department.

Shultz was furious. Despite Regan's attempts to stop him, on Sunday, December 14, Shultz met with the president in the White House family quarters. "And," he later testified, "I told the president the items on this agenda, including such things as doing something about the Da'wa prisoners. . . . And the president was astonished. And I have never seen him so mad. He's a very genial, pleasant man . . . but his jaw set, and his eyes flashed, and both of us, I think, felt the same way about it. He reacted like he'd been kicked in the belly. . . . I think, in that meeting, I finally felt that the president deeply understands that something is radically wrong here."

But according to Poindexter, the president had already been told of the Kuwaiti plan in October. Shultz knew nothing of this, and, in any case, his conclusion — that the battle for control of the Iran policy was over — was still premature. The CIA continued talking with the Iranians until January, when the Iranians, complaining that the squabbling Americans were impossible to deal with, gave up.

The day after Shultz's meeting with the president, Monday, December 15, Casey was scheduled to appear once again before the Senate Intelligence Committee for what was expected to be a more strenuous grilling than before. But that morning, as he prepared for the session in his office in Langley, the seventy-three-year-old CIA director suffered spasms in his arms and legs and was rushed by ambulance to Georgetown University Hospital. Three days later he underwent surgery for a lymphoma, a cancerous tumor, on the left side of his brain. At first the prognosis was optimistic. Casey, his doctors said, could recover completely, perhaps even resume his work as director of central intelligence. But William Casey had spun his last cover story: the promised recovery never came. Casey resigned on January 29, leaving vital questions unanswered; he died on May 6, the day after Secord named him in congressional testimony as North's chief patron.

Outwardly, at least, Reagan was determined to overcome the crisis as he always had — by projecting the image that all was well. On December 12, the same day that he quietly renewed the hostage deals, he pledged in an upbeat speech in the Old Executive Office Building that "we cannot and we will not let this thing stop us from getting on with the business of governing." He concluded with his trademark grin and gave his audience the thumbs-up sign.

But as the headlines grew bolder and bigger, the president and his staff grew increasingly unable to cope. In a desperate gambit to distract the press, they rushed to release a long-awaited welfare reform proposal, even though the president had not yet read it or endorsed it. They had planned to offer an alternative to Congress's proposal to deploy the $45 billion Midgetman missile, which much of the Defense Department opposed, but they were too preoccupied by the scandal. Important appointments, from the White House staff to the Federal Reserve Board, went unmade. Policymaking was going awry. "We're getting total flip flops from one thing to another. There's schizophrenia across the board," complained Edwin Feulner, a supporter whose conservative think tank, the Heritage Foundation, provided many ideas for the White House.

John Sears, Reagan's former campaign manager, explained the growing paralysis quite simply. "People panicked," he later said. "They thought, 'Finally we got caught, and now everyone knows that Ronald Reagan doesn't know what he's doing.' "

Increasingly, Nancy Reagan moved to fill the vacuum. Her reach extended to Reagan's legal strategy, on which she even consulted a private lawyer. It was at her urging that the president called on the Senate Intelligence Committee to give North and Poindexter "use immunity," meaning that their testimony wouldn't be held against them in a trial. A White House aide who questioned the move was surprised to get a scorching call from the First Lady, who let him know that the East Wing, not the West, was calling the shots.

She was especially concerned about the approaching State of the Union address. At this pivotal moment, when the presidency seemed to be coming apart, the speech had to be strong. In mid-December, she insisted to Regan that he bring in Kenneth Khachigian, the trusted speechwriter from California who was not on the White House staff, to put together the address.

Khachigian took the assignment, but he quickly discovered that no one could give him any guidance about what the speech should contain. "There was no leadership from the top. As far as I could tell, no one had talked to the president about any of it."

Not until New Year's Eve was Khachigian able to speak directly to the president about the address — at Mrs. Reagan's initiative. The Reagans were in Palm Springs for their annual round of parties with Walter Annenberg and their old California cronies, and at 5:13 P.M., Mrs. Reagan called Khachigian to see how he was coming with the draft. They discussed his ideas and agreed that, unlike Reagan's previous State of the Union addresses, this one should have no live American "hero" seated in the hall's balcony, ready for the president to name in a dramatic flourish. Khachigian was afraid it would look like a tired gimmick, reinforcing the notion that the president was leaning on worn-out props. More than anything else, they agreed, the speech needed to show the country that Reagan had no plans to abandon his bold foreign policy and that, despite news reports to the contrary, the president was, as Khachigian put it, "strong and vigorous."

After Mrs. Reagan and Khachigian discussed the speech for seven minutes, she handed the phone to the president, who had just returned from the golf course. Khachigian explained some of his ideas for the speech and waited for the president's response.

But Reagan wasn't in the mood to discuss the fine points of his State of the Union address. Instead, he amiably said, "I just played my annual game of golf, and George Shultz and I beat Bill Smith and Charlie Price by one hole!"

The State of the Union message was not the only subject on which the president was incommunicative during this period. Some close to the president began to wonder if he had lost the enthusiasm and focus necessary to do the job. His chief of staff, for instance, observed that "he read and signed the papers put before him and listened to his briefings, but he appeared to be in the grip of lassitude." And one old associate claimed that Reagan forgot who he was talking to in the midst of a phone conversation. On several occasions, he mirthlessly told a long joke, likening himself to a farmer who had been hit by a truck.

Reagan returned to Washington soon after New Year's, and on January 3, 1987, the president's men began trying to prepare him for his first interview with the Tower board, which was scheduled for later that month. A key point, which his aides hoped to clarify, was whether he had approved the first arms shipment in August 1985. McFarlane continued to insist that the president had approved it, while Don Regan continued to contend that he had not.

In the sitting room of the residence, with its huge fan window looking out over the snowy grounds, Don Regan, White House counsel Peter Wallison, and his deputy Jay Stephens sat with the president, trying, in the words of one of them, "to stimulate a presidential memory."

The president simply couldn't recall much about the first arms sale to Iran. Knowing that Reagan's memory on this point was spotty, Wallison had asked the president to review his diary and phone logs. Wallison had also prepared a number of visual aids that he hoped would help the president. He had drawn up a chart listing events by date in columns: on one side were the arms shipments; and on the other were the major presidential activities at the time — a speech here, a trip there. Furthermore, he soon gave Reagan copies of McFarlane's testimony; using a yellow marker, he highlighted the controversial sections, those in which McFarlane had said the president had authorized the sale before it occurred.

But it was to no avail. "I'm racking my brains, and I just can't remember," Reagan said bleakly.

"Do you remember being surprised when you first heard about the Israeli shipment?" asked Wallison. (Regan had testified under oath that the president had cursed the Israelis when he found out.)

"Well, yes, I think I was surprised," said the president.

"That would indicate that you didn't give your approval, right?" asked the counsel.

"Yes, maybe," said the president, without conviction. "But I really don't recall."

The session, the first of several like it, ended with those in the room believing that the president would have to tell the Tower board that he simply didn't remember what he had done. He seemed "embarrassed," said one participant, "because there were all these stories that he was getting old, or losing it. He really wanted to recall, in his heart of hearts I think he thought he should, but he couldn't. He was very unhappy."

Two days later, on January 5, Reagan underwent surgery for an enlarged prostate gland. It is a common but uncomfortable operation among men of his age, and one that the doctors said would require a six-week recovery period. As it turned out, the surgery proved more debilitating to the president than his aides had expected. After the surgery, Nancy Reagan was more vigilant than ever. When the White House photographer was ushered into Reagan's hospital room to document the president's recovery, Mrs. Reagan saw that the president's knees were exposed and commanded sharply, "Don't shoot!" Then she covered her husband's knees and hastily placed some papers on his lap, to make it look as if he had been working.

Meanwhile, Khachigian was still trying to piece together the State of the Union message. He met with the new NSC staff and was impressed with Carlucci. But then he met with Regan's staff in the Roosevelt Room and found them, as he put it, "just groping and scrambling, with no blueprint for 1987." They had been studying the latest polls, and had come up with what Khachigian called "mush" like a drive for "excellence in America" and an unformed program to foster "competitiveness." "The problem," Khachigian later said, "was that there was no program there. In August, September, and October, instead of working on initiatives when they should have been, they diverted their attention to the Senate races and spin control."

In despair, Khachigian, like Pat Buchanan the month before, sought presidential help from their former boss, Richard Nixon. "Competitiveness is a nonstarter," Nixon counseled. "A laundry list won't fly. Most important is that the president look good and feel good — that's more important than his words." Nixon's other advice was that Reagan should "be aggressive. Don't give any ground on the contras."

On January 15, Reagan, who had returned from the hospital but, on doctors' orders, could work only an hour or so a day, met with Khachigian and Regan about the speech. Expectations ran high that he would say something new and more meaningful about the Iran-contra affair. He hadn't made any substantive statement on the scandal since December 6, during his five-minute radio address, when he had conceded that in the policy's execution, "mistakes were made." That had satisfied no one, not even his supporters. But, as Khachigian discovered, the president didn't want to dwell on the Iran-contra failure. He wanted to talk about how the American Constitution is different from all others, because the people define the government's rights rather than the other way around, and about the limited role of the federal government. It was one of Reagan's favorite points. He had made it in speeches when he toured the lecture circuit for General Electric in the early 1960s, when he campaigned for Barry Goldwater in 1964, and through twenty years of his own campaigns. It was as if he were taking refuge in his familiar refrains. But that alone could not fill a State of the Union message.

Not long afterward, Khachigian repaired to a vacant office in the White House basement and began to write. The next day, Don Regan called, asking him to meet with Wirthlin. The pollster arrived with reams of data and a political warning that Khachigian interpreted as "no abortion, no contras." Those subjects were too controversial. On January 17, ten days before the address, Khachigian handed in his draft. Dennis Thomas, Regan's top aide, soon appeared in his provisional office. "Ken, Ken," he said with fatherly disappointment, "what's the lead?" Regan's staff was concerned that the speech didn't contain pithy newspaper leads and television sound-bites — not whether it offered a program of goals for 1987. Disgusted, Khachigian flew back to California. He wasn't entirely satisfied with the speech himself, but he thought he could rework it from home.

But after Khachigian's departure, Regan's deputy, Thomas, rewrote the speech without telling him. When it was done, he added his own name to the title page as co-author. Meanwhile, one of the White House speechwriters, Tony Dolan, had done his own different draft, and submitted that too. The speechwriting process, like so much else in the White House, had completely broken down, and in the end, three separate drafts of the State of the Union message were submitted to the president.

On January 22, five days before the speech was to be delivered, Mrs. Reagan called Khachigian's San Clemente office in a state of grave concern. The president, whose recovery from surgery was still going slowly, had told her about receiving three drafts of the same speech, and asked plaintively, "What do the fellas expect me to do?" Mrs. Reagan was insistent that Khachigian come back to Washington to take charge of the speech.

Khachigian flew back the next day and rewrote his own draft. In its final form, the speech went further than before toward acknowledging that the Iranian deals had been a bad idea. It included a paragraph saying that "serious mistakes were made" in the Iranian policy, and "one major regret" was the failure of the attempt to win the hostages' freedom "because it did not work." Still, it did not renounce the overall policy itself but instead said "the goals were worthy," nor was there any personal apology. Despite Khachigian's best efforts, the speech was a collection of vague themes and shopworn ideas, the product of the Regan staff's uncertain vision of the future. One official said the speech showed that they had "finally achieved the content-free presidency."

After rewriting the address, Khachigian joined his wife and the Reagans at Camp David. The president made no comment to Khachigian about the earlier confusion. At lunch, the conversation turned to the early days of Hollywood. Both of the Reagans told charming stories about their movie days. But the experience shocked Khachigian. He was used to a certain amount of political jockeying, but nothing like this. Rampant infighting had filled the vacuum of a White House in receivership. He concluded that Regan and his aides were taking huge liberties behind the president's back; as he put it, "The integrity of the whole process stunk."

Although the president had largely been able to avoid comment on the Iran-contra affair to the press and public, the Tower board now expected a full account from him in private. Reagan met with the board for the first time on January 26, a day when Washington was blanketed in deep snow. The streets were hushed and empty, and most of the West Wing deserted in the storm. As the snowflakes drifted steadily down outside the windows of the Oval Office, the president seemed, to one participant, "all alone in this." His recovery from surgery was still not complete, and the meeting was supposed to be his only activity that day. Scheduled to last only an hour, it ran seventy-five minutes. No transcriber was allowed to attend, but the encounter made an indelible impression on those who were present.

Reagan's aides were especially concerned about how he would handle the questions of whether he had authorized the first arms shipment. Those who had been with Reagan during the preparatory sessions expected that he would tell the three members of the board, as he had told them, that he simply had been unable to remember. But that's not what happened.

The board members began by asking about several less sensitive issues, but eventually, as expected, one of them asked, "Did you authorize the Israeli shipment of arms to Iran in August?"

"Yes," he said quite clearly, astonishing the White House aides.

Asked when, he answered, "Well, I'm still digging on that."

Further questioning about his approval led nowhere, but the Tower board felt he was definitely siding with McFarlane over Regan. "I've taken a lot of depositions," said one participant, "and I had no doubt."

The White House legal advisers, who had been through the tortuous prep sessions, were stunned. The White House counsel, Peter Wallison, interjected, "Mr. President, is that really your recollection?"

Reagan then became vague. He pointed to the briefing materials in his lap. He focused on the copy of McFarlane's testimony that Wallison had highlighted for him in yellow. Reagan then handed the underlined testimony to the board and said, "Here, you might look at this. McFarlane's laid it out very nicely."

"He read it," said one astonished aide, "and accepted it as fact."

At the same session, the president told the board that he "did not know that the NSC staff was engaged in helping the contras," even though he had been given many briefings and had met with numerous contra leaders and supporters. Furthermore, he said he had not known that the United States was sharing intelligence with the Iranians, although it was written into the January 17 finding, which he said he had never read.

On a final point, Reagan told the board he'd known nothing about the diversion.

Wallison was disturbed by the president's performance, especially by his assertion that he had given prior authorization to the August arms shipment to Iran — a statement that Wallison believed was based on a misunderstanding by the president, for it contradicted not only his earlier statements but also Regan's sworn testimony. The Tower board had indicated that it was not yet finished with its questioning of the president, and so Wallison urged the board to raise the issue of authorization again. Meanwhile, he and the former ambassador to NATO, David Abshire, who had been appointed a special counselor to the president on the Iran-contra affair, as well as Vice President Bush and Don Regan, met again with Reagan in the Oval Office to try to straighten the issue out.

"You certainly never approved the transfer of arms before the fact in my presence, Mr. President," Regan insisted.

Regan then asked Bush whether he recalled the president's making such a decision. The vice president agreed he could not.

Wallison reminded the president that he had recalled being "surprised" when he learned that the Israelis had sent the TOWs.

"Yes," said the president, "I was surprised."

"And," added Regan, who had hewn hard to this line himself, "you said 'Damn them!' of the Israelis, when you heard about the arms shipment."

"Yes," agreed the president.

"Well, doesn't this mean you didn't authorize the arms shipment in advance?" continued Regan.

"Yes," said the president hesitantly.

"Then you left the wrong impression," Regan said.

Taking no chances on the next session with the Tower board, Wallison prepared an aide-mémoire, a memo reminding the president of this version of events.

On February 9, two days before Reagan was scheduled to meet again with the board, the scope of its probe grew dramatically. The board, which had been established to conduct a limited, unthreatening inquiry, had stumbled into a cache of damning evidence, thanks largely to Kenneth J. Kreig, a twenty-six-year-old Pentagon intern who was a minor functionary on the twenty-three-member staff serving the board. Kreig had served a stint in the NSC's Crisis Management Center and, like many his age, was conversant with computer technology in a way that his elders were not. The FBI and the special prosecutor were by this time conducting their own parallel probes, but they had asked the White House only for the notes stored in Poindexter's and North's desk computers, most of which had been deliberately purged by Poindexter and his staff. But Kreig thought to ask if there were backup copies lodged in the computer's mainframe, where the NSC's purge might not have penetrated.

It was the right question. The mainframe computer spewed forth reams of information, tens of thousands of secret PROFS notes previously believed destroyed, documenting thousands of sensitive conversations between McFarlane, Poindexter, North, and others. Like the Watergate tapes fourteen years earlier, these computer transcripts provided a vivid trail of evidence. The notes were so intimate and unguarded that it was as if someone had eavesdropped on two years of private conversations at the highest levels of the NSC.

But the Tower board was almost out of time. They asked for and received a one-week extension merely to digest the new PROFS notes. But even in the little time they had, they could now see indisputably that, contrary to Poindexter's professions of absent-mindedness, he was deeply involved in both the arms deals and the diversion of funds. As Brent Scowcroft later put it, "Ollie North was not a loose cannon. He communicated extensively with Poindexter at every step." It was the first serious link upward in the chain of command.

As the investigation intensified, so did the pressure on those who were its targets. The night before the cache of PROFS notes was found, Bud McFarlane stayed up late, working at his home computer. He was scheduled to appear before the Tower board for a third session the next day, but apparently he could no longer face the panel, which included two of his former mentors, Scowcroft and Tower. He knew that he had given his word of honor to Congress that the NSC had not solicited foreign contributions for the contras, but now the truth was coming out. McFarlane brooded until almost midnight. He wrote letters to his lawyer, Leonard Garment, and to members of the House and Senate Intelligence committees, apologizing for concealing the Saudi contributions. He also wrote a note to his wife. Then he swallowed at least twenty Valium pills. His wife discovered him, unconscious, in the morning. An ambulance rushed him to nearby Bethesda Naval Hospital, where he slowly recovered. McFarlane's suicide attempt marked not only a personal tragedy but also a growing national sense that the administration's troubles ran much deeper than anyone imagined.

While he was recovering in the hospital, McFarlane got a phone call from the president that meant a great deal to him. In the White House McFarlane had anguished over his inability to win more respect and support from Reagan, but now that he had so obviously undergone a wrenching trauma, the president responded to his personal plight. "It was the first time," McFarlane later recalled, "that I felt a genuine relationship of respect."

The president was meanwhile increasingly befuddled about his own role in the affair. Two days after McFarlane's suicide attempt, on February 11, the president met again with the Tower board in the Oval Office. Again he was asked whether he had authorized the August arms shipment in advance. This time Reagan replied, "That reminds me of something." He searched the top of his desk for the aide-mémoire that Regan and Wallison had prepared for him and read aloud the portion about his surprise at learning of the Israeli shipment. The president also inadvertently read out loud the instructions his staff had included for him on the aide-mémoire: "You might want to go back over the question [of the arms shipment] for the Tower board."

It was the investigators' turn to be flabbergasted. They inspected the memo, and pressed him gently on how it had been prepared. When the president explained that Regan and Wallison had helped him with it, there was a sense of incredulity in the room. The overwhelming impression, one participant said, was "shock at the president's ignorance."

One week later, on February 18, the story of Reagan's flip-flop appeared in the *Los Angeles Times;* on the next day it ran in the *Washington Post.* The news accounts, though understated and lacking detail, conveyed a devastating picture; the public now glimpsed a president too feeble to recall his own decisions, and so malleable that he had let others push him into contradicting himself.

On February 20, Reagan sent off an unprecedented note of presidential clarification to the Tower board. (By now, David Abshire so distrusted Regan that he refused to show the chief of staff an advance copy.) It read: "I'm afraid that I let myself be influenced by others' recollections, not my own. . . . I have no personal notes or records to help my recollection on the matter. The only honest answer is that try as I might, I cannot recall anything whatsoever about whether I approved an Israeli sale in advance, or whether I approved replenishment of Israeli stocks around August of 1985. My answer therefore — and the simple truth is, 'I don't remember — period.' "

Yet another blow to the president's credibility came one day later, this time from McFarlane. Speaking to the Tower board from his hospital room, McFarlane provided new details of his actions over the past months. He explained that he had participated in a cover-up meant to aggrandize Reagan's motives as having been diplomatic; he had not told the truth, which was that for the president the Iranian initiative had been primarily an emotional attempt to get back the hostages. McFarlane's confession was expressed in his typically ponderous fashion: "It has been, I think, misleading, at least, and wrong, at worst, for me to overly gild the president's motives for his decision in this — to portray them as mostly directed toward political outcomes. The president acknowledged those and recognized that those were clearly important. However, by the tenor of his questioning, which was oriented toward the hostages and the timing of the hostages, from his recurrent, virtually daily questioning just about welfare and 'Do we have anything new?' and so forth, it is very clear that his concerns here were for the return of the hostages."

Reagan, whose leadership had rested in his ability to move the nation to suspend disbelief, now seemed to be the only one left who believed his own story.

By Valentine's Day, one former aide later said, Reagan had finally agreed with his wife that Donald Regan had to go. The president's resolve was strengthened by Regan's part in convincing him to switch his testimony to the Tower board. The publicity about the flip-flop had been excruciating. Regan could argue legitimately that he had only been trying to serve the truth, which he saw resting with him and against McFarlane; but it was also true that his preoccupation with this issue was at least in part a matter of self-interest, and it had blinded him from seeing or serving the president's broader interests.

Regan's other fatal miscalculation — underestimating the importance of Nancy Reagan — had also caught up with him by this time. The tensions between the two were now out in the open; Mrs. Reagan routinely asked the chief of staff with mock surprise, "Oh, are you still here, Don?" On February 8, the feud reached a climax. During a lengthy telephone call, the first lady and the chief of staff argued furiously about whether the president should hold a press conference. Mrs. Reagan did not believe her husband was well enough to resume his full schedule; she had always understood his physical and psychological limits best, and she did not want him to hold a press conference until March. But Regan was desperate to get the president out into broad daylight — giving speeches, holding press conferences, doing anything possible to dispel the growing perception that Reagan might not have "the mental vigor . . . to undertake the repairwork necessary," as Washington's most influential political columnist, David Broder, wrote. (Regan later declared that he suspected Mrs. Reagan's hesitation was based on her astrological beliefs, which he viewed as maddeningly irrational — and, in this instance, dangerous to the presidency. While this may have been true, it has to be noted that members of the Tower board as well as other outsiders who saw the president during this period described him as physically and psychologically drained.) The conversation between the two soon became acrimonious, and their relationship effectively ended when both parties apparently slammed their receivers down simultaneously. Mrs. Reagan soon told her husband about the fight, and he was so appalled at Regan's rudeness that some White House aides suspected that his wife had provoked the confrontation simply to sway him against the chief of staff. And swayed he was: when asked by reporters whether he thought his chief of staff should quit, the president no longer protested. Instead, he shrugged and said, "Well, this is up to him."

In many respects, Mrs. Reagan became the de facto chief of staff. She supervised a talent search for Regan's replacement. And she commandeered plans for the president's response to the Tower board report, which was to be released on February 26. Other than the occasional photo opportunity and the State of the Union address, the president had been in virtual seclusion since his operation. He hadn't answered questions from reporters on the scandal since November 25 and hadn't held a press conference since November 19. So, in Mrs. Reagan's eyes, his public reaction to what was now expected to be a devastating report was clearly of critical importance. Mrs. Reagan again insisted on a speechwriter from outside the White House to draft the president's remarks. This time she chose Landon Parvin, the young writer who had so deftly handled Bush's address in December. By now, distrust of the White House staff ran so deep that arrangements were made for the speech to be typed in a secret office in the Old Executive Office Building; the regular White House speechwriters, who were in contact with Regan, wouldn't see it. Although Regan's staff continued to hold meetings about the speech, they were not permitted to see the drafts.

Mrs. Reagan also had definite ideas about what the speech should say. As she explained her ideas to one confidant, she assumed her husband's voice, speaking in the first person as if she were the president. Notes of the conversation show her saying, "I welcome the report. I'm angry. I'm disappointed. I've been deceived by my staff." Still impersonating him, she said, "Of course I remember giving the go-ahead [for the Israeli arms sale] — I just don't remember what day it was."

Meanwhile, Regan and his aides were making a valiant attempt to look as though they were still doing business as usual. They informed Parvin that he had been chosen by Regan to do the speech — at least a week after he had already started work. The belated display of authority was faintly ridiculous. It was clear to Parvin that "at this point, there was no real power center in the White House. Things were just falling apart."

Regan was aware of the maneuvers to replace him, but he was determined to stay on for at least a few days after the release of the Tower report. Several news organizations, among them ABC News and *Newsweek* magazine, had left the strong impression that the chief of staff would be implicated by the report in a cover-up — a charge that was far from true — so Regan wanted to clear his name. His plan was to hang on unless the president fired him personally — a confrontation he knew Reagan would do almost anything to avoid. Short of that, Regan proved impervious to an assortment of hints and prods that would have shamed most men. In mid-February, Abshire forthrightly urged Regan to resign. The chief of staff heard him out politely, then asked him for "a memo" on his thoughts. On Monday morning, February 23, three days before the Tower report was expected, Bush called Regan into his office and suggested discreetly that he should "stick your head into the Oval Office and talk to the president about your situation." Bush, who had previously been loath to confront Regan directly, had not become an informal intermediary at his own instigation. He was acting at the request of Stuart Spencer, who was still working with the First Lady to dislodge Regan. Clearly, no one trusted the president to do the job himself.

Regan later said he did talk to the president about his status. Shortly after talking with Bush on that Monday, he entered the Oval Office and asked when the president wanted him to leave. After some uncomfortable shifting in his chair, Reagan shocked him by suggesting that "now" sounded fine to him. Regan, who had never let anyone thwart him in his entire professional career, exploded. "You can't do that to me!" he yelled. "I deserve better treatment than that!" The president was apparently intimidated by the display. He finally asked Regan what he thought would be a proper timetable. The two agreed that the following Monday, March 2, sounded fine.

Reagan's presidency was now completely reactive: in the first term his administration had set an entirely new political agenda, but now it waited for a group of outsiders to render a verdict. As the release date of the Tower report approached, the president's aides jockeyed furiously about who would have to brief Reagan on its contents. Those around him evidently believed that they could mold his reaction to the report by their own. Thus Abshire, working in tandem with Mrs. Reagan, was adamant that Regan should have no chance to meet alone with the president about the report before it was released, thereby cutting short Regan's opportunity to turn the president against it. Regan, who understood the value of a private chat with the president as well as anyone, was positively livid.

But Abshire won, and neither the president nor his chief of staff was given any chance to digest the report in private. Instead, at 10:00 A.M. on February 26 in the Cabinet Room, just an hour before the president was to receive the 304-page report in public, the board briefed him and an assortment of aides — including Regan — about its contents.

The board members sat in the high-backed leather chairs that flanked the long cabinet table. As they enumerated their criticisms, the president, who had downplayed every aspect of the scandal, grew "flustered," said one participant, by the harshness of their conclusions. He argued that he set policy, and his policy had never been to trade arms for hostages. One board member, Brent Scowcroft, was incredulous. "Mr. President," he said, "there were occasions when the aircraft loaded with weapons was sitting on the runway, waiting for word that the hostages had been freed." The president looked surprised and confused — "shaken," said one board member. At 11:00 A.M., the rest of the country got to see why.

In the Old Executive Office Building, another board member, Edmund Muskie, read a devastating bill of particulars to an auditorium crammed with reporters and television cameras. The report gently couched its criticisms of Reagan in terms of his "management style," and it accepted at face value many of his professions of ignorance. The board had had too little time to discover many of the specifics of the NSC's secret operations. But this unimpeachable panel of three of the country's most experienced public servants gave the nation its first irrefutable glimpse of a presidency out of control.

In Section Four of the report, "What Went Wrong," the panel described the Iranian initiative as flawed from the start by contradictory policies; indeed, the arms sales would be likely to encourage the "most radical" elements in Iran to continue terrorist actions. And it found "the president's staff doing what Congress forbade" in Nicaragua and Iran without adequate legal authority and with "no serious effort . . . to come to grips with the risks to the president." Still more damaging, the report gently but squarely pinned the responsibility on the president, concluding, "The NSC system will not work unless the president makes it work. . . . The president did not seem to be aware of the way in which the operation was implemented and the full consequences of U.S. participation. He did not force his policy to undergo the most critical review . . . at no time did he insist upon accountability." In the end, the report traced an extraordinary web of deception and incompetence. It had been spun by military men obsessed with secrecy, unchecked and indeed passively condoned by a disengaged president who, as the Republican stalwart John Tower told the assembled reporters, "clearly didn't understand the nature of this operation, who was involved, and what was happening." Summarizing the board's conclusions, Scowcroft told the press that "the problem, at the heart, was one of people, not process." Reagan, visibly crestfallen, received the report with a faltering promise to study it.

The Tower board had exceeded its original charter and diagnosed serious and chronic problems in the Reagan White House. And although it found the president ultimately responsible for the misdeeds of his own NSC, it assigned more sweeping blame to his chief of staff, Donald Regan, for failing, in essence, to act as the president's guardian. The report declared Regan responsible for the "chaos" that had descended upon the White House once the first disclosures occurred. "More than almost any Chief of Staff in recent memory," it concluded, "he asserted control over the White House staff and sought to extend this control to the National Security Adviser. He was personally active in national security affairs, and attended almost all the relevant meetings regarding the Iran initiative. He, as much as anyone, should have insisted that an orderly process be observed."

Regan had gambled that the report would exonerate him of crimes of commission, but he had again failed to see any larger responsibility for sins of omission. It would be Regan's last political miscalculation; contrary to his hopes, the report only added urgency to the search for his replacement.

Within hours of the report's release, Mrs. Reagan and a handful of friends — among them Michael Deaver, Paul Laxalt, Republican party chairman Frank Fahrenkopf, and pollster Richard Wirthlin — had all settled on Howard Baker as Regan's successor. But no one told the president until Laxalt presented the idea to him at an early afternoon meeting in the residence. Laxalt thought he could detect Reagan's enthusiasm for the idea; although the president said nothing definite, "his eyes sparkled." Save for this body language, however, Reagan was apparently no more active in choosing his new chief of staff than he had been two years earlier.

In a matter of hours, Reagan called Baker, who was vacationing in Florida. Deaver had already laid the groundwork earlier that day, but by the time Reagan called, Baker's wife, Joy, told him that her husband was at the zoo with his grandchildren. "Great," the president replied. "Wait until he sees the zoo I have in mind."

The next morning, Friday, February 27, Baker was back in Washington. He was spirited through the side gate into the White House. In the elegant privacy of the Reagans' living room, surrounded by Impressionist paintings and monogrammed pillows, the president offered him the job. He accepted it immediately. Laxalt was also there, and he and Baker both warned the president that it was almost inevitable that the news would leak out. But the president resisted making any announcement until Monday. They had been telling him for days that he had to face Regan. But, said one confidant, "he was very uncomfortable about it." Reagan insisted that any announcement would have to wait. That was the agreement.

Mrs. Reagan was still unhappy. She thought it would be disastrous if Regan tried to stay on through the president's "comeback" speech, which Landon Parvin was writing for delivery early the following week. She called David Abshire and urged him to convince her husband that the news could not hold.

Don Regan, meanwhile, remained in the dark. The same afternoon that Baker and the president met to plan Baker's promotion, Regan was obliviously putting his own "spin" on his retirement, arranging interviews with the *New York Times* and *Time* magazine to inform them that he would be resigning the following Monday. He explained to two reporters from *Time*, shortly after 3:00 P.M., that he had been determined "not to be drummed out of office." Stoutly defending his performance, he offered a mathematical analysis of the Tower report meant to quantify his own innocence: only fifteen lines mentioned him, he said, so only "2.5 percent" of the blame was his. He told the reporters that he thought "the president regrets my leaving in many ways."

But Mrs. Reagan had already ensured that his final public relations effort would be rudely preempted. By midmorning, her friends were spreading the rumor of Baker's appointment. When reporters called her office to check further, she told her press secretary that it would be fine to tell them that she wished Regan "good luck" and "welcomed Howard Baker." The fact that this deliberate leak violated the president's wishes apparently mattered little.

By the time the chief of staff finished telling the reporters from *Time* that he would stay on the job until Monday, national security adviser Frank Carlucci was in his outer office with news reports suggesting otherwise. As the reporters left, Carlucci leaped up, entered Regan's office, and closed the door. Moments later, Regan grabbed his coat and dictated a twenty-two-word letter to his secretary that was as thankless and blunt as his tenure had been:

Dear Mr. President:

I hereby resign as Chief of Staff to the President of the United States.

Respectfully yours, Donald T. Regan.

As the copies of Regan's terse letter of resignation reached the wooden bins in the press room, the stately White House complex seemed unusually exposed and uncharacteristically chaotic. Reporters were staking out every entrance and mobbing the hallways. All over the West Wing, telephones were pealing. The chief of staff's office was empty, and no one was certain which of his aides — several of whom had coincidentally resigned that day — remained behind.

Upstairs in the residence, Reagan had read about half of the Tower report. He had been particularly stunned by the appendices, where the PROFS notes were reproduced. "I had no idea these things were going on," he confessed to his wife, his political adviser Stuart Spencer, and Parvin, who had gathered to assess the damage and plan his comeback speech.

"I can see why people might think we were trading arms for hostages," Reagan said. "But we weren't —"

"You can't say that in the speech!" the others replied in unison.

The president fell silent.

The conversation turned to the subject of his former aides. Mrs. Reagan praised McFarlane as having acted the most "honorably." There were acid comments about Regan's impetuous exit. But Reagan just shrugged and said nothing.

Howard Baker, meanwhile, had returned to his law offices in downtown Washington. In deference to the president's request, he remained sequestered, ducking phone calls, particularly from the press. One caller, however, got through: on the line for Senator Baker was the attorney general of the United States.

"Howard," said the voice on the other end of the phone, "I think you better get over to the White House. Don Regan's left."

Baker listened, then tried to put Meese off: "Ed, the problem is that the president doesn't want it out until Monday. I gave him my word."

The attorney general seemed not to hear. "Howard," he said again, slowly, "I think you better get over to the White House. There's no one in charge."

Epilogue

POLITICS IS A BATTLE over public perceptions, and for Ronald Reagan the battle was all but lost. Six years into his remarkable presidency, with two years yet to go, the Reagan era seemed prematurely over. Reagan could still walk through the practiced motions of his office, but the performance would never again be as convincing. It was as if the house lights had come on too early, the artifice laid bare.

In time, Reagan would recover both his jauntiness and most of his popularity. He would send budgets to Congress, inveigh against the federal deficit, and travel to Moscow; and he would retain, throughout, a strong measure of the public's affection. But although much of his self-assurance would return, the public's confidence in his leadership, which had been essential to his success, was never completely restored. Never again did he recapture the extraordinary hold on the national imagination that he had enjoyed from 1981 through 1986. Nor did his administration ever regain the political initiative. There was no last opportunity to advance the policies that true believers had called the Reagan Revolution. Their moment was gone; the chance was lost. As a commanding political force, Ronald Reagan was unmade.

Public opinion polls, the index of performance so beloved by his aides, reflected the change. Through 1987 and most of 1988, Reagan's approval rating hovered around the 50 percent mark, a precipitous drop from his 1986 high of 70 percent but a respectable figure for a second-term president. And while a large majority still believed him to be a decent man, the number who saw him as a strong leader plunged from 75 to 56 percent. Reagan himself had not changed, yet he seemed somehow diminished. Even Republicans lost some of their enthusiasm; when GOP voters were asked in 1988 if they would vote for Reagan again if they had the chance, only 40 percent said yes. Another poll, in May 1988, found that most voters wanted the next president to "set the nation on a new direction," not to "keep the country moving in the same direction that Ronald Reagan has been taking."

The decline in Reagan's political clout was apparent in Congress as well. The White House had gradually lost control over the agenda on Capitol Hill ever since 1982, but by the end of the second term the battle turned into a rout. In 1987 and 1988, the *Congressional Quarterly* found that Reagan's success rate in the legislature — the percentage of issues on which his position carried the day — had fallen to the lowest point since ratings were first compiled in 1953. Congress began to override presidential vetoes, including one on a highway spending bill that Reagan quixotically proclaimed a test of his remaining influence. In October 1987, the Senate rejected Reagan's nomination of Robert H. Bork to the Supreme Court, the first such repudiation in seventeen years and a bitter blow to a president who had vowed to remake the court in his conservative image. And in February 1988, the House of Representatives ignored desperate pleas from the White House and killed military aid for the contras — the same action that had prompted Casey, McFarlane, and North to launch their search for off-the-books funding four years earlier.

Reagan's power also waned abroad. In Nicaragua, the contras' guerrilla campaign began to disintegrate, and the CIA quietly disengaged from its crusade to overthrow the Sandinistas. In Panama, military dictator Manuel Antonio Noriega publicly thumbed his nose at Reagan's attempts to oust him from power, a tragicomic demonstration of American impotence. In the Middle East, U.S. relations with Iran, instead of improving, deteriorated badly; far from dealing with Tehran "moderates," the United States turned to gunboat diplomacy, sending the navy into the Persian Gulf to confront — this time successfully — the same Iranian forces that Reagan had helped to rearm. And in Beirut, nine American hostages remained in helpless captivity; when Reagan began his arms deals with Iran, there had been only seven.

There were still some bright spots, especially in U.S.-Soviet relations. Reagan and Gorbachev held summit meetings in Washington and in Moscow and concluded a treaty to abolish intermediate-range nuclear weapons. The agreement was at least partly a payoff for Reagan's steadfast insistence that arms control concessions would come from the Soviet Union, not the United States. But progress in other, more critical aspects of arms control remained slow, and the new era of good feelings came only at the expense of some of the president's most cherished beliefs. During the Moscow summit of 1988, while he was strolling happily in Red Square, Reagan was asked about his once-fervent condemnation of the Soviet Union as "an evil empire." "You are talking about another time," the president replied, "another era." A presidency once known for its ideological fervor now seemed to be devolving into a series of pleasing photo opportunities.

Reagan's defeats in both the domestic and international arenas revealed his diminishing ability to exercise the most fundamental power of his office: the power to persuade. Without that power, as many of his predecessors had discovered, there was little left. ("I sit here all day trying to persuade people to do the things they ought to have sense enough to do without my persuading them," Harry Truman once groused. "That's all the powers of the president amount to.") During Reagan's first term, this had been power enough. But Reagan had never been able to match his initial legislative success again. And after the reelection, as his frustration grew and his popularity emboldened him, he instead tried to use the unilateral powers of his office to impose his policy in Nicaragua against the will of Congress and to pursue his secret policy in Iran against the will of the public. His overreaching stemmed, in part, from a misreading of his mandate; in part, from an ill-conceived staff system, which replaced the safeguards of the Baker-Meese-Deaver troika with Donald Regan's unwitting prescription for disaster: "Let Reagan be Reagan."

In 1987 and 1988, Reagan seemed the last to understand why his credibility had foundered, the last to see that the Iran-contra affair was not just an unpleasant anomaly but a reflection of his own failure of leadership. In both Iran and Nicaragua, Reagan had attempted to achieve difficult ends without incurring high political costs. In Iran, he had sought a shortcut to free American hostages without paying the high price that a serious policy against terrorism demanded. In Nicaragua, he had tried to overthrow a government without bearing the costs of war. In both cases, he bought short-term popularity at the expense of candor; in both cases, he deceived not only the public but himself as well.

Only once, in the immediate aftermath of the Tower report, did Reagan admit that he had made an error on Iran. In his March 4, 1987, speech, the one that Landon Parvin wrote at the First Lady's request, Reagan conceded, "What began as a strategic opening to Iran deteriorated, in its implementation, into trading arms for hostages. It was a mistake." But it had taken frantic arguments from his aides to get the president to deliver the speech as it was written. As soon as the heat was off, he quickly slid back into his comforting old rationalizations: he had not traded arms for hostages, he had not dealt with the followers of Ayatollah Khomeini. His stubborn insistence on these fictions was apparent during the summer of 1987, when congressional investigators unearthed a copy of the initial finding under which he had approved the November 1985 HAWK shipment to Iran. White House aides were dismayed to see the real purpose of the arms sale spelled out in black and white: "Material and munitions may be provided to the government of Iran, which is taking steps to facilitate the release of the hostages." But when they handed the document to Reagan, he read it quickly — and beamed. "It doesn't say arms are being swapped for hostages," he said triumphantly.

In later interviews, Reagan blithely rearranged the history of the Iranian deals, just as he had revised his memories of earlier episodes in his career. People had misunderstood "the Iran-contra so-called affair," he said; missiles had not gone to Khomeini. Instead, he claimed, the Iranians with whom he dealt were "individuals not in the government, not government forces of Iran."

The president also seemed to ignore the findings of the three months of hearings that Congress held on the Iran-contra affair in the summer of 1987. "Let me give you an ironic thing," he told a reporter in October of that year. "After all the weeks of this big hearing and all the hours of testimony, they still have not come up with the answer that I was seeking. Who raised the price [of the weapons]? Who got the added money? And where did it go? Not one word of evidence has ever been given on that subject." In fact, the hearings answered all three questions in exhaustive detail.

As for North and Poindexter, who had almost brought down his presidency, Reagan was astonishingly indulgent. North, he said several times, was a "hero"; Poindexter was "an honorable man." Not once did he condemn North's diversion of funds as legally or constitutionally wrong. Not once did he evince alarm that Poindexter had sold U.S. weapons at a profit to finance an unauthorized covert operation. Not once did he object to the idea of an off-the-books team that could undertake secret projects in the name of the United States without complying with the law.

"I feel that I have to recognize that whatever happened, they must have felt that somehow they were protecting me," he said of North and Poindexter. "My own personal belief is that they were not involved in anything that was breaking the law." To work for Reagan, it seemed, was to be forgiven all sins. And his endorsement of North and Poindexter appeared part of a larger rationale: if they had done nothing wrong, then he had done nothing wrong.

But the public's judgment of Reagan's role in the scandal was less forgiving. Congress's three months of hearings turned into a televised seminar on what had gone wrong inside the administration. And although the hearings produced one major piece of good news for Reagan — they saved him from the specter of impeachment on the narrow question of whether he had approved the diversion — they also provided a devastating portrait of a feckless presidency. Testifying under oath, shorn of their usual ability to evade tough questions, Reagan's closest aides described a president who bore almost no resemblance to the protean leader that had been constructed by the White House staff. McFarlane testified that Reagan's decisionmaking process was "intrinsically unworkable." Poindexter testified that the president had been obsessed with the hostages. Shultz told of endless guerrilla warfare and described the president's inability to grasp the truth of what the Iranian arms deals had become. The testimony flatly refuted White House denials that Reagan had ever swapped arms for hostages or directed fund-raising efforts for the contras. Even on the signal issue of the diversion, polls found that a majority of the public believed the president was lying.

The final judgment of the congressional committees was polite but unsparing. Even the president's staunchest defenders said they were profoundly disturbed by what they had learned. A bipartisan majority concluded that the president had, in fact, violated his oath of office. Congress had no stomach for the idea of impeaching Ronald Reagan in the last year of his tenure, but the committees gently charged him with an impeachable offense all the same.

"The Constitution requires the president to 'take care that the laws be faithfully executed.' This charge encompasses a responsibility to leave the members of his administration in no doubt that the rule of law governs," the committees' majority concluded in their final report. "It was the president's policy — not an isolated decision by North or Poindexter — to sell arms secretly to Iran and to maintain the contras 'body and soul,' the Boland amendment notwithstanding. . . . For failing to take care that the law reigned supreme, the president bears the responsibility."

On Wednesday, March 16, 1988, a federal grand jury in Washington, D.C., charged Oliver North, John Poindexter, Richard Secord, and Albert Hakim with conspiracy to defraud the United States, theft of government property, and other crimes. The four defendants pleaded not guilty.

Robert McFarlane, who had publicly confessed his own failings, pleaded guilty that same month to four counts of withholding information from Congress, a misdemeanor. The reduced charge was part of a plea bargain under which McFarlane agreed to testify against his old protégé, Oliver North.

Spitz Channell and his public relations man, Richard Miller, pleaded guilty to conspiracy to defraud the government of taxes by soliciting tax-deductible contributions for the purpose of arming the contras. One of Channell's organizations was stripped of its tax-exempt status, but the fund-raiser soon went back to work, seeking more donations for the contra cause.

At the CIA, the two senior clandestine officers who had helped the contras in the field, Joe Fernandez and Jim Adkins, were fired after a long investigation; in June 1988, Fernandez was indicted on charges of conspiracy to defraud the United States, the first CIA station chief ever indicted for exceeding his formal instructions. Four others were formally reprimanded, including Duane Clarridge, who had served as Oliver North's mentor inside the agency; Alan Fiers, who had run the contra war in 1985 and 1986; and Charles Allen, the intelligence analyst who had found himself miscast as Manucher Ghorbanifar's case officer. Deputy director Robert M. Gates, who had been nominated to succeed William Casey as director, withdrew his nomination in the face of serious opposition in Congress.

In the cabinet, Shultz, vindicated, stayed on as secretary of state. Weinberger resigned as secretary of defense; his successor, Frank Carlucci, was a former State Department official with more centrist views.

Nevertheless, the State Department and the Pentagon still did not get along on many issues, and Reagan's new national security adviser, Lieutenant General Colin L. Powell, like his predecessors, did not always have the power to break the stalemate.

Well before Reagan left office, his own former aides, Regan, Deaver, and Speakes, published a series of unflattering memoirs. Regan reported that Mrs. Reagan had turned to an astrologer to guide her decisions on the president's schedule; Deaver portrayed his longtime chief as an amiable but frequently befuddled man; Speakes confessed that he had confected bogus statements from Reagan when the Great Communicator was being outtalked by Gorbachev.

Of the indicted conspirators, North was the first to go on trial, in February 1989. At the defendant's table, in a blue civilian suit (he retired from the Marine Corps in 1988), he seemed smaller and more subdued than the cocky officer of the congressional hearings.

North's tenacious defense lawyer, Brendan V. Sullivan, Jr., forced the prosecutor to drop his main charge, conspiracy to defraud the government, by demanding the release of thousands of secret documents. Sullivan's argument was that the complete record of the Reagan administration's covert operations would show that diverting profits from Iranian arms deals hadn't been so unusual after all. But the new Bush administration refused to open the records, leaving the prosecution little choice but to drop the conspiracy charge.

North still faced twelve more counts, ranging from misleading Congress and Attorney General Meese to misusing the traveler's checks that the contras had placed in his care. He based his defense on the argument that his superiors — Reagan, Bush, McFarlane, and Poindexter — had authorized his every move. "I had been led to believe that everything I was doing was done at the direction of the president," North testified. "What's the difference between what Oliver North did and what the president did?" Sullivan demanded in his closing statement to the jury. Reagan "threw him overboard."

But Reagan and Bush refused to testify in North's defense, and in their absence, the prosecution inflicted new damage on his once-heroic image. One of North's NSC colleagues warned, "With Colonel North, you could never be certain if what he told you was true or fantasy." Perhaps most damning, an NSC administrative officer told of how North had been chronically, almost comically, short of cash until the middle of 1985 — about the same time Calero began providing him with money from Saudi Arabia's contributions. After that, North managed to buy a $7,000 horse for his daughter and an $8,000 van for cash; he explained that the money came from a "family fund" he had amassed in a tin strongbox with "change out of my pocket."

The jury was persuaded by some of North's defense, but not all. On May 4, 1989, North was convicted of three of the twelve charges: destroying government documents, aiding and abetting an attempt to mislead Congress (during the attempted cover-up of November 1986) and accepting "an illegal gratuity" in the form of a $13,800 home security system that Secord had paid for. Those were the charges on which his claim of approval from higher-ups was least credible. On the other nine, where his argument that he acted according to orders seemed plausible, he was acquitted.

On hearing the verdict, North broke into his wide, gap-toothed grin and kissed his wife. Then he told reporters that he intended to appeal his three convictions. "We are absolutely confident of the final outcome," he said. "As a marine, I was taught to fight and fight hard as long as it takes to prevail. We will continue this battle, and with the support and prayers of the American people we will be fully vindicated."

North was, indeed, winning support from at least some of the American people. His defense fund, with the help of sophisticated mailing lists and glossy photographs of North and his family, swelled to hundreds of thousands of dollars; North himself drew as much as $25,000 an appearance making patriotic speeches. A national poll found that 52 percent of the country believed he deserved a pardon.

But no pardon was forthcoming. On July 5, 1989, U.S. District Judge Gerhard A. Gesell sentenced North to a three-year suspended sentence, with two years probation, 1,200 hours of community service in drug rehabilitation, and a fine of $150,000.

Every presidential election is partly a referendum on the administration in power. George Bush, in his 1988 presidential campaign, unexpectedly found the Reagan record a burden as well as an asset. The Iran-contra affair raised the same questions about Bush's judgment and credibility as it had about Reagan's. The vice president had supported Reagan's decisions throughout the Iranian initiative; although he later said he had harbored reservations about some aspects of the deal, none of his colleagues in the cabinet remembered his raising any specific objections. And the vice president's accounts of his own knowledge of the hostage dealings raised as many questions as they answered. Bush insisted that the deals had not been driven by a simple desire to free the hostages, but said at the same time that his highest concern had been to free William Buckley, the kidnapped CIA officer. And Bush claimed that he didn't know that arms had been traded for hostages until he was informed by the Senate Intelligence Committee in December 1986, even though the minutes of earlier meetings showed convincingly that the deals were described to him in detail in both July and November of that year.

There was also the question of how deeply the vice president was involved in clandestine support for the contras. Several aides on Bush's staff left a strange trail of documents that seemed to demonstrate that they knew of North's secret operation to provide guns to the rebels, but they stoutly denied any such understanding. During the campaign year, a parade of gun runners and drug dealers claimed that Bush's associates had known of schemes to help the contras with cocaine money; the charges came with little or no supporting evidence, but they were of no help to the Bush campaign.

Like Reagan, Bush was remarkably solicitous of North and Poindexter. In 1985, Bush had written an effusive note to North, praising him for his work on the hostages and Central America; a spokesman later suggested, not very convincingly, that the vice president must have been referring to work North had done on El Salvador two years earlier. North told friends that he considered the vice president one of his chief sponsors in the White House.

After North and Poindexter had been disgraced, Bush offered them a gesture of loyalty. Echoing Reagan, he called North "a hero," and at the end of 1987, as the two former aides were heading for indictment by a federal grand jury, Bush pointedly put them on the guest list for his official Christmas party. During his 1988 presidential campaign, Bush told reporters, "My own personal hope is that they are found innocent of any wrongdoing. I think they made some mistakes, but that doesn't mean one is guilty of some crime until the system works." Asked whether he still considered North a hero, the candidate replied, "Anybody who wins three Purple Hearts and gets a Silver Star fighting for his country and bleeding for it in Vietnam is a hero, absolutely."

And after the split verdict in North's trial in May 1989, President Bush hailed the acquittals as well. "As you know, I wanted all along to see him exonerated," he said. The implicit message was clear: North and his accomplices may have lied and violated their constitutional oaths, but in Bush's eyes they had still served the nation well.

After his election in November 1988, evidence suggesting that Bush had been more deeply involved in North's exploits than he acknowledged continued to trickle from the government's secret archives. Documents released during North's trial showed that Bush was informed of Honduras's secret help for the contras in 1985 and that he may have helped persuade the Hondurans to increase their assistance to the rebels in exchange for accelerated aid and assurances of military protection. "The Hondurans seem to regard [this] as the main quid pro quo for cooperating with the FDN [contras]," McFarlane advised Reagan and Bush in a memo at the time.

Nevertheless, Bush insisted that there had never been a quid pro quo. "I can now state declaratively, without any fear of contradiction, that there wasn't," he told reporters.

Some in Congress and in the public remained skeptical. "We still need to know a lot more about then–Vice President Bush's activities," said Lee Hamilton, chairman of the House Iran-Contra Committee. "These documents . . . clearly reveal the involvement of the vice president to a greater degree than he has acknowledged heretofore." A poll taken after North's trial found that 64 percent of the public believed that Bush was "hiding something" about his actions as vice president; another found that 51 percent believed the new president had lied.

But the doubts about Bush's veracity did not seem to affect his popularity, apparently because the public's interest in the scandal had faded. And Bush easily waved off reporters' questions about the truth behind his role in the affair.

"I think it was set to rest in the last election," he said.

In fact, the 1988 presidential campaign had failed notably to illuminate Bush's role in the Iran-contra affair. In part this was because the Democratic nominee, Massachusetts Governor Michael Dukakis, largely ignored the issue. The Democrats' reticence stemmed as much from indecision as from any master plan. Some in the Dukakis campaign argued that the Iran-contra affair was a losing issue no matter how it was handled. They pointed to internal polls that showed that the public was as confused as it was outraged. And they noted that the press had largely lost interest in the scandal after concluding that it was not a replay of Watergate. As Democratic strategist Thomas Donilon later put it, "We could gain ground more quickly" with other issues. "The Iran-contra affair was complicated," he explained. "It was difficult to come up with a one-minute-and-twenty-second confrontation on it."

Yet a clutch of other campaign advisers insisted that Dukakis could use the scandal to advantage. They went so far as to hire a full-time research consultant, who helped to draft a number of potential attacks against Bush. But Dukakis resisted such "negative tactics." Eventually, in the campaign's final weeks, he agreed to press questions about Bush's credibility stemming from the scandal. But by then Dukakis was preoccupied with his own defense against being labeled a "Massachusetts liberal" and had little time to mount an offense.

John Sears, Reagan's former campaign manager, believed the Democrats' failure to attack Bush on the Iran-contra affair amounted to a serious tactical error. "It was a very powerful issue, and I couldn't understand why the Democrats weren't making something of it," he said after Bush's victory. "I think the Democrats were fooled by Reagan's personal popularity. They didn't understand that they could still point out his shortcomings. They were afraid to take Reagan on, so they dropped the whole thing."

Reagan's sullied second term nonetheless had some effect on the election returns. Compared with Walter Mondale's 1984 campaign, Dukakis did better, not just in his native New England, but also in states like Wisconsin, Iowa, Washington, and Oregon — the so-called good-government states, where there is a tradition of progressive, reform politics. Fueling the Democratic gains in these states, suggested political analyst Alan Baron, was a general concern about the so-called sleaze factor and a specific distaste for the Iran-contra affair.

Reagan's misadventures also had an effect on George Bush's campaign strategy. Although Bush ran as the candidate of Republican continuity who would maintain the successful economic policies of the Reagan era, in order to win he had to differentiate himself from Reagan and borrow some campaign themes that had traditionally belonged to the Democrats: education, environment, child care, and civil rights.

In the glory days after the 1980 and 1984 elections, Reagan's followers had dreamed of realigning the electorate for a generation to come, just as Franklin Roosevelt had done for the Democrats half a century earlier. But in 1988, the long-predicted Republican realignment remained as tentative as ever. Bush won the presidency in a near-landslide, with 54 percent of the popular vote and forty states — but those margins were closer than either of Reagan's. And the Democrats managed to increase their strength in both the Senate and the House of Representatives.

Reagan himself played a remarkably muted role in the campaign. He was seldom asked to share a stage with Bush because, according to the candidate's aides, the vice president needed to "define himself." Nor did Reagan barnstorm the country on behalf of congressional candidates as he had in 1986. After eight years of Reagan, the country was ready for a change, if only a measured one.

The same polls that buoyed Reagan's popularity now revealed a subtle shift in the public's perception of the president. After Bush's election, Reagan's popularity abruptly soared again to 63 percent — as if the public felt a wave of nostalgia once it realized he would be out of office for good. But however high his standing as a popular icon, Reagan had begun to pass, well before the end of his term, into a kind of early political retirement. His successes were celebrated in newspaper and television retrospectives, but most of the triumphs cited came from the first two years of his presidency, an era that was rapidly receding into memory. Some of his achievements appeared to be lasting, like the restoration of confidence in the office. By the end of 1988, though, Reagan himself was in no position to make use of his own legacy. "The polls showed that the public just wasn't worrying about Reagan anymore," William Schneider noted. "Increasingly, Reagan was ignored."

"The pulse of the life of the presidency moves by one rhythm: the making of decisions," Emmet John Hughes has written. "To know a presidency is to catch this rhythm. Yet there can be no secret to any presidency as difficult to discover as the riddle of precisely how even one decision came to be made." After the Iran-contra affair, the secret of the Reagan White House was out.

Although the presidency is tremendously visible, its inner workings are intensely private. And the public image of the Reagan White House was cropped especially well. The most astonishing aspect of the scandal was less its uncovering of specific misjudgments and policy failures than the unexpected glimpse it provided into the way that decisions were made in the Oval Office. As a result, a president who had personified American myth, first on the wide screen of the movies and later from the proscenium of the White House, was abruptly demythologized. He was still likable enough; he just wasn't the president many had believed him to be.

Viewed from outside as a powerful leader who had changed the course of America's political debate, Reagan showed little dynamism inside his own White House. His toughness dissolved in the face of human appeals. His decisiveness evaporated when the courtiers around him were at odds. He was strangely susceptible to the wiles of both his staff and his wife. Far from being a sophisticated manager, he rarely demanded accountability from subordinates. Too often, he crossed the line from delegation to abdication.

The Great Communicator, it turned out, was frequently incommunicative with those closest at hand. In critical policy decisions, Reagan often kept his thoughts to himself, leaving his aides to interpret his ambiguous signals as they pleased. He exuded manly bonhomie at a distance, yet seemed wooden and remote to those who worked with him. Magnetic in public and sometimes inspirational on the stump, behind the scenes he was both amiable and friendless, ill informed and incurious, trusting and careless, stubborn and passive, larger than life yet less than imagined.

Perhaps most disillusioning, the revelations showed that a president thought to possess a clear moral compass had lost his way. The core of Reagan's strength had been the public's perception that he was a man of his beliefs: he might compromise on the margins, but he would not sell out his principles wholesale. The shipments of weapons to Khomeini shook the foundations of this belief, squandering Reagan's moral authority, which by 1986 was the main asset of an administration whose intellectual energy had long since run low.

Reagan's fall from grace might have been less abrupt had his been a more conventional presidency. But Reagan had never amassed many of the tangible accomplishments of more traditional politicians. He was neither an adept administrator nor a master of the mundane intricacies of policy. His gift was for communication, particularly through television. His was a rhetorical presidency, capable at its best of uniting the country behind a common vision and moving the political center a long step to the right. But the Iran-contra affair revealed his rhetoric to be disconnected from his actions, and his actions to be disconnected from his policies. Ronald Reagan's talents had hidden his flaws too well; inevitably, his unmasking was his unmaking.

Acknowledgments

This book could not have been written without the generous help of a great many individuals who shared their time, thoughts, patience, and enthusiasm. In particular, we could not have embarked on this project without the support of both the *Wall Street Journal* and the *Los Angeles Times*. We are especially grateful to *Wall Street Journal* managing editor Norman Pearlstine and *Los Angeles Times* editor William F. Thomas as well as the papers' respective Washington bureau chiefs, Albert R. Hunt and Jack Nelson, who granted us leaves of absence and allowed us to work together despite the usual constraints of journalistic competition.

It is impossible to thank all of the colleagues who helped us along the way, but we are especially indebted to David Ignatius, who first read this work, and to Kenneth Bacon, Sidney Blumenthal, Tim Carrington, Richard T. Cooper, Thomas M. DeFrank, James Gerstenzang, Paul Gigot, Bob Greenberger, Roy Gutman, Joel Havemann, Ellen Hume, Doug Jehl, David Martin, Johanna Neuman, Ronald J. Ostrow, Barrett Seaman, Robert C. Toth, Cathy Trost, Owen Ullmann, John Walcott, and Michael Wines, all of whom took time out from their own busy beats to help this project. In addition, we are indebted to Lou Cannon, David Hoffman, and Garry Wills, on whose work we have drawn.

For this paperbound edition, we are also grateful to those readers of the hardcover edition who offered corrections, notably Cindy Arnson, A. Peter Burleigh, David Martin, Andrea Mitchell, and Peter Wallison.

In assembling this book, we have interviewed hundreds of sources, from cabinet officers to presidential relatives, many of whom cannot be publicly named; we are grateful to all of them. We owe special thanks to the several dozen current and former White House officials who talked with us, particularly those on the National Security Council staff, who provided insight into its workings. Many gave us help, although they no doubt do not share all of our assessments. Among those to whom we are especially grateful are Robert McFarlane; Donald Regan and his aides Thomas Dawson, Christopher Hicks, and Dennis Thomas; and Elliott Abrams, Cresencio Arcos, Lee Atwater, Michael Barnes, Patrick Buchanan, Mark Belnick, Adolfo Calero, James Cannon, Bruce Cameron, Linda Chavez, Charles Cooper, Iain Crawford, Arturo Cruz, Mitchell Daniels, Jr., Michael Deaver, Robert Duemling, Fred Fielding, Max Friedersdorf, Alexander Haig, William Henkel, Lee Hamilton, Ann Higgins, Mary Jo Jacobi, Robert Kagan, Kenneth Khachigian, Frederick Khedouri, Robert Kimmitt, James Lake, Arthur Liman, Bosco Matamoros, Langhorne Motley, Rodney McDaniel, Johnathan Miller, Lance Morgan, Robert Oakley, Robert Owen, Landon Parvin, William Perry, Nancy Reynolds, William Bradford Reynolds, Alfonso Robelo, Felix Rodriguez, Edward Rollins, John Sears, John Singlaub, Larry Speakes, Howard Teicher, Peter Wallison, and Richard Wirthlin. Thanks also to the president's friends, Holmes Tuttle and Paul Laxalt among them, and also to the many in Congress who helped us. We are also indebted to the Jenco family and Peggy Say. And we owe special thanks to Nelson Polsby, visiting professor at the Joan Shorenstein Barone Center for the Press, Politics and Public Policy at the John F. Kennedy School of Government, who opened to us the resources of Harvard University; to the Dartmouth College library; to Peter Kornbluh and Jeff Nason at the National Security Archive; to historians Barton Bernstein of Stanford and Theodore Mitchell of Dartmouth; and to political scholars Fred Greenstein, Richard Neustadt, Roger Porter, and William Schneider.

This work was prepared quickly, and though some errors may remain, there would be more had it not been for a talented team of research assistants, among them Aleta Embrey, Abebe Gessesse, Barclay Walsh, Barbara Yuill, and especially Karine Roesch.

We are deeply grateful to Raphael Sagalyn, who first saw the possibilities of this book and was able to make it happen. We owe tremendous thanks to our editor and partner at Houghton Mifflin, John Sterling. His unfailing creative energy brought this project to life, and he showed two daily journalists who thought they knew how to tell a story just how much more there was to learn. And special thanks as well to our manuscript editor, Luise Erdmann, who fought tirelessly to turn what passes for language in Washington into English.

Finally, our heartfelt thanks to our families and friends, especially Paula Copeland McManus and Richard Sauber, for their forbearance and humor in the face of this monumental preoccupation. They have made us understand why acknowledgments are written.

WASHINGTON, D.C.
June 1988

Notes on Sources

This book is based principally on more than two hundred interviews with Reagan administration officials, from cabinet members to White House clerks. It draws as well on the extraordinary and invaluable materials made available by the Tower Commission and the House and Senate Select committees on the Iran-contra affair, including more than 35,000 pages of testimony and more than 4,000 pages of documents; and, of course, on the body of work produced by the many reporters who have covered Ronald Reagan's second term.

We have attempted to provide clear attribution for all the information in this account. As is unavoidable in a story that touches on sensitive and sometimes officially secret government operations, some officials spoke only on the condition that they not be identified by name. In such cases, we have attempted to make it clear, at least, what prejudices and sympathies an unnamed source may bring along with his information.

President Reagan and Mrs. Reagan declined our requests for interviews, as did Rear Admiral John M. Poindexter and Lieutenant Colonel Oliver L. North.

Where dialogue is presented, the quotations have been derived from contemporaneous notes, from the participants' sworn testimony, or from interviews with several participants. No dialogue has been reconstructed from secondhand sources.

The events of the Iran-contra affair present a special problem for journalists and historians. Many of the actors' accounts differ. Some oral accounts cannot be squared with the documentary record. Some actors have admitted lying to Congress or to their colleagues, and their accounts must be taken with a grain of caution. Others have been caught in lies that they have never openly acknowledged. In such cases, we have tried our best to judge which accounts appear closest to the truth.

On the other hand, the scandal uncovered a hitherto unknown source of information about national security policymaking: the NSC's computerized archive of PROFS notes. These messages, written by officials who did not know that copies were being preserved, provide an unprecedented contemporary record of the inner workings of the NSC staff.

In the following notes, all interviews cited are with one or both of the authors unless otherwise specified. "Testimony," "depositions," *Select Committee Documents*, and *Select Committee Report* refer to the proceedings of the U.S. Senate Select Committee on Secret Military Assistance to Iran and the Nicaraguan Opposition and the U.S. House of Representatives Select Committee to Investigate Covert Arms Transactions with Iran. *Tower Commission Report* refers to the report of the President's Special Review Board, issued on February 26, 1987.

PROLOGUE

xii   Regan learned of his firing: Regan learned that he would be replaced by Baker from national security adviser Frank Carlucci, who had been told by White House personnel director Robert Tuttle, who had seen a report on the Cable News Network. Interview with *Time* reporter Barrett Seaman, who was interviewing Regan at the time, and Donald Regan, *For the Record* (San Diego: Harcourt Brace Jovanovich, 1988), p. 372.

xiii   Consideration of the Twenty-fifth Amendment: Interviews with Jim Cannon, July, August, and October 1987 and April 1988; interviews with two White House officials involved in the deliberations.

CHAPTER 1: MORNING IN AMERICA

8   Mrs. Reagan's rationing of her husband's handshakes: From the accounts of several White House officials who planned the president's trips.

8   Stuart Spencer on Nancy Reagan: Sidney Blumenthal, *The Permanent Campaign* (New York: Simon and Schuster, 1980), p. 174.

10   Reagan as governor and his legislative program: Lou Cannon, *Reagan* (New York: Putnam's, 1982), p. 120.

10   Washington's second-term woes: *Response of Presidents to Charges of Misconduct*, edited by C. Vann Woodward (New York: Delacorte Press, 1974).

10   "If he was not the greatest": Clinton Rossiter, *The American Presidency* (New York: New American Library, 1960), p. 87.

11   "Efficient government": Emmet John Hughes, *The Living Presidency* (New York: Coward, McCann & Geoghehan, 1972), p. 99.

11   Reagan's record as campaign platform: For a fuller discussion, see Albert R. Hunt, "The Campaign and the Issues," in Austin Ranney, ed., *The American Elections of 1984* (Durham, N.C.: Duke University Press, 1985).

13   Reagan meant what he said: Austin Ranney, "Reagan's First Term," in *The American Elections of 1984*, p. 35.

14   Reagan's crying at his film: Peter Goldman and Tony Fuller, *The Quest for the Presidency* (New York: Bantam Books, 1985), p. 265.

14   Mrs. Reagan's complaint about her convention film: Interviews with two campaign officials and one White House official.

15   Reagan's popularity versus that of his policies: *Washington Post*–ABC News poll, May 1984.

16   Central America not to be campaign issue: Bob Woodward, *Veil: The Secret Wars of the CIA* (New York: Simon and Schuster, 1987), p. 256.

16   The CIA manual: Prepared by the CIA in 1983, when CIA aid to the contras was legal (though assassinations were not). See, among other ac-

counts, Christopher Dickey, *With the Contras* (New York: Simon and Schuster, 1985), pp. 254–57.

17   North's meeting with contra leader: The contras wanted to "borrow" a jet fighter from Honduras, paint it with Sandinista markings, and then use it to attack Sandinista helicopter assemblies. North to McFarlane, November 7, 1984, *Select Committee Documents*.

18   They had "swallowed enough": Interview with Michael Deaver, September 1987.

18   "If you're very popular": Interview with Sears, July 21, 1987.

20   "Let's do them all!": Interviews with McFarlane, August 1987, and with another NSC official who participated in the report's formulation.

CHAPTER 2: THE NO-HANDS PRESIDENCY

21   Regan's early designs on the chief of staff's job: *Newsweek*, January 7, 1985.

21   Reagan's failure to define his economic goals: Donald T. Regan, *For the Record* (San Diego: Harcourt Brace Jovanovich, 1988), p. 142.

22   The Regan-Baker swap: Interviews with two firsthand participants and three secondhand observers.

22   "brutalizing him": The term used by Senator Paul Laxalt, who flew back to Washington with the First Lady after the first debate, in Louisville, Ky.

23   "He's tired": Interview with Regan, June 1988.

24   "Reagan nodded affably": Regan, *For the Record*, p. 228.

24   "I believe that you surround yourself": *Fortune*, September 15, 1986.

25   Reagan's following his subordinates' media plans: Larry Speakes said, "I can't think of a time when he didn't follow my advice." Reagan would often answer questions his advisers had told him not to, but otherwise he took their advice on when to do interviews and news conferences, saying openly at times that he was sorry, but his advisers had told him he was not allowed to talk about a subject. Interview with Speakes, August 1987.

26   Reagan's habits in the Oval Office: Robert Timberg, in the *Baltimore Sun*, January 29, 1984.

27   "He made almost no demands": Martin Anderson, *Revolution* (San Diego: Harcourt Brace Jovanovich, 1988), p. 290.

28   "The job was whatever": Interview with Rollins, October 1987.

28   "If you gave him too many pages": Interview with David Gergen conducted for an unfinished book by Edward J. Rollins.

28   "a lot": Interview with Regan, June 1988.

29   "We've had many years": Interview with Tuttle, September 1987.

29   "campaigning together": Interview with Laxalt, October 1987.

29   Eisenhower after his heart attack: Richard E. Neustadt, "Approaches to Staffing the Presidency: Notes on FDR and JFK," *American Political Science Review* (1963), p. 858.

30   "he makes things up": Interview with one of Reagan's children, September 1987.

30   "He has this great ability": Interview with a former senior NSC official, October 1987.

30   Deaver's walking through glass: Marjorie Williams, in a July 13, 1987, profile in the *Washington Post*, reports that Deaver's brother Bill believed Deaver was fetching Mrs. Reagan a glass of water.

31   Possibility of racist image: For a fuller account of Deaver's and Baker's efforts against Meese in the Bob Jones University case, see Lawrence I. Barrett, *Gambling with History* (New York: Penguin, 1984), p. 415.

32   "If you think that was a go-ahead": Interview with a former senior NSC official, November 1987.

32   "Reagan is like a great race horse": Interview with Miller, November 1987.

33   "Reagan arguments": One of the earliest and best accounts of Reagan's operating style appeared in *Time*, December 13, 1982, reported by Doug Brew and John Stacks.

33   Politicizing intelligence: A good example can be found in David Stockman's account of Caspar Weinberger's distorted charts, exaggerating the peril of Soviet military strength in order to convince Reagan to fully back his proposed increases in defense spending; Stockman, *The Triumph of Politics* (New York: Harper & Row, 1986), p. 290.

33   "if he went one-on-one": Interview with Lake, August 1987.

33   "he was too loose": Speakes explained in an August 1987 interview that Deaver vetoed a proposed Q and A with high school students before the Geneva summit on the theory that Reagan would be "too loose" and speak too freely. Similarly, former White House aide Judi Buckelew said, "The staff was always trying to keep him away from these high school groups that would come in to have their pictures taken, because he'd stand around and answer all their questions, saying all kinds of things. The staff would literally tug him away from these kids."

34   Ghost in the Lincoln Bedroom: Interview with Maureen Reagan, January 1987.

34   Flying saucer: In the summer of 1974, Norman C. Miller, then a reporter for the *Wall Street Journal* and now national editor of the *Los Angeles Times*, was told by Governor Reagan about his having sighted an unidentified flying object on a flight in his private plane. Reagan had convinced his pilot to follow the object, which was heading toward Bakersfield. But then, he told Miller, "it went straight up!"

      Reagan soon told his wife about what he had seen, and they did some personal research. Reagan related to Miller that they had found references to UFOs in Egyptian hieroglyphics. Reagan was extremely animated as he spoke, and it became clear to Miller that the governor really believed in flying saucers. But when Miller asked him, "Governor, are you telling me you saw a UFO?" he said that Reagan seemed to remember suddenly that he was talking to a reporter. "This look crossed his face," recalled Miller, who said that Reagan then replied, "Let's just say that I'm agnostic." This was also the answer Reagan gave in 1988 when questions arose about whether he shared his wife's belief in astrology. Interview with Miller, June 1988.

      There is much evidence that the Reagans consulted astrologers regularly at least as early as 1952. In his autobiography, Reagan noted that they considered Hollywood stargazer Carroll Righter a good friend and started each morning by looking at their horoscopes. Ronald Reagan and Richard Heubler, *Where's the Rest of Me?* (New York: Dutton, 1965), p. 283, and Martin Gardner, "Seeing Stars," *New York Review of Books*, June 30, 1988.

34   "For him to be seen": In James Thomas Flexner, *George Washington and the New Nation* (Boston: Little, Brown, 1970), p. 105.

34   Herbert Hoover: Neustadt, "Approaches to Staffing the Presidency," p. 862.

34   Press conference habits: David Broder, *Behind the Front Page* (New York: Simon and Schuster, 1987), p. 153.

35   "death sentences": Interview with Larry Speakes, August 1987.

35   "to find out who was running": Interview with Terry Arthur, October 1987.

36   "To me, the White House": Alexander M. Haig, Jr., *Caveat: Realism, Reagan and Foreign Policy* (New York: Macmillan, 1984), p. 85.

36   "I've got 'fuck you' money": Interview with Regan by Johanna Neuman of *USA Today* and Owen Ullmann of the Knight-Ridder News Service, December 7, 1986.

36    $40 million blind trust: Regan neither confirmed nor denied accounts suggesting that he came into government with a $40 million fortune. Interview with Regan, June 1988.

36   "close enough to hear the whistle blow": Reagan's press conference, June 16, 1981, in Cannon, *Reagan*, p. 22.

36   the rich grew richer: According to the November 1987 Congressional Budget Office analysis, between 1977 and 1988, 80% of U.S. families saw their incomes decline (after adjustments for inflation). But the richest 10% had income increases of 16%, the top 5% had increases on the average of 23%, and the very highest 1% of the population saw its income rise a full 50%.

37   Donald Regan: By far the best newspaper account of Regan's early years is the two-part profile by Myra McPherson, *Washington Post*, February 13 and 14, 1985.

37   "Although I could walk home": Thomas P. O'Neill, Jr., *Man of the House* (New York: Random House, 1987), p. 6.

37   "Sure, they can do it": Interview with Regan by Jane Mayer and Ellen Hume of the *Wall Street Journal*, August 1986.

37   "I was never sure": Interview with Quint, August 1987.

38   "white men, gray men": Theodore White, *In Search of History* (New York: Warner, 1979), pp. 41–42.

38   "Daddy": Chris Welles, "The Making of a Treasury Secretary," *Institutional Investor*, March 1981.

39   "an absolute dictator": Ibid.

39   Clifford's help promoting Regan: Interview with Clifford, June 1988; Peter Brimelow, "The Real Donald Regan," *Barron's*, March 9, 1981, p. 31.

39   Regan as third choice for Treasury secretary: Barrett, *Gambling with History*, p. 67. He suggests Regan's name came up only after William Simon refused to take the post unless he was guaranteed to be the administration's top economic spokesman. Walter Wriston, the chairman of Citibank, also backed out. According to one administration source, a third choice, George

Shultz, then president of Bechtel Group, Inc., also turned down the job before Regan was chosen; others say Shultz never received a firm offer.

39   Regan's doing too little: James Shannon of Massachusetts, a Democrat on the House Ways and Means Committee, said to the *Washington Post* on February 13, 1985, "Regan sat by and let a disaster happen. . . . He had to have seen that the 1981 tax bill was not going to be the smashing success that Representative Jack Kemp and Company said it would be."

40   "Chief": Regan denied that he liked to be called "Chief" once his reputation was sufficiently controversial, but at least one top assistant continued to call him this, and others believed he liked the title.

40   Roosevelt's staff: Neustadt, "Approaches to Staffing the Presidency," p. 860.

40   Reagan's less frequent attendance at meetings: Colin Campbell, S.J., *Managing the Presidency* (Pittsburgh: University of Pittsburgh Press, 1986), p. 110.

41   "It was just embarrassing": Interview with Friedersdorf, June 1987.

41   "The American people wanted": Regan, *For the Record*, p. 242.

41   "I believe in loyalty up": Interview with Regan by Jane Mayer and Ellen Hume of the *Wall Street Journal*, September 1986.

42   "Negroes . . . have such big families": Interview with Regan by Jane Mayer and Robert W. Merry of the *Wall Street Journal*, 1985.

45   The inaugural's reminding Mrs. Reagan of her wedding day: Interview of Nancy Reagan on *Good Morning America*, January 21, 1985.

45   "where will the television cameras be?": Interview with Ron Walker, October 1987.

CHAPTER 3: A DANGEROUS WORLD

47   "There's an understandable tendency": Reagan's remarks to the Executive Forum, January 25, 1985.

48   Reagan on the Sandinistas: Address to Latin American legislators, January 24, 1985.

48   But Nancy Reagan: Interviews with McFarlane, June 1988; Michael Deaver, *Behind the Scenes* (New York: William Morrow, 1987), pp. 111, 120.

49   "*We* will never retreat": Reagan speech, January 16, 1984.

49   the "sky-is-falling" cable: The full text is in David C. Martin and John Walcott, *Best Laid Plans* (New York: Harper & Row, 1988), pp. 119–20.

50   "The sad thing in Lebanon": Interview with a senior NSC official, September 1987.

51   "Few seemed willing": Garry Wills, *Reagan's America* (New York: Doubleday, 1987), p. 355.

51   Haig's memo: Alexander Haig, *Caveat* (New York: Macmillan, 1984), p. 92.

52   "Foreign policy wasn't terribly important": Interview with McFarlane, August 1987.

53   The debate on terrorism: Shultz's argument was made in a speech in New York, October 25, 1984; Weinberger's reply, in a speech in Washington, November 28; Shultz's rebuttal, in New York, December 9.

53   "If you're not willing": Shultz in Philip Taubman, "The Shultz-Weinberger Feud," *New York Times Magazine*, April 14, 1985.

54   Coaching the president: Interviews with former NSC officials, November 1987.

55   "Intrinsically unworkable": McFarlane testimony, May 13, 1987.

55   "Mr. President, you don't need": Shultz testimony, July 23, 1987.

55   walk-in privileges: Others with walk-in rights were the vice president, the national security adviser, the White House chief of staff, deputy chief of staff Michael Deaver, and, of course, Nancy Reagan. In addition, Attorney General Edwin Meese, White House spokesman Larry Speakes, personal aide David Fischer, and the president's physician and military aide had de facto walk-in privileges.

55   a private hour: Shultz soon changed his one hour-long session with Reagan to two half-hour sessions. "He saw that he wasn't keeping the president's attention for a full hour," an aide recalled.

55   Shultz's ultimatum to Reagan: Interview with McFarlane, August 1987. According to another, secondhand version of the conversation, the president gave Shultz an even stronger reassurance: "If I fired you," a former aide quoted him as saying, "I'd be left with nothing but Cap's bad advice."

57   "He's a very . . . private person": Jane Leavy, "McFarlane and the Taunting of Truth," *Washington Post*, May 7, 1987; interview with Fairbanks, June 1988.

57   McFarlane's background: See, for example, McFarlane's interview with Trude B. Feldman in *McCall's*, November 1987.

58   "The most relevant lesson": Interview with McFarlane, March 1985.

58   "It was unpredictable": Interview with McFarlane, June 1988.

58   "The NSC became operational": Martin and Walcott, *Best Laid Plans*, pp. 112–13; interview with Teicher, June 1988. See also Charles Babcock and Don Oberdorfer, "The NSC Cabal," *Washington Post*, June 21, 1987.

59   "I had no idea": This account of the abortive appointments of Deaver and Baker is based on interviews with Deaver and three other White House aides.

59   "This job is way beyond me": *New York Times*, March 28, 1984; interview with McFarlane, June 1988.

60   "My greatest frustration": David Ignatius, "Man in the Middle," *Wall Street Journal*, August 10, 1984.

60   NSC staff: White House memorandum, Hicks to Regan, October 28, 1985. The figure of 182 includes "detailees" borrowed from other agencies.

61   "FOR THE PRESIDENT: Robert C. McFarlane": Signing orders on Reagan's behalf was not unprecedented — Clark had exercised the same power during his tenure as national security adviser — but it did mark a clear increase in McFarlane's influence. Interview with McFarlane, June 1988.

63   Regan's ideology: Interview with Regan by Jane Mayer and Ellen Hume of the *Wall Street Journal*, August 1986.

64   McFarlane's New Year's Day briefing: Jody Powell, "McFarlane Bolts the Pack," *Los Angeles Times*, January 9, 1985.

CHAPTER 4: COWBOYS

66   North's proposal to seize the *Monimbo*: North to McFarlane, February 6, 1985, *Select Committee Documents*. Ironically, U.S. intelligence analysts believed that some of the weapons aboard the ship had been donated to Nicaragua by the government of Iran.

68   North and the president watching the planes return from Grenada: This story has been told in several accounts; an especially detailed version is in David Halevy and Neil C. Livingstone, "The Ollie We Knew," *Washingtonian*, July 1987.

68   North even exaggerated his official NSC biography: See Roy Gutman, *Banana Diplomacy* (New York: Simon and Schuster, 1988), p. 137.

69   "I used to keep Ollie": Interview with Deaver, June 1988.

69   "And if the commander in chief": North testimony, July 9, 1987.

69   North once plotted to remove records: Richard A. Petrino, *Los Angeles Times*, December 20, 1986. It is not clear whether North actually altered the records or not. See also Ben Bradlee, Jr., *Guts and Glory* (New York, Donald I. Fine, 1988), p. 62.

69   North's foray across the DMZ: From an excellent account of North's Vietnam years by Ari Harris, *Washington Post*, December 13, 1986.

69   He was hospitalized: The Marine Corps publicly confirmed in December 1986 that North had been voluntarily hospitalized for twenty-two days, from December 16, 1974, until January 7, 1975. White House officials said North apparently did not divulge the episode in his applications for security clearances at the NSC, nor did White House background checks discover it. Former national security adviser Richard Allen said he would not have approved North's appointment at the NSC had he known about the hospitalization. Nevertheless, not only was North appointed; both McFarlane and Poindexter extended his terms of duty at the White House. For a more exhaustive account of North's battle stress and his hospitalization, see Bradlee, *Guts and Glory*, pp. 107–10.

69   a top-secret study group: The group drafted a plan that included among its options a declaration of martial law and the suspension of some constitutional rights. Contrary to some reports, however, members of the secret panel said North himself was too junior to have any impact on the content of the plan. In 1982, Clark appointed North as staff coordinator for the Crisis Pre-Planning Group, the NSC's special operations board. See Clark memorandum, May 14, 1982, *Select Committee Documents*.

70   "rather lurid": McFarlane testimony, May 11, 1987.

70   Fawn Hall: Hall later denied that she ever used her mother's influence to aid North; see Bradlee, *Guts and Glory*, p. 272. But other NSC officials insist that North did use his connection with Wilma Hall—at least initially, until his growing relationship with McFarlane made it unnecessary.

70   "Ten thousand miles": North testimony, July 9, 1987.

71   Early years of the contra war: The best account is Christopher Dickey, *With the Contras* (New York: Simon and Schuster, 1985). See also Roy

Gutman, *Banana Diplomacy* (New York: Simon and Schuster, 1988); Bob Woodward, *Veil: The Secret Wars of the CIA* (New York: Simon and Schuster, 1988); the three-part series by Robert C. Toth and Doyle McManus, *Los Angeles Times*, March 3–5, 1985; and the two-part series by David Ignatius and David Rogers, *Wall Street Journal*, March 5–6, 1985.

72   "No . . . that would be violating": Remarks to reporters, April 14, 1983.

72   The Pentagon delivered: *Select Committee Report*, pp. 34–35. Special Interagency Working Group memo, September 23, 1983, *Select Committee Documents*.

73   "Managua by Christmas": Interviews with U.S. officials in Washington and Tegucigalpa, February 1985. Most CIA officers considered Managua a wildly unrealistic goal and said the slogan was only a motivational tool. On the other hand, one agent told Robert Owen: "If they can't make it by then, they never will."

73   The CIA's role: See "CIA Internal Report Details U.S. Role in Contra Raids in Nicaragua Last Year," *Wall Street Journal*, March 6, 1985.

73   The Managua airport raid: Casey and his Latin American operations chief, Duane "Dewey" Clarridge, disavowed that attack, insisting that contra leader Eden Pastora launched it without authorization. But the CIA had supplied the airplane; and senior U.S. officials admitted later that while the raid apparently was not formally approved in Washington, Clarridge had encouraged Pastora to try something like it.

73   The Senate's reaction to the mining: This story has been told most fully in Woodward, *Veil*, pp. 319–35. See also *Select Committee Report*, pp. 117–18.

74   "The CIA is something unique": James Conaway, "Spy Master: The File on Bill Casey," *Washington Post*, September 7, 1983.

75   Casey and the listening device: Woodward, *Veil*, p. 147.

75   "Bill Casey was the last great buccaneer": George testimony, August 6, 1987.

75   "Anyone with access to Roosevelt": William J. Casey, speech to Donovan symposium on OSS conference, September 19, 1986.

75   "the president's intelligence officer": Woodward, *Veil*, p. 92.

75   The first CIA director ever to hold a cabinet seat: Earlier directors of central intelligence, such as the Eisenhower administration's Allen Dulles, had been powerful figures and de facto members of the cabinet, but Casey was the first to win formal cabinet rank. The CIA director often kept his opinions to himself during formal NSC meetings. "Casey would mumble ten or fifteen minutes' worth of largely unhelpful intelligence analysis," said an NSC aide who attended the meetings. "The president would often turn to someone next to him and ask, 'What did Bill say?' " However, Casey pressed his views energetically in his own meetings with Reagan, White House aides said.

75   Casey's use of intelligence: Both McFarlane and former deputy CIA director John N. McMahon defend Casey on this score; for McMahon's view, see *Select Committee Report*, pp. 525–26.

76   The general and the contras' food: As told by a U.S. diplomat who heard the story from General John Galvin, September 1987.

76 Casey's using Regan as entree: Interviews with McFarlane and other officials.

76 Casey's notes: See Casey to Regan, March 20 and April 26, 1985, in *Select Committee Documents*.

77 Covert operations in 1985: Administration and congressional sources confirmed the list of targets. The Ethiopian program reportedly did not include direct military aid.

77 Shultz's interest in negotiations: Interviews with State Department officials. See also Shultz to Reagan, May 25, 1983, in *Select Committee Documents:* "In all likelihood the only way we can reestablish a peaceful Central America, free from foreign incursions into democratic countries, is by regional negotiations leading to a reciprocal and verifiable agreement." Casey on negotiations: Speech in New York, May 1, 1985.

77 Casey on Congress: Interview with U.S. official who also attended the hearings, November 1987.

77 Casey on Khrushchev: Speech, Metropolitan Club of New York, May 1, 1985.

78 Casey sent Clarridge to South Africa: Clarridge testimony, August 4, 1987. North's notebooks suggest that South Africa later sent 200 tons of weaponry to the contras and that Clarridge was aware of the shipment; but Clarridge testified that he knew of no such weapons. North notebooks, January 5, 1985, *Select Committee Documents;* Steven Emerson, *Secret Warriors* (New York: Putnam, 1988), p. 222.

78 "No, not to my knowledge": *Select Committee Report*, pp. 118–19.

78 "You can't do indirectly": Shultz was quoting chief of staff James Baker (who was not present at the NSPG meeting) on these points, but the sentiments were his own as well. Baker later said that he could not recall using the term "impeachable offense," but there is no question that Shultz did. *Select Committee Report*, p. 39; interviews with Baker aides, June 1988.

78 King Fahd's yacht: *New York Times*, April 6, 1984.

78 McFarlane-Bandar meeting: McFarlane testimony, May 11 and 12, 1987.

79 "Good News!": McFarlane recalled that Reagan responded to one Saudi contribution orally and the other in writing, but could not remember positively which was which. McFarlane did, however, recall distinctly that the president showed no surprise at learning about the 1985 contribution, which suggests that the response was oral on that occasion. The *Select Committee Report* draws the same conclusion.

79 McFarlane conceals Saudi aid from Shultz: Department of State, "Chronology of Non-USG support for Nicaraguan Opposition Forces," *Select Committee Documents*.

80 "I have a feeling": Reagan's remarks, April 4, 1985.

80 Lafayette Park meetings: According to an American and a Nicaraguan who attended some of the meetings.

81 North as "the switching point": Poindexter deposition, May 2, 1987.

81 "Where I went wrong": McFarlane testimony, May 14, 1987.

81 "I remember sitting": George testimony, August 6, 1987.

82 Pumpkin Papers dinner: North calendar, October 31, 1984, *Select Committee Documents*.

82   "Bill Casey was": North testimony, July 9 and 13, 1987.

82   "It was always the intention": North testimony, July 8, 1987.

83   Guatemalan EUCs: North to McFarlane, March 5, 1985, *Select Committee Documents*. Even when the EUCs were in hand, the shipments did not always run smoothly. One of the contras' arms dealers arranged to buy thirty SA-7 antiaircraft missiles from Communist China, but the Chinese balked when they saw certificates pledging that the missiles were for rightist Guatemala. North and Gaston Sigur, the NSC's chief Asian expert, had to take a Chinese military attaché to lunch at Washington's Cosmos Club to explain. The Guatemalan documents were only a subterfuge, North told him, adding that Calero would undoubtedly give diplomatic recognition to Peking as soon as the contras took Managua. The Chinese were more comfortable with the contras than with the Guatemalans, and the shipment went ahead.

83   Singlaub in Taiwan: Singlaub testimony, May 20, 1987. North and Sigur later gave Taiwan such a signal themselves, resulting in a $2 million contribution. McFarlane testified later that he had repeatedly warned his aides "not to solicit, encourage, coerce, or broker" financial contributions for the contras. But North, Poindexter, and three other NSC aides all say they remember no such lecture.

83   British mercenary: The plan was never carried out, because the helicopter bases were too well defended. See *Select Committee Report*, p. 44.

84   Owen's handing money to Diego: Interviews with two participants in the incident.

85   "Exercise absolute stealth": McFarlane note on North memorandum, August 28, 1984, *Select Committee Documents*.

85   "Keep mouth shut": North notebooks, November 10, 1984, *Select Committee Documents*.

85   "I didn't know who Oliver North": Fiers testimony, August 5, 1987.

85   Casey himself had told North: North memorandum to McFarlane, November 7, 1984, *Select Committee Documents*.

85   "No, I'm not operating": Fiers testimony, August 5, 1987.

86   "They are our brothers": Speech to the Conservative Political Action Conference dinner, March 1, 1985.

86   Hamilton at the White House: David Rogers, "Misinformation, Confusion on Nicaragua Issue Threaten Efforts by Reagan to Aid Guerrillas," *Wall Street Journal*, April 23, 1985.

87   Nicaraguan refugee fund-raiser: *Washington Post*, April 16, 17, 1985.

87   The $3,000 proceeds: Associated Press in *Washington Post*, September 3, 1985.

87   Arms agreements and the polls: Interview with Dennis Thomas, January 1988.

88   "pure panic": Interview with Khachigian, September 1987.

88   Regan's recommendation on the April 24 speech: Wirthlin confirmed Rollins's account. The budget speech did poorly. Reagan told the nation that growth wasn't solving all the nation's economic woes and warned that further spending cuts were needed, particularly in middle-class entitlements. The message got the worst television audience rating of any speech the president had ever given, according to Wirthlin.

88   "With all due respect": Interview with Rollins, October 1987. Regan's staff
      disputed the account, but confirmed that Regan favored the budget address.
      A third participant could not recall Rollins's exact words, but suggested
      the account sounded plausible.

89   "The administration has yet to produce": *Congressional Record*, April 17,
      1985.

89   "Abysmal handling": Woodward, *Veil*, pp. 403–4.

CHAPTER 5: A HARD-LINER'S SOFT TOUCH

91   Carter's "foreign policy helped create": Campaign statement in Kansas
      City, Mo., October 27, 1980.

91   "Where did we first go wrong?": Interview with Arnold, December 1987.

91   "swift and effective retribution": The contribution of Kenneth Adelman,
      according to David C. Walcott and John Martin, *Best Laid Plans* (New
      York: Harper & Row, 1988), p. 41.

92   "You can't help but thrill": Hedrick Smith, "Reagan's World," in *Reagan
      the Man, the President* (New York: Macmillan, 1980), p. 102.

92   Spanish Civil War scholars: Among those who said they'd never heard of
      the incident were Dr. Stanley G. Payne, Dr. Robert Wheatley at Ohio
      State University, Dr. Nicholas Sanchez-Albornez at Columbia University,
      Douglas Ford at the National Endowment for the Humanities, Dr. William
      C. Frank of Old Dominion University, William Susman, a veteran of the
      Lincoln Brigade, and Barbara Solomon, a writer on the period.

93   Reagan's hopes of making a quick deal for the hostages: Interview with
      one of those in the meeting; also, Martin and Walcott, *Best Laid Plans*,
      pp. 184–87.

95   "Regan appears taken": The private diary of a White House aide, June 18,
      1985.

95   "It was not an upbeat issue": Interview with Regan, June 1988.

95   "there were two weeks": Interview with McFarlane, June 1988.

95   Reagan and White House efforts: Reagan, who described himself as frus-
      trated enough to "pound a few walls," considered retaliation during those
      weeks but rejected the option. In the first week after the hijacking, terrorists
      in El Salvador killed four U.S. marines and nine civilians. Reagan asked
      Casey and Weinberger for a list of possible terrorist targets to be hit
      there — and announced that "our limits have been reached." Yet, after
      discussing the target list with McFarlane and hearing about the possible
      civilian casualties that might result, Reagan indefinitely deferred any de-
      cision on retaliation either there or in the Middle East. "You have to be
      able to pinpoint the enemy, you can't just start shooting without having
      someone in your gunsights," he explained.

97   Sacramento good will stories: Interview with Nancy Reynolds, October
      1987.

99   Reagan's empathy vs. his policies: Reagan made a televised appeal for a
      liver for Ashley Bailey of Clyde, Texas, on July 24, 1983. Although one
      researcher in the correspondence office devoted nearly all his time to an-
      swering organ transplant problems, the administration continuously op-

posed federal involvement in coordinating organ transplants; in its FY 1988 budget, it moved to take away funds from a national computerized organ donor network set up at the urging of Senator Albert Gore, Jr., of Tennessee.

99   "I can't stay here": Interview with Michael K. Deaver, September 1987. Deaver includes a less detailed account of this exchange in his own book, *Behind the Scenes* (New York: William Morrow, 1987).

100   Reagan called Begin: Laurence I. Barrett, *Gambling with History* (New York: Penguin, 1984), asserts that Reagan's sudden show of conviction against the Israeli invasion of Lebanon resulted from the Israelis' having underestimated his interest in the issue and having finally pushed him to anger by ignoring him (pp. 283–84). But Deaver's firsthand account suggests that the president really had not paid much attention to the issue before, as the Israelis had supposed, and was only drawn in when he was graphically exposed to the carnage.

100   "I knew that the president": Interview with McFarlane, August 1987.

101   Chicago Heights meeting: Compiled from interviews with four members of the Jenco family and with two senior White House officials present at the meeting.

101   The local official speaking of the Jencos: Ted Cormaney, Representative George M. O'Brien's press secretary, was involved in the arrangements for the meeting.

103   Beirut's deteriorating conditions: It was only after the Israeli invasion of 1982 and the Reagan administration's ill-fated attempt to enforce a U.S.-Israeli settlement upon Lebanon that the Shia militants targeted Americans and other foreigners in Beirut for terrorism at all. And it was only in the aftermath of the embassy bombings of 1983 and 1984, which prompted increases in physical security at the foreign missions, that terrorists began to find it easier and more cost-effective to kidnap individual hostages than to do anything else. See Brian Jenkins and Robin Wright, "The Kidnappers in Lebanon," *TVI Report*, vol. 7, no. 4.

104   Advance men: Theodore White, *Breach of Faith: The Fall of Richard Nixon* (New York: Atheneum, 1975), p. 91.

105   "There's only one thing missing": Interview with Henkel, June 1987.

105   Stethem service: *Washington Post*, June 21, 1985.

106   "discreet assistance": Note from Reagan to Perot, June 11, 1986.

106   Casey and Buckley: Clair George testimony, August 8, 1987; also William Safire, "Walk Back the Cat," *New York Times*, May 21, 1987.

107   Ten-point rise in polls: Wirthlin has argued that the Bitburg fiasco actually resulted in a net plus for Reagan's popularity, since it set off a backlash of sympathy, but according to the *Washington Post*–ABC News poll, Reagan's approval rating slid from the high 60s, shortly after his reelection, to the mid-50s, after the Bitburg trip in May 1985, then up to the mid-60s after the TWA hostage crisis.

107   Reagan's more "activist" image: Lou Cannon, "Reagan Agenda May Get a Lift," *Washington Post*, July 1, 1985.

107   Hostage crisis as news event: A tally of the news stories about hostages carried by the *New York Times* shows that in the six months before the

TWA hijacking, there were only 8 stories; for the two weeks of the crisis and the one after, it carried 191 stories. Interestingly, in the three months after the crisis, the paper showed a marked increase over what it had shown before, carrying 34 stories. The pattern suggests that the media didn't really discover the hostages until after the TWA spectacle.

108   "Anything new?": Regan interview at *Christian Science Monitor* breakfast, November 14, 1986.

CHAPTER 6: DRIFTING INTO A DEAL

111   Transfer of powers: The 1988 *Report of the Miller Center Commission on Presidential Disability and the Twenty-fifth Amendment* was critical of Fielding for not formally invoking the Twenty-fifth Amendment, instead using a letter as a legal disclaimer. But the report acknowledged that Fielding did so "at least to get him started down [the Twenty-fifth Amendment] route. And that is how it worked out."

112   Reagan's regaining consciousness after surgery: Interviews with White House officials and the *Report of the Miller Center Commission.*

112   Test of Reagan's faculties: Speakes later said he only vaguely remembered testing Reagan's lucidity.

113   Hospital visits after the assassination attempt: Interview with one of the troika.

113   "I noticed that he": Larry Speakes, *Speaking Out* (New York: Scribners, 1988), p. 74.

114   Regan and the helicopter: Interview with Speakes. In *For the Record* (San Diego: Harcourt Brace Jovanovich, 1988), Regan contends that he only planned to take the helicopter with Bush (p. 13). However, a former Bush aide disputed this statement and said that Bush always refused to use the South Lawn landing pad unless accompanied by the president.

114   "I've never let any broad": Ed Rollins's recollection. Regan's executive assistant, who was also supposed to be present during the exchange, denied Rollins's account.

114   Regan "built up a staff": Interview with Friedersdorf, June 1987.

114   "Regan's style was not to bother": Interview with Rollins, October 1987.

115   "We'll try to make as many decisions": in David Hoffman, "President Recovering Well," *Washington Post*, July 15, 1985. The quote was not for attribution, but another official later identified Regan as the source.

115   Reagan was deeply frustrated: *Tower Commission Report*, p. 166.

117   HAWK price of $437,700: Defense Department estimated replacement cost, in *Select Committee Report*, p. 178.

117   "a rumormonger": *Select Committee Report*, pp. 163–64.

118   "People betray me": *New York Times*, June 23, 1987.

119   "Mr. Ghorbanifar's information": Clair George testimony, August 6, 1987.

119   "The transaction would be simple": Shackley letter, *Washington Post*, February 2, 1987.

119   Adnan Khashoggi: See Anthony Sampson, *The Arms Bazaar* (New York: Viking, 1977); Ronald Kessler, *The Richest Man in the World* (New York:

1986); and William Rempel's articles in the *Los Angeles Times* May 15, 1987, March 12, 1988.

120 Ghorbanifar-Khashoggi meeting in Hamburg: Drawn principally from Khashoggi's long interview on ABC News's *20/20*, December 11, 1986; and Furmark deposition, July 22, 1987.

120 "In [Khashoggi's] mind": Furmark deposition, July 22, 1987.

121 "people's eyes lit up": The Israeli intermediary describing Peres's reaction to the arms dealer was Nimrodi.

121 Nimrodi-Ghorbanifar mortar deal: *New York Times*, February 1, 1987.

121 "Sure he is a liar": Nimrodi on selling arms, *Washington Post*, December 14, 1986.

121 Amitay and Allen: *New York Times*, November 27, 1986; *Washington Post*, August 16, 1987. Allen confirmed that the conversation occurred, but he denied that he approved any Israeli shipments; Amitay agreed that there was no explicit approval, merely a verbal wink and a nod.

121 Haig and the Israelis: Haig said his first protest to Defense Minister Ariel Sharon came during a visit to Jerusalem in 1981. "We damn near had a fistfight," Haig recalled. "Sharon was a pretty tough cookie. He wanted to send F4 tires and wheels to Iran which were U.S.-provided. I said, 'Mr. Minister, what Israel does with its own equipment is its own sovereign decision. But if it's U.S.-provided equipment with strings on it, it's against our law.' " Interview with Haig, December 1987. Haig recounted both his 1981 argument with Sharon and the 1982 shouting match in an interview with the *Los Angeles Times*, December 1987. He later said he did not know whether Egypt was, in fact, selling U.S.-made or U.S.-licensed weaponry to Iraq.

121 Haig-Sharon shouting match: Interview with Haig, December 1987.

122 Kimche on Iran's biggest problem: On a 1982 BBC broadcast, as quoted in the *Washington Post*, August 16, 1987.

122 Iranian Jewish exodus: Interviews with Iranian Jews and U.S. and Israeli officials; see also the *New York Times*, November 17, 1986; the *Financial Times* (London), November 21, 1986; and the *Los Angeles Times*, November 25, 1986. Ironically, fewer than 10,000 of the exiles chose to settle in Israel; most preferred the United States or Western Europe.

123 Buckley's condition: David C. Martin and John Walcott, *Best Laid Plans* (New York: Harper & Row, 1988), p. 217.

124 "can fill a military gap": "Iran: Prospects for Near-Term Instability," May 20, 1985, in *Tower Commission Report*, pp. B7–B8.

124 "This is almost too absurd": Handwritten note on Draft NSDD, June 17, 1985, *Select Committee Documents*.

124 "Its proposal that we permit": Shultz to McFarlane, June 29, 1985, cited in *Tower Commission Report*, p. B9.

125 McFarlane on Iranian help: Interview with McFarlane, September 1987.

125 Ledeen's role: Interviews with McFarlane and others and *Select Committee Report*, pp. 165–66.

125 Kimche's July 3 meeting: McFarlane said later that he did not believe arms came up, but Israeli officials said they did; and Weinberger's military assistant, Lieutenant General Colin Powell, told the select committees that

McFarlane mentioned both arms and hostages to Weinberger after the meeting.

126   Briefing the president: *Tower Commission Report*, p. B15.

126   McFarlane's account of the July 18 meeting with Reagan: *Tower Commission Report*, p. B15.

127   Reagan approved the deal in principle: *Select Committee Report*, p. 167.

127   "This would undercut": *Tower Commission Report*, p. B22.

127   Regan on the misuse of Latin, Regan testimony, July 30, 1987.

128   No one recalled Bush expressing an opinion: *Tower Commission Report*, p. B21.

128   August 6 discussion: Accounts differ; instead of one meeting, there may have been several with different participants. But all agreed on the arguments that were made. The *Select Committee Report* puts Reagan, Bush, Regan, Shultz, Weinberger, and McFarlane in the room, but neither McFarlane's nor Shultz's schedule includes such a meeting. McFarlane's schedule shows two meetings, one in the morning with Reagan, Bush, Regan, Weinberger, and General John Vessey, chairman of the Joint Chiefs of Staff, and a second in the afternoon, with Reagan and Shultz. Shultz's schedule has only the afternoon meeting, which he later described as one of his weekly sessions with the president. The president's official schedule agrees that Shultz was not at the morning meeting (see *Tower Commission Report*, p. B21). Finally Bush has contended that he was not present at any meeting at which Shultz or Weinberger objected to the arms deal (as both did on August 6).

128   Iranian Jews in TOW deal: Regan testimony cited in *Tower Commission Report*, p. B24.

128   Shultz's objections: Shultz testimony, July 23, 1987, and *Tower Commission Report*, p. B22.

128   The Reagan phone call: Interview with McFarlane, September 1987.

129   McFarlane's and Reagan's whereabouts, August 6–11: Drawn from White House records.

130   Reagan's denial of divorce: Lou Cannon, *Reagan* (New York: Putnam's, 1982), p. 65.

132   Reagan's isolation at the ranch in the summer of 1985: Lou Cannon, "Overprotecting the President," *Washington Post*, August 26, 1985.

132   Regan's spreading rumors about McFarlane: Interviews with two White House aides present at the Santa Barbara gathering and three journalists present at the *Newsweek* gathering.

132   McFarlane-Regan lunch: McFarlane and Regan disagree about the lunch in Montecito. According to McFarlane, he initiated the invitation and brought up his concern about the rumors. According to Regan's aides, it was the chief of staff who took the initiative. Interviews with McFarlane, August 1987, and Regan, June 1988.

133   "It's good, really good, Don": Regan, *For the Record*, p. 267.

134   "Do you want the Iranians": Ha'aretz, *Baltimore Sun*, December 7, 1988; *Los Angeles Times*, December 28, 1986.

134   "We might as well go ahead": Ledeen deposition, September 10, 1987.

134   Casey learns of the deal: Clair George testimony, August 5, 1987.

135   Djerejian and Donaldson: Interview with Djerejian, October 1987.
135   "He was delirious": NBC News interview, cited in *Los Angeles Times*, December 28, 1986.
136   Bush and the hostage families: Interviews with four hostage relatives, including Peggy Say, and one White House official, all in attendance.
137   "We staged it": Interview with Regan, June 1988.

CHAPTER 7: PROJECT DEMOCRACY

139   North's role in the *Achille Lauro* affair: Interviews with NSC officials who worked with him.
139   Reagan's reaction to the October 10, 1985, *Washington Times* editorial: Hugh Sidey in *Time*, October 28, 1985. A White House official confirmed the account.
140   The *Achille Lauro* exploit: For a more complete recounting, see David C. Martin and John Walcott, *Best Laid Plans* (New York: Harper & Row, 1988), pp. 235–57.
140   "I salute the admiral": An NSC public relations aide asked later if the details of the story could be given to the press. Poindexter thought for a moment; then, ever the organization man, he asked that the president's greeting be reported as: "I salute the navy!" And so it was.
140   "He has better judgment": Weinberger may have had a special reason for praising Reagan in public: according to more than one account, he opposed the plan to force down the Egyptair jet. See Martin and Walcott, *Best Laid Plans*, pp. 248–49.
140   October 11 morning staff meeting: From the notes of an assistant to the president who was present.
140   The message of the *Achille Lauro* incident: Interviews with four White House and NSC officials; North testimony, July 9, 1987. The officer who actually came up with the idea of intercepting the hijackers, according to three officials, was navy captain James Stark, an aide in the NSC's political-military office.
141   Casey suggested Secord: North testimony, July 8, 1987. Secord confirmed that Casey knew about his role, and Casey's office logs showed several telephone calls and meetings between the two men.
142   Secord thesis: "Unconventional Warfare/Covert Operations as an Instrument of U.S. Foreign Policy" (1972), reprinted in *Joint Iran-Contra Hearings*, 1987. See also Bob Drogin, "Secord — A Specialist in Covert Deals," *Los Angeles Times*, March 29, 1987.
142   Edwin P. Wilson: *Select Committee Report*, pp. 327–29, and Peter Maas, *Manhunt* (New York: Random House, 1986).
142   Albert Hakim: In 1976, CIA associate deputy director for operations Theodore G. Shackley recommended that the CIA's station chief in Tehran introduce Hakim to Secord. Shackley memorandum for the record, August 16, 1976, *Select Committee Documents*. But Wilson, who was in Tehran at the time, said he made the introduction.
143   The Syrian arms merchant (Manzer al Kassar): *Select Committee Report*, p. 337; *Newsday*, April 19, 1987; *Los Angeles Times*, July 17, 1987.

144   "Since funding expired": North to McFarlane, April 11, 1985, *Select Committee Documents*.

144   McFarlane briefed the president: McFarlane testimony, May 11, 1987.

144   "We have grown": Bermúdez, in Roy Gutman, *Banana Diplomacy* (New York: Simon and Schuster, 1988), p. 304.

144   "The training of the contras": Gorman deposition, March 22, 1987.

144   Secord and his partners had collected a commission: The congressional committees investigating the Iran-contra affair calculated that Secord, Hakim, and Clines retained profits of 28.7% during 1984 and 1985 when both the cost of the weapons and transportation costs were taken into account, 31.6% if the calculation was based on the cost of the weapons alone. *Select Committee Report*, p. 347.

144   Singlaub and Secord: Interviews with Singlaub and Owen, November 1987; Singlaub and Calero testimony, May 20, 1987.

145   Contras' organizational problems: Interviews with contra officers, Honduras, February 1985.

146   June 28, 1985: The date of the Miami meeting is taken from a submission of evidence to the U.S. District Court for the District of Columbia by independent counsel Lawrence E. Walsh, *U.S. v. Poindexter et al.*, May 31, 1988.

146   Secord on June 28 meeting: Secord testimony, May 5, 1987.

147   A virtually unnoticed article: The *Miami Herald* reported on January 18, 1985, that North had asked private fund-raisers to help arrange a purchase of SA-7 antiaircraft missiles for the contras. Further fragmentary accounts of North's activities were published by the *Herald*, the Associated Press, the *Washington Post*, and the *Los Angeles Times*. But the *New York Times* article was more comprehensive — and more prominently displayed — than the earlier stories.

147   Barnes letter: Barnes to McFarlane, August 16, 1985, *Select Committee Documents*.

147   Poindexter on withholding information: Poindexter testimony, July 17, 1987.

147   "My objective all along": Poindexter testimony, July 17, 1987.

148   McFarlane approved North's suggestion: McFarlane testified that North suggested altering the memos because they were susceptible to misinterpretation, and McFarlane agreed. McFarlane testimony, May 12, 1987.

148   McFarlane letters: To Hamilton, September 5, 1985, and Barnes, September 12, 1985, in *Select Committee Documents*.

148   All four denials were untrue: In his testimony before Congress's Iran-contra committees in May 1987, McFarlane acknowledged that his denials had been "too categorical." After the committees' report concluded that McFarlane had been intentionally deceptive, however, his attorneys argued that the earlier denials were "accurate as far as Mr. McFarlane knew at the time" (Leonard Garment and Peter Morgan letter to committee members, January 7, 1988). In March 1988, McFarlane pleaded guilty to four counts of withholding information from Congress, a misdemeanor, stemming in part from his letters to Hamilton and Barnes. The misdemeanor charges were part of a bargain with prosecutors.

NOTES ON SOURCES 417

148   Hamilton on McFarlane: *Select Committee Report*, p. 163. The account of Barnes's meeting with McFarlane is based on an interview with Barnes, May 1988.

149   Mary McGrory: *Washington Post*, August 13, 1985.

149   North on Casey and Project Democracy: North testimony, July 10, 1987.

150   Shultz, Abrams, and North: Shultz testimony, July 23, 1987; Abrams testimony, June 2, 1987.

150   "Monitor Ollie": Abrams testimony, June 1, 1987, citing Abrams's notebook, September 4, 1985.

150   Abrams on ambassadors: Abrams testimony, June 2, 1987. The account of the meeting with Ferch is from interviews with several State Department officials. Abrams denied any knowledge of North's orders to Tambs to open a "Southern Front."

151   The CIA's political aid to the contras: *Los Angeles Times*, April 14, 1986.

151   The Honduran government: The Hondurans were piqued for several reasons. Their president, a provincial doctor named Roberto Suazo, was annoyed that Abrams wouldn't let him ignore the Honduran constitution and run for reelection. Army officers were upset that they had not been allowed to control the contras' weapons business. The result was that the United States' closest ally in Central America was stubbornly preventing the administration from pursuing its main priority, the contra war.

152   Felix Rodriguez: Interview with Rodriguez, April 1988.

152   Owen memorandum on Costa Rican airstrip site: "T.C." (Owen) to "B.G." (North), August 25, 1985, *Select Committee Documents*.

152   Gadd, Southern Air Transport, and Airmach: Gadd deposition, May 19, 1987.

153   Project Democracy's sales, expenditures, and profits: For a precise breakdown, see *Select Committee Report*, Chapter 22.

153   Owen's wedding: Owen testimony, May 19, 1987.

154   Spitz Channell: Channell deposition, September 1, 2, 1987; interviews with four Channell associates; interview with John Roberts, October 1987.

156   Coors donation: Coors testimony, May 21, 1987.

156   North's first briefing: Described by several people who saw it; North described it himself in testimony on July 13, 1987.

156   Rich Miller is given the money: Miller's firm, International Business Communications Inc. (IBC), transferred the contributions to dummy accounts in the Cayman Islands and Switzerland. The largest part went to Secord's Geneva account, Lake Resources, Inc.; some went directly to Calero and other contra leaders. And some — just over one third, according to congressional investigators — stayed with the middlemen of IBC. Of about $5 million paid to IBC by Channell in 1985–86, $1.7 million went to Lake Resources, $1.5 million to Calero and other contra leaders, and $1.7 million to IBC for both commissions and expenses. No one quite knew how much Channell retained to help pay for his lavish offices and Lincoln town car, but he took direct compensation of $346,000 during those two years. IBC figures are from *Select Committee Report*, p. 98; "Carl Channell Affiliated Companies Statement of Operations" and "Summary of International Business Communications Account," *Select Committee Documents*.

157   Ellen Clayton Garwood: Garwood testimony, May 21, 1987, and *Los Angeles Times*, September 15, 1985.

157   Barbara Newington: Newington deposition, May 12, 1987.

157   Channell associate: Interview with Bruce Cameron, June 1987.

CHAPTER 8: SEA CHANGE

158   "spirit of détente": *New Republic*, October 14, 1985.

158   Nancy Reagan's tenacity: Deaver described Mrs. Reagan as going after the summit as tenaciously as "a dog with a bone. . . . She felt strongly it was not only in the interest of world peace, but the correct move politically. She would buttonhole George Shultz, Bud McFarlane, and others, to be sure they were moving toward that goal." Deaver, *Behind the Scenes* (New York: Random House, 1987), p. 120; interview with McFarlane, June 1988.

158   McFarlane convinced Reagan to take Shultz's side: In an August 1987 interview with the authors, McFarlane said, "By September, [Reagan] took George's position on every single decision."

158   Weinberger not invited to summit: It was not unusual for a defense secretary to be left off the list for a summit. But if Weinberger was not invited, he was heard from. On November 16, the day that Reagan left for Geneva, the *New York Times* and the *Washington Post* published complete texts of an ostensibly private letter he had sent the president, warning against any Soviet deal forcing the U.S. to comply with the 1972 Antiballistic Missile Treaty — an issue the cabinet had argued all summer. McFarlane later denounced the letter as "just a blatant, willful leak from the Defense Department," though he conceded, "Cap was trying to save the president from himself."

159   "It was the president's own idea!": Interview with William Henkel, summer 1987.

160   manufactured lines: Larry Speakes, *Speaking Out* (New York: Scribners, 1988), p. 136.

161   "We got all that support": Interview with McFarlane, August 1987.

161   Regan posing with Reagan and Gorbachev: In *For the Record* (San Diego: Harcourt Brace Jovanovich, 1988), Regan denies that he deliberately planted himself in the middle of the Geneva photograph, but others present saw it quite differently. Even Regan's ally, William Henkel, admitted that Regan's tropism toward publicity was unseemly. "Jim Baker," he concluded, "would never have been in that picture."

161   Regan's ignorance of arms control: Regan's penchant for appearing as an arms control expert, according to the NSC staff, led him to accept a TV appearance during the UN General Assembly in September. NSC aides were horrified when, before Regan went on the air, one of his aides came sprinting down the hotel corridor where they were both staying, buttonholed McFarlane, and asked breathlessly, "What do we have on the table, and what have the Russians said?" McFarlane walked him stolidly through the issues, but couldn't believe Regan intended to talk publicly on such a delicate subject with so little knowledge. And in fact the NSC aides said

Regan slipped up, revealing that McFarlane and Shultz were going to Moscow for a preparatory meeting — a piece of news that was supposed to be hush-hush.

162   Backdoor contacts: Interview with McFarlane, August 1987. In contrast, Regan's staff complained that McFarlane played the same game, particularly by slipping private messages to the president in the national security briefing papers.

163   Budget targets: The Gramm-Rudman-Hollings goals were extraordinarily ambitious: in the first fiscal year, a staggering $50 billion would have to be cut — bringing the deficit down to $144 billion for FY 1987 and supposedly balancing the budget by 1991. A measure of the scale of this goal was that even David Stockman — the former budget director who'd been accused of bleeding the federal government dry — had dared aim for no deficit smaller than $180 billion in the prior three years.

163   "Don't worry about it": Interview with McFarlane, August 1987. Regan's staff suggests that the president knew the consequences of the legislation well before he signed it, and that while it did force him to choose between two equally cherished priorities, he fully understood and supported the bill anyway. They confirm the fight between McFarlane and Regan over the legislation, but suggest the acrimony was supplied by McFarlane, who they said was late in understanding the impact of the bill. A third, high-ranking administration official involved in the Gramm-Rudman process, but working for neither McFarlane nor Regan, confirms McFarlane's account: "It's doubtful Reagan ever understood the arguments about it." Asked how the president could have missed them, given the publicity they received in the press, he said, "He wouldn't necessarily read the papers, and if he did, he wouldn't likely believe them."

165   "an utterly fictitious falsehood": Interview with McFarlane by David Ignatius and Jane Mayer of the *Wall Street Journal*, fall 1985.

165   McFarlane's "nervous breakdown": Ledeen deposition, March 11, 1987. McFarlane denied that he had suffered a nervous breakdown in the White House and attributed Ledeen's accusation to a falling out between the two, which began when McFarlane threw Ledeen out of his office. McFarlane also pointed out that Ledeen had wanted him to stay on at the NSC despite his concerns. Interview with McFarlane, June 1988.

166   "I have a bad feeling": Ledeen depositions, March 11 and June 19, 1987.

166   "live Americans": North's notebook, October 30, 1985, *Select Committee Documents*.

166   "Cross your fingers": McFarlane interview with Tower Commission, cited in *Select Committee Report*, p. 176.

166   120 HAWKs: North's notebook entry on HAWKs, November 20, 1985, *Select Committee Documents*.

166   "It was a straight-out arms-for-hostage deal": Shultz testimony, July 23, 1987.

167   Turkish overflight clearance: Permission for the HAWKs shipment was never granted because the Turks became suspicious when the CIA told them the plane contained oil drilling parts and St. Lucia Airways told them it carried medical supplies. But the pilot talked his way through anyway.

167   "I told you not to get involved": The CIA officer whom McMahon castigated for approving the St. Lucia flight was Edward Juchniewicz, associate deputy for operations. Juchniewicz deposition, April 23, 1987.

168   Casey on the warpath about leaks: After the *Achille Lauro* interception, the Senate Intelligence Committee's ranking Democrat, Vermont's Patrick Leahy, had gone directly from a private CIA briefing to a television studio, where he revealed too much, in Casey's eyes, about the kind of intelligence the U.S. had on Egypt. Then, in the beginning of November, the *Washington Post*'s Bob Woodward had revealed a CIA plan to undermine Qadhafi by financing his opponents. "See," Casey had told Reagan, "I told you congressional oversight can't work. Those bastards all leak." Bob Woodward, *Veil: The Secret Wars of the CIA* (New York: Simon and Schuster, 1987), p. 419.

168   "He wants them out by Christmas": Noel Koch testimony, June 23, 1987.

168   "the most horrible thing": Ledeen deposition, June 19, 1987.

168   The wrong missile: The HAWK for low- and medium-altitude targets. Ghorbanifar had requested the wrong missile.

169   Kimche begged McFarlane to stay: Michael Ledeen got David Kimche to beg McFarlane to stay, his doubts about McFarlane's emotional stability notwithstanding.

169   McFarlane's resignation: Interviews with his staff and reporters and editors at *Newsweek*.

170   McFarlane's immediate regrets: Expressed to Maureen Dowd, *New York Times*, March 2, 1987.

171   "everyone's second choice": Interview with Regan, June 1988, also interviews with McFarlane, June 1988, and Deaver, summer 1987.

171   "It's a big mistake": Interview with Deaver, October 1987.

172   Poindexter's fitness report: Report by Admiral James Holloway III, chief of naval operations, August 1978, *Select Committee Documents*.

172   Poindexter's mother's observations and other early details: Maura Dolan, "Clues to Poindexter Found in Early Life," *Los Angeles Times*, May 3, 1987.

175   Salinger communiqué: David Halberstam, *The Best and the Brightest* (New York: Penguin, 1984), p. 59.

177   "We are now so far down the road": North to Poindexter, December 4, 1985, *Select Committee Documents*.

177   Idea invented by Ghorbanifar: Interviews with NSC and State Department officials, November 1987.

178   Poindexter relented to pressure: He agreed to hold the December 7 meeting reluctantly, according to top officials at both State and Defense, who said he had hoped originally to go ahead with just a phone call to each of the players, avoiding face-to-face confrontation.

178   December 7 meeting: Accounts from Shultz, Weinberger, and McFarlane testimony; *Select Committee Report*; and *Tower Commission Report*.

179   "I want to leave no stone unturned": Poindexter testimony, July 15, 1987.

180   "He was being pulled": Interview with Regan, June 1988.

180   December 8 London meeting: McFarlane and North testimony, and Ghorbanifar interview, ABC News's *20/20*, December 18, 1986.

181   December 10 meeting: Weinberger, Regan, and McFarlane testimony; *Select Committee Report*; and *Tower Commission Report*.

182   Plan was audacious: North to Poindexter, December 9, 1985. The memo was addressed to both Poindexter and McFarlane, but McFarlane said he never saw it.

183   "When the president is reading something": Poindexter testimony, July 15, 1987.

183   NSC meeting, January 7, 1986: Two NSC members, Treasury Secretary James Baker and Admiral William J. Crowe, chairman of the Joint Chiefs of Staff, were not present. Poindexter apparently did not invite them.

184   "Exactly, exactly": Nixon's 1977 interview with David Frost, cited in the *New York Times*, May 22, 1987.

185   January 17 meeting: Regan deposition, July 15, 1987.

185   North's three-page memorandum: Poindexter to Reagan [drafted by North], January 17, 1986, *Select Committee Documents*. It may be just as well that Reagan did not read the memo, for in it North (with Poindexter's approval) had carefully falsified the history of the initiative, portraying it as a purely Israeli idea and omitting the earlier arms sales — presumably to protect them from discovery by Shultz or others. In November 1986, while he was still national security adviser, Poindexter publicly released the text of this previously Top Secret memorandum to prove that the initiative had been aimed at broad geopolitical goals. It thus appears to have been designed from the start as a cover document in more than one sense.

185   "Well . . . if we get all the hostages": Poindexter testimony, July 15, 1987.

186   "unwise and illegal": State Department, "Iran Chronology I," n.d., *Select Committee Documents*.

186   Leaking to the press: In *The Thirteenth Man, A Reagan Cabinet Memoir* (New York: Macmillan, 1988), Bell writes about how his aide, Bill Clohan, was successfully removed from office after having been wrongly accused of leaking to the press (p. 53).

186   Shultz on leaks: Shultz testimony, July 23, 1987.

188   "I agreed": *Select Committee Report*, p. 209.

CHAPTER 9: "A NEAT IDEA"

189   The meeting in the bathroom: North testimony, July 8 and 15, 1987.

190   North and Israeli official: North told an Israeli official about his diversion plan on December 6, 1985 — seven weeks before his meeting with Ghorbanifar in London — according to an Israeli government chronology given to Congress's Iran-contra committees.

190   Ghorbanifar and CIA officer: Ghorbanifar told Charles Allen of the idea on January 13, 1986. *Select Committee Report*, pp. 201–2, 205, 269–71, 550–51. Allen testified that he did not mention Ghorbanifar's offer to anyone else at the CIA because he did not "consider it important or even relevant to my mission," which was to evaluate Ghorbanifar's usefulness to the effort against terrorism. The transcript of the taped North-Ghorban-

ifar dialogue, January 22, 1986, is reprinted in *Select Committee Documents*.

191   "a real lie": Ghorbanifar, on ABC News's *Nightline*, July 16, 1987.

191   "On the formal level": Kissinger in *Washington Post*, July 28, 1987.

191   "You cannot spend funds": Shultz testimony, July 24, 1987.

191   "That is the path to dictatorship": *Select Committee Report*, p. 390.

191   "The power of the purse": *The Federalist Papers*, No. 58. Madison noted that the power of the purse belonged to the House of Representatives as "the immediate representatives of the people." In 1985 and 1986, it was, in fact, the Democratic House that attempted to use the power of the purse to stop U.S. aid to the contras.

191   "The point was": Poindexter testimony, July 17, 1987.

192   Poindexter's approval of the diversion plan: Poindexter deposition, May 2, 1987, and North testimony, July 8 and 10, 1987. North did not recall Poindexter's approving the scheme at the meeting in which he first proposed it, but could not remember when the admiral did approve it. "I don't [recall]," he said. "I guess it was a matter of weeks — or days or weeks." Poindexter's version, that he approved the diversion on the spot, would strengthen his contention that he never raised the issue with Reagan; North's version leaves the question open.

192   "I assumed that the president was aware": North testimony, July 7, 1987.

192   "On this whole issue": Poindexter testimony, July 15, 1987.

193   Members of Congress on impeachment: For example, Congressman Lee H. Hamilton on ABC's *This Week with David Brinkley*, June 14, 1987.

193   "If you've got [another] memo": North's story that he wrote more than one "diversion memo" was confirmed by two other NSC officials, who said they saw another.

193   "fall guy" plan: North testimony, July 13, 1987. North testified that Casey worried that North might not be senior enough to make a convincing "fall guy" and nominated Poindexter for the honor instead.

194   In their formal report: *Select Committee Report*, p. 11. The report was approved by a bipartisan majority of the Senate Select Committee, including three of the panel's five Republicans. However, all six of the House committee's Republican members and two GOP senators issued a minority report, which held: "The evidence available to these committees shows that the president did not know about the diversion." It relied primarily on Poindexter's testimony, and secondarily on Regan's description of the president's apparent surprise at the news that a diversion had been discovered, for this conclusion.

194   McFarlane on Poindexter's diversion decision: Interview with McFarlane, September 1987. "I'm sure he did not undertake it on his own authority," McFarlane testified on May 14, 1987, before Poindexter testified.

194   Shultz on the hypothesis of a vague diversion briefing: Shultz testimony, July 24, 1987.

195   Regan on Reagan's knowledge of the diversion: Regan testimony, July 30, 1987.

196   "The hostage plan": Poindexter to McFarlane, February 2, 1986, *Select Committee Documents*.

196   "Giving them TOW missiles": McMahon to Casey, January 25, 1986, *Select Committee Documents*; *Tower Commission Report*, p. B71.

197   Army TOW pricing: *Select Committee Report*, p. 215; and House Armed Services Committee, *Staff Report*, March 1987. Army officials later noticed that the price they were charging was too low for the missiles they were shipping, but apparently because hiking the price would have entailed a fight with the CIA, they never pursued the issue.

197   Frankfurt meeting, February 25–26, 1986: *Select Committee Report*, pp. 218–19; *Tower Commission Report*, p. B77.

198   Regan on the February deal: Regan testimony, July 30, 1987. However, McFarlane's impression at the time was that Regan was bullish on the arms deals. In a computer message on February 26, he told North that he sympathized with Poindexter and "the narrow path he is trying to walk between those who want to go balls out for the wrong reasons (Regan) and those who don't want to do it at all (GPS [Shultz] and Cap)."

199   North and McFarlane messages, February 27, 1986: *Select Committee Documents*.

200   A Maule: The airplane paid for by beer magnate Joseph Coors.

200   Gadd's L-100 flight: Gadd deposition, May 1, 1987. Later, when the diplomats discovered they were being charged for an ammunition drop, they refused to pay that part of the bill.

200   "Mick" and "Moe": Interview with Iain Crawford, April 1987.

200   "Sure they bent the rules": Interview with army officer, April 1987.

200   Steele and Galvin: *Select Committee Report*, p. 65. Galvin testified that he knew of the air resupply operation, but said he believed it was being run by private individuals.

201   Letters: Reagan to Channell, February 21, 1986, *Select Committee Documents*.

202   Fischer fee arrangements with Channell: Channell said the details of the arrangement had been handled by one of his assistants, Daniel Lynn Conrad; and Conrad testified that the $50,000 was indeed paid on a fee-for-service basis. *Select Committee Report*, pp. 96–97; Channell deposition, September 1–2, 1987; Conrad deposition, June 10, 1987; Fischer deposition, August 11, 1987; Miller deposition, August 21, 1987; interviews with Channell associates, October 1987.

202   Fischer followed the White House staff: Fischer deposition, August 11, 1987.

202   "I hope you're being compensated": Fischer deposition, August 11, 1987. Regan later denied knowing that Fischer was being paid for setting up the meeting with the president. "We thought he was doing it out of his concern for the contras and the goodness of his heart — sort of a pro bono publico type of thing," Regan said. "To find out he was being paid for it was a real shock, 'cause we tried to avoid that. . . . Anyone that was getting paid to get a group into the White House, we tried to block that." Regan testimony, July 30, 1987.

203   "selfless devotion": Reagan's words at the January 30 briefing are taken from his prepared "talking points" as cited in Select Committee Hearings, June 27, 1987.

203   More than $4 million: Select Committee Hearings, July 30, 1987.

203   Wirthlin's influence on the 1986 State of the Union address: Interviews with Wirthlin, four speechwriters, and two Regan aides.

204   The 1986 speech: The authors viewed a copy of Reagan's comments on the first draft of the speech.

207   "Although it may not be my place": Hicks to Regan, February 27, 1986; copy obtained by authors.

CHAPTER 10: OFF THE SHELF

208   "We wanted to dramatize": Interview with William Henkel, June 1987.

209   Buchanan's March 5 column: Interviews with Buchanan and three members of the senior staff, July 1987.

210   Reagan on Sandinista drug-running charge: Doubts first surfaced in the *Village Voice* and a *Columbia Journalism Review* story by Joel Millman; they were expanded by Jonathan Kwitny in the *Wall Street Journal*, April 22, 1987.

213   "Dick Secord's a great American": Owen testimony, May 19, 1987.

214   "Who knows?": Hakim deposition, May 22, 1987.

214   Separate accounts: A fifth account was set up for Thomas Clines, which by the spring of 1986 had received more than $597,000.

214   Arms commissions: *Select Committee Report*, p. 348. These figures reflect deposits to the profit distribution accounts only through the end of April 1986.

214   Distributions to Secord: *Select Committee Report*, p. 344.

215   Clarridge's restricting knowledge within CIA: According to one account, Clarridge instructed his man in Copenhagen to file any further reports on the ship directly to Alan Fiers, the chief of Central American operations. The effect of this curious order was to restrict knowledge within the CIA.

215   *Erria* and CIA: Michael Wines and William C. Rempel, "Evidence Points to Bigger CIA Role in Iran-Contra Network," *Los Angeles Times*, December 30, 1987; *Select Committee Report*, pp. 367–69.

216   CIA in Honduras in March 1986: After the March 22 Sandinista incursion into Honduras, the CIA advisers working for chief of base Jim Adkins started flying the first of hundreds of helicopter supply missions for the contras over the next six months, ferrying troops, guns, and ammunition. Some of the missions were inside Honduras, but most were in Nicaragua and were clearly illegal.

216   "I couldn't believe the cheapness": Interview with Iain Crawford, April 1987.

216   Southern Front: The core of the Southern Front was the men who had fought with the mercurial, charismatic hero of the Sandinista revolution, Eden Pastora. Pastora had once been funded lavishly by the CIA, but as it turned out, he had a cardinal flaw. As he acidly put it, "I had only one problem with the CIA: I didn't speak English well enough to say 'Yes, sir.' " In 1984, Pastora's war came to an abrupt end when he was badly injured by a bomb that exploded in the middle of a press conference, killing three journalists and five contras. The assassin, a saboteur posing as a Danish photographer, disappeared. During the investigation that followed,

one witness, a somewhat eccentric adventurer named Jack Terrell, said he had been present at a meeting where Calero discussed "terminating" Pastora. And a former Costa Rican intelligence officer gave a sworn statement that his superiors ordered him to provide a jeep to the assassin, who he said came to visit him in the company of John Hull, a rancher affiliated with the CIA. The mystery of the bombing was never solved. But it effectively ended Pastora's career as a contra. See Leslie Cockburn, *Out of Control* (New York: Atlantic Monthly Press, 1987). Not all reporters have accepted the witnesses in this tangled case as credible; Cockburn's account is the most complete. A handful of reporters and lawyers pursued the threads behind the Pastora bombing assiduously, with no help and occasional hindrance from the governments of Costa Rica and the United States. One of the reporters injured filed a celebrated lawsuit charging that Calero, Secord, Clines, Owen, Singlaub, Hull, and others had plotted the attack.

217   "a perfect drop": *Los Angeles Times*, April 6, 1987.

218   Project Democracy accounts: *Select Committee Report*, pp. 337, 348.

219   "The resistance account": North to McFarlane, April 22, 1986, *Select Committee Documents*.

219   Opium addict: Hakim deposition, May 25, 1987.

220   Bush's request to postpone Tehran trip: North to Poindexter, April 3, 1986, *Select Committee Documents*.

221   Libya not formidable: Syria, though also on the State Department's list of terrorist sponsors, was so formidably linked to the hopes of both the Soviet Union and the U.S. for any Middle East peace plan that the administration largely exempted it from criticism.

222   Attack on Libya: Bob Woodward, *Veil: The Secret Wars of the CIA* (New York: Simon and Schuster, 1987), p. 441; David C. Martin and John Walcott, *Best Laid Plans* (New York: Harper & Row, 1988), pp. 258–322.

223   NSC's private polls on Libya: Interview with a participant. See also Jack Anderson and Dale Van Atta's February 28, 1988, column.

224   Regan said he would take it up with the president: *Select Committee Documents*, p. 229.

225   Prices for May HAWK deal: North notebooks, May 6, 1986, *Select Committee Documents*.

226   "I'm really serious": Poindexter testimony, May 2, 1987.

CHAPTER 11: INTO TEHRAN

232   Talks in Tehran: This account is drawn from the minutes taken during the meetings by Howard Teicher, McFarlane's two cables to Poindexter from Tehran, and George Cave's report for CIA director Casey, all reproduced in the *Tower Commission Report*, pp. B103–19 and in *Select Committee Documents;* McFarlane testimony, May 11, 12, and 14, 1987; North testimony, July 9, 10, 1987; Secord testimony, May 6, 1987; Cave deposition, April 17, 1987; and interviews with members of the U.S. delegation. All quotations are taken directly from the minutes and cables written by the Americans at the time, although some have been edited slightly for the sake of clarity.

244   Poindexter and the British envoy: Interview with NSC official, December 1987.

CHAPTER 12: SUCCESS

247   *Time* on Reagan: July 7, 1986. The introduction to the magazine's cover story is worth quoting at length as an only slightly exaggerated reflection of the sense of the time: "Ronald Reagan has found the American sweet spot. The white ball sails into the sparkling air in a high parabola and vanishes over the fence, again. The 75-year-old man is hitting home runs. Winning a lopsided vote on a tax-reform plan that others had airily dismissed. Turning Congress around on the contras. Preparing to stand with a revitalized Miss Liberty on the Fourth of July. He grins his boyish grin and bobs his head in the way he has and trots around the bases.

"Reagan inhabits his moment in America with a triumphant (some might say careless or even callous) ease that is astonishing and even mysterious. It is an afternoon in early summer. The sky is a splendid blue, with great cotton clouds floating across it and the grass a vivid field of green. There are noises of celebration in the crowd. Tonight there will be fireworks.

"Ronald Reagan has a genius for American occasions. He is a Prospero of American memories, a magician who carries a bright, ideal America like a holograph in his mind and projects its image in the air. . . . Reagan, master illusionist, is himself a kind of American dream. Looking at his genial, crinkly face prompts a sense of wonder: How does he pull it off?"

248   "We've given up running": Interview with Robert Squier, July 1986.

249   Twentieth Century–Fox: Garry Wills, *Reagan's America: Innocence at Home* (Garden City, N.Y.: Doubleday, 1987), pp. 268–69, 303; and John Gregory Dunne, *The Studio* (New York: Farrar, Straus & Giroux, 1969), pp. 126–27. The studio also made Reagan rich by buying his 236-acre ranch for $8,000 an acre when he had bought it fifteen years earlier for $293 an acre. Fox later sold it for only $1,800 an acre. See Dan E. Moldea and Jeff Goldberg, "The Deal's the Thing," *Los Angeles Reader,* November 2, 1984.

249   "Astonishingly unconcerned": Barrett, *Gambling with History,* (New York: Penguin, 1984), p. 465.

250   "He seemed even more puzzled": Michael K. Deaver, *Behind the Scenes* (New York: William Morrow, 1987), p. 220.

250   "you know Ronnie and I": Interview with a close associate of Holmes Tuttle's, September 1987.

250   "she made him come to her": Interview with White House aide.

250   American politics moves in cycles: See, among others, Arthur M. Schlesinger, Jr., *The Cycles of American History* (Boston: Houghton Mifflin, 1986).

251   Airlift results: The figures are for May through August, based on the incomplete records of the supply operation's air crews; see *Select Committee Report,* pp. 79–81.

251   "Some of those bastards": Rodriguez testimony, May 27–28, 1987; interview with Rodriguez, April 1988.

252   CBS News report: The *Los Angeles Times* confirmed that Secord was involved and added that North had recruited Secord for the contra cause. On July 25, 1986, Secord's attorney, Thomas C. Green, told one of the authors: "Secord hasn't sold anything to the contras. He hasn't sold one goddamn thing to the contras. . . . They're saying that he is off on some secret mission for Oliver North. That's just baloney.

       "We may be suing," Green added. "So you might want to be careful with what you write."

252   Meese had "okayed everything": Thompson testified that he did not know the extent of North's activities in Central America; Thompson deposition, March 9, 1987.

253   "I am very concerned": North to Poindexter, June 10, 1986, *Select Committee Documents.*

253   "Now you are getting emotional": North to Poindexter and Poindexter to North, July 15, 1987, *Tower Commission Report*, pp. B125–27.

253   "Reagan's star player": Evans and Novak, *Washington Post*, July 21, 1986.

253   "For senior officials": Suzanne Garment, *Wall Street Journal*, July 18, 1986.

254   North and the House Intelligence Committee: NSC minutes of meeting, August 6, 1986, *Select Committee Documents*; Hamilton letter to Congressman Ron Coleman, August 12, 1986, *Select Committee Documents*; interview with Congressman Hamilton, July 1987. In his testimony before the congressional Iran-contra committees, North acknowledged: "I misled the Congress . . . face to face" (North testimony, July 7, 1987).

254   "In 1985, there were 45,703 deaths": *Tower Commission Report*, pp. B131–35.

255   "What the hell": Oakley had come across traces of McFarlane's mission to Tehran, and in June he tried vainly to attract his superiors' attention with a deliberately intemperate memo: "This was in direct, blatant violation of basic hostage policy approved, reapproved, stated and restated by the president and the secretary of state." The memo was apparently deflected by one of Shultz's executive assistants, known around the State Department as "the Temple Dogs" (Oakley to Armacost, June 2, 1986, *Select Committee Documents*).

255   "Of course, we have not agreed": Poindexter to McFarlane, July 26, 1986, *Select Committee Documents.*

255   "It is entirely possible": Casey to Poindexter: July 26, 1986; North to Poindexter: July 29, 1986, *Select Committee Documents.*

256   Bush meeting with Nir: Craig Fuller notes of meeting, *Tower Commission Report*, pp. B144–47. A White House official described the meeting further in an interview in July 1987. Bush said he recalled Nir's briefing as covering only Israeli actions in an interview with CBS News, January 25, 1988. He said repeatedly that he understood the contacts to be with Iranian moderates (e.g., "people in Iran more responsible than Khomeini," January 13, 1988). He implied several times that he did not know that weapons were being exchanged for hostages; "I wish with clairvoyant hindsight that

I had known that we were trading arms for hostages," Bush said on CBS on March 15, 1987. ". . . I would have weighed in more heavily with the president."

257   "As this story surfaces": July 2, 1986, *Select Committee Documents.*

257   "My understanding": Shultz testimony, July 23, 1987.

258   "Shultz must have said": Interview with Shultz's aide, December 1987.

258   "It'll be easy": Recounted by another aide who was present. In the end, Shultz said he would, in fact, submit to urinalysis, but he never actually took the test.

259   Shultz's resignation: Shultz testimony, July 23, 1987.

259   McFarlane's telephone call: Shultz testimony, July 24, 1987. McFarlane got the size of the total Saudi contribution wrong: it was $32 million, not $31 million.

260   Abrams's Brunei solicitation: Abrams testimony, June 2, 1987. General Ibnu's identity was confirmed by several U.S. officials.

261   Hakim on $10 million: Hakim testimony, June 6, 1987.

261   Calero: The relationship between Secord and Calero was sufficiently strained that Secord did not believe he could safely base his airplanes at the contras' airstrip at Aguacate, Honduras. See Secord to North, July 22, 1986, *Select Committee Documents.*

261   Rodriguez: Rodriguez complained about Secord, Tom Clines, and Rafael Quintero to Bush's national security adviser, Donald Gregg, in August 1986. Gregg asserted that he never informed Bush about the problem because, in his words, "we had never discussed the contras. We had no responsibility for it. We had no expertise in it. . . . I frankly did not think it was vice presidential level" (Gregg deposition, May 18, 1987).

261   "a red letter day": Dutton to North, September 12–13, 1986, *Select Committee Documents.*

262   "It was never resolved": Interview with former NSC official, August 1987.

262   Charles Allen: *Select Committee Report*, p. 273.

262   Gates's "first reaction": Gates testimony to Tower commission, in *Select Committee Report*, p. 381.

262   Project Democracy profits: *Select Committee Report*, p. 348. Secord disavowed any interest in the profits that Hakim set aside for his account.

262   Selling Project Democracy: North to Poindexter, July 15, 1986, *Select Committee Documents.* Also, Clair George deposition, August 6, 1987.

262   Arms sale to the CIA: *Select Committee Report*, pp. 368–69, and *Los Angeles Times*, December 30 and 31, 1987. Secord said he and his partners bought the arms for $2.4 million and sold them to arms broker James P. Atwood for $1.2 million. Atwood then sold them to the CIA proprietaries for $2.2 million. According to congressional investigators, the proprietaries then planned to sell the weapons to the CIA itself for $4 million or more — generating an "off the books" profit of at least $1.8 million. The scheme was derailed after investigators (and reporters) discovered it.

263   Israeli deal: Poindexter to North, September 1986, *Tower Commission Report*, p. C14.

263   Secord and Hakim business ventures: *Select Committee Report*, pp. 349–50.

263   Bahremani: Several U.S. officials confirmed the identity of Rafsanjani's nephew. According to some reports, Hakim was introduced to Bahremani

through Sadegh Tabatabai, a son-in-law of Ayatollah Khomeini. Tabatabai was the man who set up the secret U.S.-Iranian negotiations in 1980 that ultimately ended the Carter administration's Iranian hostage crisis.

263   Secord on Bahremani: Secord to North, August 25, 1986, *Select Committee Documents*.

264   "We are prepared": Secord notes of meeting, September 20, 1986, *Select Committee Documents*, p. 252.

265   Twetten and Allen: *Tower Commission Report*, pp. B159–60.

CHAPTER 13: SPIN CONTROL

272   Hasenfus flight: Hasenfus's interviews after the crash, Dutton's testimony, and messages in the *Select Committee Documents*.

272   "I can't believe": CBS interview, cited in Leslie Cockburn, *Out of Control* (New York: Atlantic Monthly Press, 1987), pp. 214–15.

273   North lied to Congress: On August 6, 1986, North told members of the Senate Intelligence Committee that he had "given no military advice" to the contras and that he "knew of no specific military operations."

274   "to assume responsibility": Vincent Cannistraro to Poindexter, October 7, 1986, *Select Committee Documents*.

274   "to protect George Bush": Interview with contra officials, April 1988.

274   Abrams's TV appearance: His denial on CNN specifically covered the NSC. The interviewer, Robert Novak, famous for badgering his guests, took one more swipe at the assistant secretary. "Now, you're not playing word games . . . you're not talking about the NCS [*sic*] or something else — "

"I am not playing games!" shot back Abrams.

"National Security Council?" persisted Novak.

"No government agencies, none," Abrams replied.

275   DeGraffenreid and Poindexter: Poindexter testimony, July 16, 1987.

277   More concessions: Instead of releasing all three hostages, the United States only asked for "one and a half hostages — one definitely and the second with all effective possible effort." Also, Secord would work on winning the release of Shia prisoners held by the Israeli-controlled militia in southern Lebanon. The account of the Frankfurt meetings of October 5–7 is from documents in the *Tower Commission Report*, *Select Committee Documents*, and the testimony of North, Secord, Hakim, and Cave.

278   Deal was a bargain: North not only supported the Hakim accords, he said the CIA was solidly behind them. "All seem to be convinced that this is the best [and] fastest way to get two more out," he assured the admiral. ". . . all can be managed [without] any great complications."

278   Poindexter and Reagan approval: Poindexter testimony, July 15, 1987.

278   Kuwaiti editorial: *Wall Street Journal*, November 18, 1986; interviews with U.S. officials.

279   Reagan's pitch: David Hoffman, in his excellent piece in the *Washington Post Magazine*, November 30, 1986, first wrote about the top-level political meetings where drug abuse was seized on. As Hoffman wrote, "They wanted to control the agenda by diverting attention from the difficult issues, like the budget deficit."

279   A safe focus: Reagan emphasized the drug issue especially during the early phases of the 1986 midterm election campaign, less so toward the end, when he returned from Reykjavik and spoke about SDI and the need to elect conservative judges. Reagan's campaign against drugs was short on substance. Aside from calling for drug testing of some government employees, the program consisted largely of shuffling funds from one account to another so that the White House could say that it was devoting an additional $300 million to fighting drugs.

283   "Mr. President, we've got to clear up": The account of Poindexter's conversation with Reagan about eliminating all nuclear weapons comes from an official who witnessed the exchange.

283   "We can't go back with our tails between our legs.": Thus Regan recalled his staff meeting on *Air Force One* in an interview with the *Wall Street Journal* just a few days later. In *For the Record* (San Diego: Harcourt Brace Jovanovich, 1988), he instead says he told his staff, "This summit must not be seen or portrayed as a defeat" (p. 354).

285   "He thought the speech was dumb": Poindexter's reaction to Reagan's writing his own October 13 speech is based on two eyewitness accounts from White House officials.

285   "This operation is about to spin": Charles Allen's suspicions about the diversion were more than a hunch. He explained later that Ghorbanifar had mentioned a diversion to him, and other evidence supported the notion. "Secord and Hakim were directly involved [in the Iran deals] and were also directly involved in supplying the contras," he explained. "And I could not understand this incredible price markup that we were seeing." *Tower Commssion Report*, p. B168.

286   Allen and Casey: Allen testimony, *Tower Commission Report*, p. B168.

286   Furmark and Casey: *Select Committee Report*, pp. 288–90; Furmark deposition, July 22, 1987; and interviews with Furmark by Bob Drogin of the *Los Angeles Times*.

286   North's lunch with Casey and Gates: *Senate Intelligence Committee Report*, January 29, 1987.

288   "I [have] been out there": Abrams testimony, June 2, 1987.

289   Bahremani divulged: Cave said that Khomeini himself apparently did not learn of the negotiations until August or September; Cave deposition, April 17, 1987.

CHAPTER 14: THE SHOVEL BRIGADE

292   Reagan's Twin Falls speech: October 31, 1986, at the College of Southern Idaho.

293   A leftist ayatollah: the Iranians who leaked the story were agents of Ayatollah Hossein Ali Montazeri, a political rival of the more moderate Rafsanjani, U.S. officials said. The CIA eventually discovered that Ghorbanifar and Montazeri had a longstanding relationship, giving rise to suspicions that the arms merchant himself had leaked the news. See Cave deposition, April 17, 1987.

295 "There's no way": Rodney McDaniel notes of Reagan national security briefing, November 5, 1986, *Select Committee Documents*; interview with former White House aide.

295 "We must remain absolutely close-mouthed": Shultz to Poindexter, November 4, 1986, and Poindexter to Shultz, November 5, 1986, *Select Committee Documents*. Aides to Bush confirmed that he supported the view of Reagan and Poindexter that the Iranian initiative should be kept secret at this point.

295 "I wish everybody would calm down": Poindexter to McFarlane, November 7, 1986, *Select Committee Documents*.

296 "Because it has to happen again": Nancy Reagan also opposed going public for reasons of her own. The First Lady's astrologer warned that the stars did not favor any public statement by the president during early November. "He's not going to talk to the press," Mrs. Reagan ordered, according to Regan. "My God, Nancy," the chief of staff replied, "he's going to go down in flames if he doesn't speak up"; Regan, *For the Record* (San Diego: Harcourt Brace Jovanovich, 1988), p. 28.

296 "This will be the second lie": McFarlane to Poindexter, November 7, 1986, *Select Committee Documents*.

296 NSPG meeting, November 10, 1986: Drawn from notes taken at the meeting by Regan and Poindexter's deputy, Alton Keel, and notes dictated immediately afterward by Weinberger, all in *Select Committee Documents*. Quotes from the Regan and Keel notes have been edited slightly for readability.

298 "It just always came back to the president": Weinberger notes. See also Weinberger deposition, June 27, 1987.

300 "The appearance of things": Buchanan to Regan, November 12, 1986.

300 Project Democracy was enlisting: North and Poindexter hoped to persuade Iran's Rafsanjani to help as well. North drafted a statement for the Iranian clergyman proclaiming in mock-royal style: "His Holiness the Imam . . . graciously commands that acts of terrorism are not acceptable." See North draft, November 11, 1986, *Select Committee Documents*.

300 Reagan's briefing Congress, November 12, 1986: *Select Committee Report*, p. 295; Larry Speakes, *Speaking Out* (New York: Simon and Schuster, 1988), pp. 286–87.

301 "We went over the text": Interview with Buchanan, July 1987.

301 A giant C-5A: The C-5 is designed to carry up to 220,967 pounds of cargo. No precise estimate of the weight of the eight cargoes shipped to Iran is available, but a rough estimate taken from the individual weights of the weapons adds up to 216,000 pounds, not including packing material. In other words, North's assertion may have been technically correct, but even that is uncertain. What is clear, of course, is that North's portrayal of the shipments as modest was misleading.

301 Poindexter briefing, November 13, 1986: A fuller excerpt of the exchange is in the *Tower Commission Report*, pp. D11–12. The White House also made public a complete transcript that, since the briefing was given on a "background" basis, identifies Poindexter only as a "Senior Administration

Official." The reporter who noticed the inconsistency in Poindexter's briefing was George de Lama of the *Chicago Tribune*.

303   *Newsweek* and ABC News poll: *Newsweek*, November 24, 1986. Barry Goldwater, in *Time*, November 24, 1986.

304   Regan on Iran deals: Briefing transcripts, November 14, 1986.

304   "Ollie can produce": Interview with Abrams by Michael Wines of the *Los Angeles Times*; see *Los Angeles Times*, November 8, 1986.

305   "I sought him out": Shultz testimony, July 23, 1986. Quotes from the meeting are taken from Shultz's "talking points" prepared for the November 14 meeting (undated, in the *Select Committee Documents*). A senior State Department official confirmed that they were delivered substantially as prepared.

305   Shultz at Camp David, November 15: Shultz testimony, July 23, 1987; Regan testimony, July 30, 1987.

306   "I don't know what's gotten into George": Speakes, *Speaking Out*, p. 292.

306   The president himself was grumbling: Regan, *For the Record*, p. 34.

307   "Let's not forget whose idea": *Washington Post*, November 21, 1986.

307   "Some of us are like a shovel brigade": *New York Times*, November 16, 1986.

307   "Get the message out": Interview with Buchanan, April 1988.

308   Wallison, Sofaer, and Thompson: Interview with one of the participants; Cooper testimony, June 25, 1987; Sofaer deposition, June 18, 1987.

309   Casey-Poindexter telephone call, November 18, 1986: *Select Committee Documents*.

310   Chronology: For an exhaustive history of the NSC's chronologies, see *Select Committee Report*, pp. 298–300.

310   "There's something wrong": Secord testimony, May 6, 1987.

310   "the channeling of money": McFarlane testimony, May 11, 1987.

311   Shultz-Reagan meeting, November 19: Shultz testimony, July 23, 1987, and State Department chronology, *Select Committee Documents*.

312   "reinventing the wheel": Speakes, *Speaking Out*.

313   November 19 press conference: Interviews with Speakes, Buchanan, and other aides; Speakes, *Speaking Out*, pp. 293–94.

315   "I want a correction": In fact, it was Poindexter who first acknowledged Israel's role in his November 13 briefing, but Regan also confirmed the account.

315   Regan's tantrum: Interviews with Buchanan, Speakes, and a former NSC aide.

315   "the usual crisp, clear way": Meese testimony, July 28, 1987.

315   "the talk of moderates": Earl deposition, March 30, 1987.

316   "The second-raters": Cannon, *Washington Post*, November 24, 1986.

316   79 percent: *Los Angeles Times* poll, November 18, 1986.

CHAPTER 15: BATTLE ROYAL

319   The effect . . . was to commit: In his testimony before Congress in 1987, North was asked, "Isn't it true [that] you were committing the president of the United States to a false story?" North replied, "Yes, that's true." North testimony, July 7, 1987.

319 "pandemonium": Gates deposition, July 31, 1987.

320 Lawyers' discussions, November 20, 1986: Sofaer deposition, June 18, 1987; Cooper testimony, June 25, 1987; and an interview with a senior White House official.

321 "You're shitting me": Interview with Cooper, June 1988.

321 "I didn't make a dent": Shultz testimony, July 23, 1987.

322 Problems at the NSC: Casey testimony before House Intelligence Committee, November 21, 1986, *Select Committee Documents*.

323 "There seems to be a lot of confusion": The account of the November 21 meeting of Reagan, Meese, Regan, and Poindexter is taken from Meese testimony, July 28, 1987; Cooper testimony, June 25, 1987; Regan testimony, July 30, 1987; and Regan depositions, March 3 and July 15, 1987. The reference to intercepted communications is in the classified version of the Regan deposition of March 3, 1987.

324 Meese's investigation: Meese, Cooper, North, McFarlane, and Shultz testimony; interview with William Bradford Reynolds, March 1988; and *Select Committee Documents*. The timing of events is taken from the "Chronology of Justice Department Inquiry," prepared by the staff of the Senate Select Committee and published in the *Select Committee Documents*.

325 "Don't worry": North testimony, July 7, 1987.

325 North and McFarlane at Ledeen's house: McFarlane testimony, May 11, 1987; Ledeen depositions, March 11, September 10, 1987.

325 "[I'm] worried that Ledeen might have profited": McFarlane testimony, May 11, 1987. North denied using the words "shredding party," but McFarlane said that was the phrase he recalled. North also wrote a note suggesting that he suspected Ledeen of profiting from the arms sales in February 1986. See *Tower Commission Report*, p. B78.

325 North meets with Poindexter, November 21, 1986: North testimony, July 9, 1987.

326 "I felt a little bit of uneasiness": Hall testimony, June 8, 1987.

326 North and the spiral notebook: Poindexter testimony, July 16, 1987.

327 "Can I have forty-eight hours?": Earl deposition, May 2, 1987. Earl was not certain of the precise time North told him of his conversation with Meese. The attorney general spent ten minutes in Poindexter's office after their meeting with the president ended at 12:15 P.M., and North could have talked with him then. There is no reason to doubt Earl's account of what North told him, but there is also no other evidence that a North-Meese meeting occurred.

327 "Should I go ahead": Hall testimony, June 8, 9, 1987; North testimony, July 9, 1987.

328 Earl and three phases of arms deal: Earl deposition, May 22, 1987.

329 Poindexter destroys the December 1985 finding: Poindexter testimony, July 15, 1987; Poindexter deposition, May 2, 1987; Thompson deposition, April 28, 1987.

329 "Our position is": *Washington Post*, July 11, 1987.

329 "a quid pro quo": Cooper notes of interview with McFarlane, November 21, 1986, *Select Committee Documents*.

329 Meese helpfully told him: Cooper said he did not recall Meese's telling McFarlane about Shultz's notes, but McFarlane did remember the ex-

change. State Department records show that McFarlane called Shultz's office immediately after his meeting with the attorney general to ask for a copy of the notes. See *Select Committee Report*, p. 308; also McFarlane testimony, *Tower Commission Report*, pp. 53–57.

330   "He was not a man": Interview with Cooper, June 1988.

330   "There was no urgency": Meese deposition, July 8, 1987.

331   Regan and the chronology: Regan deposition, July 15, 1987.

331   Sofaer's suspicions: Sofaer deposition, June 18, 1987.

332   Shultz on Iran-contra connection: Hill notes of Shultz interview, November 22, 1986, in *Select Committee Report*, p. 309; and Shultz testimony, July 23, 1987.

333   "I was rather bored": Interview with Reynolds, March 1988; Reynolds deposition, August 27, 1987; and Richardson deposition, July 22, 1987.

334   Lunch at the Old Ebbitt Grill: Cooper testimony, June 25, 1987; Meese testimony, July 28, 1987; Reynolds interview, March 1988; and Cooper interview, June 1988.

334   North continues shredding: North testimony, July 9, 1987, and Earl deposition, May 2, 1987. North said he shredded documents in his office while Meese's aides were looking at files at his conference table: "They were sitting in my office, and the shredder was right outside, and I walked out and shredded documents. . . . They could hear it. The shredder was right outside the door. They were working ten feet from me." But Reynolds and Richardson denied this, and Earl said he clearly recalled that North's own shredder was jammed.

335   Meese at Casey's house: Meese testimony, July 28, 1987. No written record of this meeting is known to exist. Later events provide circumstantial evidence, at least, to support Meese's claim that he did not tell Casey of the discovery of the diversion memo. If Meese had told Casey, the CIA chief would have had time to contact North and devise a cover story to explain the memo — for example, that the diversion idea was only a proposal that never got off the ground, a possibility Meese's aides were already considering. Instead, North was taken by surprise when Meese confronted him with the diversion memo, and confessed that the diversion had, in fact, occurred.

336   "Mr. President, you need a new pitcher": Casey's letter to Reagan is dated November 23, 1986, but notes that Casey wrote it on the evening of November 22. The declassified version of the letter in *Select Committee Documents* blacks out the call for "a new pitcher," but the passage was quoted in the hearings on July 24, 1987.

336   North's conversation with McFarlane, November 23, 1986: McFarlane testimony, May 11, 1987; North testimony, July 9, 1987.

337   North's interview at the Justice Department: Richardson notes of interview, November 23, 1986; interview with Reynolds, March 1988; Cooper testimony, June 25, 1987; Meese testimony, July 28, 1987; Reynolds depositions, August 27, September 1, 1987. In his own testimony, North claimed that he did not intend to say that Israel had carried out the diversion but acknowledged that he may have given that impression; North testimony, July 8, 1987.

339   "I cannot back this story": North notebook, November 23, 1986, *Select Committee Documents.*

339   "They showed me this": Earl deposition, May 2, 1987.

340   "Things are in good hands": Interview with Bruce Cameron, October 1987.

340   "It wasn't even a close call": Interview with Reynolds, March 1988.

340   Meese meetings with Regan and Reagan: Regan testimony, July 30, 1987, and Regan deposition, July 15, 1987. Meese's account differs: the attorney general said he recalled briefing both Reagan and Regan in more detail on Monday morning. However, Meese's account of the events of late November conflicts repeatedly with the testimony of others as well as the documentary record, so we have chosen to rely on Regan's version here.

342   Regan turned purple: Interviews with Regan aides.

342   Nancy Reagan was annoyed: Interviews with friends of Mrs. Reagan.

342   The negotiations would go on: Department of State, "Iran Chronology II," n.d, *Select Committee Documents.*

342   Meese tells Reagan of the diversion: Meese testimony, July 28, 1987; Regan testimony, July 30, 1987; Regan deposition, March 3, 1987.

344   Regan at Casey's office: Regan testimony, July 30, 1987. Secord's lawyer, Tom Green, also made a last-minute attempt on November 24 to stop the administration from making the diversion public. Green met with Meese's aides and told them that it wasn't North or the Israelis who had diverted money to the contras; it was Secord's business partner Albert Hakim. He added that if the diversion was made public, "Iran will kill more of the hostages — to say the United States is an asshole." See Cooper notes, November 24, 1986, *Select Committee Documents*; Cooper testimony, June 25, 1987.

345   Regan's plan of action, November 24, 1986: *Select Committee Documents.*

346   Casey's meeting with Meese: Later on the morning of November 25, at Langley, Casey rediscovered the memorandum on the diversion reports that his aides had prepared in October. Somehow, it had languished on his desk for more than a month. The spy chief wrote a letter to Meese explaining that, remarkably, the CIA had known that there was a possible diversion of funds but, through pure mischance, had failed to bring it to anyone's attention.

346   Meese's meeting with Poindexter: Donald Regan, for one, never understood why the attorney general met with Poindexter on the morning of November 25 without informing him first. "I still don't know," Regan said in a June 1988 interview.

347   Poindexter's resignation: Regan testimony, July 30, 1987, and Poindexter deposition, July 2, 1987. Poindexter's deputy, Alton Keel, was named acting national security adviser, but he only learned of the honor when he heard it on television; Keel deposition, March 18, 1987.

347   NSC meeting: Shultz testimony, July 23, 1987; *Washington Post*, February 12, 1987.

347   Reagan briefs Congress: Regan notes, November 25, 1986, *Select Committee Documents*; interviews with several members.

348   North's priorities: North notebook, *Select Committee Documents*, as cited in Stephen Emerson, *Secret Warriors* (New York: Putnam, 1988), p. 234.

351   "Ollie, you're a national hero": Reagan's characterization of North as a hero was recounted by Fawn Hall (Hall testimony, June 8, 1987, and confirmed by Reagan himself in an interview with *Time* magazine, December 8, 1986. North's recounting of Reagan's comment about the affair "making a great movie" was first reported in the *New York Times,* November 30, 1986, and later confirmed by the authors.

351   "It is important that I not know": North testified that he recalled Reagan's saying only: "I just didn't know." Earl deposition, May 22, 1987; Coy deposition, June 1, 1987.

351   "I'm very tired": Thompson deposition, July 24, 1987.

354   "I have to say": *Time,* December 8, 1986. Reagan later said the conversation was intended to be off the record.

CHAPTER 16: NO ONE IN CHARGE

357   "My God, has government failed?": Garry Wills cites Lou Cannon as writing that Reagan's despondency lasted two months; *Reagan's America: Innocence at Home* (New York: Doubleday, 1987), p. 303. But in *Reagan* (New York: Putnam's, 1982), Lou Cannon describes this lasting four months (p. 134).

359   "If there was any shredding": White House briefing, January 6, 1987.

361   "We've had far worse problems": Interview with Regan by Jane Mayer and Ellen Hume of the *Wall Street Journal,* November 1986.

361   Nancy Reagan's fears about impeachment: Interview with a friend of the Reagan family. Another source, a former White House official who dealt with her during this period, said, "Nancy was so worried about impeachment she was ready to trade anything to avert it — she would have brought a Democrat in as chief of staff if that's what it took."

362   "He did not protect": *Washington Post,* December 6, 1986.

362   Strauss and Rogers visit: Interviews with one participant in the meeting and one accessory to it.

363   "It can't look like my idea": Notes of a conversation between Mrs. Reagan and an associate.

365   "not that unusual": Reagan, about North and Poindexter pleading the Fifth Amendment, December 5, 1986.

366   "It's not my role": Interview with Bush's interlocutor. Several others, including members of Bush's staff, confirm the thrust of the story, although they were unfamiliar with the exact conversation.

366   Eagleton and Abrams: Senate Intelligence Committee, hearing transcript, December 8, 1986, *Select Committee Documents.*

367   Casey and his men: The account of the CIA inspector general's visit to Central America is based on interviews with two intelligence officials and two congressional investigators. Some of the men involved, including Jim Adkins, the chief of the contra support operation in Honduras, reportedly argued that the inspector general's questions were so imprecise that they did not clearly refer to the helicopter operation.

368   Gates kept in the dark: Gates testimony, December 4, 1986, *Select Committee Report,* p. 381.

369   Reagan agreed to overrule Shultz: Regan testimony, July 30, 1987.
369   "The president intends to continue": State Department cable, Shultz to Dunbar, December 13, 1986, *Select Committee Documents.*
369   U.S.-Iranian meeting in Frankfurt: From the State Department's Charles Dunbar, "Memorandum for the Record," December 14, 1986, *Select Committee Documents.*
369   Regan's blocking Shultz: Shultz testified that "there was a lot of back and forth, what did I want to see him about and so on. And I didn't seem to be getting an appointment right away. So I picked up the phone Sunday morning and I called the president." Shultz testimony, July 23, 1987.
369   Shultz's meeting with Reagan: Shultz testimony, July 23, 1987.
370   Minuteman Missile: "White House Decisions on Policy, Staffing Delayed as Officials' Energies Are Diverted by Iran Affair," Ellen Hume, *Wall Street Journal,* January 16, 1987. The rush of the welfare reform bill is based on an interview with a participant.
371   State of the Union address: Interviews with Khachigian and Regan's staff.
372   "he read and signed the papers": Regan, *For the Record,* p. 71.
373   "Don't shoot!": Interview with an eyewitness to the episode.
375   "finally achieved the content-free presidency": David Hoffman, *Washington Post,* January 29, 1987.
375   Reagan's sessions with the Tower board: Interviews with two participating White House officials as well as three Tower board officials.
377   Kreig and the Tower board: Charles R. Babcock and Don Oberdorfer, *Washington Post,* February 28, 1987.
377   "Ollie North . . . loose cannon": *Washington Post,* February 28, 1987.
379   "the mental vigor": David Broder, *Washington Post,* December 23, 1986.
380   "Well, this is up to him": *Washington Post,* February 19.
383   "Wait until he sees the zoo": As told by Baker, United Press International, May 18, 1988.
383   Meeting in the residence: Interview with Landon Parvin, May 1987.
384   "I had no idea": Interview with Landon Parvin, May 1987.
385   "Howard, I think you better get over": This is the account of Jim Cannon, Baker's aide, who was with Baker in the office at the time of the phone call and talked with him about it immediately afterward.

EPILOGUE

386   Reagan's approval rating: To cite only a few of the major polls, Reagan's popularity was measured in March 1987 at 46% (the Gallup poll); June 1987, 53% (Gallup); July, 50% (CBS–*New York Times* poll); September, 49% (Gallup); October, 52% (CBS–*New York Times*); November, 45% (CBS–*New York Times*); December 49% (Gallup); December, after the Washington summit meeting with Gorbachev, 56% (CBS–*New York Times*); January 1988, 50% (CBS–*New York Times*); March, 51% (Gallup); June, 54% (Gallup). From January through October 1986, by contrast, Reagan's rating never fell below 60% and reached 68% in the CBS–*New York Times* poll and 70% in the ABC–*Washington Post* poll, the highest marks since 1981.

386   Decent: Survey by Center for Political Studies, University of Michigan, May/June 1987, as cited in Jack Citrin, Donald Green, and Beth Reingold, "Confidence in the Reagan Years," *Public Opinion*, November/December 1987.

386   Even Republicans: CBS–*New York Times* poll, *New York Times*, January 26, 1988.

386   May 1988 poll: ABC–*Washington Post* poll, May 20–25, 1988.

386   *Congressional Quarterly*: See *CQ Weekly*, November 19, 1988, and January 16, 1988. The magazine measured Reagan's "success rate," defined as the percentage of votes in Congress on which his declared position won, at 43.5% in 1987 and 47.4% in 1988. The previous low had been Richard Nixon's 50.6% in 1973. Reagan's success rate slid continuously after his first-year high of 82.4% in 1981 to 72.4% in 1982, 67.1% in 1983, 65.8% in 1984, 59.9% in 1985, and 56.1% in 1986. The drop to 43.5% in 1987 was both more precipitous than any before and the first time a president's success rate had fallen below 50%. In his final year, Reagan "arrested the steady downhill slides of his fortunes on Capitol Hill," *CQ Weekly* noted. "But doing better wasn't the same as doing well. . . . Reagan lost more roll-call votes than he won."

389   "Let me give you": Interview with Fred Barnes, *The New Republic*, October 26, 1987.

389   Not once did he condemn: In a news conference on March 19, 1987, Reagan claimed that he would have objected to the diversion of funds if Poindexter had informed him of it: "You would have heard me without opening the door to the office if I had been told that at any time," he said. But he never expressed any condemnation of the scheme and never offered a judgment of any kind on its merits.

389   The president was lying: See *New York Times*, July 18, 1987. Even after Poindexter testified that Reagan did not know about the diversion, the CBS–*New York Times* poll found that 53% of the public believed that the president was lying; only 34% believed that he was telling the truth. Before Poindexter's testimony, 56% believed Reagan was lying about the diversion, and only 26% believed he was telling the truth.

390   "The Constitution requires": *Select Committee Report*, pp. 21–22.

392   A national poll: *USA Today*, May 5, 1989.

393   "The Hondurans seem to regard": McFarlane to Reagan (with copies to Bush and others), May 21, 1985, North trial documents.

394   Poll on Bush "hiding something": *New York Times*/CBS News Poll, May 12, 1989. On Bush "lying": *Los Angeles Times* Poll, April 26, 1989. The same poll found that 47% said they were still troubled by the scandal, but 51% said they were not.

Index

327–28, 339, 340, 353, 359; and North's removal, 348, 351; removes documents from office, 353
Hamadi, Mohammed Ali, 92
Hamburg, Germany: origin of arms deal in, 117, 120
Hamilton, Rep. Lee H.: on Reagan's military option in Nicaragua, 86; questions McFarlane on covert contras aid, 147, 148; questions North, 255; questions Abrams, 273; on Bush, 394
Hasenfus, Eugene H.: crash of, 271, 272, 273, 274, 282, 286–87, 288, 304
Hatch, Sen. Orrin: calls for Regan's removal, 362
HAWK missiles: cost of, 117, 320; in second arms sale to Iran, 166–67, 168–69, 178–79, 296, 297, 300, 302, 303, 309–11, 318–21, 323, 325, 329, 332–33, 335, 337–39, 342, 352, 368, 388; in third arms deal, 177–78; in fourth arms deal, 225, 231, 243–44, 245, 255, 257, 262, 333; Secord and Hakim plan to invest in producers of, 263; in fifth arms deal, 276–77
Hayes, Rutherford B., 26
Hellcats of the Navy, 14
Hemingway, Ernest, 160
Henkel, William: and Reagan's meeting with hostages' relatives, 96; on Jencos' excoriating of Reagan, 103; and reception plans for released TWA hostages, 104–5; as advance man, 104, 208; at Geneva summit, 159; and Reykjavik summit, 282, 283
Heritage Foundation, 371
Hicks, Christopher, 42; on Crisis Management Center, 61–62; and government telephone line for McFarlane, 181; on NSC staff expansion, 206–7
Higgins, Anne: and president's correspondence, 98–99
Hill, Charles, 319, 321
Hinckley, Ronald, 221
Hines, Rudy: pen pal to president, 99
Hizballah, 245; and TWA hijacking, 124–25; and treatment of hostages, 177, 255, 257; exposes McFarlane mission to Tehran, 289; statement on Jacobsen's release, 293
Hoffman, David, 34
Honduras: contra bases in, 73, 74, 151–

52, 200; and supplying of contras, 145; American embassy in, 150; Poindexter tours, 176–77; CIA agents in, 200
Hoover, Herbert: on FDR, 11; public access to, 34
Horton, John: on Reagan at NSC meeting, 52; on North, 68–69, 70
hostages: Tehran American embassy (1979), 12, 91, 94, 95, 107, 121, 122, 141, 236; TWA flight 847, 90–91, 93–94, 95–96, 99–103, 104–7, 115, 124, 136, 137, 138, 146, 277; pressure from relatives of, 95–96, 100–107, 136–38; Reagan's obsession with, 102, 107, 115–16, 180, 181, 354–55, 391; Seven Forgotten, 103–4, 106–7, 136–37; origins of arms-for-hostages exchange, 116 (*see also* arms-for-hostages exchange); release of Weir, 135, 136; yellow ribbon given to Reagan, 138; murder of British, 245; resurgence of kidnappings in Beirut, 264, 277, 297, 368, 387; *see also specific hostages*
House Foreign Affairs Committee: Shultz testifies before, 365; McFarlane testifies on Reagan's knowledge of arms deals, 367
House Intelligence Committee: and CIA aid (1981–1982) to contras, 71–72; and news of foreign funding of contras, 72; and Boland amendment, 72 (*see also* Boland amendment); on Reagan's military option in Nicaragua, 86; confronts McFarlane over contra aid, 147, 148–49; approves selective CIA aid to contras, 151; questions North, 253–54; Abrams lies to, 275; Casey testifies before, 322–23, 336; McFarlane writes to, 377
House of Representatives. *See* Congress
HPS precept, 104
Hughes, Emmet John, 395
Human Events: Reagan's reading of, 29
Hunt, Nelson Bunker: contribution to contras, 156
Hussein, Saddam, 118, 277
Hyde Park Square Corp., 213

Iacocca, Lee, 250
Ibnu, General, 260